APPLIED COMPUTATION THEORY:

Analysis, Design, Modeling

Prentice-Hall
Series in Automatic Computation

MARTIN, *Systems Analysis for Data Transmission*
MARTIN, *Telecommunications and the Computer*
MARTIN, *Teleprocessing Network Organization*
MARTIN AND NORMAN, *The Computerized Society*
MCKEEMAN, et al., *A Compiler Generator*
MEYERS, *Time-Sharing Computation in the Social Sciences*
MINSKY, *Computation: Finite and Infinite Machines*
NIEVERGELT, et al., *Computer Approaches to Mathematical Problems*
PLANE AND MCMILLAN, *Discrete Optimization:*
  Integer Programming and Network Analysis for Management Decisions
POLIVKA AND PAKIN, *APL: The Language and Its Usage*
PRITSKER AND KIVIAT, *Simulation with GASP II:*
  A FORTRAN-based Simulation Language
PYLYSHYN, ed., *Perspectives on the Computer Revolution*
RICH, *Internal Sorting Methods Illustrated with PL/1 Programs*
RUDD, *Assembly Language Programming and the IBM 360 and 370 Computers*
SACKMAN AND CITRENBAUM, eds., *On-Line Planning:*
  Towards Creative Problem-Solving
SALTON, ed., *The SMART Retrieval System:*
  Experiments in Automatic Document Processing
SAMMET, *Programming Languages: History and Fundamentals*
SCHAEFER, *A Mathematical Theory of Global Program Optimization*
SCHULTZ, *Spline Analysis*
SCHWARZ, et al., *Numerical Analysis of Symmetric Matrices*
SHAH, *Engineering Simulation Using Small Scientific Computers*
SHAW, *The Logical Design of Operating Systems*
SHERMAN, *Techniques in Computer Programming*
SIMON AND SIKLOSSY, eds., *Representation and Meaning:*
  Experiments with Information Processing Systems
STERBENZ, *Floating-Point Computation*
STOUTEMYER, *PL/1 Programming for Engineering and Science*
STRANG AND FIX, *An Analysis of the Finite Element Method*
STROUD, *Approximate Calculation of Multiple Integrals*
TANENBAUM, *Structured Computer Organization*
TAVISS, ed., *The Computer Impact*
UHR, *Pattern Recognition, Learning, and Thought:*
  Computer-Programmed Models of Higher Mental Processes
VAN TASSEL, *Computer Security Management*
VARGA, *Matrix Iterative Analysis*
WAITE, *Implementing Software for Non-Numeric Application*
WILKINSON, *Rounding Errors in Algebraic Processes*
WIRTH, *Algorithms + Data Structures = Programs*
WIRTH, *Systematic Programming: An Introduction*
YEH, ed., *Applied Computation Theory: Analysis, Design, Modeling*

APPLIED COMPUTATION

THEORY:

Analysis, Design,

Modeling

RAYMOND T. YEH, *Editor*

Department of Computer Sciences
The University of Texas at Austin

PRENTICE-HALL, INC.

ENGLEWOOD CLIFFS, NEW JERSEY

Library of Congress Cataloging in Publication Data

YEH, RAYMOND TZUU-YAU, (date)
  Applied computation theory.

  Includes bibliographies and index.
  1. Sequential machine theory. 2. Electronic
digital computers—Programming. 3. Electronic digital
computers—Design and construction. I. Title.
QA267.5.S4Y43   629.8'91   75–4517
ISBN 0–13–039305–3

10 9 8 7 6 5 4 3 2 1

Printed in the United States of America

PRENTICE-HALL INTERNATIONAL, INC., *London*
PRENTICE-HALL OF AUSTRALIA, PTY. LTD., *Sydney*
PRENTICE-HALL OF CANADA, LTD., *Toronto*
PRENTICE-HALL OF INDIA PRIVATE LIMITED, *New Delhi*
PRENTICE-HALL OF JAPAN, INC., *Tokyo*
PRENTICE-HALL OF SOUTHEAST ASIA (PTE.) LTD., *Singapore*

CONTENTS

PREFACE

The invention of calculus and the concomitant reduction of physical processes to mathematics gave birth to a new scientific discipline called physics which has revolutionized our understanding of the environment and its control. However, physics, or the study of energy changes in a system, is inadequate for modeling many complicated systems such as those having to do with living organisms. Although there have been isolated results obtained by considering living organisms as closed energy systems, most of the questions which arise in life sciences are not amenable to such restricted treatment.

During the twentieth century, we have been witnessing many breakthroughs in sciences and engineering caused by a new way of looking at things. For example, modern physiology is concerned with how information is transferred through the blood stream and nervous system by hormones. The problem of how parents pass their traits on to offsprings in genetics can be solved by reducing the problems to that of encoding information in the genes. Modern technological wonders such as radio, telephone, telegraph, and television, to name just a few, are, of course, means for *information*, rather than energy, transmission. Even in physics, the Heisenberg's Uncertainty Principle is less a statement about energy change in a system than a statement about how much information about the energy change in a system an experimenter can gather without having to take the effects of his observations into account.

Along with the aforementioned technological breakthroughs in the twentieth century is the invention of another scientific discipline called *computation theory* which reduces algorithmic processes to mathematics. Viewing a system as an algorithmic process is precisely the reason that information changes within the system can be measured discretely. Just as physics is a mathematical treatment of energy changes in a system, *computation theory is a mathematical treatment of information changes in a system*. There is already strong evidence that this treatment will result in as revolutionary a change in our relationship to the environment as physics has.

This book is strongly motivated by the need to complement the study of computation theory with practical applications. Thus, the book consists of a collection of *tutorial* papers which provides both the fundamentals of computation theory as well as methodologies for its utilization to analyze, design, and model discrete systems. Already, rudiments of computation theory form the bases of a common descriptive language for modeling and organization of a wide spectrum of disciplines in sciences and engineering. It is hoped that this book will enable better understanding and promote greater use of this common descriptive language for communication.

This book is intended to serve both as a reference for professionals in the computer field and a text book for senior or graduate students in computer science and computing engineering. Since each chapter is tutorial in nature, the reader may choose any chapter pertinent to his specific interest independent of the others. On the other hand, materials from different chapters may be quite intimately related and hence could be grouped together to form the basic material of a course. In the appendices, we give detailed course descriptions of the following three courses:

1. Introduction to the Theory of Automata and Formal Languages.
2. Design Principles of Programming Languages and Compilers.
3. Design Principles of Fault-Tolerant Computing Systems.

Let us also point out that a course on "Foundations of Finite Arithmetics" could be taught using primarily the material covered in Chapter 9, and that Chapters 5 and 11 could form the core material of a course on "Scene Analysis."

In order to help the reader to facilitate the use of this book, an editor's note is included at the beginning of each chapter (except Chapter 1). Each note briefly describes the content of that particular chapter, its prerequisites (if any), and its relation to other chapters.

The purpose of Chapter 1 is to provide the reader with fundamentals of computation theory which serve as background material to most of the other chapters. In this chapter, the concept of computation or information processing is discussed in terms of the power of two formal models: abstract machines and grammars, for characterizing languages. The grammar-machine pair are viewed as two ends of a communication channel. We are interested in knowing under what conditions language generated by a grammar is identical to that recognized by a machine. Thus, any adjustment made on one end must necessarily affect the other end as far as language characterization is concerned. This viewpoint brings out a hierarchy of grammar-machine pair. Finally, the concept of algorithmic unsolvability is also discussed.

Acknowledgment

I wish to express my sincere appreciation to all the contributing authors of this book, and to the following reviewers: R. B. Banerji, S. Basu, M. Chandy, R. Duda, A. Fleck, D. Friedman, S. Hedetneimi, S. Kundu, P. Lewis, J. Nievergelt, E. Pearson, J. Reynolds, A. Solomaa, V. M. Sorensen, S. Underwood, and T. Welch. Special thanks are due my colleague W. H. Henneman who helped greatly during the early planning stage of this book. Finally, I would like to thank Suzanne Rhoads for her excellent help in typing the manuscript.

R. T. Yeh

Austin, Texas

APPLIED COMPUTATION

THEORY:

Analysis, Design,

Modeling

PART **I** **BACKGROUND**

A BRIEF INTRODUCTION TO THE THEORY OF AUTOMATA AND FORMAL LANGUAGES

1

Raymond T. Yeh
Department of Computer Sciences
The University of Texas at Austin
Austin, Texas

The purpose of this chapter is to provide the reader with basic concepts and results of computation theory which will be used in some of the later chapters. Since the intention is to provide a tutorial guide to abstract machines and formal languages, proofs of most theorems will be intuitively motivated but compacted in such a way that the reader will have no difficulty in understanding or completing them.

1.1. INTRODUCTION

The theory of computation studies how information is processed; information changes within a system and communication of information between systems. While communications engineers were drawing the following diagram, many other people were using the same (or equivalent versions of the same) diagram, with different labels. The stimulus-response diagrams of the behavioral psychologists, the speaker-listener diagrams of the linguists, and

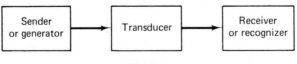

Fig. 1.1.1

3

the diagrams of natural scientists studying instinctual behavior all had the same form. When such an idea starts appearing in so many different places, it is a natural thing to ask if there isn't something common that warrants study as an abstract entity in its own right, and this is what the study of computation theory centers about. We shall formalize our notion of a communication system, and then study the interrelationships between its components.

There are two items that need to be formalized: an abstract device to process information (recognition, translation, and generation), and a language through which information can be conveyed.

Our definition of a *language L* is simply a set of strings of finite length over some finite set Σ called an *alphabet*. A language has a *vocabulary* and a *grammar*. The vocabulary forms the building-blocks of the language, and the grammar tells how to combine these building-blocks in a (syntactically) acceptable manner. In English, for example, the sentence

The man gives me a book.

is grammatically correct. Whereas the sequence

Book a gives man the me.

is not an acceptable English sentence.

How do we recognize that a sentence is grammatically correct? This is done by parsing the sentence to see if grammatical categories (subject, noun, verb, etc.) of a given sentence occur in the right places. The parsing can be expressed by means of a tree referred to as a *parse tree* of a sentence. A parse tree for the sentence "The man gives me a book" is given in Fig. 1.1.2.

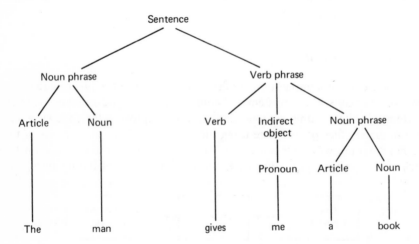

Fig. 1.1.2   Parse tree of an English sentence.

It is important to observe that the process of parsing is reversible. Hence, a grammar can be used as a device to generate acceptable sentences. For example, the parse tree in Fig. 1.1.2 can be used to generate many sentences of the same form.

> A lady gives me a kiss.
> The work gives her the headache.
> The letter brings him a check.

Thus, a grammar is simply a set together with a finite set of rules which governs how sentences can be generated.† This notion will be formalized in the next section.

Our notion of an abstract information transducer or automaton is a device which consists of a combination of the following parts: an input tape, an output tape, an auxiliary memory, and a finite set of rules which controls or regulates the flow of information as shown in Fig. 1.1.3.

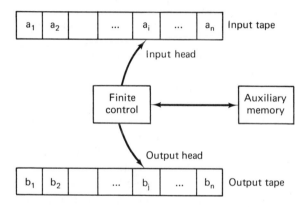

Fig. 1.1.3 An information transducer.

We usually refer to a device having all components in Fig. 1.1.3, with the possible exception of an auxiliary memory, a *transducer*. An example of this is a computer in which the finite control is a stored program. A transducer without output is called a *recognizer*. A *generator* is a transducer without input.

Both the input and output tapes are considered to be divided into squares in which exactly one symbol can be printed.

The input head can have various capabilities. It can move about in a tape,

---

†Note that our concern of a "formal" language is exclusive on its syntactic structures. The semantic structure will be ignored here. As an example, the parse tree in Fig. 1.1.2 will generate the sentence "The book gives me a man" which is of course absurd as far as its meaning goes. Nevertheless, it is grammatically correct.

one square at a time, or remain stationary. Sometimes, it also has the ability to erase an existing symbol and print a new symbol on the square it is reading.

The output head can print a sequence of output symbols at a time but is allowed only to move right.

The auxiliary memory of the automation can be any type of data store. We assume that the machine has ways of accessing data in the memory and that the contents of memory can be finitely described at any given time.

The finite control corresponds to the set of rules which describe how information within the system changes in accordance with the current input symbol and the current information accessed in the memory.

It is the intention of this chapter to review briefly some formal aspects of how these three phrases of communication—generation, translation, and recognition—are related as well as how information is processed. Our emphasis will be on the relationship between the generation and recognition phases. In particular, the following questions are answered.

Given a class of languages, what are the least powerful devices (if exist) which can recognize these languages?

Given a certain type of recognizers, how large is the class of languages it defines (or recognizes)?

Since both the grammar and the recognizer, in our view, are systems consisting of sets together with finite sets of rules to regulate the information changes in the system, our approach would be to transform generating rules to recognition rules and vice versa.

The question of how information is changed within a system brings us to the concept of "computation" or "algorithm." Relevant questions will be whether there exists an algorithm or procedure for the solution of a class of problems, and how efficient is the algorithm.

In the next few sections, we will discuss hierarchy of grammars and their corresponding recognizers. The only transducer to be mentioned is the pushdown transducer due to its important application to compiler design (see Chapter 6). In the last section, we will discuss very briefly the possibility of proving that certain classes of problems cannot be solved by any algorithm. This will be an eye opener for readers who have not been exposed to this concept before.

EXERCISES 1.1

1. Using Fig. 1.1.2 as a hint, describe a set of rules by which the sentence "The man gives me a book" can be generated from a given initial condition.

2. Describe intuitively how you would design the switchboard of an intercom system with no more than 100 extensions.

3. Consider a candy machine in which each merchandise costs 15¢. Can you fit it into the form of Fig. 1.1.3 and describe in detail its control rules?

4. Describe how you would automate a toll booth. Say the toll is 10¢ and that only a nickel or a dime will be accepted.

1.2. LANGUAGES AND GRAMMARS

This section is intended to provide basic terminologies on formal languages and grammars. A hierarchy of languages, based on the form of their grammatical rules, will also be given here.

Definition 1.2.1

An *alphabet* is a finite set. A *language* over an alphabet Σ is a set of finite sequences called *words* or *sentences*, or *tapes*, of elements of Σ. The word which contains no element of Σ is called the *empty* or *null* word and is denoted by $\wedge$. The *length* of the word is the number of elements occurring in it. The length of the empty word is zero.

Thus if $\Sigma = \{a, b\}$, then the set L which consists of all sequences having more a's than b's is a language over Σ, and the sequence $abaab$ is a word of length five in L.

Let L_1 and L_2 be two languages, the language $L_1 L_2$, called the *concatenation* of L_1 and L_2, is defined to be the set of all sequences xy, obtained by juxtaposing x on the left and y on the right, for all x in L_1 and y in L_2.

We also define the following operations on a language L:

1. $L^0 = \{\wedge\}$
2. $L^{i+1} = L^i L$
3. $L^+ = \bigcup_{i>0} L^i$
4. $L^* = \bigcup_{i\geq0} L^i$

Thus, if $L = \{a, b\}$, then L^+ consists of all finite sequences of a's and b's of length greater than 0.

Definition 1.2.2

A *grammar* G is a 4-tuple (N, Σ, P, S), where N and Σ are two finite, disjoint sets of *nonterminal symbols* (or syntactic categories) and *terminal symbols*, respectively. S is a distinguishing symbol in N called the *sentence* (or start) symbol. P is a finite set of rules called *productions*, which is a set of ordered pairs (α, β), where $\alpha \in (N \cup \Sigma)^*$ and contains at least one element of N, and $\beta \in (N \cup \Sigma)^*$. We shall denote a production (α, β) by $\alpha \rightarrow \beta$.

Let $G = (N, \Sigma, P, S)$ be a grammar. A string α is said to *directly generate* another string β (denoted by $\alpha \underset{G}{\Rightarrow} \beta$) iff $\alpha = \alpha_1 \gamma \alpha_2$, $\beta = \alpha_1 \delta \alpha_2$ and $\gamma \rightarrow \delta$ is a production in P. We will use $\underset{G}{\overset{+}{\Rightarrow}}$ to denote the transitive closure of $\underset{G}{\Rightarrow}$, and $\underset{G}{\overset{*}{\Rightarrow}}$ to denote the reflexive and transitive closure of $\underset{G}{\Rightarrow}$. When no confusion arises, we shall drop the subscript G and simply use the notations $\Rightarrow$, $\overset{+}{\Rightarrow}$, and $\overset{*}{\Rightarrow}$. The notation $\overset{k}{\Rightarrow}$ will be used to denote k-fold composition of the relation $\Rightarrow$. If $\alpha \overset{k}{\Rightarrow} \beta$, then the sequence $\alpha_0 = \alpha$, $\alpha_1, \ldots, \alpha_k = \beta$ such that $\alpha_i \Rightarrow \alpha_{i+1}$ $(0 \leq i < n)$, is called a *derivation* of length k.

Definition 1.2.3

Let $G = (N, \Sigma, P, S)$ be a grammar. The language generated by G, denoted by $L(G)$, is the set of words $x \in \Sigma^*$ such that $S \overset{*}{\Rightarrow} x$.

Example 1.2.1

Let $G = (\{S, A\}, \{a, b\}, P, S)$, where P consists of

$S \rightarrow aS$	$A \rightarrow aA$
$S \rightarrow bA$	$A \rightarrow bS$
$S \rightarrow a$	$A \rightarrow b$

It is easily seen that $L(G)$ consists of words having any number of a's and an even number of b's. A derivation of the string *aabbaa* is illustrated in the following:

$$S \Rightarrow aS \rightarrow aaS \Rightarrow aabA \Rightarrow aabbS \Rightarrow aabbaS \Rightarrow aabbaa \qquad (1.2.1)$$

Grammars can be classified by imposing restrictions on the forms of their productions. The following classification is due to Chomsky [2].

Definition 1.2.4

Let $G = (N, \Sigma, P, S)$ be a grammar. G is said to be of *type i,* for $0 \leq i \leq 3$, if and only if P satisfies restriction (i) given in the following:

0. No restrictions.
1. Each production in P is either of the form $\alpha A \beta \rightarrow \alpha \gamma \beta$, where $A \in N$, α, $\beta \in (N \cup \Sigma)^*$ and $\gamma \in (N \cup \Sigma)^+$, or of the form $A \rightarrow \wedge$, where A does not occur on the right-hand side of any productions in P.
2. Each production is of the form $A \rightarrow \alpha$, where $A \in N$ and $\alpha \in (N \cup \Sigma)^*$.
3. Each production is of the form $A \rightarrow xB$ or $A \rightarrow x$, where $A, B \in N$, $X \in \Sigma^+$, and $x \in \Sigma^*$.

A type 1 grammar is also referred to as *context-sensitive grammar* (or CSG for short) because a nonterminal A can be replaced by a word γ only in the context of α and β. If $\alpha = \beta = \wedge$, i.e., if replacement can be done independent of any context, we arrive at a type 2 grammar, which is also referred to as *context-free grammar* (CFG for short). A type 3 grammar is called a *right-linear* grammar. It is also called a *regular* grammar since the class of languages generated by right-linear grammars coincide with the class of languages each of which can be expressed by a "regular expression." This fact will be shown in Section 1.4.

Definition 1.2.5

A language is said to be *context-sensitive, context-free,* or *right-linear* if it can be generated by a context-sensitive grammar, a context-free grammar, or a right-linear grammar, respectively.

Example 1.2.2

Let $G = (\{S\}, \{a, b\}, P, S)$ be a context-free grammar where P consists of the productions:
$$S \longrightarrow aSb, \qquad S \longrightarrow ab$$
G generates a context-free language $\{a^n b^n \mid n > 1\}$.

Example 1.2.3

Let $G = (\{S, A, B\}, \{a, b, c\}, P, S)$ be a context-sensitive grammar, where P consists of the following productions:

$S \longrightarrow aSAB$	$aA \longrightarrow ab$
$S \longrightarrow aAb$	$bA \longrightarrow bb$
$BA \longrightarrow BA'$	$bB \longrightarrow bc$
$BA' \longrightarrow AA'$	$cB \longrightarrow cc$
$AA' \longrightarrow AB$	

G generates a context-sensitive language $\{a^n b^n c^n \mid n \geq 1\}$.

Example 1.2.4

Let $G = (\{S, A, B, C, D, E\}, \{0, 1\}, P, S)$ be a type 0 grammar, where P consists of the following productions:

$S \longrightarrow ABC$	$E1 \longrightarrow 1E$
$AB \longrightarrow 0AD$	$C \longrightarrow \wedge$
$AB \longrightarrow 1AE$	$DC \longrightarrow B0C$
$AB \longrightarrow \wedge$	$EC \longrightarrow B1C$
$D0 \longrightarrow 0D$	$0B \longrightarrow B0$
$D1 \longrightarrow 1D$	$1B \longrightarrow B1$
$E0 \longrightarrow 0E$	

G generates a type 0 language $\{xx \mid x \in \{0, 1\}^*\}$.

Let $\mathscr{L}_i$ denote the family of languages generated by type i grammars. As a direct consequence of Definition 1.2.4 we see that $\mathscr{L}_{i+1} \subseteq \mathscr{L}_i (0 \leq i < 3)$. In-

deed, it will be shown in this chapter that $\mathscr{L}_3 \subset \mathscr{L}_2 \subset \mathscr{L}_1 \subset \mathscr{L}_0$
The hierarchy of grammars and their corresponding recognizers is illustrated
in Fig. 1.2.1.

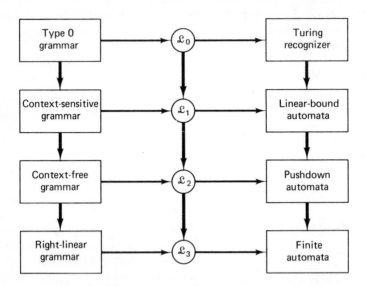

Fig. 1.2.1 The Chomsky hierarchy of grammars and their corresponding languages and recognizers.

EXERCISES 1.2

1. Find the highest type number which can be applied to each of the following
   grammars.
   (a) $G = (\{S, A, B\}, \{a, b, c, d\}, P, S)$, where P consists of the following pro-
        ductions:
        $S \rightarrow AsB$
        $S \rightarrow a$
        $A \rightarrow dA$
        $A \rightarrow acb$
        $A \rightarrow b$
        $ddA \rightarrow ddBC$
   (b) $G = (\{s\}, \{a, b\}, P, S)$, where P consists of the following productions:
        $S \rightarrow Sa$
        $S \rightarrow a$
   (c) $G = (\{S, A\}, \{a, b\}, P, S)$, where P consists of the following productions:
        $S \rightarrow aA$
        $A \rightarrow bS$
        $A \rightarrow a$

2. For each of the following languages, find a grammar which will generate it.

   (a) $L_1 = \{x\$x \mid x \in \{0, 1\}\}$

   (b) $L_2 = \{a^n b \mid n \geq 1\}$

   (c) $L_3 = \{a^{n2} \mid n \geq 1\}$

   (d) $L_4 = \{x \mid x$ contains more 1's than 0's$\}$

3. Prove that the grammar G in Example 1.2.3 does generate the language $\{a^n b^n c^n \mid n \geq 1\}$ as claimed.

4. Show that the language generated by the type 0 grammar in Example 1.2.4 is context-sensitive.

1.3. RIGHT-LINEAR GRAMMARS AND FINITE AUTOMATA

In this section, we will discuss some simple properties of regular languages and define recognizers for this class of languages.

Recall that our notion of a recognizer is a device which can parse sentences generated by a grammar. To motivate the definition of such a device, let us look at the grammar given in Example 1.2.1. A sentence *aabbaa* can be parsed by tracing the derivation sequence (1.2.1) replacing terminals by nonterminals. If the trace ends up with no terminal to be replaced at the end of the sentence, then the sentence is correctly generated. So, what do the nonterminals do in this grammar? They retain some information about the nature of the history of the sentence being generated. Hence, intuitively, a recognizer can be constructed such that its control simply keeps track of which production is to be applied based on the current input and the nonterminal it last remembered. This gives motivation for the following definition.

Definition 1.3.1

A *finite automaton* (or FA for short) is a 5-tuple $M = (Q, \Sigma, \delta, q_0, F)$, where

1. Q is a finite set of *states*.

2. Σ is a finite set of *input symbols*.

3. $\delta: Q \times \Sigma \rightarrow 2^Q$ is the *transition function,* where 2^Q denotes the family of subsets of Q.

4. $q_0 \in Q$ is the initial state of M.

5. $F \subseteq Q$ is the set of *final states* of M.

We say that M is *deterministic* if $\delta(q, a)$ is a singleton set for each $q \in Q$ and $a \in \Sigma$. Otherwise, it is called *nondeterministic*. We say M is *complete* if $\delta(q, a) \neq \emptyset$. Otherwise, it is said to be *incomplete*.

In the context of our general model discussed in Section 1.1, the input head of an FA is read-only and always moves to the right.

It is natural to raise the question as to whether a deterministic processor is in general a less powerful tool than a nondeterministic one. In the case of a finite automaton defined above, this is not the case. This is so since a finite automaton has no additional auxiliary memory other than its states. Therefore, the nondeterminancy, contributed by the finite choices of next states, can always be simulated using a finite amount of memory in a deterministic fashion. This fact will be proven later.

A finite automaton $M = (Q, \Sigma, \delta, q_0, F)$ may be expressed graphically by a directed graph whose vertices are labelled by states in Q, and arcs labelled by elements of Σ such that (q, q') is an arc with label a if $q' \in \delta(q, a)$. All vertices labelled by elements of F are doublecircled, and start state q_0 is indicated by an arrow pointing to it. Such a graph is referred to as the *transition graph* or *state diagram* of M.

Example 1.3.1

Let $M = (\{S, A\}, \{a, b\}, \delta, S, \{S\})$ be a finite automaton such that δ is defined by the following table

δ	a	b
S	S	A
A	A	S

The transition graph of M is given in Fig. 1.3.1.

Definition 1.3.2

Let $M = (Q, \Sigma, \delta, q_0, F)$ be a given finite automaton. A *configuration* of M is a pair (q, w) in $Q \times \Sigma^*$.

A *move* by M is denoted by a binary relation $\vdash_{\overline{M}}$ (or simply $\vdash$ when M is understood) on configurations such that $(q, ax) \vdash (q', x)$ if $q' \in \delta(q, a)$.

We will denote by $\vdash^+$, $\vdash^*$, and $\vdash^k$ the transitive closure, the reflexive and transitive closure, and the k-fold composition of $\vdash$, respectively.

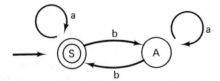

Fig. 1.3.1 Transition graph of a finite automaton.

For the automaton in Example 1.3.1, we see that M reads the tape *aabbaa* in a sequence of moves illustrated in the following:

$$(S,\ aabbaa)\ |\!\!-\!(S,\ abbaa)\ |\!\!-\!(S,bbaa)\ |\!\!-\!(A,baa)\ |\!\!-\!(S,aa)\ |\!\!\stackrel{2}{-}\!(S,\ \wedge)$$

Definition 1.3.3

A string $x \in \Sigma^*$ is said to be *recognizable* (or *acceptable*) by a finite automaton $M = (Q, \Sigma, \delta, q_0, F)$ if and only if $(q_0, x) \mid\!\stackrel{*}{-} (q, \wedge)$, for some $q \in F$. The language recognizable by M, denoted by $L(M)$, is defined to be the set of all strings in Σ^* recognizable by M.

It follows from the above definition that a tape t is recognized by M if starting in initial state, M begins reading the symbol in the leftmost square of t and eventually falls off the right-hand side of tape while entering a final state. Note that a nondeterministic automaton recognizes a sequence x if there *exists* one sequence of moves from the initial configuration (q_0, x) to a terminal configuration $(q, \wedge)$, $q \in F$, although there may be other sequences of moves which will cause x to be rejected.

In order to show that finite automata defined above recognize precisely the class of right-linear languages, we note that our motivation for an FA is based on grammar in Example 1.2.1, which is rather simple since all terminal sequences occurring in its productions are of length 1. It is easily seen that all right-linear grammars can be reduced to a right-linear grammar whose productions are of the form in Example 1.2.1 as stated in the following lemma.

Definition 1.3.4

Two grammars G_1 and G_2 are said to be *equivalent* iff $L(G_1) = L(G_2)$.

Lemma 1.3.1

Every right-linear grammar G is equivalent to a right-linear grammar $G' = [N, \Sigma, P', S']$ whose productions have the following forms:

$$A \longrightarrow aB, \qquad A \longrightarrow a, \qquad S' \longrightarrow \wedge$$

where A, B are nonterminals, and a is a terminal.

Proof: For each production of the form $A \longrightarrow a_1 a_2 \ldots a_n B$, we replace it by productions $\{A \longrightarrow a_1 B_1,\ B_1 \longrightarrow a_2 B_2,\ \ldots,\ B_{n-1} \longrightarrow a_n B\}$, where $B_1, \ldots, B_{n-1}$ are new nonterminal symbols. Similarly, we can replace a production of the form $A \longrightarrow x$, $x \in \Sigma^+$, by a set of productions of the desired forms. ∎

Theorem 1.3.1

A language is right-linear if and only if it is recognizable by some finite automaton.

Proof: Let $M = (Q, \Sigma, \delta, q_0, F)$ be a given finite automaton. Define a regular grammar $G = (Q, \Sigma, P, q_0)$ as follows:

$$q \rightarrow ap, \quad \text{if } p \in \delta(q, a)$$
$$q \rightarrow a, \quad \text{if } q' \in \delta(q, a) \text{ for some } q' \in F$$
$$q_0 \rightarrow \wedge, \quad \text{if } q_0 \in F$$

It is easily proved by induction on the length of input strings that $x \in L(M) \Longleftrightarrow x \in L(G)$. The converse can be proved similarly. ∎

We note that $L(G) = L(M)$ for the grammar G in Example 1.2.1 and the *FA* in M Example 1.3.1.

We will now answer the question we raised about determinism vs. non-determinism.

Theorem 1.3.2

To every finite automaton M there is a deterministic finite automaton M' such that $L(M) = L(M')$.

Proof: Let $M = (Q, \Sigma, \delta, q_0, F)$ be a (nondeterministic) finite automaton. Denote by 2^Q the family of all subsets of Q. We construct a deterministic and complete finite automaton $M' = (2^Q, \Sigma, \delta', \{q_0\}, F')$ where F' consists of all subsets K of Q such that $K \cap F \neq \varnothing$, and δ' is defined by the following rule:

$$\delta'(K, a) = \begin{cases} \{q'\}, & \text{if there exists } q \in K \text{ such that } q' \in \delta(q, a) \\ \varnothing, & \text{if } \delta(q, a) \text{ is not defined, or } K = \varnothing \end{cases}$$

It is easily seen that $L(M) = L(M')$. ∎

Example 1.3.2

The state diagram of an incomplete, nondeterministic finite automaton M is given in Fig. 1.3.2(a). The state diagram of the corresponding complete, deterministic finite automaton M which is constructed according to the procedure given in the proof of Theorem 1.3.2 is shown in Fig. 1.3.2(b).

Although we have given two characterizations of a regular language in terms of a generating device, the grammar, and a recognition device, the automaton, they are in general not very effective means in determining whether a given language is regular or not. A tool is given in the following

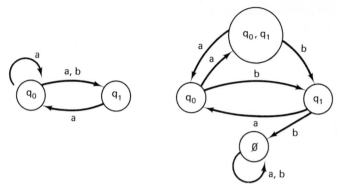

(a) State diagram of an incomplete, nondeterministic finite automaton.

(b) State diagram of a complete, deterministic finite automaton.

Fig. 1.3.2 State diagrams of two finite automata.

theorem for this purpose. The theorem is referred to as a "pumping lemma" which utilizes a property characteristic of right-linear languages: If a sufficiently long string is given in a right-linear language, then one can always select a substring in it which can be repeated (or pumped) indefinitely such that the resulting string is still in the set. The result is immediate by looking at the diagram if Fig. 1.3.3 in which xyz is a string in a right-linear language. Clearly, xy^iz is also in the language, for $i \geq 0$.

Fig. 1.3.3 Illustration of the pumping lemma.

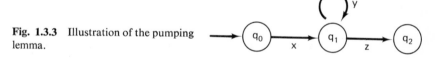

With the above illustration, the following result may be stated without proof.

Theorem 1.3.3

For each regular language L, there exists a nonnegative integer p such that if $w \in L$ and $|w| \geq p$, then w can be written as xyz, where $0 < |y| \leq p$ and $xy^iz \in L$ for all $i \geq 0$.

Example 1.3.3

We will show that the language $L = \{a^nb^n \,|\, n \geq 1\}$ is not regular by utilizing the pumping lemma. Suppose that L is regular. Consider a string $w = a^nb^n$ in L such that $|w| \geq p$. By Theorem 1.3.3, $w = xyz$ such that $y \neq \Lambda$. y can be only in one of the three forms, a^k, b^k, a^ib^j. If y is of either the form

a^k or b^k, then $xy^0z \notin L$. If $y = a^ib^j$, then $xyyz \notin L$. Hence, we have a contradiction and L cannot be regular.

The following result is a direct consequence of Examples 1.2.2 and 1.3.3.

Corollary 1.3.1

The family of right-linear languages is a proper subset of the family of context-free languages.

EXERCISES 1.3

1. For each of the following languages, either give the transition graph of a finite automaton recognizing it, or prove that it is not regular.
   (a) $L_1 = \{x \,|\, x$ contains k more a's than b's$\}$
   (b) $L_2 = \{a^p \,|\, p$ is a prime$\}$
   (c) $L_3 = \{x \,|\, x$ contains kn more a's than b's, for a fixed k and $n \geq 1\}$

2. Show that regular languages are closed under the following operations:
   (a) Boolean operations
   (b) concatenation
   (c) reversal of sentences in the language
   (d) star (if L is regular, so is L^*)

3. Let G be a right-linear grammar. Give an algorithm which can check whether a word x is in $L(G)$ or not.

4. Show that there is an algorithm to decide whether a right-linear language is empty or not.

5. A grammar is said to be *left-linear* if each of its productions is either of the form $A \rightarrow Bx$, or of the form $A \rightarrow y$, for $A, B \in N$, $x \in \Sigma^+$ and $y \in \Sigma^*$. Show that a language is generated by a left-linear grammar if and only if it is generated by a right-linear grammar.

*6. A two-way finite automaton is a FA M in which the input head is allowed to move in both directions, one step at a time, or stay stationary. M accepts a sentence x if the input head of M begins at the leftmost symbol of x and eventually falls off the right-hand side of x in a final state. Show that every two-way FA is equivalent to a (one-way) FA.

7. A k-marker finite automaton (or K-FA for short) is a two-way FA M which has k markers the input head can drop, pick up, or move about on its input tape. (For convenience, it is assumed that the input tape is bounded on both sides by special symbols to prevent the input head from falling off.) We assume here that M has two special states, s_a and s_r, such that it halts upon entering either

*The more difficult exercises are denoted by an asterisk.

one of these two states. Recognition of a sentence is denoted by entering the state s_a. Show that:

(a)   2-FA can recognize the language $\{a_1^n a_2^n \ldots a_k^n \mid n \geq 1\}$

*(b)   Give an intuitive argument for the equivalence of 1-FA to 0-FA.

1.4. REGULAR EXPRESSIONS

An important problem associated with automata theory concerns efficient description of languages.

Consider the transition graph in Fig. 1.3.1. After tracing the graph for a while, we can say that the language it recognizes consists of all strings having an even number of b's and any number of a's. Of course, it will be more difficult to trace a state diagram having a large number of states and even more difficult to describe the language it recognizes. Therefore, it is natural to ask whether (1) there exists a compact way to describe a right-linear language, and (2) there exists a procedure to obtain this compact representation in a systematic fashion.

One way to represent a language is by means of an expression in some language. Looking at transition graphs, we see that in order to develop a formal language of expressions for the representation of right-linear languages, we need the following three types of operations: One operation describes the sequential ordering of paths; one operation represents branching; and one operation denotes looping. These ideas will now be formalized in the following.

Definition 1.4.1

Let A be an alphabet and $A' = \{\varnothing, \wedge, +, \cdot, *, (,)\}$. A *regular expression* over A is a word over $A \cup A'$ defined recursively as follows:

1. $\varnothing$ and $\wedge$ are regular expressions.

2. If α and β are regular expressions, so are $(\alpha + \beta)$, $(\alpha \cdot \beta)$, and $(\alpha)^*$.

3. A regular expression can be obtained only by a finite number of applications of steps (1) and (2) above.

The language represented by a regular expression, denoted by $|\alpha|$, is defined in the following:

1. $\varnothing$ represents the empty set.

2. $|\wedge| = \{\wedge\}$

3. $|(\alpha + \beta)| = |\alpha| \cup |\beta|$, $|(\alpha \cdot \beta)| = |\alpha| \, |\beta|$, $|(\alpha)^*| = |\alpha|^*$

A language L is called *regular* iff $L = |\alpha|$ for some regular expression.

Example 1.4.1

The regular expression 101(101)* describes the set consisting of these strings which can be formed by concatenating one or more 101 component strings, i.e.,

$$|101(101)^*| = \{101\} \cup \{101101\} \cup \{101101101\} \cup \cdots$$

The set of strings over $\{0, 1\}$ which contains exactly two occurrences of 0's can be represented by the regular expression 1*01*01*.

It should be noted here that regular expression representations of a language are not unique. For instance,

1. $|1^*1^*| = |(1^*)^*|$
2. $|(1^*(011)^*| = |(1 + 011)^*|$

However, an algebra of regular expression is beyond the scope of this chapter.

In order to obtain a regular expression systematically from a state diagram, consider again Fig. 1.3.1. The set of strings recognized by this FA consists of all strings which are labels on paths emanating from vertex S to itself. These paths can be broken into two parts, those passing through vertex A and those which do not. Let α_S and α_A denote, respectively, the set of strings representing paths from S to S and S to A, then we have the following system of two simultaneous equations with two unknowns.

$$\alpha_S = \wedge + \alpha_S a + \alpha_A b$$
$$\alpha_A = \alpha_S b + \alpha_A a \tag{1.4.1}$$

The following result will allow us to solve this system of equations.

Lemma 1.4.1

If α, β, and γ are regular expressions over a finite alphabet A and $|\gamma|$ does not contain $\wedge$, then the equation

$$\alpha = \beta + \alpha\gamma \tag{1.4.2}$$

has a unique solution in

$$\alpha = \beta\gamma^*$$

Proof: $\alpha = \beta\gamma^*$ is clearly a solution to (1.4.2). To prove the uniqueness, pick some arbitrary string $\omega \in |\alpha|$. If length $(\omega) = k$, then expand (1.4.2) by repeated substitution of (1.4.2) for α on the right-hand side, we have

$$\alpha = \beta(\wedge + \gamma + \gamma^2 + \ldots + \gamma^k) + \alpha\gamma^{k+1}$$

Since $|\alpha|$ does not contain $\wedge$, the shortest word in $|\alpha\gamma^{k+1}|$ is of length at least $k + 1$, hence $\omega \in |\beta(\wedge + \gamma + \ldots + \gamma^k)| \subseteq |\beta\gamma^*|$.

Conversely, if $\omega \in |\beta\gamma|$ then $\omega \in |\beta(\wedge + \gamma + \ldots + \gamma^i)|$ for some i. Hence, the solution (1.4.3) is unique. ∎

Example 1.4.2

Using Lemma 1.4.1, we can obtain the solution of (1.4.1). First we obtain the solution $\alpha_S ba^*$ for the equation:

$$\alpha_A = \alpha_S b + \alpha_A a$$

Substituting the solution into the second equation, we have

$$\alpha_S = \wedge + \alpha_S a + \alpha_S ba^* b$$
$$= \wedge + \alpha_S(a + ba^* b)$$

One more application of Lemma 1.4.1 gives the unique solution

$$(a + ba^* b)^*$$

The following result can be proved easily with the aid of Example 1.4.2 and Lemma 1.4.1, and hence will be stated without proof.

Lemma 1.4.2

Every right-linear language is regular.

The converse of the Lemma 1.4.2 is also true. Although we will not prove this result here, the following example will provide an instance of the so called "top-down" design technique which systematically transforms a regular expression α to the state diagram of a FA M such that $L(M) = |\alpha|$.

Example 1.4.3

Consider the regular expression $\alpha = (11 + 01(10)^*)^*$. We first obtain a "crude" extended transition graph in Fig. 1.4.1(a) recognizing $\alpha = \alpha_1^*$, where $\alpha_1 = 11 + 01(10)^*$, with the aid of some "empty transitions," i.e., arcs labelled by $\wedge$. In later steps, these empty transitions will be deleted.

The next step is to break α_1 into $11 + \alpha_2$, where $\alpha_2 = 01(10)^*$ and expand the graph in Fig. 1.4.1(a) appropriately into that in Fig. 1.4.1(b). Repeating the same procedure on α_2, etc., we reach the fully expanded graph in Fig. 1.4.1(d). Finally, the arcs with $\wedge$ labels are deleted to obtain a transition graph in Fig. 1.4.1(e) which recognizes $|\alpha|$.

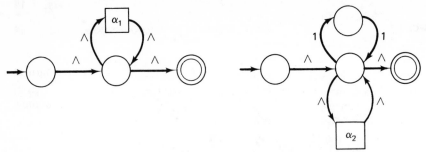

(a) Extended transition graph recognizing $\alpha = \alpha_1^*$, where $\alpha_1 = 11 + 01\ (10)^*$.

(b) Extended transition graph recognizing $\alpha = (11 + \alpha_2)^*$, where $\alpha_2 = 01\ (10)^*$.

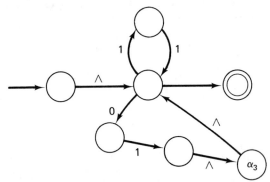

(c) Extended transition graph recognizing $\alpha = (11 + 01\ \alpha_3)^*$, where $\alpha_3 = (10)^*$.

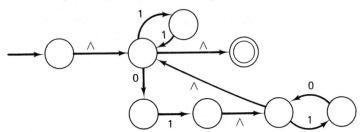

(d) Extended transition graph recognizing α.

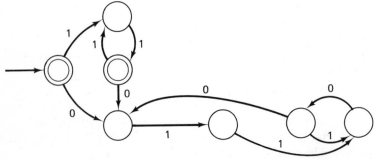

(e) Transition graph recognizing α.

Fig. 1.4.1 Diagrammatical illustration of "top-down" design technique to construct transition graphs from regular expressions.

It is easily seen that the design techniques illustrated in Example 1.4.3 can be applied to any regular expression. We therefore state the following result without proof.

Theorem 1.4.1

A language is right-linear if and only if it is regular.

EXERCISES 1.4

1. For each of the following sets, find the transition graph of FA which recognizes the set, and obtain the regular expression representing the language.
   (a) The set of strings over the alphabet {0, 1} which begins and ends with a 0, and every 1 is immediately followed by at least three 0's.
   (b) The set of strings over the alphabet {0, 1} each of which consists of at least two 1's and five 0's.

2. For each of the following regular expressions, find a FA that recognizes the corresponding language.
   (a) $1(0 + 1)^* 101$
   (b) $1(1010^* + 1(010)^*1)^*0$
   (c) $(11 + (00)^*01)^*1$

3. Two regular expressions α and β are said to be *equal*, denoted by $\alpha = \beta$, if $|\alpha| = |\beta|$. Show that the following identities hold.
   (a) $\alpha + \alpha = \alpha$
   (b) $\alpha(\beta + \gamma) = \alpha\beta + \alpha\gamma$
   (c) $(\alpha^*)^* = \alpha^*$
   (d) $\alpha^* = \wedge + \alpha\alpha^*$
   (e) $(\alpha\beta)^*\alpha = \alpha(\beta\alpha)^*$
   (f) $(\alpha + \beta)^* = (\alpha^*\beta^*)^* = (\alpha^* + \beta^*)^*$
   (g) Apply (d) and (f) to show that

$$\wedge + 1^*(011)^*(1^*(011)^*)^* = (1 + 011)^*$$

4. Prove Lemma 1.4.2.

5. Prove Theorem 1.4.1.

1.5. ADDITIONAL PROPERTIES OF FINITE AUTOMATA AND REGULAR LANGUAGES

The concept of equivalence between automata and closure properties of regular languages will be discussed in this section.

Sometimes there are many finite automata recognizing the same languages. Consider the FA M specified by its transition graph in Fig. 1.5.1(a). This FA recognizes precisely the same language as the FA M of Example 1.3.1 whose transition graph is redrawn in Fig. 1.5.1(b) for convenience. How are these two FA related? We note that states q_0 and q_1 in Fig. 1.5.1(a) behave very similarly in that for any $x \in \Sigma^*$, if $(q_0, x) \vdash^* (q, \wedge)$ and $(q_1, x) \vdash^* (q', \wedge)$, then q is a final state if and only if q' is a final state. States q_2, q_3 and A are related in the same way. This example gives motivation for the following definition.

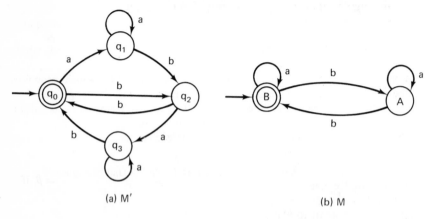

(a) M'   (b) M

Fig. 1.5.1   Transition graph of two finite automata.

Definition 1.5.1

Let $M = (Q, \Sigma, \delta, q_0, F)$ and $M' = (Q', \Sigma, \delta', q_0', F')$ to two FA over the same alphabet Σ. The states $q \in Q$ and $q' \in Q'$ are said to be *equivalent* if and only if for any sequence $x \in \Sigma^*$, if $(q, x) \vdash^* (q_1, \wedge)$ and $(q', x) \vdash^* (q_1', x)$, then $q_1 \in F$ if and only if $q_1' \in F'$.

M and M' are said to be *equivalent* if and only if for each state $q \in Q$ there corresponds an equivalent state $q' \in Q'$, and for each state $q_1' \in Q'$, there corresponds an equivalent state $q \in Q$. M and M' are called *initial-equivalent* if and only if q_0 and q_0' are equivalent.

It follows immediately from the previous definition that M and M' are initial-equivalent if and only if they recognize precisely the same language.

Example 1.5.1

Consider the FA in Fig. 1.5.1. States q_0, q_1 and B are equivalent. This means that for any given input string, the computation sequence started from either q_0 or q_1 is identical whether states in the corresponding portions are final states or not. Thus, as far as recognition goes, q_0 and q_1 are *indistinguishable*. Similarly, states q_2, q_3, and A are equivalent. Hence, M and M' are equivalent.

We observe from the previous example that M can be obtained from M' by collapsing indistinguishable states.

Definition 1.5.2

A FA $M = (Q, \Sigma, \delta, q_0, F)$ is called *initial-connected* if and only if for each state $q \in Q$, there exists an input sequence x such that $(q_0, x) \vdash^* (q, \wedge)$.

Example 1.5.2

The FA specified in Fig. 1.5.2 is not initial-connected since q_2 is not reachable from q_0.

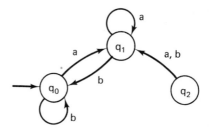

Fig. 1.5.2 An example of a FA which is not initial-connected.

Theorem 1.5.1

Corresponding to each FA $M = (Q, \Sigma, \delta, q_0, F)$, there is a unique (up to relabelling of states) FA $M' = (Q', \Sigma, \delta', q_0', F')$ called the *reduced* FA of M, such that

1. M' is equivalent to M.
2. If M'' is equivalent to M, then $\#(Q') \leq \#(Q'')$.
3. M' is initial-connected.

Proof: We will only prove (1) here since (2) and (3) are fairly straightforward. We construct the state set of M' by grouping all indistinguishable states of M by the following procedure.

Define a sequence of relations R_i on Q as follows.

1. $R_0 = \{(q_1, q_2) \mid$ either q_1 and q_2 are both in F or both not in $F\}$.
2. If R_i has been defined, then define R_{i+1} as follows.
$$R_{i+1} = \{(q_1, q_2) \mid (q_1, q_2) \in R_i \text{ and for each } a \in \Sigma$$
$$\delta(q_1, a) \in F \text{ if and only if } \delta(q_2, a) \in F$$

Let R be the relation R_j, where j is the smallest number such that $R_j = R_{j+1}$. Clearly such a j exists since Q is a finite set. It is also easily seen that each R_i is an equivalence relation. Let the equivalence classes of R be $[q_1]$, . . ., $[q_k]$, where q_i is any element in the equivalence class $[q_i]$.

Further, R has the property that for any q_1, $q_2 \in [q]$, and $a \in \Sigma$, $\delta(q_1, a) \in [q^*]$ if and only if $\delta(q_2, a) \in [q^*]$. This property, referred to as the *substitution property*, allows us to define a transition function on these equivalence classes to obtain M' as follows.

Construct M' such that $Q' = \{[q_1] \ldots [q_k]\}$. $F' = \{[q] \mid [q] \cap F \neq 0\}$. $q_0' = [q_0]$, and δ' is defined in the following.

$$\delta'([q], a) = [\delta(q, a)] \tag{1.5.1}$$

Clearly, (1.5.1) is well defined by the substitution property. Furthermore, M' is equivalent to M through the correspondence between states q and $[q]$.   ∎

Example 1.5.3

Let M be a FA specified in Fig. 1.5.3(a). Apply the procedure given in the proof of Theorem 1.5.1. The partitions of equivalence relation R_0, R_1, and R_2 are:

$$P_{R_0} = \left\{ \overline{q_0, q_1},\ \overline{q_2, q_3, q_4, q_5} \right\}$$

$$P_{R_1} = \left\{ \overline{q_0, q_1},\ \overline{q_2, q_4},\ \overline{q_3, q_5} \right\}$$

$$P_{R_2} = \left\{ \overline{q_0, q_1},\ \overline{q_2, q_4},\ \overline{q_3, q_5} \right\}$$

Hence $R = R_1$ and the resulting reduced automaton is specified in Fig. 1.5.3(b).

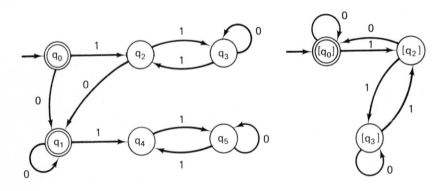

(a) Transition graph of M.   (b) Transition graph of M_R.

Fig. 1.5.3 Illustration of the reduced automaton.

An interesting question related to the equivalence concept is whether there is a decision procedure to tell whether two given automata are equivalent. The answer is affirmative. In fact, one can prove this result by observing that we can test the equivalence of two states by feeding input sequences to the automata and compare the resulting induced state sequences. Now, just as in the case of the pumping lemma (Theorem 1.3.3), if a test sequence is too long, the resulting state sequence will contain at least one state occurring more than once. Hence, a shorter test sequence will do the job. We will leave the proof of the following theorem as an exercise for the reader.

Theorem 1.5.2

There is an algorithm which can decide whether two states of a given automaton with n states ($n \geq 2$) are equivalent by testing only those input sequences of length less than or equal to $n - 1$.

Another natural question concerns the nature of the class of regular languages. In other words, what this class of languages consists of.

Theorem 1.5.3

The class of all regular languages over an alphabet is the smallest class which contains all finite languages and is closed under the operations of union, intersection, complementation, concatenation, and star (the transitive closure of concatenation).

Proof: Certainly all finite languages are regular. Let L_1 and L_2 be two regular languages recognized by $M_1 = (Q_1, \Sigma, \delta_1, q_0^{(1)}, F_1)$ and $M_2 = (Q_2, \Sigma, \delta_2, q_0^{(2)}, F_2)$, respectively. Then the complement $\bar{L}_1$ of L_1 is recognized by $\bar{M}_1 = (Q_1, \Sigma, \delta_1, q_0^{(1)}, Q_1 - F_1)$ and hence is regular. $L_1 \cap L_2$ is recognized by the automaton $M = (Q_1 \times Q_2, \Sigma, \delta, (q_0^{(1)}, q_0^{(2)}), F_1 \times F_2)$, where

$$\delta((q_1, q_2), a) = (\delta_1(q_1, a), \delta_2(q_2, a)).$$

Hence, $L_1 \cap L_2$ is regular. Since $L_1 \cup L_2 = (\overline{\bar{L}_1 \cap \bar{L}_2})$, we see that $L_1 \cup L_2$ is also regular.

Let α_1 and α_2 be the respective regular expressions representing L_1 and L_2, respectively. Then $L_1 L_2 = |\alpha_1 \alpha_2|$ and $L_1^* = |\alpha_1^*|$ and hence are regular.

Since every regular language is representable as a regular expression, we conclude that the theorem holds. ∎

EXERCISES 1.5

1. Find the reduced automaton of an FA specified in Fig. 1.5.4.

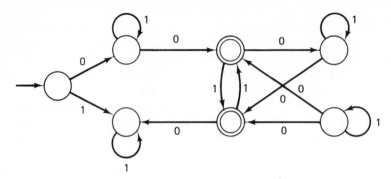

Fig. 1.5.4   Transition graph of a FA.

2. Complete the proof of Theorem 1.5.1.

3. Prove Theorem 1.5.2.

4. Show that there is an algorithm for deciding the equivalence between a state q in a FA with m states and a state q' in a FA with n states by testing input sequences of length less than or equal to $m + n - 1$.

5. If $x = a_1 a_2 \ldots a_n$ is a sequence, denote by x^{-1} the sequence $a_n a_{n+1} \ldots a_1$. Show that L is regular if and only if $L^{-1} = \{x^{-1} \mid x \in L\}$ is regular.

1.6.   CONTEXT-FREE GRAMMARS AND PUSHDOWN AUTOMATA

In this section, we will explore the properties of context-free languages and their corresponding recognizers.

We have seen in Section 1.2 that parsing of an English sentence can be expressed in terms of a tree. Such graphical representation is a powerful aid to the understanding of syntactic structures of context-free grammar and will be formalized in the following.

Definition 1.6.1

Let $G = (N, \Sigma, P, S)$ be a context-free grammar. A *derivation tree D* of G is a pair (T, γ), where T is an oriented, rooted tree (V, R) and $\gamma: V \rightarrow N\Sigma \cup \{\wedge\}$ such that

1. $\gamma(v_0) = S$, if v_0 is the root of T.
2. If v is a vertex such that $(v, u) \in R$ for some u, then $\gamma(v) \in N$.
3. If $\gamma(v) = A$, and $v_1, v_2, \ldots, v_n$ are immediate successors of v, in order from left to right, such that $\gamma(v_i) = A_i$, then $A \rightarrow A_1 A_2 \ldots A_n$ is a production in P.

If D is a derivation tree, the *frontier* of D is defined to be the strings of symbols, from left to right, of these vertices of D which has out-degree zero.

Example 1.6.1

Consider the grammar $G = \{\{S, A, B\}, \{0, 1\}, P, S\}$, where P consists of the following productions:

$S \rightarrow 0B$

$S \rightarrow 1A$ $B \rightarrow 0BB$

$A \rightarrow 0$ $B \rightarrow 1S$

$A \rightarrow 0S$ $B \rightarrow 1$

$A \rightarrow 1AA$

A derivation tree whose frontier is 001101 is given in Fig. 1.6.1.

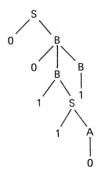

Fig. 1.6.1   A derivation tree.

The following result is intuitively clear and hence is stated without proof.

Theorem 1.6.1

Let $G = (N, \Sigma, P, S)$ be a context-free grammar. Then $S \xRightarrow{*} \alpha$ if and only if there is a derivation tree D of G such that frontier of D is α.

The following straightforward simplifications of context-free grammar will be of considerable aid.

Theorem 1.6.2

Let L be a nonempty language generated by a CFG G', there is an equivalent grammar $G = (N, \Sigma, P, S)$ such that for nonterminals A and B in N,

1. There is a string $x \in \Sigma^*$ such that $A \xRightarrow{*} x$.
2. There exists a derivation

$$S \xRightarrow{*} xAz \xRightarrow{*} xyz$$

where, x, y, and z are in Σ^*.

3. P does not contain any productions of the form $A \rightarrow B$.
4. If $A \rightarrow \wedge$ is a production in P, then $A = S$.

It was shown in the previous section that the language $\{0^n 1^n \mid n \geq 1\}$ is context-free but not regular. The reason that a finite automaton cannot parse sentences of context-free language is that it cannot keep track of its position in a derivation tree in general. The derivation trees for a regular grammar look essentially like a string. However, this is not the case for context-free grammar due to the following property.

Definition 1.6.2

A CFG is said to be *self-embedding* if there exists a nonterminal A and nonempty sequences α and β such that $A \overset{*}{\Rightarrow} \alpha A \beta$.

Clearly, a regular grammar in the form stated in Lemma 1.3.1 cannot be self-embedding. Indeed, it is the property of self-embedding which separates context-free grammars from regular grammars as stated in the following theorem.

Theorem 1.6.3

A context-free grammar G is regular if and only if G is not self-embedding.

Proof: It suffices to show that if a CFG $G = (N, \Sigma, P, S)$ is not self-embedding, then it is regular. We consider two cases.

1. For each $A \in N$, $A \overset{*}{\Rightarrow} \alpha S \beta$, for some $\alpha, \beta \in (N \cup \Sigma)^*$. We note that every production in P containing nonterminals on the right-hand side must be in one of the following forms:
   (1) $A \longrightarrow xBy$,
   (2) $A \longrightarrow xB$, and
   (3) $A \longrightarrow By$, where $A, B \in N$ and $x, y \in (\Sigma \cup N)^+$ Clearly, productions of type (1) or type (2) and type (3) together cannot be allowed since it will violate the non-self-embedding assumption. Hence, G must be either left-linear or right-linear and therefore, is regular.
   2. Assume now that there is a nonterminal A such that A can never reach S.

If $\#(N) = 1$, then $L(G)$ is clearly regular. Assume that $L(G)$ is regular for $\#(N) = k \geq 1$. Let $G' = (N', \Sigma, P', S')$ be a CFG satisfying the assumption such that $\#(N') = k + 1$. Construct two grammars $G_1 = (N - \{S'\}, \Sigma, P_1, A)$, where P_1 is obtained from P' by deleting all productions containing S', and $G_2 = (N - \{A\}, \Sigma \cup \{A\}, P_2, S')$, where P_2 is obtained from P' by deleting all productions with A on the left-hand side. We see that both $L(G_1)$ and $L(G_2)$ are regular either by case 1 or by the inductive hypothesis. Let M_1 and M_2 be the corresponding automata recognizing $L(G_1)$ and $L(G_2)$, respectively. We construct another automaton M such that the transition graph is obtained from the transition graph G_2 of M_2 by replacing each subgraph in G_2 of the form

by the graph

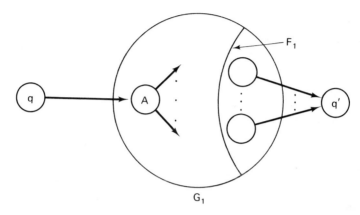

In other words, the arc with label A is replaced by the transition graph G_1 of M_1. Clearly, the resulting graph is the transition graph of some automaton M such that $L(M) = L(G')$. ∎

As a consequence of the previous theorem, it is necessary to add auxiliary memory to a finite automaton before it can parse sentences generated by a CFG. To motivate for the type of such additional memory, let us look at the derivation tree for the sequence 001101 in Fig. 1.6.1. A derivation for this sequence is given in the following.

$$S \Rightarrow 0B \Rightarrow 0BB \Rightarrow 001SB \Rightarrow 0011AB \Rightarrow 00110B \Rightarrow 001101 \qquad (1.6.1)$$

We note that in the above derivation, the nonterminal being replaced in each step has no nonterminal to its left. This is usually referred to as a *leftmost* derivation. Clearly, if a sentence has a derivation, then it has a leftmost derivation.

How does one parse the sequence 001101 in the context of the given grammar? One way to do it is to trace a leftmost derivation through a derivation tree by observing, for example, that an input symbol 0 may be generated by the production $S \Rightarrow 0B$ and proceed in this fashion down the tree. This technique is usually referred to as *top-down* parsing. Note that using the top-down procedure, we need to remember certain nonterminals occurring in the middle of the tree before converting them to terminals. In the derivation given in

(1.6.1), the second B in the third step needs to be remembered. It is important to observe that in the top-down parsing, the first nonterminal to be remembered is the last one in the list of remembered nonterminals to be converted into a terminal sequence. With this observation, a natural candidate for the auxiliary memory is the device used in a cafeteria for stacking plates on a spring. The main characteristic of such a stack is "first in-last out;" i.e., plates can only be removed at the top of the stack.

Definition 1.6.3

A pushdown automaton (or PDA for short) is a 6-tuple $P = (Q, \Sigma, \Gamma, \delta, q_0, Z_0)$, where

1. K is a finite set of *states*.
2. Σ is a finite set of *input symbols*.
3. Γ is a finite set of *stack symbols*.
4. $\delta: Q \times (\Sigma \cup \{\wedge\}) \times \Gamma \rightarrow$ finite subsets of $Q \times \Gamma^*$ is called the *transition function* of P.
5. $q_0 \in Q$ is the *initial state* of P.
6. $z_0 \in \Gamma$ is the *start symbol* of the pushdown stack.

A PDA is said to be *deterministic* if

1. For each q and Z, $\delta(q, \wedge, Z) \neq \varnothing$ implies that $\delta(q, a, Z) = \varnothing$ for all $a \in \Sigma$.
2. $\delta(q, a, Z)$ contains at most one element for any (q, a, Z) in $Q \times \{\Sigma \cup \{\wedge\}\} \times \Gamma$.

It follows from the previous definition that a pushdown automaton is a one-way (nondeterministic) automaton consisting of a one-way infinite pushdown stack as depicted in Fig. 1.6.2.

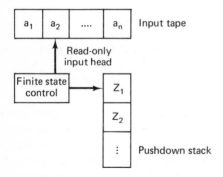

Fig. 1.6.2   A pushdown automaton.

We note that from the definition it is possible for a pushdown automaton to manipulate its pushdown stack without advancing its input head.

Definition 1.6.4

Let $P = (Q, \Sigma, \Gamma, \delta, q_0, Z_0)$ be a pushdown automaton. A *configuration* of P is a triple (q, x, α) in $Q \times \Sigma^* \times \Gamma^*$, where q denotes the current state, x the unread portion of input tape such that the leftmost symbol of x is under the input head, and α is the content of pushdown stack from top to bottom.

A *move* of P is represented by a binary relation $\vert_{\overline{P}}$ ($\vert\!-$ if P is understood) on configurations such that

$$(q, ax, Z\alpha) \vert\!- (q', x, \gamma\alpha)$$

if $(q', \gamma) \in \delta(q, a, Z)$, for $q \in Q$, $a \in \Sigma$, $x \in \Sigma^*$, $Z \in \Gamma$ and $\gamma\alpha \in \Gamma^*$.

If $a = \wedge$, then the input head will not advance. If $\gamma = \wedge$, then Z is popped (or erased).

A string $x \in \Sigma^*$ is *recognizable* by P if and only if

$$(q_0, x, Z_0) \vert^{*}\!- (q, \wedge, \wedge)$$

The language recognizable by P, denoted by $L(P)$, is the set of all recognizable strings of P.

It should be noted here that recognition by PDA via a final set of states, as in the case of FA, can also be defined and is equivalent to the one defined above (see Exercise 1.6.6).

We are now ready to show that every CFL is recognizable by a PDA and that all PDA recognizable languages are context-free.

The way a PDA can parse a string in a CFL is to perform a leftmost derivation of its input string in its pushdown stack.

Theorem 1.6.4

Let $G = (N, \Sigma, P, S)$ be a CFG. Then we can construct a PDA P such that $L(G) = L(P)$.

Proof: Construct $P = (\{q\}, \Sigma, N \cup \Sigma, \delta, q, S)$ such that δ is defined as follows:

1. If $A \to \alpha$ is in P, then $(q, \alpha) \in \delta(q, \wedge, A)$.
2. $\delta(q, a, a) = \{(q, \wedge)\}$ for all a in Σ.
3. $\delta(q, a, Z) = \varnothing$, otherwise. ∎

Note that if $x \in L(G)$, then there exists a leftmost derivation for x in G, and hence all symbols in x will find a match with the topmost symbol of the pushdown stack in the right order. This of course implies that when the last match occurs, the input head will fall off the right-hand side of the tape while the pushdown stack becomes empty.

Example 1.6.2

Let G be the grammar given in Example 1.6.1. The corresponding PDA P is specified by δ defined below.

$$\delta(q, \wedge, S) = \{(q, 0B), (q, 1A)\}$$
$$\delta(q, \wedge, A) = \{(q, 0), (q, 0S), (q, 1AA)\}$$
$$\delta(q, \wedge, B) = \{(q, 1), (q, 1S), (q, 0BB)\}$$
$$\delta(q, 0, 0) = \delta(q, 1, 1) = \{(q, \wedge)\}$$

The following moves indicate how the sequence 0011101 is recognized by the PDA P.

$$(q, 001101, S) \vdash (q, 001101, 0B) \vdash (q, 01101, B)$$
$$\vdash (q, 01101, 0BB) \vdash (q, 1101, BB) \vdash (q, 1101, 1SB)$$
$$\vdash (q, 101, SB) \vdash (q, 101, 1AB) \vdash (Q, 01, AB)$$
$$\vdash (q, 01, 0B) \vdash (q, 1, B) \vdash (q, 1, 1) \vdash (q, \wedge, \wedge)$$

We note in the PDA P constructed in Theorem 1.6.4 has only one state. In this case, the parameter of state is discounted and a PDA can parse a string in much the same fashion as a finite automaton. This is evident from the construction in the following theorem.

Lemma 1.6.1

If P is a one-state PDA, then $L(P)$ is context-free.

Proof: Let $P = (\{q\}\ \Sigma,\ \Gamma,\ \delta,\ q,\ Z_0)$. Construct a CFG $G = (\Gamma',\ \Sigma,\ P,\ Z_0)$ such that $A' \rightarrow aA'_1 \ldots A'_k$ is a production in P if $(q, A_1 \ldots A_k) \in \delta(q, a, A)$. Note that if $k = 0$, then $A' \rightarrow a$ is a production. ∎

Clearly, every PDA is equivalent to a one-state PDA, since it is possible to keep a record of state information in the pushdown stack as shown in the following theorem.

Lemma 1.6.2

Every PDA P is equivalent to a one-state PDA P' in the sense that $L(P) = L(P')$.

Proof: Let $P = (Q, \Sigma, \Gamma, \delta, q_0, Z_0)$. Construct another PDA $P' = (\{q^*\}, \Sigma, Q \times \Gamma, \delta', q^*, (q_0, z_0))$ such that whenever $(q', A_1 \ldots A_K) \in \delta(q, a, z)$, then $(q^*, (q_1, A_1)) \ldots (q_k, A_k)) \in \delta'(q^*, a, (q, z))$, where $q_1, \ldots, q_k$ range over Q. ∎

It should be noted that the construction in Lemma 1.6.2 works because of the nondeterministic nature of a PDA.

As an immediate consequence of Lemmas 1.6.1 and 1.6.2, and Theorem 1.6.4, we have the following theorem.

Theorem 1.6.5

A language L is context-free if and only if it is recognizable by some PDA.

Again, it is proper now to ask whether these are abstract tools which would aid in deciding effectively whether a string is context-free or not. It turns out that context-free languages also possess properties like that of regular languages as described in the next section.

EXERCISES 1.6

1. Prove Theorem 1.4.1.

2. Prove Theorem 1.4.2.

3. Show that in a given CFG G, if $S \overset{*}{\Rightarrow} x$, then there is a leftmost derivation of x in G.

4. Find a self-embedding CFG.

5. Show that every CFL over an alphabet consisting of only one symbol is regular.

6. Let $P = (Q, \Sigma, \Gamma, \delta, q_0, Z_0)$ and let $F \subseteq Q$. A sentence $x \in \Sigma^*$ is said to be recognizable by P with respect to F, if $(q_0, x, Z_0) \vdash^* (q, \wedge, \alpha)$, for some $q \in F$. Let L_F (P) denote all sentences recognizable by P with respect to F. Show that for each PDA P, there is a PDA P' such that $L(P) = L_F(P')$, and vice versa.

7. Construct PDA recognizing each of the following languages:
   (a) $L_1 = \{x\$x^{-1} \,|\, x \in \{0, 1\}^*\}$
   (b) $L_2 = \{x \,|\, x \text{ consists of an equal number of 1's and 0's}\}$
   (c) $L_3 = \{a^i b^j \,|\, j > i\}$

8. Give an algorithm to determine if the language generated by a CFG is empty.

9. Show that the class of CFL's are closed under the operations of union, and intersection with regular sets. However, it is not closed under intersection and complementation.

1.7. PUMPING LEMMA FOR CONTEXT-FREE LANGUAGE

The pumping lemma for regular languages can be extended to the context-free case. The proof of this lemma is simplified using a normal form for context-free grammar.

Theorem 1.7.1   Chomsky normal form

Any context-free language can be generated by a grammar in which all productions are of the form

$$A \to BC \quad \text{or} \quad A \to a \quad \text{or} \quad S \to \wedge$$

Proof: Let G be a CFG. We may assume, by Theorem 1.6.1, that G does not contain any production of the form $A \to B$. Let P' denote a new set of productions which include all productions of desired form in P. If $A \to A_1 \ldots A_k$ is a production in P for $k > 2$, then first introduce a new nonterminal A'_i for any terminal A_i and replace $A \to A_1 \ldots A_k$ by the productions $A \to A_1 \ldots A_{i-1} A'_i A_{i+1} \ldots A_k$ and $A'_i \to A_i$.

Now, the only nondesirable productions left are of the form $A \to B_1 \ldots B_j$, where each B_i is a nonterminal (old or newly introduced). In this case, we introduce new nonterminals $C_1, C_2, \ldots, C_{j-2}$ and replace $A \to B_1 \ldots B_j$ by the set of productions

$$A \to B_1 C_1, \qquad C_1 \to B_2 C_2, \qquad \ldots, \qquad C_{j-2} \to B_{j-1} B_j$$

Clearly, the new grammar generates the same language as G.   ∎

Example 1.7.1

Let G be the context-free grammar given in Example 1.6.1. An equivalent Chomsky normal form grammar has the productions

$S \to 0B$ $B \to B'B_1$
$S \to 1A$ $B_1 \to BB$
$A \to 0$ $B' \to 0$
$A \to 0S$ $B \to 1S$
$A \to A'A_1$ $B \to 1$
$A_1 \to AA$
$A' \to 1$

To motivate the following results, let us consider a CFG G in Chomsky normal form having the following productions.

$S \to BC$ $S \to a$
$B \to CS$ $B \to b$
$C \to SB$ $C \to c$

A derivation tree for the sequence $cbbcbab$ is given in Fig. 1.7.1(a). We observe that in the path indicated by thick edges the nonterminal C occurs twice (one of the occurrences is as the immediate predecessor of the terminal vertex c). Consider the subtree with the root labeled by the first occurrence of C shown in Fig. 1.7.1(b). It is easily seen that no matter how many times this subtree is duplicated, the resulting tree is still a derivation tree of the grammar since all we have done is to apply the valid productions repeatedly.

This subtree, duplicated twice, is given in Fig. 1.7.1(c). We now state the "pumping" lemma for context-free language.

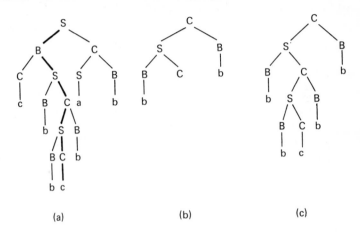

Fig. 1.7.1   Derivation trees.

Theorem 1.7.2

For any context-free language L, there exists two positive integers p and q such that if $z \in L$ and $|z| > p$, then z can be written as $z = uvwxy$, where $|vwx| \leq q$ and $|vx| > 0$. Furthermore, for each $i > 0$, uv^iwx^iy is in L.

Proof: Let $G = (N, \Sigma, P, S)$ be a grammar in Chomsky normal form generating L. If $\#(N) = k$, then let $p = 2^{k-1}$ and $q = 2^k$. Let $z \in L$ such that $|z| > p$. Then a path P of maximum order must contain two vertices v_1 and v_2 having the same label, say A, in a derivation tree T for z and the order of path from one of the two vertices, say v_1, to the terminal vertex is at most $k + 1$. This is illustrated in Fig. 1.7.2. Let T_1 and T_2 denote subtrees of T

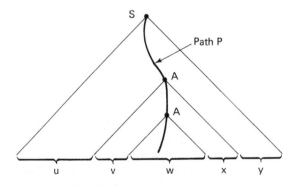

Fig. 1.7.2   A derivation tree for illustrating the proof of Theorem 1.7.1.

with roots v_1 and v_2, respectively. If z' and w are the frontiers of T_1 and T_2, respectively, then z' can be written as vwx (see Fig. 1.7.2) since the first productions used in the derivation of z' must be of the form $A \to BC$. Hence, we must have $A \overset{*}{\Rightarrow} vAx$ and $A \overset{*}{\Rightarrow} vwx$, where $|vwx| \leq q$. But it follows that $A \overset{*}{\Rightarrow} v^i w x^i$. Hence, $S \overset{*}{\Rightarrow} uAy \overset{*}{\Rightarrow} uv^i w x^i y$, for $i \geq 0$. ∎

Example 1.7.2

We will use Theorem 1.7.1 to show that the language $L = \{a^n b^n c^n \,|\, n \geq 1\}$ is not context-free. Assume that L is context-free, then let p and q be the integers given in Theorem 1.7.1. Consider the sequence $z = a^q b^q c^q$. Then z can be written as $uvwxy$. Since $|vwx| < q$, it is not possible that vx can have all three occurrences of a, b, and c. This implies that uwy will have either q a's or q c's but not enough b's. Hence, $uwy \notin L$.

The following result is a direct consequence of Examples 1.2.3 and 1.7.2.

Theorem 1.7.3

The class of languages generated by context-free grammars is a proper subset of that generated by context-sensitive grammars.

EXERCISES 1.7

1. Convert the CFG specified by the following production rules into Chomsky normal form.

$S \to 0S1$	$A \to 1B0$
$S \to 0SB$	$A \to SB$
$S \to 0$	$B \to 1BA$
$S \to 1A0$	$B \to SA$

2. Use Theorem 1.7.1 to show that each of the following languages is not context-free.
   (a) $L_1 = \{a^p \,|\, p \text{ is a prime}\}$
   (b) $L_2 = \{a^{n^2} \,|\, n \geq 1\}$

1.8. ADDITIONAL PROPERTIES OF PUSHDOWN AUTOMATA AND CONTEXT-FREE LANGUAGES

The nonequivalence between deterministic and nondeterministic PDA, the concept of ambiguity of languages, and closure properties of context-free languages will be discussed in this section.

Intuitively, a nondeterministic finite automaton, though having more choices for next states, is confined to finite amount of memory and hence can be "simulated" deterministically. In the case of PDA, the amount of memory is not finite, but is linearly proportional to the length of the input tapes. Therefore, freedom of choices at each move could conceivably accumulate to something nontrivial. As an example, consider the language $L = \{\omega\omega^{-1} | \omega \in \{0, 1\}^*\}$. It is easily seen that L is recognizable by a PDA. However, it is intuitively clear that L probably cannot be recognized by a deterministic PDA because it does not have the ability to guess whether it has reached the "center" of the input tape. On the other hand, the language $L' = \{\omega\$\omega^{-1} | \omega \in \{0, 1\}^*\}$ is clearly recognizable by a deterministic PDA. A neat way to prove that nondeterministic PDA is more powerful than deterministic PDA is by means of the closure properties of CFL as shown in the later part of this section.

The following result can be proved in a fashion similar to the proof of Theorem 1.5.3 and hence is stated without proof.

Theorem 1.8.1

The class of context-free languages is closed under the operations of union, concatenation, and star.

Theorem 1.8.2

The class of context-free languages is not closed under intersection and complementation.

Proof: The languages $L_1 = \{a^n b^n c^i | n \geq 1$ and $i \geq 0\}$ and $L_2 = \{a^j b^n c^n | j \geq 0$ and $n \geq 1\}$ are context-free. But $L_1 \cap L_2 = \{a^n b^n c^n | n \geq 1\}$ is context-sensitive by Example 1.7.2. Hence CFL's are not closed under intersection.

Since $L_1 \cap L_2 = \overline{\bar{L_1} \cup \bar{L_2}}$ and CFL's are closed under union but not intersection, we must conclude that CFL's do not close under complementation. ∎

We would like to show that the class of language recognized by deterministic PDA is closed under complementation. This can be done by interchanging the final states and nonfinal states of a given deterministic PDA if the following two problems can be taken care of. The first problem comes from the fact that after reading all of the input tape and in a final state, the PDA uses a number of moves on $\wedge$ input to reach a nonfinal state. It is intuitively clear that one can always find an equivalent PDA in which no $\wedge$ input is allowed to use when in final states. The second problem comes from the fact that the PDA may never finish reading the whole input tape either because it is in a configuration in which no move is possible or it makes an infinite number of moves on $\wedge$ input. One can take care of the first case by creating a "dead" state and forcing the PDA to finish reading the input in configurations whose state component is the dead state. By observing that there are only a finite number of distinct configurations, we can detect "looping" and hence remove the second problem. With these remarks, we will state the following result without proof (which is quite tedious and long).

Lemma 1.8.1

The class of languages recognized by deterministic pushdown automata is closed under complementation.

Corollary 1.8.1

There exists a context-free language which cannot be recognized by a deterministic pushdown automata.

Proof: Let $L = \{a^n b^n c^n \mid n \geq 1\}$ and let L_1 and L_2 be the CFL's given in the proof of Theorem 1.8.2. Since $\bar{L} = L_1 \cup L_2$, hence, by Theorem 1.8.1. L is context-free. If L were recognized by a deterministic PDA, then so would $\bar{L}$ by Lemma 1.8.1. But L is not even context-free and hence the corollary holds. ∎

One of the important applications of CFG lies in defining programming languages. An important characteristic of a programming language is that the meaning of its sentences are well defined or unambiguous. The use of CFG to define programming languages and compilers are discussed in detail in Chapter 6 and 7. We will only provide here the definition of ambiguity.

Definition 1.8.1

A context-free grammar G is said to be *ambiguous* if there is a sentence in $L(G)$ with more than one distinct leftmost derivation. A context-free language L is *ambiguous* if there is an ambiguous grammar G such that $L = L'(G)$. Otherwise, L is said to be *unambiguous*.

Example 1.8.1

Consider the grammar G in Example 1.6.1. A different derivation tree for the sentence $x = 001101$ is given in Fig. 1.8.1. Since both derivation trees in Figs. 1.6.1 and 1.8.1 give rise to a leftmost derivation for x, the grammar is ambiguous.

The following result is straightforward and is stated without proof.

Theorem 1.8.3

Every regular language is unambiguous.

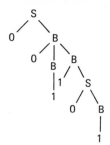

Fig. 1.8.1 A derivation tree.

EXERCISES 1.8

1. Prove Theorem 1.8.1.

2. Show that the language $L = \{x\$x^{-1} \mid x \in \{0,1\}^*\}$ is recognizable by a deterministic PDA.

3. Show that the language $L = \{xx^{-1} \mid x \in \{0, 1\}^*\}$ is recognizable by a PDA.

4. Show that the language $L = \{0^i 1^j \mid j > i\}$ is unambiguous.

5. Prove Theorem 1.8.3.

1.9. PUSHDOWN TRANSDUCERS

In this section we will discuss very briefly a class of transducers which has important applications to compiler design as discussed in Chapter 6.

Definition 1.9.1

A *pushdown transducer* (or PDT for short) P is a 7-tuple $(Q, \Sigma, \Gamma, \Delta, \delta, q_0, z_0)$, where $Q, \Sigma, \Gamma, q_0, z_0$ are as defined in Definition 1.6.3, Δ is a finite set of *output symbols* and δ is a function mapping $Q \times (\Sigma \cup \{\wedge\}) \times \Gamma$ to finite subsets of $Q \times \Gamma^* \times \Delta^*$.

A *configuration* of P is a 4-tuple (q, x, α, y), where $q \in Q, x \in \Sigma^*, \alpha \in \Gamma^*$, and $y \in \Delta^*$. A *move* is defined by a binary relation $\vdash$, similar to that given in Definition 1.6.4, such that

$$(q, ax, z\gamma, y) \vdash (q', x, \alpha\gamma, yy')$$

if $(q', \alpha, y') \in \delta(q, a, z)$.

We say $y \in \Delta^*$ is an *output* for $x \in \Sigma^*$ if $(q_0, x, z_0, \wedge) \vdash^* (q, \wedge, \wedge, y)$.

The *translation* defined by P denoted by $\tau(P)$ is the set

$$\{(x, y) \mid (q_0, x, z_0, \wedge) \mid^{*} (q, \wedge, \wedge, y), \text{ for some } q \in Q\}$$

The *input language* of P is $L_i(P) = \{x \mid (x, y) \in \tau(P) \text{ for some } y \in \Delta^*\}$, and the *output language* of T is $L_O(P) = \{y \mid (x, y) \in \tau(P) \text{ for some } x \in \Sigma^*\}$.

Example 1.9.1

Let $P = (\{q\}, \{a, +, *\}, \{z_0, +, *\}, \{a, +, *\}, \delta, q, z_0)$ be a PDT such that δ is defined in terms of the following moves:

$$(q, +, z_0) \mid\!- (q, z_0 + z_0, \wedge)$$
$$(q, *, z_0) \mid\!- (q, z_0*z_0, \wedge)$$
$$(q, a, z_0) \mid\!- (q, \wedge, a)$$
$$(q, \wedge, +) \mid\!- (q, \wedge, +)$$
$$(q, \wedge, *) \mid\!- (q, \wedge, *)$$

It is easily seen that T maps arithmetic expression in prefix representation into its infix representation.

It is natural to raise the question as to whether the pair of languages $L_i(T)$ and $L_O(T)$ can completely specify a PDT. Let us take another look at the translation defined by the PDT given in Example 1.9.1. We see that segments of prefix expression of the form $+aa$ or $*aa$ is translated into $z_0 + z_0$ or z_0*z_0 in the pushdown stack and then output as $a + a$ or $a * a$. Now $L_i(T)$ and $L_O(T)$ can be generated by grammars G_i and G_O with the following productions:

$S_1 \rightarrow + S_1 \ S_1$	$S_2 \rightarrow S_2 + S_2$
$S_1 \rightarrow A$	$S_2 \rightarrow A'$
$A \rightarrow *BB$	$A' \rightarrow B'*B'$
$B \rightarrow a$	$B' \rightarrow a$
$B \rightarrow + S_1 S_1$	$B' \rightarrow S_2 + S_2$
$B \rightarrow A$	$B' \rightarrow A'$
G_i	G_O

We see that there is a one-to-one correspondence between nonterminals as well as productions of G_i and G_O. Furthermore, we see that corresponding nonterminals occurring in the same order in corresponding productions. It is now quite clear to see that if given a pair of grammars G_1 and G_2 satisfying the conditions mentioned above, then a PDT P can be constructed in a straightforward fashion such that $\tau(P)$ consists precisely of those pairs (x, y) such that $S_1 \overset{*}{\Rightarrow} x$ and $S_2 \overset{*}{\Rightarrow} y$. Furthermore, in each step of the generation of x and y, corresponding productions are applied to corresponding nonterminals.

The previous discussion gives motivation for the following definition.

Definition 1.9.2

A *syntax-directed translation schema* (or SDTS for short) is a 5-tuple $T = (N, \Sigma, \Delta, R, S)$, where

1. N is a finite set of *nonterminals*.
2. Σ is a finite set of *input symbols*.
3. Δ is a finite set of *output symbols*.
4. S is a distinguished nonterminal called the *start symbol*.
5. R is a finite set of rules of the form $A \longrightarrow \alpha, \beta$, where $\alpha \in (N \cup \Delta)^*$ and $\beta \in (N \cup \Delta)^*$ such that to each nonterminal in α, there is an identical nonterminal in β.

T is called a *simple* SDTS if for each rule $A \longrightarrow \alpha, \beta$ in T, associated nonterminals occur in the same order in α and β.

A *translation form* of T is a pair $(\alpha A \beta, \alpha' A \beta')$ defined recursively as follows:

1. (S, S) is a translation form.
2. If $(\alpha A \beta, \alpha' A \beta')$ is a translation form, and $A \longrightarrow \gamma, \gamma'$ is a rule in R, then $(\alpha \gamma \beta, \alpha' \gamma' \beta')$ is a translation form.

If two translation forms are related as in (2) above, then we write $(\alpha A \beta, \alpha' A \beta') \underset{T}{\Rightarrow} (\alpha \gamma \beta, \alpha' \gamma' \beta')$. As usual, the subscript T will be omitted when no confusion arises. Also, the symbols $\overset{+}{\Rightarrow}$, $\overset{*}{\Rightarrow}$, and $\overset{k}{\Rightarrow}$ will stand for transitive closure, reflexive and transitive closure, and k-fold composition of the relation $\Rightarrow$.

A *translation* defined by T, denoted by $\tau(T)$, is the set

$$\{(x, y) \mid (S, S) \overset{*}{\Rightarrow} (x, y), x \in \Sigma^* \text{ and } y \in \Delta^*\}$$

We conclude this section with the following results which are consequences of the previous discussion.

Lemma 1.9.1

Let $T = (N, \Sigma, \Delta, R, S)$ be a simple SDTS. Then there is a PDT P such that $\tau(T) = \tau(P)$.

Proof: Construct $P = (\{q\}, \Sigma, N \cup \Sigma \cup \Delta', \Delta, \delta, q, S)$, where $\Delta' = \{a' \mid a \in \Delta\}$, and δ is defined as follows:

1. If $A \longrightarrow x_0 B_1 x_1 \ldots B_k x_k, y_0' B_1' y_1' \ldots B_k y_k'$ is in R, then $(q, \wedge, A) \vdash (q, x_0 y_0' B_1 x_1 y_1' B_2 \ldots B_k x_k y_k', \wedge)$, where for $y_i = a_1 \ldots a_n$, $y_i' = a_1' \ldots a_n'$.
2. $(q, a, a) \vdash (q, \wedge, \wedge)$, for each $a \in \Sigma$.

3. $(q, \wedge, a') \vdash (q, \wedge, a)$, for each $a \in \Delta$.

We left it as an exercise for the reader to show that $(S, S) \overset{*}{\Rightarrow} (x, y)$ if and only if $(q, x, S, \wedge) \vdash^{*} (q, \wedge, \wedge, y)$. ∎

The proofs of the following two results closely parallel that of Lemmas 1.6.1 and 1.6.2, and hence they are given without proofs.

Lemma 1.9.2

To every PDT P there exists a one-state PDT P' such that $\tau(P) = \tau(P')$.

Lemma 1.9.3

Let P be a PDT. Then there is a simple SDTS T such that $\tau(P) = \tau(T)$.

As a consequence of the previous three lemmas, we have the following theorem.

Theorem 1.9.1

Let $L \subseteq \Sigma^* \times \Delta^*$. Then $L = \tau(P)$ for some PDT P if and only if $L = \tau(T)$ for some simple SDTS T.

EXERCISES 1.9

1. Let $P = (Q, \Sigma, \Gamma, \Delta, \sigma, q_0, z_0)$ be a given PDT. The *translation defined by P with respect to* $F \subseteq Q$, denoted by $\tau_F(P)$, is defined to be the set $\{(x, y) | (q_0, x, z_0, \wedge) \vdash^{*} (q, \wedge, \alpha, y)$, for some $q \in F$. Show that for each PDT P, there exists a PDT P' such that $\tau(P) = \tau_F(P')$, for some F, and vice versa.

2. For each of the following conditions, construct a SDTS T.
    (a) Map $x \in \{0, 1\}^*$ to x^{-1}.
    (b) Map Boolean expression in infix notation to postfix notation.

3. Let G and G' be two CFG such that there is a one-to-one correspondence between nonterminals as well as productions of G and G'. Show that there is a PDT P such that $(x, y) \in \tau(P)$ implies that $S \overset{n}{\Rightarrow} x$ and $S' \overset{n}{\Rightarrow} y$ for some n. Is the converse true? If not, what are the additional constraints necessary to make it true?

*4. Let P be a PDT. Show that $L_i(P)$ is context-free if and only if $L_0(P)$ is context-free.

1.10. CONTEXT-SENSITIVE GRAMMARS AND PUSHDOWN AUTOMATA WITH TWO LINEAR-BOUNDED STACKS

This section is intended to be a very brief exposition of the relationship between context-sensitive grammars and their recognizers. The results in this section will not be used in later chapters. They are included here for the sake of completeness.

To motivate for recognizers of CSL, let us consider first a derivation "tree" of sentence *aabbcc*, generated by the grammar of Example 1.2.3, given in Fig. 1.10.1 The dotted lines indicate context.

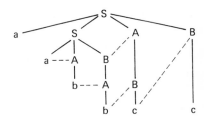

Fig. 1.10.1 Derivation tree of the sentence *aabbcc* in context-sensitive language.

We see that as in the case of CFG, it is necessary to take care of self-embedding which requires a pushdown stack. (Note that the amount of stack space used in parsing a word x in a CFL is linearly proportional to the length of x.) In addition, in order to replace a nonterminal, it is necessary to check its context first. This amounts to traversing the derivation tree, and hence can be done by a pushdown stack. To see this, we note that if $x \neq \wedge$, then x is generated by "length-preserving" productions. Therefore, the height of the derivation tree is linearly proportional to the length of its frontier. The discussions provide motivation for the following definition.

Definition 1.10.1

A *2-pushdown automaton* (2-PDA for short) is an 8-tuple $P = (Q, \Sigma, \Gamma_1, \Gamma_2, \delta, q_0, z_0^{(1)}, z_0^{(2)})$, where

1. Q is a finite set of *states*.
2. Σ is a finite set of *input symbols*.
3. Γ_1 and Γ_2 are finite sets of *pushdown stack alphabets*.
4. δ is a function mapping $Q \times \{\Sigma \cup \{\wedge\}\} \times \Gamma_1 \times \Gamma_2$ to finite subsets of $Q \times \Gamma_1^* \times \Gamma_2^*$.
5. $q_0 \in Q$ is a distinguished state called the *initial state*.
6. $z_0^{(1)}$ and $z_0^{(2)}$ are the respective *starting symbols* (of the two pushdown stacks).

P is said to be *linearly bounded* if at any time, the length of each pushdown stack used is linearly proportional to the length of the input tape.

Recognizability of a 2-PDA is defined similar to that of a PDA by emptying both stacks. The concepts of a configuration and the relation "yield" for 2-PDA are also similar to that of a PDA and hence will not be formally defined here.

In order to show that 2-PDA can recognize only CSL, it is convenient to consider a normal form for CSG stated in the following.

Theorem 1.10.1

To every context-sensitive grammar G, there corresponds an equivalent grammar G' such that each production in G' is in one of the following forms:

1. $S' \to \wedge$, and S' does not occur on the right-hand side of any production
2. $A \to \zeta$, where $\zeta \in N \cup \Sigma$
3. $A \to BC$, A, B, $C \in N$
4. $AB \to CD$, A, B, C, $D \in N$

Proof: First, transform G into an equivalent grammar in which the only productions involving terminal symbols are of the form $A \to a$. Second, for each production of the form $A \to BCD\alpha$, replace it by

$$A \to B_1 C_1, \qquad B_1 \to B, \qquad C_1 \to CD\alpha$$

For each production of the form $AB\alpha \to BCD\beta$, replace it by

$$AB \to A_1 A_2, \qquad A_1 \to B \qquad A_2\alpha \to CD\beta.$$

G' is obtained by repeating the replacement procedure outline above. ∎

Theorem 1.10.2

Let G be a CSG, then we can construct a one-state linear-bounded 2-PDA P such that $L(G) = L(P)$.

Proof: Let $G = (N, \Sigma, P, S)$ be given in the form of Theorem 1.11.2. Define a 2-PDA $P = (\{q\}, \Sigma, N \cup \Sigma \cup \{S_1, S_2\}, N \cup \Sigma \cup \{S'\}, \delta, q, S', S_1)$ as follows:

$$(q, x, S', S) \vdash (q, x, \wedge, \wedge), \qquad \text{if } S \to \wedge \text{ is in } P$$

$$\left. \begin{array}{l} (q, x, A\alpha, \beta) \vdash (q, x, \delta\alpha, \beta) \\ (q, x, \alpha, A\beta) \vdash (q, x, \alpha, \delta\beta) \end{array} \right\}, \qquad \text{if } A \to \delta \text{ is in } P$$

$$(q, x, A\alpha, B\beta) \vdash (q, x, C\alpha, D\beta), \qquad \text{if } AB \to CD \text{ is in } P$$

$$\left. \begin{array}{l} (q, x, A\alpha, \beta) \vdash (q, x, CB\alpha, \beta) \\ (q, x, \alpha, A\beta) \vdash (q, x, \alpha, BC\beta) \end{array} \right\}, \qquad \text{if } A \to BC \text{ is in } P$$

$$\left. \begin{array}{l} (q, ax, a\alpha, \beta) \vdash (q, x, \alpha, \beta) \\ (q, ax, \alpha, a\beta) \vdash (q, x, \alpha, \beta) \end{array} \right\}, \qquad \text{if } A \to a \text{ is in } P$$

$$\left. \begin{array}{l} (q, x, \alpha, Z\beta) \vdash (q, x, Z\alpha, \beta) \\ (q, x, Z\alpha, \beta) \vdash (q, x, \alpha, Z\beta) \end{array} \right\}, \qquad \text{for } Z \in N \cup \Sigma$$

$$(q, x, S', S_1) \vdash (q, x, S', SS_2)$$

$$(q, \wedge, S', S_2) \vdash (q, \wedge, \wedge, \wedge)$$

We leave it to the reader to show that $L(G) = L(P)$. ∎

As an example, we will illustrate how the linear bounded 2-PDA recognizes the sentence $a^2b^2c^2$ generated by the grammar given in Example 1.2.3. The formal construction of the automaton will be left for the reader.

$$(q, a^2b^2c^2, S', S_1) \mathrel{|\!\!-} (q, a^2b^2c^2, S', SS_2) \mathrel{|\!\!-} (q, a^2b^2c^2, S', aSABS_2)$$
$$\mathrel{|\!\!-} (q, ab^2c^2, S, SABS_2) \mathrel{|\!\!-} (a, ab^2c^2, S', aABABS_2)$$
$$\mathrel{|\!\!\overset{*}{-}} (q, ab^2c^2, BbaS', ABS_2) \mathrel{|\!\!-} (q, ab^2c^2, BbaS', A'BS_2)$$
$$\mathrel{|\!\!-} (q, ab^2c^2, AbaS', A'BS_2) \mathrel{|\!\!-} (q, ab^2c^2, AbaS', BBS_2)$$
$$\mathrel{|\!\!-} (q, ab^2c^2, aS', bAA'BS_2) \mathrel{|\!\!-} (q, b^2c^2, S', bAA'BS_2)$$
$$\mathrel{|\!\!\overset{*}{-}} (q, bc^2, bS', BBS_2) \mathrel{|\!\!-} (q, bc^2, bS', cBS_2)$$
$$\mathrel{|\!\!\overset{*}{-}} (q, c, S', cS_2) \mathrel{|\!\!-} (q, \wedge, S', S_2) \mathrel{|\!\!-} (q, \wedge, \wedge, \wedge).$$

Lemma 1.10.1

If P is a one-state linear-bounded 2-PDA, then $L(P)$ is context-sensitive.

Lemma 1.10.2

Every linear bounded 2-PDA is equivalent to a one-state linear-bounded 2-PDA.

As a consequence of the previous results, we have the following theorem.

Theorem 1.10.3

A language L is context-sensitive if and only if it can be recognized by a linear-bounded 2-PDA.

We now ask the question as to what are the properties which separate the class of CSL's from that of type 0 languages. The property is that in a CSG, all productions, with the possible exception of $S \rightarrow \wedge$, are length preserving.

Definition 1.10.2

A language L is called *recursive* if there is an algorithm which can decide whether any sentence belongs to L or not.

Theorem 1.10.4

Every CSL is recursive.

Proof: Let $L = L(G)$ for some CSG $G = (N, \Sigma, P, S)$. Clearly, we know whether $\wedge \in L$ or not. Let $x \in \Sigma^*$ and $|x| > 0$. Consider sequences of the following form

$$x_0 = S, x_1, x_2, \cdots, x_n = x \tag{1.10.1}$$

such that $x_i \in (N \cup \Sigma)^*$ and $|x_i| \leq |x_{i+1}|, 0 \leq i < n$. There are only a finite number of sequences of the form (1.10.1) for each $k = |x|$. Therefore, for each such sequence, one can check whether (1.10.1) is a derivation in G, i.e.,

$$S \Rightarrow x_1 \Rightarrow x_2 \Rightarrow \cdot \cdot \cdot \Rightarrow x \quad \blacksquare$$

We will prove in Section 1.13 that there are recursive languages which are not context-sensitive.

We conclude this section by stating two open problems:

1. Is a (nondeterministic) linear-bounded 2-PDA more powerful than a deterministic linear-bounded 2-PDA in general?

2. Is the class of context-sensitive languages closed under complementation?

EXERCISES 1.10

1. Construct a 2-PDA to recognize the language $\{a^n b^n c^n | n \geq 1\}$.

2. Complete the proof of Theorem 1.11.3.

3. Prove Lemma 1.10.1.

4. Prove Lemma 1.10.2.

5. A grammar $G = (N, \Sigma, P, S)$ is called *length preserving* if every production $\alpha \to \beta$, except possibly $S \to \wedge$ and S does not occur on the righthand side of any production, satisfies the condition $|\alpha| \leq |\beta|$. Show that every CSG is length preserving and vice versa.

6. Show that the class of CSL's is closed under the operation of union, concatenation, and star.

7. Show that every CFL is recognizable by a deterministic 2-PDA.

8. Show that a language is recursive implies that its complement is also recursive.

*9. A k-PDA is a pushdown automaton with k pushdown stacks.
   (a) Formalize the definition of a 3-PDA.
   (b) Are linear-bounded 3-PDA's more powerful than linear-bounded 2-PDA's?
   (c) Are 3-PDA's more powerful than 2-PDA's?

10. Formalize a definition for 2-PDA to recognize sentences by final states.

1.11. TYPE 0 GRAMMARS AND TURING MACHINES

In this section, we will introduce the concept of a Turing machine which is one of the most important mathematical concepts discovered in the twentieth century. The importance of this concept lies in that it is one of the several equivalent formalizations of the intuitive concept of an effective procedure or algorithm.

To motivate for the recognition device of type 0 languages, let us observe that a grammar is context-sensitive if no shrinking productions, except $S \rightarrow \wedge$, is allowed. If productions of the form $\alpha \rightarrow \wedge$ are allowed in a context-sensitive derivation, then we see that the height of a derivation tree no longer is in linear proportion to the length of its frontier. Indeed, the height (or the width) could be arbitrarily large. This indicates that removing the corresponding restriction of linear-boundedness in 2-PDA should provide recognizers for type 0 languages. To prove this fact, the following normal form is useful.

Lemma 1.11.1

To every type 0 grammar G, there corresponds an equivalent grammar G' such that each production in G' is in one of the following forms.

1. $A \rightarrow \delta, \delta \in N \cup \Sigma$
2. $A \rightarrow BC, \ A, \ B, \ C \in N$
3. $AB \rightarrow CD, \ A, \ B, \ C, \ D, \ \in N$
4. $A \rightarrow \wedge, \ A \in N$
5. $AB \rightarrow \wedge, \ A, \ B \in N$

Proof: From Theorem 1.10.2, we need only to consider productions of the form $\alpha \rightarrow \beta$, where $|\alpha| > |\beta|$. If $\beta \neq \wedge$, then introduce a sequence of new nonterminals γ such that $|\gamma| = |\alpha| - |\beta|$, and replace $\alpha \rightarrow \beta$ by $\alpha \rightarrow \beta\gamma$ and $\gamma \rightarrow \wedge$. Clearly, productions of the form $\alpha \rightarrow \beta\gamma$ can be converted to productions of the forms (1), (2), and (3) by Theorem 1.10.1, and any production of the form $\gamma \rightarrow \wedge$ for $|\gamma| > 0$ can be replaced by productions of the form $AB \rightarrow \wedge$ or $A \rightarrow \wedge$. ∎

The derivation of a type 0 grammar can also be described in "tree" form as illustrated in the following example.

Example 1.11.1

Productions of the normal form grammar for the grammar given in Example 1.2.4 are listed in the following. A derivation tree for the sentence 01 01 is illustrated in Fig. 1.11.1

$S \rightarrow A_1A_2$	$DA_8 \rightarrow A_8D$
$A_1 \rightarrow A$	$EA_7 \rightarrow A_7E$
$A_2 \rightarrow BC$	$EA_8 \rightarrow A_8E$
$A_3 \rightarrow 0$	$C \rightarrow \wedge$
$AB \rightarrow A_3A_4$	$DC \rightarrow A_{11}A_{12}$
$A_4 \rightarrow AD$	$A_{11} \rightarrow B$

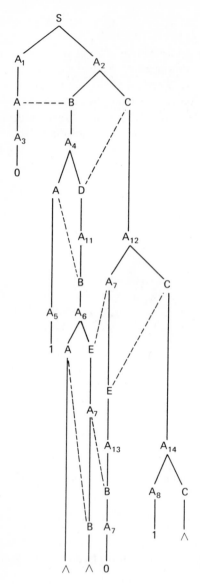

Fig. 1.11.1 Illustration of a derivation tree in a type 0 grammar.

$$A_5 \rightarrow 1 \qquad\qquad A_{12} \rightarrow A_7 C$$
$$AB \rightarrow A_5 A_6 \qquad\qquad EC \rightarrow A_{13} A_{14}$$
$$A_6 \rightarrow AE \qquad\qquad A_{13} \rightarrow B$$
$$AB \rightarrow \wedge \qquad\qquad A_{14} \rightarrow A_8 C$$
$$A_7 \rightarrow 0 \qquad\qquad A_7 B \rightarrow BA_7$$
$$DA_7 \rightarrow A_7 D \qquad\qquad A_8 B \rightarrow BA_8$$
$$A_8 \rightarrow 1$$

The following theorem can be proved in the same fashion as Lemmas 1.10.1 and 1.10.2 and Theorem 1.10.3 and hence is given without proof.

Theorem 1.11.1

A language L is generated by a type 0 grammar if and only if it is recognizable by a 2-PDA.

It is usually more convenient to discuss the following equivalent version of a 2-PDA by considering the two semi-infinite stacks of a 2-PDA as halves of an infinite tape.

Definition 1.11.1

A Turing machine (or TM for short) Z is a 6-tuple $(Q, \Sigma, \Gamma, \delta, q_0, F)$, where

1. Q is a finite set of *states*.
2. Σ is a finite set of *input symbols*.
3. Γ is a finite set of *tape symbols* which contains Σ and a special symbol B called the *blank* symbol.
4. $q_0 \in Q$ is a distinguished state called the *initial state;*
5. $F \subseteq Q$ is a set of *final states*.
6. δ is a partial function mapping $Q \times \Sigma$ to subsets of $Q \times \{\Gamma - \{B\}\} \times \{-1, 0, 1\}$.

Z is said to be deterministic if the range of Z consists of only singleton sets.

Thus, a Turing machine in a particular state and reading a particular symbol can change its state, erase the symbol being read and write another symbol on the same square, and move its input head either one square to the left (denoted by -1), or to the right (denoted by 1) or stay stationary (denoted by 0). Observe that a TM may never halt. We use the convention in this book that a TM halts in a state q reading a symbol a if $\delta(q, a)$ is not defined. Note that an empty or blank tape $\wedge$ is the tape consisting of all blanks —*BBB*—.

Schematically, a Turing machine is illustrated in Fig. 1.11.2.

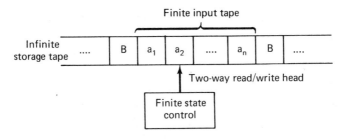

Fig. 1.11.2 A Turing machine.

Definition 1.11.2

Let $Z = (Q, \Sigma, \Gamma, \delta, q_0, F)$ be a given TM. A *configuration* of Z is a sequence $(\alpha, q, \beta) \in \Gamma^* \times Q \times \Gamma^*$, where a represents the nonempty portion of the tape to the left of the input head, and β the nonempty portion of the tape located beneath and to the right of the input head. A *move* of Z is represented by the binary relation $\vdash_{\overline{Z}}$ (or $\vdash$ when Z is understood) defined as follows:

$$(\alpha, q_1, a\beta) \vdash (\alpha, q_2, b\beta) \qquad \text{if } (q_2, b, 0) \in \delta(q_1, a)$$
$$(\alpha, q_1, \wedge) \vdash (\alpha, q_2, b) \qquad \text{if } (q_2, b, 0) \in \delta(q_1, B)$$
$$(\alpha, q_1, a\beta) \vdash (\alpha b, q_2, \beta) \qquad \text{if } (q_2, b, 1) \in \delta(q_1, a)$$
$$(\alpha, q_1, \wedge) \vdash (\alpha b, q_2, \wedge) \qquad \text{if } (q_2, b, 1) \in \delta(q_1, B)$$
$$(\alpha a, q_1, b\beta) \vdash (\alpha, q_2, ac\beta) \qquad \text{if } (q_2, c, -1) \in \delta(q_1, b)$$
$$(\wedge, q_1, a\beta) \vdash (\wedge, q_2, Bb\beta) \qquad \text{if } (q_2, b, -1) \in \delta(q_1, a)$$
$$\left.\begin{array}{l}(\alpha a, q_1, \wedge) \vdash (\alpha, q_2, ab) \\ (\wedge, q_1, \wedge) \vdash (\wedge, q_2, Bb)\end{array}\right\} \qquad \text{if } (q_2, b, -1) \in \delta(q_1, B)$$

As usual, we will denote by $\vdash^k$, $\vdash^+$, and $\vdash^*$, the k-fold composition, transitive closure, and reflexive-transitive closure of the relation $\vdash$.

Definition 1.11.3

Let Z be a TM. The *translation* defined by Z, denoted by $\tau(Z)$, is the set

$$\{(x, yaz) | (\wedge, q_0, x) \vdash^* (y, q, az) \text{ for some } q \in F \text{ such that } \delta(q, a) = \varnothing.$$

Example 1.11.2

Let $Z = (\{q_0, q_1, q_2, q_3\}, \{0, 1, *\}, \{0, 1, *, B\}, \delta, q_0, \{q_3\})$, where δ is defined as follows:

$$(q_0, B) \vdash (q_0, B, 1) \qquad (q_1, B) \vdash (q_0, B, 0)$$
$$(q_0, 1) \vdash (q_2, B, 1) \qquad (q_1, *) \vdash (q_1, *, -1)$$
$$(q_0, *) \vdash (q_3, B, 0) \qquad (q_1, 1) \vdash (q_2, 1, 1)$$
$$(q_1, 1) \vdash (q_1, 1, -1) \qquad (q_1, *) \vdash (q_2, *, 1)$$
$$(q_2, B) \vdash (q_1, 1, 0)$$

we see that Z is a transducer which maps unary representations of two integers m and n, separated by a special symbol *, into the unary representation of the integer $m + n$ as illustrated in Fig. 1.11.3.

The TM given in the previous example is deterministic. Indeed, since a TM has infinite storage capacity, a nondeterministic TM can always be simulated by a deterministic TM. This is stated as a theorem.

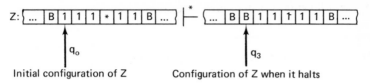

Fig. 1.11.3 Illustration of a Turing transducer.

Theorem 1.11.2

Every TM Z is equivalent to a deterministic TM Z' in that $\tau(Z) = \tau(Z')$.

As a consequence of the previous theorem, every TM can be represented by a sequence of 5-tuples of the form (q, a, q', a', d), where $\delta(q, a) = (q', a', d)$, such that if $(q_1, a_1, q_1', a_1', d_1)$ and $(q_2, a_2, q_2', a_2', d_2)$ are two arbitrary distinct 5-tuples, then $(q_1, a_1) \neq (q_2, a_2)$.

Definition 1.11.4

Let Z be a TM. The language *recognizable* by Z, denoted by $L(Z)$, is the set

$$\{x \,|\, (\wedge, q_0, x) \mathrel{\vdash^*} (\wedge, q, a), \text{ for some predetermined symbol } a, q \in F \text{ and }$$
$$\delta(q, a) = \varnothing\}.$$

Example 1.11.3

Let Z be a TM represented by the following 5-tuples.

$$(q_0, 0, q_0, B, 1) \qquad (q_1, 0, q_1, B, 1)$$
$$(q_0, 1, q_1, B, 1) \qquad (q_1, 1, q_0, B, 1)$$
$$(q_0, B, q_4, 0, 0) \qquad (q_1, B, q_3, 1, 0)$$

We see that Z is a recognizer which accepts a sequence having an even number of occurences of 1's. Z indicates the acceptance by leaving a 0 in the tape when it halts.

The following results are stated without proofs.

Theorem 1.11.3

To every 2-PDA P, there is a TM Z, such that $L(P) = L(Z)$, and vice versa.

Corollary 1.11.1

A language L is recognizable by a TM if and only if it is generated by some type 0 grammar.

In the following, we shall give an example of a TM which never halts.

Example 1.11.4

Let Z be a TM represented by the following 5-tuples.

$$
\begin{array}{ll}
(q_0, B, q_1, 1, 0) & (q_3, \$, q_3, \$, 1) \\
(q_0, \$, q_1, 1, 0) & (q_3, B, q_4, B, 1) \\
(q_0, 1, q_1, 1, 0) & (q_4, 1, q_4, 1, 1) \\
(q_1, 1, q_1, 1, -1) & (q_4, \$, q_4, \$, 1) \\
(q_1, \$, q_1, \$, -1) & (q_4, B, q_5, 1, 0) \\
(q_1, B, q_2, B, 1) & (q_5, B, q_5, B, -1) \\
(q_2, \$, q_2, \$, 1) & (q_5, 1, q_5, 1, -1) \\
(q_2, 1, q_3, \$, 0) & (q_5, \$, q_2, 1, 1) \\
(q_2, B, q_6, B, 1) & (q_6, 1, q_6, 1, 1) \\
(q_3, 1, q_4, 1, 1) & (q_6, B, q_0, B, 0) \\
& (q_6, \$, q_6, \$, 1)
\end{array}
$$

Z is a generator in the sense that, beginning with the blank tape, it will generate the unary representations of all positive integers, separated by a blank, in succession (see Fig. 1.11.4).

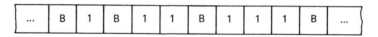

Fig. 1.11.4   An infinite tape containing unary representations of positive integers.

EXERCISES 1.11

1. Prove Theorem 1.11.1.

2. Show that every 2-PDA is equivalent to a Turing recognizer and vice versa.

3. Show that every Turing recognizer is equivalent to one which has a oneway infinite tape.

4. Show that every Turing recognizer is equivalent to one which has a finite number of infinite tapes.

5. Construct Turing machines accepting the following languages:
    (a) $L_1 = \{a^n b^n c^n \mid n \geq 1\}$
    (b) $L_2 = \{a^{n^2} \mid n \geq 1\}$

(c) $L_3 = \{a^p \mid p \text{ a prime}\}$.

6. Estimate the amount of tapes used and number of moves made by a Turing machine in recognizing each of the languages in Exercise 1.12.5.

7. A partial function of n arguments $f: (\Sigma^*)^n \to \Delta^*$ is said to be *computable* if there exists a TM $Z = (Q, \Sigma \cup (\$), \Gamma, q_0, \delta, F)$ such that

$$f(x_1, x_2, \ldots, x_n) = \begin{cases} \alpha a \beta & \text{if } (\wedge, q_0, x_1\$x_2\$ \ldots \$x_n) \overset{*}{\vdash} (\alpha, q, a\beta) \\ & \text{for some } q \in F \text{ and } \delta(q, a) = \varnothing \\ \text{not defined}, & \text{otherwise} \end{cases}$$

(a)   Show that the function which performs the multiplication of two binary numbers is computable.

*(b)   Can you think of a function which is not computable?

***8.** A real number $0 \leq N \leq 1$ is said to be *computable* if there exists a TM such that given a representation of k as input, it will halt with the representation of the kth digit of N. Show that any rational number is computable.

***9.** A TM is called a *linear-bounded* automaton if the length of its storage tape is a linear function of the length of its input tape.
(a)   Show that a language is context-sensitive if and only if it can be recognized by a linear-bounded automaton.
(b)   If the storage tape of a TM is quadratically bounded, is it more powerful than a linear-bounded automaton?

***10.** A language is called *recursive enumerable* if and only if it is the range of a computable function whose domain is the set of positive integers.
(a)   Show that union and intersection of recursive enumerable languages are recursive enumerable.
(b)   Can you find a non-recursive-enumerable language whose complement is also not recursive enumerable?

1.12.   THE CONCEPT OF ALGORITHMIC UNSOLVABILITY

What we intend to do in this section is to illustrate that there are classes of problems which cannot be solved by any algorithm. Such problems are called algorithmically *unsolvable*.

All unsolvable problems are *paradoxical* in nature. We will illustrate this point by a popular version of Russell's paradox which is stated below.

"A barber shaves only those persons who do not shave themselves." The question then is "Does the barber shave himself?" This question can never be decided, since from the given statement, we can conclude that the barber shaves himself if and only if he does not shave himself. This is clearly a contradictory statement.

The usual technique to show that a class of problems is unsolvable is by means of the so-called "diagonalization technique" which was first used by the mathematician Cantor to prove the existence of irrational numbers. This method will be demonstrated in the following.

From the experience of tracing the operations of Turing machines in previous examples, it is easily seen that any person who has a precise understanding of how to interpret the description (or transition table) of a Turing machine can imitate the machine given the initial data and the description of the machine and storage medium, say pencil and paper. The imitation process involves no more than looking up the transition table of the machine to find out what symbol to write, which way to move, and which row to look at next. Thus, the very process of imitating a machine can itself be given as an exact sequence of instructions. In view of our assertion in the previous paragraph, such an imitation procedure can be realized by a Turing machine U. Such a machine U is called a *Universal* Turning machine since it can imitate the behavior of any other Turing machine given the initial data and the description of the machine. We shall not go into the construction of a Universal Turing machine, but merely assert here that Universal machines have been constructed.

A Universal Turing machine is a fixed machine having a fixed number of tape symbols and states. Thus, in order to imitate the operations of other Turing machines (some of which will have more states and more tape symbols than the Universal machine in question), we need to code the data as well as the description of a given machine by means of the tape symbols of the Universal machine. Once the input data, coded description, and the initial state of Z are given, a Universal Turing machine U will simulate Z one step at a time by looking at the description of Z to see what Z is supposed to do next and do it. We will not give a detailed construction here. Interested readers are referred to Minsky's book [6].

We will now consider the problem "Given any TM Z and any tape t, will Z eventually halt on t?" This problem is referred to as the *halting problem* of Turing machines.

Let us suppose that there is indeed an effective decision procedure for the halting problem. Then there must exist a Universal Turing machine U_1 such that, given a copy of the tape t of the machine Z and the description d_Z of Z on its tape, U_1 will eventually halt and decide as to whether Z will eventually halt. (Notice that both Z and t are arbitrary.) Let us adopt the convention that if Z eventually halts, then U_1 also halts and prints a "1" on the tape after erasing all other symbols. If Z will never halt, then U_1 halts and prints a "0" on the tape after erasing all other symbols. The transformation of tape configurations performed by U_1 is illustrated in Fig. 1.12.1. Since t could be any tape, we now select a specific tape for consideration, namely, d_Z. We shall now construct a new Turing machine U_2 from U_1 such that U_2 is composed of two machines Z' and U_1, where Z' is a machine which simply duplicates

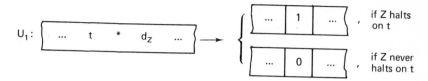

Fig. 1.12.1   An illustration of the transformation performed by the Turing machine U_1.

the nonblank portion of the tape. Thus U_2 is a machine which when started with a tape $\boxed{\text{t } * \text{ t}}$ will convert it into $\boxed{\text{t}}$ and then transfer control to U_1. The transformation of the tape configuration as performed by U_2, is illustrated in Fig. 1.12.2.

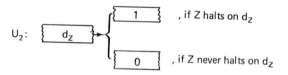

Fig. 1.12.2   Transformation performed by the machine U_2.

Since the machine U_2 must halt eventually and output a "1" or a "0" depending on whether Z halts or not, it must have the following two transitions:

$$(q_1, a, q, \ 0, 0) \qquad (q_2, b, q, 1, 0) \tag{1.12.1}$$

for some states q_1, q_2, q and tape symbols a and b. We construct a new machine U_3 from U_2 by adding two new state symbols q_1' and q_2', and replace the transition in (1.12.1) by the following set of transitions:

$$(q_2, b, q_1, ', 1, 0)$$
$$(q_1', 1, q_2', 1, 1)$$
$$(q_2', B, q_1', B, -1)$$

The newly introduced transitions in U_3 have the effect of causing U_3 to move back and forth on two squares of the tape without ever coming to a halt. In other words,

U_3 halts on d_Z if Z does not halt on d_Z; U_3 does

not halt on d_Z if Z halts on d_Z.

Since Z was arbitrary, so is d_Z; therefore, let us consider the application of

U_3 to d_{U_3}. With the appropriate substitutions we have the following result:

$$U_3 \text{ halts on } d_{U_3} \text{ if } U_3 \text{ does not halt on } d_{U_3}; U_3 \text{ does} \atop \text{not halt on } U_3 \text{ if } U_3 \text{ halts on } d_{U_3}. \tag{1.12.2}$$

This statement is clearly contractory and we must conclude that U_3 and hence U_2 and hence Z cannot exist. This demonstrates the algorithmic unsolvability of the halting problem.

As another illustration of the diagonalization technique, we will prove in the following therorem the existence of non-context-sensitive recursive languages.

Theorem 1.12.1

There exists a recursive language which is not context-sensitive.

Proof: Consider CSG's with terminals 0, 1 and nonterminals A_i, $i \geq 0$. If G is a given CSG with productions $\alpha_1 \rightarrow \beta_1, \ldots, \alpha_n \rightarrow \beta_n$, then it is completely specified by the word

$$\alpha_1 \rightarrow \beta_1 \$ \alpha_2 \rightarrow \beta_2 \$ \ldots \$ \alpha_n \rightarrow \beta_n \tag{1.12.3}$$

Define an encoding function f: $\{0, 1, \$, \rightarrow, A_i \ (i \geq 0)\} \rightarrow \{0, 1\}$ as follows:

$$f(0) = 101, \quad f(1) = 10^2 1, \quad f(\rightarrow) = 10^3 1, \quad f(\$) = 10^4 1,$$
$$f(A_i) = 10^{i+5} 1, \quad i \geq 0.$$

Clearly, to every CSG, there corresponds a sentence in $\{0,1\}^*$ and vice versa.

Let us introduce a linear ordering Π on $\{0, 1\}^*$. This induces an ordering $\{L(G_1), L(G_2), \ldots\}$ on the family of CSF's. Define a language L as follows:

$$L = \{x \mid \Pi(x) = i \text{ and } x \notin L(G_i) \text{ for some } i > 0\} \tag{1.12.4}$$

By Therorem 1.10.5, L is recursive. Assume that L is also context-sensitive. Then $L = L(G_i)$ for some i. Consider the ith sentence x_i; we have

1. $x_i \notin L$ implies $x_i \in L(G_i)$, and hence $x_i \in L$.
2. $x_i \in L$ implies $x_i \notin L(G_i)$, and hence $x_i \notin L$.

In both cases, we have arrived at a contradiction. Hence, L cannot be recursive. ∎

Corollary 1.12.1

The class of context-sensitive languages is a proper subclass of the class of type 0 languages.

EXERCISES 1.12

1. Show that the question "Does a Turing machine Z halt if started on a blank tape?" is unsolvable by showing that it is equivalent to the halting problem.

2. Show that the set of all recursively enumerable languages can be effectively enumerated.

*3. Show that there exists recursive enumerable sets which are not recursive.

REFERENCES

1. AHO, A. V. and J. D. ULLMAN, *The Theory of Parsing, Translation, and Compiling, Vol. 1: Parsing,* Prentice-Hall, Inc., Englewood Cliffs, N. J., 1972.

2. CHOMSKY, N., "Formal Properties of Grammars, "*Handbook of Mathematical Psychology 2,* John Wiley & Sons, New York, 1963, pp. 323–418.

3. HOPCROFT, J. E. and J. D. ULLMAN, *Formal Languages and Their Relation to Automata,* Addison-Wesley Publishing Co., Inc., Reading, Mass., 1969.

4. HSIA, P. and R. T. YEH, "Finite Automata with Markers," *Information Sciences,* 1975.

5. KOHAVI, Z., *Switching and Finite Automata Theory,* McGraw-Hill Book Co., New York, 1970.

6. MINSKY, M. *Computation: Finite and Infinite Machines,* Prentice-Hall, Inc., Englewood Cliffs, N. J. 1967.

7. SALOMAA, A. *Formal Languages,* Academic Press, Inc., New York, 1973.

PART **II** **ANALYSIS**

2

INTRODUCTION TO THE COMPLEXITY OF ALGORITHMS

Eugene Lawler
*Department of Electrical Engineering
and Computer Sciences
University of California at Berkeley
Berkeley, California*

Editor's Note:

This chapter provides a first introduction to the notion of algorithmic complexity. Various ways of combinatorially measuring the complexity of an algorithm are discussed and illustrated by examples. Two elegant proofs are given to establish a lower bound for computing the median, and for estimating the running time in context-free language recognition.

The material given here together with that of Chapter 3 presents a clear picture on combinatorial approach to algorithm analysis.

Prerequisites for the understanding of this chapter will be the notion of context-free language, introduced in Chapter 1, and some basic knowledge in combinatorics. Readers who have no knowledge of combinatorics are referred to Chapter 6 of the following book.

Preparata, F. P. and R. T. Yeh, Introduction to Discrete Structures, *Addison-Wesley Publishing Company, 1973.*

The complexity of algorithms is one of the most important and rapidly developing areas of computation theory. The purpose of this chapter is to provide a very brief and elementary introduction to the subject. A few examples of interesting and useful algorithms are presented as case studies.

2.1. AN INTUITIVE INTRODUCTION TO COMPUTATIONAL COMPLEXITY

To give an intuitive idea of what computational complexity is all about, we begin by giving some examples.

2.1.1. Insertion of an Element in Ordered Sequence

We are given distinct real numbers $x_1, x_2, \ldots, x_{n-1}$, and x, with $x_1 < x_2 < \ldots < x_{n-1}$. We wish to insert x into the ordered sequence by comparing it with elements of that sequence.

Algorithm 2.1.1   Sequential Search

Compare x with $x_1, x_2, \ldots, x_{n-1}$ in turn, until either an x_i is found such that $x < x_i$, or else $x > x_{n-1}$.

In the worst case, this algorithm requires $n - 1$ comparisons, as can clearly be seen from the algorithm.

Algorithm 2.1.2   Binary Search

Compare x with $x_{\lceil n/2 \rceil}$, an element closest to the middle of the sequence $x_1, x_2, \ldots, x_{n-1}$. If $x > x_{\lceil n/2 \rceil}$, throw away $x_1, x_2, \ldots, x_{\lceil n/2 \rceil}$; if $x < x_{\lceil n/2 \rceil}$, throw away $x_{\lceil n/2 \rceil}, x_{\lceil n/2 \rceil+1}, \ldots, x_{n-1}$. Repeat, each time throwing away half the elements, until the position for x is located.

This algorithm requires $\lceil \log_2 n \rceil$ comparisons in the worst case, which is better than the worst case performance for sequential search. But what distinguishes binary search is its optimality; every algorithm to insert x must require at least $\lceil \log_2 n \rceil$ comparisons in some cases.

To establish the optimality of the algorithm, we may make a simple information theoretic argument. There are n possible outcomes to the computation, corresponding to the possible positions of x in the sequence. The number of bits of information required to specify one of n alternatives is $\lceil \log_2 n \rceil$. Each comparison yields one bit of information. Hence $\lceil \log_2 n \rceil$ comparisons are required in the worst case.

2.1.2. Evaluation of a Polynomial

Suppose we wish to compute

$$P(x) = a_n x^n + a_{n-1} x^{n-1} + \ldots + a_0$$

with a minimum number of multiplications and divisions.

By Horner's method,

$$P(x) = ((a_n x + a_{n-1}) x + a_{n-2})x + \ldots + a_0$$

and the evaluation can be accomplished in n multiplications. It can be shown that this method is optimal.

2.1.3. Multiplication of Matrices

Suppose we wish to multiply two $n \times n$ real matrices A and B. The obvious and traditional form of matrix multiplication requires n^3 scalar multiplications. However, a clever scheme due to Strassen permits the matrix multiplication to be accomplished with approximately $n^{\log_2 7}$ scalar multiplications.

For example, in the 2×2 case, let

$$A = \begin{pmatrix} a_{11} & a_{12} \\ a_{21} & a_{22} \end{pmatrix}, \qquad B = \begin{pmatrix} b_{11} & b_{12} \\ b_{21} & b_{22} \end{pmatrix}$$

and $C = AB$. Then Strassen computes C with only seven (instead of eight) scalar multiplications as follows:

$$
\begin{aligned}
\text{I} &= (a_{11} + a_{22})(b_{11} + b_{22}) \\
\text{II} &= (a_{21} + a_{22}) b_{11} \\
\text{III} &= a_{11}(b_{12} - b_{22}) \\
\text{IV} &= a_{22}(-b_{11} + b_{21}) \\
\text{V} &= (a_{11} + a_{12}) b_{22} \\
\text{VI} &= (-a_{11} + a_{21})(b_{11} + b_{12}) \\
\text{VII} &= (a_{12} - a_{22})(b_{21} + b_{22})
\end{aligned}
$$

Then

$$
\begin{aligned}
c_{11} &= \text{I} + \text{IV} - \text{V} + \text{VII} \\
c_{12} &= \text{III} + \text{V} \\
c_{21} &= \text{II} + \text{IV} \\
c_{22} &= \text{I} + \text{III} - \text{II} + \text{VI}
\end{aligned}
$$

EXERCISES 2.1

1. Apply an information theoretic argument to show that $0(n \log_2 n)$ comparisons are required to sort n numbers in the worst case. *Note:* There are $n!$ possible outcomes to the computation. Stirling's formula asserts

$$\sqrt{2\pi}\, n^{n+1/2}\, e^{-n} < n! < \sqrt{2\pi}\, n^{n+1/2}\, e^{-n}(1 + 1/4n).$$

2. The polynomial

$$P(x) = x^2 + y^2 - z^2 - t^2$$

can obviously be evaluated with 4 multiplications. By suitable factoring, show how the evaluation can be accomplished with only two multiplications.

2.2. TYPES OF COMPLEXITY ANALYSES

All types of complexity analyses are concerned with the "amount of work" done by algorithms. Depending upon the situation at hand, work may be measured in terms of computation time, the number of operations of a particular type which must be performed, the amount of storage space required, or some other measure.

There are various types of investigations of interest. Among these are the following.

Analysis of a Specific Algorithm. For a given class of inputs, we may ask what the worst case behavior of an algorithm is, i.e., the maximum amount of work done. Or, alternatively, we may wish to determine the average amount of work done.

Worst case analyses appear to be more common than probabilistic analyses, at least in part because worst case estimates are generally easier to obtain. Another difficulty with probabilistic analyses is that it is often difficult to specify a meaningful probability distribution over inputs.

In Sections 2.3 and 2.5 we shall analyze two specific algorithms, one for computing the median of a set of numbers, and another for recognizing context-free languages.

Optimality of Algorithms. A particularly challenging type of investigation is to show that an algorithm is optimal. Ordinarily, optimality is specified with respect to a well defined class of algorithms, e.g., "decision tree algorithms" or "chains of rational operations."

The reader should have little difficulty in showing that the binary search algorithm minimizes the maximum number of comparisons required for insertion. We have also commented that Horner's method is optimal. The median algorithm described in the next section requires an optimal number of comparisons, within a linear scale factor.

Inherent Complexity of Problems. It is often the case that we are not able to exhibit an optimal algorithm for solving a particular problem, but we may still be able to establish a useful lower bound in its complexity. In the next section, we give an example of such a lower bound, by showing that at least $\frac{3}{2} n$ comparisons are required to find the median of n numbers.

Another type of investigation of the inherent complexity of problems is concerned with the demonstration that two problems have equivalent complexity with respect to some criterion, even though we do not know what that complexity is. The discussion of so-called "polynomial complete problems" later in this chapter is an example of an investigation of this type.

Discovery of Efficient Algorithms. Generally speaking, questions of optimality and of inherent complexity are quite difficult. The next best thing to finding an algorithm which is optimal, is finding one which is substantially better than the traditional method of solution. Many such algorithms have been developed recently. Strassen's algorithm for matrix multiplication, cited above, and the median algorithm described in the next section are two such examples.

Of course, any algorithm provides an upper bound on the inherent complexity of a problem. Thus, in the next section, we show that no more than about $6n$ comparisons are sufficient to find the median of n numbers. This compares with a lower bound of $\frac{3}{2}n$. (Recent investigations have reduced the gap substantially.)

2.3. COMPUTING THE MEDIAN

Suppose we wish to find the median of n unordered numbers $x_1, x_2, \ldots, x_n$. Our objective is to minimize the number of comparisons which must be made in the worst case.

Clearly, it is possible to sort the numbers into a sequence $x_{i(1)} \leq x_{i(2)} \leq \ldots \leq x_{i(n)}$ in order to find the median. But this will require something like $n \log_2 n$ comparisons. Is it possible to find the median in a linear number of comparisons, i.e., Kn, for some K? Somewhat surprisingly, the answer is in the affirmative, as can be demonstrated by an algorithm due to Blum, Floyd, Tarjan, Pratt, and Rivest [1].

We shall generalize the problem of finding the median to that of finding an arbitrary quantile, i.e., finding the kth largest element, for some specified k.

Quantile Finding Algorithm. We wish to find the kth largest element for given k. First break up the set of n elements into subsets of 15. Then completely sort the elements in each subset. This yields a number of "strips," and we know the median of each strip:

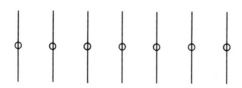

Now find the median of the medians of the strips (using this same algorithm recursively). Let x be the median of the medians. We know that x is larger than all of the elements in A but smaller than all of the elements in B:

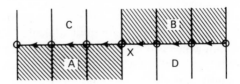

(Note: Any set of comparisons sufficient to determine x will tell us which of the other medians it is larger than, and which it is smaller than.)

Now find out the exact rank of x in the complete set of elements. (At this point we know only that x is somewhere in the second or third quantile.) Do this by performing binary insertion of x into each of the strips in C and D. (Since each of the strips contains seven elements, each insertion requires three comparisons.)

It is now known whether the rank of x is greater or less than k. If the rank of x is greater than k, throw away all of the elements in B; otherwise throw away all of the elements in A.

We are now left with approximately $\frac{3}{4} n$ elements, and we seek the k'th element of this smaller set, for some known k' (determined from the original value of k and the exact number of elements larger or smaller than it which were thrown out.)

We now recursively apply the algorithm to the smaller set of elements. In doing so, we note that it is possible to reconstitute strings of 15 out of strings of seven remaining after the $(\frac{1}{4})n$ elements were thrown out.

When the number of remaining elements is reduced to 64 or less, we find the desired quantile by sorting, which can be accomplished by no more than $6 n$ comparisons, for $n \leq 64$.

We carry out an analysis of the number of comparisons required by the algorithm as follows. Let

$Q(n) = $ the maximum number of comparisons required to find
a quantile from among n elements (from scratch)

$Q'(n) = $ the maximum number of comparisons required to find a
quantile from among n elements after they have been broken
into sorted strings of length 15

We have the relation:

$$Q(n) = 42 \left(\frac{n}{15}\right) + Q'(n) \qquad (2.3.1)$$

(It takes 42 comparisons to sort a string of length 15.)

It is further asserted that

$$Q'(n) = Q\left(\frac{n}{15}\right) + 3\left(\frac{n}{15}\right) + \frac{13}{2}\left(\frac{n}{30}\right) + Q'\left(\frac{3}{4}n\right) \qquad (2.3.2)$$

The terms in the sum come from the algorithm as follows:

$Q\left(\dfrac{n}{15}\right)$ is the number of comparisons to find the median of the medians (call it x).

$3\left(\dfrac{n}{15}\right)$ is the number of comparisons to insert x into each of $n/15$ "half strings" of length 7.

$\dfrac{13}{2}\left(\dfrac{n}{30}\right)$ is the number of comparisons to merge $n/30$ strings of length 7 into strings of length 15 (a dummy element being added after each pair of strings is merged.)

$Q'\left(\dfrac{3}{4}n\right)$ is the number of comparisons to find an arbitrary quantile for the new problem with $\left(\dfrac{3}{4}n\right)$ elements.

Substituting (2.3.1) into (2.3.2) we obtain

$$Q'(n) = .6033\,n + Q'\left(\frac{n}{15}\right) + Q'\left(\frac{3}{4}n\right)$$

Assuming $Q'(n)$ is of the form $Q'(n) = Kn$, we obtain:

$$Kn = .6033\,n + K\left(\frac{n}{15}\right) + K\left(\frac{3}{4}\right)n$$

so that

$$K \approx 3.29$$

and

$$Q'(n) \leq 3.29\,n$$

(A more exact analysis reduces this bound to $3.22\,n$; see exercises.)
Substitution of $Q'(n)$ into (2.3.1) yields

$$Q(n) \leq 2.8\,n + 3.29\,n = 6.09\,n$$

Blum and Floyd [1] have obtained $Q(n) \leq 5.43\,n$ by analyzing the more complicated strategy of throwing away everything greater (or less) than the discriminator x and reconstituting strings of length 15 from the irregular substrings that remain.

Very recent results have shown that by other, more complicated techniques, a worst case of approximately $3n$ comparisons is attainable.

EXERCISES 2.3

1. Carry out a more detailed analysis in which it is assumed that $n = 15(2t + 1)$, where t is odd, so that

$$Q'(n) = Q\left(\frac{n}{15}\right) + 6t + 13\left(\frac{(t+1)}{2}\right) + Q'\left(15\left(t + \left(\frac{(t+1)}{2}\right)\right)\right).$$

Show that this results in a bound of $Q'(n) \leq 3.22\,n$.

2. Analyze the algorithm for the case that the numbers are separated into strips of 7, instead of 15.

3. Carry out a general analysis in which it is assumed that the n elements are separated into strips of m, and find the value of m for which $Q(n)$ is minimum.

2.4. A LOWER BOUND ON THE MEDIAN COMPUTATION

It is clear that any method for computing the median (or other quantile) of n numbers must "look at" each of those numbers, i.e., each number must enter into at least one comparison. Thus, any algorithm must require at least Kn comparisons, for some K, in the worst case. How large must K be?

Any set of comparisons which determines $x_{(k)}$, the kth largest element, can be represented diagrammatically as seen at the top of page 69.

There are $(k - 1)$ elements larger than $x_{(k)}$ and $n - k$ elements smaller than $x_{(k)}$. Any element known to be larger (smaller) than $x_{(k)}$ must have been found to be larger (smaller) than $x_{(k)}$ by means of a direct comparison with an element already known to be larger (smaller) than $x_{(k)}$. Hence, for any $x_i \in \{x_1, x_2, \ldots, x_n\}$ and different from $x_{(k)}$, a comparison has taken place with some $y \in \{x_1, x_2, \ldots, x_n\}$ and the outcome of the comparison was

$$x_{(k)} \leq y < x_i$$

or

$$x_{(k)} \geq y > x_i$$

This is called a *crucial* comparison for x_i. Every $x_i \neq x_{(k)}$ must enter into a crucial comparison and no comparison is crucial for more than one element. Therefore, at least $n - 1$ crucial comparisons must be made.

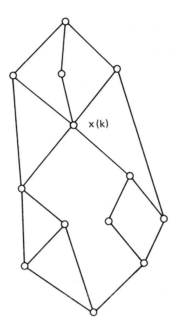

Now let us obtain a stronger result.

Theorem 2.4.1

Given a set $\{x_1, x_2, \ldots, x_n\}$ of n unordered elements, any algorithm to compute the kth largest element requires at least

$$n - 1 + \min (k - 1, n - k) \tag{2.4.1}$$

comparisons in the worst case (thus $\frac{3}{2} n$ comparisons, to find the median).

Proof: We shall assume that after each comparison the diagram of comparisons is of the simple form:

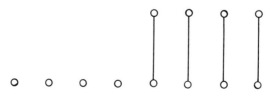

If at any point in the sequence of comparisons the diagram threatens to look different, we shall assume that an oracle (or "birdie") provides us with additional information sufficient to simplify the diagram. If, even with the extra information provided by the oracle, a certain number of comparisons is neces- sary, then surely that number of comparisons is necessary in the absence of the oracle.

We can parameterize the problem as follows. We are given n elements, of which we are looking for the kth largest, and we have s pairs in the diagram, where $s \leq n/2$. At any point in the algorithm we refer to the situation by (n, k, s).

Consider the following situation. A comparison is made between x and y:

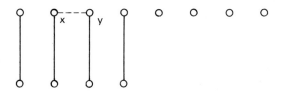

If x is found to be greater than y, then the oracle tells us that x is greater than all other elements. Therefore, x can be thrown away and the problem is re- duced to an $(n - 1, k - 1, s - 1)$ problem.

Suppose that a comparison is made between x and y:

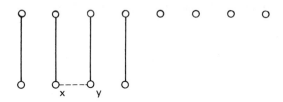

If x is found to be less than y, then the oracle tells us that x is less than all other elements. Therefore, x can be thrown away and the problem reduces to an $(n - 1, k - 1, s - 1)$ problem.

Suppose that a comparison is made between x and y as shown in any of the ways shown on page 71. In each of these situations, as well, the oracle enables us to make similar simplifications.

Given that the state of the computation is (n, k, s) one more comparison always yields one or another of the following states:

$$(n, k, s + 1)$$
$$(n - 1, k, s - 1)$$
$$(n - 1, k - 1, s - 1)$$

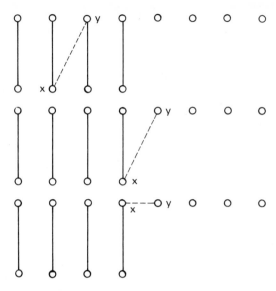

(We consider only worst case outcomes, eliminating others that are dominated, e.g. $(n - 1, R, D)$ is dominated by $(n, k, s - 1)$.)

Let $F(n, k, s)$ be the number of comparisons required to finish the algorithm, given state (n, k, s). We want to prove that

$$F(n, k, s) \geq n - s - 1 + \min \{k - 1, n - k\} \tag{2.4.2}$$

This can be established by induction on the value of $p = 2n - s$.

Relation (2.4.2) can easily be established for small values of p. For example $p = 2$ implies $n = 1$, $s = 0$ and (2.4.2) is valid in this case.

Now, by induction hypothesis, to finish from state $(n, k, s + 1)$ requires at least $F(n, k, s + 1)$ comparisons, where

$$F(n, k, s + 1) \geq n - s - 2 + \min \{k - 1, n - k\}$$

Hence, to finish from state (n, k, s) by going to state $(n, k, s + 1)$ requires at least $F(n, k, s + 1) + 1$ comparisons, where

$$F(n, k, s + 1) + 1 \geq n - s - 1 + \min \{k - 1, n - k\}$$

To finish from state $(n - 1, k, s - 1)$ requires at least $F(n - 1, k, s - 1)$ comparisons. Hence, to finish from state (n, k, s) by going to state $(n - 1,$

$k, s - 1$) requires at least $F(n - 1, k, s - 1) + 1$ comparisons, where

$$F(n - 1, k, s - 1) + 1 \geq n - s - 1 + \min \{k - 1, n - k - 1\}$$
$$+ 1 \geq n - s - 1 + \min \{k - 1, n - k\}$$

A similar demonstration holds for the case of finishing from state (n, k, s) by going to state $(n - 1, k - 1, s - 1)$. Hence, relation (2.4.2) is established and the theorem is proved. ∎

A rather different proof is obtained by assuming the existence of a demon, instead of an oracle. The demon attempts to frustrate the algorithm by determining the outcome of each successive comparison in such a way that the number of crucial comparisons in minimized.

2.5. CONTEXT-FREE LANGUAGE RECOGNITION

Let us now turn to the analysis of an algorithm due to Cocke, Younger, and Kasaimi, for recognizing context-free languages. For any specified grammar G, we wish to determine whether or not a given string x belongs to $L(G)$. We shall show that this can be accomplished in $0(n^3)$ running time, where n is the number of symbols in x.

2.5.1. Recognition Algorithm

We first recall Theorem 1.7.1.

Theorem 1.7.1 Chomsky normal form

Every context-free grammar G is equivalent to a grammar $G' = [N', \Sigma', P', S']$ in Chomsky normal form whose productions have the following forms:

$$A \rightarrow BC, \qquad A \rightarrow a, \qquad S' \rightarrow \wedge$$

where A, B, C are nonterminals, a is a terminal symbol, and $\wedge$ is the empty string.

Hereafter we shall assume that any grammar G is in Chomsky normal form.

If a string α can be generated from the nonterminal A we say that α *reduces to* A. The problem of recognition is that of determining whether or not x reduces to S, the sentence nonterminal. We shall do this by first finding the sets of nonterminals to which substrings of length one reduce, then the sets of nonterminals to which substrings of length two reduce, etc., until finally we find the set of nonterminals to which the complete string x itself reduces.

If $x = \wedge$, then $x \in L(G)$ if and only if $S \rightarrow \wedge$ is a production, and clearly this is very easily checked. Hence assume that x is nonempty and of the form $a_1 a_2 \ldots a_n$ where $n \geq 1$.

Let $N(i, j)$ denote the set of nonterminals to which the substring $a_i a_{i+1} \ldots a_j$ reduces. It is easy to determine $N(i, i)$, for $i = 1, 2, \ldots, n$. Let $L(a_i)$ denote the set of all nonterminal symbols on the left-hand side of productions which have a_i on the right. That is,

$$L(a_i) = \{A \mid A \rightarrow a_i \in P\}$$

Then clearly,

$$N(i, i) = L(a_i) \tag{2.5.1}$$

Now consider how to find $N(i, i + 1)$ for $i = 1, 2, \ldots, n - 1$. If $B \in N(i, i)$, $C \in N(i + 1, i + 1)$, and $A \rightarrow BC$ is a production, then $A \in N(i, i + 1)$. Formally, we indicate this as follows. Let $N(i, i)N(i + 1, i + 1)$ denote the set of all strings of the form BC, where $B \in N(i, i)$, $C \in N(i + 1, i + 1)$. Let

$$L(N(i, i)N(i + 1, i + 1)) = \{A \mid A \rightarrow BC \in P,$$
$$BC \in N(i, i)N(i + 1, i + 1)\}.$$

Then clearly,

$$N(i, i + 1) = L(N(i, i)N(i + 1, i + 1))$$

For $N(i, i + 2)$, $i = 1, 2, \ldots, n - 2$, we have the relation

$$N(i, i + 2) = L(N(i, i)N(i + 1, i + 2)) \cup L(N(i, i + 1)$$
$$N(i + 2, i + 2))$$

And, more generally, we have, for $i < j$, the relation

$$N(i, j) = \bigcup_{k=0}^{j-i-1} L(N(i, i + k)N(i + k + 1, j)) \tag{2.5.2}$$

The relations (2.5.1) and (2.5.2) provide a sufficiently complete characterization of the recognition algorithm for our purposes.

2.5.2.　Ground Rules for the Complexity Analysis

It is clear that the running time of the algorithm depends upon the computer which is to be used, and how the algorithm is programmed for that computer.

We shall assume a hypothetical computer with the following general characteristics. The computer has unlimited random access memory. Input data reside in this memory at the beginning of the computation and output data are left in it at the end. Thus, there is no need to consider input-output operations. The memory stores logical constants and integers in words of any required size. The access time for these words is constant, unaffected by the size of the words, and the number of words stored.

The hypothetical computer is capable of executing instructions of a conventional and mundane type, e.g., integer arithmetic operations, numerical comparisons and branching operations, etc. It is not necessary to indicate explicitly what these instructions are.

Ordinarily, we assume that each executed instruction requires one unit of time, regardless of the size of the operands involved. However, we should take care that this assumption does not lead to an unrealistic complexity estimate because of the size of operands.

We are able to bypass the question of instruction timing, because we are not interested in estimating the actual running time of the algorithm, but only the asymptotic *order* of the running time. That is, when we assert that the running time is $O(n^3)$, where n is the number of symbols in x, we are simply declaring that the running time is given by some polynomial of the form

$$P(x) = a_3 n^3 + a_2 n^2 + a_1 n + a_0$$

If the speed of the computer is, say, doubled, or the execution times of the individual instructions are changed, the coefficients in the polynomial will be modified, but the running time will remain $O(n^3)$.

Similarly, we are able to avoid nagging details of the programming implementation of the algorithm. We will assume that the algorithm will be programmed in a fairly straightforward, obvious way, with neither clever tricks nor unnecessary inefficiencies.

2.5.3. Estimate of Running Time

Let us now estimate the running time of the algorithm, as a function of n, the number of symbols in x.

There are n sets $N(i, i)$ to be computed by relation (2.5.1). Each set $N(i, i)$ is determined by simply checking for all productions of the form $A \rightarrow a_i$. The number of computational steps required for each set $N(i, i)$ is dependent only on the number of productions in the grammar, and can thus be considered to be bounded by a constant. Thus the total running time attributable to relation (2.5.1) is $O(n)$.

There are exactly $n(n - 1)/2$ or $0(n^2)$ sets $N(i, j)$, where $i < j$, to be computed by relation (2.5.2). The size of each of the sets $N(i, i + k)$, $N(i + k + 1, j)$ depends only on the number of nonterminal symbols in the grammar and is thus independent of n. The number of computational steps required to determine $L(N(i, i + k)N(i + k + 1, j))$ depends only on the size of $N(i, i + k)N(i + k + 1, j)$ and on the number of productions in the grammar, and can thus be considered to be bounded by a constant. There are $0(n)$ values of k over which the union must be taken in (2.5.2) and hence there are $0(n)$ steps to be performed for the computation of each set $N(i, j)$ by (2.5.2). And since there are $0(n^2)$ sets to be computed, the total running time attributable to relation (2.5.2) is $0(n^2) \times 0(n)$ or $0(n^3)$ overall.

The total running time for the algorithm is thus $0(n)$, for (2.5.1), plus $0(n^3)$, for (2.5.2), or $0(n^3)$ overall.

The amount of storage required by the algorithm is $0(n^2)$. By contrast, there are other algorithms requiring exponential running time, but as little as $0((\log n)^2)$ space. Clearly, there are many tradeoffs possible between running time and storage, for this problem and most others.

EXERCISE 2.5

1. A *linear* grammar is a context-free grammar in which each production contains at most one nonterminal symbol on the right-hand side. Every linear grammar G is equivalent to a grammar $G' = \{N', \Sigma', P', S'\}$ in which productions have the following forms:

$$A \to aB, \qquad A \to Ba, \qquad A \to a, \qquad S' \to \wedge$$

where A, B are nonterminals, a is a terminal symbol, and $\wedge$ is the empty string. Develop relations analogous to (2.5.1) and (2.5.1) for linear grammars and show that the recognition problem can be solved in $0(n^2)$ running time.

2.6. POLYNOMIAL-BOUNDED COMPUTATIONS

We have seen that the recognition of context-free languages can be accomplished in $0(n^3)$ running time. In general, we say that any algorithm is *polynomial-bounded* if its worst case running time is bounded by a function in order n^k, where n is an appropriate measure of the size of the input.

In the realm of combinatorial computations, it has come to be accepted that an algorithm is "good" or "efficient" if it is polynomial-bounded, and "inefficient" otherwise. Thus, a combinatorial problem is "solved" when a polynomial-bounded algorithm has been found for it.

2.6.1. Justification of Polynomial-Bounded Criterion

The reader may question the appropriateness of equating polynomial-boundedness with computational efficiency. And there is, of course, good reason to ask why one should prefer an algorithm requiring, say $10^{20} \times n^{100}$ steps to one requiring $(1.01)^n$ steps. In answer, we give the following justifications:

Machine Independence.   The notion of polynomial-boundedness is essentially machine independent. That is, an algorithm which is polynomial-bounded for one type of computer, e.g., an idealized UNIVAC 1108, will be polynomial-bounded when executed on virtually any other computer, e.g., an idealized ILLIAC 4 or a Turing machine.

Asymptotic Behavior.   A polynomial-bounded algorithm requires fewer computational steps than a nonpolynomial-bounded one, for all but a finite number of problem instances. (Admittedly, those values of n for which $(1.01)^n < 10^{20} \times n^{100}$ may be precisely those of practical interest, but in practice this situation is unlikely.)

Accordance with Experience.   Experience tends to indicate that polynomial-bounded algorithms do indeed tend to be preferable to those which are not.

Susceptability to Theoretical Analysis.   The notion of polynomial-boundedness lends itself well to theoretical analysis, as indicated below.

2.6.2. Combinatorial Problems Formulated as
Recognition Problems

One very good way to proceed with a theoretical analysis of the inherent complexity of combinatorial optimization problems is to view these problems as recognition problems for formal languages.

For example, consider the notorious "traveling salesman" problem. A network with n nodes is given, in which each arc has a specified length. One is asked to find a cycle of minimum length which contains each of the nodes of the network.

A recognition problem related to the traveling salesman problem can be formulated as follows. Let the matrix of integer arc lengths of the network be encoded as a single string of symbols. (Take the first row of the matrix, follow it by the second, etc., with appropriate punctuation.) Concatenate to this string a number k which is an upper bound on the length of a shortest tour in the network.

Consider the formal language consisting of all strings formed as in the above paragraph. The recognition problem for this language now amounts to the following. Given a string of symbols, interpret (if possible) this string as a matrix of arc lengths and an integer k. Accept this string as a sentence of the language if the network contains a tour of length not greater than k; otherwise reject the string.

2.6.3. Cook's Theorem

Now consider a very simple and basic recognition problem known as the *satisfiability problem*. A Boolean expression in conjunctive normal form, or "product of sums" form, e.g., $(A + \bar{B})(\bar{A} + \bar{B})(\bar{A} + \bar{B} + C)$, is said to be *satisfiable* if there is some assignment of "true" and "false" values to its variables, such that the expression evaluates to "true." For example, let $A =$ true, $B =$ false, $C =$ true (or false) and the expression above is seen to be satisfiable.

There is no known polynomial-bounded algorithm for solving the recognition problem for the formal language consisting of all satisfiable Boolean expressions in conjunctive normal form. That is, no known algorithm requires only a polynomial-bounded number of steps when execution is to be performed by a physically realizable computing device. There is, however, such an algorithm, if execution is performed by a physically unrealizable computer known as the *nondeterministic* Turing machine.

The reader is assumed to be familiar with the notion of an ordinary (deterministic) Turing machine, with its finite set of symbols, infinite tape, finite-state reading head, etc. A nondeterministic Turing machine is like an ordinary Turing machine, except that state transitions are not necessarily uniquely determined. That is, for any state-symbol combination, a multiplicity of state transitions may be possible.

A nondeterministic Turing machine is said to *accept* an input tape if there exists some permissible sequence of state transitions leading to an accepting state.

There is no recognition problem which can be solved by a nondeterministic Turing machine that cannot also be solved by a deterministic Turing machine, if the latter is permitted enough time. There are, however, problems which the nondeterministic Turing machine can solve much more efficiently. Roughly speaking, this is because the nondeterministic machine is capable of "guessing" the correct solution, whereas the deterministic machine must, in effect, try all possible solutions to find the correct one. For example, in the case of the satisfiability problem, the nondeterministic Turing machine can guess at a set of values for the Boolean variables and then simply verify that this guess does in fact result in satisfiability.

We make the following two conjectures:

Conjecture A

The satisfiability problem cannot be solved in a polynomial-bounded number of steps by any deterministic Turing machine. (It is known that this is possible for a nondeterministic machine.)

Conjecture B

There are recognition problems which can be solved in a polynomial-bounded number of steps by nondeterministic Turing machines which cannot be solved in a polynomial-bounded number of steps by any deterministic Turing machine.

We label the above as conjectures because we cannot prove them to be true. However, we do have the following important theorem of Stephen Cook:

Theorem 2.6.1

Conjectures A and B are equivalent, i.e., they are either both true or both false.

The proof of this theorem is beyond the scope of this chapter.

2.6.4. NP-Complete Problems and Karp's Reductions

There are many so-called "NP-complete" problems which are equivalent to the satisfiability problem with respect to the notion of polynomial-boundedness. That is, if a polynomial-bounded algorithm can be devised for any one of these NP-complete problems, then a polynomial-bounded algorithm exists for each of the other NP-complete problems, including the satisfiability problem, and by Cook's theorem, Conjecture B will be false.

The following list was compiled principally by Richard Karp, but also partly by Robert Tarjan, by the present author, and by others. In each case, NP-completeness is demonstrated by appropriate problem reductions some of which are quite intricate in nature. An example of such a problem reduction is given below.

Satisfiability Problem.   This was discussed above. The specialization of this problem in which each clause (i.e., sum) of the expression contains no more than two letters can, however, be solved in a polynomial-bounded number of steps by the so-called "resolution" technique.

Hamiltonian Cycle Problem.   The problem of determining whether or not a given graph contains a Hamiltonian cycle is NP-complete. Moreover, this problem is NP-complete even when the problem is restricted to the class of regular graphs of degree three. This situation can be contrasted with the very easy problem of determining whether or not a graph contains a Euler tour.

Clique Problem. Given a graph and an integer k, does the graph contain a complete subgraph with k nodes? This *NP*-complete problem can be contrasted with the following polynomial-bounded problem: Given a graph and an integer k, does the graph contain a subgraph with node-connectivity k? A solution to this latter problem has been found by David Matula.

3-D Assignment Problem. Given a three-dimensional matrix of 0's and 1's and an integer k, does there exist a selection of k 1's within the matrix no two of which are in a line (row, column, or "file")? This *NP*-complete problem contrasts with the classical (two-dimensional) assignment problem which is certainly polynomial bounded.

Covering Arcs with Nodes. Let us say that a node "covers" all the arcs incident to it. Given a graph and an integer k, does there exist a selection of k nodes which will cover all the arcs? This *NP*-complete problem contrasts with the problem of covering nodes with arcs, which can be solved in a polynomial-bounded member of steps by matching theory.

Chromatic Number Problem. Given a graph and an integer k, is it possible to paint the nodes of the graph with k colors, such that no two nodes with the same color are adjacent (connected by an arc)? The author must admit that, at the time this is written, he does not know whether or not the corresponding coloring problem for arcs is *NP*-complete.

Steiner Network Problem. Given an arc weighted graph, a specified subset of nodes, and an integer k, is it possible to connect together all of the nodes in the specified subset by means of a selection of arcs whose total weight does not exceed k? If the specified subset of nodes contains *all* the nodes of the graph, we simply have the simple spanning tree problem, which can be solved by the so-called "greedy" algorithm.

A Sequencing Problem. Given a set of jobs, each with a known processing time, deadline, and penalty, and an integer k, is it possible to sequence the jobs on a single machine in such a way that the sum of the penalties for the late jobs does not exceed k? If all processing times are equal, or if all penalties are the same, or if all deadlines are the same, the problem can be solved in a polynomial-bounded number of steps.

Feedback Arc Set Problem. Given a strongly connected directed graph and an integer k, is it possible to delete k arcs from the graph so as to render it acyclic? This problem is *NP*-complete, whereas the following problem is polynomial-bounded, as shown by Eswaran and Tarjan. Given an acyclic directed graph and an integer k, is it possible to add k arcs to the graph so as to render it strongly connected?

2.6.5. Example of a Problem Reduction

As an example of the sort of problem reduction that is employed to compile the list of NP-complete problems in the previous section, we illustrate the reduction of the satisfiability problem to the clique problem.

For a given Boolean expression in conjunctive normal form, we form a graph with one node for each letter in the given expression. This graph is complete, i.e., contains all possible arcs, except that (1) it does not contain an arc between two nodes associated with letters from the same clause and (2) it does not contain an arc between nodes associated with a letter X and its complement $\bar{X}$. We assert (and the reader is invited to prove) that the Boolean expression is satisfiable if and only if the corresponding graph contains a complete subgraph with k nodes, where k is the number of clauses in the expression.

An example of this construction for the expression

$$(A + B) (\bar{B} + C + D) (\bar{A})$$

is indicated below:

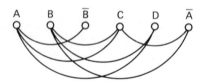

The reader will easily see that the expression is satisfiable and that the corresponding graph contains many 3-cliques.

The reduction in the reverse direction, i.e., from the clique problem to the satisfiability problem, can be carried out by the formulation of an appropriate Boolean expression, or by a uniform encoding technique for NP-complete problems devised by Cook.

2.6.6. Comments

Although we are not yet able to prove it, it seems very unlikely that polynomial-bounded algorithms will ever be found for the NP-complete problems, such as those listed above. The very size and diversity of the list of these problems seems, of itself, to be strong circumstantial evidence in this direction. However, this is not to say that eminently practical solution methods are not possible, including some algorithms which may be far superior to those known at the present time.

It should also be noted that the nonexistence of polynomial-bounded algorithms does not necessarily imply that the only possible algorithms are those which require an exponentially growing number of steps. There are, of course, many possible growth rates between polynomial and exponential, e.g., $n^{\log n}$.

Moreover, the inherent difficulties of the NP-complete problems may actually be quite different.

Acknowledgement

The author is indebted to Professor R. M. Karp for material adapted from his class notes, particularly with respect to the median problem.

REFERENCES

1. BLUM, M., R. W. FLOYD, V. PRATT, R. L. RIVEST, and R. E. TARJAN, "Time Bounds for Selection," *J. Computer and System Sciences* 7 (1973), 448–461.

2. BOOK, R. V. "On Languages Accepted in Polynomial Time," *SIAM J. Computing* 1 (1972), 281–287.

3. BORODIN, A., "Computational Complexity: Theory and Practice," to appear in *Current Trends in the Theory of Computing,* ed. by A. Aho, Prentice Hall, Inc., Englewood Cliffs, N. J.

4. COOK, S. A., "The Complexity of Theorem Proving Procedures," *Proc. 3rd Annual ACM Symposium on Theory of Computing* (1971), 151–158.

5. COOK, S. A., "A Hierarchy of Nondeterministic Time Complexity," *Proc. 4th Annual ACM Symposium on Theory of Computing* (1972), 187–192.

6. ESWARAN, K. and R. TARJAN, "Minimal Augmentation of Graphs," to appear in *SIAM J. Computing.*

7. KARP, R. M., "Reducibility among Combinatorial Problems," *Proc. IBM Symposium on Complexity of Computer Computations.* Plenum Press, N.Y., 1973.

8. KARP, R. M., Mimeographed Notes for Computer Science 230, University of California, Berkeley, Spring 1971 and Fall 1972.

9. LAWLER, E. L., "The Complexity of Combinatorial Computations," *Proc. of 1971 Polytechnic Institute of Brooklyn Symposium on Computers and Automata,* Polytechnic Institute of Booklyn Press, New York, 1971.

10. STRASSEN, V., "Gaussian Elimination is Not Optimal," *Numerische Mathematik* 13 (1969), 354–356.

11. TARJAN, R., "An Efficient Planarity Algorithm," *STAN-CS-244–71,* Ph. D. dissertation, Computer Science Dept., Stanford University, Nov. 1971.

12. TARJAN, R., "Depth First Search and Linear Graph Algorithm," *SIAM J. Computing* 1 (1972), 146–160.

13. WINOGRAD, S., "On the Number of Multiplications Required to Compute Certain Functions," *Comm. Pure and Applied Math.* 23 (1970), 165–179.

14. YOUNGER, D. H., "Recognition and Parsing of Context Free Languages in Time n^3," *Information and Control* 10 (1967), 189–208.

15. AHO, A. V., J. E. HOPCROFT, and J. D. ULLMAN, *The Design and Analysis of Computer Algorithms,* Addison-Wesley, Reading, Mass., 1974.

3

A COMBINATORIAL STUDY
OF SOME SCHEDULING
ALGORITHMS†

C. L. Liu
Department of Computer Science
University of Illinois
Urbana, Illinois

Editor's Note:

This chapter is a tutorial introduction to combinatorial analysis of scheduling algorithms. Although proofs for some of the theorems were not given here, examples to illustrate the results and pointers to literature containing the proofs are carefully provided.

The material presented here and that of Chapter 2 provides a clear picture on combinatorial approach to algorithmic analysis.

The chapter is written so that readers with only a basic knowledge in combinatorics can understand it. For readers who have no knowledge or who want to refresh their memory on combinatorics, they are referred to Chapter 6 of the following book.

Preparata, F. P. and R. T. Yeh, Introduction to Discrete Structures, *Addison-Wesley Publishing Company, 1973.*

3.1. INTRODUCTION

A topic of significant interest in the study of computation algorithms is that of algorithms producing optimal results. An algorithm that determines

†This work was partly supported by NSF Grant GJ31222.

how traffic should be directed to maximize the total traffic flow and an algorithm that determines how workmen should be assigned to jobs to maximize the efficiency are examples of such algorithms. From a mathematical point of view, to be able to obtain a best possible result is an ultimate goal one always tries to reach. From a practical point of view, a best possible result would invariably mean an increase in efficiency or a reduction in cost. In this chapter, we shall present several examples, all drawn from the general area of job sequencing and scheduling, to illustrate some of the concepts concerning algorithms that produce results that are optimal according to some chosen criteria.

It should be noted, however, that there are many problems for which no algorithm for producing an optimal result is known. Furthermore, there are also many instances in which although such an algorithm is available, to carry out the algorithmic steps to obtain the optimal result might be prohibitively tedious or expensive. A simple example is the case in which there is only a finite number of ways to perform a certain task. Clearly, we can always examine all the possible ways of performing the task and then pick the one that yields the best result. However, to exhaustively examine all possible ways to perform the task might not be a practical proposition at all. Consequently, in many occasions one might wish to settle for algorithms that produce only suboptimal results. Indeed, settling for something that is short of the very best is a very attractive idea as will be illustrated in our subsequent discussion.

In evaluating the performance of an algorithm, we can consider either its average performance or its worst case performance. Since an algorithm works on different sets of input data, the performance of an algorithm can either be measured by its expected performance on the basis of a given statistical distribution of the input data or be measured by its performance corresponding to the most unfavorable (with respect to the algorithm) set of input data. To study the average performance of algorithms is known as a *statistical analysis* and to study the worst case performance of algorithms is known as a *combinatorial analysis* of the algorithms. Our discussion in this chapter will be restricted to combinatorial analysis of the performance of algorithms.

3.2.   A SCHEDULING PROBLEM IN MULTI-PROCESSOR COMPUTING SYSTEMS

We consider the problem of scheduling a set of jobs on a multiprocessor computing system that has a set of identical processors capable of independent operation on independent jobs. Let $P_1, P_2, \ldots, P_n$ denote the n identical processors in a multiprocessor computing system. Let $\mathcal{J} = \{ J_1, J_2, \ldots, J_r \}$ denote a set of jobs to be executed on the computing system. We assume that the execution of a job occupies one and only one processor. Moreover, since the processors are identical, a job can be executed on any one of the processors. Let $\mu(J_i)$ denote the *execution time* of task J_i, that is, the amount of time it takes to execute J_i on a processor. There is also a partial ordering $<$ specified over $\mathcal{J}$. It is required that if $J_i < J_j$ then the execution of job J_j cannot begin until the execution of job J_i has been completed. (J_i is said to be a *predecessor* of J_j, and J_j is said to be a *successor* of J_i.) Formally, a set of tasks is specified by an ordered triple ($\mathcal{J}, \mu, <$) where μ is a function from $\mathcal{J}$ to the reals. A set of jobs can be described by a directed graph such as that in Fig. 3.2.1(a). (Since the meaning of such a graphical description is amply clear, we shall not attempt to give an explanation.)

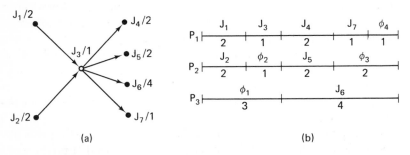

(a)   (b)

Fig. 3.2.1

By *scheduling* a set of jobs on a multiprocessor computing system we mean to specify for each job J_i the time interval within which it is to be executed and the processsor P_k on which execution will take place.[†] (Without loss of generality, we assume that execution of the set begins at $t = 0$.) An explicit way to describe a schedule is a *timing diagram,* which is also known as the *Gantt chart.* As an example, the timing diagram of a schedule for the execution of the set of jobs in Fig. 3.2.1(a) on a three-processor computing system is shown in Fig. 3.2.1(b). In a given schedule, an *idle period* of a processor is defined to be a time interval within which the processor is not executing a job (while at least one other processor is executing some job). We use $\phi_1, \phi_2, \ldots$ to denote idle periods of the processors as shown in Fig. 3.2.1(b). Also, with a slight abuse in notations, we use $\mu(\phi_1), \mu(\phi_2), \ldots$ to denote the lengths of the idle periods. Notice that in a schedule, a processor might be left idle for a period of time either because there is no executable job within that time period or because it is an intentional choice. (A job is said to be *executable* at a certain time instant if the execution of its predecessors have all been completed at that time.) Clearly, it is never necessary nor beneficial in a schedule to leave all processors idle at the same time.

The *completion time* of a schedule is the total time it takes to execute all the jobs according to the schedule. We shall use completion time as the criterion for comparing different schedules. Consequently, for a given set of

---

[†]Throughout our discussion in this section, we assume that once the execution of a job begins on a processor, it will continue until completion without any interruption.

jobs an optimal schedule is one with minimal completion time. It is evident that optimal schedules and algorithms that yield optimal schedules are of significant interest to us. Unfortunately, there is no algorithm (short of exhaustion) that will produce an optimal schedule for an arbitrary set of jobs. As a matter of fact, algorithms that produce optimal schedules are known only for the following cases:

1. All jobs have the same execution time and the partial ordering $<$ is such that either every job has at most one successor or every job has at most one predecessor.
2. All jobs have the same execution time and there are only two processors in the computing system.

As an illustration, we shall discuss case (1) here.

3.2.1. An Optimal Scheduling Algorithm

For a given set of jobs ($\mathscr{J}$, μ, $<$), we define the *level* of a job as follows:

1. The level of a job that has no successor is equal to 1.
2. The level of a job that has one or more successors is equal to one plus the maximal value of the levels of the successors of the job.

As an example, for the jobs in Fig. 3.2.2 the level of J_1 is 4, the levels of J_2 and J_3 are 3, the levels of J_4, J_5, J_6, and J_7 are 2, and the levels of J_8 and J_9 are 1. For a given set of jobs, we shall use h to denote the value of the highest level and use $N_i, i = 1, 2, \ldots, h$, to denote the number of jobs at level i.

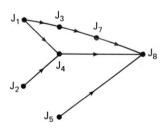

Fig. 3.2.2

Theorem 3.2.1

Let ($\mathscr{J}$, μ, $<$) be a set of jobs with execution times all equal to 1.† A neces-

---

†Clearly, when the execution times of all the jobs are equal, there is no loss of generality in assuming them to be 1.

sary condition for completing the execution of the jobs in time t, where t is an integer, is

$$N_h + N_{h-1} + \ldots + N_i \leq n(t - i + 1) \qquad (3.2.1)$$

for $i = h, h - 1, \ldots, 1$, where n is the number of processors in the computing system.

Proof: If we are to complete the execution of all jobs at time t, we must complete the execution of all the jobs at levels $h, h - 1, \ldots, i$ by $t - i + 1$. Because if this is not the case, there will be a chain of i jobs to be executed in the remaining $i - 1$ time units, which is an impossibility. Since the computing system can execute at most $n(t - i + 1)$ jobs in $t - i + 1$ units of time, the inequalities in (3.2.1) follows immediately. ∎

It should be pointed out that Theorem 3.2.1 has a clear physical interpretation. Since an n-processor computing system can execute n jobs of unit execution time in each time unit, it can execute at most $n\tau$ jobs altogether in τ time units. Consequently, in any schedule the total number of jobs to be executed in $n\tau$ time units can never exceed $n\tau$ for any integer τ.

Theorem 3.2.2

Let $(\mathscr{J}, \mu, <)$ be a set of jobs with execution times all equal to 1. Moreover, the partial ordering $<$ is such that every job has at most one successor. If for some integer t

$$N_h + N_{h-1} + \ldots + N_i \leq n(t - i + 1) \qquad (3.2.2)$$

for $i = h, h - 1, \ldots, 1$, then the jobs can be executed in time t.

Proof: We shall give an explicit construction of a schedule that executes the jobs in time t. Let us label the jobs in the following manner:

1. Initially, a job at level i is labelled with the integer $t - i + 1$.
2. Let M_j denote the number of jobs that are labelled j. If $M_j \leq n$ for $j = 1, 2, \ldots, t$, stop.
3. Suppose that $M_j \leq n$ for $j = 1, 2, \ldots, k - 1$ but $M_k > n$. Since $M_k > M_{k-1}$, there is a job labelled k that is not a successor of the jobs labelled $k - 1$. Change the label of this job from k to $k - 1$, and repeat step (2).

Because of the inequalities in (3.2.2), at the termination of the labelling process the labels of the jobs are within the range $[1, t]$. (No jobs will have a label

0 or a negative label.) Moreover, it is clear that jobs with the same label are independent of each other. Consequently, if we execute all jobs labelled j in the jth time unit, we shall complete the execution of the jobs in time t. ∎

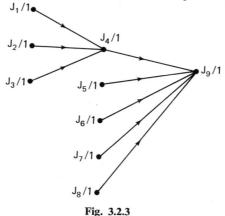

Fig. 3.2.3

For example, consider the set of jobs shown in Fig. 3.2.3. For $t = 5$ and $n = 3$ in Theorem 3.2.2, we obtain the labels:

Job	J_1	J_2	J_3	J_4	J_5	J_6	J_7	J_8	J_9
Label	2	2	3	4	3	3	4	4	5

and the schedule shown in Fig. 3.2.4.

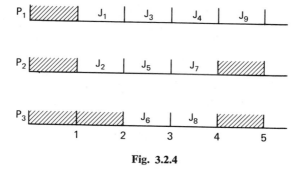

Fig. 3.2.4

It follows immediately from Theorem 3.2.2 that if we choose a smallest integer t such that the inequalities in (3.2.2) are satisfied, then the schedule we obtained according to the labelling procedure is an optimal schedule. A slight modification of the labelling procedure will enable us to determine the smallest value of t. Let us change step (1) in the labelling procedure to

1. Initially, a job at level i is labelled with the integer $h - i + 1$.

Note that at the termination of the labelling procedure, no job will have a label larger than h. Let a denote the smallest label. (Clearly, $a \leq 1$.) Then $h - a + 1$ will be the value of the smallest t that satisfies the inequalities in (3.2.2). We leave it to the reader to confirm the validity of this claim. Furthermore, it is straightforward to obtain an optimal schedule from the labels.

As an example, for the set of jobs in Fig. 3.2.3 and for $n = 3$ we obtain the labels

Job	J_1	J_2	J_3	J_4	J_5	J_6	J_7	J_8	J_9
Label	0	0	1	2	1	1	2	2	3

Since $h = 3$ and $a = 0$ in this case, the minimal time for completing the execution of this set of jobs is 4.

3.2.2. Lower Bounding the Performance of Algorithms

In view of the difficulty of obtaining an optimal schedule for an arbitrary set of jobs we turn to the possibility of employing algorithms that are easy to implement although they do not necessarily yield optimal schedules. We study now a class of scheduling algorithms in which processors will not be left idle intentionally. That is, a processor is left idle for a certain period of time if and only if no job is executable within that period. In this case, a scheduling algorithm can be specified by merely giving the rules on how jobs are to be chosen for execution at any instant when one or more processor is free. (Of course, the choice is only among jobs that are executable at that instant.) A simple way to spell out the rule is to assign priorities to the jobs so that jobs with higher priorities will be executed instead of jobs with lower priorities when they are competing for processors. (If two or more processors are available, we shall make an arbitrary choice.) Consequently, we call such algorithms *priority-driven scheduling algorithms*. Thus, for example, for the set of jobs in Fig. 3.2.1(a), the list (in the order of decreasing priorities)

$$L = (J_1, J_2, J_3, J_4, J_5, J_6, J_7)$$

yields the schedule in Fig. 3.2.1(b). Note however, the list

$$L' = (J_4, J_5, J_6, J_1, J_7, J_3, J_2)$$

also yields the same schedule, because at any time instant only jobs that are *executable* at that instant will compete for processors. In other words, whenever a processor is available, we search the priority list from left to right and will execute the first executable job encountered.

It should be pointed out that leaving a processor idle intentionally might be desirable in terms of minimizing the completion time. Figure 3.2.5 shows an example in which between $t = 9$ and $t = 10$, processor P_2 is left idle although J_3 is executable at $t = 9$. The reader can convince himself easily that the schedule in Fig. 3.2.5(b) is better than any schedule obtained by a priority-driven scheduling algorithm.

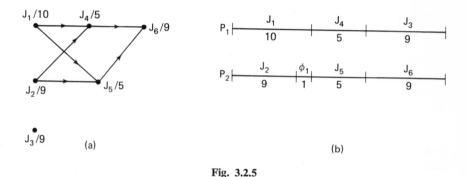

(a)   (b)

Fig. 3.2.5

We also wish to point out several anomalies in priority-driven schedules which are not intuitively obvious at all. Consider the set of tasks specified in Fig. 3.2.6. Let

$$L = (J_1, J_2, J_3, J_4, J_5, J_6, J_7, J_8, J_9)$$

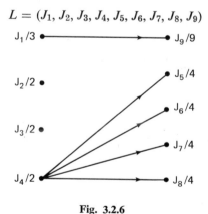

Fig. 3.2.6

With three processors, the completion time for the execution of this set of jobs will be 12. Suppose we relax the constraints on job-sequencing by removing the arrow between J_4 and J_5, and the arrow between J_4 and J_6. The reader can check that the completion time will *increase* to 16. Suppose we reduce the execution time of *each* job by 1 unit. Again the completion time will *increase* to 13. Suppose we execute this set of jobs on four processors. Surprisingly enough, the completion time will *increase* to 15. Note that all these "strange" phenomena are due to the simple fact that we are not willing to leave a processor idle when it can be used to execute a job at a certain time.

Theorem 3.2.3

Let $(\mathscr{J}, \mu, <)$ be a given set of jobs to be executed on an n-processor computing system. Let L and L' be two priority lists, and ω and ω' be the corresponding completion time when the jobs are executed according to these lists. Then

$$\frac{\omega'}{\omega} \leq \frac{2n-1}{n}$$

Moreover, the bound is best possible.

Proof: To simplify the presentation, we prove the theorem for $n = 2$. The proof for the general case is analogous. Consider the timing diagram for the execution of the set of jobs according to the priority list L' as illustrated in Fig. 3.2.7. We observe first that the termination of an idle period in one processor coincides with the completion of the execution of a job in another processor. (Otherwise, the idle period would not have been terminated.) Let ϕ_i be an idle period in a processor. A job J_{ij} is said to overlap with ϕ_i if

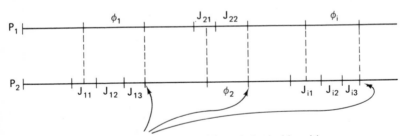

Termination of an idle period coincides with
the completion of the execution of a task

Fig. 3.2.7

the execution of J_{ij} in the other processor overlaps with ϕ_i. For example, in Fig. 3.2.7, J_{11}, J_{12}, J_{13}, overlap with ϕ_1. Let $J_{i1}, J_{i2}, J_{i3}, \ldots, J_{il}$ be jobs that overlap with ϕ_i. We claim that

$$J_{i1} < J_{i2} < J_{i3} < \ldots < J_{il}$$

Because if this is not the case the jobs $J_{i1}, J_{i2}, \ldots, J_{il}$ will not have to be executed sequentially. Similarly, let ϕ_j be another idle period. Let $J_{j1}, J_{j2},$

$J_{j3}, \ldots, J_{jm}$ be jobs that overlap with ϕ_j. Repeating the argument, we have

$$J_{j1} < J_{j2} < J_{j3} < \ldots < J_{jm}$$

Moreover, if ϕ_i occurs before ϕ_j, we have

$$J_{i1} < J_{i2} < \ldots < J_{il} < J_{j1} < J_{j2} < \ldots < J_{jm}$$

because every job executed after the completion of J_{il} must be a successor of J_{il}. Consequently, there is a subset of jobs $\mathscr{C}$ overlapping with the idle periods such that

1. $\mathscr{C}$ is a chain.
2. $\sum\limits_{J_k \in \mathscr{C}} \mu(J_k) \geq \sum\limits_{\phi_i \in \Phi} \mu(\phi_i)$

where Φ is the set of all idle periods in the schedule according to the priority list L'. We note that

$$\omega' = \tfrac{1}{2} [\sum\limits_{J_j \in \mathscr{J}} \mu(J_j) + \sum\limits_{\phi_i \in \Phi} \mu(\phi_i)]$$
$$\leq \tfrac{1}{2} [\sum\limits_{J_j \in \mathscr{J}} \mu(J_j) + \sum\limits_{J_k \in \mathscr{C}} \mu(J_k)]$$

Since

$$\omega \geq \tfrac{1}{2} \sum\limits_{J_j \in \mathscr{J}} \mu(J_j)$$

and

$$\omega \geq \sum\limits_{J_k \in \mathscr{C}} \mu(J_k)$$

(3.2.3) becomes

$$\omega' \leq \omega + \tfrac{1}{2} \omega$$

or

$$\frac{\omega'}{\omega} \leq \frac{3}{2}$$

That this bound is best possible can be demonstrated by the example in Fig. 3.2.8. ∎

The significance of the result in Theorem 3.2.3 is as follows: Although it is desirable to have a priority list such that the completion time is minimal,

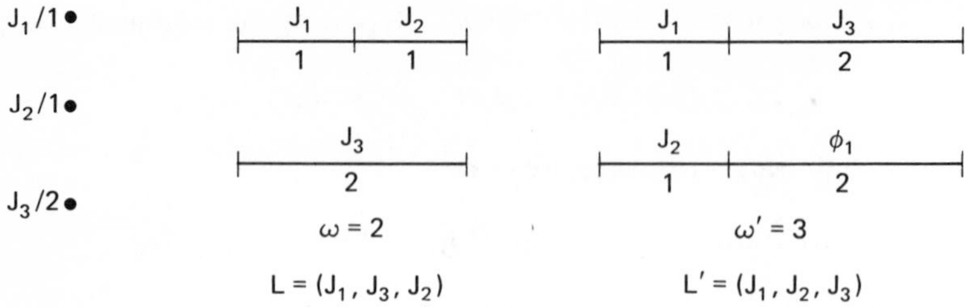

$J_1/1 \bullet$

$J_2/1 \bullet$

$J_3/2 \bullet$

Fig. 3.2.8

any arbitrary priority list will not lead to an increment of more than 100% of the minimal completion time. Since searching for an optimal priority list is quite time-consuming (as a matter of fact, there is no general algorithm short of exhaustion), the result in Theorem 3.2.3 is indeed comforting.

Theorem 3.2.3 can be stated in a slightly more general form.

Theorem 3.2.4

Let $(\mathcal{J}, \mu, <)$ and $(\mathcal{J}, \mu', <')$ be two sets of jobs such that

1, $J_i < J_j$ implies that $J_i <' J_j$ for any $J_i, J_j \in \mathcal{J}$
2. $\mu(J) \geq \mu'(J)$ for any $J \in \mathcal{J}$

Let ω and ω' be the completion times when these two sets of tasks are executed according to some priority lists on an n-processor and an n'-processor computing system, respectively. Then

$$\frac{\omega'}{\omega} \leq 1 + \frac{n-1}{n'}$$

3.3.   A PROBLEM OF SCHEDULING JOBS WITH PERIODIC REQUESTS

To further illustrate some of the concepts related to optimal and subopti-mal schedules, we study now another scheduling problem in which a time-shared single-processor computing system is to execute a set of jobs each of which consists of a sequence of periodic requests. That is, each job demands a certain amount of computation time within a certain time interval periodi-cally. Let $\mathcal{J} = \{J_1, J_2, \ldots, J_r\}$ denote a set of jobs with periodic requests. We shall use T_i to denote the request period and C_i to denote the computa-tion time of job J_i for $i = 1, 2, \ldots, r$. As an example, consider a computer used in a process control system. At regular intervals, the computer must determine the adjustments in the amounts of chemicals to be mixed as well as that in the temperature and the pressure inside of the reaction tank on the basis of various measurements. Moreover, it is the case that adjustment in the amounts of chemicals should be carried out more frequently, and adjustments in temperature and pressure can be carried out less frequently. Let J_1, J_2, J_3 denote the three computation jobs of determining the adjustments in ingredients, temperature, and pressure. Suppose that $T_1 = 4$, $C_1 = 1$; $T_2 = 5$, $C_2 = 2$; and $T_3 = 10$, $C_3 = 1$. It means that in every four time units, one unit of computation time is needed to determine the adjustment in the amounts of chemicals to be mixed; in every five time units, two units of computation time is needed to determine the adjustment in temperature; and in every ten time units, one unit of computation time is needed to determine the adjustment in pressure. Our problem is to schedule the usage of the processor so that all the requests will be satisfied.

We define the *deadline* of a request to be the time at which the next request of the same job occurs. By scheduling a set of jobs with periodic requests we mean to specify which of the requests is to be executed at every time instant so that all requests will be satisfied before their deadlines. Throughout our discussion, we assume that the execution of a request can be interrupted if it is so desired. A schedule can be described by a timing diagram such as that in Fig. 3.3.1 where shaded areas indicate the time intervals within which requests are executed in the processor. Note that Fig. 3.3.1 shows a schedule for the three jobs in the example on process control mentioned above.

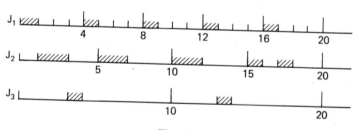

Fig. 3.3.1

For a given scheduling algorithm, a set of jobs is either schedulable, meaning that all the requests will be satisfied before their deadlines, or not schedulable, meaning that one or more of the requests will not be satisfied before the deadlines. Consequently, the performance of a scheduling algorithm will be measured by the "varieties" of jobs that it is capable of scheduling. To be precise about what we mean, we define the *processor utilization factor* of a set of jobs as the fraction of processor time spent in the execution of the set. Since C_i/T_i is the fraction of processor time spent in executing job J_i, the utilization factor of a set of jobs $\{J_1, J_2, \ldots, J_r\}$ will be

$$U = \sum_{i=1}^{r} \frac{C_i}{T_i}$$

We shall measure the effectiveness of a scheduling algorithm by the process utilization factor it can attain in the worst case, that is, the minimum of the processor utilization factors among all sets of jobs that the algorithm can schedule. Consequently, a best possible scheduling algorithm is one that attains a process utilization factor of 100%.

In general, the decision rules of a scheduling algorithm can be quite complicated. Here, we study a class of scheduling algorithms which assign priorities to the jobs. At any instant, the current request of the job with the highest priority will be executed.

3.3.1. The Deadline Driven Scheduling Algorithm

We study now a scheduling algorithm which we call the *deadline driven scheduling algorithm*. Using this algorithm, priorities are assigned to jobs according to the deadlines of their current requests. A job will be assigned the highest priority if the deadline of its current request is the nearest, and will be assigned the lowest priority if the deadline of its current request is the furthest. At any instant, the job with the highest priority and yet unfulfilled request will be executed. Such a method of assigning priorities to the jobs is a dynamic one, in contrast to a static assignment in which priorities of jobs do not change with time. We want now to show that the deadline driven scheduling algorithm is a best possible one. To this end, we show first the following lemma.

Lemma 3.3.1

When the deadline driven scheduling algorithm is used to schedule a set of jobs on a processor, there is no processor idle time prior to an overflow.†

Proof: Suppose that there is processor idle time prior to an overflow. To be specific, starting at time 0, let t_3 denote the time at which an overflow occurs, and let t_1, t_2 denote the beginning and the end, respectively, of the processor idle period closest to t_3 (i.e., there is no processor idle time between t_2 and t_3.) The situation is illustrated in Fig. 3.3.2 where the times of the first request for each of the r jobs after the processor idle period $[t_1, t_2]$ are denoted $a, b, \ldots, r$.

Suppose that from t_2 on we move all requests of J_1 up so that a will coincide with t_2. Since there was no processor idle time between t_2 and t_3, there will be no processor idle time after a is moved up. Moreover, an overflow will occur either at or before t_3. Repeating the same argument for all other jobs, we conclude that if all jobs are initiated at t_2, there will be an overflow with no pro-

---

†We say that an overflow occurs at time t if t is the deadline of an unfulfilled request.

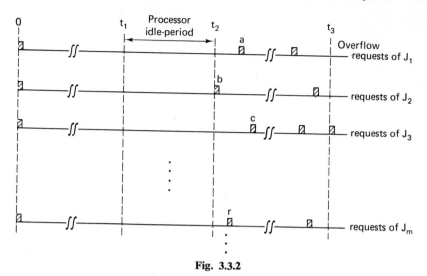

Fig. 3.3.2

cessor idle period prior to it. However, this is a contradiction to the assumption that starting at time 0 there is a processor idle period prior to an overflow. ∎

Lemma 3.3.1 will be used to establish the following theorem:

Theorem 3.3.1

Any set of jobs with a processor utilization factor not exceeding 100% can be scheduled by the deadline driven scheduling algorithm.

Proof: We want to show that any set of jobs $\mathscr{J} = \{J_1, J_2, \ldots, J_r\}$ satisfying the condition

$$\frac{C_1}{T_1} + \frac{C_2}{T_2} + \ldots + \frac{C_r}{T_r} \leq 1 \tag{3.3.1}$$

can be scheduled by the deadline scheduling algorithm. Let us assume the contrary is true. That is, there is a set of jobs satisfying the condition in (3.3.1) which cannot be scheduled by the deadline driven scheduling algorithm. In other words, there is an overflow between $t = 0$ and $t = T_1 T_2 \ldots T_r$. Moreover, according to Lemma 3.3.1 there is a $t = T (0 \leq T \leq T_1 T_2 \ldots T_r)$ at which there is an overflow with no processor idle time between $t = 0$ and $t = T$. To be specific, let $a_1, a_2, \ldots, b_1, b_2, \ldots$, denote the request times of the r jobs immediately prior to T, where $a_1, a_2, \ldots$ are the request times of jobs with deadlines at T, and $b_1, b_2, \ldots$ are the request times of jobs with deadlines beyond T. This is illustrated in Fig. 3.3.3.

Two cases must be examined.

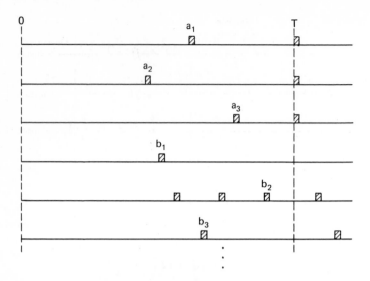

Fig. 3.3.3

Case 1: None of the computations requested at b_1, b_2, . . . was carried out before T. In this case, the total demand of computation time between 0 and T is

$$\left\lfloor \frac{T}{T_1} \right\rfloor C_1 + \left\lfloor \frac{T}{T_2} \right\rfloor C_2 + \ldots + \left\lfloor \frac{T}{T_r} \right\rfloor C_r$$

Since there is no processor idle period,

$$\left\lfloor \frac{T}{T_1} \right\rfloor C_1 + \left\lfloor \frac{T}{T_2} \right\rfloor C_2 + \ldots + \left\lfloor \frac{T}{T_r} \right\rfloor C_r > T$$

Also, since $x \geq \lfloor x \rfloor$ for all x,

$$\left(\frac{T}{T_1} \right) C_1 + \left(\frac{T}{T_2} \right) C_2 + \ldots + \left(\frac{T}{T_r} \right) C_r > T$$

and

$$\left(\frac{C_1}{T_1} \right) + \left(\frac{C_2}{T_2} \right) + \ldots + \left(\frac{C_r}{T_r} \right) > 1$$

which is a contradiction to (3.3.1).

Case 2: Some of the computations requested at b_1, b_2, . . . were carried out before T. Since an overflow occurs at T, there must exist a point T' such that none of the requests at b_1, b_2, . . . was carried out within the interval $T' \leq t \leq T$. In other words, within $T' \leq t \leq T$, only those requests with deadlines at or before T will be executed, as illustrated in Fig. 3.3.4. Moreover, the fact

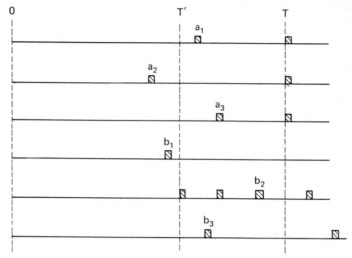

Fig. 3.3.4

that one or more of the jobs having requests at the b_i's is executed until $t = T'$ means that all those requests initiated before T' with deadlines at or before T have been fulfilled before T'. Therefore, the total demand of processor time within $T' \leq t \leq T$ is less than or equal to

$$\left\lfloor \frac{(T - T')}{T_1} \right\rfloor C_1 + \left\lfloor \frac{(T - T')}{T_2} \right\rfloor C_2 + \ . \ . \ . \ + \left\lfloor \frac{(T - T')}{T_r} \right\rfloor C_r.$$

That an overflow occurs at T means that

$$\left\lfloor \frac{(T - T')}{T_1} \right\rfloor C_1 + \left\lfloor \frac{(T - T')}{T_2} \right\rfloor C_2 + \ . \ . \ . \ + \left\lfloor \frac{(T - T')}{T_r} \right\rfloor C_r > T - T'$$

which implies again

$$\left(\frac{C_1}{T_1}\right) + \left(\frac{C_2}{T_2}\right) + \ . \ . \ . \ + \left(\frac{C_r}{T_r}\right) > 1$$

and which is a contradiction to (3.3.1). ∎

We have thus shown that the deadline driven scheduling algorithm is a best possible algorithm in the sense that if a set of jobs can be scheduled by any algorithm, it can be scheduled by the deadline driven scheduling algorithm.

3.3.2.   The Rate Monotonic Priority Assignment

Although the deadline driven scheduling algorithm is relatively simple to implement, it still requires a certain amount of work to determine and to keep track of the deadlines of unfulfilled requests. A class of simpler algorithms will be those that assign fixed priorities to jobs. That is, if a job J_i is assigned a higher priority than a job J_j then all requests of J_i will preempt all requests of J_j. We shall state two theorems concerning the class of algorithms without proof. The interested reader is referred to Liu and Layland [11]. Let $\mathscr{J} = \{J_1, J_2, \ldots, J_r\}$ be a set of jobs with periodic requests. We shall assign priorities to the jobs according to their request periods such that jobs with shorter periods will have higher priorities. Such an assignment of priorities is known as the *rate monotonic priority assignment*. (The reciprocal of the request period of a job is known as its request rate.)

Theorem 3.3.2

Among all possible ways of assigning *fixed* priorities to jobs, the rate monotonic priority assignment is a best possible one.

Theorem 3.3.2 says that if a set of jobs can be scheduled by a certain assignment of fixed priorites to the jobs, it can also be scheduled by the rate monotonic assignment of priorities. Intuitively, it is reasonable to expect that we assign higher priority to jobs with higher request rate. Yet on the other hand, that a best possible assignment can be made independent of the computation times of the jobs is not totally obvious. As a simple example, let $\mathscr{J} = \{J_1, J_2\}$ and $T_1 = 2, C_1 = 1; T_2 = 5, C_2 = 2$. If we assign higher priority to J_2 and lower priority to J_1, it can readily be checked if there will be an overflow at $t = 2$ because the first request of T_1 will not be fulfilled at that time. On the other hand, this set of jobs can be scheduled by the rate monotonic priority assignment as the schedule in Fig. 3.3.5 shows.

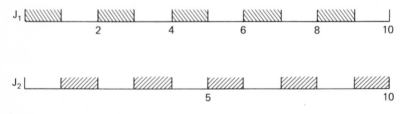

Fig. 3.3.5

However, the rate monotonic priority assignment is not a best one among all priority driven scheduling algorithms in that there are sets of jobs whose utilization factors are less than 1 and cannot be scheduled by such an algorithm. For example, the set $\mathscr{J} = \{J_1, J_2\}$ with $T_1 = 2, C_1 = 1.1$ and $T_2 = 5$,

$C_2 = 2$ cannot be scheduled by the rate monotonic priority assignment. However, the performance of the rate monotonic priority assignment can be lower bounded as stated in the following:

Theorem 3.3.3

A set of r jobs whose utilization factor is less than or equal to

$$r(2^{1/r} - 1) \tag{3.3.2}$$

can always be scheduled by the rate monotonic priority assignment.

For example, for $r = 2$, the lower bound in (3.3.2) becomes

$$2(\sqrt{2} - 1) = 0.83$$

The reader can check that the lower bound is tight by examining the set of tasks $\mathscr{J} = \{J_1, J_2\}$ where $T_1 = 1, C_1 = \sqrt{2} - 1; T_2 = \sqrt{2}, C_2 = 2 - \sqrt{2}$.

3.4. A DRUM SCHEDULING ALGORITHM

As another example, we study the problem of processing information on a magnetic drum or a fixed-head magnetic disk. The surface of the drum is

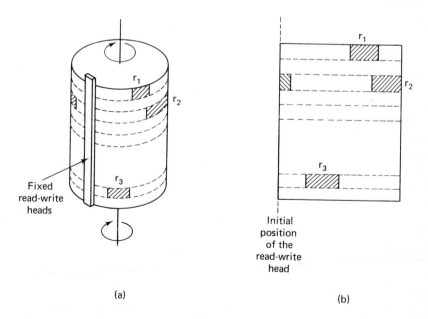

(a)

(b)

Fig. 3.4.1

divided into parallel tracks. Blocks of data are to be stored on the drum, each of which is called a *record*. A record might occupy a portion of a track, a whole track, or several tracks. Figure 3.4.1(a) shows a drum unit and Fig. 3.4.1(b) shows the surface of the drum where shaded strips represent records stored on the drum. The drum has a fixed set of read-write heads. Consequently, a record can be read from the drum only when the record is positioned directly under a read-write head. At any instant only one of the read-write heads can read from the surface of the drum. Thus, only one record can be retrieved at a time. Also, the reading of a record must commence at the beginning of the record, and shall not be interrupted until completion. Given a set of records to be retrieved from the drum and the initial angular position of the read-write heads, we want to schedule the order in which these records will be read. A schedule can be described by a timing diagram which exhibits the records to be processed in successive revolutions of the drum. As an example, Fig. 3.4.2(a) shows a sched-

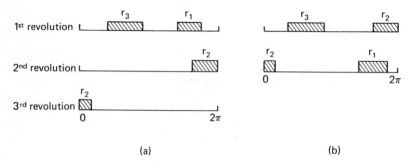

(a)   (b)

Fig. 3.4.2

ule for the records shown in Fig. 3.4.1(b). Specifically, according to this schedule, record r_3 and then r_1 are to be read in the first revolution, record r_2 is to be read in the second and the third revolutions. Figure 3.4.2(b) shows another schedule for processing the same set of records. Clearly, if the order of processing the records is carelessly chosen, considerable time can be wasted waiting for the drum to rotate from the end of one record to the beginning of the next record. This delay is referred to as *latency*. An optimal schedule is one in which the total latency is minimal. Equivalently, it is one that minimizes the total rotational distance of the drum. Fuller [4] and Gill [6] studied algorithms that produce optimal schedules. Unfortunately, these algorithms are quite complicated. Instead of describing these algorithms, we shall study one that produces optimal or almost optimal schedules.

Instead of presenting these algorithms here, we study a scheduling algorithm known as the shortest latency time first (SLTF) scheduling algorithm. Such a scheduling algorithm simply means that whenever the processing of a record is completed, the record (among the unprocessed ones) that comes under a read-write head first will be the next one to be processed. A schedule obtained according to the SLTF scheduling algorithm is known as an SLTF schedule. For example, the schedule in Fig. 3.4.2(a) is an SLTF schedule for the set of records shown in Fig. 3.4.1(b). Although an SLTF schedule is not necessarily optimal, it is a reasonably good schedule as the following theorem shows.

Theorem 3.4.1

For any given set of records to be processed on a drum, an SLTF schedule takes k_0 or $k_0 + 1$ revolutions, where k_0 is the number of revolutions in an optimal schedule.

Proof: Suppose that the SLTF schedule for a given set of records takes k revolutions. We examine two cases: The first case is that one or more complete records is processed in the kth revolution as illustrated in Fig. 3.4.3(a). Let θ_0

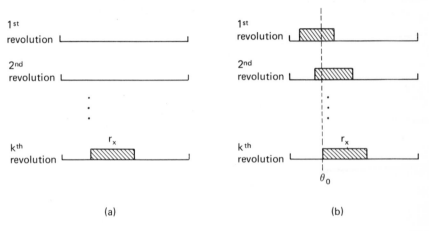

(a)   (b)

Fig. 3.4.3

be the angular position at which a read-write head begins to read a record r_x during the kth revolution. We note that at the angular position θ_0 the read-write heads must be reading a record during each of the 1st, 2nd, . . ., $(k-1)$st revolutions as illustrated in Fig. 3.4.3(b). Because if this is not the case, the record r_x would have been processed in an earlier revolution. Consequently, an optimal schedule must also take k revolutions. The second case is that only a portion of a record is processed in the kth revolution as illustrated in Fig. 3.4.4(a). Let θ_0 be the angular position at which a read-write head begins to read the last record in the schedule as illustrated in Fig. 3.4.4(b). We note that at the angular position θ_0, the read-write heads must be reading a record during each of the 1st, 2nd, . . ., $(k-1)$st revolutions. Consequently, an optimal schedule takes at least $k - 1$ revolutions. The example in Fig. 3.4.1(b) shows that indeed an SLTF schedule might take one more revolution than an optimal one. ∎

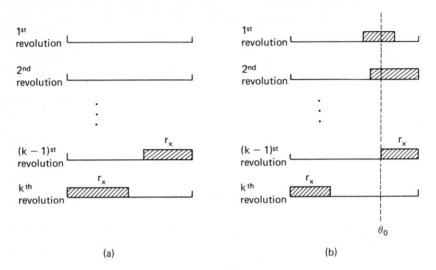

(a)   (b)

Fig. 3.4.4

Corollary 3.4.1

For any given set of records to be processed on a drum, let ω and ω_0 denote the total rotational distance of the drum for an SLTF schedule and an optimal schedule, respectively, then

$$\omega \leq \omega_0 + l$$

where l is the length of longest record in the set.

The set of records in Fig. 3.4.1 shows that the upper bound on ω in Corollary 3.4.1 is tight.

A problem equivalent to the retrieval problem is that of transferring records from one track to another on the drum. Suppose the tracks on the drum are divided into *cells* of equal length. Each cell can hold a record of fixed length, which we shall call a *word*. Let there be a group of tracks, called the source tracks, and another group of tracks, called the destination tracks. To transfer a word from a source track to a destination track, the read-write heads read from the source track the word to be transferred, save the word in a storage register, and then write the word into the destination cell. We assume that the drum is equipped with only one storage register. Consequently, before the word in the register is transferred to the destination cell, the read-write heads cannot attempt to read another word from the drum. For example, Fig. 3.4.5(a) shows a set of words $w_1, w_2, \ldots, w_6$ in the source tracks with their corresponding destination cells labelled as $d_1, d_2, \ldots, d_6$ in the destination tracks. By scheduling the transfer of a set of words, we mean to determine an order in which the words are to be transferred. We note that as far as the usage of the read-write heads is concerned, transferring a word from one cell to another cell is equivalent to retrieving a (variable-length) record as illustrated in Fig. 3.4.5(b) where $r_1, r_2, \ldots, r_6$ are the records corresponding to the words $w_1, w_2, \ldots, w_6$. Therefore, we conclude that the scheduling problem for transferring words is equivalent to the scheduling problem for retrieving records.

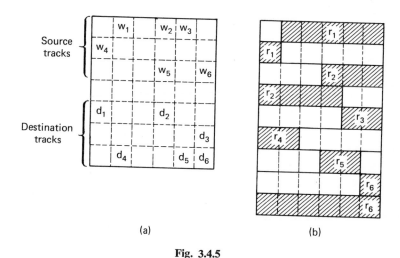

(a)   (b)

Fig. 3.4.5

Although the results in Theorem 3.4.1 and Corollary 3.4.1 can be applied directly to the word transfer problem, we can show that for a special case of the word transfer problem, the SLTF schedule is actually optimal. Suppose there is one source track and one destination track, each of which is divided into n cells. There are n words in the source track to be transferred to the n cells in the destination track. We refer to this problem as that of *permuting* n words. As it turns out, we were able to prove:

Theorem 3.4.2

An SLTF schedule for the permutation of n words minimizes the total rotational distance of the drum.

REFERENCES

A general reference for the material in Section 3.2 is Chapter 3 of Coffman and Denning [2]. An optimal scheduling algorithm for jobs with unit execution time and a partial ordering such that each job has at most one successor was first published by Hu [10]. See also Hsu [9] and Schindler [13]. For optimal scheduling algorithms for jobs with unit execution time when there are only two processors see Coffman and Graham [3]. A variation of Coffman and Graham's algorithm will appear in Chen and Liu [1]. The material in Sec. 3.2.2 is based on Graham's work [7, 8]. For some further results on lower bounding the performance of multiprocessor computing systems, see Garey and Graham [5] and Liu and Liu [12].

The material in Section 3.3 is based on the work by Liu and Layland [11] and Serlin [14]. The material in Section 3.4 is based on a paper by Wong, Liu, and Apter [16]. Theorem 3.8 also appeared in Stone and Fuller [15].

1. CHEN, N. F. and C. L. LIU, "Scheduling Algorithms for Multiprocessor Computing Systems," to appear.

2. COFFMAN, E. G. and P. J. DENNING, *Operating Systems Theory*, Prentice-Hall, Inc., Englewood Cliffs, N.J. 1973.

3. COFFMAN, E. G. and R. L. GRAHAM, "Optimal Scheduling for Two-Processor Systems, "*Acta Informatica* 1 : 3 (1972), 200–213.

4. FULLER, S. H., "An optimal drum scheduling algorithm," *IEEE Trans. on Computers* C–21 : 11 (Nov. 1972), 1153–1165.

5. GAREY, M. R. and R. L. GRAHAM, "Bounds on Scheduling with Limited Resources," *Proc. 4th SIGOPS Symposium on Operating Systems Principles* (Oct. 1973), 104–111.

6. GILL, A., "The optimal organization of serial memory transfers," *IRE Trans. on Electronic Computers* EC–9 (Mar. 1960), 12–15.

7. GRAHAM, R. L., "Bounds on Multiprocessing Timing Anomalies, "*SIAM J. Applied Math.* 17 : 2 (1969), 263–269.

8. GRAHAM, R. L., "Bounds on Multiprocessing Anomalies and Related Packing Algorithms," *AFIPS Conf. Proc.* 40 (1972), 205–217.

9. HSU, N. C., "Elementary Proof of Hu's Theorem on Isotone Mapping," *Proc. American Math. Society* 17 (1966), 111–114.

10. HU, T. C., "Parallel Scheduling and Assembly Line Problems," *Oper. Res.* 9 : 6 (1961), 841–848.

11. LIU, C. L. and J. W. LAYLAND, "Scheduling Algorithms for Multiprogramming in a Hard-Real-Time Environment," ACM 20 : 1 (1973), 46–61.

12. LIU, JANE W. S. and C. L. LIU, "Bounds on Scheduling Algorithms for Heterogeneous Computing Systems," to appear.

13. Schindler, S., "On Optimal Schedules for Multiprocessor Systems," *Proc. 6th Annual Princeton Conference on Information Sciences and Systems* (Mar. 1972), 219–223.

14. SERLIN, O., "Scheduling of Time Critical Processes, "*AFIPS Conf. Proc.* 40 (1972), 925–932.

15. STONE, H. S. and S. H. FULLER, "On the Near-Optimality of the Shortest-Latency-Time-First Drum Scheduling Discipline," *Comm. ACM* 16:6, (June 1973), 352–353.

16. WONG, C. K., C. L. LIU, and J. APTER "A Drum Scheduling Algorithm," *Proc. Conference on Automata Theory and Formal Languages* (July 1973), Bonn, Germany.

4

LINGUISTIC APPROACH
TO PATTERN RECOGNITION

K. S. Fu
Department of Electrical Engineering
Purdue University
West Lafayette, Indiana

Editor's Note:

This chapter is a delightful guided tour, illustrated with a great number of examples, to the wide spectrum of techniques utilizing the formal language theory for pattern recognition or, more generally, scene analysis.

Material covered in this chapter together with that of Chapter 11 could form the core for a course in syntactic scene analysis.

The only prerequisite for this chapter is the notion of context-free grammar introduced in Chapter 1.

4.1. LINGUISTIC (STRUCTURAL) APPROACH TO PATTERN RECOGNITION

The many different mathematical techniques used to solve pattern recognition problems may be grouped into two general approaches; namely, the decision-theoretic (or discriminant) approach and the linguistic (or structural) approach. In the decision-theoretic approach, a set of characteristic measurements, called features, are extracted from the patterns; the recognition of each pattern (assignment to a pattern class) is usually made by partitioning the feature space [1]. Most of the developments in pattern recognition research during the past decade deal with the decision-theoretic approach [1–11] and

its applications. In some pattern recognition problems, the structural information which describes each pattern is important, and the recognition process
includes not only the capability of assigning the pattern to a particular class
(to classify it), but also the capacity to describe aspects of the pattern which
make it ineligible for assignment to another class. A typical example of this
class of recognition problem is picture recognition or more generally speaking,
scene analysis. In this class of recognition problems, the patterns under consideration are usually quite complex and the number of features required is
often very large, which make the idea of describing a complex pattern in terms
of a (hierarchical) composition of simpler subpatterns very attractive. Also,
when the patterns are complex and the number of possible descriptions is
very large it is impractical to regard each description as defining a class (for
example in fingerprint and face identification problems, recognition of continuous speech, Chinese characters, etc.). Consequently, the requirement of
recognition can only be satisfied by a description for each pattern rather than
the simple task of classification.

Example 4.1.1

   The pictorial patterns shown in Fig. 4.1.1 can be described in terms of the
hierarchical structures shown in Fig. 4.1.2.

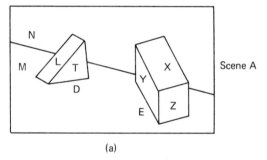

(a)

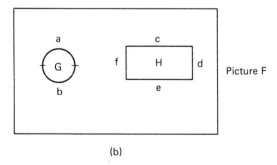

(b)

Fig. 4.1.1   The pictorial pattern for Example 4.1.1.

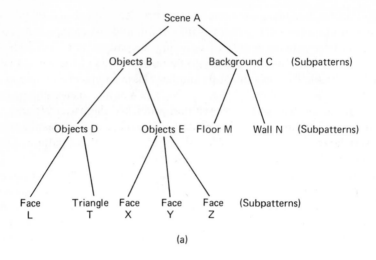

(a)

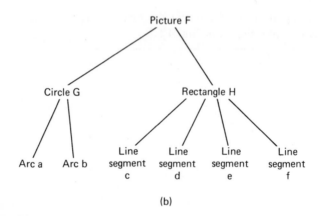

(b)

Fig. 4.1.2 Hierarchical structural descriptions of (a) scene A
and (b) picture F.

In order to represent the hierarchical (tree-like) structural information of
each pattern, that is, a pattern described in terms of simpler subpatterns and
each simpler subpattern again described in terms of even simpler subpatterns,
etc., the linguistic or structural approach has been proposed [12–16]. This approach draws an analogy between the (hierarchical, tree-like) structure of patterns and the syntax of languages. Patterns are specified as building up out of
subpatterns in various ways of composition just as phrases and sentences are
built up by concatenating words and words are built up by concatenating characters. Evidently, for this approach to be advantageous, the simplest subpatterns selected, called *pattern primitives,* should be much easier to recognize
than the patterns themselves. The "language" which provides the structural

description of patterns in terms of a set of pattern primitives and their composition operations, is sometimes called *pattern description language*. The rules governing the composition of primitives into patterns are usually specified by the so-called "grammar" of the pattern description language. After each primitive within the pattern is identified, the recognition process is accomplished by performing a syntax analysis or parsing of the "sentence" describing the given pattern to determine whether or not it is syntactically (or grammatically) correct with respect to the specified grammar. In the meantime, the syntax analysis also produces a structural description of the sentence representing the given pattern (usually in the form of a tree structure).

The linguistic approach to pattern recognition provides a capability for describing a large set of complex patterns using small sets of simple pattern primitives and of grammatical rules. As can be seen later, one of the most attractive aspects of this capability is the use of the recursive nature of a grammar. A grammar (rewriting) rule can be applied any number of times, so it is possible to express in a very compact way some basic structural characteristics of an infinite set of sentences. Of course, the practical utility of such an approach depends upon our ability to recognize the simple pattern primitives and their relationships represented by the composition operations.

The various relations or composition operations defined among subpatterns can usually be expressed in terms of logical and/or mathematical operations. For example, if we choose concatenation as the only relation (composition operation) used in describing patterns, then for the pattern primitives shown in Fig. 4.1.3(a) the rectangle in Fig. 4.1.3(b) would be represented by the string *aaabbcccdd*.

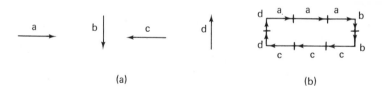

(a)   (b)

Fig. 4.1.3 A rectangle and its pattern primitives.

More explicitly, if we use "$+$" for the "head-to-tail concatenation" operation, the rectangle in Fig. 4.1.3(b) would be represented by $a + a + a + b + b + c + c + c + d + d$, and its corresponding tree-like structure would be

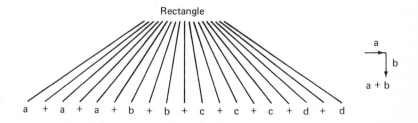

Similarly, a slightly more complex example is given in Fig. 4.1.4 using the pattern primitives in Fig. 4.1.3(a).

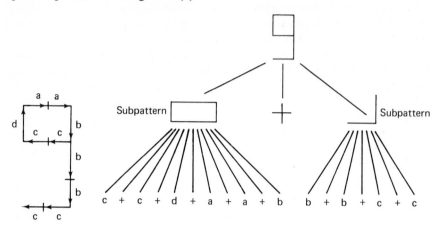

Fig. 4.1.4 Pattern ⊐ and its structural description.

An alternative representation of the structural information of a pattern is to use a *relational graph*. For example, a relational graph of Picture F in Fig. 4.1.1(b) is shown in Fig. 4.1.5. Since there is a one-to-one corresponding relation between a linear graph and a matrix, a relational graph can certainly also be expressed as a *relational matrix*. In using the relational graph for pattern description, we can broaden the class of allowed relations to include any re-

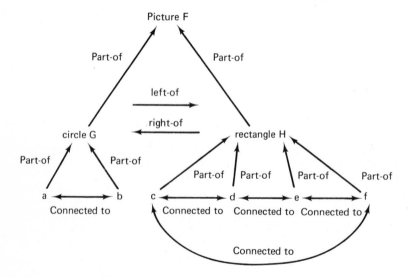

Fig. 4.1.5 A relational graph of picture F.

lation that can be conveniently determined from the pattern. (Notice that (1) the concatenation is the only natural operation for one-dimensional languages, and (2) a graph, in general, contains closed loops whereas a tree does not.) With this generalization, we may possibly express richer descriptions than we can with tree structures. However, the use of tree structures does provide us a direct channel to adapt the techniques of formal language theory to the problem of compactly representing and analyzing patterns containing a significant structural content.

4.2. LINGUISTIC PATTERN RECOGNITION SYSTEM

A linguistic pattern recognition system can be considered as consisting of three major parts; namely, preprocessing, pattern description or representation, and syntax analysis†. A simple block diagram of the system is shown in Fig. 4.2.1. The functions of preprocessing include (1) pattern encoding, and

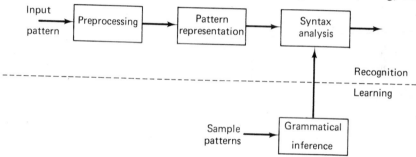

Fig. 4.2.1 Block diagram of a linguistic pattern recognition system.

approximation, and (2) filtering, restoration, and enhancement. An input pattern is first coded or approximated by some convenient form for further processing. For example, a black-and-white picture can be coded in terms of a grid (or a matrix) of 0's and 1's, or a waveform can be approximated by its time samples or a truncated Fourier series expansion. In order to make the processing in the later stages of the system more efficient, some sort of "data compression" is often applied at this stage. Then, techniques of filtering, restoration, and/or enhancement will be used to clean the noise, to restore the degradation, and/or to improve the quality of the coded (or approximated) patterns [9, 21–28]. At the output of the preprocessor, presumably, we have patterns with reasonably "good quality." Each preprocessed pattern is then

---

†The division of three parts is for convenience rather than necessity. Usually, the term "linguistic pattern recognition" refers primarily to the pattern representation (or description) and the syntax analysis.

represented by a language-like structure (for example, a string). The operation of this pattern-representation process consists of (1) pattern segmentation, and (2) primitive (feature) extraction. In order to represent a pattern in terms of its subpatterns, we must segmentize the pattern and, in the meantime, identify (or extract) the primitives in it. In other words, each preprocessed pattern is segmentized into subpatterns and pattern primitives based on pre-specified syntactic or composition operations; and, in turn, each subpattern is identified with a given set of pattern primitives. At this point, each pattern is represented by a set of primitives with specified syntactic operations.† For example, in terms of "concatenation" operation, each pattern is represented by a string of (concatenated) primitives. The decision on whether or not the representation (pattern) is syntactically correct (i.e., belongs to the class of patterns described by the given syntax or grammar) will be performed by the *syntax analyzer* or *parser*. When performing the syntax analysis or parsing, the analyzer can usually produce a complete syntactic description, in terms of a parse or parsing tree, of the pattern provided it is syntactically correct. Otherwise, the pattern is either rejected or analyzed on the basis of other given grammars, which presumably describe other possible classes of patterns under consideration.

Conceptually, the simplest form of recognition is probably *template-matching*. The string of primitives representing an input pattern is matched against strings of primitives representing each prototype or reference pattern. Based on a selected matching or similarity criterion, the input pattern is classified in the same class as the prototype pattern which is the "best" to match the input. The hierarchical structural information is essentially ignored. A complete parsing of the string representing an input pattern, on the other hand, explores the complete hierarchical structural description of the pattern. In between, there are a number of intermediate approaches. For example, a series of tests can be designed to test the occurrences or nonoccurrence of certain subpatterns (or primitives) or certain combinations of subpatterns or primitives. The result of the tests (for example, through a table look-up, a decision tree, or a logical operation) is used for a classification decision. Notice that each test may be a template-matching scheme or a parsing for a subtree representing a subpattern. The selection of an appropriate approach for recognition usually depends upon the problem requirement. If a complete pattern description is required for recognition, parsing is necessary. Otherwise, a complete parsing could be avoided by using other simpler approaches to improve the efficiency of the recognition process.

In order to have a grammar describing the structural information about the class of patterns under study, a grammatical inference machine is required

---

†Presumably, more sophisticated systems should also be able to detect the syntactic relations within the pattern.

which can infer a grammar from a given set of training patterns in language-like representations.† This is analogous to the "learning" process in a decision-theoretic pattern recognition system [1–11, 17–20]. The structural description of the class of patterns under study is learned from the actual sample patterns from that class. The learned description, in the form of a grammar, is then used for pattern description and syntax analysis (see Fig. 4.2.1). A more general form of learning might include the capability of learning the best set of primitives and the corresponding structural description for the class of patterns concerned.

Practical applications of linguistic pattern recognition include the recognition of English and Chinese characters, spoken digits, and mathematical expressions, and the classification of bubble chamber and spark chamber photographs and chromosome and fingerprint images [29–42].

4.3. SELECTION OF PATTERN PRIMITIVES

As was discussed in Section 4.1, the first step in formulating a linguistic model for pattern description is the determination of a set of primitives in terms of which the patterns of interest may be described. This will be largely influenced by the nature of the data, the specific application in question, and the technology available for implementing the system. There is no general solution for the primitive selection problem at this time. The following requirements usually serve as a guideline for selecting pattern primitives.

1. The primitives should serve as basic pattern elements to provide a compact but adequate description of the data in terms of the specified structural relations (e.g., the concatenation relation).
2. The primitives should be easily extracted or recognized by existing nonlinguistic methods, since they are considered to be simple and compact patterns and their structural information not important.

For speech patterns, phonemes are naturally considered as a "good" set of primitives with the concatenation relation.†† Similarly, strokes have been suggested as primitives in describing handwriting. However, for general pictorial patterns, there is no such "universal picture element" analogous to phenomes in speech or strokes in handwriting. Sometimes, in order to provide an adequate description of the patterns, the primitives should contain the information which is important to the specific application in question. For example, if the size (or shape or location) is important in the recognition prob-

---

†At present, this part is performed primarily by the designer.
††The view of continuous speech as composed of one sound segment for each successive phoneme is, of course, a simplification of facts.

lem, then the primitives should contain information relating to size (or shape or location) so that patterns from different classes are distinguishable by whatever method is to be applied to analyze the descriptions. This requirement often results in a need for semantic information in describing primitives, which will be discussed in Section 4.5. The following simple example is used to illustrate that, for the same data, different problem specifications would result in different selections of primitives.

Example 4.3.1

Suppose that the problem is to discriminate rectangles (of different sizes) from nonrectangles. The following set of primitives is selected:

a' 0° horizontal line segment

b' 90° vertical line segment

c' 180° horizontal line segment

d' 270° vertical line segment

The set of all rectangles (of different sizes) is represented by a single sentence or string $a'b'c'd'$.

If, in addition, the problem is also to discriminate rectangles of different sizes, the above description would be inadequate. An alternative is to use unit-length line segments as primitives:

The set of rectangles of different sizes can then be described by the language

$$L = \{a^n b^m c^n d^m \,|\, n, m = 1, 2 \ldots \} \tag{4.3.1}$$

Requirement (2) may sometimes conflict with requirement (1) due to the fact that the primitives selected according to requirement (1) may not be easy to recognize using existing techniques. On the other hand, requirement (2) could allow the selection of quite complex primitives as long as they can be recognized. With more complex primitives, simpler structural descriptions (e.g., simple grammars) of the patterns could be used. This tradeoff may become quite important in the implementation of the recognition system. An example is the recognition of two-dimensional mathematical expressions in which characters and mathematical notations are primitives [33, 34]. However, if we consider the characters as subpatterns and describe them in terms of simpler primitives (e.g., strokes or line segments), the structural descriptions of mathematical expressions would be more complex than the case of using characters directly as primitives.

Another example is the recognition of Chinese characters [30–32]. From the knowledge about the structure of Chinese characters, a small number of simple segmentation operations such as

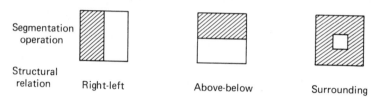

| Segmentation operation | | | |
| Structural relation | Right-left | Above-below | Surrounding |

can be used. Each operation also generates a particular structural relation between the two neighboring subpatterns or primitives. Applying these operations recursively, that is, segmentizing each subpattern again by any one of the three operations, we can segmentize a Chinese character into its subpatterns and primitives. If the primitives can be extracted or recognized by existing techniques, a Chinese character can be described syntactically with the given set of structural relations. It is anticipated that the resulting structural descriptions will be much more complex if we choose basic strokes as the primitives.

One of the earliest papers describing the decomposition of pictorial patterns into primitives [43] presented a conceptually appealing method which allows the recognition system to (heuristically) determine the primitives by inspection of training samples. A pattern is first examined by a programmed scan. The result of the scan is to produce descriptions of segments of the picture (subpictures) which are divisions conveniently produced by the scanning process, and not necessarily true divisions. The scanning process also includes preprocessing routines for noise-cleaning, gap-filling, and curve-following. The subpictures obtained in the scan are analyzed and connected, when appropriate, into true picture parts; a description is given in terms of the length and slope of straight-line segments and the length and curvature of curved segments. The structural relations among various segments (primitives) of a picture is expressed in terms of a connection table (Table of Joins). The assembly program produces a "statement" which gives a complete description of the pattern. The description is independent of the orientation and the size of the picture, the lengths of the various parts being given relative to one another. It is, in effect, a coded representation of the pattern and may be regarded as a one-dimensional string consisting of symbols chosen from a specified alphabet. The coded representation gives the length, slope, and curvature of each primitive, together with details of the ends and joins to other primitives. No explicit consideration is given to formalizing the pattern syntax.

A formal model for the abstract description of English cursive script has been proposed by Eden and Halle [44]. The primitives are four distinct line segments in the form of a triple:

$$\sigma_j = [(x_{j_1}, y_{j_1}), (x_{j_2}, y_{j_2}), \theta_j] \qquad (4.3.2)$$

where (x_j, y_j)'s represent the approximate location of the end-points of the line segment, and θ_j refers to the sense of rotation from the first to the second end-point. θ_j is positive if the sense of rotation is clockwise and negative if counterclockwise. The four primitives are:

$\sigma_1 = [(1, 0), (0, 0), +]$ "bar"

$\sigma_2 = [(1, 1), (0, 0), +]$ "hook"

$\sigma_3 = [(0, 0), (0, 1), +]$ "arch"

$\sigma_4 = [(1, \in), (0, 0), +], \quad 0 < \in < 1,$ "loop"

They can be transformed by changing the sign of θ or by reflection about the horizontal or vertical axis. These transformations generate 28 strokes (because of symmetry, the arch generates only four strokes), but only nine of them are of interest in the English script commonly used.

A word is completely specified by the stroke sequence comprising its letters. A word is represented by the image of a mapping of a finite sequence of strokes into the set of continuous functions, the mapping being specified by concatenation and tracing rules applied in specific order. Only two concatenation rules are required. The first specifies stroke locations within a letter. The rule prescribes that two consecutive strokes are concatenated by identifying the abscissa of the terminal end-point of the first stroke with that of the initial end-point of the second stroke. The second rule states that across a letter boundary, the leftmost endpoint of the stroke following the boundary is placed so as to be to the right of the rightmost end-point of the penultimate stroke before the letter boundary. The simple cursive strokes of the word "globe" are shown in Fig. 4.3.1 and their concatenation in Fig. 4.3.2. These concatenation rules are not sufficient to specify all sequences of English letters unambiguously. Nevertheless, the ambiguities are intrinsic to the writing system, even in careful handwriting.

No formal syntax was attempted for the description of handwriting. Interesting experimental results on the recognition of cursive writing were ob-

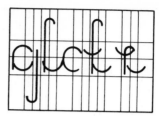

Fig. 4.3.1   Cursive strokes of "globe."

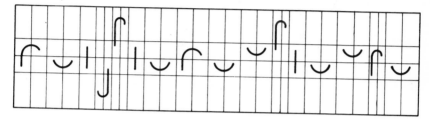

Fig. 4.3.2   Stroke sequence representation of the word "globe."

tained by Earnest [45] and Mermelstein [46] using a dictionary and rather heuristic recognition criteria. In addition, the dynamics of the trajectory (in space and time) that the point of the pen traces out as it moves across the paper has also been studied [47]. The motion of the pen is assumed to be controlled by a pair of orthogonal forces, as if one pair of muscles controls the vertical displacement and another the horizontal.

More general methods for primitive selection may be grouped roughly into methods emphasizing boundaries and methods emphasizing regions. These methods are discussed in the following.

4.3.1. Primitive Selection Emphasizing Boundaries or Skeletons

A set of primitives commonly used to describe boundaries or skeletons is the chain code given by Freeman [48, 49]. Under this scheme, a rectangular grid is overlaid on the two-dimensional pattern, and straight-line segments are used to connect the grid points falling closest to the pattern. Each line segment is assigned an octal digit according to its slope. The pattern is thus represented by a chain (or string) or chains of octal digits. Fig. 4.3.3 illustrates the primitives and the coded string describing a curve. This descriptive scheme has some useful properties. For example, patterns coded in this way can be rotated through multiples of 45° simply by adding an octal digit (modulo 8) to every digit in the string (however, only rotations by multiples of 90° can be accomplished without some distortion of the pattern). Other simple manipulations such as expansion, measurement of curve length, and determination of pattern self-intersections are easily carried out. Any desired degree of resolution can be obtained by adjusting the fineness of the grid imposed on the

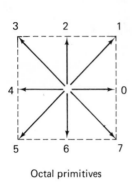

Octal primitives

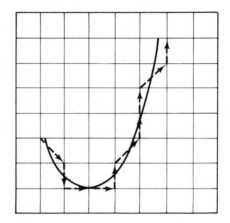

Coded string of the curve = 7600212212

Fig. 4.3.3 Freeman's chain code.

patterns. This method is, of course, not limited to simply-connected closed boundaries; it can be used for describing arbitrary two-dimensional figures composed of straight or curved lines and line segments.

Notable work using Freeman's chain code include efforts by Knoke and Wiley [50] and by Feder [51]. Knoke and Wiley attempted to demonstrate that linguistic approaches can usually be applied to describe structural relationships within patterns (hand-printed characters, in this case). Feder's work considers only patterns which can be encoded as strings of primitives. Several bases for developing pattern languages are discussed, including equations in two variables (straight lines, circles, and circular arcs, etc.), pattern properties (self-intersections, convexity, etc.), and various measures of curve similarity. The computational power (automaton complexity) required to detect the elements of these pattern languages is studied. However, this problem is complicated considerably by the fact that (1) these languages are mostly context-sensitive and not context-free, (2) the chain code yields only a piecewise linear approximation of the original pattern, and (3) the coding of a typical curve is not unique, depending to a degree on its location and orientation with respect to the coding grid.

Other applications of the chain code include description of contour maps [52], shape matching [53], and identification of high energy particle tracks in bubble chamber photographs [54]. Contour lines can be encoded as chains. Contour map problems may involve finding the terrain to be flooded by a dam placed at a particular location, the water shed area for a river basin, the terrain visible from a particular mountain-top location, or the determination of optimum highway routes through mountainous terrain. In shape matching, two or more two-dimensional objects having irregular contours are to be matched for all or part of their exterior boundary. For some such problems the relative orientation and scale of the objects to be matched may be known and only translation is required. The problem of matching aerial photographs to each other as well as to terrain maps falls into this category. For other problems either orientation, or scale, or both may be unknown and may have to be determined as part of the problem. An example of problems in which relative orientation has to be determined is that of the computer assembly of potsherds and jigsaw puzzles [55].

Other linguistic pattern recognition systems using primitives with the emphasis on boundary, skeleton, or contour information include systems for hand-printed character recognition [56–58], bubble chamber and spark chamber photograph classification [35, 59, 60], chromosome analysis [37, 61], fingerprint identification [38, 62–64], face recognition [65, 66], and scene analysis [67–69].

4.3.2. Pattern Primitives in Terms of Regions

A set of primitives for encoding geometric patterns in terms of regions has been proposed by Pavlidis [70]. In this case, the basic primitives are halfplanes in the pattern space† (or the field of observation). It can be shown that any figure (or arbitrary polygon) may be expressed as the union of a finite number of convex polygons. Each convex polygon can, in turn, be represented as the intersection of a finite number of halfplanes. By defining a suitable ordering (a sequence) of the convex polygons composing the arbitrary polygon, it is possible to determine a unique minimal set of maximal (in an appropriate sense) polygons, called primary subsets, the union of which is the given polygon. In linguistic analogy, a figure can be thought of as a "sentence," the convex polygons composing it as "words," and the halfplanes as "letters." This process is summarized in this section.

Let A be a bounded polygon and let $s_1, s_2, \ldots, s_n$ be its sides. A point x in the plane will be said to be positive with respect to one side if it lies on the same side of the extension of a side as the polygon does with respect to the side itself. Otherwise, it will be said to be negative with respect to that side.

Example 4.3.2

For the polygon A given in Fig. 4.3.4, the point x is positive with respect to the sides s_5 and s_6, but negative with respect to s_7. Similarly, y is positive with respect to s_4 and s_7, but negative with respect to s_5. Extending all the sides of A on both directions, A is intersected by some of these extensions, and it is subdivided into $A_1, A_2, \ldots, A_9$ convex polygons.

Obviously, the points which are positive with respect to a side form a half-

†This could be generalized to halfspaces of the pattern space.

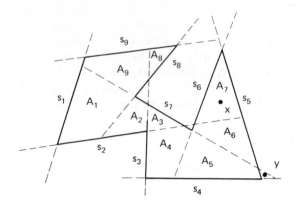

Fig. 4.3.4   Polygon A of Example 4.3.2.

plane whose boundary is the extension of the side. Let h_i denote the halfplane corresponding to the side s_i, and let Q denote the intersection of all the half-planes $h_1, h_2, \ldots, h_n$ in A. If A is convex, then $A = Q$. If A is not convex then Q may be empty or simply different from A. Let Q_I represent the inter-section of all the halfplanes except $s_{i_1}, \ldots, s_{i_k}$ where $I = \{i_1, \ldots, i_k\}$ index set. Then we can define a sequence of Q_I as follows:

$$Q \quad = \bigcap_{i=1}^{n} h_i$$

$$Q_j \quad = \bigcap_{\substack{i=1 \\ i \neq j}}^{n} h_i \qquad\qquad (4.3.3)$$

$$Q_{jk} = \bigcap_{\substack{i=1 \\ i \neq j, i \neq k}}^{n} h_i$$

$$\cdots$$

This is an increasing sequence since $Q \subset Q_j \subset Q_{jk} \ldots$. The last element of the sequence will be the whole plane, and it is obtained for $I = (1, \ldots, n)$. If a sequence of the above form has a maximal element, then that set is called a primary (convex) subset of A. A nonempty member of such a Q-sequence which is also a subset of A is called a nucleus of A if all the previous elements of the sequence are empty. Consequently, it can be shown that the union of the primary subsets of A precisely equals A.

For a given polygon the primary subsets can be found by forming all the sequences $Q, Q_j, Q_{jk}, \ldots$ and searching for their maximal elements. This is a well-defined procedure and, hence, the primary subsets of A are unique.

If the original figure (polygon) has not been approximated by an arbitrary polygon but by one whose sides were parallel to certain prespecified directions ϕ_1, ϕ_2, . . ., ϕ_k, then the figure can be represented by a finite number convex polygons. Any one of the halfplanes determined by the sides of the polygon will actually be a parallel translation of the halfplanes H_i determined by the chosen directions. These halfplanes play the role of primitives. If G denotes the group of parallel translations, then each primary subset R_j can be expressed as

$$R_j = \bigcap_{i=1}^{2k} g_i^j H_i, \qquad g_i^j \in G \tag{4.3.4}$$

where the intersection goes over $2k$ because each direction defines two halfplanes. If a halfplane does not actually appear in the formation of R_j, it will still be included in the above expression with an arbitrary transformation g which will be required only to place its boundary outside the field of observation. The original polygon A can then be represented as

$$A = \bigcup_{j=1}^{l} R_j = \bigcup_{j=1}^{l} \bigcap_{i=1}^{2k} g_i^j H_i \tag{4.3.5}$$

If a similarity measure between two convex polygons A and B, denoted by $S(A, B)$, can be appropriately defined, we may be able to find a finite set B of convex polygons B_1, . . ., B_N such that for every convex polygon A of interest there will exist a member of B and a member of G to satisfy

$$S(A, gB) < \delta$$

for a prespecified δ. The members of B will be referred to as the basic components, and, consequently, we can write

$$A = \bigcup_{i=1}^{l} g_i B_{k(i)} \tag{4.3.6}$$

It is noted that this approach provides a formalism for describing the syntax of polygonal figures and more general figures which can be approximated reasonably well by polygonal figures. The analysis or recognition procedure requires the definition of suitable measures of similarity between polygons. The similarity measures considered so far are quite sensitive to noise in the patterns and/or are difficult to implement practically on a digital computer. A somewhat more general selection procedure of pattern primitives based on regions has been recently proposed by Rosenfeld and Strong [71].

Another form of representing polygonal figures is the use of primary graphs [72, 73]. The primary graph of a polygon A is one whose nodes correspond to the nuclei and the primary subsets of A, and its branches connect each nucleus to all the primary subsets containing it. An example is given in Fig. 4.3.5. Primary subsets and nuclei of polygons approximating the figures are shown in

Fig. 4.3.5(a). (Shaded areas are nuclei.) Primary graphs for the corresponding polygons in Fig. 4.3.5(a) are given in Fig. 4.3.5(b). This form of representation may not characterize a figure uniquely; however, it does provide information describing it, and, in particular, about its topology. Also, as will be seen later in this chapter, patterns represented by graphs can be formally described by graph grammars.

Another approach to the analysis of geometric patterns using regions is discussed primarily in the problem of scene analysis [9, 68]. Minsky and Papert [74] have considered the direct transformation of a gray scale picture to regions, bypassing the edge-finding, line-fitting procedures. Regions are constructed as the union of squares whose corners have the same or nearly the same gray

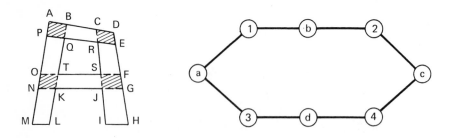

Primary subset or nucleus	Label
ABLM	a
ADEP	b
CDHI	c
OFGN	d
ABQP	1
CDER	2
OTKN	3
SFGJ	4

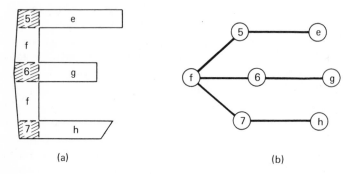

(a)   (b)

Fig. 4.3.5   (a) Polygon figures and (b) corresponding primary graphs.

scale. The method proposed by Guzman [75] assumes that a picture can be reduced by preprocessing to a list of vertices, lines, and surfaces. Various heuristics, based on the analysis of types of intersections of lines and surfaces, are applied to this list to compose its elements into two- or three-dimensional regions. Some candidate pattern recognition schemes have been investigated, all of which involve methods for matching the reduced pattern descriptions against a prototype dictionary. The procedure studied by Brice and Fennema [76] decomposes a picture into atomic regions of uniform gray scale. A pair of heuristics is used to join these regions in such a way as to obtain regions whose boundaries are determined more by the natural lines of the scene than by the artificial ones introduced by quantization and noise. Then a simple line-fitting technique is used to approximate the region boundaries by straight lines and finally, the scene analyzer interprets the picture using some simple tests on object groups generated by a Guzman-like procedure.

4.4. PATTERN GRAMMAR

Assume that a satisfactory solution of the "primitive selection" problem is available for a given application. The next step is the construction of a grammar (or grammars) which will generate a language (or languages) to describe the patterns under study. Ideally, it would be nice to have a grammatical inference machine which would infer a grammar from a set of given strings describing the patterns under study. Unfortunately, such a machine has not been available except for some very special cases [77]. In most cases so far, the designer constructs the grammar based on the a priori knowledge available and his experience. It is known that increased descriptive power of a language is paid for in terms of increased complexity of the analysis system (recognizer or acceptor). Finite-state automata are capable of recognizing or accepting finite-state languages although the descriptive power of finite-state languages is also known to be weaker than that of context-free and context-sensitive languages. On the other hand, nonfinite, nondeterministic devices are required, in general, to accept the languages generated by context-free and context-sensitive grammars. Except for the class of deterministic languages, nondeterministic parsing procedures are usually needed for the analysis of context-free languages. The tradeoff between the descriptive power and the analysis efficiency of a grammar for a given application is, at present, almost completely justified by the designer. (For example, a precedence language may be used for pattern description in order to obtain good analysis efficiency; or, on the other hand, a context-free programmed grammar generating a context-sensitive language may be selected in order to describe the patterns effectively.) The effect of the theoretical difficulty may not be serious, in practice, as long as some care is exercised in developing the required grammars. This is especially true when the languages of interest are actually finite-state, even though the form of the grammars may be context-sensitive, or when the languages may be approximated by finite-state languages. The following simple examples illustrate some of the points discussed above, particularly the increased power of the productions of the more general classes of grammars.

Example 4.4.1

It is desired to construst a grammar to generate the finite-state language $L = \{a^n b^n c^n \mid 1 \leq n \leq 3\}$. This might be the language describing, say, the set of equilateral triangles of side length one, two, or three units. In order for the grammar to be compatible with a top-down goal-oriented analysis procedure, the grammar must produce terminals in a strictly left-to-right order, and, at most, one terminal may be produced by a single application of any production. Nonterminals may not appear to the left of terminal symbols, but the generation of nonterminals is otherwise unrestricted.

1. A finite-state grammar:

$$G_1 = (N, \ \Sigma, \ P, \ S)$$

where

$$N = \{S, A_1, A_2, B_{10}, B_{20}, B_{30}, B_{21}, B_{31}, B_{32}, C_1, C_2, C_3\}$$

$$\Sigma = \{a, b, c\}$$

$$
\begin{array}{ll}
P: S \ \rightarrow aA_1 & B_{21} \rightarrow bC_2 \\
 S \ \rightarrow aB_{10} & B_{30} \rightarrow bB_{31} \\
 A_1 \ \rightarrow aA_2 & B_{31} \rightarrow bB_{32} \\
 A_1 \ \rightarrow aB_{20} & B_{32} \rightarrow bC_3 \\
 A_2 \ \rightarrow aB_{30} & C_1 \ \rightarrow c \\
 B_{10} \rightarrow bC_1 & C_2 \ \rightarrow cC_1 \\
 B_{20} \rightarrow bB_{21} & C_3 \ \rightarrow cC_2
\end{array}
$$

2. A context-free grammar (in Greibach Normal Form):

$$G_2 = (N, \ \Sigma, \ P, \ S)$$

where

$$N = \{S, A_1, A_2, B_1, B_2, B_3, C\}$$

$$\Sigma = \{a, b, c\}$$

$$P: S \rightarrow aA_1C \qquad B_3 \rightarrow bB_2$$
$$A_1 \rightarrow b \qquad B_2 \rightarrow bB_1$$
$$A_1 \rightarrow aB_2C \qquad B_1 \rightarrow b$$
$$A_1 \rightarrow aA_2C \qquad C \rightarrow c$$
$$A_2 \rightarrow aB_3C$$

3. A context-free programmed grammar:

$$G_3 = (N, \ \Sigma, \ J, \ P, \ S)$$

where

$$N = \{S, \ B, \ C\}$$

$$\Sigma = \{a, \ b, \ c\}$$

$$J = \{1, \ 2, \ 3, \ 4, \ 5\}$$

P: Label	Core	Success Field	Failure Field
1	$S \rightarrow aB$	$\{2, 3\}$	$\{\phi\}$
2	$B \rightarrow aBB$	$\{2, 3\}$	$\{\phi\}$
3	$B \rightarrow C$	$\{4\}$	$\{5\}$
4	$C \rightarrow bC$	$\{3\}$	$\{\phi\}$
5	$C \rightarrow c$	$\{5\}$	$\{\phi\}$

Even for this simple case, the context-free grammar is considerably more compact than the finite-state grammar. For this example, a context-sensitive grammar would not be much different from the context-free grammar and, hence, has not been given. However, the context-free programmed grammar is still more compact than the context-free grammar.

Example 4.4.2

The language

$$L = \{a^n b^n c^n d^n \,|\, n \geq 1\}$$

could be interpreted as the language describing squares of side length $n = 1$, 2, ...

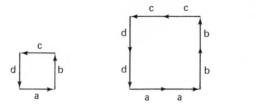

L is known as a context-sensitive language, and can be generated in the following two ways:

1. A context-sensitive grammar:

$$G_1 = (N, \Sigma, P, S)$$

where

$$N = \{S, A, B, C, D, E, F, G\}$$

$$\Sigma = \{a, b, c, d\}$$

$P:$	$S \rightarrow aAB$	$dG \rightarrow Gd$
	$A \rightarrow aAC$	$aG \rightarrow abcD$
	$A \rightarrow D$	$bG \rightarrow bbcD$
	$Dc \rightarrow cD$	$dFB \rightarrow dFd$
	$Dd \rightarrow dD$	$dFd \rightarrow Fdd$
	$DC \rightarrow EC$	$cF \rightarrow Fc$
	$EC \rightarrow Ed$	$bF \rightarrow bbc$
	$DB \rightarrow FB$	$aF \rightarrow ab$
	$Ed \rightarrow Gd$	$bB \rightarrow bcd$
	$cG \rightarrow Gc$	

2. A context-free programmed grammar:

$$G_2 = (N, \Sigma, P, S, J)$$

where

$$N = \{S, A, B, C, D\}, \quad \Sigma = \{a, b, c, d\}, \quad J = \{1, 2, 3, 4, 5, 6, 7\}$$

$P:$Label	Core	Success Field	Failure Field
1	$S \rightarrow aAB$	$\{2, 3\}$	$\{\phi\}$

2	$A \to aAC$	$\{2, 3\}$	$\{\phi\}$
3	$A \to D$	$\{4\}$	$\{\phi\}$
4	$C \to d$	$\{5\}$	$\{\phi\}$
5	$D \to bDc$	$\{4\}$	$\{\phi\}$
6	$B \to d$	$\{7\}$	$\{\phi\}$
7	$D \to bc$	$\{0\}$	$\{\phi\}$

It is noted that if n is finite, then $L = \{a^n b^n c^n d^n \mid n = 1, \ldots, N\}$ can certainly also be generated by a finite-state or context-free grammar.

It should be remarked that a grammar is most appropriate for description when the pattern of interest is built up from a small set of primitives by recursive application of a small set of production rules. Also, the "primitive selection" and the "grammar construction" should probably be treated simultaneously rather than in two different stages. There is no doubt that a different selection of pattern primitives will result in a different grammar for the description of a given set of patterns. Sometimes, a compromise is necessary in order to develop a suitable grammar. Example 4.3.2 may also be used to illustrate this point. Referring to the example, it is evident that the grammar which generates $L = \{a^n b^m c^n d^m \mid n, m = 1, 2, \ldots\}$ will be much more complex than the grammar generating $a'b'c'd'$.

Although many classes of patterns appear to be intuitively context-sensitive, context-sensitive (but not context-free) grammars have rarely been used for pattern description simply because of their complexity. Context-free languages have been used to describe patterns such as English characters [29], chromosome images [37], spark chamber pictures [35], chemical structures [78], and spoken digits [40, 41].

In addition to (1) the tradeoff between the language descriptive power and the analysis efficiency, and (2) the compromise sometimes necessary between the primitives selected and the grammar constructed, the designer should also be aware of the need to control the excessive strings generated by the constructed grammar. The number of pattern strings available in practice is always limited. However, in most cases, the grammar constructed would generate a large or infinite number of strings.† It is hoped that the excessive strings generated are similar to the available pattern strings. Unfortunately, this may not be true since the grammar, in many cases, is constructed heuristically. The problem may become very serious when the excessive strings include some pattern strings which should belong to other classes. In this case, adjustments should be made to exclude these strings from the language generated by the

---

†It may be argued that, in practice, a pattern grammar can always be finite-state since it is constructed from a finite number of pattern strings. However, the finite-state grammar so constructed may require a large number of productions. In such a case, a context-free or a context-free programmed pattern grammar may be constructed for the purpose of significantly reducing the number of productions.

constructed grammar.

Recently, probably due to their relative effectiveness in describing natural language structures, transformational grammars have been proposed for pattern description [79, 80]. Transformational grammars would allow the possibility of determining from the pattern generative mechanism a simple base grammar (deep structure) which generates a certain set of patterns and a problem-oriented set of transformations. Through the base grammar and the transformations, the original set of patterns can be described.

From the above discussion, it might be concluded that, before efficient grammatical inference procedures are available, a man-machine interactive system would be suitable for the problem of grammar construction. The basic grammar and the various tradeoffs and compromises have to be determined by the designer. The results of any adjustment on the grammar constructed can be easily checked and displayed through a computer system.

4.5. HIGH-DIMENSIONAL PATTERN GRAMMARS

4.5.1. General Discussion

In describing patterns using a string grammar, the only relation between subpatterns and/or primitives is the concatenation; that is, each subpattern or primitive can be connected only at the left or right. This one-dimensional relation has not been very effective in describing two-or three-dimensional patterns. A natural generalization is to use a more general formalism including other useful relations [29, 81–86]. Let R be a set of n-ary relations $(n \geq 1)$. A relation $r \in R$ satisfied by the subpatterns and/or primitives X_1, . . ., X_n is denoted $r(X_1, . . ., X_n)$. For example, TRIANGLE (a, b, c) means that the ternary relation TRIANGLE is satisfied by the line segments a, b, and c, and ABOVE (X, Y) means that X is above Y. The following examples illustrate pattern descriptions using this formalism of relations.

Example 4.5.1

The mathematical expression

$$\frac{a + b}{c}$$

can be described by

ABOVE (ABOVE (LEFT $(a$, LEFT $(+, b))$, ——), $c)$

where LEFT (X, Y) means that X is to the left of Y.

Example 4.5.2

The following grammar will generate sentences describing houses.

$$G = (N, \Sigma, P, S)$$

where

$N = \{$ ⟨house⟩, ⟨side view⟩, ⟨front view⟩, ⟨roof⟩, ⟨gable⟩, ⟨wall⟩, ⟨chimney⟩, ⟨windows⟩, ⟨door⟩ $\}$

$\Sigma = \{$ ▯ , ⃰ , ▮ , ⊞ , △ , ▭ , ▱ , → (,)

⊙ , ◔ , ↑ , ↦ $\}$

$S = $ ⟨house⟩   ▮

P : ⟨door⟩ →

⟨window⟩ → ⊞ , ⟨windows⟩ → → (⟨windows⟩, ⊞)

⟨chimney⟩ → ▯ , ⟨chimney⟩ → ⃰

⟨wall⟩ → ▭ , ⟨wall⟩ → ◔ (⟨door⟩, ▭)

⟨wall⟩ → ⊙ (⟨windows⟩, ▭)

⟨gable⟩ → △ , ⟨gable⟩ → ↑ (⟨chimney⟩, △)

⟨roof⟩ → ▱ , ⟨roof⟩ → ↑ (⟨chimney⟩, ▱)

⟨front view⟩ → ↑ (⟨gable⟩, ⟨wall⟩)

⟨side view⟩ → ↑ (⟨roof⟩, ⟨wall⟩)

⟨house⟩ → ⟨front view⟩

⟨house⟩ → ↦ (⟨house⟩, ⟨side view⟩)

The notation

→ (X, Y) means that X is to the right of Y

⊙ (X, Y) means that X is inside of Y

◔ (X, Y) means that X is inside on the bottom of Y

↑ (X, Y) means that X rests on top of Y

↦ (X, Y) means that X rests to the right of Y

House	Description
	↑(△ , ▯)
	↑ (↑ (⃰ , △), ◔ (▮ , ▭))
	↦ (↑ (↑ (▯ , ▱), ◔ (⊞ , ▭)), ↑ (△ , ⊙ (▮ , ▭)))

A simple two-dimensional generalization of string grammars is to extend grammars for one-dimensional strings to two-dimensional arrays [87, 88]. The primitives are the array elements and the relation between primitives is the two-dimensional concatenation. Each production rewrites one subarray by another, rather than one substring by another. Relationships between array grammars and array automata (automata with two-dimensional tapes) have been studied recently [89].

4.5.2. Special Grammars

Shaw, by attaching a "head" (hd) and a "tail" (tl) to each primitive, has used the four binary operators $+$, $\times$, $-$, and $*$ for defining binary concatenation relations between primitives [90, 91].

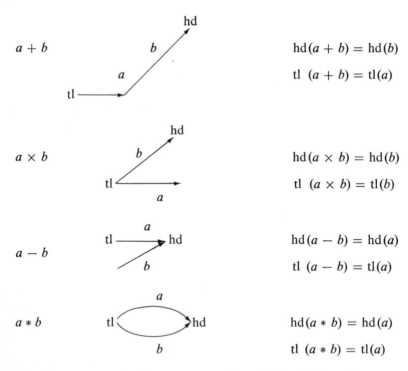

$a + b$
$$hd(a + b) = hd(b)$$
$$tl\ (a + b) = tl(a)$$

$a \times b$
$$hd(a \times b) = hd(b)$$
$$tl\ (a \times b) = tl(b)$$

$a - b$
$$hd(a - b) = hd(a)$$
$$tl\ (a - b) = tl(a)$$

$a * b$
$$hd(a * b) = hd(a)$$
$$tl\ (a * b) = tl(a)$$

For string languages, only the operator $+$ is used. In addition, the unary operator $\sim$ acting as a tail/head reverser is also defined; i.e.,

$\sim a$
$$hd(\sim a) = tl(a)$$
$$tl\ (\sim a) = hd(a)$$

In the case of describing patterns consisting of disconnected subpatterns, the "blank" or "don't care" primitive is introduced. Each pictorial pattern is represented by a *labelled branch-oriented graph* where branches represent primitives.

The grammar which generates sentences (PDL expressions) in PDL (picture description language) is a context-free grammar

$$G = (N, \Sigma, P, S)$$

where

$$N = \{S, SL\}$$

$$\Sigma = \{b\} \cup \{+, \times, -, /, (,)\} \cup \{l\}, b \text{ may be any primitive (including}$$
the null point primitive λ which has identical tail and head)

and

$$S \rightarrow b, \; S \rightarrow (S \, \phi_b \, S), \; S \rightarrow (\sim S), \; S \rightarrow SL, \; S \rightarrow (/SL),$$

$$SL \rightarrow S^l, \; SL \rightarrow (SL \, \phi_b \, SL), \; SL \rightarrow (\sim SL), \; SL \rightarrow (/SL),$$

$$\phi_b \rightarrow +, \phi_b \rightarrow \times, \phi_b \rightarrow -, \phi_b \rightarrow *$$

l is a label designator which is used to allow cross reference to the expressions S within a description. The / operator is used to enable the tail and head of an expression to be arbitrarily located.

Example 4.5.3

The following grammar illustrates the operations of PDL for pattern structural description.

$$G = (N, \Sigma, P, S)$$

where

$$N = \{S, A, \text{house, triangle}\}$$

$$\Sigma = \left\{ \xrightarrow{a}, \quad \overset{b}{\diagup}\overset{c}{\diagdown}, \quad \downarrow e, (,), +, \times, -, *, \sim \right\}$$

and P:

$$S \rightarrow A, \; S \rightarrow \text{house}$$

$$A \rightarrow (b + (\text{triangle} + c))$$

$$\text{House} \rightarrow ((e + (a + (\sim e))) * \text{triangle})$$

$$\text{Triangle} \rightarrow ((b + c) * a)$$

$$L(G) = \{(b + (((b + c) * a) + c)), ((e + (a + (\sim e))) * ((b + c) * a))\}$$

The structural description in terms of a parse tree of the patterns "*A*" and "house" is shown in Fig. 4.5.1. A top-down parsing procedure was used for the recognition of PDL expressions describing pictorial patterns [91].

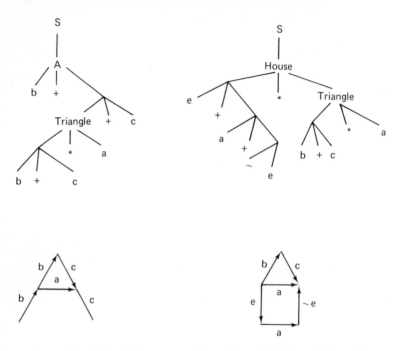

Fig. 4.5.1   PDL structural description of "A" and "House."

Once we include relations more than just concatenations, the description of a pattern may be more conveniently represented by a relational graph, where nodes represent subpatterns or primitives and branches denote (binary) relations.† (Refer to Section 4.1.) When *n*-ary relations are involved, a graph-representable description can be obtained by transforming all relations into binary ones. A unary relation $r(X)$ can be changed to a binary one $r'(X, \lambda)$ where λ denotes the "null" primitive. $r(X_1, \ldots, X_n)$ $(n > 2)$ can be transformed into a composition of binary relations, such as

$$r_1(X_1, r_2(X_2, \ldots, r_{n-1}(X_{n-1}, X_n)))$$

or into a conjunction of binary relations

$$r_1(X_{11}, X_{12}) \wedge r_2(X_{21}, X_{22}) \wedge \cdots \wedge r_k(X_{k1}, X_{k2})$$

or into a combination of these. For example, the ternary relation TRIANGLE (a, b, c) could be transformed into either one of the following equivalent

---

†This straightforward representation is called a *labelled node-oriented directed graph.* See [50] for examples using a tree-representable description.

binary relations:

$$CAT(a, b) \land CAT(b, c) \land CAT(c, a)$$

or

$$\varDelta(b, CAT(a, c))$$

where $CAT(X, Y)$ means that hd (X) is concatenated to tl(Y), i.e., $CAT(X, Y)$ $= X + Y$, and $\varDelta(X, Y)$ means that the line X is connected to form a triangle with the object Y consisting of two concatenated segments. In general, replacement of an n-ary relation with binary ones using composition requires the addition of more levels in the description.

Based on an idea in [56], Feder has formalized a "plex" grammar which generates languages with terminals having an arbitrary number of attaching points for connecting to other primitives or subpatterns [78]. The primitives of the plex grammar are called N-attaching point entity (NAPE). Each production of the plex grammar is in context-free form in which the connectivity of primitives or subpatterns is described by using explicit lists of labelled concatenation points (called loint lists). While the sentences generated by a plex grammar are not directed graphs, they can be transformed by either assigning labelled nodes to both primitives and concatenation points as suggested by Pfaltz and Rosenfeld [92] or by transforming primitives to nodes and concatenations to labelled branches. Figure 4.5.2 gives an example to illustrate such transformations [63].

Pfaltz and Rosenfeld have extended the concept of string grammars to grammars for labelled graphs called webs. Labelled node-oriented graphs are explicitly used in the productions. Each production describes the rewriting of a graph α into another graph β and also contains an "embedding" rule E which specifies the connection of β to its surrounding graph (host web) when α is rewritten. A web grammar G is a 4-tuple

$$G = (N, \Sigma, P, S)$$

where N is a set of nonterminals, Σ is a set of terminals, S is a set of "initial" webs, and P is a set of web productions. A web production is defined as†

$$\alpha \rightarrow \beta, E$$

where α and β are webs, and E is an embedding of β. If we want to replace the subweb α of the web ω by another subweb β, it is necessary to specify how to "embed" β in ω in place of α. The definition of an embedding must not depend on the host web ω since we want to be able to replace α by β in any web containing α as a subweb. Usually E consists of a set of logical functions which specify whether or not each vertex of $\omega - \alpha$ is connected to each vertex of β.

---

†In a most general formulation, the contextual condition of the production is added.

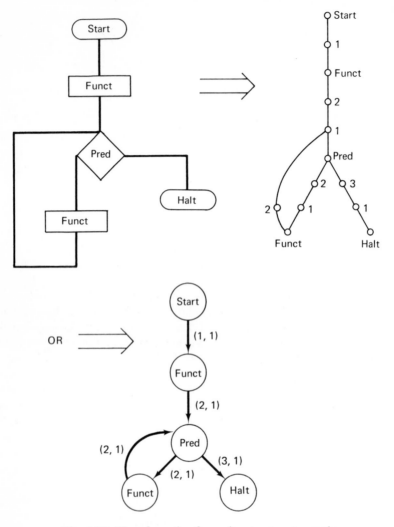

Fig. 4.5.2 Transformation from plex structure to graphs.

Example 4.5.4

Consider the web grammar

$$G = (N, \Sigma, P, S)$$

where

$$N = \{A\}, \quad \Sigma = \{a, b, c\}, \quad S = \{A\}$$

and

$$P: (1)\ A \rightarrow a \overset{b}{\underset{c}{\big\langle}} \qquad E = \{(p,\ a)\,|\,(p,\ A)\ \text{an edge in the host web}\}$$

$$(2)\ A \rightarrow a \diamondsuit A \qquad E \text{ is the same as in (1)}$$

The language of this grammar is the set of all webs of the form

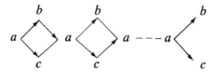

It is noted that web grammars are vertex-or node-oriented compared with the branch- or edge-oriented grammars (e.g., PDL, plex grammars, etc.). That is, terminals or primitives are represented as vertices in the graph rather than as branches.

An important special case of a web grammar is that in which the terminal set Σ consists of only a single symbol. In this case, every point of every web in the language has the same label, so that we can ignore the labels and identify the webs with their underlying graphs. This type of web grammar is called a "*graph grammar*," and its language is called *graph language* [95]. The formalism of web grammars has been rather extensively analyzed [92]. The relations among PDL grammars, plex grammars and web grammars have been discussed by Shaw [93] and Rosenfeld [94].

Pavlidis [95, 96] has generalized string grammars to graph grammars by including nonterminal symbols which are not simple branches or nodes. An mth order nonterminal structure is defined as an entity which is connected to the rest of the graph by m nodes. In particular, a second-order structure is called a branch structure and a first-order structure a node structure. Then an mth order context-free graph grammar G_g is a quadruple

$$G_g = (N,\ \Sigma,\ P,\ S)$$

where

    N is a set of mth order nonterminal structures: nodes, branches, triangles, . . ., polygons with m vertices;

Σ is a set of terminals: nodes and branches;

P is a finite set of productions of the form $A \rightarrow \alpha$, where A is a nonterminal structure and α a graph containing possibly both terminals and nonterminals. α is connected to the rest of the graph through exactly the same nodes as A;

S is a set of initial graphs.

The expression $A * B$ denotes that the two graphs A and B are connected by a pair of nodes (Fig. 4.5.3(a)), and $N(A + B + C)$ denotes that the graphs A, B, and C are connected through a common node N(Fig. 4.5.3(b)). Thus the production $A \rightarrow B * C$ where A, B, and C are branch structures should be interpreted as: Replace branch structure A by branch structures B and C connected to the graph through the same nodes as A. No other connection exists between B and C. Similarly, the production $N \rightarrow M(A + B)$ should be interpreted as: Replace node structure N by a node structure M and two other structures A and B connected to the rest of the graph by the same node as N. When no ambiguity occurs, we can use simple concatenations, e.g., ANB to denote a nonterminal subgraph consisting of a branch structure A with nodes X and Y connected to the node structure N through Y and a branch structure B with nodes Y and Z connected to N through Y (Fig. 4.5.3 (c)). The subgraph is connected to the rest of the graph through the nodes X and Z.

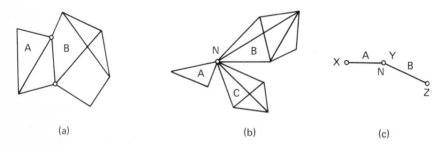

(a)   (b)   (c)

Fig. 4.5.3 Illustration of (a) $A * B$, (b) $N(A + B + C)$, and (c) ANB.

The following examples illustrate the use of graph grammars for pattern description:

Example 4.5.5

The following grammar describes graphs representing two terminal series-parallel networks (TTSPN)

$$G_g = (N, \Sigma, P, S)$$

where

$$N = \{S, B\}, \qquad \Sigma = \{\overset{b}{—}, \overset{n}{\cdot}\}, \qquad S = \{nBn\}$$

and

P: (1) $B \longrightarrow BnB$

    (2) $B \longrightarrow B * B$

    (3) $B \longrightarrow b$

A typical generation would be

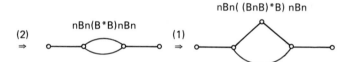

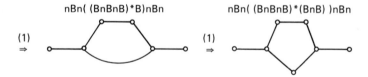

Example 4.5.6

The following graph grammar describes connected trees

$$G_g = (N, \Sigma, P, S)$$

where

$$N = \{N\}, \qquad \Sigma = \{\overset{b}{\text{---}}, \overset{n}{\cdot}\}, \qquad S = \{N\}$$

and

$$P: N \longrightarrow NbN$$
$$N \longrightarrow n$$

A typical generation would be

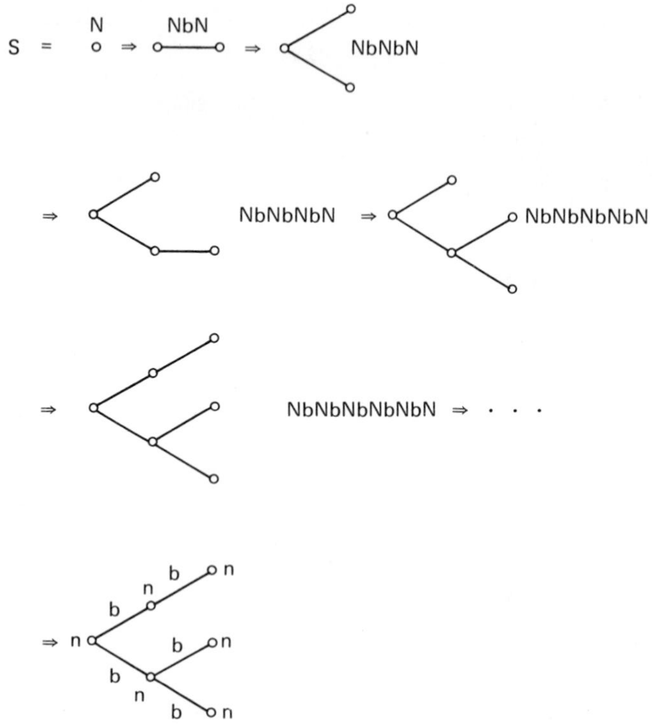

By extending one-dimensional concatenation to multi-dimensional concatenation, strings are generalized to trees. Tree grammars and the corresponding recognizers, tree automata, have been studied recently by a number of authors [97, 98]. Naturally, if a pattern can be conveniently described by a tree, it will easily be generated by a tree grammar. For example, in Fig. 4.5.4, patterns and their corresponding tree representations are listed in (a) and (b), respectively [99].

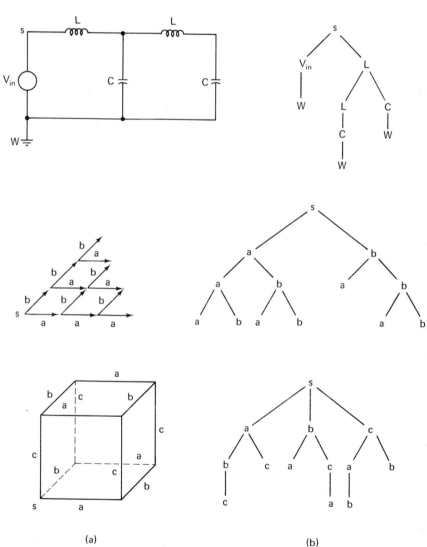

(a)   (b)

Fig. 4.5.4 (a) Patterns and (b) corresponding tree representations.

4.6. CONCLUDING REMARKS

In this chapter, we have demonstrated that languages can be used to describe complex patterns. Consequently, syntax analysis procedures can be used to implement the pattern recognition process. In some practical applications, however, a certain amount of uncertainty exists in the process under study. For example, due to the presence of noise and variations in the pattern measurements, ambiguities often occur in the languages describing real-data patterns. In order to describe and recognize noisy patterns under possible ambiguous situations, the use of stochastic languages has been recently suggested [100–102]. A stochastic grammar is a 4-tuple $G_s = (N, \Sigma, P_s, S)$ where P_s is a finite set of stochastic productions and all the other symbols are the same as defined in Section 4.1. For a stochastic context-free grammar, a production in P is of the form

$$A_i \xrightarrow{\quad P_{ij} \quad} \alpha_j, \qquad A_i \in N, \qquad \alpha_j \in (N \cup \Sigma)^*$$

where P_{ij} is called the production probability. The probability of generating a string x, called the string probability $p(x)$, is the product of all production probabilities associated with the productions used in the generation of x. The language generated by a stochastic grammar consists of the strings generated by the grammar and their associated string probabilities.

By associating probabilities with the strings, we can impose a probabilistic structure on the language to describe noisy patterns. The probability distribution characterizing the patterns in a class can be interpreted as the probability distribution associated with the strings in a language. Thus, statistical decision rules can be applied to the classification of a pattern under ambiguous situations (for example, use the maximum-likelihood decision rule). Furthermore, because of the availability of the information about production probabilities, the speed of syntactic analysis can be improved through the use of this information [103, 104]. Of course, in practice, the production probabilities will have to be inferred from the observation of relatively large numbers of pattern samples [105].

E X E R C I S E S   4.6

1. Describe the following pictorial pattern by:
    (a) a tree structurre
    (b) a relational graph
    (c) a relational matrix

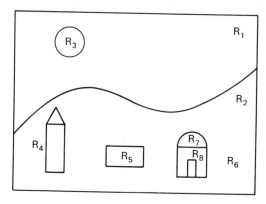

2. For the polygon shown in the following, determine its primary subsets and nuclei.

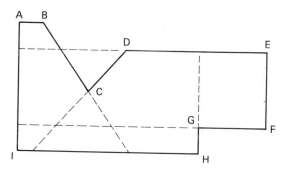

3. For each class of patterns given below, construct a grammar to describe the patterns:
    (a)   a set of squares from size 1 to $k (= 10)$
    (b)   a set of squares of different sizes
    (c)   a set of rectangles of different sizes

4. Construct a PDL grammar to describe the class of $L\text{-}C$ networks shown below. Use V_{in}, L, and C as primitives.

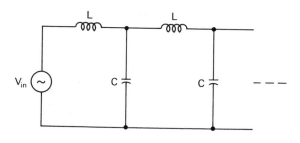

5. Construct (a) a tree grammar, (b) a web grammar to describe the class of *L-C* networks in Problem 4.

6. Describe the following flow chart using
   (a) PDL
   (b) WEB grammar
   (c) graph grammar

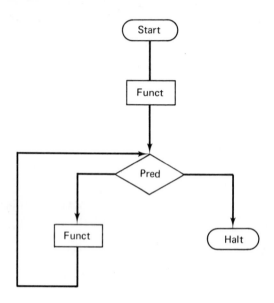

REFERENCES

1. Fu, K. S., *Sequential Methods in Pattern Recognition and Machine Learning,* Academic Press, Inc, New York, 1968.

2. Sebestyen, G. S., *Decision Processes in Pattern Recognition,* The Macmillan Company, New York, 1962.

3. Nilsson, N. J., *Learning Machines—Foundations of Trainable Pattern-Classifying Systems,* McGraw-Hill Book Co., New York, 1965.

4. Mendel, J. M. and K. S. Fu (eds.), *Adaptive Learning and Pattern Recognition Systems: Theory and Applications,* Academic Press Inc., New York, 1970.

5. Meisel, W., *Computer-Oriented Approaches to Pattern Recognition,* Academic Press, Inc., New York, 1972.

6. Fukunaga, K., *Introduction to Statistical Pattern Recognition,* Academic Press, Inc., New York, 1972.

7. PATRICK, E. A., *Fundamentals of Pattern Recognition*, Prentice-Hall, Inc., Englewood Cliffs, N.J., 1972.

8. ANDREWS, H. C., *Introduction to Mathematical Techniques in Pattern Recognition*, John Wiley & Sons, New York, 1972.

9. DUDA, R. O. and P. E. HART, *Pattern Classification and Scene Analysis*, John Wiley & Sons, New York, 1973.

10. CHEN, C. H., *Statistical Pattern Recognition*, Hayden Book Co., Washington, D.C., 1973.

11. YOUNG, T. Y. and T. W. CALVERT, *Classification, Estimation, and Pattern Recognition*, American Elsevier, New York, 1974.

12. FU, K. S. and P. H. SWAIN, "On Syntactic Pattern Recognition," *Software Engineering*, Vol. 2, ed. by J. T. Tou, Academic Press, Inc, New York, 1971.

13. MILLER, W. F. and A. C. SHAW, "Linguistic Methods in Picture Processing— A Survey," *Proc. AFIPS Fall Joint Computer Conference*, 1968.

14. NARASIMHAN, R., "A Linguistic Approach to Pattern Recognition," *Report 121*, Digital Computer Laboratory, University of Illinois, Urbana, Illinois, 1962.

15. Special issues of *Pattern Recognition* on Syntactic Pattern Recognition, 3:4 (1971) and 4:1 (1972).

16. ZAVALISHIN, N. V. and I. B. MUCHNIK, "Linguistic (Structural) Approach to the Pattern Recognition Problem," *Automatika i Telemekhanika* (Aug. 1969), 86–118.

17. TSYPKIN, YA. Z., *Foundations of the Theory of Learning System*, Nauka, Moscow, 1970.

18. AISERMAN, M. A., E. M. BRAVERMAN and L. I. ROZONOER, *Potential Function Method in Theory of Learning Machines*, Nauka, Moscow, 1970.

19. Fu, K. S. (ed.), *Pattern Recognition and Machine Learning*, Plenum Press, 1971.

20. ARKADEV, A. G. and E. M. BRAVERMAN, *Learning in Pattern Classification Machines*, Nauka, Moscow, 1971.

21. ROSENFELD, A., *Picture Processing by Computer*, Academic Press, Inc, New York, 1969.

22. HAWKINS, J. K., "Image Processing: A Review and Projection," *Automatic Interpretation and Classification of Images*, ed. by A. Grasselli, Academic Press, Inc., New York, 1969

23. ANDREWS, H. C., *Computer Techniques in Image Processing*, Academic Press, Inc, New York, 1970.

24. Special issue of *Pattern Recognition* on Image Enhancement 2:2 (1970)

25. HUANG T. S., et al., "Image Processing," *Proc. IEEE*, 59:11 (Nov. 1971)

26. PRESTON, JR., K., *Coherent Optical Computers,* McGraw-Hill Book Company, New York, 1972.

27. Special issue of *IEEE Trans. on Computers* on Two-Dimensional Digital Signal Processing, C-21:7 (July 1972).

28. Special issue of *Proc. IEEE* on Digital Picture Processing 60:7 (July 1972).

29. NARASIMHAN, R., "On the Description, Generation, and Recognition of Classes of Pictures," in *Automatic Interpretation and Classification of Images,* ed. by A. Grasselli, Academic Press, Inc., New York, 1969.

30. STALLINGS, W., "Recognition of Printed Chinese Characters by Automatic Pattern Analysis," *Computer Graphics and Image Processing,* 1:1 (1972), 47–65.

31. SAKAI, T., M. NAGAS, and H. TERAI, "A Description of Chinese Characters Using Subpatterns," *Information Processing* (Japan), 10 (1970), 10–14.

32. CHANG, S. K., "An Interactive System for Chinese Character Generation and Retrieval," *IEEE Trans. on Systems, Man, and Cybernetics,* SMC-3 (May 1973).

33. ANDERSON, R. H., "Syntax-Directed Recognition of Hand-Printed Two-Dimensional Mathematics," Ph. D. thesis, Harvard University, Cambridge, Mass., Jan. 1968.

34. CHANG, S. K., "A Method for the Structural Analysis of Two-Dimensional Mathematical Expressions," *Information Sciences* 2 (July 1970).

35. SHAW, A. C., "The Formal Description and Parsing of Pictures," *Report SLAC-84,* Stanford Linear Accelerator Center, Stanford, California, March 1968.

36. BHARGAVA, B. K., and K. S. FU, "Application of Tree System Approach to Classification of Bubble Chamber Photographs," *Tech. Rept. TR-EE 72–30,* School of Elec. Eng., Purdue University, West Lafayette, Indiana, Nov. 1972.

37. LEDLEY R. S., et al., "FIDAC: Film Input to Digital Automatic Computer and Associated Syntax-Directed Pattern Recognition Programming System," *Optical and Electro-Optical Information Processing,* ed. by J. T. Tippett et al., Massachusetts Institute of Technology Press, Cambridge, Mass., 1965.

38. MOAYER, B. and K. S. FU, "A Syntactic Approach to Fingerprint Pattern Recognition," Proc. First Int'l. Joint Conf. on Pattern Recognition, Washington, D.C. Oct. 30–Nov. 1, 1973.

39. HANKLEY, W. J. and J. T. TOU, "Automatic Fingerprint Interpretation and Classification via Contextual Analysis and Topological Coding," *Pictorial Pattern Recognition,* ed by G. C. Cheng et al., Thompson Books Co., 1968.

40. DeMORI, R., "A Descriptive Technique for Automatic Speech Recognition," *IEEE Trans. on Audio and Electroacoustics,* AU-21 (Apr. 1973).

41. KUREMATSU, A., M. TAKEDA, and S. INOUE, "A Method of Pattern Recognition Using Rewriting Rules," Second International Joint Conference on Artificial Intelligence, London, Sept. 1971, pp. 248–257.

42. ANDERSON, R. H., "Syntax-Directed Recognition of Hand-Printed Two-Dimensional Mathematics," *Interactive Systems for Experimental Applied Mathematics,* ed. by M. Klerer and J. Reinfelds, Academic Press, Inc., New York, 1968.

43. GRIMSDALE, R. L., F. H. SUMMER, C. J. TUNIS, and T. KILBURN, "A System for the Automatic Recognition of Patterns," *Proc. IEEE,* 106:B: No. 26, (Mar. 1959), 210–221; reprinted in *Pattern Recognition,* ed. by L. Uhr, John Wiley & Sons, New York, 1966, pp. 317–338.

44. EDEN, M. and M. HALLE, "The Characterization of Cursive Writing," *Proc. 4th London Symposium on Information Theory,* ed. by C. Cherry, Butterworth & Co., London, 1961, pp. 287–299.

45. EARNEST, L. D., "Machine Recognition of Cursive Writing," *Information Processing, Proc. IEEE Congress 1962,* ed. by C. M. Poplewell, North-Holland Publishing Co., Amsterdam, 1963, pp. 462–466.

46. MERMELSTEIN, P. and M. EDEN, "Experiments on Computer Recognition of Connected Handwritten Words," *Information and Control,* 7 (1964), 255–270.

47. EDEN, M. and P. MERMELSTEIN, "Models for the Dynamics of Handwriting Generation," *Proc. 16th Annual Conference on Engineering in Medicine and Biology* (1963), 12–13.

48. FREEMAN, H., "On the Encoding of Arbitrary Geometric Configurations," *IEEE Trans. on Electronic Computers,* EC-10 (1961), 260–268.

49. FREEMAN, H., "On the Digital-Computer Classification of Geometric Line Patterns," *Proc. National Electronics Conference,* 18 (1962), 312–324.

50. KNOKE, P. J. and R. G. WILEY, "A Linguistic Approach to Mechanical Pattern Recognition," *Proc. IEEE Computer Conference* (Sept. 1967), 142–144.

51. FEDER, J., "Languages of Encoded Line Patterns," *Information and Control,* 13 (1968), 230–244.

52. FREEMAN, H. and S. P. Morse, "On Searching a Contour Map for a Given Terrain Elevation Profile," *Journal of Franklin Institute,* 284 (1967), 1–25.

53. FEDER, J. and H. FREEMAN, "Digital Curve Matching Using a Contour Correlation Algorithm" *IEEE International Convention Record,* Part 3 (1966), 69–85.

54. ZAHN, C. T., "Two-Dimensional Pattern Description and Recognition via Curvature Points," *SLAC Rept. No. 72,* Stanford Linear Accelerator Center, Stanford, Calif., Dec. 1966.

55. FREEMAN H. and J. GARDER, "Pictorial Jig-saw Puzzles: The Computer Solution of a Problem in Pattern Recognition," *IEEE Trans. on Electronic Computers,* EC-13 (1964), 118–127.

56. NARASIMHAN, R., "Syntax-Directed Interpretation of Classes of Picurtes," *Comm. ACM,* 9 (1966), 166–173.

57. SPINRAD, R. J., "Machine Recognition of Hand Printing," *Information and Control,* 8 (1965), 124–142.

58. O'CALLAGHAN, J. F., "Problems in On-Line Character Recognition," *Picture Language Machines,* ed. by S. Kaneff, Academic Press, Inc., New York, 1970.

59. NIR, M., "Recognition of General Line Patterns with Application to Bubble-Chamber Photographs and Handprinted Characters," Ph. D. thesis, Moore School of Electrical Engineering, University of Penn., Phila., Penn., Dec. 1967.

60. NARASIMHAN, R., "Labeling Schemata and Syntactic Description of Pictures," *Information and Control,* 7 (1964), 151–179.

61. BUTLER, J. W., M. K. BUTLER, and A. STROUD, "Automatic Classification of Chromosomes," *Proc. Conference on Data Acquisition and Processing in Biology and Medicine,* New York, 1963.

62. HANKLEY, W. J. and J. T. TOU, "Automatic Fingerprint Interpretation and Classification via Contextual Analysis and Topological Coding," *Pictorial Pattern Recognition,* ed. by G. C. Cheng et al., Thompson Book Co., Washington, D.C., 1968.

63. GRASSELLI, A., "On the Automatic Classification of Fingerprints," *Methodologies of Pattern Recognition,* ed. by S. Watanabe, Academic Press, Inc., New York, 1969.

64. LEVI, G. and F. SIROVICH, "Structural Description of Fingerprint Images," *Information Sciences,* 4:4 (1972), 327–356.

65. NAGAO, M., "Picture Recognition and Data Structure," *Graphic Languages,* ed. by F. Nake and A. Rosenfeld, North-Holland Publishing Co., Amsterdam, London, 1972.

66. KELLEY, M. D., "Visual Identification of People by Computer," Ph. D. thesis, Dept. of Computer Science, Stanford University, Stanford, Calif., June 1970.

67. ROBERTS, L. G., "Machine Perception of Three-Dimensional Solids," *Optical and Electro-Optical Information Processing,* ed. by J. T. Tippett et. al., MIT Press, Cambridge, Mass., 1965, pp. 159–197.

68. DUDA, R. O. and P. E. Hart, "Experiments in Scene Analysis, "*Proc. First National Symposium on Industrial Robots,* Chicago, Apr. 1970.

69. FELDMAN, J. A. et al., "The Stanford Hand-Eye Project," *Proc. First International Joint Conference on Artificial Intelligence,* Washington, D.C., May 1969.

70. PAVLIDIS, T., "Analysis of Set Patterns," *Pattern Recognition,* 1 (1968), 165–178.

71. ROSENFELD, A. and J. P. STRONG, "A Grammar for Maps," *Software Engineering,* Vol. 2, ed. by. J. T. Tou, Academic Press, Inc., New York, 1971.

72. PAVLIDIS, T., "Representation of Figures by Labeled Graphs," *Pattern Recognition*, 4: 1 (1972), pp. 5–17.

73. PAVLIDIS, T., "Structural Pattern Recognition: Primitives and Juxtaposition," *Frontiers of Pattern Recognition*, ed. by S. Watanabe, Academic Press, Inc., New York, 1972.

74. MINSKY, M. L. and S. PAPERT, *Project MAC Progress Report IV*, MIT Press, Cambridge, Mass., 1967.

75. GUZMAN, A., "Decomposition of Scenes into Bodies," *Proc. AFIPS* Fall Joint Computer Conference 33:1 (Dec. 1968), 291–304.

76. BRICE, C. R. and C. L. FENNEMA, "Scene Analysis Using Regions," *Artificial Intelligence*, 1 (1970), 205–226.

77. FU, K. S. and T. L. BOOTH, "Grammatical Inference—Introduction and Survey," Parts I and II, *IEEE Trans. on Systems, Man and Cybernetics*, SMC-5, Jan. and July 1975.

78. FEDER, J., "Plex Languages," *Information Sciences*, 3 (July 1971).

79. CLOWES, M. C., "Transformational Grammars and the Organization of Pictures," in *Automatic Interpretation and Classification of Images,* ed. by A. Grasselli, Academic Press, Inc., New York, 1969,

80. KANAL, LAVEEN and B. CHANDRASEKARAN, "On Linguistic, Statistical and Mixed Models for Pattern Recognition," in *Frontiers of Pattern Recognition*, ed. by S. Watanabe, Academic Press, Inc., New York, 1972.

81. NARASIMHAN, R., "Picture Languages," in *Picture Language Machines*, ed. by S. Kaneff, Academic Press, Inc, New York, 1970.

82. EVANS, T. G., "A Formalism for the Description of Complex Objects and Its Implementation," *Proc. Fifth International Congress on Cybernetics*, Namur, Belgium, Sept. 1967.

83. MINSKY, M. L., "Steps Toward Artificial Intelligence," *Proc. IRE*, 49: 1 (1961), 8–30.

84. CLOWES, M. B., "Pictorial Relationships—A Syntactic Approach," in *Machine Intelligence IV*, ed. by B. Meltzer and D. Michie, American Elsevier, New York, 1969.

85. EVANS, T. G., "Descriptive Pattern Analysis Techniques," in *Automatic Interpretation and Classification of Images*, ed. by A. Grasselli, Academic Press, Inc., New York, 1969.

86. BARROW, H. G., and J. R. POPPLESTONE, "Relational Descriptions in Picture Processing," *Machine Intelligence 6*, ed. by B. Meltzer and D. Michie, Edinburgh University Press, Edinburgh, 1971, pp. 377–396.

87. KIRSCH, R. A., "Computer Interpretation of English Text and Patterns," *IEEE Trans. on Electronic Computers*, EC-13 (1964), 363–376.

88. DACEY, M. F., "The Syntax of a Triangle and Some Other Figures," *Pattern Recognition*, 2 (1970), 11–31.

89. MILGRAM, D. M. and A. ROSENFELD, "Array Automata and Array Grammars," Booklet TA-2, *IFIP Congress 71*, North-Holland Publishing Co., Amsterdam, Aug. 1971, pp. 166–173.

90. SHAW, A. C., "A Formal Picture Description Scheme as a Basis for Picture Processing Systems," *Information and Control*, 14 (Jan. 1969).

91. SHAW, A. C., "Parsing of Graph-Representable Pictures," *J. ACM*, 17 (June 1970).

92. PFALTZ, J. L. and A. ROSENFELD, "Web Grammars," *Proc. First International Joint Conference on Artificial Intelligence*, Washington, D.C, May 1969, pp. 609–619.

93. SHAW, A. C., "Picture Graphs, Grammars, and Parsing," in *Frontiers of Pattern Recognition*, ed. by S. Watanabe, Academic Press, Inc., New York, 1972.

94. ROSENFELD, A., "Picture Automata and Grammars: An Annotated Bibliography," *Proc. Symposium on Computer Image Processing and Recognition*, 2, Columbia, Mo., (Aug. 24–26, 1972).

95. PAVLIDIS, T., "Linear and Context-Free Graph Grammars," *J. ACM*, 19: 1 (1972), 11–22.

96. PAVLIDIS, T., "Graph Theoretic Analysis of Pictures," in *Graphic Languages*, ed. by F. Nake and A. Rosenfeld, North-Holland Publishing Co., Amsterdam, 1972.

97. BRAINERD, W. S., "Tree Generating Regular Systems," *Information and Control*, 14 (1969), 217–231.

98. DONAR, J. E., "Tree Acceptors and Some of Their Applications," *J. Computer and System Sciences*, 4: 5 (1970).

99. FU, K. S. and B. K. BHARGAVA, "Tree Systems for Syntactic Pattern Recognition," *IEEE Trans. on Computers*, C-22 (Dec. 1973).

100. GRENANDER, V., "Syntax-Controlled Probabilities," Tech. Dept., Division of Applied Math., Brown University, Providence, Rhode Island, 1967.

101. FU, K. S., "Syntactic Pattern Recognition and Stochastic Languages," in *Frontiers of Pattern Recognition*, ed. by S. Watanabe, Academic Press, Inc., New York, 1972.

102. FU, K. S., "Stochastic Languages for Picture Analysis," *U.S.–Japan Seminar on Picture and Scene Analysis*, Kyoto, Japan, July 23–27, 1973.

103. LEE, H. C. and K. S. FU, "A Stochastic Syntax Analysis Procedure and Its Application to Pattern Classification," *IEEE Trans. on Computers*, C-21 (1972).

104. HUANG, T. and K. S. FU, "Stochastic Syntactic Analysis for Programmed Grammars and Syntactic Pattern Recognition," *Computer Graphics and Image Processing*, 1 (Nov. 1972).

105. LEE, H. C. and K. S. FU, "A Syntactic Pattern Recognition System with Learning Capability," *Proc. COINS-72*, Dec. 1972.

106. NAKE, F. and A. ROSENFELD (eds.), *Graphic Languages*, North-Holland Publishing Co., Amsterdam, 1973.

107. KANEFF, S. (ed.), *Picture Language Machines*, Academic Press, Inc., New York, 1970.

108. ROSENFELD, A., "Isotonic Grammars, Parallel Grammars, and Picture Grammars," *Machine Intelligence VI*, Edinburgh University Press, Edinburgh, 1971.

109. PAVLIDIS, T., "Structural Pattern Recognition: Primitives and Juxtaposition Relations," *Frontiers of Pattern Recognition*, ed. by S. Watanabe, Academic Press, Inc., New York, 1972.

110. FU, K. S., *Syntactic Methods in Pattern Recognition*, Academic Press, Inc., New York, 1974.

111. AHO, A. V. and J. D. ULLMAN, *The Theory of Parsing, Translation, and Compiling, Vol. I: Parsing*, Prentice-Hall, Inc., Englewood Cliffs, N.J., 1972.

112. BANERJI, R. B., "A Language for Pattern Recognition," *Pattern Recognition*, 1 (1968), 63–74.

113. SHERMAN, R. and G. W. ERNST, "Learning Patterns in Terms or Other Patterns," *Pattern Recognition*, 1 (1969), 301–313.

114. MICHAELSKI, R. S., "Discovering Classification Rules Using Variable-Valued Logic System VL₁," *Proc. Third International Joint Conference on Artificial Intelligence* (1973), 162–172.

5 A FORMALIZATION AND ANALYSIS OF SIMPLE LIST STRUCTURES

R. K. Guha
Department of Computer Science
Southern Illinois University
Carbondale, Illinois

R. T. Yeh
Department of Computer Sciences
Software Engineering and Systems Laboratory and
Electronics Research Center
University of Texas at Austin
Austin, Texas

Editor's Note:

This chapter formalizes the semantics of simple list structures. Various data representations are analyzed based on this formalization. The chapter is written with the assumption that the reader is familiar with the notion of simple data structures. Therefore, although most of the definitions and results are illustrated with examples, the chapter proceeds reasonably fast.

Basic knowledge in combinatorics and the concepts of finite automata and context-free grammar is all that is needed in order to comprehend this chapter.

5.1. INTRODUCTION

In order for a computer to process information properly and efficiently, it is necessary to be able to represent and manipulate data representing information being processed within a computer. Therefore, we need to understand the structural relationships present within data and to acquire formal tools and techniques in describing these structures and how to handle them in a computer's memory. First of all, we need to come up with semantics to describe the structural relationship among data elements, and how data can be accessed, altered, created, and destroyed. With semantics of data structures defined, it is then possible to realize it in a particular machine, and evaluate the specific implementation with measurement under various constraints.

It is quite clear that the most important aspects of understanding data structures is how to define its semantics formally. The formalization of the semantics of data structure not only helps toward better understanding of the structures themselves, but may lead to systematic implementation and evaluation of data structures. As an example, it was shown by Fleck [4] that there is a correspondence between representations of list structures and context-free languages. Such a correspondence provides us more insights in the analysis and limitations of data representations.

In this chapter, semantics of simple list structures will be formalized. Based on the formalization, various data representations are analyzed, and a method of estimating storage requirement of a list environment using the concept of "operation automata" is also given.

5.2. CONCEPT OF A LIST

Formal definitions of data structure will be given in this section. To define data structure formally, one should consider the storage where the data elements are stored. The storage might be computer memory and/or external storage device such as disk, drum, or tape, etc. In any case, the amount of storage available is finite. The place where the data element is stored is usually identified by a unique address. At this point, the amount of storage space required for each data element (which is an important consideration in implementation) may be ignored and it can be assumed that each element needs only a unit of space identified by an address. Hence, a finite set of addresses (say A) is available for representing data structure. This finite set A will be called the address space. Any data element will use an element of A for its representation. A data element in a data structure is usually logically related to several data elements. These relations are either implicitly or explicitly represented with the data elements. When the data element along with the logical relations are represented in the element of the address space A, an order (explicit or implicit) is imposed among the logical relations. With these in mind, we now proceed to define a data structure formally as a list.

Definition 5.2.1

A *list* L over an address space A is a 7-tuple $L = (N, \Gamma, \Sigma, M, Z, \delta, E)$, where

1. $N \subseteq A$.
2. Γ is a finite set of *information items*.
3. $\Sigma \subseteq \Gamma$ is called the *alphabet set* or the set of *data information*.
4. M is a subset of the set of *nodes* $N \times (\Gamma \cup \{\wedge\})$ where $\wedge$ corresponds to null information, such that for any two nodes (n_1, a_1) and (n_2, a_2) in M, $n_1 = n_2$ implies $a_1 = a_2$, and for each $n \in N$, there exists a node (n, a) in M. In the event $M = \varnothing$, then L is called an *empty list*.
5. Z is a finite ordered set of *link labels*.
6. δ is a partial function, called the *link function*, mapping $M \times Z$ to N.
7. $E \subseteq N$ is a finite set of *entry addresses* (or entry points).

A node (n, a) is referred to as an *entry node* if n *is* an entry point. We will denote the set of all entry nodes of L by $\bar{E}$.

Example 5.2.1

$L = (N, \Gamma, \Sigma, M, Z, \delta, E)$ is a list where $N = \{1, 3, 5, 7, 9\}$; $\Gamma = \{a, b, c\}$; $\Sigma = \{a, b\}$; $M = \{(1, c), (3, a), (5, c), (7, b), (9, \wedge)\}$; $Z = \{\text{NXT1, NXT2, BACK}\}$; $E = \{1\}$; and δ is given as

$$\delta((1, c), \text{NXT1}) = 3, \qquad \delta((1, c), \text{NXT2}) = 9$$
$$\delta((3, a), \text{NXT1}) = 5$$
$$\delta((5, c), \text{NXT1}) = 7, \qquad \delta((5, c), \text{BACK}) = 1$$

A list may conveniently be represented by a diagram. For example, the diagrammatic representation of the list L in Example 5.2.1 is given in Fig. 5.2.1.

Definition 5.2.2

A *record r* of a list L is a set consisting of a node (n, a) followed by elements of the set $\{(z_i, n_j) \mid \delta((n, a), z_i) = n_j\}$.

For example, $r_1 = [(5, c); (\text{NXT1}, 7), (\text{BACK}, 1)]$ and $r_2 = [(7, b);]$ are two records of the list L in Example 5.2.1

Let $f = \{(n, (n, a)) \mid n \in N$ and $(n, a) \in M\}$ be a one-to-one correspondence between N and M. Let θ be a partial function mapping $\theta: M \times Z \to M$ such that $\theta((n_i, a_i), z_j) = (n_k, a_k)$ if and only if $\delta((n_i, a_i), z_j) = n_k$ and $(n_k, (n_k, a_k)) \in f$. In order to simplify the notations later on, for each $z \in Z$, we define a partial function $\theta_Z: M \to M$ such that

$$\theta_Z = \{((n_i, a_i), (n_k, a_k)) \mid \theta((n_i, a_i), z) = (n_k, a_k)\}$$

We can further extend the notation for each $\alpha \in Z^+$ such that if $\alpha = z_1 z_2 \cdots z_k$ then

$$\theta_\alpha = \theta_{z_1}\theta_{z_2} \cdots \theta_{z_k}$$

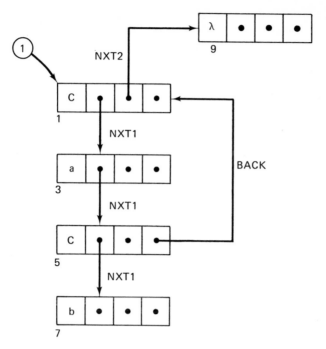

Fig. 5.2.1 Diagrammatic representation of the list L in Example 5.2.1.

We let $\theta_{\wedge}$ denote the *identity function*, and denote the set $\{\theta_z\}$ $z \in Z$ by $\bar{\theta}$.

Definition 5.2.3

A node m_j is said *directly accessible* from another node m_i in a list L if either $m_i = m_j$ or there exists a link label z such that $\theta_z(m_i) = m_j$. We say m_j is *accessible* from m_i if there exists a sequence $\alpha = z_1 z_2 \ldots z_n$ of link labels such that $\theta_\alpha(m_i) = m_j$. α is also referred to as a *path* from m_i to m_j.

Thus node $(7, b)$ is accessible from node $(3, a)$ in Example 5.2.1, whereas node $(9, \wedge)$ is not accessible from $(7, b)$.

Notation

Let L be a list. We will create a special node called the *empty node*, denoted by e, such that whenever $\theta_z(m)$ is not defined in L, we let $\theta_z(m) = e$. Therefore, θ_z is now a total function.

Definition 5.2.4

A list $L = (N, \Gamma, \Sigma, M, Z, \delta, E)$ is said to be *connected* if every nonentry node is accessible from some entry node.

The list given in Example 5.2.1 is clearly connected.

In the following we will assume that all lists are connected unless otherwise specified.

Definition 5.2.5

A finite set of lists over an address space A having the same set of information items Γ, the same alphabet set Σ, and the same set of link labels Z is called a *list set* and is denoted by the symbols $L(\Gamma, \Sigma, Z)$.

We assume here that only one list will be in address space A at any one time. If a list L_i is initially in the address space, a different list L_j is obtained whenever L_i is altered.

Definition 5.2.6

Let m_i and m_j be two nodes in a list L such that $m_j = \theta_z(m_i)$. We say $m_j(m_i)$ is a *successor* (*predecessor*) of $m_i(m_j)$ via z. We refer to θ_z and θ_z^{-1} a *successor function* and *predecessor function*, respectively. A node m is called a *terminal node with respect to z* if $\theta_z(m) = e$. it is called a *terminal node* if it is a terminal node with respect to z for all z.

EXERCISES 5.2

1. (a) Give an example of a list which is not connected.
   (b) Draw the diagrammatic representation of the list in (a).

2. $L = (N, \Gamma, \Sigma, M, Z = \{z_1, z_2\}, \delta, E)$ is a list which need not be connected.
   (a) If $M = \{m_1, m_2, m_3\}$, $\bar{E} = \{m_1, m_3\}$, $\theta_{z_1} = \{(m_1, m_1), (m_1, m_2)\}$ and $\theta_{z_2} = \{(m_3, m_1)\}$, can L be considered to be a list? Justify your answer.

3. Let $L_1 = (N_1, \Gamma_1, \Sigma_1, M_1, Z_1, \delta_1, E_1)$ and $L_2 = (N_2, \Gamma_2, \Sigma_2, M_2, Z_2, \delta_2, E_2)$ are two lists over the address space A. Assume $L = L_1 \cup L_2 = (N_1 \cup N_2, \Gamma_1 \cup \Gamma_2, \Sigma_1 \cup \Sigma_2, M_1 \cup M_2, Z_1 \cup Z_2, \delta_1 \cup \delta_2, E_1 \cup E_2)$ and $N_1 \cap N_2 = \phi$.
   (a) Is L a list? A connected list?
   (b) If $N_1 \cap N_2 \neq \phi$, is L always a list?

4. $L(\Gamma, \Sigma, Z)$ is a list set over A where $A = \{1, 3\}$, $\Gamma = \Sigma = \{a, b\}$ and $Z = \{z_1, z_2\}$. How many different connected lists can there be in $L(\Gamma, \Sigma, Z)$?

5. Let $z_1 = NXT1$, $z_2 = NXT2$, $z_3 = BACK$. Define θz_1, θz_2 and θz_3 for the list L in Example 5.2.1. For this list L, find the languages
   $L_1 = \{\alpha \,|\, \alpha \in \{z_1, z_2, z_3\}^*$ and each $m \in M, \theta_\alpha(m) \in M\}$ and
   $L_2 = \{\beta \,|\, \beta \in \{z_1, z_2, z_3,\}^*$ and there exist $m \in M; \theta_\beta(m) = e\}$.

5.3. GRAPH REPRESENTATION OF LISTS

In this section, we will introduce the concept of a labelled, directed graph and use it to represent the structure of a list.

Definition 5.3.1

A *labelled, directed graph* (LDG) is a 4-tuple $G = (V, R, Y, \Phi)$ where V, R, and Y are finite sets of *vertices*, *arcs*, and ordered *arc labels*, respectively, and Φ is a partial function mapping $V \times V$ to $R \times Y$.

Example 5.3.1

Let $G = (V, R, Y, \Phi)$ be an LDG which is drawn in Fig. 5.3.1.

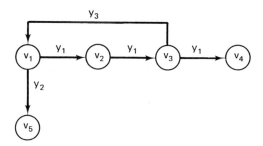

Fig. 5.3.1　An example of LDG.

It is easily seen from the previous example that a path in an LDG can also be represented by the sequence of arc labels of the arcs in the path. For example, the path $(V_1, V_2) (V_2, V_3) (V_3, V_4)$ may be represented by $y_1 y_1 y_1$. Indeed, for notational convenience, for each $y \in Y$, we denote by $\Phi_y : V \longrightarrow V$ such that $\Phi_y = \{(V_i, V_j) \mid \Phi(V_i, V_j) = (\alpha, y)$, for some $\alpha \in R\}$. For $\beta = y_1 y_2 \ldots y_n \in Y^*$, let $\Phi_\beta = \Phi_{y_1} \Phi_{y_2} \ldots \Phi_{y_n}$, and let Φ_λ be the identity function.

Definition 5.3.2

Let U be a subset of the vertex set V of an LDG $G = (V, R, Y, \Phi)$. G is said to be *initially connected* (ICLDG) by U if each vertex of V is reachable by a path from some vertex in U.

For example, the LDG in Example 5.3.1 is an ICLDG by $\{v_1\}$, since every vertex is reachable by v_1. We will usually denote an ICLDG by U as $G = (V, Y, \Phi, U)$.

Definition 5.3.3

A function g mapping an ordered set $(X, \le)$ to an ordered set $(Y, \le)$ is said to be *order preserving* if $x_1 \le x_2$ implies $g(x_1) \le g(x_2)$.

Definition 5.3.4

Two ICLDG $G_1 = (V_1, Y_1, \Phi, U_1)$ and $G_2 = (V_2, Y_2, \psi, U_2)$ are said to be *isomorphic* if and only if

1. There exists a one-to-one correspondence h between V_1 and V_2 and between U_1 and U_2;

2. There exists an order preserving one-to-one correspondence $g: Y_1 \to Y_2$; such that $(\forall y \in Y_1) [\Phi_y h = h\psi_{g(y)}]$.

Example 5.3.2

The ICLDG's given in Figs. 5.3.2(a) and 5.3.2(b) are isomorphic.

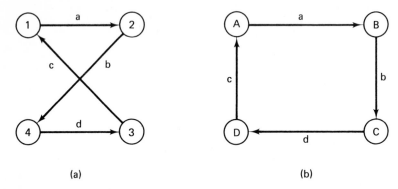

(a)   (b)

Fig. 5.3.2   Two isomorphic ICLDG's.

Definition 5.3.5

An ICLDG $G = (V, Y, \Phi, U)$ is said to be a *structural representation* of a list $L = (N, \Gamma, \Sigma, M, Z, \delta, E)$ if and only if

1. There exists a one-to-one correspondence η between M and V and between E and U;.
2. There exists an order preserving one-to-one correspondence $\mu: Z \to Y$ such that $(\forall z \in Z) [\theta_z \eta = \eta \Phi_{\mu(z)}]$.

The following results are quite straightforward and, hence, will be stated without proofs.

Theorem 5.3.1

Corresponding to each list L, an ICLDG G can be constructed such that G is a structural representation of L.

Theorem 5.3.2

If G_1 and G_2 are two structural representations of a list L, then G_1 and G_2 are isomorphic.

Definition 5.3.6

Two lists L_1 and L_2 are said to be *structurally equivalent* if and only if their corresponding structural representations G_1 and G_2 are isomorphic.

Theorem 5.3.3

Two lists $L_1 = (N_1, \Gamma_1, \Sigma_1, M_1, Z_1, \delta_1, E_1)$ and $L_2 = (N_2, \Gamma_2, \Sigma_2, M_2, Z_2, \delta_2, E_2)$ are structurally equivalent if and only if

1. There exists a one-to-one correspondence ξ between M_1 and M_2 and between $\bar{E}_1$ and $\bar{E}_2$.

2. There exists an order preserving one-to-one correspondence ζ between Z_1 and Z_2 such that

$$(\forall z \in Z_1) \, [\theta_z^1 \, \xi = \xi \, \theta_{\zeta(z)}^2] \tag{5.2.1}$$

Proof: Assume that L_1 and L_2 are structurally equivalent. This means that their corresponding structural representations $G_1 = (V_1, Y_1, \Phi_1, U_1)$ and $G_2 = (V_2, Y_2, \Phi_2, U_2)$ are isomorphic. By Theorems 5.3.1 and 5.3.2, there exist one-to-one and onto functions $\mu_1 : Z_1 \to Y_1$, $\eta_1 : M_1 \to V_1$, $g : Y_1 = Y_2$, $h : V_1 \to V_2$, and $\mu_2 : Z_2 \to Y_2$, $\eta_2 : M_2 \to V_2$. Clearly, $\eta_1 h \eta_2^{-1}$ and $\mu_1 g \mu_2^{-1}$ are one-to-one and onto functions satisfying conditions (1) and (2) in the statement of the theorem.

Conversely, assuming conditions (1) and (2) are satisfied, then, with the aid of Theorem 5.3.1, ξ and ζ induces two one-to-one and onto functions $h : V_1 \to V_2$ and $g : Y_1 \to Y_2$ satisfying conditions listed in Definition 5.3.4. ∎

EXERCISES 5.3

1. Prove Theorem 5.3.1.

2. Prove Theorem 5.3.2.

3. Is ICLDG $G = (V, Y, \Phi, \{v_i\})$ in Example 5.3.1 a structural representation of L in Example 5.2.1? Prove your answer.

4. (a) How many ICLDG's can there be if $\# \, V = 2$ and $\# \, Y = 2$? Enumerate them.

   (b) How many nonisomorphic ICLDG can there be if $\# \, V = 2$ and $\# \, Y = 2$? Enumerate them.

5. Prove Theorem 5.3.3 in detail.

5.4. LINEAR LISTS

Formal definitions of various classes of linear lists will be discussed.

Definition 5.4.1

A *linear list* (or L-list for short) is a nonempty list $L = (N, \Gamma, \Sigma, M, Z, \delta, E)$ such that

1. $1 \leq \# E \leq 2$ and $1 \leq \# \bar{Z} \leq 2$.

2. There exists a linear order $m_1, m_2, \ldots, m_k$ on nodes of M such that
   (a) m_1 is an entry node and is called the *front* node.
   (b) m_k is called the *rear* node, and is also an entry node if $\# \bar{E} = 2$.

3. If $Z = \{z_1\}$, then $\theta_{z_1}(m_i) = m_{i+1}$, for $1 \leq i \leq k$, and the value of $\theta_{z_i}(m_k)$ is either e or m_1.

4. If $Z = \{z_1, z_2\}$, then $\theta_{z_2} = \theta_{z_1}^{-1}$.

5. For $1 < i \leq k, m_i \in N \times \Sigma$.

If $m_1 \in N \times (\Gamma - \Sigma)$, then it is called a *list head*. In this case, L is referred to as an L-*list with list head* (or L-list with LH for short).

Different types of L-lists will be defined in the following.

Definition 5.4.2

Let $L = (N, \Gamma, \Sigma, M, Z, \delta, E)$ be a nonempty L-list (with LH) such that $m_1, m_2, \ldots, m_k$ is a linear order of its nodes. L is a

1. *1-way 1-entry L-list* (with LH) if and only if $Z = \{z_1\}, \bar{E} = \{m_1\}$ and $\theta_{z_1}^{-1}(m_1) = e$.

2. *1-way circular L-list* (with LH) if and only if $Z = \{z_1\}, \bar{E} = \{m_1\}$ and $\theta_{z_1}(m_k) = m_1$.

3. *2-way 1-entry L-list* (with LH) if and only if $Z = \{z_1, z_2\}, \bar{E} = \{m_1\}$, $\theta_{z_1}^{-1}(m_1) = e$ and $\theta_{z_2} = \theta_{z_1}^{-1}$.

4. *1-way 2-entry L-list with end-pointer* (with LH and end-pointer) if and only if $Z = \{z_1\}, \bar{E} = \{m_1, m_k\}$ and $\theta_{z_1}^{-1}(m_1) = e$.

5. *2-way 2-entry L-list* (with LH) if and only if $z = \{z_1, z_2\}, \bar{E} = \{m_1, m_k\}, \theta_{z_1}^{-1}(m_1) = e$ and $\theta_{z_2} = \theta_{z_1}^{-1}$.

6. *2-way circular L-list* (with LH) if and only if $z = \{z_1, z_2\}, \bar{E} = \{m_1\}$, $\theta_{z_1}(m_k) = m_1$ and $\theta_{z_2} = \theta_{z_1}^{-1}$.

It should be noted here that if $m_1, m_2, \ldots, m_k$ is the linear order of nodes of an L-list with LH, then m_1 is the list head. Thus, an L-list with LH cannot be an empty list. Since, in implementation, only entry nodes are available at all times, a 2-entry L-list provides access immediately to both ends of the list; whereas, a 1-entry L-list has access to only one end. All types of L-lists are illustrated in Fig. 5.4.1. If $(2, a)$ is the list head, then it illustrates all types of L-lists with LH.

We shall discuss several representations of L-lists in the rest of this section.

Definition 5.4.3

Let L be an L-list with $m_1 = (n_1, a_1), m_2 = (n_2, a_2), \ldots, m_k = (n_k, a_k)$ a linear ordering of its nodes. Sequences $n_1 n_2 \ldots n_k$, and $m_1 m_2 \ldots m_k$, are called the *address representation*, and *node representation*, respectively, of

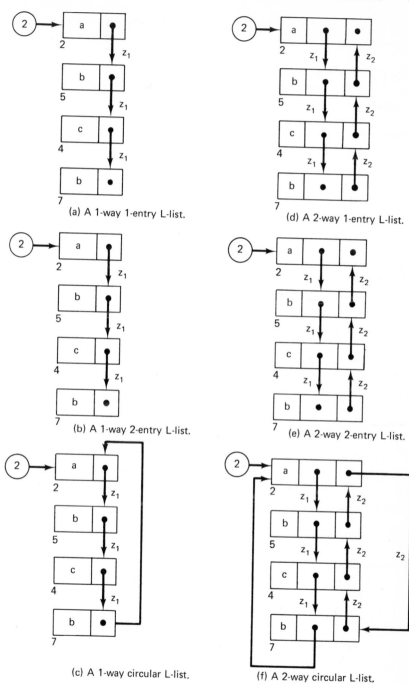

(a) A 1-way 1-entry L-list.

(d) A 2-way 1-entry L-list.

(b) A 1-way 2-entry L-list.

(e) A 2-way 2-entry L-list.

(c) A 1-way circular L-list.

(f) A 2-way circular L-list.

Fig. 5.4.1 Diagrammatic representation of different types of L-lists.

L. The sequence $a_1 a_2 . . . a_k$ ($a_2 . . . a_k$) is the *data representation* of L if L is an L-list (L-list with LH).

We will use the notations $AR(L)$, $DR(L)$, and $NR(L)$, to denote, respectively, the *address representation*, *data representation*, and *node representation* of L. Clearly, if L is empty, then $AR(L) = DR(L) = NR(L) = \wedge$.

Example 5.4.1

Let L be an L-list given in Fig. 5.4.1(a). Then

$$AR(L) = 2547$$
$$DR(L) = abcb$$
$$NR(L) = (2, a)\ (5, b)\ (4, c)\ (7, b)$$

If L is an L-list with LH, then $DR(L) = bcb$.

Definition 5.4.4

Two L-lists L_1 and L_2 of the same type are

1. *identical* if and only if $NR(L_1) = NR(L_2)$;
2. *data equivalent* if and only if $DR(L_1) = DR(L_2)$;
3. *address equivalent* if and only if $AR(L_1) = AR(L_2)$;
4. *structurally equivalent* if and only if their respective structural representations are isomorphic.

Example 5.4.2

Four 1-way L-lists L_1, L_2, L_3 and L_4 are given in Fig. 5.4.2. Then L_1 and L_2 are identical, L_1 and L_3 are address and structurally equivalent but not identical or data equivalent. L_3 and L_4 are data and structurally equivalent but not address equivalent or identical, and L_1 and L_4 are structurally equivalent but not data, address equivalent or identical.

The following theorems, being simple, are stated without proof.

Theorem 5.4.1

Let L_1 and L_2 be two L-lists (with the same list head) in a list set. Then

1. L_1 and L_2 are identical if and only if L_1 and L_2 are data and address equivalent.
2. L_1 and L_2 are data or address equivalent implies that L_1 and L_2 are structurally equivalent.

Theorem 5.4.2

It is decidable whether two L lists L_1 and L_2 in a list set are structurally, data, address equivalent or identical.

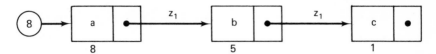

(a) 1-way 1-entry L-list L_1.

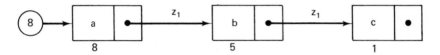

(b) 1-way 1-entry L-list L_2.

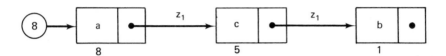

(c) 1-way 1-entry L-list L_3.

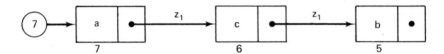

(d) 1-way 1-entry L-list L_4.

Fig. 5.4.2 Diagrammatic representation of lists given in Example 5.4.2.

Definition 5.4.5

A *list set* $L(\Gamma, \Sigma, Z)$ over an address space A is called an *L-list set* if all of its elements are L-lists.

Definition 5.4.6

The node, address, data, and structural representations of an L-list set $L(\Gamma, \Sigma, Z) = \{L_i\}$ $i \in I$ are the sets of the node, address, data, and structural representations of each L-list in $L(\Gamma, \Sigma, Z)$ and will be denoted respectively by $NR[L(\Gamma, \Sigma, Z)]$, $AR[L(\Gamma, \Sigma, Z)]$, $DR[L(\Gamma, \Sigma, Z)]$, and $SR[L(\Gamma, \Sigma, Z)]$.

The following three results which provide bounds on the number of nonequivalent L-lists in a list set are quite simple and hence their proofs are left as exercises.

Theorem 5.4.3

Let A be an address space with k elements. The number of nonstructurally equivalent 1-way L-lists is bounded by $(k + 1)$.

Theorem 5.4.4

Let A be an address space with k elements. The number of nondata equivalent 1-way L-lists is bounded by

$$\sum_{j=0}^{k} l^j = \frac{l^{k+1} - 1}{l - 1} \qquad \text{where } l = \# \, \Sigma$$

Theorem 5.4.5

Let A be address space with k elements. The number of nondata equivalent 1-way L-lists with LH is bounded by

$$\sum_{j=0}^{k-1} l^j = \frac{l^k - 1}{l - 1} \qquad \text{where } l = \# \, \Sigma$$

Theorem 5.4.6

Let A be an address space with k elements. The number of nonaddress equivalent 1-way L-lists is $\sum_{j=0}^{k} k^p j$ where $k^p j$ $(1 \leq j \leq k)$ is the number of permutations of k elements taken j at a time.

Proof: Let $L_i = (N_i, \Gamma, \Sigma, M_i, Z, \delta_i, E_i)$ be a 1-way L-list. Since there are k elements in A, there are

$$\binom{k}{j} = \frac{k^p j}{j!}$$

subsets of A such that the cardinality of each subset is j. For each such subset N_i of A, there are $j!$ distinct linear order of N_i. Hence the number of nonaddress equivalent lists L_i, such that $|\mathrm{AR}(L_i)| = j$, is

$$\binom{k}{j} \times j! = \frac{k^p j}{j!} \times j! = k^p j$$

Since $\# \, A = k$, the number of nonaddress equivalent 1-way L-lists is bounded by $\sum_{j=0}^{k} k^p j$. ∎

The following results are immediate consequences of Theorems 5.4.4 and 5.4.6.

Theorem 5.4.7

Let A be an address space with k elements. The number of nonidentical 1-way L-lists is bounded by $\sum_{j=0}^{k} (k^p j \times l^j)$ where $\# \, \Sigma = l$.

Theorem 5.4.8

Let A be an address space with k elements. Then the number of nonidentical 1-way L-lists with LH in the 1-way L-list with LH set $L(\Gamma, \Sigma, Z)$ is bounded by $\sum_{j=1}^{k} (k^p j \times l_1^{j-1} \times l_2)$ where $\# \Sigma = l_1$, $\#(\Gamma - \Sigma) = l_2$.

EXERCISES 5.4

1. (a) Enumerate all nonstructurally equivalent 1-way L-lists where $\# A = 3$.
   (b) Enumerate all nonaddress equivalent 1-way L-lists where $\# A = 3$.
   (c) Enumerate all nondata equivalent 1-way L-lists where $\# A = 3$ and $\# \Sigma = 2$.

2. (a) Prove Theorems 5.4.3, 5.4.4, 5.4.5, 5.4.7, and 5.4.8.

5.5. OPERATIONS ON L-LIST SET

Operations performed on lists can generally be classified into two categories according to whether an operation changes or does not change a given list. For example, operations such as those which gain access to a node, count the number of nodes in a list, etc., do not change the list being operated on. In this section, we will be concerned with the formalization of two operations which change the list being operated on, namely, insertion and deletion of nodes on L-lists.

Definition 5.5.1

A *configuration* of a list $L = (N, \Gamma, \Sigma, M, Z, \delta, E)$ is a triple $c = [M, \bar{\theta}, \bar{E}]$. If L is empty, then its configuration is called the *empty configuration* and is denoted by $c = [\varnothing, \varnothing, \varnothing]$. The *configuration set* of a list set $L(\Gamma, \Sigma, Z)$ is the set of all configurations of elements in $L(\Gamma, \Sigma, Z)$.

Definition 5.5.2

Let $L(\Gamma, \Sigma, Z)$ be an L-list set containing all L-lists of the same type, and C the configuration set of $L(\Gamma, \Sigma, Z)$. For each L-list $L_i = (N_i, \Gamma, \Sigma, M_i, Z, \delta_i, E_i)$ in the L-list set, let c_i denote its configuration. The *insertion function* I on $L(\Gamma, \Sigma, Z)$ is a partial function

$$I: \quad C \times \{A \times \Sigma\} \times \{A \times \Sigma \cup \{e\}\} \times \{A \times \Sigma \cup \{e\}\} \rightarrow C$$

such that if $I(c_i, m, m_1, m_2) = c_j$, then $f^{-1}(m) \notin N_i$, and $(m_1, m_2) \in \theta_z$ for some z in Z if $m_1 \neq e$ and $m_2 \neq e$.

It follows from the-definition that $I(c_i, m, m_1, m_2) = c_j$ means that the node m is inserted into the list L_i between nodes m_1 and m_2 and the configuration changes from c_i to c_j. Insertion function may be formalized for different types of L-list sets in a straightforward fashion. For example, consider a 1-way 1-entry L-list Li with $C_i = [M_i, \bar{\theta}^{(i)}, \bar{E}_i]$. In this case

$$\bar{\theta}^{(i)} = \{\theta_{z_1}^{(i)}\} \qquad \text{since} \qquad Z = \{z_1\}, \# E_i = 1$$

1. $m_1 = e, m_2 = e \Rightarrow \theta_{z_1}^{(j)} = \theta_{z_1}^{(i)} ; \bar{E}_j = \{m\}$
2. $m_1 = e, m_2 \neq e \Rightarrow \theta_{z_1}^{(j)} = \theta_{z_1}^{(i)} \cup \{(m, m_2)\} ; \bar{E}_j = \{m\}$
3. $m_1 \neq e, m_2 = e \Rightarrow \theta_{z_1}^{(j)} = \theta_{z_1}^{(i)} \cup \{(m_1, m)\} ; \bar{E}_j = \bar{E}_i$
4. $m_1 \neq e, m_2 \neq e \Rightarrow \theta_{z_1}^{(j)} = \theta_{z_1}^{(i)} \cup \{(m_1, m), (m, m_2)\}$
   $- \{(m_1, m_2)\} ; \bar{E}_j = \bar{E}_i$

Definition 5.5.3

The *deletion function* D on $L(\Gamma, \Sigma, Z)$ defined in Definition 5.5.2 is a partial function

$$D: C \times \{A \times \Sigma \cup \{e\}\} \times \{A \times \Sigma \cup \{e\}\} \times \{A \times \Sigma \cup \{e\}\} \to C$$

such that if $D(c_i, m, m_1, m_2) = c_j$ is defined, then

1. $m = e$ $\Rightarrow c_i = [\Phi, \varnothing, \Phi]$ and $m_1 = e, \quad m_2 = e$ for any L-list.

   $m = e$ $\Rightarrow c_i = [\{m_1\}, \bar{\theta}^{(i)}, \bar{E}_i]$ and $m_2 = e$ for any L-list with LH.
2. $m_1 = e, m_2 = e$ and $m \neq e \Rightarrow M = \{m\}$.
3. $m_1 = e, m_2 \neq e \Rightarrow (m, m_2) \in \theta_z^{(i)}$ for some $z \in Z$ and m is the front node.
4. $m_1 \neq e, m_2 = e \Rightarrow (m_1, m) \in \theta_z^{(i)}$ for some $z \in Z$ and m is the rear node.
5. $m_1 \neq e, m_2 \neq e \Rightarrow (m_1, m), (m, m_2) \in \theta_z^{(i)}$ for some $z \in Z$.

It will be assumed that if $c_i = [\varnothing, \varnothing, \varnothing]$, then $c_j = [\varnothing, \varnothing, \varnothing]$. Furthermore, if $c_i = [\{m_1\}, \bar{\theta}^{(i)} \bar{E}_i]$ for an L-list with LH, then $c_j = c_i$. Formalizations of the deletion function for L-list sets of different types is straightforward and will be left as exercises.

Definition 5.5.4

A *1-way L-list system* $\mathscr{L}$ over an address space A is a triple $\mathscr{L} = \langle L(\Gamma, \Sigma, Z), I, D \rangle$, where $L(\Gamma, \Sigma, Z)$ is a 1-way L-list set, I and D are insertion and deletion functions as defined before.

An L-list system can be considered as a formalization of some practical system with dynamic behavior. To cite an example, one might think of an L-list system as a formalization of the behavior of a program in a paging environment with dynamic storage allocation where each node is considered as a page with information (part of data or program). Thus, insertion implies assigning a new page to the program; whereas, deletion implies removing a page from the program which is not needed anymore.

We now define three important special types of L-list systems where the insertion and deletion operations are restricted only to front and rear nodes of the L-list.

Definition 5.5.5

A *1-way stack list system* is a 1-way L-list system $\mathscr{L} = \langle L(\Gamma, \Sigma, Z),$ $I, D \rangle$ such that whenever $I(C_i, m, m_1, m_2)$ or $D(C_i, m, m_1, m_2)$ are defined, then $m_1 = e$ (or $m_2 = e$).

Thus, in a 1-way stack list system, the insertion and deletion operations are restricted either to the front nodes or to the rear node but both ends of the 1-way L-lists.

Definition 5.5.6

A *1-way queue list system* is a 1-way L-list system $\mathscr{L} = \langle L(\Gamma, \Sigma, Z),$ $I, D \rangle$ such that whenever $I(c_i, m, m_1, m_2)$ is defined, then $m_2 = e$ ($m_1 = e$), and whenever $D(c_i, m, m_1, m_2)$ is defined, then $m_1 = e$ ($m_2 = e$).

Hence, in a 1-way queue list system, when the insertion operation is restricted to rear node (front node) only, the deletion operation is restricted to front node (rear node) only.

Definition 5.5.7

A *1-way deque list system* is a 1-way L-list system $\mathscr{L} = \langle L(\Gamma, \Sigma, Z),$ $I, D \rangle$ such that the insertion and deletion operations can be in both the front and rear nodes.

We have defined different types of L-list systems only for 1-way L-list set. One can similarly define systems for different types of L-list sets. It should be pointed out here that if there is only one entry node in a 1-way L-list, the entry node is the front node, whereas, the rear node is not an entry node and so is not immediately accessible. Since in a 1-way 1-entry stack list system, the insertion and deletion are done only at the front node, the implementation of 1-way 1-entry stack list system poses no problem. In a 1-way 1-entry queue or deque list system, the rear node is used, the implementation of such a system is usually difficult whereas it may be easier to implement 1-way 2-entry queue (deque) list system since the rear node is immediately available.

EXERCISES 5.5

1. Formally define the insertion and deletion functions for L-list sets of different types.

2. Express Definition 5.5.7 formally.

3. Let $\mathscr{L}_i = \langle L_i(\Gamma, \Sigma, Z), I_i, D_i \rangle, i = 1, 2, 3$ where $Z = \{z_1\}$ be a three stack list system over address space A. Initially, the lists of the list sets $L_1(\Gamma, \Sigma, Z)$ and $L_2(\Gamma, \Sigma, Z)$ in address space A are empty. Furthermore, the $\theta_{z_1}^3$ of the list with entry node m_1, of $L_3(\Gamma, \Sigma, Z)$ initially is given by

$$\theta_{z_1}^3 = \{(m_1, m_2), (m_2, m_3), (m_3, m_4), (m_4, m_5), (m_5, m_6)$$

When an element is deleted from the list of $\mathscr{L}_3$, the deleted element is finally inserted in the list of $\mathscr{L}_1$. No element can be deleted from the list of $\mathscr{L}_1$ and no element can be inserted in the list of $\mathscr{L}_3$.

(a) Is it possible to have the list with $\theta_{z_1}^1$ and entry node m_3 (in the address space A) in $\mathscr{L}_1$ where

$$\theta_{z_1}^1 = \{(m_3, m_2), (m_2, m_5), (m_5, m_6), (m_6, m_4), (m_4, m_1)\}$$

by the restricted operations mentioned above?

(b) It is possible to have the list with $\theta_{z_1}^1$ and entry node m_1 (in the address space A) in $\mathscr{L}_1$ where

$$\theta_{z_1}^1 = \{(m_1, m_5), (m_5, m_4), (m_4, m_6), (m_6, m_2), (m_2, m_3)\}$$

(c) In case it is possible, give the sequence of operations done in $\mathscr{L}_1$, $\mathscr{L}_2$, and $\mathscr{L}_3$.

5.6. TREE LISTS

In this section, we will define and analyze several representations of tree lists. We will also show that every forest list is weakly node equivalent to a binary tree list.

Definition 5.6.1

A *tree list* (or T-list for short) is a nonempty list $L = (N, \Gamma, \Sigma, M, Z, \delta, E)$ such that $\bar{E} = \{m\}$ and every node is accessible from m by a unique path. Furthermore, m is not accessible from any node in $M - \{m\}$.

The node m is referred to as the *root* of the tree list.

A *binary tree list* (or B-list for short) is either empty or a nonempty tree list L such that $\#Z = 2$.

Example 5.6.1

Diagrammatic representation of a B-list is given in Fig. 5.6.1.

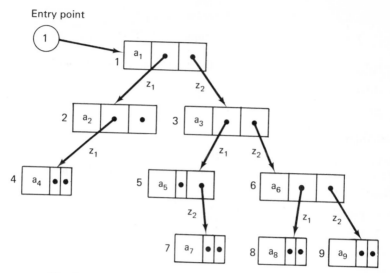

Fig. 5.6.1   Diagrammatic representation of a binary tree list.

Definition 5.6.2

Let $L = (N, \Gamma, \Sigma, M, Z, \delta, E)$ be a tree list with root m. If $m_i = \theta_\alpha(m)$, then the *level* of the node m_i is $|\alpha| + 1$. Thus, the root m has level 1. The tree list is said to have level r if there exists at least one node with level r and no node with level greater than r. The *degree* of the node m_i is $\#Z_1$ where $Z_1 \subseteq Z$ such that $\theta_z(m_i) \neq e$ for $z \in Z_1$.

It follows from the definition that a node is a terminal node if and only if it has degree 0.

The level and degree of $(7, a_7)$ in the B-list in Example 5.6.1 are 4 and 0, respectively.

Definition 5.6.3

Let L be a binary tree list. The *preorder representation* of a node m denoted by $\mathrm{PR}(m)$ is a sequence of nodes $m_1 m_2 \ldots m_k = (n_1, a_1)(n_2, a_2) \ldots (n_k, a_k)$ defined as follows:

1. $\mathrm{PR}(e) = \wedge$
2. $\mathrm{PR}(m) = m \, \mathrm{PR}\theta_{z_1}(m) \, \mathrm{PR}\theta_{z_2}(m)$, if m is not a terminal node.

If m is the root of L, then we say $\mathrm{PR}(m)$ is a *preorder node representation* of L, denoted by $\mathrm{NP}(L)$. The sequence $a_1 a_2 \ldots a_k$ is called the *preorder data representation* of L, denoted by $\mathrm{DP}(L)$, and the sequence $n_1 n_2 \ldots n_k$ is called the *preorder address representation* of L, denoted by $\mathrm{AP}(L)$.

Example 5.6.2

Let L be the B-list given in Example 5.6.1. Then

$\text{NP}(L) = (1, a_1) (2, a_2) (4, a_4) (3, a_3), (5, a_5) (7, a_7) (6, a_6) (8, a_8) (9, a_9)$

$\text{DP}(L) = a_1 a_2 a_4 a_3 a_5 a_7 a_6 a_8 a_9$

$\text{AP}(L) = 124357689$

Definition 5.6.4

Let L be a B-list. The *endorder representation* of a node m, denoted by $\text{EN}(m)$, is a sequence of nodes $m_1 m_2 \ldots m_k = (n_1, a_1) (n_2, a_2) \ldots (n_k, a_k)$ defined as follows:

1. $\text{EN}(e) = \wedge$
2. $\text{EN}(m) = \text{EN}(\theta_{z_1}(m)) \, \text{EN}(\theta_{z_2}(m)) \, m$.

If m is the root of L, then we say $\text{EN}(m)$ is the *endorder node representation* of L, denoted by $\text{NE}(L)$. The sequence $a_1 a_2 \ldots a_k$ is called the *endorder data representation* of L, denoted by $\text{DE}(L)$, and the sequence $n_1 n_2 \ldots n_k$ is called the *endorder address representation* of L, denoted by $\text{AE}(L)$.

Example 5.6.3

Let L be the B-list given in Example 5.6.1. Then

$\text{NE}(L) = (4, a_4) (2, a_2) (7, a_7) (5, a_5) (8, a_8) (9, a_9) (6, a_6) (3, a_3) (1, a_1)$.

$\text{DE}(L) = a_4 a_2 a_7 a_5 a_8 a_9 a_6 a_3 a_1$

$\text{AE}(L) = 427589631$

Definition 5.6.5

Let L be a B-list. The *postorder representation* of a node m, denoted by $\text{PS}(m)$, is a sequence of nodes $m_1 m_2 \ldots m_k = (n_1, a_1) (n_2, a_2) \ldots (n_k, a_k)$ defined as follows:

1. $\text{PS}(e) = \wedge$
2. $\text{PS}(m) = \text{PS}(\theta_{z_1}(m)) \, m \, \text{PS}(\theta_{z_2}(m))$.

If m is the root of L, then we say $\text{PS}(m)$ is the *postorder node representation* of L, denoted by $\text{NS}(L)$. The sequence $a_1 a_2 \ldots a_k$ is called the *postorder data representation* of L, denoted by $\text{DS}(L)$, and the sequence $n_1 n_2 \ldots n_k$ is called the *postorder address representation* of L, denoted by $\text{AS}(L)$.

Example 5.6.4

Let L be the B-list given in Example 5.6.1. Then

$NS(L) = (4, a_4) (2, a_2) (1, a_1) (5, a_5) (7, a_7) (3, a_3) (8, a_8) (6, a_6) (9, a_9)$

$DS(L) = a_4a_2a_1a_5a_7a_3a_8a_6a_9$

$AS(L) = 421573869$

Let

$$b_i = \frac{1}{i + 1}\binom{2i}{i} \quad \text{for } i > 0 \text{ and } b_o = 1.$$

The following result is due to Knuth [7].

Theorem 5.6.1

Let A be an address space with k elements. The number of nonstructurally equivalent B-lists in A is bounded by $\sum_{i=0}^{k} b_i$.

Definition 5.6.6

Two nonempty B-lists L_1 and L_2 are said to be *data equivalent* if and only if L_1 and L_2 are structurally equivalent and $DP(L_1) = DP(L_2)$, $DS(L_1) = DS(L_2)$, and $DE(L_1) = DE(L_2)$.

Examples 5.6.5

Consider the B-lists L_1 and L_2 given in Fig. 5.6.2. The B-lists L_1 and L_2 are data equivalent.

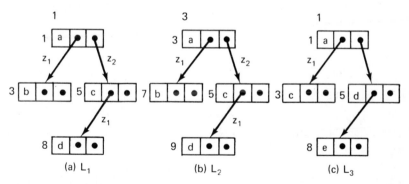

Fig. 5.6.2 Diagrammatic representation of B-lists L_1, L_2, L_3.

Theorem 5.6.2

Let A be an address space with k elements. The number of nondata equivalent B-lists in A is bounded by $\sum_{i=0}^{k} b_i \times l^i$, where $l = \#\Sigma$.

Proof: Let L_j be any B-list such that $|DP(L_j)| = i$. Since $\#\Sigma = l$, there are l^i distinct sequences over Σ of length i. Hence there are at most $b_i \times l^i$ nondata equivalent tree lists with i nodes by Theorem 5.6.1. $\blacksquare$

Definition 5.6.7

Two nonempty B-lists L_1 and L_2 are *address equivalent* if and only if L_1 and L_2 are structurally equivalent and $AP(L_1) = AP(L_2)$, $AS(L_1) = AS(L_2)$, and $AE(L_1) = AE(L_2)$.

For example, the B-lists L_1 and L_3 in Fig. 5.6.2 are address equivalent.

Theorem 5.6.3

Let A be an address space with k elements. The number of nonaddress equivalent B-lists in A is bounded by

$$\sum_{i=0}^{k} b_i \times k^p i$$

Proof: Let L_j be any B-list such that $|NP(L_j)| = i$. Since $\#A = k$, there are $\binom{k}{i}$ subsets of A such that each subset contains i elements. For each subset with i elements, there are $i!$ distinct sequences of length i such that each element appears only once in a particular sequence. Thus there are at most $\binom{k}{i} \times i! = k^p i$ nonaddress equivalent B-lists such that $|NP(L_j)| = i$ and structurally equivalent to L_j. Hence, by Theorem 5.6.1, the number of nonaddress equivalent B-lists in A is bounded by

$$\sum_{i=0}^{k} b_i \times k^p i$$

Definition 5.6.8

Two nonempty binary tree lists L_1 and L_2 are *identical* if and only if L_1 and L_2 are structurally equivalent and $NP(L_1) = NP(L_2)$, $NS(L_1) = NS(L_2)$, and $NE(L_1) = NE(L_2)$.

The following result is a consequence of Theorems 5.6.2 and 5.6.3.

Theorem 5.6.4

Let A be an address space with k elements. The number of nonidentical B-lists in A with $\#\Sigma = l$ is bounded by

$$\sum_{i=0}^{k} k^p i \times l^i \times b_i$$

Definition 5.6.9

A *forest list* F is an order set of tree lists $[L_1, L_2, \ldots, L_k]$ where $L_i = (N_i, \Gamma, \Sigma, M_i, Z, \delta_i, E_i)$, $1 \leq i \leq k$ and $i \neq j$ implies $N_i \cap N_j = \varnothing$.

Definition 5.6.10

Let $F = [L_1, L_2, \ldots, L_k]$ be a forest list such that the root of each $L_i = (N_i, \Gamma, \Sigma, M_i, Z, \delta_i, E_i)$ is m_i and $Z = \{z_1, z_2, \ldots, z_l\}$.

The *preorder node representation* of F, denoted by $\mathrm{NP}(F)$ or $\mathrm{NP}(m_1, m_2, \ldots, m_k)$, is defined recursively as follows:

1. $\mathrm{NP}(e) = \wedge$

2. $\mathrm{NP}(m_1, \ldots, m_k) = \begin{cases} \mathrm{NP}(m_2, \ldots, m_k), & \text{if } m_1 = e \\ m_1 \mathrm{NP}(\theta_{z_1}(m_1), \ldots, \theta_{z_l}(m_1)) \, \mathrm{NP}(m_2, \ldots, m_k), \\ \quad \text{otherwise} \end{cases}$

Let $\mathrm{NP}(F) = (n_1, a_1) (n_2, a_2) \ldots (n_q, a_q)$. The sequence $a_1 a_2 \ldots a_q$ is called the *preorder data representation* of F, denoted by $\mathrm{DP}(F)$, and the sequence of $n_1 n_2 \ldots n_q$ is called the *preorder address representation* of F, denoted by $\mathrm{AP}(F)$.

Example 5.6.6

Diagrammatic representation of a forest $F = [L_1, L_2, L_3, L_4]$ is given in Fig. 5.6.3. Then

$\mathrm{NP}(F) = (1, a_1) (2, a_2) (4, a_4) (3, a_3) (5, a_5) (7, a_7) (6, a_6) (8, a_8) (9, a_9)$

$\mathrm{DP}(F) = a_1 a_2 a_4 a_3 a_5 a_7 a_6 a_8 a_9$

$\mathrm{AP}(F) = 124357689$

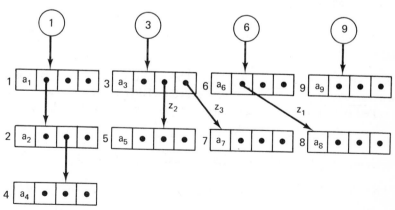

Fig. 5.6.3 Diagrammatic representation of a forest list $F = [L_1, L_2, L_3, L_4]$.

Definition 5.6.11

Let F be a forest list satisfying the condition given in Definition 5.6.10. The *endorder node representation* of F, denoted by $NE(F)$ or $NE(m_1, m_2, \ldots, m_k)$, is defined as follows:

1. $NE(e) = \wedge$

2. $NE(m_1, m_2, \ldots, m_k) = \begin{cases} NE(m_2, \ldots, m_k), \text{ if } m_1 = e \\ NE(\theta_{z_1}(m_1), \ldots, \theta_{z_l}(m_1)) NE(m_2, \ldots, \\ \quad m_k) m_1, \text{ otherwise} \end{cases}$

Let $NE(F) = (n_1, a_1)(n_2, a_2) \ldots (n_q, a_q)$. The sequence $a_1 a_2 \ldots a_q$ is called the *endorder data representation* of F, denoted by $DE(F)$. The sequence $n_1 n_2 \ldots n_q$ is called the *endorder address representation* of F, denoted by $AE(F)$.

Example 5.6.7

Consider the forest list $F = [L_1, L_2, L_3, L_4]$ given in Fig. 5.6.3. Then,

$NE(F) = (4, a_4)(2, a_2)(7, a_7)(5, a_5)(8, a_8)(9, a_9)(6, a_6)(3, a_3)(1, a_1)$

$DE(F) = a_4 a_2 a_7 a_5 a_8 a_9 a_6 a_3 a_1$

$AE(F) = 427589631$

Definition 5.6.12

Let F be a forest list satisfying the condition given in Definition 5.6.10. The *postorder node representation* of F, denoted by $NS(F)$ or $NS(m_1, m_2, \ldots, m_k)$ is defined as follows:

1. $NS(e) = \wedge$

2. $NS(m_1, m_2, \ldots, m_k) = \begin{cases} NS(m_2, \ldots, m_k), \text{ if } m_1 = e \\ NS(\theta_{z_1}(m_1), \ldots, \theta_{z_l}(m_1)) m_1 NS(m_2, \ldots, \\ \quad m_k), \text{ otherwise} \end{cases}$

Let $NS(F) = (n_1, a_1) \ldots (n_q, a_q)$. The sequence $a_1 \ldots a_q$ is called the *postorder data representation* of F, denoted by $DS(F)$. The sequence $n_1 \ldots n_q$ is called the *postorder address representation* of F, denoted by $AS(F)$.

Example 5.6.8

Consider the forest list $F = [L_1, L_2, L_3, L_4]$ given in Fig. 5.6.3. Then,

$NS(F) = (4, a_4)(2, a_2)(1, a_1)(5, a_5)(7, a_7)(3, a_3)(8, a_8)(6, a_6)(9, a_9)$

$DS(F) = a_4 a_2 a_1 a_5 a_7 a_3 a_8 a_6 a_9$

$AS(F) = 421573869$

Definition 5.6.13

Let F be a forest list and L be a B-list. F and L are said to be

1. *weakly node equivalent* if and only if $NP(F) = NP(L), NS(F) = NS(L)$, and $NE(F) = NE(L)$;

2. *weakly data equivalent* if and only if $DP(F) = DP(L), DS(F) = DS(L)$, and $DE(F) = DE(L)$;

3. *weakly address equivalent* if and only if $AP(F) = AP(L), AS(F) = AS(L)$, and $AE(F) = AE(L)$.

Example 5.6.9

Consider the B-list in Fig. 5.6.1 and the forest list $F = [L_1, L_2, L_3, L_4]$ in Fig. 5.6.3. From previous computations it follows that F and L are weakly node equivalent, weakly data equivalent, and weakly address equivalent.

Theorem 5.6.5

Corresponding to each forest list F, there exists a B-list $B(F)$ such that F and $B(F)$ are weakly node equivalent.

Proof: Let $F = [L_1, L_2, \ldots, L_k]$ be a forest list such that m_i is the root of $L_i = (N_i, \Gamma, \Sigma, M_i, Z, \delta_i, E_i), 1 \le i \le k$, where $i \ne j$ implies $N_i \cap N_j = \varnothing$. Now we construct a binary tree list $B(F)$ from F as follows:

If F is empty, then $B(F)$ is empty. Otherwise, let $B(F) = (N, \Gamma, \Sigma, M, Z', \delta, E)$

Then $N = \bigcup\limits_{i=1}^{k} N_i, M = \bigcup\limits_{i=1}^{k} M_i, Z' = (z_1', z_2')$, and $\bar{E} = \{m_1\}$.

Instead of defining δ, we define $\bar{\theta}$.

$\bar{\theta} = \{\theta_{z_1'}, \theta_{z_2'}\}$ where

$\theta_{z_1'} = \{(m, \theta_{z_i}^{(p)}(m)) | m \in M$ and $\forall\ 1 \le j < i$,

$\quad \theta_{z_j}^{(p)}(m) = e$ and $\theta_{z_i}^{(p)}(m)$

$\quad \ne e$ for some $p, 1 \le p \le k\}$

$\theta_{z_2'} = \{(m_i, m_{i+1}) | 1 \le i < k\} \cup \{(\theta_{z_i}^{(p)}(m), \theta_{z_{i+j}}^{(p)}(m)) | m \in M, 1 \le i < l, 1 \le p \le k, \theta_{z_i}^{(p)}(m) \ne e$ and j is the smallest positive integer such that $\theta_{z_{i+j}}^{(p)}(m) \ne e\}$.

The theorem is proved by induction. Let F be a forest list or k ordered tree lists such that the level of each tree list is at most 1. Let $m_1, m_2, \ldots, m_k$ be the roots of those ordered tree lists.

Then $NP(F) = NS(F) = m_1 m_2 \ldots m_k$ and $NE(F) = m_k m_{k-1} \ldots m_1$.

It follows directly from the construction that

$NP(B(F)) = m_1 m_2 \ldots m_k = NS(B(F))$ and $NE(B(F)) = m_k m_{k-1} \ldots m_1$.

Hence, the theorem holds in this case.

Assume that the theorem is true for a forest F consisting of k (> 0) tree lists each of level at most k_1 with at least one ordered tree list of level k_1. Without any loss of generality, we may assume $1 \leq k \leq l = \#Z$. Let $F = [L_1, L_2, \ldots, L_k]$ where $L_i = (N_i, \Gamma, \Sigma, M_i, Z, \delta_i, E_i)$ is the ordered tree list with root m_i, $1 \leq i \leq k$.

Now construct a new T-list L from F by including all lists in F and introduce a new node m as the root of L such that m is connected to m_i by z_i, $1 \leq i \leq k$. By construction we see that L has level $k_1 + 1$.

Let $F_1 = [L]$ be the forest list consisting of L alone. It is easily seen that

$$NP(F_1) = mNP(F) = mNP(B(F)) = NP(B(F_1)).$$

Similarly, $NS(F_1) = NS(B(F_1))$, and $NE(F_1) = NE(B(F_1))$.

Thus, if the theorem is true for a forest list with k ($1 \leq k \leq l$) ordered tree lists each of level at most k_1 with at least one of level k_1, then the theorem is also true for a forest list of one tree list of level $k_1 + 1$.

Now assume that the theorem holds for both lists $F_1 = [L_1]$ and $F_2 = [L_2, \ldots, L_k]$. We will show that it also holds for list $F = [L_1, L_2, \ldots, L_k]$. Let m_i be the root of list L_i, $1 \leq i \leq k$. We have

$$NP(F) = m_1 NP(\theta_{z_1}^{(1)}(m_1), \ldots, \theta_{z_l}^{(1)}(m_1)) NP(m_2, \ldots, m_k)$$
$$= NP(F_1) NP(F_2).$$

$$NP(B(F)) = m_1 NP(\theta_{z_1}'(m_1) NP(\theta_{z_2}'(m_1)) = NP(B(F_1)) NP(B(F_2)).$$

By inductive hypothesis, $NP(F_i) = NP(B(F_i))$, $1 \leq i \leq 2$. We conclude that $NP(F) = NP(B(F))$.

Similarly, we can conclude that $NS(F) = NS(B(F))$ and $NE(F) = NE(B(F))$.

Thus, if the theorem holds for a forest list with k T-lists, it also holds for forest lists with $k + 1$ T-lists. Hence, the theorem is proved. ∎

The following result is a direct consequence of the previous theorem, and, hence, is stated without proof.

Theorem 5.6.6

Let F be a forest list and L a B-list.

1. If $B(F)$ and L are node equivalent, then F and L are weakly node equivalent.

2. If $B(F)$ and L are data equivalent, then F and L are weakly data equivalent.

3. If $B(F)$ and L are address equivalent, then F and L are weakly address equivalent.

EXERCISES 5.6

1. Construct two B-lists which are data equivalent but not address equivalent.

2. Prove Theorem 5.6.1.

3. Let $F = [L_1, L_2]$ be a forest list where L_1 and L_2 are given in Fig. 5.6.2. Apply Theorem 5.6.5 to obtain a B-list $B(F)$ which is weakly node equivalent to F.

4. (a) Give an example of a B-list L with the property that for any node m,

$$\theta_{z_1}(m) = e \Rightarrow \theta_{z_2}(m) = e$$

and

$$\theta_{z_2}(m) = e \Rightarrow \theta_{z_1}(m) = e$$

    (b) Let $F = [L]$ be a forest list. Apply Theorem 5.6.5 to obtain a B-list $B(F)$ which is weakly node equivalent to F.

    (c) Compute $NP(L)$, $NE(L)$ and $NS(L)$.

    (d) Compute $NP(B(F))$, $NE(B(F))$ and $NS(B(F))$ and verify that $NP(L) = NP(B(F))$ and $NE(L) = NB(B(F))$.

    (e) Prove that if a B-list L has the property given in (a), then

$$NP(L) = NP(B(F))$$

and

$$NE(L) = NS(B(F))$$

where $F = [L]$ is an F-list and $B(F)$ is the B-list constructed from F using Theorem 5.6.5.

5.7. OPERATIONS ON TREE LISTS

As in linear lists, we consider only insertion and deletion operations on tree list sets. Since the number of elements in the label set Z for a tree list set is usually greater than one, when a node is inserted to a tree list, it is necessary to have the node to which the new node is linked and the label by which the new node is linked. We restrict ourselves only to the simplest type of operations such as insertion of a node or deletion of a node, since the insertion of a tree list in a tree list or deletion of a subtree list from a tree list can be considered as compositions of simplest type operations. Since the deletion of an interior node may change the characteristics of the tree list, the deletions are restricted only to terminal nodes. Similarly, for insertion operation, we insert a new node by $z \in Z$ only to a terminal node with respect to z.

Definition 5.7.1

The *insertion function* $\bar{I}$ on a T-list set $L(\Gamma, \Sigma, Z)$ with configuration set C is a partial function

$$\bar{I}: C \times \{\{A \times \Sigma\} \cup \{e\}\} \times \{A \times \Sigma\} \times Z \rightarrow C$$

such that $\bar{I}(c_i, m_1, m, z) = c_j$ means that node m is linked to node m_1 of a T-list with configuration c_i by label z, and that the configuration is changed from c_i to c_j.

It follows from the above definition that if $I(c_i, m_1, m, z)$ is defined then (1) $m \notin M_i$, (2) $m_1 = e$ implies that $c_i = [\emptyset, \emptyset, \emptyset]$, (3) $m_1 \neq e$ implies that $m_1 \in M_i$, and (4) $\theta_z(m_1) = e$.

Definition 5.7.2

The *deletion function* $\bar{D}$ on a T-list $L(\Gamma, \Sigma, Z)$ with configuration set C is a partial function

$$\bar{D}: \quad C \times \{\{A \times \Sigma\} \cup \{e\}\} \times \{A \times \Sigma\} \times Z \rightarrow C$$

such that $\bar{D}(c_i, m_1, m, z) = c_j$ means that node m is deleted from the T-list with configuration c_i such that $\theta_z(m_1) = m$ if $m_1 \neq e$ and the configuration is changed from c_i to c_j.

Although we have only defined insertion and deletion of nodes with reference only to terminal nodes, other types of insertion and deletion operations can be obtained by a composition of two simple operations defined previously as demonstrated by the following example.

Example 5.7.1

Let L be a B-list given in Fig. 5.7.1(a). Insertion of a node $(6, a_6)$ to node $(2, a_2)$ by z_1, can be accomplished by first deleting node $(4, a_4)$ and then insert it back after the insertion of node $(6, a_6)$.

In other words, we perform the following operations.

$$\bar{I}(\bar{I}(\bar{D}(c_1, (2, a_2), (4, a_4), z_1), (2, a_2), (6, a_6), z_1), (6, a_6), (4, a_4), z_1)$$

The resulting B-list is shown in Fig. 5.7.1(b).

EXERCISES 5.7

1. Let $L(\Gamma, \Sigma, Z)$ be a B-list set with configuration C. Suppose $c_i = [M_i, \bar{\theta}^{(i)}, \bar{E}_i]$ and $c_j = [M_j, \bar{\theta}^{(j)}, \bar{E}_j]$, and $\bar{I}(c_i, m_1, m, z) = c_j$. Specify $M_j, \bar{\theta}^{(j)}, \bar{E}_j$ in terms of components of c_i.

2. Can you perform deletion of an interior node in a T-list in terms of insertion and deletion operations defined in Definitions 5.7.1 and 5.7.2?

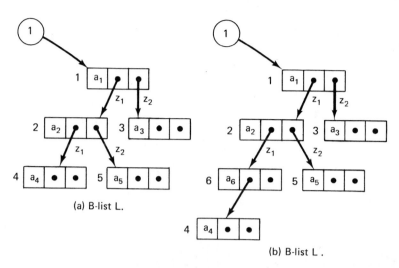

(a) B-list L.

(b) B-list L'.

Fig. 5.7.1 Diagrammatic representation of two B-lists.

5.8. SIMPLE ENVIRONMENT LIST SYSTEM

In this section, we create an environment in the address space A in which several simple lists are defined and are operated on with the assumption that operations are performed to only one list at any time. Whenever a node is to be inserted in a list, the space (an element of A) for creating the node is taken from available address space. The element of A used for the creation of a new node cannot be used by any other list for insertion until it is released by a deletion operation. In other words, that element of A is not available for any insertion operation to other lists. However, when a node is deleted, the element of A used by the node is available to other lists for insertion operation at subsequent time. Thus, it is necessary to keep track of the number of elements in A not used by any list. When all the elements of A have been used, no insertion operation can be performed further. In the following, we formalize the notion of such an environment and characterize the sequence of operations that can be performed. Probabilistic estimation of the number of elements in A not used by any list and the number of nodes in each list will also be given. For simplicity, we assume no list consists of list heads.

Definition 5.8.1

A *simple list system* over an address space A is a triple $\mathscr{S} = \langle L(\Gamma, \Sigma, Z),$ $I', D' \rangle$, where $L(\Gamma, \Sigma, Z)$ is either an L-list set of a T-list set, and I' and D' are the appropriate insertion and deletion operations defined on $L(\Gamma, \Sigma, Z)$.

Definition 5.8.2

A *simple environment list system* (SELS) T over an address space A is a 5-tuple $T = (\{\mathscr{L}_i\}_{1 \leq i \leq k}, Q, \hat{I}, \hat{D}, q_0)$ where

1. Each $\mathscr{L}_i = \langle L_i(\Gamma_i, \Sigma_i, Z_i), I_i, D_i \rangle$ is a simple list system.
2. $Q \subseteq L_1(\Gamma_1, \Sigma_1, Z_1) \times L_2(\Gamma_2, \Sigma_2, Z_2) \times \ldots \times L_k(\Gamma_k, \Sigma_k, Z_k)$ is a set of *states*.
3. If $(L_1, L_2, \ldots, L_k) \in Q$ where N_i is the set of addresses of nodes in L_i, $1 \leq i \leq k$, then $\bigcup\limits_{i=1}^{k} N_i \subseteq A$ and $i \neq j$ implies that $N_i \cap N_j = \varnothing$.
4. $\hat{I}$ is a set of insertion operations $\{\hat{I}_i\}_{1 \leq i \leq k}$.
5. $\hat{D}$ is a set of deletion operations $\{\hat{D}_i\}\ 1 \leq i \leq k$.
6. $q_0 \in Q$ is called the initial state of T.

Definition 5.8.3

Let $T = (\{\mathscr{L}_i\}_{1 \leq i \leq k}, Q, \hat{I}, \hat{D}, q_0)$ be an SELS. For each $q = (L_1, \ldots, L_k)$, the *status* of q, denoted by $S(q)$, is a $k + 1$-tuple $(l_1, l_2, \ldots, l_{k+1})$ where for each $1 \leq j \leq k$, l_j is the number of nodes in list L_j and $l_{k+1} = A - \sum\limits_{i=1}^{k} l_i$. If $\hat{I}_i(q, (n, a)) = Q'$ or $\hat{D}_i(q, (n, a)) = Q'$ then $\forall q_i, q_j \in Q'$, $S(q_i) = S(q_j)$.

For each operation $\hat{I}_i$ or $\hat{D}_i$, we define two relations $\stackrel{\hat{I}_i}{\vert\!-\!-}$ and $\stackrel{\hat{D}_i}{\vert\!-\!-}$ on the set of status as follows:

$$S(q) = (l_1, \ldots, l_{k+1}) \stackrel{\hat{I}_i}{\vert\!-\!-} S(q') = (l_1, \ldots, l_{i-1}, l_i + 1, l_{i+1}, \ldots, l_{k+1} - 1)$$

if $q' \in I_i(q, (n, a))$ for some (n, a).

Similarly,

$$S(q) = (l_1, \ldots, l_{k+1}) \stackrel{\hat{D}_i}{\vert\!-\!-} S(q') = (l_1, \ldots, l_{i-1}, l_i - 1, l_{i+1}, \ldots, l_{k+1}$$

$+ 1)$ if $q' \in D_i(q, (n, a))$ for some (n, a) and $S(q) \stackrel{D_j}{\vert\!-\!-} S(q)$ where $S(q) = S(q')$ if $q' \in \hat{D}_i(q, e)$.

If $\alpha \in (\hat{I} \cup \hat{D})^*$, then we define $\stackrel{\alpha}{\vert\!-\!-}$ as follows:

1. $S(q) \stackrel{\alpha}{\vert\!-\!-} S(q)$, if $\alpha = \wedge$.
2. If $\alpha = \sigma_1 \ldots \sigma_n$ then $S(q) \stackrel{\alpha}{\vert\!-\!-} S(q')$ if there exists a sequence of status $S(q_0) = S(q), S(q_1), \ldots, S(q_n) = S(q')$ such that $S(q_{i-1}) \stackrel{\sigma_i}{\vert\!-\!-} S(q_i)$, for $0 < i \leq n$.

Theorem 5.8.1

To each SELS $T = (\{\mathscr{L}_i\}_{1 \leq i \leq k}, Q, \hat{I}, \hat{D}, q_0)$ there exists a finite automaton M such that

$$L(M) = \{ \alpha \in (\hat{I} \cup \hat{D})^* | \exists q \in Q[S(q_0) \mid \underline{\alpha} \; S(q)]\}$$

Proof: We construct a finite automaton $M = (S, \hat{I} \cup \hat{D}, \delta, s_0, F)$ called an *operation automaton* of T as follows:

1. $S = \{S(q) | q \in Q\} \cup \{(l_1, \ldots, l_{k+1}) | \sum_{i=1}^{k} l_i = \#A + 1$ and $l_{k+1} = 0\}$
   $\cup \{s^*\}$

2. $\delta(s, \sigma) = \begin{cases} S(q') \text{ if } s = S(q) \text{ and } S(q) \mid \underline{\sigma} \; S(q') \\ (l_1, \ldots, l_{i-1}, l_i + 1, l_{i+1}, \ldots, l_{k+1}) \text{ if } \sigma = \hat{I}_i \text{ and} \\ \quad s \in \{S(q) | q \in Q\} \text{ and } s = (l_1, \ldots, l_{k+1}) \text{ with } l_{k+1} = 0 \\ s^*, \text{ otherwise} \end{cases}$

3. $s_0 = S(q_0)$
4. $F = \{S(q) | q \in Q\}$

We leave it to the reader to verify that $L(M) = \{\alpha \mid S(q_0) \mid\!\!- S(q)$, some $q \in Q\}$. ∎

If one is interested only in the number of the addresses used by a simple list of a simple list set while several simple list systems are operating in the same address space, then the structure of the list becomes unimportant; and this motivates the creation of operation automaton. Each state of the operation automaton reflects the number of addresses used by each of k simple lists and the remaining number of addresses in A. If one considers a simple list system as the formalization of a computer system in paging environment with dynamic storage allocation such that at most parts of k programs are in the memory space for execution, then one's interest, besides the system overhead, lies in the page usage for each program and not in the structure of the program, although it may be possible that some structured program is more suitable in paging environment in the sense of minimizing system overhead. The operation automaton reflects the usage of pages in memory. Furthermore, the fact that computer systems usually gather statistics for estimating the performance, including memory usage, of the computer system motivates the concept of a probabilistic (operation) automaton for estimating the usages of addresses (pages) if the operations (page in, page out) are probabilistic in nature.

Definition 5.8.4

A *probability vector* of the state set of the operation automaton M of a SELS T is a column vector $P = (P_1, P_2, \ldots, P_n)$ where n is the number of states of the operation automaton and for each $1 \leq i \leq n$, P_i is the probability that the automaton is in the ith state.

Definition 5.8.5

A *probabilistic transition matrix* $H' = [h_{ij}]$ of an operation automaton M of a SELS T is an $n \times n$ matrix where n is the number of states in the state set of operation automaton. The (i, j)th element h_{ij} is the probability of the transition from ith state to jth state of the operation automaton. If ith state is an overflow state, we define $h_{ii} = 1$ and $h_{ij} = 0$, $i \neq j$ since the operations are undefined for any overflow state. We note that $\sum_{j=1}^{n} h_{ij} = 1$ and $0 \leq h_{ij} \leq 1$.

For example, let us consider an operation automaton M, with four states, of a SELS T where T contains only one list system $\mathcal{L}_1$. The transition diagram of M is given in Fig. 5.8.1.

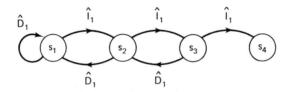

Fig. 5.8.1   Transition diagram of an operation automaton.

Let p_i and p'_i, $1 \leq i \leq 3$ be the probabilities of the occurrences of $\hat{I}_1$ and $\hat{D}_1$, respectively, when the operation automaton is in the ith state. Then, $p_i + p'_i = 1$, $1 \leq i \leq 3$. The probabilistic transition matrix H' is given in the following

$$
H' = \begin{array}{c} \\ s_1 \\ s_2 \\ s_3 \\ s_4 \end{array}
\begin{array}{cccc} s_1 & s_2 & s_3 & s_4 \\ \end{array}
\left[\begin{array}{cccc} p'_1 & p_1 & 0 & 0 \\ p'_2 & 0 & p_2 & 0 \\ 0 & p'_3 & 0 & p_3 \\ 0 & 0 & 0 & 1 \end{array} \right].
$$

s_4 is an "overflow" state, so $h_{44} = 1$. It is assumed whatever the input is, it would always remain there. After one operation, the new probability vector is given by $p^1 = HP$ where H is the transpose of H'.

The following theorem being similar to theorem proved in [6] is stated without proof.

Theorem 5.8.2

Let H' and p^0 be the transition probability matrix and initial probability vector of the state set of an operation automaton of a SELS T. The probability vector of the state set after a large number of operations converges to a constant probability vector.

Corollary 5.8.1

Let H' and $p^0 = (\underline{\sigma}_1^0, \underline{\sigma}_2^0)$ be the transition probability matrix and initial probability vector of the state set of an operation automaton M of a SELS T. $\underline{\sigma}_2^0$ and $\underline{\sigma}_1^0$ are the initial probability vectors of the overflow state set and the rest of the states, respectively. After a large number of operations, σ_1, the probability vector of the set of states excluding the overflow states when normalized to 1, converges to a constant probability vector.

Theorem 5.8.2 and its corollary implies that the probability of having a fixed number of pages in a program in memory space of a computer system with dynamic page allocation scheme is constant. Similarly the probability of having the fixed number of unused pages in memory space is constant. Finally, if the page is requested by a program (page in), the probability that there is no unused page in memory is constant.

5.9. CONCLUDING REMARKS

In previous sections, the formal semantics for simple list structures are defined. The formalization leads to the various notions of equivalence between data structures as well as providing tools for analysis of various systems as demonstrated in Section 5.8. It is hoped that this chapter will provide motivation toward the development of a theory of formal semantics for data structures.

REFERENCES

1. CHILDS, D. L., "Description of a Set Theoretic Data Structure," *Proc. AFIPS Fall Joint Computer Conference*, 33 (1968), 557–564.

2. CHILDS, D. L., "Feasibility of a Set Theoretic Data Structure–A General Structure based on a Reconstituted Definition of a Relation," *Proc. IFIP Congress*, North-Holland Publishing Co., Amsterdam, 1968, pp. 162–172.

3. EARLEY, J., "Towards an Understanding of Data Structures," *Comm. ACM*, 14 (Oct. 1971), 617–627.

4. FLECK, A. C., "Towards a Theory of Data Structures," *J. Computer and System Sciences*, 5 (1971), 475–488.

5. FLORES, I., *Data Structure and Management*, Prentice-Hall, Inc., Englewood Cliffs, N.J., 1970.

6. HSU, W. L., "Formalization of Simple List and Probabilistic Estimation of Storage for Simple List System," *Tech. Report.*, Computer Science Department, Southern Illinois University, Aug. 1973.

7. KNUTH, D. E., *The Art of Computer Programming, Vol. 1: Fundamental Algorithms,* Addison-Wesley Publishing Co., Inc., Reading, Mass., 1968.

8. MEALY, G., "Another Look at Data," *Proc. AFIPS Fall Joint Computer Conference,* 31 (1967), 525–534.

9. DODD, G. E., "Elements of Data Management Systems," *Computing Surveys* (June 1969).

10. ROSENBERG, A., "Data Graphs and Addressing Schemes," *J. Computer and System Sciences,* 5 (1971), 193–238.

PART **III** **DESIGN**

6 LANGUAGE THEORY IN COMPILER DESIGN

Alfred V. Aho
Bell Laboratories
Murray Hill, New Jersey

Editor's Note:

This chapter discusses how formal language theory can aid in the specification and design of compilers. By separating a compiler into functional components such as a lexical analyzer, syntactic analyzer, code optimizer, error recovery, code generator, etc., the author proceeds to introduce various algorithmic techniques for constructing some of these components. Formal results in the chapter are discussed, motivated, and illustrated with many examples. Therefore, the fact that proofs for most of the theorems are omitted does not present any problem in understanding the chapter. On the other hand, pointers to literature containing proofs of theorems presented in this chapter are carefully provided.

The material given in this chapter and that of Chapter 7 could form the core of a course in "Design of Algorithmic Languages and Compilers."

The only prerequisites for this chapter are the notions of context-free language and pushdown transducer introduced in Chapter 1.

6.1. INTRODUCTION

Formal language theory was born during the late 1950's in the work of Noam Chomsky, searching for an adequate grammatical model for natural languages such as English [15, 16]. Shortly thereafter, research in formal language theory was given a great stimulus by the use of a context-free grammar (BNF) in the specification of the influential programming language ALGOL 60 [56]. Since that time, formal language theory has been an active area of research in computer science, and considerable knowledge has been amassed about the properties of various classes of grammars and the classes of languages they define. Certain aspects of this theory have had a significant impact on the specification of programming languages and the implementation of compilers for these languages. In this article we shall touch upon some of these aspects.

Formal language theory is primarily concerned with the specification of sets. Certain formalisms studied by language theorists, such as regular expressions, context-free grammars, and syntax-directed translation schemes, are also useful to programming language designers in the specification of programming languages. In addition, from certain classes of specifications of this nature it is possible to generate mechanically the corresponding compiler components; in so doing, it is possible to provide a better guarantee that a compiler agrees with a given language specification.

An important area of application for theory in compiler design is to warn a compiler writer that certain algorithms are expensive or even may not exist. For example, an unwitting compiler designer might want to specify that a compiler detect every error in every source program or produce a truly optimal object code for every source program. Theory warns him that algorithms to perform these tasks for programming languages such as FORTRAN or ALGOL simply do not exist, so specifications of this nature are generally impossible to satisfy.

A useful application of language theory along these lines is in providing a characterization of the descriptive power of various formalisms. We can prove that certain types of syntactic constructs cannot be specified by regular expressions or context-free grammars; we can prove that certain types of translations cannot be performed by syntax-directed translation schemes. Characterizations such as these help the compiler builder to understand better some of the tradeoffs that occur in language and compiler design.

6.2.   PROGRAMMING LANGUAGES AND
THEIR COMPILERS

A complete specification of a programming language must describe (at the very least) what symbols are to be permitted in valid programs (the terminal *character set*), what strings of symbols are to be deemed syntactically well-formed programs (the *syntax* of the language), and what meaning is to be attributed to each syntactically well-formed program (the *semantics* of the language).

The only easy task of these three is specifying the terminal character set. It is very difficult to specify exactly those strings which are to be considered valid programs. As a consequence it is customary (and easier) to define the class of valid programs by a set of rules that, in addition to generating all valid programs, permits some programs of questionable validity to be specified. For example, the ALGOL 60 report permits syntactically valid ALGOL programs to contain statements of the form

loop: **goto** loop

In this article we shall restrict ourselves to syntactic specifications consisting of context-free grammars. But we shall mention some of the syntactic constructs often found in programming languages that cannot be specified solely by means of context-free grammars.

Perhaps the most difficult task in the specification of a language is the assignment of a meaning to each valid program. Several approaches are possible. One is to assign to each valid program a sentence of another language, such as predicate calculus, whose meaning is universally "understood." Another approach is to specify the meaning of a valid program in terms of its effect on the state of some well-defined machine. However, an approach that is suitable both for specification and for mechanical implementation is still the subject of current research.

A compiler for a programming language is in itself the ultimate specification of the language. Thus, it is desirable that the specification embodied in the compiler agree with the specification stated by the language designer. This is one of the reasons why algorithmic techniques for constructing compiler components are particularly important.

To place the ideas in the remainder of this article in perspective, let us consider the basic model of a compiler shown in Fig. 6.2.1. The input to a compiler is a string of characters. The first component of the model, the lexical analyzer (or scanner as it is sometimes called), partitions the input string into a sequence of *tokens* where a token is a string of characters that forms a single logical unit. Some typical examples of tokens are identifiers, constants, keywords, and operator symbols (including composite symbols such as :=, . EQ., and **).

In addition to partitioning the input string into a sequence of tokens, the lexical analyzer does some bookkeeping activity by entering certain of the tokens into a *symbol table*. The lexical analyzer and later components of the compiler gather information about these tokens and store this information into the symbol table. For example, after seeing the declaration **integer** *num*

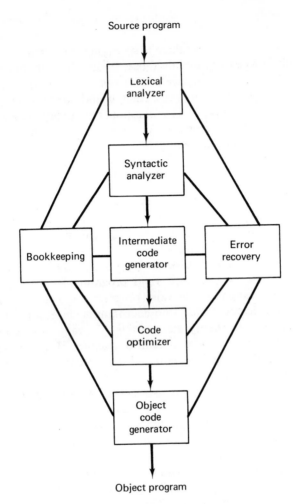

Fig. 6.2.1 Model of a compiler.

a compiler would have entered the identifier *num* into a symbol table and stored along with the name of the identifier an indication that it is of type "integer."

We can view a token as a pair of the form

(token type, pointer)

where the first component identifies the nature of the token (i.e., whether it is an identifier, keyword, constant, etc.) and the second component is a pointer into a portion of the symbol table that contains the string of characters making up the token along with information about the token. Not all tokens need to be stored in the symbol table so the second component may sometimes be null.

We should mention that certain language constructs complicate lexical analysis. For example, in PL/I upon seeing the input string of the form

$$\text{DECLARE } (X1, X2, \ldots, Xn)$$

a lexical analyzer cannot determine whether DECLARE is a keyword or a function identifier without seeing what comes after the right parenthesis.

The syntactic structure of most tokens can be represented by regular expressions and regular definitions. Thus techniques from the theory of finite automata are useful in the design of lexical analyzers. We shall not discuss lexical analysis further. The interested reader is referred to Johnson et al. [38], Gries [33], and Aho and Ullman [7] for more details.

The main output of the lexical analyzer is the string of tokens, which forms the input to the next phase of the compiler, the syntactic analyzer, or parser as it is often called. The syntactic analyzer performs two functions. It checks that the source program obeys the syntactic rules of the source language. It also places a grammatical structure on the source program and makes this structure explicit, usually in the form of a tree.

If a context-free grammar is used to specify the syntax of a programming language, then a syntactic analyzer that parses the string of tokens (actually the string of first components of the tokens) according to this grammar would perform both functions. For if the string of tokens has a derivation tree in the grammar, then the compiler would have verified that the source program is syntactically well-formed. In addition, the compiler could use the derivation tree itself to represent the underlying grammatical structure of the source program.

Not surprisingly, it is in the specification and implementation of syntactic analyzers that language theory has its greatest impact on compiler design. Much of this article is concerned with the design and implementation of parsers for various classes of context-free grammars.

. The output of the syntactic analyzer is some representation of a derivation tree. The next phase of the compiler, the intermediate code generator, takes the derivation tree and maps it onto some intermediate language representation of the source program, such as three-address code. This type of representation resembles machine language, but retains the relevant syntactic information present in the derivation tree and permits the collection of information which is useful in performing certain types of code optimization.

The term "code optimization" is actually a misnomer in that it is generally impossible to design an algorithm that will generate optimal object code for most programming languages. The term "code improvement" would be far more accurate. Improvements are directed at reducing either the running time or the length of the resulting object language program. Although we have shown the code optimization phase occurring immediately after intermediate code generation, code improvements can be performed throughout the compilation process.

Code improvement techniques can be classified as being machine independent or machine dependent. The machine independent techniques can be further classified as being local or global. An example of a local improvement would be to replace a time-consuming computation such as A**2 (i.e., A^2) by the equivalent but faster computation A*A. Examples of global code improvements are the elimination of redundant computations and the movement of invariant computations out of loops.

Machine dependent improvements are generally techniques which recognize language constructs for which special hardware instructions exist. For example, if a machine has an "add one to storage" instruction, then recognizing statements of the form $I = I + 1$ would be a part of machine dependent code optimization.

We can view the code improvement process as one in which a sequence of semantics-preserving transformations is applied to the intermediate language representation of a source program in an effort to map the intermediate language program into one from which a faster or smaller object language program can be produced. The transformations to be applied depend on the source language, the object language, and the environment in which the compiler resides. Code optimization is discussed in more detail in Cocke and Schwartz [17], Aho and Ullman [10], Shaefer [64], and Wulf [74].

The final phase of the compiler model, the object code generator, takes as input an "optimized" intermediate language program and produces as output an object language program. For most compilers the object language is assembly or machine language. However, some compilers (e.g., SNOBOL) produce as output an object language program that is to be interpreted.

The information that has been collected in the symbol table about tokens is used during the code generation phase. For example, different object code will be generated for the expression A + B when A and B are integers than when A and B are floating point numbers. Also, questions of register and storage allocation must be solved prior to or during the final code generation phase. Optimal register allocation is very difficult (it belongs to the class of NP-complete problems, a class of problems renowned for their computational intractability [65]).

Certain compilers which do little code optimization may have no explicit code optimization phase. Some such compilers generate object code as they perform syntactic analysis. In these compilers, each time a new vertex of the derivation tree is found, instead of creating the vertex, the syntactic analyzer calls a semantic routine to generate object code. In such compilers the syntactic analyzer constructs the derivation tree only in a figurative sense. The derivation tree is represented only as a sequence of calls to semantic routines.

Error recovery is another important, but difficult and often neglected, aspect of compiler design. Errors in the source program can be discovered during all phases of the compilation process. For example, misspellings can be found during lexical analysis, syntactic errors (such as missing parentheses) can be detected during syntactic analysis, and semantic errors (such as illegal mixed mode expressions) can be uncovered during code generation. A good compiler cannot cease processing its input once the first error is found; it must find some way to recover from the error in such a fashion that subsequent errors can also be detected. We shall describe some ways of recovering from syntactic errors. Treatment of misspellings is covered by Freeman [29] and Morgan [54]. There are some compilers that go to extraordinary lengths to provide good diagnostic messages, such as CORC (Conway and Maxwell [18]), DITRAN (Moulton and Muller [55]), IITRAN (Dewar et al. [22]), and PL/C (Conway and Wilcox [19]).

6.3. CONTEXT-FREE GRAMMARS

Context-free grammars, hereafter simply called *grammars*, are useful in helping specify the syntax of programming languages. In this section we shall review some basic terminology concerning context-free grammars and show what syntatic features of programming languages can or cannot be specified by grammars.

A grammar $G = (N, \Sigma, P, S)$ is said to be *admissible* if each grammar symbol in $N \cup \Sigma$ can be used in the derivation of at least one sentence in $L(G)$. Given a grammar G, we can eliminate all useless grammar symbols and productions from G to obtain an equivalent admissible grammar. From now on we assume that the term *grammar* means *admissible grammar*.

Grammars are ideally suited for describing nested structures in languages as the following two examples show.

Example 6.3.1

Consider the grammar G_1 with productions

$$S \to S(S) \mid \wedge$$

$L(G_1)$ consists of all strings of balanced parentheses, including $\wedge$, the empty string.

Example 6.3.2

Consider the grammar G_2 having the productions

$$S \longrightarrow \textbf{if } b \textbf{ then } S \textbf{ else } S$$
$$S \longrightarrow \textbf{if } b \textbf{ then } S$$
$$S \longrightarrow a$$

$L(G_2)$ consists of sentences representing **if-then** and **if-then-else** statements, where b represents a Boolean expression and a an assignment statement.

Definition 6.3.1

Let $G = (N, \Sigma, P, S)$ be a grammar. We shall write $\alpha \underset{\text{lm}}{\Rightarrow} \beta$ if $\alpha = wA\gamma$, $\beta = w\delta\gamma$, and $A \longrightarrow \delta$ is a production. That is, we have rewritten the leftmost nonterminal in α to obtain β. A derivation of the form

$$\alpha_0 \underset{\text{lm}}{\overset{*}{\Rightarrow}} \alpha_1 \underset{\text{lm}}{\overset{*}{\Rightarrow}} \ldots \underset{\text{lm}}{\overset{*}{\Rightarrow}} \alpha_n$$

is said to be a *leftmost* derivation of α_n from α_0 in G. If $S \underset{\text{lm}}{\overset{*}{\Rightarrow}} \alpha$, then α is called a *left sentential form*. We can make the analogous definition for *rightmost* derivation and *right sentential form*.

Let λ be the sequence of productions used in a leftmost derivation of a sentence w from S in G. We say λ is a *left parse* for w.

Let ρ be the sequence of productions used in a rightmost derivation of a sentence w from S in G. The reversal of ρ is a *right parse* for w.

Example 6.3.3

Consider the grammar G_3 with the three productions

1. $S \longrightarrow bSeS$
2. $S \longrightarrow bS$
3. $S \longrightarrow a$

(G_3 is isomorphic to G_2.) A leftmost derivation for the sentence $bbaea$ is:

$$S \overset{1}{\Rightarrow} bSeS$$
$$\overset{2}{\Rightarrow} bbSeS$$
$$\overset{3}{\Rightarrow} bbaeS$$
$$\overset{3}{\Rightarrow} bbaea$$

The superscript to the left of each arrow indicates the production used. Thus 1233 is a left parse for $bbaea$.

The corresponding rightmost derivation is:

$$S \Rightarrow^1 bSeS$$
$$\Rightarrow^3 bSea$$

$$\Rightarrow^2 bbSea$$

$$\Rightarrow^3 bbaea$$

Thus 3231 is a right parse for *bbaea*. The derivation tree corresponding to these two derivations is shown in Fig. 6.3.1.

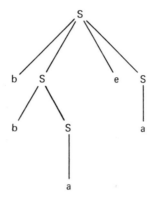

Fig. 6.3.1 Derivation tree for *bbaea*.

Definition 6.3.2

Let T be a rooted tree with root r and subtrees $T_1, T_2, \ldots, T_k, k \geq 0$, in order from left to right. A *prefix Polish* (sometimes called *preorder*) *traversal* of T is defined recursively as follows:

1. Visit the root r.
2. Visit each of $T_1, T_2, \ldots, T_k$ in a prefix Polish traversal.

Intuitively, a prefix Polish traversal is a top-down, left-to-right traversal of a tree.

A *postfix Polish* (sometimes called *postorder*) *traversal* of T is defined recursively as follows:

1. Visit each of $T_1, T_2, \ldots, T_k$ in a postfix Polish traversal.
2. Visit the root r.

Intuitively, a postfix Polish traversal is a bottom-up, left-to-right traversal of a tree.

Example 6.3.4

The vertices of the tree in Fig. 6.3.2 are numbered in the order in which they would be visited in a prefix Polish traversal. The vertices of the tree in Fig. 6.3.3 are in postfix Polish order.

We say production $A \rightarrow X_1 X_2 \ldots X_k$ *is associated with vertex v of a*

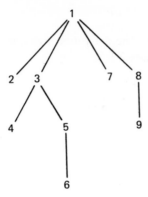

Fig. 6.3.2. Prefix Polish order.

derivation tree if v is labeled A and v has exactly k direct descendants labelled $X_1, X_2, \ldots, X_k$ (in left-to-right order). No production is associated with a leaf labelled by a terminal.

The following theorem shows the correspondence between left parses and prefix traversals, and between right parses and postfix Polish traversals.

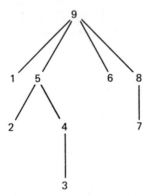

Fig. 6.3.3 Postfix Polish order.

Theorem 6.3.1

Let T be a derivation tree with frontier w.

1. The sequence of productions associated with the prefix Polish traversal of T is a left parse for w.

2. The sequence of productions associated with the postfix Polish traversal of T is a right parse for w.

(Proofs of all unproved theorems in this paper can be found in Aho and Ullman [7] and [10].)

A *left parser* for a grammar G is an algorithm that takes as input a string x and produces as output a left parse of x if x is in $L(G)$, and an error indication if x is not in $L(G)$. A *right parser* is defined analogously. Much of this chapter will be concerned with the construction of efficient left and right parsers for various classes of grammars.

Before we discuss parsers, however, let us examine some of the issues involved in using grammars to describe the syntax of programming languages. The first such issue concerns ambiguity.

Definition 6.3.3

A grammar G is *ambiguous* if there is at least one sentence in $L(G)$ with two or more distinct leftmost derivations.

Theorem 6.3.2

The following statements about a grammar G are equivalent:

1. G is ambiguous.
2. There are two or more distinct derivation trees of G having the same frontier.
3. There is a sentence in $L(G)$ with two or more left parses.
4. There is a sentence in $L(G)$ with two or more right parses.

Example 6.3.5

The grammar G_3 is ambiguous because the sentence *bbaea* has the derivation tree shown in Fig. 6.3.4 in addition to the one shown in Fig. 6.3.1.

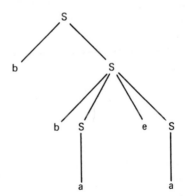

Fig. 6.3.4   Another derivation tree for *bbaea*.

Grammar G_2, which is essentially the same as G_3, illustrates the famous "dangling **else**" ambiguity of programming languages. The sentence

if b **then if** b **then** a **else** a

has the two phrasings

1. **if** b **then (if** b **then** a **else** a**)**
2. **if** b **then (if** b **then** a**) else** a

In virtually all programming languages with **if-then** and **if-then-else** statements the first phrasing is the preferred phrasing.

It is undesirable to have undetected ambiguities in the specification of a programming language. Thus, if we use the productions in grammar G_2 to specify **if-then** and **if-then-else** statements, we must provide a disambiguating rule which will state how the ambiguity is to be resolved. One such rule would be to state that in every sentence each **else** is to be matched with the closest unmatched **then**. Another alternative would be to use an equivalent unambiguous grammar such as G_4 having productions:

$$S \longrightarrow B \,|\, U$$
$$B \longrightarrow \textbf{if } b \textbf{ then } B \textbf{ else } B \,|\, a$$
$$U \longrightarrow \textbf{if } b \textbf{ then } S \,|\, \textbf{if } b \textbf{ then } B \textbf{ else } U$$

As the following theorem states, there is no general algorithm to determine if a grammar is ambiguous.

Theorem 6.3.3

It is undecidable whether an arbitrary grammar is ambiguous.

However, Theorem 6.3.3 is not as discouraging as one might think at first. Certain classes of grammars have been found, such as the LL and LR grammars, which we can prove contain only unambiguous grammars. Moreover, there is an algorithm to test whether a grammar is LL or LR. If on testing a grammar for membership in the LL or LR class of grammars, we find the grammar does not belong to the class, then we can isolate the places in the grammar in which all non-LL or non-LR constructs occur. These constructs must include all ambiguous constructs in the grammar. Theorem 6.3.3 is not violated because we cannot provide an algorithm to tell whether a recalcitrant construct in the grammar is ambiguous or merely an unambiguous non-LL or non-LR construct. As a practical matter, it is usually quite easy to recognize the ambiguous constructs when a grammar has been run through a well-designed deterministic parser generator.

In some situations it is more natural to use ambiguous grammars in the specification of a programming language, provided the ambiguities can be easily recognized and resolved by simple disambiguating rules [4]. Grammar G_2 with the "match each **else** with the closest unmatched **then**" disambiguating rule was one example. Here is another.

Example 6.3.6

Consider the following commonly used grammar G_0 for arithmetic expressions:

$$E \rightarrow E + T \,|\, T$$
$$T \rightarrow T * F \,|\, F$$
$$F \rightarrow (E) \,|\, a$$

This grammar is unambiguous. It enforces a left-to-right associativity of the operators + and *, and it makes * of higher precedence than +.

The following grammar G_5 generates the same language:

$$E \rightarrow E + E \mid E * E \mid (E) \mid a$$

However, G_5 is ambiguous because the sentence $a + a * a$, for example, has the two derivation trees shown in Fig. 6.3.5. The first tree makes * of higher precedence than +; the second tree makes + of higher precedence than *. We can resolve all ambiguities in G_5, if we state that:

1. + is left-associative.
2. * is left-associative.
3. + has lower precedence than *.

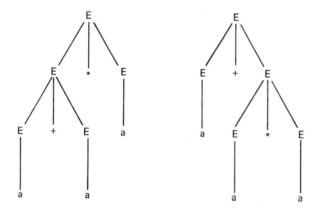

Fig. 6.3.5 Two derivation trees for $a + a * a$.

This method of specifying the syntax of arithmetic expressions has several advantages over the conventional grammar G_0. The ambiguous grammar is more concise, and, as we shall see, more efficient parsers can be constructed directly from the ambiguous grammar than from G_0.

Certain syntactic constructs that appear in programming languages cannot be specified by grammars. We shall give some examples.

Theorem 6.3.4

The language $L_1 = \{wcw \mid w \text{ is in } \{a, b\} *\}$ is not a context-free language.

Proof: If we intersect L_1 with the regular set $a^*b^*ca^*b^*$, we obtain the language $\{a^m b^n c a^m b^n \mid m, n \geq 0\}$, which by an application of the pumping lemma for context-free languages, can be easily shown to be non-context-free. Since the context-free languages are closed under intersection with regular sets, this implies L_1 is also not a context-free language. ∎

Theorem 6.3.4 can be generalized to show that if a language requires that an arbitrarily long string (containing two or more symbols) be repeated in a sentence, then such a language cannot be context-free. This type of syntactic construction occurs in programming languages that permit identifiers to be of arbitrary length and that require identifiers to be declared. ALGOL 60 is an example of such a language. For example, in the ALGOL program

begin integer w; $w := 1$ **end**

the identifier w can be of arbitrary length. If identifiers cannot be arbitrarily long, then all identifiers could, in principle, be enumerated and specified by a grammar. However, this would not be a practical solution. In practice, specifying that identifiers must be declared is always done by some non-context-free means.

There are several other examples of non-context-free constructs in the syntax of some programming languages. Here are two more well-known examples:

1. Usually, a procedure must have the same number of arguments every time it is mentioned. If the number of arguments procedures can have is arbitrary, then a grammar cannot specify that multiple occurrences of the same procedure must have the same number of arguments.

2. FORTRAN Hollerith statements include the construct nHw where n is a decimal number and w is any string of FORTRAN characters of length n. For arbitrary n this construct cannot be specified by a grammar.

These examples show that context-free grammars are not totally adequate to specify all of the syntax of major programming languages. However, grammars can be used to specify a large portion of the syntax of a language in such a natural and elegant way that a grammar is invariably included as part of the specification of any new language. The non-context-free aspects of the languages are usually specified by qualifications on the grammar.

Within a compiler the non-context-free aspects of the language are usually checked outside of the syntactic analyzer. For example, checking that identifiers have been declared is usually done by the lexical analyzer with the help of the symbol table. Thus, it is reasonable to consider a syntactic analyzer within a compiler as a parser for a grammar.

A number of formalisms that can specify some of the non-context-free aspects of programming languages have been defined. Aho [1], Fischer [25], Rosenkrantz [61], Stearns and Lewis [68], and Van Wijngaarden [70] are but a few examples. However, the mechanical construction of efficient parsers for these classes of grammars is not as well understood as for context-free grammars.

EXERCISES 6.3

1. Prove that G_1 is unambiguous.

2. Give an algorithm to construct (a) a left parse from a right parse and (b) a right parse from a left parse.

3. Use Post's correspondence problem to prove that there is no algorithm to determine if a grammar is ambiguous.

4. Prove that $\{a^m b^n c a^m b^n \mid m, n \geq 0\}$ is not a context-free language.

*5. Prove that $\{nHw \mid n$ is a decimal integer and w is in $\{a, b\}^n$ is not a context-free language.

6.4. LL PARSING

We shall first consider the problem of trying to construct an efficient left parser for a given grammar. Unfortunately, we do not known how to construct such parsers for all grammars. In this section we shall describe an algorithm that will construct efficient left parsers for an important subclass of grammars known as the $LL(k)$ grammars. These grammars, first defined by Lewis and Stearns [50], are the largest natural class of unambiguous grammars for which we can construct deterministic "top-down" parsers. The term $LL(k)$ stands for scanning the input from *l*eft to right, producing a *l*eft parse, using k-symbol lookahead to make parsing decisions. We shall describe the parser generation algorithm only for the case where $k = 1$.

We shall retrict ourselves to a class of left parsers called *predictive parsers*. A model of a predictive parser is shown in Fig. 6.4.1.

A predictive parser is merely a special type of pushdown transducer. It uses an input tape to hold the string to be parsed. The last square of the input tape contains a unique right endmarker $. The pushdown stack holds grammar symbols during the parsing process. Initially, the stack contains only the start symbol of the grammar and a unique bottom marker $. The output tape will hold the sequence of productions emitted by the parser. Initially, the output tape is empty.

The parser behaves in the following manner. The control examines the symbol X on top of the pushdown stack and the current input symbol a (the symbol under the input head). These two symbols determine the three possible moves the parser may make.

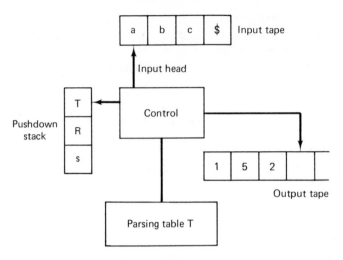

Fig. 6.4.1   Model of predictive parser.

1. If X is a terminal symbol and $X = a$, the control pops X off the stack and moves the input head one square right.

2. If X is a nonterminal symbol, the control consults $M(X, a)$, the entry for X and a in the parsing matrix M. This entry will be either a production of the grammar, or error. If $M(X, a) = \{X \rightarrow \alpha\}$, the parser replaces X on top of the stack by α and writes the production $X \rightarrow \alpha$ on the output tape. If $M(X, a) = \{\text{error}\}$, the parser announces it has found a syntactic error and it transfers control to an error recovery routine. In either case, the input head is not advanced.

3. If $X = a = \$$, the parser halts and accepts the input string.

The parser starts from an initial configuration in which the pushdown list contains the start symbol of the grammar, the input contains the string to be parsed with the input head on the leftmost square of the input tape, and the output tape is empty. The parser then continues to make moves until it either accepts the input or announces error.

Example 6.4.1

Consider the grammar G_6 with start symbol E:

$$E \rightarrow aTR$$
$$R \rightarrow +aTR \mid \wedge$$
$$T \rightarrow *aT \mid \wedge$$

A predictive parsing table for G_6 is shown in Fig. 6.4.2.

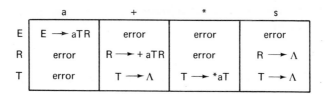

Fig. 6.4.2 Predictive parsing matrix for G_6.

With input $a + a * a$ the predictive parser using the matrix of Fig. 6.4.2 would make the following moves. Here $\wedge$ indicates the location of the input head on the input. The top of the stack is on the left. For example, on the first move the symbol on top of the stack is E and the current input symbol is a. Since E is a nonterminal, the parser consults the parsing matrix entry for E and a to determine that it should replace E by aTR on the stack, and emit the production $E \rightarrow aTR$ as output.

Input	Stack	Output
$\hat{a} + a * a\$$	$E\$$	
$\hat{a} + a * a\$$	$aTR\$$	$E \rightarrow aTR$
$\hat{+}\, a * a\$$	$TR\$$	
$\hat{+}\, a * a\$$	$R\$$	$T \rightarrow \wedge$
$\hat{+}\, a * a\$$	$+aTR\$$	$R \rightarrow +aTR$
$\hat{a} * a\$$	$aTR\$$	
$\hat{*}\, a\$$	$TR\$$	
$\hat{*}\, a\$$	$*aTR\$$	$T \rightarrow *aT$
$\hat{a}\$$	$aTR\$$	
$\hat{\$}$	$TR\$$	
$\hat{\$}$	$R\$$	$T \rightarrow \wedge$
$\hat{\$}$	$\$$	$R \rightarrow \wedge$
		accept

Note that at all times the input symbols that have already been scanned followed by the grammar symbols on the stack make up a left sentential form. Thus, the predictive parser above traces out a leftmost derivation for the input string and the sequence of productions emitted is a left parse for the input string. We can prove that this parser accepts an input string w if and only there is a leftmost derivation for w in G_6. In so doing, we would prove the parser is a left parser for G_6.

We say that a parsing matrix M is *valid* for grammar G if the predictive parser using M is a left parser for G. Thus the problem of constructing a predictive parser for a grammar is really one of constructing a valid parsing matrix for the grammar. We shall show how to construct valid parsing matrices for LL(k) grammars.

Definition 6.4.1

Let $G = (N, \Sigma, P, S)$ be a grammar and α a string in $(N \cup \Sigma)^*$. We define two set-valued functions on α.

1. $\text{FIRST}_k(\alpha) = \{x \mid x \text{ is in } \Sigma^*, \alpha \overset{*}{\Rightarrow} xy \text{ and } |x| = k\}$
   $\cup \{x \mid x \text{ is in } \Sigma^*, \alpha \overset{*}{\Rightarrow} x \text{ and } |x| < k\}$
2. $\text{FOLLOW}_k(\alpha) = \{x \mid x \text{ is in } \Sigma^*, S \overset{*}{\Rightarrow} w\alpha xy \text{ and } |x| = k\}$
   $\cup \{x \mid x \text{ is in } \Sigma^*, S \overset{*}{\Rightarrow} w\alpha x \text{ and } |x| < k\}$

Roughly speaking, a terminal string x is in $\text{FIRST}_k(\alpha)$ if α can derive a string beginning with x. A terminal string x is in $\text{FOLLOW}_k(\alpha)$ if αx is a substring of some sentential form of the grammar. For example, for G_6, $\text{FIRST}_1(R) = \{+, \wedge\}$, $\text{FOLLOW}_1(T) = \{+, \wedge\}$, and $\text{FIRST}_2(aTR) = \{a, a^*, a+\}$.

Definition 6.4.2

A grammar G is LL(k) if whenever we have two derivations of the form

1. $S \overset{*}{\underset{\text{lm}}{\Rightarrow}} xA\gamma \underset{\text{lm}}{\Rightarrow} x\alpha\gamma \overset{*}{\Rightarrow} xy$
2. $S \overset{*}{\underset{\text{lm}}{\Rightarrow}} xA\gamma \underset{\text{lm}}{\Rightarrow} x\beta\gamma \overset{*}{\Rightarrow} xz$

such that $\text{FIRST}_k(y) = \text{FIRST}_k(z)$, then $\alpha = \beta$.

If G is an LL(k) grammar, then we say $L(G)$ is an *LL(k) language*. A language L is said to be an *LL language* if $L = L(G)$ for some LL(k) grammar G.

The LL(k) definition can be best understood in the context of trying to construct a leftmost derivation for a given input string xy. Suppose we have already constructed the derivation up to the left sentential form $xA\gamma$, that is, we have generated the prefix x of the input string xy. The LL(k) definition says that at this point in the derivation the two strings $A\gamma$ and $\text{FIRST}_k(y)$ uniquely determine the production to be used to rewrite A to obtain the next left sentential form in the derivation. That is, there must be in the grammar at most one production for A, namely $A \rightarrow \alpha$, such that

$$\text{FIRST}_k(\alpha\gamma) = \text{FIRST}_k(y)$$

It may appear that the production does not depend on x. However, we can show that the string y in the left sentential form $xA\gamma$ is uniquely determined by the prefix xA. Thus, the LL(k) definition says that the production used to rewrite A in the left sentential form $xA\gamma$ depends on x and $\text{FIRST}_k(y)$. The next theorem follows directly from this discussion.

Theorem 6.4.1

Every LL(k) grammar is unambiguous.

If we want the production to depend only on the nonterminal A, rather than $A\gamma$ (or equivalently xA), then we should restrict ourselves to strong LL(k) grammars.

Definition 6.4.3

A grammar G is a *strong* LL(k) grammar if whenever $A \rightarrow \alpha$ and $A \rightarrow \beta$ are two distinct productions, the condition

$$\text{FIRST}_k(\alpha y) \text{ and } \text{FIRST}_k(\beta z) \text{ are disjoint}$$

holds for all y and z in $\text{FOLLOW}_k(A)$.

It can be shown that every LL(k) language has a strong LL(k) grammar (see Rosenkrantz and Lewis [62]), although not every LL(k) grammar is a strong LL(k) grammar.

Example 6.4.2

The grammar G_7 with productions

$$S \rightarrow aAaa \mid bAba$$
$$A \rightarrow b \mid \wedge$$

is an LL(2) grammar but not a strong LL(2) grammar since $\text{FOLLOW}_2(A) = \{aa, ba\}$, and $\text{FIRST}_2(baa)$ and $\text{FIRST}_2(ba)$ are not disjoint.

We shall consider only LL(1) grammars since we do not want to construct predictive parsers that require the input head to look at more than one input symbol in one move. Our task is somewhat simplified because every LL(1) grammar is a strong LL(1) grammar. The following characterization for LL(1) grammars is a direct consequence of the definition of an LL(k) grammar when $k = 1$ (See Knuth [42]).

Theorem 6.4.2

$G = (N, \Sigma, P, S)$ is an LL(1) grammar if and only if whenever $A \rightarrow \alpha$ and $A \rightarrow \beta$ are two distinct productions in P the following three conditions hold:

1. There is no terminal α such that both α and β derive strings beginning with a.

2. α and β cannot both derive the empty string.

3. If $\beta \overset{*}{\Rightarrow} \wedge$, then there is no terminal a in $\text{FOLLOW}_1(A)$ such that α derives a string beginning with a.

The following procedure can be used to try to construct a predictive parsing matrix for a grammar G. Theorem 6.4.2 guarantees that when G is an LL(1) grammar, the algorithm produces a valid parsing matrix for G.

Algorithm 6.4.1

Construction of a Predictive Parsing Matrix
Input: A grammar $G = (N, \Sigma, P, S)$.
Output: M, a predictive parsing matrix for G.
Method:

1. Consider each production $A \longrightarrow \alpha$ in P in turn.
   (a) For each terminal a in $\text{FIRST}_1(\alpha)$, add $A \longrightarrow \alpha$ to $M(A, a)$.
   (b) If $\wedge$ is in $\text{FIRST}_1(\alpha)$, add $A \longrightarrow \alpha$ to $M(A, b)$ for each terminal symbol b in $\text{FOLLOW}_1(A)$. If $\wedge$ is in $\text{FOLLOW}_1(A)$, also add $A \longrightarrow \alpha$ to $M(A, \$)$.
2. After all productions in P have been considered, make each undefined entry of M an error entry.

Example 6.4.3

Let us apply Algorithm 6.4.1 to G_6. Production $E \longrightarrow aTR$ makes

$$M(E, a) = \{E \longrightarrow aTR\}$$

Production $R \longrightarrow +aTR$ makes $M(R, +) = \{R \longrightarrow +aTR\}$. Since $\text{FOLLOW}_1(R) = \{\wedge\}$, production $R \longrightarrow \wedge$ makes $M(R, \$) = \{R \longrightarrow \wedge\}$. Continuing in this fashion, we obtain the parsing matrix shown in Fig. 6.4.2.

The following theorem is a direct consequence of Theorem 6.4.2 and Algorithm 6.4.1.

Theorem 6.4.3

The parsing matrix produced by Algorithm 6.4.1 for an LL(1) grammar G is a valid parsing matrix in which no entry is multiply-defined.

The time complexity of LL(1) parsing is embodied in the following theorem.

Theorem 6.4.4

A predictive parser using the predictive parsing matrix produced by

Algorithm 6.4.1 for an LL(1) grammar will parse an input string in a number of moves that is linearly proportional to the length of the input string.

It is interesting to ask what happens if we apply Algorithm 6.4.1 to a grammar G that is not LL(1). It is not hard to show that at least one entry of the parsing matrix will acquire two or more productions if and only if G is not LL(1). Thus Algorithm 6.4.1 can also be used to test if a grammar is LL(1). If Algorithm 6.4.1 succeeds in producing a parsing matrix in which each entry is uniquely defined, then by Theorem 6.4.3, the given grammar is LL(1). For example, G_6 is an LL(1) grammar.

What should we do if a grammar is not LL(1)? Several courses of action are possible. We could try to use another deterministic parsing technique such as the LR method of the next section. Or we could attempt to rewrite the grammar so it becomes LL(1). Neither approach, however, may be successful.

A grammar is *left-recursive* if it contains a nonterminal A such that $A \overset{+}{\Rightarrow} Ax$ for some x. No left-recursive grammar can be LL(k) for any k. However, every left-recursive grammar can be rewritten to eliminate all left-recursion. The following example illustrates the technique.

Example 6.4.4

Consider the grammar G_8:

$$S \rightarrow Aa$$
$$A \rightarrow BB$$
$$B \rightarrow Sb \,|\, c$$

Since $S \overset{+}{\Rightarrow} SbBa$, we see this grammar is left-recursive. To eliminate this left-recursion, we first remove the B-productions by substituting Sb and c for all occurrences of B in the remaining productions. We obtain:

$$S \rightarrow Aa$$
$$A \rightarrow SbSb \,|\, Sbc \,|\, cSb \,|\, cc$$

We then eliminate the A-productions in a similar fashion to obtain:

$$S \rightarrow SbSba \,|\, Sbca \,|\, cSba \,|\, cca$$

We can now eliminate the direct left-recursion by rewriting the S-productions right-recursively in the following manner:

$$S \rightarrow cSbaS' \,\,|\,\, ccaS'$$
$$S' \rightarrow bSbaS' \,\,|\,\, bcaS' \,\,|\,\, \wedge$$

Here S' is a new nonterminal. The last grammar is not left-recursive. (Note, however, the last grammar is not LL(1).) Algorithms for eliminating left-recursion are given in Rosenkrantz [60] and Aho and Ullman [7].

Another useful technique for trying to make a grammar LL(1) is *left-factoring*. The transformation is to factor out common prefixes of right sides of productions with the same left side (see Stearns [67] and Wood [73]). For example, consider the grammar G_3:

$$S \longrightarrow bSeS \quad | \quad bS \quad | \quad a$$

Left-factored, the grammar becomes G_9:

$$S \longrightarrow bSS' \quad | \quad a$$
$$S' \longrightarrow eS \quad | \quad \wedge$$

Again, S' is a new nonterminal. G_9 is not LL(1) since it is still ambiguous. In fact, $L(G_3)$ is not an LL language, so any effort to try to transform G_3 into an LL(1) grammar is futile.

However, it is interesting to note that G_9 can be parsed by a predictive parser. If we try to construct a predictive parsing matrix for G_9, we find that $M(S', e) = \{S' \longrightarrow eS, S' \longrightarrow \wedge\}$ since $\text{FOLLOW}_1(S') = \{e, \wedge\}$. If we choose to make $M(S', e) = \{S' \longrightarrow eS\}$, then the resulting predictive parser using M would be a valid left parser for G_9 that would match each e with the closest unmatched b. This example shows that a predictive parser is capable of parsing non-LL grammars and languages. We can identify one such class of grammars.

Definition 6.4.4

Let A be a nonterminal symbol in a grammar $G = (N, \Sigma, P, S)$. We define the set-valued function $F(A)$ to be $\{X \mid X$ is in $(N \cup \Sigma)$ and there exists a left sentential form $wA\gamma X\delta$ such that $\gamma \overset{*}{\Rightarrow} \wedge\}$. G is said to be an *extended LL(1) grammar* if whenever $A \longrightarrow \alpha$ and $A \longrightarrow \beta$ are two distinct productions in P, the following three conditions are satisfied:

1. There is no terminal a such that both α and β derive strings beginning with a.
2. α and β cannot both derive $\wedge$.
3. If $\beta \overset{*}{\Rightarrow} \wedge$ and $\alpha \overset{*}{\Rightarrow} ax$ for some a in $\text{FOLLOW}_1(A)$, then for all X in $(F(A) - \{A\})$, X does not derive a string beginning with a.

Condition (3) says that the only reason a can appear in $\text{FOLLOW}_1(A)$ is that A appears in $F(A)$ and $A \overset{*}{\Rightarrow} ax$. Every LL(1) grammar is an extended

LL(1) grammar and G_9 is an example of a non-LL grammar that is an extended LL(1) grammar.

If we apply Algorithm 6.4.1 to an extended LL(1) grammar G we may get conflicts in the parsing action matrix involving pairs of productions of the form $A \rightarrow \alpha$ and $A \rightarrow \beta$ such that a is in $FOLLOW_1(A)$, $\alpha \overset{*}{\Rightarrow} ax$, and $\beta \overset{*}{\Rightarrow} \wedge$. If we always use the production $A \rightarrow \alpha$ for $M(A, a)$, then because of condition (3) a predictive parser using the resulting parsing matrix will be a valid left parser for G. See Aho, Johnson and Ullman [4] for more details.

EXERCISES 6.4

1. Construct a predictive parser for the grammar

$$S \rightarrow (S)\,S \quad | \quad \wedge$$

2. A grammar is said to be *simple* if each side of each right production begins with a terminal symbol and for each nonterminal A and for each terminal a there is at most one production of the form $A \rightarrow a\alpha$. Prove that every simple grammar is an LL(1) grammar.

3. Left factor G_2 and show that the resulting grammar is extended LL(1). Construct a valid parsing matrix for the extended grammar.

4. Show that the grammar

$$S \rightarrow A \quad | \quad B$$
$$A \rightarrow aAb \quad | \quad \wedge$$
$$B \rightarrow aBc \quad | \quad \wedge$$

is not LL(k) for any k.

5. Show that

$$\{a^n b^n \quad | \quad n \geq 0\} \cup \{a^n c^n \quad | \quad n \geq 0\}$$

is not an LL language.

6. Give an algorithm that will determine, given two LL(k) grammars G_1 and G_2, whether $L(G_1) = L(G_2)$.

6.5. LR PARSERS

Let us now consider the problem of trying to construct a right parser for a given grammar. This task is easier in that we can construct efficient right parsers for a larger class of grammars than for which we can construct efficient left parsers. However, as with left parsing, there is no known way to construct efficient right parsers for all grammars. In this section we shall describe an algorithm that will construct efficient right parsers for a subclass of grammars called the LR(k) grammars. These grammars, first defined by Knuth [40], generate precisely the deterministic context-free languages. They are also the largest natural class of unambiguous grammars for which we can construct deterministic "bottom-up" parsers. The term LR(k) stands for scanning the input from *left*-to-right, producing a *r*ight parse, using k-symbol lookahead to make parsing decisions.

We shall restrict ourselves to a special class of right parsers called LR(1) parsers. An LR(1) parser is shown schematically in Fig. 6.5.1. The parsing action table f and the goto table g dictate the moves of the parser.

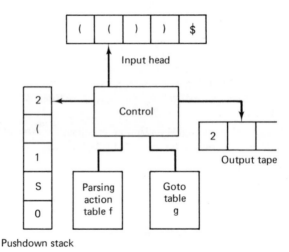

Fig. 6.5.1 Model of an LR(1) parser.

An LR(1) parser is a pushdown transducer that can pop a string of symbols off the pushdown list in one move. It has an input tape, a pushdown stack, and an output tape. The contents of the stack will at all times be a string of the form

$$s_0 X_1 s_1 X_2 s_2 \ldots X_m s_m$$

where each s_i is a *state* symbol and each X_i a grammar symbol.

An LR(1) parser behaves in the following manner. Suppose the stack contains $s_0 X_1 s_1 \ldots X_m s_m$. The control determines s_m, the state on top of the stack, and a, the current input symbol. The control then examines $f(s_m, a)$, the entry for s_m and a in the parsing action table. This entry can produce one of four different types of actions:

1. If $f(s_m, a) = \{$shift $s\}$, the parser first shifts the input symbol a to the top of the stack and then places state s on top of the stack. The input head is moved one square right. After this move the stack contains

$$s_0 X_1 s_1 \ldots X_m s_m \; as$$

2. If $f(s_m, a) = \{$reduce by production $A \rightarrow Y_1 Y_2 \ldots Y_r\}$, the parser pops $2r$ symbols from the stack, exposing state s_{m-r}. The control then consults $g(s_{m-r}, A)$, the entry for s_{m-r} and A in the goto table. If $g(s_{m-r}, A) = s$, the parser pushes As on top of the stack. The production $A \rightarrow Y_1 Y_2 \ldots Y_r$ is printed on the output tape. The input head is not moved. After this move, the stack contents are $s_0 X_1 s_1 \ldots X_{m-r} s_{m-r} As$.

3. If $f(s_m, a) = \{$accept$\}$, the parser halts and accepts the original input string.

4. If $f(s_m, a) = \{$error$\}$, or if the parser cannot excute one of the moves above, the parser declares error and transfers control to an error recovery routine.

An LR(1) parser starts off in an initial configuration in which the input tape contains the string to be parsed followed by \$, a right endmarker. The input head is over the leftmost square of the input tape. The stack contains only the initial state s_0 and the output tape is empty. The parser then makes moves until it either accepts the input or finds an error.

There is some terminology that is useful for describing the behavior of LR(k) parsers.

Definition 6.5.1

Let $S \overset{*}{\underset{rm}{\Rightarrow}} \alpha Ax \underset{rm}{\Rightarrow} \alpha\beta x$ be a rightmost derivation in a grammar G. The string β in the position shown is said to be a *handle* of the right sentential form $\alpha\beta x$. A prefix of $\alpha\beta$ is said to be a *viable prefix* of G.

Note that if G is unambiguous, the handle of each right sentential form is unique.

Example 6.5.1

Consider the grammar G_1 with productions

1. $S \rightarrow S(S)$
2. $S \rightarrow \wedge$

Parsing action and goto tables for G_1 are shown in Fig. 6.5.2. State 0 is the initial state.

	(	)	$
0	red 2	err	red 2
1	sh 2	err	acc
2	red 2	red 2	err
3	sh 4	sh 5	err
4	red 2	red 2	err
5	red 1	err	red 1
6	sh 4	sh 7	err
7	red 1	red 1	err

	S
0	1
1	err
2	3
3	err
4	6
5	err
6	err
7	err

Parsing Action Table *f*   Goto Table *g*

Fig. 6.5.2   LR parsing tables.

The notation sh *i* stands for shift and stack state *i*, red *i* for reduce by production numbered *i*, acc for accept, and err for error.

An LR parser operates by shifting symbols onto the stack until a handle β is on top of the stack. The parser then reduces the handle according to some production $A \rightarrow \beta$ by replacing β by A. The parser then shifts some more input symbols until a handle is again on top of the stack at which point the handle is reduced. The parser continues operating this way until it discovers an error or until it has reduced the entire input string to the start symbol.

Let us consider the LR parser using the table in Fig. 6.5.2 on input string (( )). The parser would make the following sequence of moves. The top of the stack is on the right. The position of the input head is indicated by ^.

	Stack	Unexpended Input	Output
Initially.	0	^(( ))$	
1.	0S1	^(( ))$	$S \rightarrow \wedge$
2.	0S1(2	(^( ))$	
3.	0S1(2S3	(^( ))$	$S \rightarrow \wedge$
4.	0S1(2S3(4	^))$	
5.	0S1(2S3(4S6	^))$	$S \rightarrow \wedge$
6.	0S1(2S3(4S6)7	^)$	
7.	0S1(2S3	^)$	$S \rightarrow S(S)$
8.	0S1(2S3)5	^$	
9.	0S1	^$	$S \rightarrow S(S)$
			accept

The derivation tree for (( )) is shown in Fig. 6.5.3. The subscripts on the vertices refer to the moves made by the LR parser above.

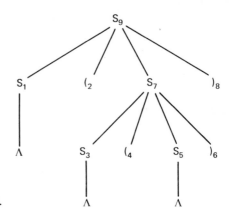

Fig. 6.5.3 Derivation tree for (( )).

Let us go through the moves made by the parser.

0. On input (, state 0 knows that the empty string on top of the stack is the handle. Thus on the first move the parser reduces the empty string to S using production $S \longrightarrow \wedge$. The parser then places state 1 on top of the stack.

1. The parser shifts the current input symbol (onto the stack and enters state 2.

2. On input (, state 2 knows that the empty string on top of the stack is the handle of the viable prefix S (. Thus the parser reduces the empty string to S and enters state 3.

3. The parser shifts (onto the stack and enters state 4.

4. The parser reduces the empty string to S and enters state 6.

5. The parser shifts) onto the stack and enters state 7.

6. The stack now contains the viable prefix S (S (S). State 7 knows that the top four grammar symbols on the stack form the handle of the viable prefix S (S (S). Thus the parser pops eight symbols off the stack, exposing state 2. Since $g(2, S) = 3$, the parser places S and then state 3 on the stack.

7. The parser shifts) onto the stack and enters state 5.

8. The parser reduces the handle $S(S)$ to S. Since $g(0, S) = 1$, the parser pushes state 1 on the stack.

9. On input $, state 1 calls for the accept action.

As is evident, the LR(1) parser constructs the derivation tree for (( )) in postfix Polish order. Each time a reduction is made, a production is output so if the parser accepts the input, it will have printed out a right parse.

Note that at all times, the grammar symbols on the stack make up a viable prefix. This viable prefix followed by the input symbols to the right of the input head (including the symbol under the input head) make up a right sentential form. Thus, this LR parser traces out in reverse a rightmost derivation for the input string. We can prove that this parser accepts an input string w if and only if there is a rightmost derivation for w in G_1. Doing so, we would prove the parser is a right parser for G_1.

Let f be a parsing action table and g a goto table. We say f and g are *valid* for grammar G if the LR(1) parser with f and g is a right parser for G.

We shall now show how to construct valid action and goto tables for a large class of grammars called the LR(1) grammars.

Definition 6.5.2

Let $G = (N, \Sigma, P, S)$ be a grammar. G', the *augmented grammar,* is the grammar $(N \cup \{S'\}, \Sigma, P \cup \{S' \rightarrow S\}, S')$. G' is merely G with a new start symbol S' and a new starting production $S' \rightarrow S$. A reduction according to this production serves to signal successful completion of parsing.

G is said to be LR(k) if whenever we have in G' two rightmost derivations of the form

1. $S' \underset{rm}{\overset{*}{\Rightarrow}} \alpha A x \underset{rm}{\Rightarrow} \alpha \beta x$
2. $S' \underset{rm}{\overset{*}{\Rightarrow}} \gamma B y \underset{rm}{\Rightarrow} \gamma \delta y$

such that $\gamma \delta y = \alpha \beta z$ for some z and $\text{FIRST}_k(x) = \text{FIRST}_k(z)$, then $\gamma B y = \alpha A z$ (i.e., $\gamma = \alpha$, $B = A$, and $y = z$).

Stated less formally, this definition says three things.

1. It says that the handle β of a right sentential form $\alpha \beta x$ is uniquely determined by $\alpha \beta$ and $\text{FIRST}_k(x)$.
2. It says that the production $A \rightarrow \beta$ which is to be used to reduce the handle is uniquely determined by $\alpha \beta$ and $\text{FIRST}_k(x)$.
3. It says that if $\alpha \beta x = S$, then we can announce completion of parsing.

If $\alpha \beta x$ and $\alpha \beta z$ are two right sentential forms in an LR(k) grammar in which $\text{FIRST}_k(x) = \text{FIRST}_k(z)$, and if β is the handle of $\alpha \beta x$, then we know that β is also the handle of $\alpha \beta z$. Moreover, if $A \rightarrow \beta$ is used to reduce the handle in $\alpha \beta x$, then $A \rightarrow \beta$ is also the production to use to reduce the handle in $\alpha \beta z$. From these observations we can prove:

Theorem 6.5.1

Every LR(k) grammar is unambiguous.

An LR(k) *item* for a grammar G is an object of the form

$$[A \rightarrow \alpha.\beta, w]$$

where $A \longrightarrow \alpha\beta$ is a production of the augmented grammar G', and w is a string of terminal symbols of length at most k called the "lookahead" string.

Intuitively, an item of this form will be used to indicate that when an LR parser is in a state associated with this item, the parser has just seen a portion of the input string derivable from α and that the parser now expects the input string to contain a substring derivable from βw.

We define two functions on sets of items. The first of these is the "closure" of a set of items.

If I is a set of items for a grammar G, CLOSURE(I) is the smallest set of items that contains I and has the following property. If $[A \longrightarrow \alpha . B\gamma, x]$ is in CLOSURE(I) and $B \longrightarrow \beta$ is a production, then $[B \longrightarrow .\beta, y]$ is also an item in CLOSURE(I) for all y in $\text{FIRST}_k(\gamma x)$.

An easy way to compute CLOSURE(I) is the following:

1. For each item of the form $[A \longrightarrow \alpha.B\gamma, x]$ currently in I, for each production $B \longrightarrow \beta$ in G, and for each string y in $\text{FIRST}_k(\gamma x)$, add the item $[B \longrightarrow .\beta, y]$ to I, provided this item is not already in I.

2. Continue adding items to I according to (1) until no more new items can be added.

3. The resulting set is CLOSURE(I).

The second function, called the GOTO function, takes two arguments, a set of items and a grammar symbol.

If I is a set of items and X a grammar symbol, then GOTO$(I, X) = J$, where J is the closure of the set of items

$$\{[A \longrightarrow \alpha X.\beta, x] \,|\, [A \longrightarrow \alpha.X\beta, x] \text{ is in } I\}$$

Computing GOTO(I, X) is straightforward. We take each item in I with the grammar symbol X immediately to the right of the dot. We move the dot to the right of the X and add the resulting item to J. We then compute CLOSURE(J).

To construct parsing action and goto tables for a given grammar G, we first construct a collection of sets of items for G. The following algorithm can be used to construct what is known as the canonical collection of sets of items for G.

Algorithm 6.5.1   Construction of the Canonical Collection of Sets of LR(k) Items

Input: A grammar $G = (N, \Sigma, P, S)$.
Output: A collection C of sets of $LR(k)$ items for G.
Method:

1. Augment G with the new starting production $S' \longrightarrow S$.

2. Let C initially contain the set of items $I_0 = \text{CLOSURE}(\{[S' \longrightarrow .S,$ $\wedge]\})$.

3. For each set of items I currently in C and for each grammar symbol X, compute $J = \text{GOTO}(I, X)$. Add J to C if it is not already there.

4. Repeat step (3) until no more new sets of items can be added to C.

Example 6.5.2

Let us compute the canonical collection of sets of LR(1) items for G_1. We begin the computation by forming the closure of the initial set of items $I_0 = \{[S' \longrightarrow .S, \wedge]\}$. Since $S \longrightarrow S(S)$ and $S \longrightarrow \wedge$ are S-productions, we must add the items $[S \longrightarrow .S(S), \wedge]$ and $[S \longrightarrow ., \wedge]$ to I_0. Because $[S \longrightarrow .S(S), \wedge]$ is now in I_0, we must add $[S \longrightarrow .S(S), (]$ and $[S \longrightarrow ., (]$ to I_0. No more new items can be added to I_0.

We now compute $I_1 = \text{GOTO}(I_0, S)$, and so on. The resulting collection of sets of items is shown in Fig. 6.5.4. The notation $[A \longrightarrow \alpha.\beta, x/y]$ is short for the two items $[A \longrightarrow \alpha.\beta, x]$ and $[A \longrightarrow \alpha.\beta, y]$. The GOTO function is shown in Fig. 6.5.5.

I_0:	$[S' \rightarrow .S,$	$\wedge]$
	$[S \rightarrow .S(S),$	$\wedge/(]$
	$[S \rightarrow .,$	$\wedge/(]$
I_1:	$[S' \rightarrow S.,$	$\wedge]$
	$[S \rightarrow S.(S),$	$\wedge/(]$
I_2:	$[S \rightarrow S(.S),$	$\wedge/(]$
	$[S \rightarrow .S(S),$	$)/(]$
	$[S \rightarrow .,$	$)/(]$
I_3:	$[S \rightarrow S(S.),$	$\wedge/(]$
	$[S \rightarrow S.(S),$	$)/(]$
I_4:	$[S \rightarrow S(.S),$	$)/(]$
	$[S \rightarrow .S(S),$	$)/(]$
	$[S \rightarrow .,$	$)/(]$
I_5:	$[S \rightarrow S(S).,$	$\wedge/(]$
I_6:	$[S \rightarrow S(S.),$	$)/(]$
	$[S \rightarrow S.(S),$	$)/(]$
I_7:	$[S \rightarrow S(S).,$	$)/(]$

	S	$($	$)$
I_0	I_1	—	—
I_1	—	I_2	—
I_2	I_3	—	—
I_3	—	I_4	I_5
I_4	I_6	—	—
I_5	—	—	—
I_6	—	I_4	I_7
I_7	—	—	—

Fig. 6.5.4 Canonical collection of sets of LR(1) items for G_1.

Fig. 6.5.5 GOTO function.

From a collection of sets of LR(1) items for a grammar G, we can construct parsing action and goto tables for G using the following algorithm. The algorithm may cause some entries of the parsing action table to be multiply defined. However, if the collection of sets of items is the canonical collection of sets of items for an LR(1) grammar, then each entry of the parsing action table and goto table will be uniquely defined.

Algorithm 6.5.2   Construction of LR(1) Parsing Action and Goto Tables

Input: C, a collection of sets of LR(1) items for a grammar G.

Output: A parsing action table f, and a goto table g.

Method: Let $C = \{I_0, I_1, \ldots, I_n\}$. With set of items I_i we shall associate state i. For $i = 0, 1, \ldots, n$ we construct the parsing actions for state i from I_i as follows:

1. If $[A \longrightarrow \alpha.a\beta, x]$ is in I_i and $\text{GOTO}(I_i, a) = I_s$, then add "shift s" to $f(i, a)$. (a is a terminal here.)

2. If $[A \longrightarrow \alpha., a]$ is in I_i and $A \neq S'$, then add "reduce by $A \longrightarrow \alpha$" to $f(i, a)$. If $a = \wedge$, then instead add "reduce by $A \longrightarrow \alpha$" to $f(i, \$)$.

3. If $[S' \longrightarrow S., \wedge]$ is in I_i, then add "accept" to $f(i, \$)$.

4. If $f(i, a)$ is not defined by (1)–(3) above, then make $f(i, a) = \{\text{error}\}$.

The goto table g is constructed as follows:

1. If $\text{GOTO}(I_i, A) = I_s$, then $g(i, A) = s$.

2. Otherwise, $g(i, A) = $ "error."

The initial state is the one constructed from the set containing the item $[S' \longrightarrow .S, \wedge]$.

If Algorithm 6.5.2 is applied to the canonical collection of sets of LR(1) items for G, then the resulting parsing action and goto tables are called *canonical*.

Example 6.5.3

The parsing action and goto tables shown in Fig. 10 are the canonical tables for G_1.

Theorem 6.5.2

Algorithm 6.5.2 produces a parsing action table and a goto table with unique entries if and only if the given grammar G is LR(1).

Thus, Algorithm 6.5.2 can be used to test whether a grammar is LR(1). Note that G_1 is LR(1) but G_1 is not LL(k) for any k since it is left-recursive.

An LR(1) parser that uses the canonical parsing action and goto tables for an LR(1) grammar G is said to be the *canonical LR(1) parser* for G.

Theorem 6.5.3

A canonical LR(1) parser for LR(1) grammar G is a right parser for G.

Canonical LR(1) parsers are fast, in that they will parse an input string of length n in cn moves for some constant c. In addition canonical LR(1) parsers possess good error detecting capabilities. They can find an error in an input string at the earliest possible opportunity.

Theorem 6.5.4

Suppose $wabx$ is a sentence in $L(G)$ for some $LR(1)$ grammar $G = (N, \Sigma, P, S)$, but for all y in Σ^*, $wacy$ is not. With input wac a canonical $LR(1)$ parser announces error as soon as it sees the erroneous input symbol c.

Unfortunately canonical $LR(1)$ parsers tend to be extremely large even for medium sized grammars (grammars with 40 nonterminals and 100 productions, say) and the amount of computation and memory space needed to produce the canonical action and goto tables is excessive. Because of these difficulties, a number of people have considered alternate methods of producing more practical $LR(1)$ parsers. For programming language grammars these techniques require substantially less computation and produce parsers that have significantly fewer states than the canonical $LR(1)$ parsers. Although many of these techniques work only on proper subsets of the $LR(1)$ grammars, the classes of grammars on which they do work include many grammars of practical interest. In this section we shall consider the Lookahead LR (LALR for short) and Simple LR (SLR for short) techniques of DeRemer [21]. The SLR technique is recommended for hand computation.

Definition 6.5.3

Let I be a set of items. $\mathrm{CORE}(I)$ is the set

$$\{[A \rightarrow \alpha.\beta] \mid [A \rightarrow \alpha.\beta, w] \text{ is in } I\}$$

i.e., the set of first components of items in I.

Definition 6.5.4

An *LALR(1) collection of sets of items* for grammar G is one that would be produced by Algorithm 6.5.1 if we replaced step (3) by the following:

3'. For each set of items I currently in C and for each grammar symbol X, we compute $J = \mathrm{GOTO}(I, X)$. If $\mathrm{CORE}(J) \neq \mathrm{CORE}(I')$ for all I' currently in C, we add J to C. If $\mathrm{CORE}(J) = \mathrm{CORE}(I')$ for some I' in C, we replace I' in C by $I' \cup J$.

If Algorithm 6.5.2 produces a parsing action table and a goto table with unique entries from the LALR(1) collection of sets of items for grammar G, then G is said to be an *LALR(1) grammar*.

Grammar G_1 is an LALR(1) grammar. Clearly, every LALR(1) grammar is an $LR(1)$ grammar, but the converse is not true.

Example 6.5.4

Grammar G_{10} with productions

$$S \longrightarrow Aa \mid dAb \mid Bb \mid dBa$$
$$A \longrightarrow c$$
$$B \longrightarrow c$$

is an LR(1) grammar that is not LALR(1). See [10].

An *SLR (1) collection of sets of items* for G is one produced by the following algorithm.

Algorithm 6.5.3   Construction of SLR(1) Collection of Sets of Items

Input: Grammar $G = (N, \Sigma, P, S)$.
Output: The SLR(1) collection of sets of items for G.
Method:

1. Construct C the canonical collection of LR(0) items for G. (The second component of an LR(0) item is always the empty string.)
2. Let I be a set of items in C. Let $I' = \{[A \longrightarrow \alpha.\beta, a] \mid [A \longrightarrow \alpha.\beta, \wedge]$ is in I and a is in $FOLLOW_1(a)\}$.
3. Let $C' = \{I' \mid I$ is in $C\}$.

If Algorithm 6.5.2 produces a parsing action table and a goto table with unique entries from the SLR(1) collection of sets of items for G, then G is said to be an SLR(1) grammar.

Example 6.5.5

The SLR(1) collection of sets of items for G_1 is shown in Fig. 6.5.6. The second components of the items are computed from $FOLLOW(S') = \{\wedge\}$ and $FOLLOW_1(S) = \{(,), \wedge\}$. The SLR(1) parsing action and goto tables for G_1 are shown in Fig. 6.5.7.

An SLR parser will have the same number of states as an LALR parser. The primary distinction between the LALR technique and the SLR technique is the manner in which the lookahead symbols of items are computed. In the

I_0: $S' \rightarrow .S$
      $S \rightarrow .S(S)$
      $S \rightarrow .$
I_1: $S' \rightarrow S.$ *
      $S \rightarrow S.(S)$
I_2: $S \rightarrow S(.S)$
      $S \rightarrow .S(S)$
      $S \rightarrow .$
I_3: $S \rightarrow S(S.)$
      $S \rightarrow S.(S)$
I_5: $S \rightarrow S(S).$

Fig. 6.5.6   SLR(1) collection of sets of items for G.

	(	)	$
0	red 2	red 2	red 2
1	sh 2	err	acc
2	red 2	red 2	red 2
3	sh 2	sh 5	err
5	red 1	red 1	red 1

	$
0	1
1	err
2	3
3	err
5	err

Parsing Action Table f Goto Table g

Fig. 6.5.7   SLR(1) parsing action and goto tables.

SLR method we always use $FOLLOW_1(A)$ as the lookahead set for a completed item of the form $[A \rightarrow \alpha.]$. $FOLLOW_1(A)$ however may contain input symbols on which the reduction by this production is not applicable in certain states. In the LALR technique the set of lookahead symbols for each completed item contains only symbols on which the reduction is applicable. The following example shows a grammar for which the SLR(1) technique will fail to produce an LR parser but for which the LALR(1) technique will succeed.

Example 6.5.6

Grammar G_{11} with productions

$$S \rightarrow Aa \mid dAb \mid cb \mid dca$$
$$A \rightarrow c$$

is an LALR(1) grammar that is not SLR(1). The reason for this is that the SLR(1) collection will contain the set of items with core

$$S \rightarrow c.b$$
$$A \rightarrow c.$$

Since $FOLLOW_1(A) = \{a, b\}$, this set of items will give rise to a shift-reduce conflict. The LALR(1) algorithm will not put b into the lookahead set of the completed item $[A \rightarrow c.]$ in this set of items.

If G is an LALR(1) grammar or SLR(1) grammar, respectively, then an LALR(1) or SLR(1) parser is a right parser for G. It can be shown that, like the canonical LR(1) parser, both the LALR(1) and SLR(1) parsers will always have only a viable prefix of grammar symbols on the stack. Thus, an LALR(1) and an SLR(1) parser will also always detect an error at the earliest possible position in an input string. However, unlike the canonical LR(1) parser, an LALR(1) and an SLR(1) parser may make several reductions before reporting error.

Example 6.5.7

Let us consider the behavior of an LR(1) parser on the erroneous input string ( )), first using the canonical tables of Fig. 6.5.2, and second the SLR(1) tables of Fig. 6.5.7.

1. *With tables of Fig. 6.5.2:*

Stack	Unexpended Input	Output
0	( ))$	—
0S1	( ))$	$S \rightarrow \wedge$
0S1(2	))$	—
0S1(2S3	))$	$S \rightarrow \wedge$
0S1(2S3)5	)$	—
		error

2. *With tables of Fig. 6.5.7:*

Stack	Unexpended Input	Output
0	( ))$	—
0S1	( ))$	$S \rightarrow \wedge$
0S1 (2	))$	—
0S1 (2S3	))$	$S \rightarrow \wedge$
0S1 (2S3)5	)$	—
0S1	)$	$S \rightarrow S(S)$
		error

Note that in the second case, the LR parser calls for a reduction by the production $S \rightarrow S(S)$ before announcing error.

Korenjak [43] considers a somewhat more general technique to construct practical LR(1) parsers. His method is based on partitioning a grammar into smaller subgrammars, constructing LR(1) parsers for the subgrammars, and then combining the parsers to derive a parser for the entire grammar. The details of his method are described in [43] and [10].

EXERCISES 6.5

1. Construct the canonical LR(1) and LALR(1) parsers for G_0.

2. Show that G_2 is not an LR(1) grammar.

3. Show that G_{10} is an LR(1) grammar that is not LALR(1).

4. Show that G_{11} is an LALR(1) grammar that is not SLR(1).

*5. Show that every LL(k) grammar is LR(k).

6.6. OPTIMIZATION OF LR(1) PARSERS

A number of methods have been developed to make LR parsers smaller and faster. Some of these methods are extensions of state minimization techniques for finite automata. For instance, we can define a notion of compatibility on the states of an LR parser and then merge states in the same compatibility class (see Pager [57], Aho and Ullman [8] and Jolliat [39]).

The number of compatible states can be increased if we notice that all error entries in a canonical LR(1), LALR(1), or SLR(1) goto table are never consulted by an LR(1) parser. We call such error entries *don't care entries*. Certain of the error entries in a canonical LR(1), LALR(1), or SLR(1) parsing action table are also don't cares. For example, in a canonical LR(1) parsing action table, all error actions that arise only after reduce moves are don't cares. In an LALR(1) or SLR(1) parsing action table, a certain subset of these error entries are don't cares (see Aho and Ullman [11]).

Another technique for increasing the number of compatible states is to replace certain error entries in the parsing action table by reduce entries. For example, suppose $f(i, a) = \{$reduce by $A \longrightarrow \alpha\}$ in some canonical LR(1), LALR(1), or SLR(1) parsing action table. Then we may replace all error entries for state i in that parsing action table by "reduce by $A \longrightarrow \alpha$." This may cause the modified LR(1) parser to make a sequence of reductions, where the unmodified parser announced error. However, the parser will announce error before it shifts another input symbol on to the stack. Thus, by occasionally postponing error detection in time (but not in space) we can often increase the number of compatible states. In fact, we can show that both the LALR(1) parser and the SLR(1) parser can be obtained from the canonical LR(1) parser by delaying error detection and merging compatible states. Details of the proof can be found in Aho and Ullman [8].

Jolliat [39] considers a further extension of this approach by replacing all error entries by don't cares. On each move his parser consults a Boolean function to determine if an entry is an error entry.

Another optimization technique which is useful in practice is to eliminate reductions by productions of the form $A \longrightarrow B$ where A and B are nonterminals. Productions of this form are called *single* productions. If no semantic action is associated with a single production, then we do not care whether a parser actually carries out the reduction according to the single production.

A large number of single productions arise in a grammar when a grammar is used to describe the associativities and precedence levels of operators. Apart from enforcing these associativities and precedence levels, such single productions serve no other function. We can cause an LR(1) parser to avoid making reductions by these semantically insignificant single productions, and by doing so we make the parser faster and reduce the number of states.

For example, let us consider the simple LR(1) parser for G_0. It would parse the input string $a + a * a$, making the reductions shown in Fig. 6.6.1.

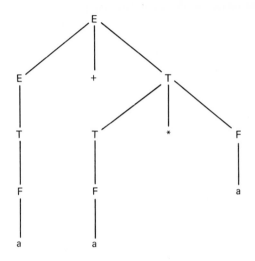

Fig. 6.6.1   Derivation tree for $a + a * a$.

The leading a is reduced to an E by a sequence of three reductions. The second a is reduced to a T by a sequence of two reductions.

We can modify the LR parser so it will reduce the leading a to an E in one reduction. The second a would be reduced to T in one reduction. By making these modifications, the parser would run faster since it makes fewer reductions.

To appreciate the significance of this type of optimization, we should bear in mind that many programming languages have operators on ten or more different precedence levels. If an LR(1) grammar is used to specify the associativities and precedence levels of the operators, the grammar would have ten or more single productions for this purpose. Since expressions are usually the basic building blocks of statements in a programming language, an unoptimized parser for such a language would spend a significant portion of its time just making reductions by single productions.

There is an algorithmic way to modify the parsing action and goto tables to eliminate reductions by single productions of this nature (see Aho and Ullman [11]). However, by using an ambiguous grammar to specify expressions, we can directly construct from this grammar parsing action and goto tables that perform no unnecessary reductions by single productions. We shall illustrate this technique by means of an example.

We recall that the grammar G_5 with productions:

1. $E \longrightarrow E + E$
2. $E \longrightarrow E * E$
3. $E \longrightarrow (E)$
4. $E \longrightarrow a$

is ambiguous but generates the same language as G_0. Suppose we attempt to construct an SLR(1) parser for G_5. We would obtain the SLR(1) sets of items shown in Fig. 6.6.2. The second components, not shown, can be computed from $FOLLOW_1(E') = \{\wedge\}$ and $FOLLOW_1(E) = \{+, *,), \wedge\}$.

I_0:	$E' \rightarrow .E$	I_5:	$E \rightarrow E * .E$
	$E \rightarrow .E + E$		$E \rightarrow .E + E$
	$E \rightarrow .E * E$		$E \rightarrow .E * E$
	$E \rightarrow .(E)$		$E \rightarrow .(E)$
	$E \rightarrow .a$		$E \rightarrow .a$
I_1:	$E' \rightarrow E.$	I_6:	$E \rightarrow (E.)$
	$E \rightarrow E. + E$		$E \rightarrow E. + E$
	$E \rightarrow E. * E$		$E \rightarrow E. * E$
I_2:	$E \rightarrow (.E)$	I_7:	$E \rightarrow E + E.$
	$E \rightarrow .E + E$		$E \rightarrow E. + E$
	$E \rightarrow .E * E$		$E \rightarrow E. * E$
	$E \rightarrow .(E)$	I_8:	$E \rightarrow E * E.$
	$E \rightarrow .a$		$E \rightarrow E. + E$
I_3:	$E \rightarrow a.$		$E \rightarrow E. * E$
I_4:	$E \rightarrow E + .E$	I_9:	$E \rightarrow (E).$
	$E \rightarrow .E + E$		
	$E \rightarrow .E * E$		
	$E \rightarrow .(E)$		
	$E \rightarrow .a$		

Fig. 6.6.2 SLR(1) sets of items for G_5.

We can try to construct the parsing action and goto tables from these sets of items. However, I_7 and I_8 give rise to entries in the action table with more than one action. These multiply-defined entries are in the parsing action table in states 7 and 8 on inputs $+$ and $*$.

	Action Table						Goto Table
	$+$	$*$	$($	$)$	a	$\$$	E
0	err	err	sh 2	err	sh·3	err	1
1	sh 4	sh 5	err	err	err	acc	
2	err	err	sh 2	err	sh 3	err	6
3	red 4	red 4	err	red 4	err	red 4	
4	err	err	sh 2	err	sh 3	err	7
5	err	err	sh 2	err	sh 3	err	8
6	sh 4	sh 5	err	sh 9	err	err	
7	sh 4, red 1	sh 5, red 1	err	red 1	err	red 1	
8	sh 4, red 2	sh 5, red 2	err	red 2	err	red 2	
9	red 3	red 3	err	red 3	err	red 3	

Fig. 6.6.3 Parsing action and goto tables for G_5.

Each of the multiply defined-entries in the action tables represents a shift-reduce conflict. Since G_5 is ambiguous, these multiply-defined entries represent the different possible associativities and precedence levels of the operators + and *.

For example, let us consider the entry $f(7, +)$. The LR parser will enter state 7 when it has just seen a portion of the input string that has been reduced into $E + E$. When the next input symbol is +, the parser does not know whether to reduce the $E + E$ it has already seen into an E, or to shift + onto the stack and continue looking for another E. The decision to reduce would be correct if + were left-associative; the shift decision would be correct if + were right-associative. For example, if we use the entry

$$\text{reduce by } E \to E + E$$

for $f(7, +)$, then the input string $a + a + a$ would be parsed left-associatively as shown in Fig. 6.6.4. On the other hand if we used the entry "shift 4" for $f(7, +)$, the same input string would be parsed right-associatively as shown in Fig. 6.6.5. We could also make $f(7, +) = \{\text{error}\}$. Doing so would make + a nonassociating operator like .LT. in FORTRAN. The input string $a + a + a$ would be syntactically invalid.

Thus, the question of how we should resolve the parsing action conflicts in the entry $f(7, +)$ can be answered once we know the associativity of the + operator.

Let us now examine the entry $f(7, *)$. Similar reasoning shows that if we wish to make + of lower precedence than *, i.e., we want $a + a * a$ to be parsed as $a + (a * a)$, then $f(7, *)$ should be "shift 5"; if we want $a + a * a$ to be treated as $(a + a) * a$, then $f(7, *)$ should be "reduce 1." We also have the option of forbidding * from following + by making $f(7, *) = \{\text{error}\}$.

State 8 will be on top of the stack when the parser has seen a portion of the

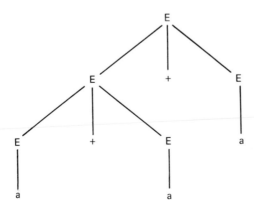

Fig. 6.6.4　Left-associative parsing.

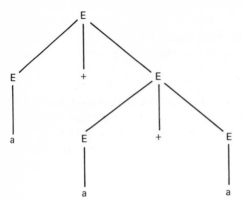

Fig. 6.6.5   Right-associative parsing.

input that is reducible to $E * E$. The resolution of the entry $f(8, *)$ is dictated by the associativity of the $*$ operator; the resolution of the entry $f(8, +)$ by the relative precedence of $*$ followed by $+$.

Thus, if we use G_5 to specify arithmetic expressions along with the disambiguating rule:

1. $+$ is left-associative
2. $*$ is left-associative
3. $+$ has lower precedence than $*$

then we can construct a deterministic LR(1) parser for G. The multiply-defined entries would be resolved in the following manner:

$$f(7, +) = \{\text{reduce by } E \rightarrow E + E\}$$
$$f(7, *) = \{\text{shift 5}\}$$
$$f(8, +) = \{\text{reduce by } E \rightarrow E * E\}$$
$$f(8, *) = \{\text{reduce by } E \rightarrow E * E\}$$

The resulting parser is shown in Fig. 6.6.6.

| | \multicolumn{6}{c}{Action Table} | Goto Table |
	$+$	$*$	$($	$)$	a	$\$$	E
0	err	err	sh 2	err	sh 3	err	1
1	sh 4	sh 5	err	err	err	acc	
2	err	err	sh 2	err	sh 3	err	6
3	red 4	red 4	err	red 4	err	red 4	
4	err	err	sh 2	err	sh 3	err	7
5	err	err	sh 2	err	sh 3	err	8
6	sh 4	sh 5	err	sh 9	err	err	
7	red 1	sh 5	err	red 1	err	red 1	
8	red 2	red 2	err	red 2	err	red 2	
9	red 3	red 3	err	red 3	err	red 3	

Fig. 6.6.6   Parsing action and goto tables for G_5.

We can show that the resulting parser behaves as an SLR(1) parser for G_0 in which reductions by chains of single productions have been eliminated. For example, we would parse the input string $a + a * a$ as follows:

Stack	Unexpended Input	Output
0	$\hat{a} + a * a\$$	
$0a3$	$\hat{+} a * a\$$	
$0E1$	$\hat{+} a * a\$$	$E \rightarrow a$
$0E1 + 4$	$\hat{a} * a\$$	
$0E1 + 4a3$	$\hat{*} a\$$	
$0E1 + 4E7$	$\hat{*} a\$$	$E \rightarrow a$
$0E1 + 4E7 * 5$	$\hat{a}\$$	
$0E1 + 4E7 * 5a3$	$\hat{\$}$	
$0E1 + 4E7 * 5E8$	$\hat{\$}$	$E \rightarrow a$
$0E1 + 4E7$	$\hat{\$}$	$E \rightarrow E * E$
$0E1$	$\hat{\$}$	$E \rightarrow E + E$
		accept

The corresponding derivation tree is the one in Fig. 6.3.5 (right). We see that we have the parsing we want, and that reductions by chains of single productions have been eliminated.

Aho, Johnson and Ullman [4] discuss some of the advantages of using ambiguous grammars in the specification of certain syntactic constructs in programming languages. Demers [20] discusses in more depth the construction of LR parsers for certain ambiguous grammars.

We shall mention one other optimization of LR parsers which concerns the physical representation of the parsing action and goto tables. Representing the parsing action and goto tables directly as tables requires a large amount of space. Since many of the entries in parsing action and goto tables are don't cares, we can reduce the space requirement if we encode the entries in the tables as lists.

One convenient encoding is to represent each row of the parsing action table as a sequence of pairs of the form

$$\text{if input} = a \text{ parsing action}$$

For example, the first row of the parsing action table of Fig. 6.6.6 can be represented in the following manner.

0:	if input = +	error
	if input = *	error
	if input = (	shift 2
	if input =)	error
	if input = a	shift 3
	if input = \$	error

To utilize this representation of the action table, the LR parser would use a linear search to find the appropriate action. For example, if the parser had state 0 on top of the stack and the current input symbol was a, then the parser would scan down the first components of the pairs of the list for state 0 until it had found the pair with input symbol a. The parser would then take the action specified by the second component of the pair.

With this type of behavior, there are several simple techniques for saving sizeable amounts of space. One such technique is to rearrange the order of the pairs in a list and to combine pairs with the same parsing action into one common entry. Applying this strategy to state 0 we obtain:

> 0:   if input = (shift 2
>
>   if input = a shift 3
>
>   error

Here the nonerror entries have been listed first. All error entries have been collected into one simple statment "error" which is an abbreviation for the unconditional statement

> if input = any symbol   error

States that have reduce actions can be subject to more extensive modifications. Recall that if a state contains at least one reduce action, then all error entries in that state can be replaced by that reduce action without affecting the position in the input string at which errors are detected. Thus, state 3, for example, can be simply encoded as

> 3:   reduce by $E \longrightarrow a$

which is an abbreviation for

> 3:   if input = any symbol reduce by $E \longrightarrow a$

Thus, a good general rule is to list for each state first the shift actions, then the accept actions, then the reduce actions, and finally the error actions. If there is at least one reduce action, then the last entry in the state can be an unconditional reduce action and no error entries need be listed.

States with the same actions can be identified. With these guidelines, we can produce the following representation for the parsing action table of Fig. 6.6.6.

Now let us consider the representation of the goto table as a list of pairs. One advantageous way is to represent each column of the goto table as a list. Since all error entries in an SRL(1) goto table are don't cares, only the nonerror entries need be listed. For example, the goto table of Fig. 6.6.6 would become

E: if current state $= 0$ new state becomes 1

                 if current state $= 2$ new state becomes 6

                 if current state $= 4$ new state becomes 7

                 if current state $= 5$ new state becomes 8

Entries can be rearranged if desired. In addition, whenever the goto table is consulted in an SLR parser, the entry found will never be an error entry. Thus, the final entry can be made an unconditional entry.

A number of other optimizations can be applied to this type of representation of a parser. Some of these are mentioned in Aho and Johnson [3] and Ichbiah and Morse [34].

Several other ways of representing LR parsers have been studied. The interested reader is referred to DeRemer [20], Lalonde, Lee and Horning [45] Aho and Ullman [11], Anderson, Eve and Horning [12].

5:4:2:0:	if input $= ($	shift 2
	if input $= a$	shift 3
	error	
1:	if input $= +$	shift 4
	if input $= *$	shift 5
	if input $= \$$	accept
	error	
3:	reduce by E → a	
6:	if input $= +$	shift 4
	if input $= *$	shift 5
	if input $=)$	shift 9
	error	
7:	if input $= *$	shift 5
	reduce by E → E + E	
8:	reduce by E → E * E	
9:	reduce by E → (E)	

Fig. 6.6.7 Representation of parsing action table of Fig. 6.6.6.

EXERCISES 6.6

1. Construct (a) a canonical LR(1), (b) an LALR(1), and (c) an SLR(1) parser for G_0. Identify the don't care entries in each parser.

2. We say two states s and s' are *compatible* if whenever the parsing action table or goto table entries of s and s' disagree, one of the entries is a don't care. Find all compatible states in the parsers of Exercise 1.

3. By replacing certain error entries by reduce entries and then merging compatible states, show that:
   (a) The LALR(1) parser for G_0 can be obtained from the canonical LR(1) parser for G_0.
   (b) The SLR(1) parser for G_0 can be obtained from the LALR(1) parser for G_0.

4. Devise an algorithm to eliminate reductions by single productions in an LR parser. Apply your algorithm to one of the parsers of Exercise 1.

5. Devise other optimizations that can be used to reduce the size of an LR parser.

6.7. ERROR RECOVERY

When a parser finds an error, it transfers control to an error recovery routine that attempts to resynchronize the parser so that normal parsing can resume. In this section we shall very briefly examine some of the strategies that such an error recovery routine might use.

We shall assume that there are three different types of syntax error: replacement errors, insertion errors, and deletion errors. Each of these errors can be considered as transformations on input strings. A replacement error is the substitution of an erroneous symbol for a correct symbol, an insertion error the introduction of an extraneous character, and a deletion error the removal of a symbol. Other types of errors could be defined (e.g., transposition errors) but these three types of errors are sufficient for our purposes here.

We say that a syntactically incorrect string x has k errors if a sequence of k replacements, insertions, or deletions transforms x into a syntactically valid string. The positions at which these transformations are applied to x define (nonuniquely) the positions of the errors in x. Of course, for certain erroneous input strings, we can never be certain what errors have been made and where they have been made without knowing what input string was intended. For example, presented with an erroneous expression such as $a +)$, we cannot be sure of even how many errors have been made.

When a canonical LL or LR parser for a grammar G announces an error at some position i in an input string x, we know that the first $i - 1$ symbols of x form a prefix of some sentence in $L(G)$ but that the first i symbols of x are the prefix of no sentence in $L(G)$. We also know with certainty that at least one error has occurred somewhere within the first i symbols of x, but unfortunately we do not know where the error or errors have occurred nor do we know what type of errors they are.

We would like an error recovery routine, when presented with an error situation, to restore the parser to a configuration from which normal parsing can resume. This is usually accomplished by modifying the contents of the parser stack and the input tape. Ideally we would like the corrective action to be such that no subsequent errors are hidden and that no spurious errors are introduced. Although there is an $O(n^3)$ parsing algorithm which will do minimum distance error correction (see Aho and Peterson [5]), there is no known $O(n)$ error recovery routine with these characteristics.

However, in an LL or LR parsing table we can, if we wish, hand tailor a different error recovery action for each error entry in the table. These hand-tailored actions can take into account the statistics of commonly occurring syntax errors in the source language. There are also a number of general error recovery algorithms that can be used.

We shall consider first a general recovery technique for LL parsing, then one for LR parsing. Suppose a canonical LL(1) parser, having read the first $i - 1$ symbols of the input string $a_1a_2\ldots a_n$, has $X_1X_2\ldots X_m$ on the stack with X_1 on top. Suppose the parsing action for X_1 and a_i, the current input symbol, is error. That is, either X_1 is a terminal and $X_1 \neq a_i$ or X_1 is a nonterminal and the entry in the parsing matrix for X_1 and a_i is error.

A simple way to resynchronize the parser is to scan forward in the input until the first input symbol a_j is found such that the parser has a nonerror action with X_k on top of the stack for some $k \geq 1$. Since $X_m = \$$, we are always guaranteed that such an a_j exists. Effectively, this says that we look for an input symbol a_j such that $\text{FIRST}_1(X_kX_{k+1}\ldots X_m) = a_j$. Once we have located a_j and X_k, we advance the input head to position j, pop symbols $X_1X_2\ldots X_{k-1}$ off the stack, and then resume normal parsing. (In fact, Irons [36] suggests that instead of popping $X_1X_2\ldots X_{k-1}$ from the stack, we replace $a_ia_{i+1}\ldots a_{j-1}$ by a shortest string w such that $X_1X_2\ldots X_{k-1} \overset{*}{\Rightarrow} w$.) This method of recovery assumes that the input symbol a_i is in error and that $X_1X_2\ldots X_{k-1}$ derives a string that was mutated into $a_ia_{i+1}\ldots a_{j-1}$. Any errors present in $a_{i+1}\ldots a_{j-1}$ will not be caught.

Let us now consider the LR case. Suppose that an LR(1) parser, having read the first $i - 1$ symbols of the input string $a_1a_2\ldots a_n$, has $s_0X_1s_1\ldots X_ms_m$ on the stack with s_m on top. Suppose that the parsing action of state s_m on input a_i is error. To resynchronize the parser Leinius [46] suggests that we scan forward on the input tape until we reach a symbol a_j such that there is a state s_k in the stack, $k \leq m$, and a nonterminal A such that:

1. $g(s_k, A) = s$, and
2. $f(s, a_j) \neq$ error.

If these conditions are satisfied, we reset the parser by advancing the input head to position j and by replacing $X_{k+1}s_{k+1}\ldots X_ms_m$ on the stack with As.

This method of recovery assumes that the input symbol a_i is in error and that the nonterminal A should derive that portion of the input that was mutated into $a_{h+1}a_{h+2}\ldots a_{j-1}$ where a_h is the rightmost symbol that was derived from X_k. Errors in the portion of the input from positions $i + 1$ to $j - 1$ are not caught.

Obviously, these two methods of error recovery can be quite bad in some situations (for example, if a keyword or left parenthesis had been left out earlier, or if a right parenthesis had been put in too soon). However, these two methods are simple to implement and they do encompass the so-called "panic mode" of error recovery used in many compilers. In such a scheme, special terminal symbols such as "end-of-line", ";", and "END" are identified. On encountering an error, the parser advances its input head until one of these symbols is found. The stack is appropriately modified and parsing resumes. Details of these and other error recovery techniques for parsing are discussed by Graham and Rhodes [30], James [37], La France [44], Levy [47], McGruther [52], Peterson [58], and Wirth [71].

EXERCISES 6.7

1. Construct an LL(1) grammar G that generates $L(G_0)$. Construct an LL(1) parser for G. How does the LL(1) error recovery algorithm of this section behave on the following input strings:

   (a) $a + a\ (a + a)$

   (b) $(a +)a * a$

   (c) $a + * (a +)$

2. Construct an SLR(1) parser for G_0. How does the LR(1) error recovery algorithm of this section behave on the input strings in Exercise 1?

3. In what ways can the information in the symbol table be used to help in error recovery?

6.8. OTHER PARSING METHODS

There are a vast number of parsing algorithms in addition to the LL and LR techniques. In this section we shall survey some of the more popular other techniques.

A parsing algorithm is said to be *nonbacktracking* (or *deterministic one-pass*) if the input head of the parser can never move backwards over the input tape. The LL and LR parsing methods are nonbacktracking. Some limited, and full, backtracking parsing methods have been proposed. However, unless there is good reason, full backtracking parsing algorithms should be shunned for programming language applications since these algorithms are usually exponential in time complexity.

In this article we have concentrated on the LL and LR techniques for several reasons. The classes of grammars on which these techniques work are two natural subclasses of context-free grammars. The LL grammars are the largest class of unambiguous grammars that can be parsed "naturally" in a deterministic top-down fashion; the LR grammars are the largest class of unambiguous grammars that can be parsed "naturally" in a deterministic bottom-up fashion. The LL and LR parsing methods are also suitable for practical use. We have seen that fast compact parsers can be mechanically generated for LL(1) and LR(1) grammars. Parsers of this nature have been used in several compilers. For example, Lewis and Rosenkrantz [48] used a 29 by 37 predictive parsing matrix in an LL(1) based ALGOL 60 compiler. Many commercial compilers have used a limited backtracking version of LL parsing called recursive descent.

The chief virtue of LL(1) parsers is that they are fast and easy to construct, even by hand. The primary drawback to trying to use an LL(1) parser is that it is hard (and sometimes impossible) to construct an LL(1) grammar for a given language (see [4]).

LR(1) parsing does not have this disadvantage. It is relatively easy to find an LR(1) grammar for a given language. However, it is rather tedious to construct an LR(1) parser by nonmechanical means. Nevertheless, LR parsing is the single most promising parsing technique known at this time.

There are a number of other nonbacktracking bottom-up parsing algorithms that require less work to construct a parser from a grammar. However, these techniques work only on subsets of the LR grammars. We shall mention a few of the more important techniques here.

There are several precedence oriented schemes. Perhaps the most fundamental of these is the simple precedence technique of Wirth and Weber [72]. In this scheme, three precedence relations are defined on the vocabulary of a grammar. These precedence relations are used to locate the handle in a right sentential form.

Definition 6.8.1

A grammar is *proper* if it has no productions of the form $A \rightarrow \wedge$ and no derivations of the form $A \overset{+}{\Rightarrow} A$ for any nonterminal A.

Let $G = (N, \Sigma, P, S)$ be a proper grammar and $\$$ a new symbol not in $N \cup \Sigma$. We define three precedence relations $\lessdot, \doteq, \gtrdot$ on $N \cup \Sigma \cup \{\$\}$ as follows:

1. $X \lessdot Y$ if there is a production $A \rightarrow \alpha X B \beta$ in P such that $B \overset{+}{\Rightarrow} Y\gamma$ for some γ.
2. $X \doteq Y$ if there is a production $A \rightarrow \alpha X Y \beta$.
3. $X \gtrdot Y$, Y a terminal, if there is a production $A \rightarrow \alpha B Z \beta$ such that $B \overset{*}{\Rightarrow} \gamma X$ and $Z \overset{*}{\Rightarrow} Y\delta$ for some γ and δ.
4. $\$ \lessdot Y$ if $S \overset{+}{\Rightarrow} Y\alpha$ for some α.
5. $X \gtrdot \$$ if $S \overset{+}{\Rightarrow} \alpha X$ for some α.

Definition 6.8.2

A grammar $G = (N, \Sigma, P, S)$ is a *simple precedence grammar* if:

1. G is proper.
2. At most one precedence relation is defined between every pair of symbols in $N \cup \Sigma \cup \{\$\}$.

3. No two productions have the same right side (i.e., G is *uniquely invertible*).

We can define a simple precedence parser for a grammar G as a device consisting of an input tape with an input head, a pushdown stack, and a matrix of precedence relations for G. The input string $x = a_1 a_2 \ldots a_n$ to be parsed is placed on the input tape followed by a right endmarker $. Initially, the parser has its input head over the leftmost square of the input tape and the pushdown stack contains $. The parser then makes a sequence of moves until it either accepts the input string or finds an error.

A move of the parser is determined by the precedence relation between the symbol on top of the stack and the current input symbol. Suppose symbols $X_1 X_2 \ldots X_m$ appear on the stack with X_m on top and a_i is the current input symbol (we assume $a_{n+1} = $). To make its next move, the parser examines its precedence matrix to determine the precedence relation between X_m and a_i.

1. If $X_m <\!\!\cdot\ a_i$ or $X_m \doteq a_i$, the parser shifts a_i on to the stack.

2. If $X_1 X_2 \ldots X_m = \$S$ and $a_i = \$$, the parser halts and accepts the input.

3. If $X_m \cdot\!\!> a_i$, the parser scans down the stack to find the symbol X_k such that $X_{k-1} <\!\!\cdot\ X_k \doteq X_{k+1} \doteq \ldots \doteq X_m$. The parser then determines the production of the form $A \to X_k X_{k+1} \ldots X_m$ and replaces $X_k X_{k+1} \ldots X_m$ on the stack by A. Since the grammar G is uniquely invertible, there can be at most one such production. If there is no production with $X_k X_{k+1} \ldots X_m$ on the right side or if for some $j \leq m$, $X_j \doteq X_{j+1} \doteq \ldots \doteq X_m$ and no precedence relation exists between X_{j-1} and X_j, the parser announces error.

4. If there is no precedence relation between X_m and a_i, the parser announces error.

Every simple precedence grammar is an SLR(1) grammar. However, the class of languages generated by simple precedence grammars is a proper subset of the deterministic context-free languages (see Fischer [26]). For example, the deterministic language

$$L = \{a0^n 1^n \mid n \geq 1\} \cup \{b0^n 1^{2n} \mid n \geq 1\}$$

cannot be generated by a simple precedence grammar. ([10] also has a proof.)

A simple precedence grammar for a given programming language is often not as clean as an equivalent LALR(1) or SLR(1) grammar. The three chief difficulties are not being able to use a given string as the right side of more than one production, not being able to use $\wedge$-productions, and not being able to have more than one precedence relation hold between any pair of grammar symbols. This last criterion precludes even G_0 from being a simple precedence grammar since ($<\!\!\cdot\ E$ and ($\doteq E$ for G_0.

The weak precedence grammars, first defined by Ichbiah and Morse [34], remove some of the awkwardness of simple precedence grammars, without sacrificing parsing ease.

Definition 6.8.3

A proper grammar G is a *weak precedence grammar* if:

1. The precedence relation $\cdot >$ is disjoint from the union of $<\cdot$ and $\doteq$.
2. If $A \rightarrow \alpha X \beta$ and $B \rightarrow \beta$ are productions, then neither of the precedence relations $X <\cdot B$ nor $X \doteq B$ holds. (This condition says that X cannot appear immediately to the left of B in any sentential form of G.)

A parser for a uniquely invertible weak precedence grammar operates in much the same shift-reduce way as a simple precedence parser. Suppose a weak precedence parser has $X_1 \ldots X_m$ on its stack and a_i is the current input symbol. To make its next move, the parser examines the precedence relation that holds between X_m and a_i.

1. If $X_m <\cdot a_i$ or $X_m \doteq a_i$, the parser shifts a_i on to the stack.
2. If $X_1 \ldots X_m = \$S$ and $a_i = \$$ (the right endmarker for the input), the parser halts and accepts the input.
3. If $X_m \cdot > a_i$, the parser scans the list of productions in the grammar to find the longest right side that matches a suffix of $X_1 \ldots X_m$. If

$$A \rightarrow X_k \ldots X_m$$

is the production with this right side, the parser replaces $X_k \ldots X_m$ on the stack by A.
4. If none of conditions (1)–(3) holds, the parser announces error.

The uniquely invertible weak precedence grammars are a proper superset of the simple precedence grammars and a proper subset of the SLR(1) grammars (see [10], e.g.). However, the class of languages generated by the uniquely invertible weak precedence grammars is no larger than the class of languages generated by the simple precedence grammars (see Aho, Denning, and Ullman [2]). For example, G_0 is a uniquely invertible weak precedence grammar that is not a simple precedence grammar. However, there is a simple precedence grammar for $L(G_0)$.

Using a uniquely invertible weak precedence grammar to describe a programming language is still awkward. A number of further generalizations of precedence grammars have been discussed. These include the mixed strategy precedence grammars [53], the extended precedence grammars [72] and [31] and the T-canonical precedence grammars [32].

A very popular early version of precedence parsing, called operator precedence, was formalized by Floyd [27]. In this scheme the precedence relations are defined only on the terminal symbols of the grammar.

Definition 6.8.4

An *operator* grammar is one in which the right side of every production does not have two adjacent nonterminal symbols.

For a proper operator grammar $G = (N, \Sigma, P, S)$ we can define operator precedence relations $<\cdot$, $\cdot>$, and $\doteq$ on $\Sigma \cup \{\$\}$ as follows:

1. $a <\cdot b$ if $A \rightarrow \alpha a B \beta$ is a production such that $B \stackrel{+}{\Rightarrow} \gamma b \delta$ for some γ in $N \cup \{\wedge\}$.
2. $a \doteq b$ if $A \rightarrow \alpha a \beta b \gamma$ is a production such that β is in $N \cup \{\wedge\}$.
3. $a \cdot> b$ if $A \rightarrow \alpha B b \beta$ is a production such that $B \stackrel{+}{\Rightarrow} \gamma a \delta$ for some δ in $N \cup \{\wedge\}$.
4. $\$ <\cdot b$ if $S \stackrel{+}{\Rightarrow} \alpha b \beta$ for some α in $N \cup \{\wedge\}$.
5. $a \cdot> \$$ if $S \stackrel{+}{\Rightarrow} \alpha a \beta$ for some β in $N \cup \{\wedge\}$.

We say a grammar $G = (N, \Sigma, P, S)$ is an *operator precedence grammar* if:

1. G is a proper operator grammar.
2. At most one operator precedence relation holds between every pair of symbols in $\Sigma \cup \{\$\}$.

The *skeletal grammar* G_s for an operator precedence grammar G is the grammar obtained by substituting the start symbol S for every nonterminal in every production and removing the production $S \rightarrow S$ if it is created. For example, G_0 is an operator precedence grammar. Its skeletal grammar is G_5.

An operator precedence parser works in essentially the same shift-reduce manner as a simple precedence parser. However, the parser is for the skeletal grammar rather than the original grammar. The skeletal grammar can be ambiguous, but the operator precedence relations will select exactly one parse for any input string. By substituting the correct nonterminals for S and filling in single productions, we can recover the parse according to the original grammar if we wish. Finally, we note that $L(G_s)$ may be a proper superset of $L(G)$ and the operator precedence parser for G recognizes a language that contains $L(G)$ and is contained in $L(G_s)$.

Example 6.8.1

G_0 is an operator precedence grammar with the operator precedence relation shown in Fig. 6.8.1.

	$\$$	$($	$+$	$*$	a	$)$
$\$$		$<\cdot$	$<\cdot$	$<\cdot$	$<\cdot$	
$)$		$<\cdot$	$<\cdot$	$<\cdot$	$<\cdot$	$\doteq$
$+$	$\cdot>$	$<\cdot$	$\cdot>$	$<\cdot$	$<\cdot$	$\cdot>$
$*$	$\cdot>$	$<\cdot$	$\cdot>$	$\cdot>$	$<\cdot$	$\cdot>$
a	$\cdot>$		$\cdot>$	$\cdot>$		$\cdot>$
$)$	$\cdot>$		$\cdot>$	$\cdot>$		$\cdot>$

Fig. 6.8.1   Operator precedence relations for G_0.

The input string $a + a * a$ would be parsed by an operator precedence grammar using these precedence relations in the following manner.

Stack	Unexpended Input	Type of Move
$\$$	$\hat{a} + a*a\$$	shift a
$\$a$	$\overset{\cdot}{+} a*a\$$	reduce by $E \to a$
$\$E$	$\overset{\cdot}{+} a*a\$$	shift $+$
$\$E +$	$\hat{a}*a\$$	shift a
$\$E + a$	$\overset{\cdot}{*}a\$$	reduce by $E \to a$
$\$E + E$	$\overset{\cdot}{*}a\$$	shift $*$
$\$E + E*$	$\hat{a}\$$	shift a
$\$E + E*a$	$\hat{\$}$	reduce by $E \to a$
$\$E + E*E$	$\hat{\$}$	reduce by $E \to E * E$
$\$E + E$	$\hat{\$}$	reduce by $E \to E + E$
$\$E$	$\hat{\$}$	accept

Note that this is exactly the way the LR parser of Fig. 6.6.6 would parse this input.

Precedence oriented parsing methods require large tables of precedence information. The storage requirements can be considerably reduced if the relevant information in a precedence table T can be represented by two integer-valued functions f and g, called *linear precedence functions*, such that

1. $f(X) < g(Y)$ if $T[X, Y]$ is $<\cdot$
2. $f(X) = g(Y)$ if $T[X, Y]$ is $\doteq$
3. $f(X) > g(Y)$ if $T[X, Y]$ is $\cdot>$

If a precedence table T can be represented by linear precedence functions of this nature (not all can), then the storage requirements are reduced from $O(n^2)$ to $O(n)$ where n is the number of symbols in the grammar vocabulary. For example, the following functions serve as linear precedence functions for the precedence table in Fig. 6.8.1.

	$\$$	$($	$+$	$*$	a	$)$
f	0	0	2	4	4	4
g	0	5	1	3	5	0

A method of computing linear precedence functions and determining when they exist was proposed by Floyd [27]. Newer techniques for computing linear precedence functions are discussed by Aho and Ullman [9], Bell [13] and Martin [51].

Instead of using the precedence relation between the top symbol on the stack and the next input symbol to make shift-reduce parsing decisions, some authors have proposed using a string of symbols on top of the stack and the next k input symbols to make the decision of whether to shift or reduce. This idea is behind the definition of (m, k)–bounded right context (BRC) grammars (see Floyd [28]).

The ultimate generalization of this idea is to use the entire contents of the stack and the next k input symbols to make each parsing decision. This generalization coincides with the class of LR(k) grammars. In an LR parser the state on top of the stack summarizes all relevent parsing information about the viable prefix on the stack. Each state in an LR(k) parser is just a representative of an equivalence class of viable prefixes.

The classes of grammars we have discussed can be arranged into the hierarchy shown in Fig. 6.8.2. We can show all containments in Fig. 6.8.2

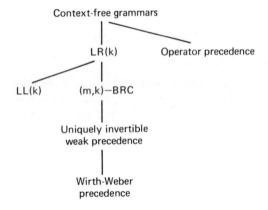

Fig. 6.8.2   Hierarchy of grammars.

are proper. The classes of languages generated by these classes of grammars are shown in Fig. 6.8.3. All inclusions shown in Fig. 6.8.3 are proper. We can also show that every deterministic language can be generated by an SLR(1) grammar or by a (1, 1)–BRC grammar.

All of the techniques discussed so far work only for a subset of the context-free grammars (and languages). Two "universal" parsing algorithms are the Cocke-Younger-Kasami algorithm and Earley's algorithm. Each of these is a tabular, dynamic programming technique that uses O(n^3) time to parse an input string of length n according to an arbitrary grammar. Earley's algorithm will work in O(n^2) time if the grammar is unambiguous, and it can be made to work in O(n) time if the grammar is LR(k). L. Valiant has recently proposed an O$(n^{2.81})$ universal parsing algorithm.

Complete descriptions of all parsing methods mentioned in this chapter and characterizations of the classes of grammars and languages for which they work can be found in Aho and Ullman [7, 8].

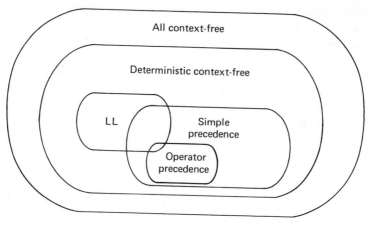

Fig. 6.8.3   Hierarchy of languages.

EXERCISES 6.8

1. Construct
   (a) an LL(1) parser
   (b) an SLR(1) parser
   (c) a simple precedence parser
   (d) a weak precedence parser
   (e) an operator precedence parser for arithmetic expressions.
   Compare the size and speed of your parsers.

2. Show that for every context-free language without ∧ there is
   (a) a proper grammar
   (b) an operator grammar
   (c) a uniquely invertible grammar
   (d) a weak precedence grammar.

3. Find a context-free language for which there is no
   (a) LL(1) grammar
   (b) LR(1) grammar
   (c) operator precedence grammar

4. Show that there is an LR(1) parser for every operator precedence grammar.

6.9. TRANSLATION SCHEMES

We can consider code generation as a process of mapping a derivation tree into a string of output code. Often, the output generated at one vertex of a derivation tree is a function of the output associated with the immediate ancestors and descendants of that vertex.

In this section we shall consider several schemes for specifying mappings on derivation trees. All of the schemes to be discussed use a grammar to specify the derivation trees. The output mapping is specified by a set of translation rules associated with the productions of the grammar. The schemes are classified according to the format of the translation rules.

The schemes basically work in the following manner. Given an input string, we construct a derivation tree for the input string according to the grammar. As we construct the derivation tree, we use the translation rules to compute values for various translation elements at the vertices of the derivation tree. The values can be strings, numbers, calls to bookkeeping routines, or whatever is necessary for the application at hand. The important point is that the values of the translation elements at one vertex v of the derivation tree depend only on values of translation elements at the sons or the father of v. The output string is usually the value of one of the translation elements at the root of the tree.

The simplest scheme of this nature is the syntax-directed translation scheme (SDTS) introduced in Chapter 1. (Here $A \rightarrow \alpha, A = \beta$ is used, where in Chapter 1 $A \rightarrow \alpha, \beta$ was used.)

Example 6.9.1

Consider the following syntax-directed translation scheme T_1 with start symbol W.

Production	Translation Rule
1. $W \rightarrow C\ V\ L$	$W = V\ L\ C$ ay
2. $W \rightarrow V\ L$	$W = V\ L$ yay
3. $C \rightarrow C$ consonant	$C = C$ consonant
4. $C \rightarrow$ consonant	$C =$ consonant
5. $L \rightarrow L\ M$	$L = L\ M$
6. $L \rightarrow \wedge$	$L = \wedge$
7. $M \rightarrow$ consonant	$M =$ consonant
8. $M \rightarrow$ vowel	$M =$ vowel
9. $V \rightarrow$ vowel	$V =$ vowel

The terminal symbol **consonant** matches any consonant and the terminal **vowel** matches any vowel. (We could have supplied the productions and translation rules to do this.) This translation scheme maps English words into their "Pig Latin" equivalent according to the following rule:

1. If a word begins with a vowel, we add the suffix "yay."
2. If a word begins with a string of one or more consonants, we move all leading consonants to the end of the word and append the suffix "ay."

For example, "ink" is translated into "inkyay" and "pig" into "igpay." In this SDTS there is one string-valued translation element for each interior vertex of the derivation tree. For example, production (1) has associated with it the translation rule

$$W = V L C \text{ ay}$$

This rule defines a translation element W for each vertex associated with production (1) in a derivation tree. The value of W at that vertex is constructed by taking the value of the translation element V at the first son of W, appending to it the value of the translation element L at the second son of W, appending to the result the value of the translation element C at the third son of W, and finally appending the string "ay" to the result.

Figure 6.9.1 shows a derivation tree for the input string "pig." At each interior vertex of the derivation tree we have indicated in braces the value of the associated translation element. The output of the tree is the value of the translation element W at the root. We see "pig" is translated into "igpay" by this scheme.

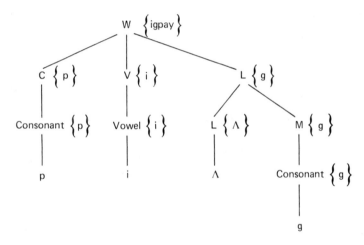

Fig. 6.9.1   Derivation tree with translation elements.

Note that an SDTS has the following properties:

1. There is one translation element for each nonterminal symbol in the grammar.
2. The value of each translation element is a string of output symbols.
3. Each translation rule defines the value of a translation element in terms of a permutation of the translation elements for the nonterminals appearing on the right side of the associated production.

We shall make the following classifications of SDTS's.

Definition 6.9.1

An SDTS is *simple* if no translation rule rearranges the order of the nonterminal symbols appearing on the right side of the associated production.

For example, T_1 is not simple since the translation rule for production (1) uses $V L C$ rather than $C V L$.

Simple SDTS's generate some interesting translations.

Example 6.9.2

Consider the following SDTS T_2 which maps arithmetic expressions in infix notation into expressions in postfix Polish notation. The input grammar is LL(1).

Production	Translation Rule
$E \to T E'$	$E = T E'$
$E' \to + T E'$	$E' = T + E'$
$E' \to \wedge$	$E' = \wedge$
$T \to F T'$	$T = F T'$
$T' \to * F T'$	$T' = F * T'$
$T' \to \wedge$	$T' = \wedge$
$F \to (E)$	$F = E$
$F \to a$	$F = a$

In Fig. 6.9.2 we show a tree with frontier $a + a * a$. The values of the translation elements at each interior vertex are shown in braces. The output is the value of E at the root. Thus, $a + a * a$ is mapped into $aaa*+$.

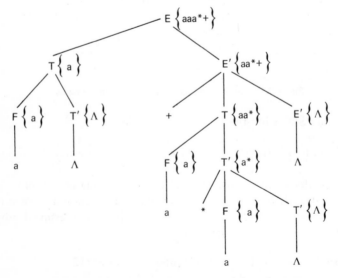

Fig. 6.9.2 Derivation tree with translation elements.

This input-output mapping can be implemented by a modified predictive parser in the following manner. Consider the "translation" grammar G_{12}:

$$E \rightarrow T E'$$
$$E' \rightarrow + T \oplus E' \mid \wedge$$
$$T \rightarrow F T'$$
$$T' \rightarrow * F * T' \mid \wedge$$
$$F \rightarrow (E)$$
$$F \rightarrow a \, \text{a}$$

We can construct an LL(1) parser for G_{12} in the usual manner. However, the symbols a, $\oplus$, and $*$ are treated as output symbols; the only parsing action associated with these symbols is that when one of these symbols appears on top of the stack, that symbol is to be emitted as output. (There is no other type of output.) We can easily show that, if the parser accepts an input string x, the output string emitted will be a postfix Polish representation for x.

Theorem 6.9.1

Every simple SDTS on an LL(k) grammar can be implemented by a deterministic pushdown transducer.

Definition 6.9.2

An SDTS is *postfix* if in each translation rule no output symbols appear before any translation elements. For example, T_1 is a postfix SDTS but T_2 is not.

Theorem 6.9.2

Every simple postfix SDTS on an LR(k) grammar can be implemented by a deterministic pushdown transducer.

Example 6.9.3

Consider the simple postfix SDTS T_3:

Production	Translation Rule
$E \rightarrow E + E$	$E = E E +$
$E \rightarrow E * E$	$E = E E *$
$E \rightarrow (E)$	$E = E$
$E \rightarrow a$	$E = a$

$+$ and $*$ are left-associative.
$+$ is of lower precedence than $*$.

This translation can be performed by the LR parser of Fig. 6.8.1 if we make the change that instead of emitting a production number, the parser emits the following output symbols:

Production	Output
1	+
2	*
3	$\wedge$
4	a

For Theorem 6.9.1 we required the SDTS to be simple, not simple postfix as in Theorem 6.9.2. Thus, it may appear that a larger class of SDT's can be implemented by a deterministic pushdown transducer parsing in an LL rather than LR manner. However, this is not the case. It can be shown that every simple SDTS on an LL(1) grammar G can be implemented by a deterministic pushdown transducer that parses G in an LR(1) fashion.

A number of generalizations of SDTS's have been proposed [59], [41], [63], [6]. The first extension we shall discuss is called a generalized SDTS (GSDTS for short). A GSDTS permits several translation elements for each nonterminal, and the translation rule for an element at a vertex v in a derivation tree can use any of the translation elements at the sons of v.

Definition 6.9.3

A GSDTS is a system $T = (N, \Sigma, \Delta, \Gamma, R, S)$ where:

1. N, Σ, and Δ are the sets of nonterminals, input symbols, and output symbols, respectively.

2. Γ is a finite set of translation elements of the form A_i, where A is a nonterminal and i an integer. We assume S_1 is in Γ.

3. R is a set of rules of the form

$$A \longrightarrow \alpha \qquad \qquad \begin{aligned} A_1 &= \beta_1 \\ A_2 &= \beta_2 \\ &\cdot \\ &\cdot \\ &\cdot \\ A_m &= \beta_m \end{aligned}$$

subject to the following conditions:

(a) A_i is in Γ for $1 \leq i \leq m$.
(b) Each symbol of each β_i is either an output symbol in Δ or a translation element β_j in Γ such that B is a nonterminal that appears in α.

4. S is the start symbol in N.

If the same nonterminal appears in α more than once, then we shall use superscripts to distinguish the occurrences.

Example 6.9.4

Let us generate assembly code for a simple function call with a GSDTS. We assume we have an assembly language statement of the form CALL f, which transfers control to location f and places the current location in a machine register reserved for returning from a function call. A source statement of the form

$$f(x_1, x_2, \ldots, x_n)$$

is to be translated into a sequence of assembly code of the form

$$
\begin{array}{l}
\text{code for } x_1 \\
\text{STORE } t_1 \\
\text{code for } x_2 \\
\text{STORE } t_2 \\
\quad \cdot \\
\quad \cdot \\
\quad \cdot \\
\text{code for } x_n \\
\text{STORE } t_n \\
\text{CALL } f \\
\text{ARG } t_1 \\
\text{ARG } t_2 \\
\quad \cdot \\
\quad \cdot \\
\quad \cdot \\
\text{ARG } t_n
\end{array}
$$

In this sequence, "code for x_i" means assembly language statements which will evaluate x_i. The statment STORE t_i stores the value of x_i just evaluated in temporary register t_i. The statement ARG t_i serves as a pointer to t_i, so that the function called will know that it can find its ith argument via the ith statement following the CALL statement.

The following GSDTS generates such a translation.

$$
\begin{array}{ll}
S \rightarrow f(L) & S = L_1\text{'}; \text{CALL} f' L_2 \\
L \rightarrow L, E & L_1 = L_1\text{'};' E_1\text{'}; \text{STORE'} E_2 \\
& L_2 = L_2\text{'}; \text{ARG'} E_2
\end{array}
$$

$L \rightarrow E$ $\qquad\qquad L_1 = E_1\text{'; STORE' } E_2$

$\qquad\qquad\qquad\qquad L_2 = \text{'; ARG' } E_2$

In this GSDTS we have surrounded output strings in quotes. The semi-colon is used to separate assembly language statements. The nonterminal E stands for an expression; E_1 stands for assembly code to evaluate E; E_2 stands for a new temporary location in which the value of E is to be stored. For simplicity we have not shown the productions or translation rules for E.

A function call of the form $f(x, y)$ would be translated into the sequence

code for x

STORE t_x

code for y

STORE t_y

CALL f

ARG t_x

ARG t_y

A translation of this nature cannot be performed by an ordinary syntax-directed translation scheme.

A GSDTS on an LL(1) grammar or LR(1) grammar can be implemented by using an LL(1) parser or LR(1) parser to construct the derivation tree and using an explicit tree structure to keep track of the values of the translation elements at each vertex. Details of such an implementation are in Aho and Ullman [11].

Knuth [41] earlier proposed an extension of a GSDTS in which the values of translation elements at a vertex v in a derivation tree can depend on the values of translation elements at the father of v (these are called *inherited* translations) or at the sons of v (these are called *synthesized* translations). Translation schemes of this nature are very powerful but we must be careful to avoid circular definitions.

For example, consider the rule

$A \rightarrow B\ C$ $\qquad\qquad A = B\ C$

$\qquad\qquad\qquad\qquad B = A$

The translation element A is a synthesized translation since its value depends only on values of translation elements at the sons of A in a derivation tree. The translation element B is an inherited translation because its value depends on A, which is defined at the father of B. This translation scheme as it stands is circular. An algorithm to test if a translation scheme is circular is given by Bruno and Burkhard [14] and Knuth [42].

The ultimate generalization of a translation scheme is to attach an arbitrary program to each production of a context-free grammar. That program is executed when a vertex associated with that production is visited. This type of translation scheme has been used as the basis of several translator writing systems (see Feldman and Gries [24] or [53], e.g.).

EXERCISES 6.9

1. Construct a simple SDTS that maps every string in $L(G_0)$ into (a) a left parse and (b) a right parse.

2. Prove that a deterministic pushdown transducer cannot map arithmetic expressions in infix notation into expressions in prefix Polish notation.

3. Prove that the set of output strings of a SDTS is a context-free language.

4. Find a translation on a context-free grammar that cannot be defined by any GSDTS.

5. Construct a translation scheme to map arithmetic expressions into assembly code for your favorite computer.

REFERENCES

1. Aho, A. V., "Indexed Grammars—an Extension of Context-Free Grammars," *J. ACM* 15: 4 (1968), 647–671.

2. Aho, A. V., P. J. Denning, and J. D. Ullman, "Weak and Mixed Strategy Precedence Parsing," *J. ACM* 19: 2 (1972), 225–243.

3. Aho, A. V. and S. C. Johnson, "LR Parsing," *Computing Surveys* 6: 2 (1974), 99–124.

4. Aho, A. V., S. C. Johnson, and J. D. Ullman, "Deterministic Parsing of Ambiguous Grammars," *Conference Record ACM Symposium on Principles of Programming Languages* (1973), 1–21.

5. Aho, A. V. and T. G. Peterson, "A Minimum Distance Error-Correcting Parser for Context-Free Languages," *SIAM J. Computing* 1: 4 (1972), 305–312.

6. Aho, A. V. and J. D. Ullman, "Translations on a Context-Free Grammar," *Information and Control* 19: 5 (1971), 439–475.

7. Aho, A. V. and J. D. Ullman, *The Theory of Parsing, Translation, and Compiling. Vol. 1: Parsing,* Prentice-Hall, Inc., Englewood Cliffs, N.J., 1972.

8. Aho, A. V. and J. D. Ullman, "Optimization of LR(k) Parsers," *J. Computer and System Sciences* 6: 6 (1972), 573–602.

9. Aho, A. V. and J. D. Ullman, "Linear Precedence Functions for Weak Precedence Grammars," *International J. Computer Mathematics* 3 (1972), 149–155.

10. Aho, A. V. and J. D. Ullman, *The Theory of Parsing, Translation, and Compiling, Vol. 2: Compiling.* Prentice-Hall, Inc., Englewood Cliffs, N.J., 1973.

11. AHO, A. V. and J. D. ULLMAN, "A Technique for Speeding up LR (k) Parsers," *SIAM J. Computing* 2: 2 (1973), 106–127.

12. ANDERSON, T., J. EVE, and J. J. HORNING, "Efficient LR (1) Parsers," *Acta Informatica* 2 (1973), 12–39.

13. BELL, J. R., "A New Method for Determining Linear Precedence Functions for Precedence Grammars," *Comm. ACM* 12: 10 (1969), 316–333.

14. BRUNO, J. L. and W. A. BURKHARD, "A Circularity Test for Interpreted Grammars." *TR 88,* Dept. of Electrical Engineering, Princeton University, Princeton, N.J., 1970.

15. CHOMSKY, N., *Syntactic Structures,* Mouton and Co., The Hague, 1957.

16. CHOMSKY, N., "Formal Properties of Grammars," in *Handbook of Mathematical Psychology, Vol. 2,* ed. by R. D. Luce, R. R. Bush, and E. Galanter, John Wiley & Sons, New York, 1963, pp. 323–418.

17. COCKE, J. and J. T. SCHWARTZ, *Programming Languages and their Compilers* (2nd ed.), Courant Institute of Mathematical Sciences, New York University, New York, 1970.

18. CONWAY, R. W. and W. L. MAXWELL, "CORC: the Cornell Computing Language," *Comm. ACM* 6: 6 (1963), 317–321.

19. CONWAY, R. W., and T. R. WILCOX, "Design and Implementation of a Diagnostic Compiler for PL/I," *Comm. ACM* 16: 3 (1973), 169–179.

20. DEMERS, A. J., "Skeletal LR parsing," *IEEE Conference Record of 15th Annual Symposium on Switching and Automata Theory* (1974), 185–198.

21. DEREMER, F. L., "Simple LR (k) Grammars," *Comm. ACM* 14: 7 (1971), 453–460.

22. DEWAR, R. B. K., R. R. HOCHSPRUNG, and W. S. WORLEY, "The IITRAN Programming Language," *Comm. ACM* 12: 10 (1969), 569–575.

23. EARLEY, J., "An Efficient Context-Free Parsing Algorithm," *Comm. ACM* 13: 2 (1970), 94–102.

24. FELDMAN, J. A., and D. GRIES, "Translator Writing Systems," *Comm. ACM* 11: 2 (1968), 77–113.

25. FISCHER, M. J., "Grammars with Macro-Like Productions," *IEEE Conference Record 9th Annual Symposium on Switching and Automata Theory* (1968), 131–142.

26. FISCHER, M. J., "Some Properties of Precedence Languages," *Proc. ACM Symposium on Theory of Computing* (1969), 181–190.

27. FLOYD, R. W., "Syntactic Analysis and Operator Precedence," *J. ACM* 10: 3 (1963), 316–333.

28. FLOYD, R. W., "Bounded Context Syntactic Analysis," *Comm. ACM* 7: 2 (1964), 62–67.

29. FREEMAN, D. N., "Error Correction in CORC, the Cornell Computing Lan-

guage," *Proc. AFIPS Fall Joint Computer Conference,* Vol. 26. Spartan, New York, 1964, pp. 15–34.

30. GRAHAM, S. L., and S. P. RHODES, "Practical Syntactic Error Recovery in Compilers," *Conference Record ACM Symposium on Principles of Programming Languages* (1973), 52–58.

31. GRAY, J., "Precedence Parsers for Programming Languages," Ph. D. thesis, Dept. of Computer Science, University of California, Berkeley, 1969.

32. GRAY, J. N., and M. A. Harrison, "Single Pass Precedence Analysis," *IEEE Conference Record 10th Annual Symposium on Switching and Automata Theory,* (1969), 106–117.

33. GRIES, D., *Compiler Construction for Digital Computers,* John Wiley & Sons, New York, 1971.

34. ICHBIAH, J. D., and S. P. MORSE, "A Technique for Generating Almost Optimal Floyd-Evans Productions for Precedence Grammars," *Comm. ACM* 13: 8 (1970), 501–508.

35. IRONS, E. T., "A Syntax-Directed Compiler for ALGOL 60," *Comm. ACM* 4: 1 (1961), 51–55.

36. IRONS, E. T., "An Error-Correcting Parse Algorithm," *Comm. ACM* 6: 11 (1963), 669–673.

37. JAMES, L. R., "A Syntax-Directed Error Recovery Method," *TR CSRG-13,* Computer Systems Research Group, University of Toronto, Toronto, 1972.

38. JOHNSON, W. L., J. H. PORTER, S. I. ACKLEY, and D. T. ROSS, "Automatic Generation of Efficient Lexical Analyzers Using Finite State Techniques," *Comm. ACM* 11: 12 (1968), 805–813.

39. JOLLIAT, M. L., "On the Reduced Matrix Representation of LR (k) Parser Tables," Ph. D. thesis, University of Toronto, Toronto, 1973.

40. KNUTH, D. E., "On the Translation of Languages from Left to Right," *Information and Control,* 8: 6 (1965), 607–639.

41. KNUTH, D: E., "Semantics of Context-Free Languages," *Mathematical Systems Theory* 2: 2 (1968), 127–145, and 5: 1, 95–96.

42. KNUTH, D. E., "Top Down Syntactic Analysis," *Acta Informatica* 1: 2 (1971), 79–110.

43. KORENJAK, A. J., "A Practical Method of Constructing LR (k) Processors," *Comm. ACM* 12: 11 (1969), 613–623.

44. LAFRANCE, J., "Syntax-Directed Error Recovery for Compilers," Ph. D. thesis, Computer Science Dept., University of Illinois, Urbana, 1971.

45. LALONDE, W. R., E. S. LEE, and J. J. HORNING, "An LALR(k) Parser Generator." *Proc. IFIP Congress 71, TA-3,* North-Holland Publishing Co., Netherlands, 1971, pp. 153–157.

46. LEINIUS, P., "Error Detection and Recovery for Syntax-Directed Compiler Systems," Ph. D. thesis, University of Wisconsin, Madison, 1970.

47. LEVY, J. P., "Automatic Correction of Syntax Errors in Programming Languages." *TR 71–116*, Dept. of Computer Science, Cornell University, Ithaca, New York, 1971.

48. LEWIS, P. M., II, and D. J. ROSENKRANTZ, "An ALGOL Compiler Designed Using Automata Theory," *Proc. Symposium on Computers and Automata*, Polytechnic Institute of Brooklyn, New York, 1971, pp. 75–88.

49. LEWIS, P. M., II, D. J. ROSENKRANTZ, and R. E. STEARNS, "Attributed Translations," *Proc. 5th Annual ACM Symposium on Theory of Computing* (1973), 160–171.

50. LEWIS, P. M., II, and R. E. STEARNS, "Syntax directed transduction," *J. ACM* 15: 3 (1968), 464–488.

51. MARTIN, D. F., "A Boolean matrix method for the computation of linear precedence functions," *Comm. ACM* 15: 6 (1972), 448–454.

52. MCGRUTHER, T., "An approach to automating syntax error detection, recovery, and correction for LR(k) grammars," Masters thesis, Naval Postgraduate School, Monterey, California, 1972.

53. MCKEEMAN, W. M., J. J. HORNING, and D. B. WORTMAN, *A Compiler Generator.* Prentice-Hall, Inc., Englewood Cliffs, N.J., 1970.

54. MORGAN, H. L., "Spelling Correction in Systems Programs," *Comm. ACM* 13: 2 (1970), 90–93.

55. MOULTON, P. G., and M. E. MULLER, "A Compiler Emphasizing Diagnostics," *Comm. ACM* 10: 1 (1967), 45–52.

56. NAUR, P. (ed.), "Revised Report on the Algorithmic Language ALGOL 60." *Comm. ACM* 6: 1 (1963), 1–17.

57. PAGER, D., "A solution to an open problem by Knuth," *Information and Control* 17: 5 (1970), 462–473.

58. PETERSON, T. G., "Syntax Error Dectection, Correction and Recovery in Parsers," Ph. D. thesis, Stevens Institute of Technology, Hoboken, N.J., 1972.

59. PETRONE, L., "Syntax-Directed Mapping of Context-Free Languages," *IEEE Conference Record 9th Annual Symposium on Switching and Automata Theory* (1968), 160–175.

60. ROSENKRANTZ, D. J., "Matrix Equations and Normal Forms for Context-Free Grammars," *J. ACM* 14: 3 (1967), 501–507.

61. ROSENKRANTZ, D. J., "Programmed Grammars and Classes of Formal Languages," *J. ACM* 16: 1 (1968), 107–131.

62. ROSENKRANTZ, D. J., and P. M. LEWIS, II, "Properties of Deterministic Top-Down Grammars," *Information and Control* 17: 3 (1970), 226–256.

63. ROUNDS, W. C., "Mappings and Grammars on Trees," *Mathematical Systems Theory* 4: 3 (1970), 257–287.

64. SCHAEFER, M., *A Mathematical Theory of Global Flow Analysis,* Prentice-Hall, Inc., Englewood Cliffs, N.J., 1973.

65. SETHI, R., "Complete Register Allocation Problems," *Proc. 5th Annual ACM Symposium on Theory of Computing* (1973) 182–195.

66. SETHI, R., and J. D. ULLMAN, "The Generation of Optimal Code for Arithmetic Expressions," *J. ACM* 17:4 (1970), 715–728.

67. STEARNS, R. E., "Deterministic Top-Down Parsing." *Proc. 5th Annual Princeton Conference on Information Sciences and Systems* (1971), 182–188.

68. STEARNS, R. E., and P. M. LEWIS, II, "Property Grammars and Table Machines," *Information and Control* 14:6 (1969), 524–549.

69. ULLMAN, J. D., "Applications of Language Theory to Compiler Design," in *Currents in the Theory of Computing,* ed. by A.V. Aho (1973), pp. 173–218.

70. VAN WIJNGAARDEN, A. (ed.), "Report on the Algorithmic Language ALGOL 68," *Numerische Mathematik* 14 (1969), 79–218.

71. WIRTH, N., "PL 360–A Programming Language for the 360 Computers," *J. ACM* 15:1 (1968), 37–74.

72. WIRTH, N., and H. WEBER, "EULER–A Generalization of ALGOL and its Formal Definition," Parts 1 and 2, *Comm. ACM* 9:1 (1966), 13–23, and 9:2 (1966), 89–99.

73. WOOD, D., "The Theory of Left Factored Languages," *Computer J.* 14:4 (1969), 349–356, and 13:1 (1970), 55–62.

74. WULF, W., R. K. JOHNSON, C. B. WEINSTOCK, S. O. HOBBS, and C. M. GESCHKE, *The Design of an Optimizing Compiler,* American Elsevier, New York, 1975.

7 APPLICATION OF FORMAL GRAMMARS AND AUTOMATA TO PROGRAMMING LANGUAGE DEFINITION†

Terrence W. Pratt
Department of Computer Sciences,
Computation Center and
Software Engineering and Systems Laboratory
University of Texas at Austin
Austin, Texas

Editor's Note:

This chapter describes a technique for formal definition of programming languages utilizing concepts in formal grammars and automata. The definition consists of two parts. In the first part, a "pair grammar" is used to translate a source program into its graph representation which forms the initial state of an automaton. In the second part, an automaton executes the translated program. This definitional technique allows intuitive representation for programs, data, translators, and run-time structures as well as the construction of realistic models of program execution.

The material presented in this chapter together with that of Chapter 6 could form the core of a course in "Design of Algorithmic Language and Compilers."

This chapter is self-contained with only the notion of context-free grammar as its prerequisite.

7.1. INTRODUCTION

The concepts of formal grammars and automata find natural application

†This work supported in part by the National Science Foundation through grants GJ–778 and GJ–36424.

in the definition of programming languages. Precise and complete formal definitions of programming language syntax and semantics have been a long standing goal in computer science. The most well-known early definition attempts are seen in the definition of Algol 60 (see Naur [12]) and in the Lisp interpreter definition (see McCarthy [9]). The Algol definition represents the first major application of context-free grammars to the definition of programming language syntax. In the Lisp interpreter we see a simple definition of an abstract machine capable of executing any Lisp program.

A precise programming language definition is of use both to the language user and the language implementor. For the implementor the definition provides a precise specification of exactly what must be implemented—including the handling of subtle details which otherwise often become an implementor's decision and thus vary between implementations. For the programmer, the definition provides a firm basis for his coding. Questions of syntactic structure or meaning may be resolved by reference to the definition, before an error is coded into the program.

In this chapter a technique for formal definition of programming languages is described. The definition takes two parts. In the first part, a formal grammar, called a *pair grammar,* is used to define a translation from programs in their ordinary character string written form into directed graph structures, which represent the logical organization of the program. The result of translation is a set of directed graphs that represent the initial state of an automaton. The automaton, when begun in this initial state, moves through a sequence of states (each represented as a set of directed graphs) that corresponds to the execution sequence of the original program. The chief difference between the automaton here and the more usual automata models lies in the use of a highly structured state and a correspondingly complex transition function for moving from state to state.

The two stage translator-automaton definition is a direct abstraction from the common structure of a programming language implementation. In the usual implementation of a language, a compiler (or other translator) translates the input program in the source language into an "executable program" either in machine language or in some intermediate form such as a "Polish prefix code string." The translated program is then executed either directly by the hardware machine language interpreter (usually augmented by some run-time support programs) or by a software (programmed) interpreter.

A number of other programming language definition techniques based on this same translator-automaton paradigm have been suggested. The most widely known is the "Vienna Definition Language" (VDL), a definitional technique developed by the IBM Vienna Laboratory for the formal definition of PL/I (see Lucas [8], Wegner [16], and Lee [6]). VDL definitions of a number of other languages have also been produced, e.g., Algol 60 (see Lauer [5]) and Basic (see Lee [6]). Using the Vienna Definition Language, a programming language formal definition takes the form of a translator and an automaton.

The translator defines a mapping between programs represented as character strings and programs represented by trees (parse trees appropriately extended to include implicit information). The automaton which "executes" these tree-form programs is defined in terms of (1) an initial state, (2) a transition rule, and (3) a set of primitive instructions (tree transformations). The automaton moves through a sequence of states (each represented by a tree structure) by applying its transition rule to the current state. The transition rule determines a primitive instruction to be executed to transform the current "state tree" into the state tree representing the next automaton state.

Landin, in a series of papers [3, 4], proposes a similar translator-automaton structure based on programs represented as expressions in the lambda-calculus rather than as trees. Both of these approaches have roots in early work by McCarthy [10].

The technique described in this paper differs from these other techniques in its use of hierarchies of directed graphs (*H*-graphs) for program representations and automaton "states," in its use of the formal "pair grammar" definition of the translator, and in most of the details of the automaton, but the gross organization of the definitions is quite similar.

The strength of this definitional technique lies largely in its use of intuitive representations for programs, data, translators, and run-time structures which are also simple mathematically. *H*-graphs and *H*-graph automata allow construction of realistic models of program execution. *H*-graphs also admit a simple formal definition, but more importantly for the analysis of programs the *H*-graph models have a basis in hierarchies and directed graphs that corresponds closely to the intuitive structures on which programs and data are usually analyzed: program control structures are represented by flowcharts, data elements and data linkages by graph nodes and arcs, subprogram hierarchies by hierarchies of graphs, recursion by a recursive graph hierarchy, etc. These structures allow straightforward formal analysis of many important properties of programs. The definitions of *H*-graph automata are also structured so as to simplify analysis: Instructions may have no implicit operands or side effects, and instruction graphs are constructed so that instruction dependencies are readily observable.

Pair grammar definitions of translators (compilers) provide simple definitions of the mapping between a program and its associated graph representation. Pair grammars are constructed from two context-free grammars, one an ordinary "string" grammar and one a simple form of "graph" grammar. Many of the known results concerning context-free grammars apply directly to pair grammars.

In the next three sections the basic formal constructs supporting the technique are defined: directed graphs and *H*-graphs, pair grammars, and *H*-graph automata. In the following section and in Appendices A and B a complete formal definition of a simple programming language *Q* is given.

7.2. HIERARCHICAL GRAPHS (H-GRAPHS)

A *hierarchical graph* or *H-graph* is a finite set of directed graphs over a common set of nodes, organized into a hierarchy. Assume a base set N of nodes, a set A of basic data "atoms," and a set L of arc labels.

Definition 7.2.1

An *extended directed graph* G over N and L is a triple $G = (M, E, S)$,

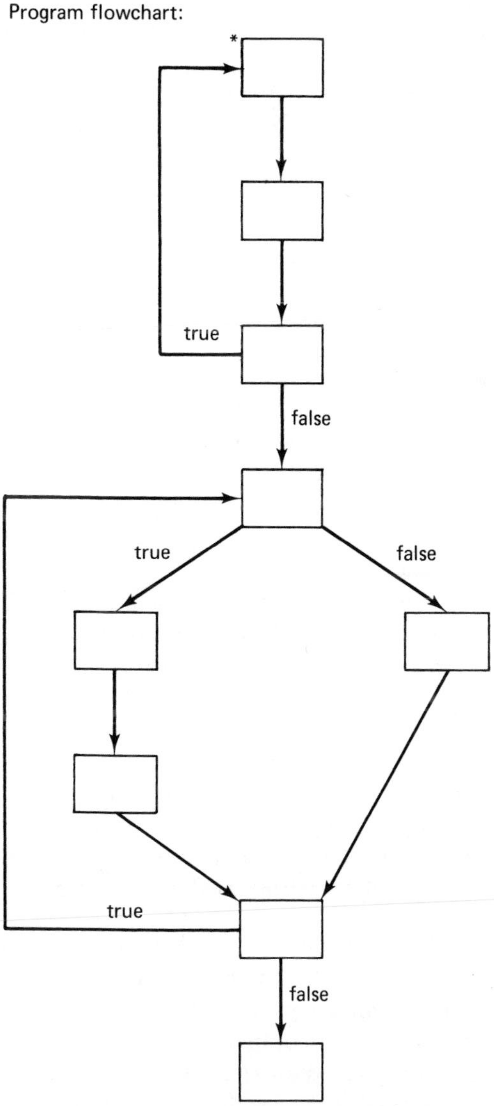

Program flowchart:

Fig. 7.2.1 Examples of extended directed graphs.

1. Arcs whose labels are not significant are labelled with the null label (blank).
2. *indicates the initial node of the graph.

List:

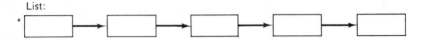

List structure with shared sublists (Lisp):

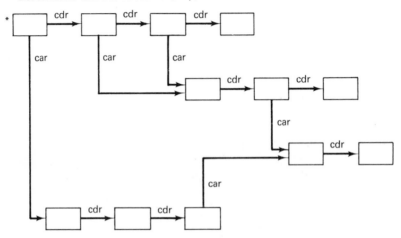

Fig. 7.2.1 (continued).

where M is a finite nonempty subset of N, E is a finite set of triples of the form (n, a, m) where $n, m \in M$ and $a \in L$, and $S \in M$, M is termed the *node set*, S is the *initial node*, and E is the *arc set* of G. If $(n, a, m) \in E$ there is said to be *an arc labelled a from node n to node m of G*.

Definition 7.2.2

An *H-graph H* over N, A, and L is a pair $H = (M, V)$, where M, the *node set*, is a finite nonempty subset of N, and V, the *value* or *contents function*, is a function mapping M into $A \cup \{X \mid X$ is an extended directed graph over M and $L\}$. If n is a node in M, then $V(n)$ is called the *value* or *contents* of n.

H-graphs are the formal structures used here to model programs and data structures. Figures 7.2.1 and 7.2.2 illustrate extended directed graphs and *H*-graphs representing common programming constructs. In the definition of a programming language the output of the translator (which is also the initial state of the automaton) is an *H*-graph, as are each of the other states through which the automaton passes during program execution.

One characteristic of *H*-graphs is particularly important but rather subtle: A single node may appear in a number of different graphs within an *H*-graph.

Note for example the *H*-graph of Fig. 7.2.3. Each node labeled STK represents the same node, and similarly for each node labeled *X*. Intuitively nodes are considered "global" objects with a unique value that is independent of the graph in which they occur. Any node may be a part of a number of different graphs representing different program and data structures. As a result an *H*-

Stack:
(represented
hierarchically)

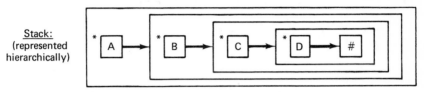

Instruction:

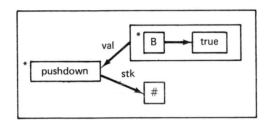

Flowchart with instructions:

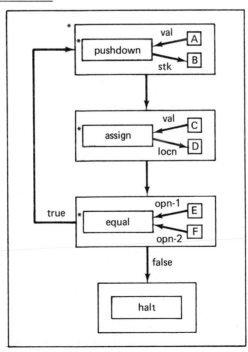

Fig. 7.2.2   Examples of *H*-graphs.

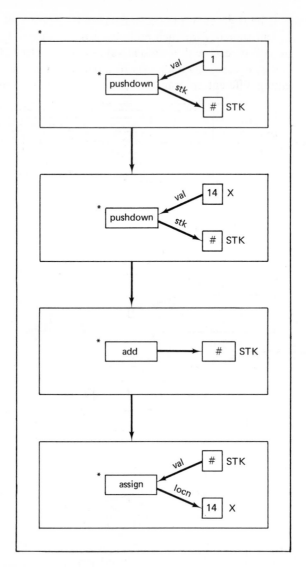

Fig. 7.2.3 An *H*-graph representation of $X: = X + 1$ using a stack for temporary storage.

graph represents a rather novel sort of hierarchy of graphs. Beginning with any given node of the *H*-graph we may "descend a level" to the value of that node by applying the value function *V*. The value is either an atom in *A* or a graph. Choosing any node in that graph we may again descend a level to its value, which again is either an atom or a graph. In this sense an *H*-graph is organized into a hierarchy of levels. However an odd thing may happen.

In descending a level to a graph we may find nodes in that graph which also appeared in graphs at "higher levels." In fact the seeming hierarchy may even be "recursive"—a node in the graph just reached may be a node through which we descended at a higher level. This facet of the H-graph definition allows natural modeling of many programming language constructs, including such structures as shared data nodes and recursive subprogram hierarchies (see the language Q for examples).

EXERCISES 7.2

1. Give a formal definition of each of the extended directed graphs of Fig. 7.2.1. Designate the nodes by unique integers.

2. Give a formal definition of the H-graph of Fig. 7.2.2.

3.˙ Give a formal definition of the H-graph of Fig. 7.2.3.

4. Give a precise formal definition of the concept of "level of a node" in an H-graph. For which nodes is the concept of level not well-defined? Your definition should assign these nodes the level "undefined."

7.3. PAIR GRAMMARS: FORMAL DEFINITIONS OF LANGUAGE TRANSLATORS

In our formal definition of Q, the syntax of Q programs and their corresponding H-graph representations are defined by a *pair grammar*, a generalization of the "syntax-directed translation schema" of Chapter 1. The pair grammar may be thought of as a formal definition of a *Q-compiler*, which translates Q programs into their H-graph representations. The complete pair grammar for Q is found in Appendix A. In this section we develop the formal concept of pair grammar and explain informally its application to the definition of programming language translators.

7.3.1.   Pair Grammars

A *pair grammar*, as the name implies, is composed of a pair of formal grammars whose productions and nonterminals are in one-to-one correspondence. The two grammars are termed the *left grammar* and the *right grammar*, respectively. Each is a context-free "string" grammar (an ordinary context-free grammar) or a *context-free graph grammar* (defined below).

Definitions 7.3.1

A *pair grammar* G is a quadruple $G = (K, T, S, P)$ where
K is a finite set of *non-terminal symbols*

T is a finite set of *terminal symbols*
$S \in K$, the *start symbol*
P is a set of *productions*.

Each production of P is composed of a pair of context-free graph or string grammar productions that rewrite the same nonterminal symbol and whose right-hand side nonterminals are in 1–1 correspondence. The two productions paired in each production of G are termed the *left production* and the *right production*, respectively. The set of all left productions of G defines a context-free grammar, termed the *left grammar* of G. This left grammar in turn defines the *left language* of G. The *right grammar* and *right language* of G are defined similarly.

The *language* $L(G)$ defined by a pair grammar G consists of a set of ordered pairs of elements from the left and right languages, respectively, of G. To generate a pair in $L(G)$, one begins with the pair (S, S), consisting of the start symbol of G in both left and right positions. A production $(S \rightarrow \alpha, S \rightarrow \alpha')$ of G is chosen. Application of this production to the pair (S, S) produces a new pair (α, α') where α and α' each contain the same nonterminal symbols in 1–1 correspondence. A pair of corresponding nonterminals in α and α' are chosen for the next rewriting, say for example, the nonterminal C. A production $(C \rightarrow \gamma, C \rightarrow \gamma')$ of G is chosen and the instances of C in α and α' are replaced by γ and γ' in the usual way, giving a new pair (δ, δ'). Since nonterminals in α and α' and nonterminals in γ and γ' are in 1–1 correspondence, we are assured that δ and δ' have a 1–1 correspondence of nonterminals. Continuing in this manner we ultimately derive a terminal pair (ω, ω') containing no nonterminal symbols, (ω, ω') is then an element of $L(G)$, with ω in the left language and ω' in the right language of G.

For programming language definition the pairs (ω, ω') in the language defined by a pair grammar may be thought of as an input program ω and its graph representation ω'. The pair grammar G then defines a translation between programs and their corresponding graph representations. In fact, the translation of ω into ω' may be done directly using G as follows. Given ω we parse it according to the left grammar of G in the usual way. This parse gives us a derivation of ω from S, the start symbol, using a sequence of rules from the left grammar. Now we may generate ω', the translation of ω, by applying the corresponding sequence of right grammar rules to the initial nonterminal S. Thus G directly defines a translation from left language elements to right language elements.

7.3.2. Graph Grammars

For programming language definitions using H-graphs we wish the right grammar of a pair to define a language composed of H-graphs, while for the left grammar the language defined should be a set of character strings representing syntactically correct programs in the language. An ordinary context-free grammar suffices for the left grammar. The right grammar, however, requires an extension of the concept of context-free grammar to that of *context-free graph grammar*, a context-free grammar which defines a "language" composed of a set of *H*-graphs.

The extension, in fact, is simple to make. Recall that an ordinary context-free grammar generates a string in its language as follows. First take the start symbol of the grammar, and find a grammar rule with that nonterminal on the left. Replace the nonterminal by the right side of the rule. Now pick a nonterminal in the resulting string, find a rule with that nonterminal on the left, replace the nonterminal by the string on the right of the chosen rule, and repeat the process. When all nonterminals have been replaced by terminal strings, the resulting string is a string in the language.

Nothing about the above process of string generation using grammar rules requires a restriction to strings. A context-free graph grammar works in just the same manner to generate a graph in its "language." You begin with a node having the start symbol of the grammar as its value. Each graph grammar rule specifies a nonterminal on the left and an *H*-graph on the right. In generating a graph using the grammar, nodes with nonterminal values are replaced by right side graphs using the appropriate grammar rules. These right side graphs may contain other nodes with nonterminal values. When all such nodes have been replaced by terminal nodes, then the resulting graph is in the "graph language" defined by the grammar. The only extra complexity in this generation process comes from the need to specify how to "hook up" the replacement graph to the existing graph when a nonterminal valued node is replaced by a graph according to a rule of the grammar. In the simple graph grammars used here this is done by simply specifying an *initial node* and a *final node* in the right side graph of each grammar rule. When a nonterminal node is replaced by a graph, each arc leading into that nonterminal node is connected to the initial node of the new graph, and each arc leading out of the nonterminal node is connected to the final node of the new graph. This is entirely analogous in generation of a string using an ordinary context-free grammar to the replacement of a nonterminal by a string according to a grammar rule and the implicit concatenation of the original string to the left of the nonterminal onto the replacement string, and likewise for the string to the right of the original nonterminal.

Definition 7.3.2

A *context-free graph grammar* F is a quadruple $F = (K, A, S, R)$ where K is a finite set of *nonterminals*, A is a set of *terminals*, $S \in K$ is the *start symbol*, and R is a finite set of *productions*. Each production in R is quintuple (C, H, G, I, O) where $C \in K$ (the *left-hand nonterminal*) and $H, G, I,$ and O form the

Left production

⟨statement⟩ ::= ⟨conditional⟩
⟨statement⟩ ::= ⟨while⟩

Right production

⟨statement⟩ ::= ⟨conditional⟩

⟨statement⟩ ::= ⟨while⟩

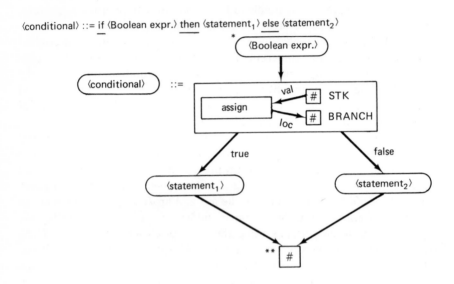

⟨conditional⟩ ::= if ⟨Boolean expr.⟩ then ⟨statement₁⟩ else ⟨statement₂⟩

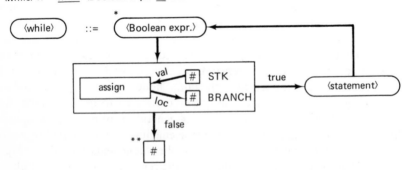

⟨while⟩ :: = while ⟨Boolean expr⟩ do ⟨statement⟩

Fig. 7.3.1   Four-pair grammar productions.

right-hand side of the production. $H = (M, V)$ is an H-graph with atoms chosen from the set $K \cup A$, G is an extended directed graph over M and A, with initial node I. O, the *final node*, is a node in G also.

An example will clarify the concepts of pair and graph grammar and also serve to introduce the notation used in the pair grammar of Appendix A, which defines the translation from Q programs into H-graphs. Consider the productions for *while* and conditional statements in Appendix A, reproduced in Fig. 7.3.1. In the left and right productions the Backus-Naur notation of the Algol 60 report is used: Nonterminals are words enclosed in "$<$. . .$>$" brackets and the symbol "$::=$" separates the two parts of the production (necessary since the usual " $\rightarrow$ " is used within the H-graphs). In graph grammar rules, nodes with nonterminal values are drawn as ovals, while nodes with terminal or graph values are shown as rectangles. Initial and final nodes in each graph grammar production are tagged "$*$" and "$**$", respectively. Figure 7.3.2 illustrates the use of these productions in the partial parse of a Q program and generation of its corresponding H-graph representation.

7.3.3.   Node Labels and Reduced H-graphs

Because both left and right grammars in a pair grammar are context-free, the translations defined by pair grammars cannot be made to depend on context. In programming language translation there typically are various context-dependent elements which need to be taken into account in the translation. An ordinary compiler uses a *symbol table* to keep track of context, so that the translation of an expression such as "$X + Y$" depends on the context—in particular on the declarations for X and Y. Other cases include the association of each *goto* control transfer with the labeled statement which is the object of the *goto*, and association of subprogram calls with subprogram definitions.

In the definition of the language Q, four such cases arise:

1. *Goto* statements need to be translated into arcs leading to the graph node representing the beginning of the appropriately labelled statement.

2. Subprogram calls need translation into a graph form "call instruction," one of whose operands is the node containing the graph representation of the subprogram.

3. References to local variables within subprograms must be translated into arcs leading to a common node containing the variable value.

4. References to global temporary storage nodes (such as STK) in the graph instructions must be represented by arcs leading to a common node.

Each of these cases represents a situation in which the global nature of nodes in an H-graph is utilized to allow many different parts of a graph to have access to common data through a node which appears in many graphs. This is precisely the sort of context-dependent connection which cannot be handled directly with a pair grammar.

A simple technique provides sufficient machinery to allow the necessary connections to be made. We allow the terminal nodes (nodes with terminal symbols as values) in H-graphs generated by a graph grammar to be *labelled*

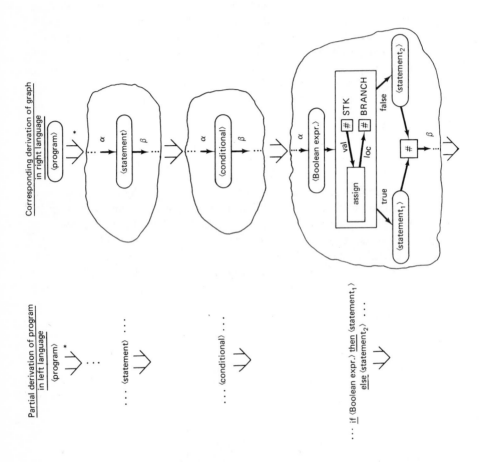

Fig. 7.3.2

262

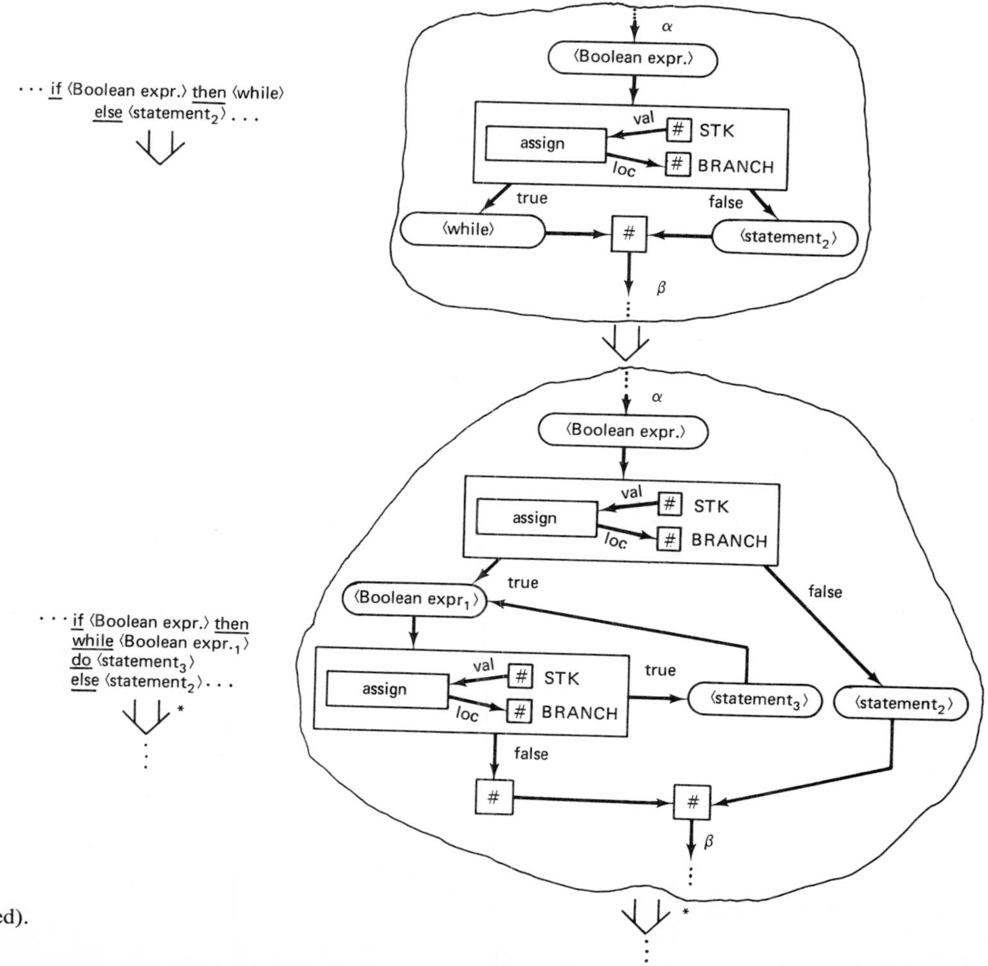

· · · if ⟨Boolean expr.⟩ then ⟨while⟩
else ⟨statement$_2$⟩ . . .
α
⟨Boolean expr.⟩
val
STK
assign
loc
BRANCH
true
false
⟨while⟩
⟨statement$_2$⟩
β
· · · if ⟨Boolean expr.⟩ then
while ⟨Boolean expr.$_1$⟩
do ⟨statement$_3$⟩
else ⟨statement$_2$⟩ . . .
α
⟨Boolean expr.⟩
val
STK
assign
loc
BRANCH
true
false
⟨Boolean expr$_1$⟩
val
STK
assign
loc
BRANCH
true
false
⟨statement$_3$⟩
⟨statement$_2$⟩
β

Fig. 7.3.2 (continued).

with an identifier (an arbitrary character string). Typically many nodes in an *H*-graph produced by a pair grammar will have the same label. In the terminal *H*-graph resulting from translation of a program *all nodes with the same label are coalesced into a single node* (leaving all arcs attached to any of the original nodes attached to the resulting composite node). The value of the composite node is either null (#) if all the original nodes had null values, or if a single node has a nonnull value then the composite node takes on that value. We term the rule of coalescing all nodes with identical labels the *basic reduction rule*, and the resulting *H*-graphs are termed *reduced H-graphs*. This use of node labels has already appeared in the example of Fig. 7.2.3 and in Fig. 7.3.1 without explicit mention. In Fig. 7.3.2 note the labelled nodes STK and BRANCH within the ASSIGN instruction graph of the two statement graph structures. These labels designate common nodes used to communicate data between these instructions and earlier or later instructions.

Yet a further problem arises in this regard, which is characteristic of programming languages also: Some of the labelled nodes represent *globally* accessible structures—structures accessible from both main program and all subprograms, such as subprogram definitions and global data structures (e.g., STK)—while other labelled nodes represent only *local* structures—statement labels and local variables. The basic reduction rule handles all labelled nodes globally, i.e., coalescing is done considering all nodes in the *H*-graph. To allow the global-local distinction to be made, certain node labels may be prefixed by "local-" Coalescing of such nodes takes place considering only the sub-*H*-graph consisting of a single subprogram or main program definition. We term this *global-local reduction*. This is the reduction rule used in the definition of language *Q*.

In this brief discussion of pair and graph grammars many interesting aspects of the formal structure of these grammars have been ignored. A more complete development of the formal concepts may be found in Pratt [14], along with examples of pair grammars for Lisp and Algol 60 translation. The basic concept underlying the pair grammar, the use of a pair of formal grammars to define a translation between two formal languages, has been studied by a number of authors interested in translations between languages of strings, e.g., Donovan [1] and Lewis [7]. Similarly various forms of graph grammars, formal grammars generating sets of directed (or undirected) graphs, have also been investigated, often for purposes outside the definition of programming languages such as the definition of classes of pictures (see e.g., Narasimhan [11], Pfaltz [13], and Ehrig [2]).

EXERCISES 7.3

1. Construct a pair grammar which translates simple Lisp lists of integers as defined by the context-free grammar:

LIST → ( )
LIST → (SEQ)
SEQ → ⟨integer⟩
SEQ → SEQ, ⟨integer⟩

into linked sequences of nodes whose values are integers.

2. Extend the simple lists of Exercise 1 to trees by adding the rules:

SEQ → LIST
SEQ → SEQ, LIST

to the grammar. The H-graph resulting from the translation should consist of a linked sequence of nodes whose values are either integers or other linked sequences, etc.

3. Describe a class of graphs which cannot be generated by a context-free graph grammar.

4. Construct a pair grammar which translates arithmetic expressions in infix notation into expressions in prefix notation.

7.4. H-GRAPH AUTOMATA

The reduced H-graphs resulting from the pair grammar "translator" represent "executable" programs and data. Execution is defined in terms of an "H-graph automaton" capable of following a path through a program graph and executing the operations encountered along that path. Ordinarily we think of an automaton as defined by a tape, head position, and internal state, together with a transition function which defines how the automaton may move through a sequence of *states*, where each state consists of a triple: tape contents, head position, and internal state. In our *H-graph automaton* each state is represented instead by an H-graph. The H-graph automaton begins in an *initial state* which consists of a reduced H-graph as output from the pair grammar. The automaton moves through a sequence of states, each representing execution of one primitive operation in the original program. Ultimately the automaton may halt. If it does then the final state (the final transformed H-graph) represents the result of execution of the original program.

Definition 7.4.1

An *H-graph automaton B* is a quintuple $B = (N, A, S, S_o, \delta)$, where N is the universe of *nodes*, A is the set of *atoms*, S is the *state set*, a set of H-graphs over N and A, $S_o \subseteq S$ is the set of *initial states*, and $\delta : S \rightarrow S$ is the *transition function*.

Various specialized forms of H-graph automata may be constructed by restrictions on the class of H-graphs S and the transition function δ. For the definition of the language Q in the next section a particular rather specialized δ is used. In this restricted definition δ is defined in terms of (1) a basic *instruction-fetch-and-execute* two-step *transition cycle*, and (2) a set of *primitive instruction schema*, each defined as a "strictly local" *H*-graph transformation. The transition cycle utilizes two nodes, labeled FETCH and CUR-INSTR, which are assumed part of each state *H*-graph.

Definition 7.4.2   Transition Cycle

If the automaton is in state *K* (represented by *H*-graph *K*), then the next state *K'* (represented by *H*-graph *K'*) is found by application of the following two-step transition cycle to state *K*:

Step 1.   (*Fetch next instruction.*) Apply the instruction schema named in the initial node of the graph in node FETCH to the graph in node FETCH, and replace the value of FETCH by the result, giving the *H*-graph *K''*. If application of the schema is undefined, halt (execution complete).

Step 2.   (*Execute next instruction.*) Apply the instruction schema named in the initial node of the graph in node CUR-INSTR (in the H-graph *K''*) to the graph in node CUR-INSTR, and replace the value of CUR-INSTR by the result, giving the new state *H*-graph *K'*. If application of the schema is undefined, halt (error). If CUR-INSTR in *K''* contains the null value (#), then *K'* is just *K''*.

The instruction schema are defined as transformations on *H*-graphs. The argument to a schema is always an "instruction *H*-graph." The schema specifies a set of changes to values of nodes in the *H*-graph. The schema is "strictly local" in that its effects are confined to its argument *H*-graph, and it may not modify other nodes in the state. Two typical instruction schema from Appendix B are shown in Fig. 7.4.1. The first stacks a "value" found in one

pushdown: add new element to stack.

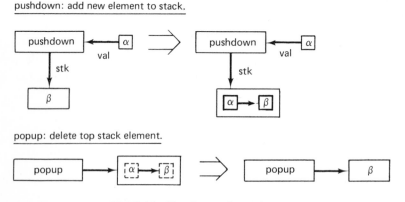

popup: delete top stack element.

Fig. 7.4.1   Two instruction definitions.

node onto a stack, represented as the value of another node. The second deletes the top stack element. In definitions of instruction schema the entire instruction graph is shown, although the structure of the "top level" of this

H-graph is never modified by application of the schema. Only the values of operand nodes of the schema are modified by its application. In the definitions of these schema in Fig. 7.4.1 and Appendix B the following notation is used:

1. Arbitrary node values are indicated by lower-case Greek letters.
2. New nodes added to a graph by application of a schema are drawn in boldface.
3. Nodes deleted by application of a schema are drawn with dotted lines.

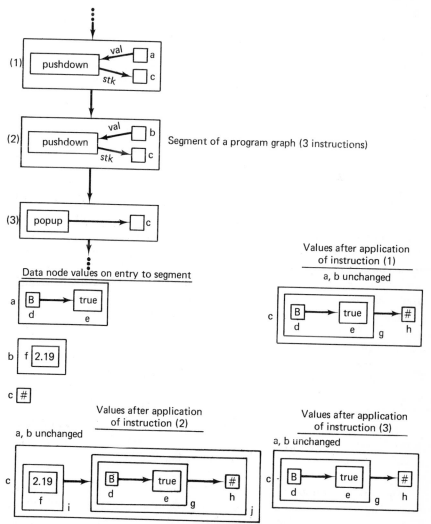

Fig. 7.4.2   Result of execution of a program segment.

4. The instruction graph schema to the left of "$\Rightarrow$" defines the inital form the instruction graph must have (with arbitrary actual node values where Greek letters appear in the schema). The instruction is undefined if the instruction graph does not have this structure.

5. The schema to the right of "$\Rightarrow$" shows the result of application of the schema.

Figure 7.4.2 shows the result of application of a sequence of these instruction schema in an actual program graph.

EXERCISES 7.4

1. Define an instruction schema for the operation which concatenates a new element to the beginning of a simple linked list (the Lisp CONS operation).

2. Define an H-graph representation for a queue (a sequence of elements to which elements are added at one end and deleted at the other) and define instruction schema for the operations of *insert an element* and *delete an element*.

7.5. DEFINITION OF THE LANGUAGE Q

Q is a simple programming language which contains a number of features found in FORTRAN and ALGOL 60. A Q program consists of a main program and a set of "separately compiled" subprograms. Subprograms may be functions or procedures. Parameters are transmitted by value. Each subprogram consists of a set of statements: assignment, conditional, *goto, while* (iteration), subprogram call, return, or compound. Data is restricted to numbers or Boolean constants and FORTRAN-like (or in ALGOL, *own*) simple variables. Variables are untyped and type checking is done entirely during execution. Expressions may compute numbers or Boolean values using the usual arithmetic, logical, and relational operators.

The complete formal definition of the syntax of Q is found in Appendix A. Q programs are translated into H-graphs, which represent the "executable form" of programs. This translation is formally defined by the pair grammar of Appendix A. The H-graph representation of programs resembles a "machine language" program for an abstract computer (the H-graph automaton). A brief outline of the structure of this H-graph automaton and its H-graph "machine language" will help to clarify the definitions of Appendices A and B.

The abstract computer is organized around four "system data nodes," each of which represents a data structure important in program execution. The four nodes are labeled FETCH, CUR-INSTR, CIS, and STK. FETCH contains the basic fetch-next-instruction primitive of the H-graph automaton.

CUR-INSTR (current instruction) always contains the instruction currently being executed. CIS (current instruction stack) acts as a "next instruction pointer" and a stack of subprogram return points. STK acts as a stack of temporaries for expression evaluation and parameter transmission. A fifth node, labelled BRANCH, serves as a link between the fetch instruction which determines an arc to follow at branch points and primitives which control program branching.

An example will clarify the details of the definition of Q. Figure 7.5.1

```
main procedure;
  begin J: = 5; K: = 0;
  L1: K: = K + FACT(J);
      J: = J + 2;
      if J<12 then goto L1 else return K
  end;
  procedure FACT(M);
    begin R: = 1; I: = 1;
    while I < M do
      begin I: = I + 1; R: = R*I end;
    return R
  end
```

Fig. 7.5.1

is a Q language program, consiting of a subprogram FACT which computes the factorial of its argument and a main program which uses FACT to compute the sum of the factorials of the four numbers 5, 7, 9, 11. Since Q contains no input-output primitives, the result of the main program is left as the top value in STK at the end of execution.

Figure 7.5.2 shows the (reduced) H-graph resulting from the translation of the program of Fig. 7.5.1 according to the pair grammar of Appendix A. Node labels are used informally in Fig. 7.5.2 to indicate nodes appearing in more than one graph; they are not actually part of the reduced H-graph.

Figure 7.5.3 shows the H-graph representing the state of the automaton at various points during execution of the program. Execution proceeds according to the transition cycle (defined in the preceding section) and the instruction schemata of Appendix B.

Most of the notational conventions used in Appendices A and B have been explained in the various examples of the preceding sections. One additional convention is seen in production 5 of the pair grammar. The two nodes labelled a designate a single node. Each time this rule is applied during graph generation a new node with null value is created for the node tagged a, which appears in the two designated graphs at the specified position. This node labelling is just a notational convenience within the grammar production and is unrelated to the node labelling associated with the reduction rule.

Productions 20, 21 and 22 illustrate how the program graph for a program

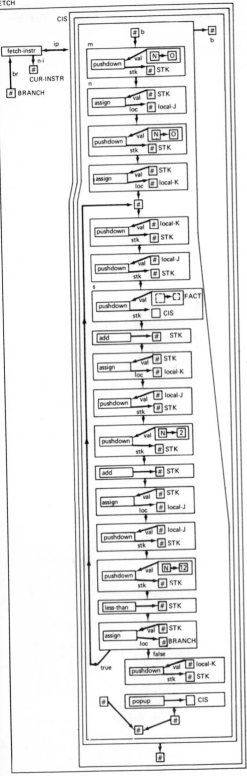

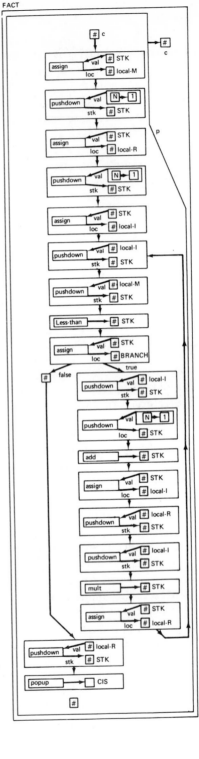

Fig. 7.5.2

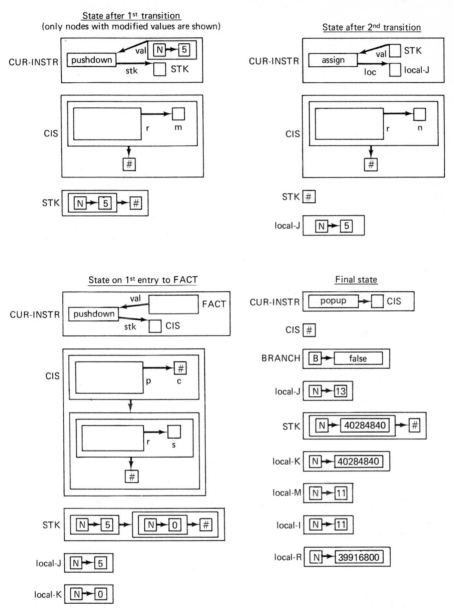

Fig. 7.5.3 Four states during program execution.

containing *goto* or *return* statements may be disconnected at appropriate points by the use of a separate null valued node as the output node in the rule. The result of application of these productions is seen in Fig. 7.5.2.

EXERCISES 7.5

1. In rule (7) of Appendix A, why is the order of assignment to formal parameters reversed?

2. Extend the definition of Q to include a unary minus operation (negation) by adding an instruction schema and appropriate pair grammar rules.

7.6. CONCLUSION

In extending the concepts of formal grammars and automata to the domain of H-graph structures and programming languages, the goal is ultimately to find a satisfactory formal theory which allows real programming languages to be defined and analyzed with the mathematical tools developed for more theoretical work in formal grammars and automata. We have already realized this desirable union of theory and practice in the area of syntactic description and analysis, as discussed in Chapter 6. This chapter illustrates how the concepts may be extended to encompass the more complex "semantic" aspects of programming languages as well.

The language Q used for illustration here is a rather simple language and does not include many common programming language constructs such as structured data, block structure, declarations, and more complex parameter transmission techniques. For the reader interested in the application of the technique to a more complex language, a complete formal definition of the language ALGOL 60 using pair grammars and H-graphs may be found in Pratt [15].

REFERENCES

1. DONOVAN, J. and LEDGARD, H. "A Formal System for the Specification of the Syntax and Translation of Computer Languages," *AFIPS Conf. Proc.* 31 (1967), 553–569.

2. EHRIG, H., M. PFENDER, and H. SCHNEIDER, "Graph Grammars: An Algebraic Approach," *IEEE Switching and Automata Theory Conference Record* (1973).

3. LANDIN, P., "The Mechanical Evaluation of Expressions," *Computer Journal* 6:4 (1964), 308–320.

4. LANDIN, P., "A Correspondence between ALGOL 60 and Church's Lambda Notation," *Comm. ACM*, 8:2 (1965), 89–101 and 8:3 (1965), 158–165.

5. LAUER, P., "Formal Definition of ALGOL 60, " *Report 25.088,* IBM Laboratory Vienna, Dec. 1968, 63 pp.

6. LEE, J., *Computer Semantics,* Van Nostrand Reinhold Company, New York, 1972.

7. LEWIS, P. and R. STEARNS, "Syntax-Directed Transduction," *J. Assoc. Comp. Mach.* 15 (1968), 464–488.

8. LUCAS, P. and WALK, K. "On the Formal Description of PL/I," *Annual Review in Auto. Prog.* 6 (1969), 105–183.

9. McCARTHY, J. et al. The *LISP 1.5 Programmer's Manual,* Massachusetts Institute of Technology Press, Cambridge, Mass., 1962.

10. McCARTHY, J. "Towards a Mathematical Science of Computation," *Proc. IFIP Congress, 1962.* North-Holland Publishing Co., Amsterdam, 1963, pp. 21–28.

11. NARASIMHAN, R., "Syntax-Directed Interpretation of Classes of Pictures," *Comm. ACM,* 9 (1966), 166–173.

12. NAUR, P. (ed.), "Revised Report on the Algorithmic Language ALGOL 60," *Comm. ACM,* 6 (1963), 1–23.

13. PFALTZ, J. and ROSENFELD, A. "Web Grammars," *Proc. International Joint Conference on Artificial Intelligence* (1969).

14. PRATT, T. "Pair Grammars, Graph Languages, and String-to-Graph Translations," *J. Computer and System Sciences* 5:6 (1971), 560–595.

15. PRATT, T., "A Formal Definition of ALGOL 60 Using Hierarchical Graphs and Pair Grammars," *Report UTEX-CC-TSN-33,* Computation Center, University of Texas, Austin, Texas, Jan. 1973, 82 pp.

16. WEGNER, P., "The Vienna Definition Language," *Computing Surveys* 4:1 (1972), 5–63.

APPENDIX A. PAIR GRAMMAR DEFINING THE TRANSLATION OF Q PROGRAMS INTO H-GRAPHS

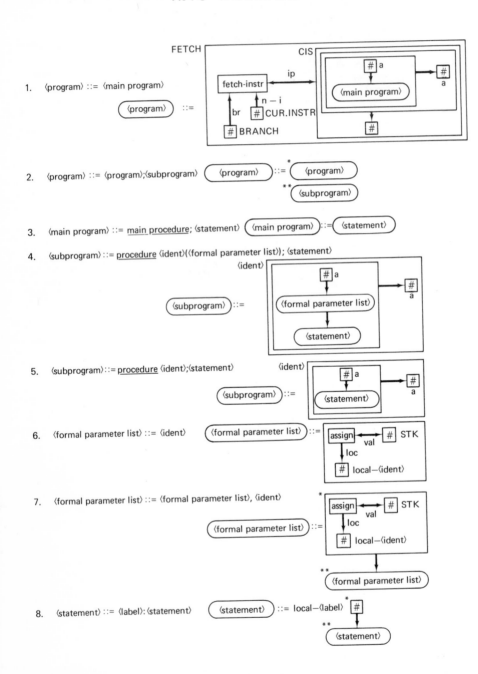

1. ⟨program⟩ ::= ⟨main program⟩

2. ⟨program⟩ ::= ⟨program⟩;⟨subprogram⟩

3. ⟨main program⟩ ::= main procedure; ⟨statement⟩

4. ⟨subprogram⟩ ::= procedure ⟨ident⟩(⟨formal parameter list⟩); ⟨statement⟩

5. ⟨subprogram⟩::= procedure ⟨ident⟩;⟨statement⟩

6. ⟨formal parameter list⟩ ::= ⟨ident⟩

7. ⟨formal parameter list⟩ ::= ⟨formal parameter list⟩, ⟨ident⟩

8. ⟨statement⟩ ::= ⟨label⟩: ⟨statement⟩

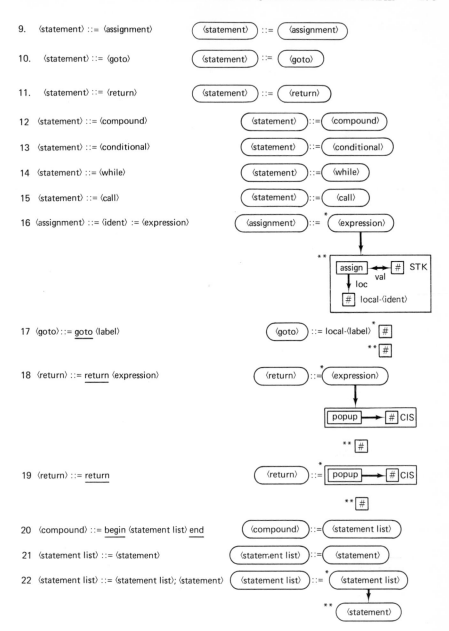

9. ⟨statement⟩ ::= ⟨assignment⟩

10. ⟨statement⟩ ::= ⟨goto⟩

11. ⟨statement⟩ ::= ⟨return⟩

12 ⟨statement⟩ ::= ⟨compound⟩

13 ⟨statement⟩ ::= ⟨conditional⟩

14 ⟨statement⟩ ::= ⟨while⟩

15 ⟨statement⟩ ::= ⟨call⟩

16 ⟨assignment⟩ ::= ⟨ident⟩ := ⟨expression⟩

17 ⟨goto⟩ ::= goto ⟨label⟩

18 ⟨return⟩ ::= return ⟨expression⟩

19 ⟨return⟩ ::= return

20 ⟨compound⟩ ::= begin ⟨statement list⟩ end

21 ⟨statement list⟩ ::= ⟨statement⟩

22 ⟨statement list⟩ ::= ⟨statement list⟩; ⟨statement⟩

23 ⟨conditional⟩ ::= if ⟨Boolean expr.⟩ then ⟨statement₁⟩ else ⟨statement₂⟩

24 ⟨while⟩ ::= while ⟨Boolean expr.⟩ do ⟨statement⟩

25 ⟨call⟩ ::= call ⟨ident⟩ (⟨actual parameter list⟩)

26 ⟨call⟩ ::= call ⟨ident⟩

27 ⟨actual parameter list⟩ ::= ⟨expression⟩

28 ⟨actual parameter list⟩ ::= ⟨actual parameter list⟩, ⟨expression⟩

29 ⟨expression⟩ ::= ⟨Boolean expr.⟩

30 ⟨expression⟩ ::= ⟨arithmetic expr.⟩

31 ⟨Boolean expr.⟩ ::= ⟨Boolean term⟩

32 ⟨Boolean expr.⟩ ::= ⟨Boolean expr.⟩ V ⟨Boolean term⟩

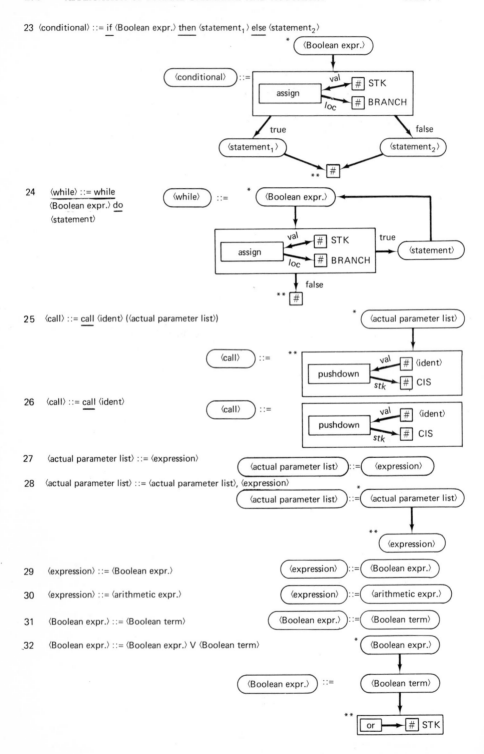

33   〈Boolean term〉 ::= 〈Boolean factor〉

34   〈Boolean term〉 ::= 〈Boolean term〉 ∧ 〈Boolean factor〉

35   〈Boolean factor〉 ::= 〈Boolean primary〉

36   〈Boolean factor〉 ::= ⌐〈Boolean primary〉

37   〈Boolean primary〉 ::= 〈relation〉

38   〈Boolean primary〉 ::= 〈function call〉

39   〈Boolean primary〉 ::= (〈Boolean expr.〉)

40   〈Boolean primary〉 ::= 〈ident〉

41   〈Boolean primary〉 ::= true | false

42   〈relation〉 ::= 〈arithmetic expr.$_1$〉 $\overset{=}{<}$ 〈arithmetic expr.$_2$〉

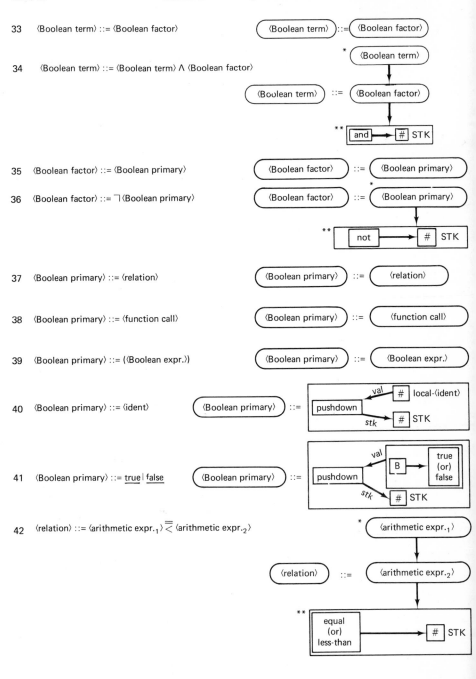

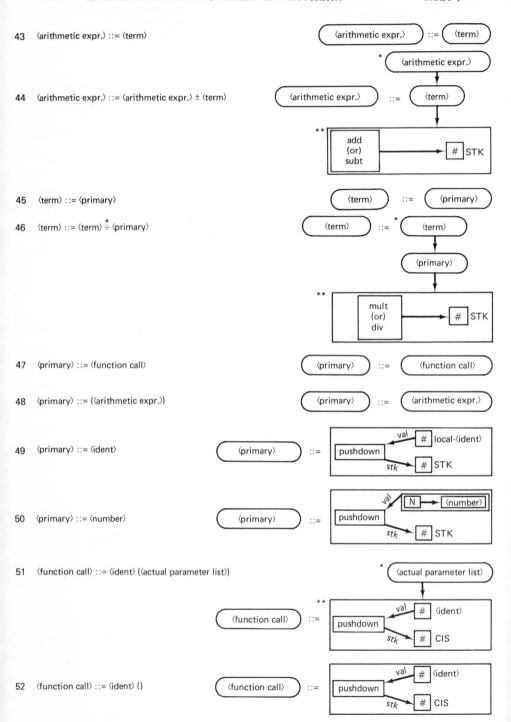

43 ⟨arithmetic expr.⟩ ::= ⟨term⟩

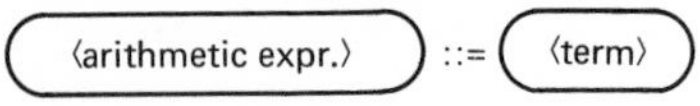

44 ⟨arithmetic expr.⟩ ::= ⟨arithmetic expr.⟩ ± ⟨term⟩

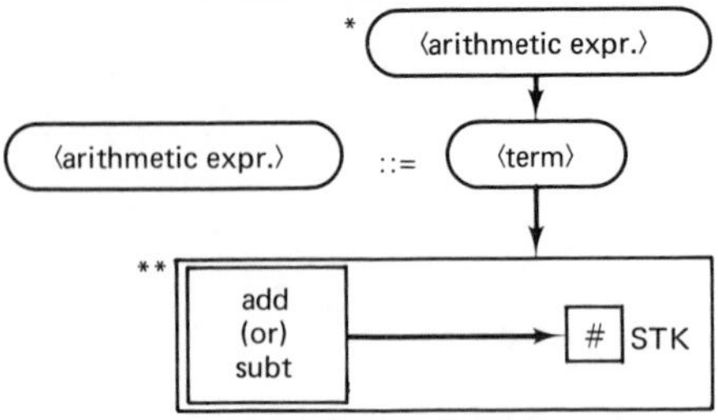

45 ⟨term⟩ ::= ⟨primary⟩

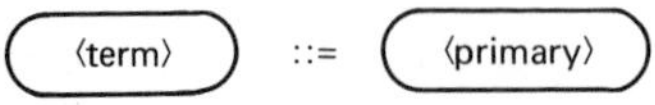

46 ⟨term⟩ ::= ⟨term⟩ $\overset{*}{\div}$ ⟨primary⟩

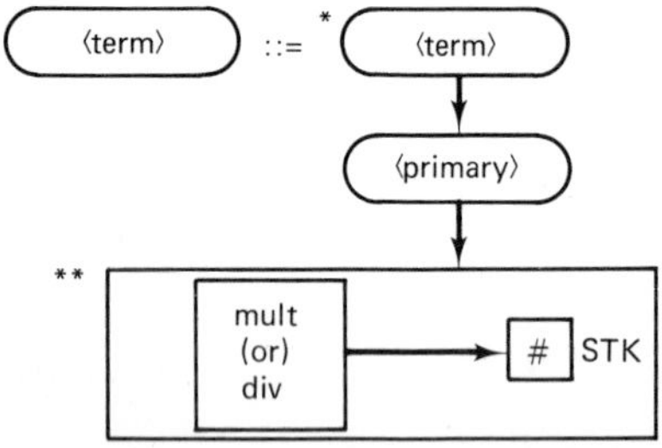

47 ⟨primary⟩ ::= ⟨function call⟩

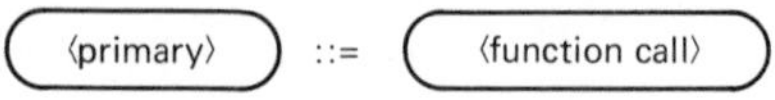

48 ⟨primary⟩ ::= (⟨arithmetic expr.⟩)

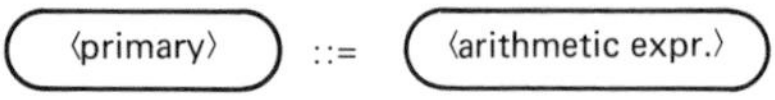

49 ⟨primary⟩ ::= ⟨ident⟩

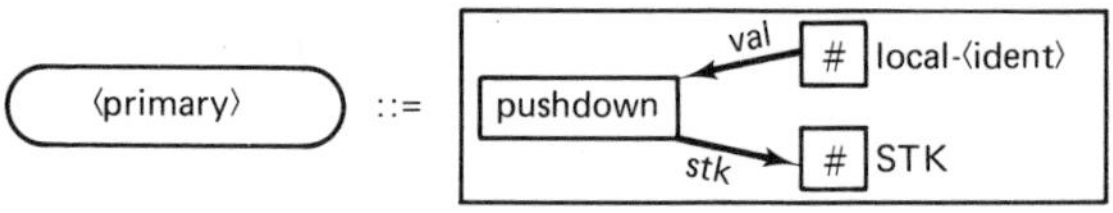

50 ⟨primary⟩ ::= ⟨number⟩

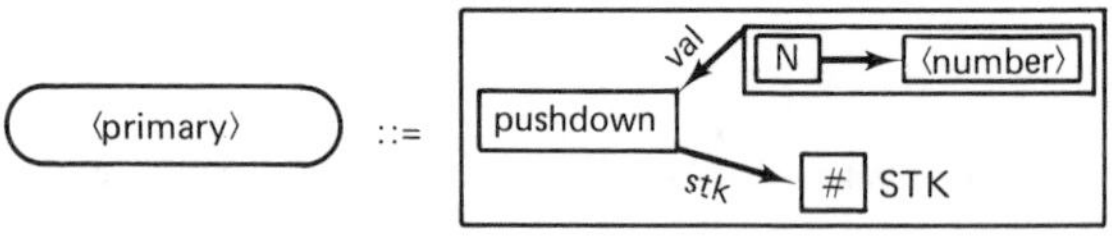

51 ⟨function call⟩ ::= ⟨ident⟩ (⟨actual parameter list⟩)

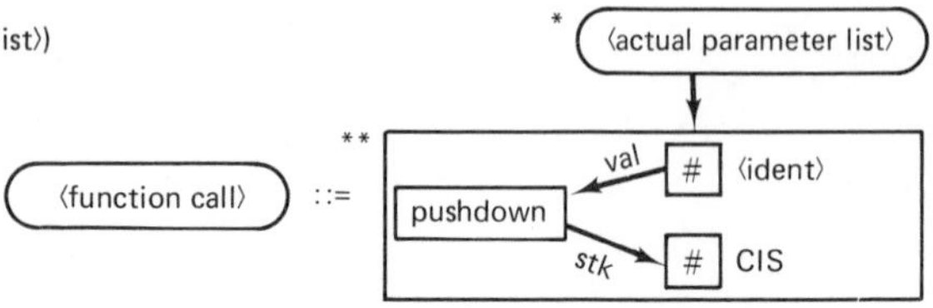

52 ⟨function call⟩ ::= ⟨ident⟩ ()

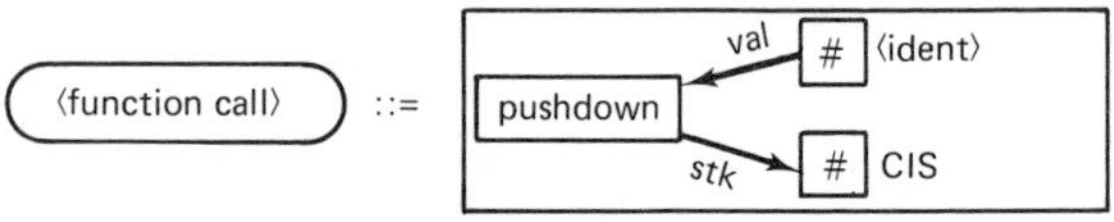

⟨ident⟩, ⟨label⟩ and ⟨number⟩ are defined as character strings in the usual way.
* and ** are omitted when the top-level graph in the right rule consists of only a single node.

APPENDIX B. INSTRUCTION SCHEMA FOR THE Q LANGUAGE AUTOMATON

1 fetch-instr: fetch next instruction and update current instruction pointer.

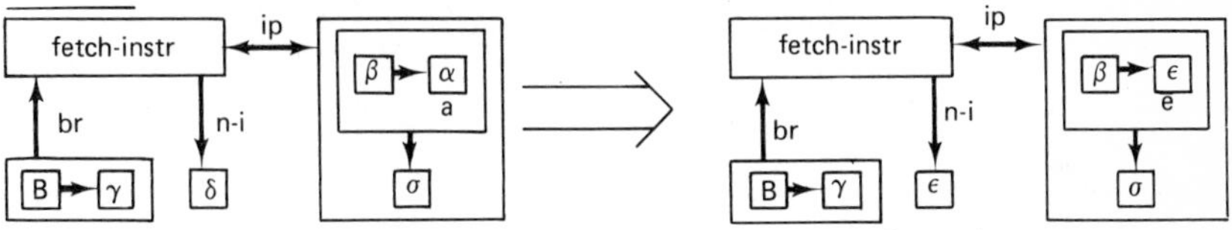

where β contains the subgraph

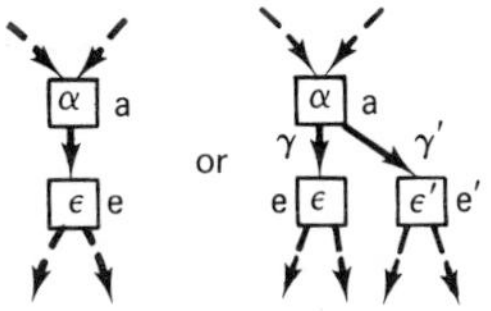

2 assign: assign top stack value and pop stack.

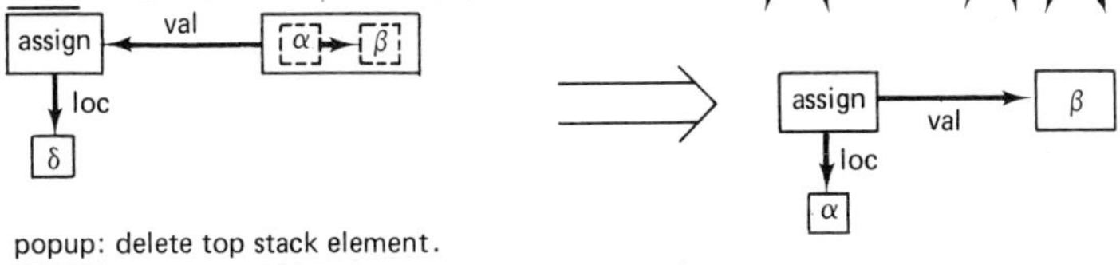

3 popup: delete top stack element.

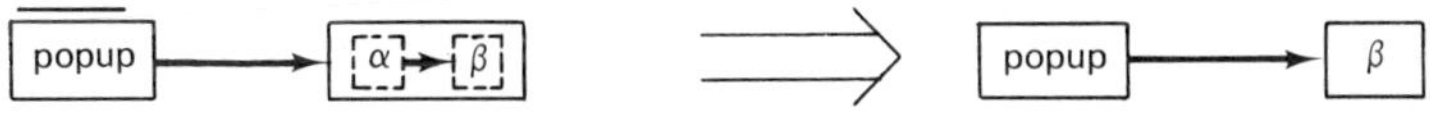

4 pushdown: add new element to stack.

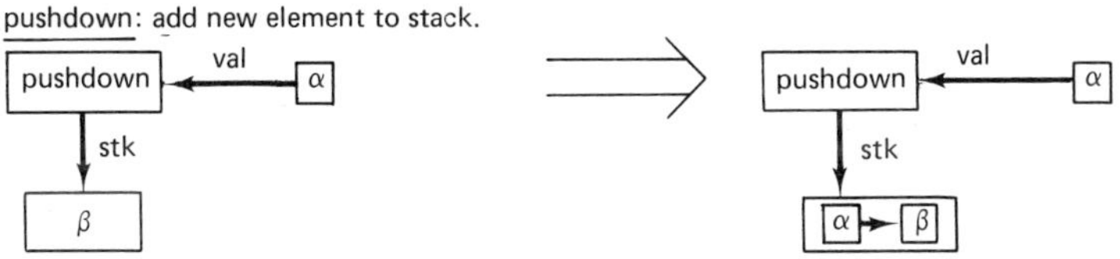

5 or/and

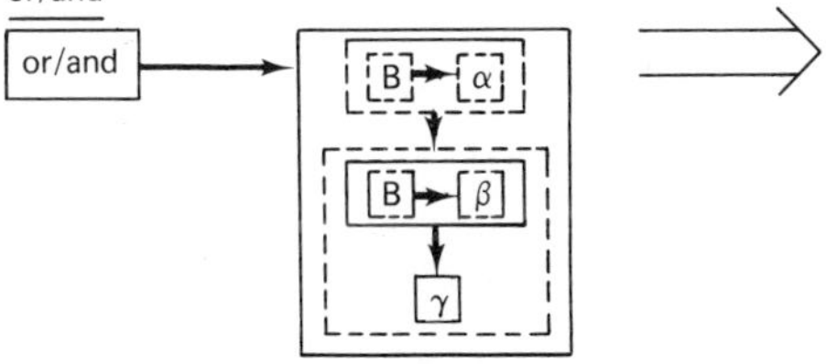

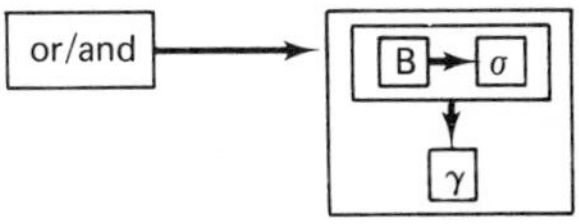

where $\sigma = \alpha \vee \beta$ (operator = or)
$= \alpha \wedge \beta$ (operator = and)

6 not

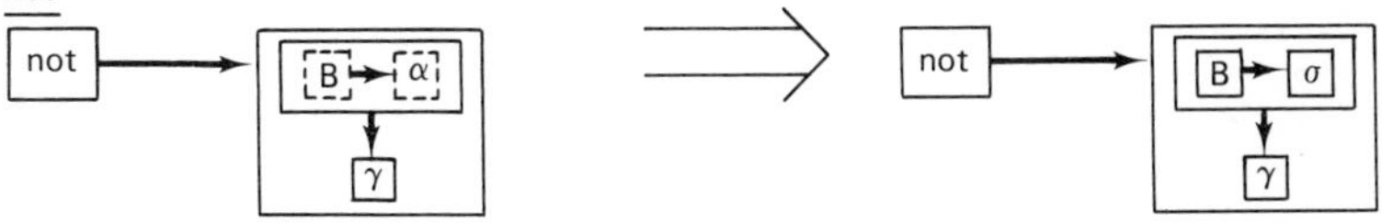

where $\sigma = \neg \alpha$

7   equal/less-than

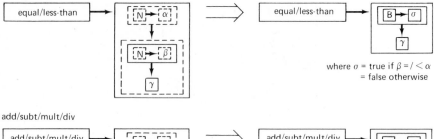

where σ = true if β = / $<$ α
= false otherwise

8   add/subt/mult/div

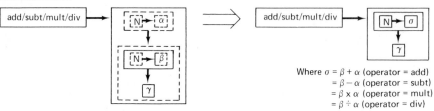

Where $\sigma = \beta + \alpha$ (operator = add)
$= \beta - \alpha$ (operator = subt)
$= \beta \times \alpha$ (operator = mult)
$= \beta \div \alpha$ (operator = div)

8 DESIGNS OF FAULT-TOLERANT COMPUTING SYSTEMS

C. V. Ramamoorthy and R. C. Cheung
*Departments of Electrical Engineering and Computer
Science
University of California at Berkeley
Berkeley, California*

Editor's Note:

This chapter surveys most of the pertinent techniques for fault-tolerant computing. Written for breadth and conciseness, this chapter has omitted many details and has placed its emphasis on motivating the reader to explore further by reading the references. The fact that many existing real computing systems were used as examples greatly enhances the reader's appreciation of the design principles and techniques introduced in the chapter.

The material presented in this chapter supplemented by that of Chapter 9 and some original literature should be sufficient for a one semester course on fault-tolerant computing.

Although the chapter is reasonably self-contained, some knowledge in switching theory and logical design is a desirable prerequisite.

The purpose of this chapter is to survey and present some of the techniques and principles used in the design of fault-tolerant computing systems. Emphasis is placed on the tutorial value rather than the extensiveness of coverage of current literature.

8.1. INTRODUCTION

8.1.1. Faults and Fault-Tolerance

8.1.1.1. Definition of Fault-Tolerance. A *fault-tolerant computer* is defined as one which executes a set of programs (algorithms) correctly in presence of certain specified faults in the system, which include hardware failures and software errors. This implies the correct execution of programs by the computer system when there are no software errors in the programs. By correct execution of the program we mean that (1) the programs are not halted or modified by faults in the computer; and that (2) the results do not contain errors caused by system faults. Fault-tolerant computing can be achieved by *protective redundancy* [1]. Protective redundancy consists of additional circuits (hardware redundancy), additional programs (software reduncancy), additional data (information redundancy), and repetition of operations (time redundancy). For practical purposes, additional constraints are also introduced. The amount of extra execution time in the presence of system faults must be within reasonable bounds. The redundant hardware and software introduced in the fault-tolerant system must be kept at a minimum so that the total storage capacity and resources required must be within feasible limits.

8.1.1.2. Levels of Fault Tolerance. Fault tolerance can be incorporated in different levels with different methods:

1. *Total system level.* In the architectural level hardware and software means can be implemented for the system to reconfigure itself after the detection of faults in the system. Usually the faulty functional unit is switched off and a spare part is used to replace it or the system simply reconfigures itself with a degraded performance, without replacing the faulty unit.

2. *Machine language level.* Diagnostic programs can be written to check a set of machine instructions by another set which will do the same operation on the operand. For example, complicated machine functions like MULTI-PLY can be checked by a program written with simpler machine instructions such as ADD and SHIFT. Also checking of the validity of the operation codes and operands can be used in fault diagnosis.

3. *Microprogram level.* Specialized microprograms written to diagnosis faults has become popular. This allows fine resoluton of the fault location with little hardware overhead for computers with microprogram features.

4. *Hardware logic level.* Redundant logic modules are usually used to mask internal faults. Simple voting schemes [2], interwoven logic [6], and adaptive voting [6] schemes can be used.

8.1.1.3. Types of Faults
1. *Hardware faults:*

(a) *Logic faults:* Failures of components can cause deviation from design-specified values of logic variables. A *logical fault* is said to occur if the logical value of one or more logical functions become opposite to the specified values. Logic faults can be further classified into two classes: *permanent* or *hard* fault and *transient* or *soft* fault. Usually permanent faults are caused by an open-circuit or short-circuit, due to solid component failures, causing "stuck-at" type of faults. Transient faults are usually caused by critical timing, noise, and overly close tolerances. They can be caused by intermittent component malfunctions or external interference with the operation of the computer. Aging or manufacturing defects can also cause gradual deterioration and marginal faults. Many soft faults can eventually become hard.

(b) *Other hardware faults.* Besides component failures there are also other hardware faults. A common fault is the clock malfunction, caused by the asynchronization of the clock pulse or the degradation of the magnitude, rise time, or width of the clock pulse. The design of a fault-tolerant digital clocking system using an array of identical oscillator modules to produce a number of phase-locked clock signals has been proposed [5]. Another common hardware failure is the power supply failure. Power supply failure will usually affect the contents of the registers and the volatile memory devices.

2. *Software faults:* These faults will cause deviations from correct program implementations in the computer, such as an incorrect translation of the source program into the machine language program. These faults can occur in different functional modules of the operating system software, such as the compiler, the assembler, the loader, etc. Software faults are usually more difficult to locate than hardware faults. Although these faults may be considered as "permanent" in nature, they are extremely data-sensitive. Program validation, using time redundancy and program redundancy, is still in an infant stage.

8.1.1.4. Causes of Faults

1. *Faults due to design errors.* Design faults are usually due to (a) imperfect or incomplete specifications; and (b) imperfect implementation of specifications. The former is especially common in software faults. There are many "special" cases that the programmer will overlook or handle improperly. There are many ways that the user can make the operating system behave in an undesirable way. (a) is not very common in the logical design of the hardware because of the existence of systematic ways of design and validation. However, (a) is common in the circuit design of the computer because of unforeseen interference between different circuit components and in the transmission line, such as cross-coupling, etc. (b) is not a common cause of software fault but is a common cause of hardware fault in the initial stage. In building a piece of hardware with thousands of components as com-

plicated as a computer, it is inevitable that some human error will occur, such as a bad soldering, a wiring error, or an unintentional short-circuit. To eliminate design errors, verification is required before it is used. Different parts of the design have to be checked out first. Then the behavior of the computer with all the individual parts coupled together has to be checked out by either simulation on another computer or by building a small experimental bench-version of the machine.

2. *Faults due to component failures.* No component can last forever. Aging, manufacturing defects, or undesirable transient power supply behavior can cause some components to deteriorate and others to fail. These faults will occur after the machine is put into operation. They are unpredictable and so some fault-tolerant features must be incorporated into the computer, either to mask off the faults or to detect the faults. Obviously, complete tolerance to all conceivable faults is impossible and we can only hope to achieve a reasonable level of fault-tolerance. The coverage of a system is the conditional probability that the system will recover given that the system has failed due to some faults. It is a measure of the proportion of faults from which the system can recover automatically, i.e., the faults that are "covered" by the system.

8.1.1.5.   Fault Characterization.   The characteristics of a fault can be classified as follows:

1. *Duration.* A fault can be *permanent* or *transient.* A *permanent fault* does not change its behavior with time until it is repaired. They can be detected by periodic checks. The behavior of a *transient fault* can vary with time, even under the same input conditions. The inability to reproduce the same environment makes transient faults very difficult to detect.

2. *Extent.* Faults can be classified as *local* or *catastrophic.* A *local,* or *independent, fault* can only affect the behavior of one logical circuit of the computer. A *catastrophic,* or *related, fault* affects other parts besides the location of the fault. For example, a logical fault is usually a local fault while the malfunction of the clock is a catastrophic fault.

3. *Value.* The value of a logical fault can be *fixed,* e.g., stuck-at-0 (s-a-0), or stuck-at-1 (s-a-1), and the value can also be *indeterministic,* e.g., stuck-at-x (s-a-x), where x can vary between 0 and 1. A stuck-at-x variable fault can randomly generate zeros and ones and are very difficult to detect.

4. *Nature.* The nature of a fault can be classified as *logical* and *nonlogical.* A logical fault causes a logical variable to malfunction, usually s-a-0 or s-a-1. Nonlogical faults cover the rest of the faults such as power failure, etc.

5. *Failure rates.* The characteristic of the *failure rate* of each class of fault can be specified by how often the fault occurs (the maximum rate of fault incidence for that class in faults per second) and how long the fault lasts (the maximum duration of the fault specified). The faults that last for a long time

can be viewed as permanent faults. Usually an exponential failure rate is assumed for component failures.

8.1.2. The Use of Redundancy in Ultra-Reliable Computer Design

Two strategies are commonly employed in the design of highly reliable, highly available computers: the selection of highly reliable components, and the introduction of redundancy. Usually both of these approaches are taken together. Redundancy enables us to make reliable computers out of unreliable parts. It has been shown by Pierce [6] that if only a fixed fraction of a redundant system need be operable in order to prevent system failure, and if errors are statistically independent, then when additional system cost is spent in adding redundancy, the log of the system's failure probability decreases linearly with cost. Therefore a system's failure probability decreases exponentially with cost! Although this is only a limit that we want to achieve (under some idealistic assumptions), it shows that redundancy theory is a promising approach to increase both the reliability and availability of the system.

Although widely used, the term "redundancy" has never been rigorously defined in the field of fault-tolerant computing design. Historically, the term "redundancy" has been used as a measure for the extra structure useless for conveying information and was restricted to describe symbolic structures such as language and codes, rather than material structures like hardware. For example, in the field of communication theory, Shanon defined redundancy as one minus the relative entropy of the source. In fault-tolerant computer design, what is implied in most cases is that the reliability of the system is increased through the use of "redundancy" being discussed. A computer system is said to contain *protective redundancy* if the effects of component failures or program errors can be controlled by the use of additional hardware or programs, or the use of additional time for the computational tasks. The techniques of functional redundancy may be divided into two main categories: *static* (*massive* or *masking*) redundancy and *dynamic* (or *selective*) redundancy.

The static redundancy approach provides continuous computation by masking out the effect of a faulty component, circuit, program, signal, subsystem, or system with permanently connected and concurrently operating redundant copies of the faulty element. The level at which replication occurs ranges from individual circuit components (component quadding [7], interwoven logic [6], etc.) to the entire system with majority voting at selected interfaces, e.g., triple modular redundancy [2]. Error-correcting codes (information redundancy) can also be considered as a form of static redundancy as continuous computation is provided.

The dynamic redundancy approach involves three steps: *fault detection, fault isolation*, and *fault recovery*. Fault detection may consist of *concurrent diagnosis* (using error-detecting codes or special monitoring circuits) or *periodic diagnosis* (interrupting the operation of the system for diagnostic tests). The completeness of fault coverage and the minimization of diagnostic time should be emphasized in the fault detection procedures. After a fault has been detected, the fault should be located and isolated to prevent the unbounded propagation of erroneous data or control information. For fault location, the system is exercised under a set of test patterns and the results are analyzed. To ensure a correct diagnosis using a faulty computer, a hardcore is needed. (The *hardcore* is that section of a system that is assumed faultless or is pre-checked independently so that it can be used with certainty as a basis for further diagnostic procedures. The hardcore is usually heavily protected with static redundancy.) A bootstrap procedure is usually employed, using successively tested subsystems to check the other unreliable parts, starting with the hardcore. Maximum distinguishability should be emphasized in the fault isolation procedures to minimize the overhead for recovery. The recovery step begins with the replacement of the faulty element or system by a standby spare (*self-repair*) or the reorganization of the system into a different computer configuration to bypass the faulty component, with a possible degradation of performance (*graceful degradation*). Afterwards an assessment of the damage to critical information (programs and data), reconstruction of this information and the restarting of the critical tasks are performed. Program rollback or program restart are usually needed. Although the computer hardware is usually better utilized in dynamic redundancy than static, the operation of the computer is constantly interrupted for diagnostic procedures, creating considerable overhead. The recovery procedure is slow and usually only permanent faults can be controlled. Thus static redundancy is still popular in some real-time systems. Usually a combination of both forms of redundancy are used.

Following this brief introduction, we will discuss in the following sections some of the fault diagnosis techniques, coding techniques, and various design philosophies to facilitate easy diagnosis and quick recovery. Afterwards quantitative evaluation and analysis of different configurations of fault-tolerant computers are performed by means of reliability models. Some examples of fault-tolerant computers will also be examined.

8.2. FAULT DIAGNOSIS OF DIGITAL SYSTEMS

8.2.1. Introduction

After a digital system has been put into operation, some components may change its performance because of physical deterioration or damage. Redundancy has to be introduced in order to ensure correct system operation. Extra components can be provided so that the failure does not affect the overall operation (*fault masking*). However no component can last forever. The system will fail eventually no matter how much redundancy we put in, unless we have a technique for detecting and locating the failed component (*fault diagnosis*) so that it can be replaced, thus restoring the fault-tolerant capability of the system. (Sometimes redundancy is introduced to the data by coding techniques for fault masking or fault diagnosis.)

Fault diagnosis includes both fault detection and fault location. *Fault detection* is the process of determining whether the system is operating correctly. *Fault location* is the process of distinguishing the fault to certain components, sets of components, functional modules, or subsystems depending on the requirement of resolution.

Testing of a logic network is carried out by applying a sequence of inputs and observing the resulting outputs. The cost of testing includes the generation of the test sequence and actually applying the test. Since the test sequence is usually applied many times while it has to be calculated only once for a given circuit, efforts must be made to minimize the test sequence.

Many types of faults can exist in a digital system and it is important for us to concentrate our attention only on the most common types of faults. The most commonly used fault models to represent system failures is the class of faults whose logical effects can be represented as constant binary signals forced on circuit leads—the so called "stuck-at" faults. This assumes that the fault results in a line permanently stuck at the logical 1 or logical 0 level, denoted by s-a-1 and s-a-0, respectively. This is a practical model because it includes the most common circuit failures due to an "open line" or a "shorted line" that does not induce feedback as a result of the short.

Digitial networks can be divided into different classes for fault-diagnosis purposes. Typical classifications are whether the network is *combinatorial* or *sequential* (which can be subclassified into *synchronous* and *asynchronous*), whether the network has *single* or *multiple outputs*, whether there is *fan-out* or not, whether *reconvergent fan-out* exists or not, and whether the network is *redundant* or *irredundant*. We can consider the case of single or multiple faults for a network and the method used can be characterized as *heuristic* or *algorithmic*.

In this study we always assume that only single "stuck-at" fault has occurred, unless specified. The problem is to construct a test or a set of tests that detects the fault by utilizing only the normal circuit inputs and outputs. This excludes the diagnosis of redundancy in the logic circuit which has undetectable faults, i.e., the output of the circuit is independent of the faulty part.

8.2.2. Diagnosis Techniques for Combinational Circuits

8.2.2.1. One-Dimensional Path Sensitizing. The concept of path sensitizing was introduced by Armstrong [8]. The basic idea is to choose some path from the site of failure, say gate G_0, through a sequence $G_1, \ldots, G_n$ of gates leading to a circuit output. The path is said to be *sensitized* if the inputs to $G_1, \ldots, G_n$ are selected so that complementing the output of G_0 causes the value of *all* leads on the path to be complemented. Thus the output of G_0 can be inferred from observation of the output of G_n. Therefore any failure in G_0 can be detected by specifying the inputs of G_0 so that the presence or absence of the failure can be inferred from the output of G_0, which will then propagate in a prescribed way to the output of the circuit, i.e., the output of G_n. This part of the process is the *forward-trace phase* of the method.

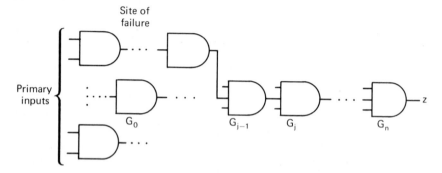

Fig. 8.2.1   Selection of a path.

Since we are restricted to applying only the normal inputs to the circuit, we must find a primary input vertex V that will realize all the necessary gate inputs of $G_0, G_1, \ldots, G_n$. This is done by tracing backwards from the prescribed values of the inputs of $G_0, G_1, \ldots, G_n$ to the circuit primary inputs. This is known as the *backward-trace* phase of the method.

An example can now be given to illustrate this method. Consider the combinational circuit in Fig. 8.2.2.

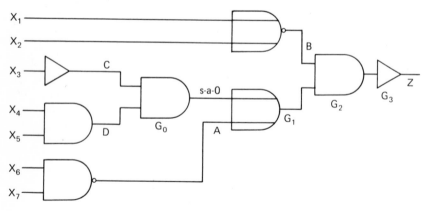

Fig. 8.2.2   Example for one-dimensional path sensitizing.

Let us suppose that we want to detect G_0 output s-a-0. In order that the output of G_1 is complemented when the output of G_0 is complemented, input A to G_1 must be 0. Similarly input B of G_2 must be set at 1 so that the output of G_2 depends solely on G_1. In order to test for G_0 s-a-0, the output of G_0 must be set at 1 if the fault is absent. Hence the leads C and D must be both set at 1. This completes the forward-trace part. The backward-trace part can now proceed. In order to set A to 0, the primary inputs X_6 and X_7 must both be 1. In order for B to be 1, X_1 and X_2 must both be 0. For C to be 1, X_3 must be 0. Similarly, X_4 and X_5 must be 1. Therefore the input vector $X = (0, 0, 0, 1, 1, 1, 1)$ can detect the failure G_0 s-a-0. When the failure is absent, the output z of the circuit is 0. The output z is 1 when the failure is present. Note that if lead i is sensitized by an input vertex X, then all leads on a single sensitized path from i to an output of the circuit are also sensitized by X. Therefore in the sensitized path in the example, X can also detect the errors G_1 s-a-0, G_2 s-a-0, and also G_3 s-a-1. Note that the above statement is not true when there is a *reconvergent fan-out*, i.e., two or more paths fan out from the site of failure and subsequently reconverge. In fact, when there is a reconvergent fan-out, a solution may not even exist to sensitize a path. A simple counterexample has been given by Schneider [9]. The circuit is shown in Fig. 8.2.3.

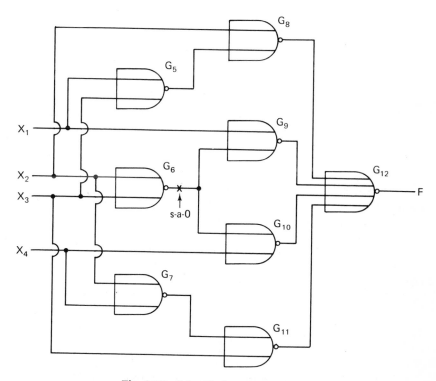

Fig. 8.2.3 Schneider's counterexample.

The failure to be tested in G_6 is s-a-0. It is impossible to generate a test for this failure by strictly one-dimensional path sensitizing. Any path must pass through G_9 or G_{10} (but not both). A sensitized path through G_9 and G_{12} requires that G_{10} and G_{11} to be both 0.

For $G_6 = 1$, $X_2 = 0$ and $X_3 = 0$.

For $G_{10} = 0$, $X_4 = 1$.

For $G_{11} = 0$, $G_7 = 1$ (since $X_3 = 0$ to make $G_6 = 1$).

Therefore, $X_2 = 0$ and $X_4 = 0$, $G_7 = 0$. Contradiction!

By symmetry of the circuit, the same argument applies to a path through G_{10} and G_{12}. Hence the method of one-dimensional path sensitizing fails while the input vector $X = (0, 0, 0, 0)$ is a valid test.

The following obvious theorem can be stated [16].

Theorem 8.2.1

A set of primary input vertices V detects all single s-a-0 and s-a-1 faults in the network if it has the following properties:

1. For all inputs i to the network, there exists $\bar{v} \in V$ such that $\bar{v}$ sensitizes input i for s-a-0, and there exists $\bar{v}' \in V$ such that $\bar{v}'$ sensitizes input i for s-a-1.

2. For all leads m in the network, there exists $\bar{v} \in V$ such that lead m is 0 when v is applied and lead m is on a single path sensitized by $\bar{v}$; and there exists $\bar{v}' \in V$ such that lead m is 1 when $\bar{v}'$ is applied and lead m is on a single path sensitized by $\bar{v}'$.

From Schneider's counterexample the reader can notice the flaw in the one-dimensional method is that only one path is allowed to be sensitized at a time, even in case of reconvergent fan-outs with equal inversion parity. The key to an algorithmic method is to sensitize all possible paths from the failure site to the output simultaneously. This approach is known as the D-algorithm or two-dimensional path sensitizing, discovered by J. P. Roth [10].

8.2.2.2. The D-Algorithm. The D-algorithm is the first algorithmic method for generating tests for nonredundant combinational circuits, i.e., if a test exists for detecting a failure then the D-algorithm is guaranteed to find this test. The D-algorithm was first formulated by J. Roth [10] in terms of calculus of cubical complexes. The D-algorithm has then been programmed and used to generate tests in practical cases. It has also been extended to apply to sequential circuits by transforming the problem of finding a single fault to that of finding multiple faults in an iterative combinational circuit constructed from the sequential model by the cutting of all its feedback lines.

The basic idea of the D-algorithm is as follows. First, generate a test for the fault f in terms of the inputs and output of the failed gate. Next, sensitize all possible paths from the site of failure to the circuit outputs simultaneously. At each step, check for cancellation caused by reconvergent fan-out, and eliminate the cancelled paths. Roth called this forward-trace phase the D-*drive*. Then proceed with the backward-trace phase of finding a consistent primary input vector which realizes all of the conditions generated during the D-drive. Roth calls this the *consistency operation*.

Before the D-algorithm can be discussed in detail, some notations and terminologies have to be introduced [11].

1. *Specification of the network behavior*—the singular cover. The *singular cover* is a rearranged compact form representation of a truth table. The single cover of an AND gate is shown in Fig. 8.2.4. (An x is used to denote that the corresponding variable may be a 1 or 0.) Each row is called a *cube* and represents the relationship between the inputs and output of the gate.

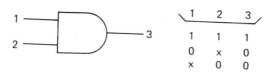

1	2	3
1	1	1
0	x	0
x	0	0

Fig. 8.2.4   An AND gate and its singular cover.

The singular cover of a network is just the set of singular covers of each of its gates on separate rows in the table. This is illustrated by the example in Fig. 8.2.5. Note that a "blank" and an x have the same meaning in the table.

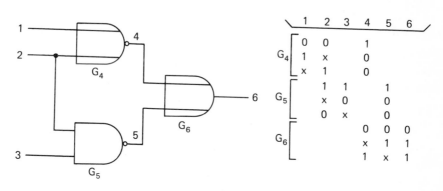

	1	2	3	4	5	6
G_4	0	0		1		
	1	x		0		
	x	1		0		
G_5			1	1		1
			x	0		0
			0	x		0
G_6				0	0	0
				x	1	1
				1	x	1

Fig. 8.2.5   A network and its singular cover.

2. *Representation of a sensitized path—D-cubes.* *D-cubes* represent the input-output behavior of the failing and the good circuit. The *propagation D-cube* of a gate tells how one gate input can be made to "bear the sole re-

sponsibility" for determining the gate output. To systematically construct propagation D-cubes, we intersect cubes with different output values in the gate's singular cover. The input values are intersected according to the following rules:

$$0 \cap 0 = 0 \cap x = x \cap 0 = 0$$
$$1 \cap 1 = 1 \cap x = x \cap 1 = 1$$
$$x \cap x = x$$
$$1 \cap 0 = D, \quad 0 \cap 1 = \bar{D}$$

Note that since we intersect cubes with different outputs, the propagation D-cubes always have a D or $\bar{D}$ on the output coordinates.

For example, the propagation D-cube of the two-input AND gate can be formed from the singular cover table as follows:

	1	2	3
$C1 = $	1	1	1
$C2 = $	0	x	0
$C3 = $	x	0	0

	1	2	3
$C1 \cap C2 = $	D	1	D
$C1 \cap C3 = $	1	D	D

Singular cover of the AND gate.   Propagation D-cube of the AND gate.

The next step is to form the *primitive D-cube of a failure*. This is the particular propagation D-cube of the faulty gate that we are interested in. However, it is conceptually different from the case of the propagation D-cube. The primitive D-cube of a failure is used to express the conditions on the inputs in order to test the failed gate. As an example, the primitive D-cube for the AND gate s-a-0 is

1	2	3
1	1	D

The primitive D-cubes for the AND gate s-a-1 is

1	2	3
0	x	$\bar{D}$
x	0	$\bar{D}$

There exists an algorithmic way to determine the primitive D-cube of failure which proceeds as follows. First we form the singular covers of the correct gate and the failed gate. Then select one cube from the singular cover of the correct gate and intersect it with the corresponding cube from the singular cover of the failed gate, with the same rules of intersection as the propagation D-cube. A vertex of the intersection has value $\bar{D}$ if the vertex has value 0 in the cube of the failure-free block, and value 1 in the cube of the failed block. All other cases are assigned values D. The primitive D-cubes of failure consist of those D-cubes having a D or $\bar{D}$ on the output coordinate. The reader should be able to use this algorithm to derive the primitive D-cubes of failure for the AND gate and compare them with the results given.

Now that the notation and terminology have been presented, we are ready to discuss the D-algorithm (DALG-II). There is a useful convention to label the circuit. Each vertex of the circuit is assigned an integer label. Each gate has the name of the vertex corresponding to its output. Therefore each vertex corresponds to either a primary input signal or a gate output signal. Finally, the vertex numbers are assigned by a "levelling rule." A gate is assigned a number greater than the integers of all vertices which feed the gate.

3. *D-Algorithm (DALG-II)*. Starting with a primitive D-cube of failure at the failing gate, we proceed with the D-drive to construct a D-path (sensitized path), or set of D-paths, from the failed gate to a primary output. Initially the *D-frontier* [12] (defined to consist of all the gates in the circuit that have D's or $\bar{D}$'s on some of their inputs and x's on their outputs) consists of the successors of the faulty gate. The D-frontier is then moved towards the primary outputs by applying suitable propagation D-cubes to the gates in the D-frontier, thus advancing the D-frontier itself. The "suitable" propagation D-cube can be chosen by inspection or algorithmically by the D-intersection of the output of the gate with all the propagation D-cubes of the successor gate. The definition of the D-intersection operator $\underset{d}{\cap}$ is given in Table 8.2.1. Any intersection that does not extend a sensitized path is discarded. In general, for a gate with d fan-out, we have to consider the propagation D-cubes of all the gates that belong to the d fan-out of the gate.

Table 8.2.1 DEFINITION OF D-INTERSECTION OPERATOR

$\underset{d}{\cap}$	0	1	x	D	$\bar{D}$
0	0	$\varnothing$	0	ψ	ψ
1	$\varnothing$	1	1	ψ	ψ
x	0	1	x	D	$\bar{D}$
D	ψ	ψ	D	μ	λ
$\bar{D}$	ψ	ψ	$\bar{D}$	λ	μ

In the table, $\varnothing$ means that the D-intersection is empty. ψ means that the D-intersection is undefined. μ is generated by the intersection of D and D, or $\bar{D}$ and $\bar{D}$. This means that the sensitized path can be consistently extended because the output of the second gate is still sensitive. λ is generated by the intersection of a pair of D and $\bar{D}$ of two cubes. However, the D-cube of the second gate (successor gate) can be complemented (by changing D's into $\bar{D}$'s, and $\bar{D}$'s into D's) independent of the first gate without changing its meaning. Hence this is the same as μ by complementing the second D-cube. However, when both μ and λ occur in an intersection, there is no way we can achieve consistency. (This is usually caused by a reconvergent fan-out.) Hence the sensitized path is blocked. Now the definitions of μ and λ can be stated as follows:

1. If only μ (but not λ) occurs in the D-intersection, then for these coordinates let $D \underset{d}{\cap} D = D$, $\bar{D} \underset{d}{\cap} \bar{D} = \bar{D}$.

2. If only λ (but not μ) occurs, then in the second D-cube (the successor gate) change all those coordinates which are D to $\bar{D}$, and those which are $\bar{D}$ to D.

3. If both μ and λ occur, the D-intersection is undefined.

The D-drive is continued until a D or $\bar{D}$ has been imposed on a primary output. Now a connected D path has been established from the site of failure to the primary output, and the D-drive is terminated. Note that in the D-drive phase of pushing the D-frontier to the output the D-intersection is carried out with all the successor gates. Hence all possible paths are sensitized simultaneously.

After the D-drive, the 0, 1 values imposed have to be justified in terms of the primary input values. This is accomplished by the consistency operation by tracing backwards to the primary inputs.

The algorithm can be better understood with the aid of an illustrative example. In order to demonstrate the power of the D-algorithm over the one-dimensional path sensitizing method, let us consider Schneider's example. Please refer to Fig. 8.2.3.

The single propagation D-cubes of the above network is shown in Table 8.2.2. Each D-cube is given an alphabetical label. We begin by writing down a primitive D-cube of the failure, G_6 s-a-0, which we label as test cube 0, T_0.

$$T_0 = \begin{array}{cccccccccccc} 1 & 2 & 3 & 4 & 5 & 6 & 7 & 8 & 9 & 10 & 11 & 12 \\ \hline & 0 & 0 & & & D & & & & & & \end{array}$$

Now the D-frontier consists of G_9 and G_{10}. Therefore we have to perform D-intersection of T with all the propagation D-cubes of G_9 and G_{10}. The intersection of T_0 with I (the first D-cube of G_9) gives

$$\begin{array}{cccccccccccc} 1 & 2 & 3 & 4 & 5 & 6 & 7 & 8 & 9 & 10 & 11 & 12 \\ \hline 0 & 0 & 0 & & D & & & \bar{D} & & & & \end{array}$$

This is a realizable D-cube. Let us call it test cube $T_{0,1}$.

Table 8.2.2   SINGLE PROPAGATION D-CUBES FOR SCHNEIDER'S EXAMPLE

		1	2	3	4	5	6	7	8	9	10	11	12
G_5	A	0		D		$\bar D$							
	B		D	0		$\bar D$							
G_6	C		0	D			$\bar D$						
	D		D	0			$\bar D$						
G_7	E		0		D			$\bar D$					
	F		D		0			$\bar D$					
G_8	G		0		D				$\bar D$				
	H		D		0				$\bar D$				
G_9	I	0			D					$\bar D$			
	J	D			0					$\bar D$			
G_{10}	K				0	D					$\bar D$		
	L				D	0					$\bar D$		
G_{11}	M			0			D					$\bar D$	
	N			D			0					$\bar D$	
	O								D	0	0	0	$\bar D$
G_{12}	P								0	D	0	0	$\bar D$
	Q								0	0	D	0	$\bar D$
	R								0	0	0	D	$\bar D$

The intersection of T with J gives

1	2	3	4	5	6	7	8	9	10	11	12
D	0	0	ψ					$\bar D$			

The presence of ψ indicates that the D-cube cannot be extended the sensitized path any more. Therefore this cube is discarded.

Similarly the intersection of T_0 with L of G_{10} is discarded and the intersection of T_0 and K gives the test cube $T_{0,2}$.

	1	2	3	4	5	6	7	8	9	10	11	12
$T_{0,2} =$		0	0	0	D					$\bar D$		

Now we have to intersect $T_{0,1}$ and $T_{0,2}$ with all the propagation D-cubes of G_{12} since G_9 and G_{10} feeds G_{12}. By discarding all the results that do not yield a sensitized path, we will obtain

	1	2	3	4	5	6	7	8	9	10	11	12
$T_{0,1} \cap_d P = T_{0,1,1} =$	0	0	0	D				0	$\bar D$	0	0	D
$T_{0,2} \cap_d Q = T_{0,2,1} =$		0	0	0	D			0	0	$\bar D$	0	D

$T_{0,1,1}$ and $T_{0,2,1}$ represents two single sensitized paths from G_6 to the output. However, since G_9 and G_{10} reconverges at G_{12}, we have to check the two paths for consistency. The intersection of these two cubes yield an undesirable case.

Since G_9 and G_{10} are fed by G_6, we have to intersect $T_{0,1}$ and $T_{0,2}$ to check for consistency. The intersection of $T_{0,1}$ and $T_{0,2}$ gives

$$
\begin{array}{cccccccccccc}
1 & 2 & 3 & 4 & 5 & 6 & 7 & 8 & 9 & 10 & 11 & 12 \\
\end{array}
$$
$$
T_{0,1,2} = \begin{array}{cccccccccccc}
0 & 0 & 0 & 0 & & & D & & \bar{D} & \bar{D} & & \\
\end{array}
$$

Now we want to attempt to propagate $T_{0,1,2}$ through G_{12}. But coordinates 9 and 10 of $T_{0,1,2}$ are both inputs to G_{12} and both have the value $\bar{D}$. Therefore these inputs must jointly determine G_{12} output. All the propagation cubes in Table 8.2.2 are single D-cubes involving only one controlling input. Therefore we must generate the double D-cubes for G_{12} in which inputs 9 and 10 jointly control the output. By trial and error, we get the following useful D-cube for G_{12}.

$$
\begin{array}{cccccccccccc}
1 & 2 & 3 & 4 & 5 & 6 & 7 & 8 & 9 & 10 & 11 & 12 \\
 & & & & & & & 0 & \bar{D} & \bar{D} & 0 & D \\
\end{array}
$$

The intersection of this double D-cube with $T_{0,1,2}$ yields

$$
\begin{array}{cccccccccccc}
1 & 2 & 3 & 4 & 5 & 6 & 7 & 8 & 9 & 10 & 11 & 12 \\
\end{array}
$$
$$
T_{0,1,2,1} = \begin{array}{cccccccccccc}
0 & 0 & 0 & 0 & & & D & & 0 & \bar{D} & \bar{D} & 0 & \bar{D} \\
\end{array}
$$

Now this is a consistent sensitized path from G_6 to the output G_{12}.

We then have to proceed with the consistency operation phase of the algorithm by back-tracing to the primary inputs of the circuit. In this example, the values of the primary inputs x_1, x_2, x_3, and x_4 are already specified by $T_{0,1,2,1}$. Hence the valid test is

$$
\begin{array}{cccccccccccc}
1 & 2 & 3 & 4 & 5 & 6 & 7 & 8 & 9 & 10 & 11 & 12 \\
\end{array}
$$
$$
\text{Valid Test} = \begin{array}{cccccccccccc}
0 & 0 & 0 & 0 & 1 & D & 1 & 0 & \bar{D} & \bar{D} & 0 & D \\
\end{array}
$$

8.2.2.3. Boolean Difference Algorithm. The Boolean difference method was first applied to fault diagnosis by Sellers et al. [13]. The Boolean difference is a function which permits one to compute all those vertices which "sensitize a path" by an elegant equation-solving procedure.

Let $F(x_1, \ldots, x_n)$ be a switching function of the n variables $x_1, \ldots, x_n$ then the *Boolean difference* of F with respect to x_i is defined as

$$
\frac{dF(x_1, \ldots, x_n)}{dx_i} = \frac{dF}{dx_i} \triangleq F(x_1, \ldots, x_i, \ldots, x_n) \oplus F(x_1, \ldots, \bar{x}_i, \ldots, x_n)
$$

which is equivalent to $F(x_1, \ldots, 1, \ldots, x_n) \oplus (x_1, \ldots, 0, \ldots, x_n)$. This implies the Boolean difference is in general a Boolean function of $(n - 1)$ variables $x_1, \ldots, x_{i-1}, x_{i+1}, \ldots, x_n$.

Note that the exclusive-or connective implies that the Boolean difference of F with respect to x_i has the value 1 at precisely all those vertices where the value of F is different for the two possible values of x_i. When $dF/dx_i = 1$, a change at x_i always causes a change at F. Hence $dF/dx_i = 1$ is a sufficient condition for the path from x_i to F to be sensitized.

The Boolean difference can be used to generate fault-detection tests. One has only to write an expression for the output in terms of (1) the lead to be tested, call if X_t, and (2) the set of primary inputs $x_1, \ldots, x_n$. (For a multi-output network, we write an expression for each output that depends on X_t.) Then one computes the Boolean difference of the expression with respect to X_t. To test for X_t s-a-0, we have to find all the input vertices for which X_t $(dF/dX_t) = 1$. Similarly to test for X_t s-a-1 we solve for $\bar{X}_t(dF/dX_t) = 1$. (Note that in general X_t is not a primary input and is therefore a function of the set of primary inputs $x_1, \ldots, x_n$). Note that the Boolean difference with respect to X_t is always independent of X_t. The Boolean difference approach can also be used in detecting inversion type faults $(1 \rightarrow 0, 0 \rightarrow 1)$ in addition to the conventional stuck-at faults.

Let us now consider an illustrative example. The Schneider example will again be used to show how different algorithms can solve the same problem. Please refer to Fig. 8.2.3.

The failure to be tested is G_6 s-a-0. First we have to write an expression of the output in terms of X_6 and the inputs x_1, x_2, x_3, and x_4, where X_6 is the output of G_6.

$$F = \bar{X}_6 x_1 x_2 x_3 x_4 + X_6(x_2 x_3 + \bar{x}_1 \bar{x}_2 \bar{x}_3 \bar{x}_4)$$

Next, the Boolean difference of F with respect to X_6 is

$$\frac{dF}{dX_6} = x_1 x_2 x_3 x_4 \oplus (x_2 x_3 + \bar{x}_1 \bar{x}_2 \bar{x}_3 \bar{x}_4)$$

$$= \bar{x}_1 \bar{x}_2 \bar{x}_3 \bar{x}_4 + \bar{x}_1 x_2 x_3 + x_2 x_3 \bar{x}_4$$

Since

$$X_6 = \bar{x}_2 \bar{x}_3$$

$$X_6 \frac{dF}{dX_6} = \bar{x}_2 \bar{x}_3(\bar{x}_1 \bar{x}_2 \bar{x}_3 \bar{x}_4 + \bar{x}_1 x_2 x_3 + x_2 x_3 \bar{x}_4)$$

$$= \bar{x}_1 \bar{x}_2 \bar{x}_3 \bar{x}_4$$

the equation

$$X_6 \frac{dF}{dX_6} = 1$$

has only one solution, i.e.,

$$(x_1, x_2, x_3, x_4) = (0, 0, 0, 0)$$

The Boolean difference is a powerful concept that can be extended into many applications. For example, to test for "stuck-at" faults of a lead X_i in a multiple-output network with output functions $F_1, \ldots, F_m$ one simply has to solve the equation

$$\sum_j x_i^* \frac{dF_j}{dX_i} = 1$$

where $X_i^* = X_i(\bar{X}_i)$ if we test for lead X_i stuck in $0(1)$, and the "OR" sum is taken over all the outputs.

To generate a test which simultaneously tests the "stuck-at" faults of a set of leads $\{X_k\}$, one has to solve the equation

$$\prod_k \left(\sum X_k^* \frac{dF_j}{dX_k} \right) = 1$$

where the "AND" product is taken over all the leads that we want to test.

The Boolean difference can also be used to find diagnostic tests under the single-fault assumption, i.e., tests that can distinguish the fault from a set of possible failures if only a single fault is assumed to have occurred. For this we find, for each pair of faults, the set of vertices which can distinguish between them. This is done by solving the equation

$$X_i^* \frac{dF}{dX_i} \oplus X_j^* \frac{dF}{dX_j} = 1$$

This constraint assures that for the applied test, the response to failure X_i^* is different from the response to failure X_j^*. To complete the diagnostic test, we have to solve the above equation for every one of the $n(n - 1)/2$ lead pairs and for each pair we have four ways of assigning X_i^* and X_j^*.

Other extensions of the Boolean difference include the partial Boolean difference, Boolean difference chains, and Boolean difference of multiple variables.

8.2.2.4 Equivalent Normal Form (enf).

The *equivalent normal form* is an equivalent two-level circuit representation of the circuit. This method of test generation, originated by Armstrong [8], can generate efficient (near minimal) test sets but unfortunately becomes unmanageable for large circuits.

The enf of a single output combinational circuit can be constructed as follows:

1. Write the Boolean expression of the circuit in terms of the input variables as literals. Each subexpression corresponding to a gate G will be enclosed by a pair of parentheses, which is labelled with the subscript j.

2. Expand to sum-of-products form. When a pair of parentheses is removed, its associated label will be attached to each literal inside the parentheses as a subscript. No redundant terms are removed.

We can see that each literal appearance in the final enf corresponds to a path from a circuit input to the output, the path being specified by the string of subscripts. Therefore a test for a literal appearance in the enf sensitizes the corresponding path. Multiple paths can also be sensitized. If we can find a set of literal appearances whose corresponding paths cover every vertex of the circuit and a set of tests to test each literal, this set of tests detects every fault of the circuit. The enf method is therefore more powerful than one-dimensional path sensitizing. Although it has not been proven to be algorithmic, neither has a counterexample been found.

8.2.2.5. Multiple Fault Test Generation. The detection of all multiple faults in a circuit is an extremely difficult problem. A reasonable approach is to identify networks for which a single-fault test set can also detect all multiple faults. A two-level network with primary input fan-out is such a network. This result can be generalized to networks that are *restricted fan-out-free*, i.e., networks that do not contain the network of Fig. 8.2.6 (or its equivalent) as a subnetwork.

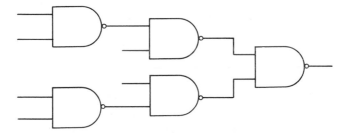

Fig. 8.2.6   Nonrestricted fan-out-free network.

Schertz and Metze [15] have outlined a heuristic procedure to design multiple-output combinational networks so that multiple faults can be detected by the single-fault test set, by transforming subnetworks to restricted fan-out-free form. First, a given m-output network N can be transformed into m equivalent single-output networks $(N_1, N_2, \ldots, N_m)$, each realizing an output of N.

Any of these networks, say N_i, which contains reconvergent fan-out of internal lines can be transformed into an equivalent fan-out-free network N_i' by duplicating the portions of the network which precede the fan-out points [16]. The transformed fan-out-free networks can then be divided into two groups: N_R' (restricted networks) and N_N' (nonrestricted). All faults in N_R' can be tested by single-fault test sets. For a network N_i' belonging to N_N', any portion of N_i' that is shared with a network N_j' in N_R' in the original network has already been tested through the corresponding output of N_j' and therefore can be removed from N_i'. The removal may convert N_i' from N_N' to N_R'. If so, the portions shared by N_i' and any other networks in N_N' can be similarly removed after the diagnosis of N_i'. If successive steps of diagnosis and removal of shared subnetworks eventually cover all output networks, multiple faults in the original network can be tested easily by single-fault test sets. Note that the order of applying the tests is very important. Also different faults in the shared portion of the network may have to be detected by different outputs.

If the procedure above still leaves some networks that are nonrestricted, these networks have to be transformed into N_R' by replacing a multilevel non-restricted subnetwork with a functionally equivalent and restricted one with fewer levels (with possibly more inputs and more fan-ins for each gate) [15]. In the worst case, a two-level network can be used. Therefore we can design a network easily diagnosable for multiple faults.

8.2.3. Fault Diagnosis of Sequential Circuits

For a sequential circuit the behavior of the network depends not only on the present values of the inputs but also on the set of past inputs. The state of the machine must be identified first before any prediction of the correct machine behavior can be made. This can be achieved by performing Gedanken experiments on the finite-state machine. A *Gedanken experiment* is the process of applying one or more input sequences to the machine, observing the corresponding output sequences, and drawing conclusions about the structure or state of the machine. In order to predict the future behavior of a correct machine, sometimes it is sufficient to put the machine into a prescribed final state. This is known as a *homing experiment*. Sometimes it is necessary to identify the machine's initial state. This is known as a *distinguishing experiment*.

The generation of tests for sequential circuits is very difficult. With an algorithmic approach, each candidate test input must be evaluated for each possible circuit state. The amount of computation required easily becomes unmanageable. There is also the problem of performing a homing experiment to put the machine into a known state. A second approach is to physically open all the feedback lines of the machine to make it combinational. It is valid for synchronous circuits but has problems with asynchronous circuits. Besides, additional hardware and signal lines have to be introduced, which may sometimes create problems. Some heuristic methods have been developed by Seshu [17], which is based on the assumption that a small change in the primary input space of the machine will give rise to only a small change in the state space. However there is no guarantee that an optimal test sequence, or even a complete test sequence, will be generated.

An algorithmic method has been proposed by Poage and McCluskey [18], which assumes that a fault in a machine simply changes the state table of the machine. Thus from the state tables of all possible failed machines under the class of known faults and the fault-free machine, an experiment is performed to identify the particular unknown failed machine by applying a suitable input sequence which differentiates the good machine from each faulty machine.

The requirement of the state table of every faulty version of the machine makes the above method impractical. Hennie [19] instead adopted the approach of "verifying" the correct behavior of the machine by "touring" through all its states. His method depends on the existence of distinguishing sequences, which identifies the initial starting state. If every state of the machine has a distinguishing sequence, we can verify every transition in the state table by performing the transition and then doing a distinguishing experiment on the final state of the transition. Hennie's procedure yields good results for machines that have distinguishing sequences, and when the actual circuit has no more states than the correctly operating machine. Kohavi and Lavallee [20] have developed a method to obtain for any arbitrary sequential machine a corresponding machine which contains the original one and which is definitely diagnosable, meaning that every input sequence of a specified length is a distinguishing sequence. When sequential machines are designed to be definitely diagnosable, the diagnosis problem using Hennie's approach becomes much easier.

8.2.4. Functional Testing Techniques

The techniques of fault diagnosis discussed so far resolve the fault to a logic gate. The complexity of these diagnostic procedures grows very rapidly with the size of the circuit and may become unmanageable even for a minicomputer. Therefore it seems advantageous to have techniques which are applicable for a wide range of fault resolution requirements. We would like to resolve the fault first to a subsystem level of manageable size and then use some of the techniques discussed above to pinpoint the error within the subsystem. In this section we will discuss some general techniques of fault diagnosis using a black-box approach. These techniques deal with the input-output relationship of the system and require no detail information about the internal structure of the system. Therefore they are applicable to subsystems of different complexities and can be generalized down to the gate level, if so desired. Some design principles for ease of maintenance and diagnostics are also discussed.

8.2.4.1.   Generation of Efficient Test Sets at Subsystem Level.   The advent of microelectronics enhanced the need for general-purpose fault diagnosis techniques applicable to a higher level than logic gates. Seshu [21] used a method based on a digital computer simulation of the good machine and N faulty versions under the class of known faults. Inputs (distinguishing sequences) are applied and the response of each is used to effect a partitioning of the $(N + 1)$ systems. The resulting partitioning tree will enable us to isolate the good system from the rest (for fault detection) and to identify each faulty version uniquely (for fault location). An adaptive procedure can also be used to speed up the diagnosis.

Another approach uses the notion of a *fault matrix*, which relates a set of tests to their associated faults. The D-matrix of Chang [22] has a 1 in the d_{ij}th entry if a fault f_i is detected by a test t_j, otherwise 0. Kautz [23] used a similar matrix for fault detection, fault location, and fault location to a module. The generation of the optimal test set then reduces to a covering problem using row and column dominance techniques.

8.2.4.2.   Structural Theory of Machine Diagnosis.   Any digital system can be viewed as the superposition of the behavioral characteristics of the components on its structural form [24]. An understanding of the structure of the machine helps us to segment a complex machine into smaller subsystems of manageable size. A *directed graph* in which *nodes* represent functional elements and the *directed arcs* indicate the information flow or connections between the elements can be used conveniently to model the structure of a digital system since it can be applied uniformly to represent systems at different complexity levels. A *directed graph* consists of a finite nonempty set of vertices (*nodes*) and a prescribed collection of ordered pairs of distinct vertices (*arcs*). In this model, the arc from i to j describes the functional relation that the output of node i enters as an input to the node j. The computer system can be considered as a multilevel structure where each level can be analyzed using a graph model. Any discrete sequential system can be shown to be isomorphic to a directed graph [25].

1. *Fault diagnosis with test points.*   Let t_i and t_j be two nodes in the system graph. The ordered pair (t_i, t_j) is defined as a *test point pair* if some input test sequence at node t_i can provoke a distinguishable output at another node t_j. A test point on a node can provide entry for input patterns from an external source and means of monitoring the outputs of the node. The introduction of test points provides isolation of selected subsystems from the rest of the system for fault diagnosis purpose and the means for injecting test sequences at the primary test points (entrances to a subsystem) and monitoring the re-

sulting outputs at the output test points (exits of the subsystem). The necessary condition for test points t_i and t_j to be a valid test point pair (t_i, t_j) is that there must exist at least one directed path from t_i to t_j. The *range* of a test point pair (t_i, t_j), denoted by $V(t_i, t_j)$, is defined as the unique set of vertices that can be tested by (t_i, t_j). In this section, we will assume the range of (t_i, t_j) to be all the nodes on the paths from t_i to t_j, including the nodes t_i and t_j. Note that test points can be placed on designated arcs as well as nodes. When an input test point is placed on an arc, (t_p, t_q) and the corresponding output test point is placed on the arc (t_m, t_n), the test point pair will be defined as (t_q, t_m).

Let N be the set of nodes of the system graph. By inserting test patterns at t_i and examining the output test patterns at t_j one can determine if the fault exists in $V(t_i, t_j)$ or $N - V(t_i, t_j)$. Therefore (t_i, t_j) induces a partition on the set of nodes in the system. By intersecting the partitions induced by all test point pairs belonging to a given set T, we will obtain a unique partition called the *D partition* under T [26]. Each block in this partition will contain a set of indistinguishable vertices from a structural point of view. The *structural resolution* at a given element is defined as the total number of elements indistinguishable from it from a structural testing viewpoint, i.e., the number of elements in the block containing the element in the D partition. If the largest block in the D partition under T contains k elements, the graph is defined to be *k-distinguishable* with respect to T. In order to resolve the fault to a single element, we must find a set of test points T such that the system graph is 1-distinguishable under T. For complete fault detection we must find a set of test points T such that the range of T will cover all vertices (elements) of the directed graph (system). Therefore the optimal choice of test point pairs reduces to a covering problem similar to that of the selection of prime implicants.

Let us illustrate this test points insertion approach with an example. Consider a system whose system graph is shown in Fig. 8.2.7. The test point pairs are (t_6, t_8), (t_6, t_9), (t_6, t_{10}), (t_7, t_8), (t_7, t_9), and (t_7, t_{10}). Since we assume that the range of a test point pair (t_i, t_j) consists of all the nodes on the paths from t_i to t_j, $V(t_i, t_j)$ is determined by intersecting the reachability vector of node t_i (the set of nodes that can be reached from t_i) and the reaching vector of node t_j (the set of nodes that can reach t_j), plus the nodes t_i and t_j. For example, the range of the test point pair (t_7, t_9) is determined as

$$V(t_7, t_9) = (R_7 \cap R_9^T) \cup (v_7 \cup v_9)$$
$$= (1101101111) \cap (1011111010) \cup (0000001000) \cup (0000000010)$$
$$= (1001101010)$$

By the same procedure the range vectors of all the test point pairs are determined and shown in the following range matrix M.

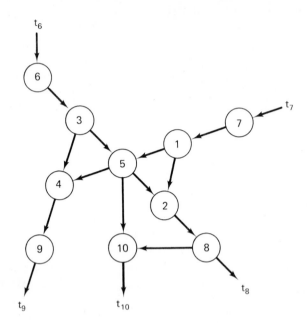

Fig. 8.2.7   A system graph.

$$
\begin{array}{cccccccccc}
 & v_1 & v_2 & v_3 & v_4 & v_5 & v_6 & v_7 & v_8 & v_9 & v_{10}
\end{array}
$$

$$
M = \begin{bmatrix} V(t_6, t_8) \\ V(t_6, t_9) \\ V(t_6, t_{10}) \\ V(t_7, t_8) \\ V(t_7, t_9) \\ V(t_7, t_{10}) \end{bmatrix} = \begin{bmatrix}
0 & 1 & 1 & 0 & 1 & 1 & 0 & 1 & 0 & 0 \\
0 & 0 & 1 & 1 & 1 & 1 & 0 & 0 & 1 & 0 \\
0 & 1 & 1 & 0 & 1 & 1 & 0 & 1 & 0 & 1 \\
1 & 1 & 0 & 0 & 1 & 0 & 1 & 1 & 0 & 0 \\
1 & 0 & 0 & 1 & 1 & 0 & 1 & 0 & 1 & 0 \\
1 & 1 & 0 & 0 & 1 & 0 & 1 & 1 & 0 & 1
\end{bmatrix}
$$

$V(t_i, t_j)$ represents the set of nodes that can be tested by (t_i, t_j). To determine the minimal set of test points to test all nodes is equivalent to finding
the minimal cover of all the nodes by the range vectors. The well-known
methods of solving prime implicant tables can be applied to the range matrix
to determine this minimal set. For this example, (t_6, t_{10}) and (t_7, t_9) is such a
set, while (t_6, t_9) and (t_7, t_{10}) is another.

To find the structural resolution, we have to determine the D partition
under the set of valid test point pairs. This is obtained by intersecting all the
partitions $(V(t_i, t_j), N - V(t_i, t_j))$ induced by the valid test point pairs. For

example, the partition induced by the test point pair (t_7, t_9) is $(\overline{1,4,5,7,9}, \overline{2,3,6}, \overline{8,10})$. By intersecting the partitions induced by the six test point pairs, we will obtain the D partition $(\overline{1,7}, \overline{2,8}, \overline{3,6}, \overline{4,9}, \overline{5}, \overline{10})$. (We also notice that nodes that are indistinguishable from each other have identical column vectors in the range matrix. Therefore the D partition can also be obtained so that all nodes belonging to the same block of the D partition have the same column vectors in the range matrix.) The largest block of the D partition contains two elements. Therefore the graph is 2-distinguishable.

2. *Structural segmentation of a complex system.* The structural segmentation of a large system into smaller subsystems can be carried out by partitioning the graph into *maximal strongly connected* (M.S.C.) subgraphs (subsystems). (An M.S.C. subgraph is a subgraph that includes all possible nodes that can be reached from one another.) Each M.S.C. subsystem can be represented by a single node, possibly with multiple inputs or outputs. The graph resulted will be called the *reduced graph.* After the analysis of the reduced graph, each node corresponding to an M.S.C. subgraph can be expanded separately into a subgraph and analyzed independently, using similar techniques as in the reduced graph.

If the subsystem is still too large, we can segment the subsystem further by providing controlled "breaks" in the information flow during system diagnostics. This can be implemented by inserting a blocking gate [27] on the arc. We define a *blocking gate* on an edge (arc) as one which merely blocks or unblocks the flow of signals through it.

By using blocking gates we can reduce the complexity of a large M.S.C. segment by reducing the number of feedback paths within it. We would like to make the system an "open-loop" (loop-free) system with a minimum number of arc removals such that all nodes in the subsystem can be reachable from the primary input nodes. (An arc can be removed in a controlled fashion by implementing a blocking gate on the arc.) This is achieved by removing all the directed arcs entering the entry node of the M.S.C. graph and then partitioning the altered subgraph into M.S.C. subgraphs. Then the procedure is repeated until no more loops exist.

So far we have defined a blocking gate as one which blocks the flow of signals through the edge on which it is located. This over-simplified definition needs more explanation. A blocking gate on an edge e can be externally controlled so that in its blocking state, the vertex v at the output end of e could receive and transmit responses based only on signals reaching it from the other edges incident on it. In the other state the blocking gate has no effect at all on the signal passing through the edge e. Thus the blocking gate masks off the effect of faults reaching the edge e while the effects of any faults reaching v through other edges may be steered towards the output vertices. Diagnosis can be conducted by injecting proper test patterns at primary entry nodes and at the same time controlling the blocking gates to steer the signals through some specific paths within the system, monitoring the output signals at the exit nodes. By the proper insertion of blocking gates, maximum distinguish-ability of the graph (from a structural viewpoint) can be achieved [27]. When-ever the elements cannot be distinguished by this method, the test point approach can be applied.

Some preliminary results of the blocking gate approach to computer diag-nosis have been reported by Ramamoorthy and Mayeda [27]. There appears a very close relationship between the path sensitizing methods, Roth's D-algorithm, etc., and the blocking gate approach. Much fruitful work re-mains to be done in order to develop a unified theory of fault diagnosis.

The problem of inserting blocking gates can be illustrated by an example. Consider the system graph shown in Fig. 8.2.8. Define the *vertex-range* of a vertex v in a single-entry-single-exit (SEC) graph as the union of the vertices on all the paths from the entry to the exit of the SEC graph after deleting the vertex v. The *edge-range* of an arc e is similarly defined for the deletion of the arc e. The first step is to find the D partition of maximum distinguishability of the graph from the vertex-range matrix by a procedure as outlined in the last subsection. For this example, the D partition is given as

$$D = \{D_1, D_2, D_3, D_4, D_5\}$$
$$= \{\overline{v_1, v_6}, \overline{v_2, v_7}, \overline{v_3}, \overline{v_4}, \overline{v_5}\}$$

and the vertex-range matrix is shown in Fig. 8.2.9.

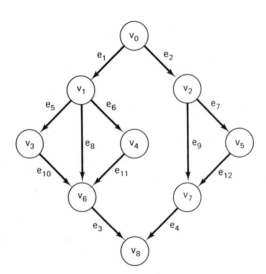

Fig. 8.2.8   A SEC graph G.

	v_1	v_2	v_3	v_4	v_5	v_6	v_7
$\bar{v}_1$	0	1	0	0	1	0	1
$\bar{v}_2$	1	0	1	1	0	1	0
$\bar{v}_3$	1	1	0	1	1	1	1
$\bar{v}_4$	1	1	1	0	1	1	1
$\bar{v}_5$	1	1	1	1	0	1	1
$\bar{v}_6$	0	1	0	0	1	0	1
$\bar{v}_7$	1	0	1	1	0	1	0

Fig. 8.2.9　The vertex-range matrix of G.

The next step is the construction of the edge-range matrix with respect to the blocks of vertices in the D partition, as shown in Fig. 8.2.10. The same D partitioning procedure is applied to this matrix to get the F partition of the arcs.

$$F = \{F_1,\ F_2,\ F_3,\ F_4,\ F_5,\ F_6\}$$
$$= \{\overline{e_1,\ e_3},\ \overline{e_2,\ e_4},\ \overline{e_5,\ e_{10}},\ \overline{e_6,\ e_{11}},\ \overline{e_7,\ e_{12}},\ \overline{e_8,\ e_9}\}$$

A reduced-range matrix is then formed, as shown in Fig. 8.2.11.

	D_1	D_2	D_3	D_4	D_5
$\bar{e}_1$	0	1	0	0	1
$\bar{e}_2$	1	0	1	1	0
$\bar{e}_3$	0	1	0	0	1
$\bar{e}_4$	1	0	1	1	0
$\bar{e}_5$	1	1	0	1	1
$\bar{e}_6$	1	1	1	0	1
$\bar{e}_7$	1	1	1	1	0
$\bar{e}_8$	1	1	1	1	1
$\bar{e}_9$	1	1	1	1	1
$\bar{e}_{10}$	1	1	0	1	1
$\bar{e}_{11}$	1	1	1	0	1
$\bar{e}_{12}$	1	1	1	1	0

Fig. 8.2.10　The edge-range matrix of G.

	D_1	D_2	D_3	D_4	D_5
F_1	0	1	0	0	1
F_2	1	0	1	1	0
F_3	1	1	0	1	1
F_4	1	1	1	0	1
F_5	1	1	1	1	0
F_6	1	1	1	1	1

Fig. 8.2.11　The reduced-range matrix of G.

From the reduced-range matrix we can follow an algorithm derived by Chang [22], to find a set of blocking gates for maximum distinguishability. Such a set is $\{e_1, e_5, e_6, e_7\}$. Costs can also be added to the arcs for implementing blocking gates and a minimal cost set may be found. To include diagnosis of the information lines (arcs), pseudo-nodes can be added to each arc and the same procedure is applicable to the equivalent graph. For proofs and more detailed discussion, the readers are referred to Ramamoorthy and Mayeda [27]. The blocking gate approach can generate the maximum distinguishability generated by any other method. Note that v_1 and v_6 are indistinguishable and a test point has to be inserted on arc e_8 if we want to distinguish between them.

We would also like to segment the system into mutually noninteracting subsystems so that many of these can be tested independently and concurrently. The required test sequences will be shorter while the fault resolutions are better, since the size of the subsystem is much smaller. The effects of multiple faults, in case they do occur, will also be diminished. Segmentation can be achieved by introducing either blocking gates (which isolate a subsystem from another) or test points (which provide means of injecting test patterns and monitoring outputs) to the appropriate arcs. Test points are much more expensive than blocking gates and should be introduced only if absolutely necessary.

The optimal location of blocking gates for *parallel segmentation* has been investigated by Ramamoorthy and Chang [28]. Parallel segmentation aims to segment the graph into a number of subgraphs that can be tested in parallel. This is achieved by first transforming the system graph into its associated "ladder graph" by adding pseudo-nodes and pseudo-edges. Then blocking gates are inserted at appropriate locations, keeping in mind that arcs that are the only entry or exit to a vertex cannot be broken. A system graph, its "ladder graph," and the resultant segmented graph are shown in Fig. 8.2.12.

An alternate approach, called *serial segmentation*, which breaks up the graph into "stages" by inserting test points, has also been proposed by the same authors [28]. It is assumed that there is an upper bound P on the number of vertices that can be tested at a time. An algorithm to insert the minimum number of test points so that the size of the subgraph between two test points is smaller than P by a form of dynamic programming has been proposed [28]. An example of a system graph and its serially segmented form is shown in Fig. 8.2.13, for the case $P = 3$. (The system graph has been converted to an SEC graph for convenience.) For a more detailed explanation of these two algorithms, the readers are referred to Ramamoorthy and Chang [28].

3. *Combined fault detecting and locating procedures.* We will first present a procedure for debugging newly built equipment in which each step depends on the correct operation of elements previously tested. This implies dividing the system into stages so that each stage will depend on the previous stages.

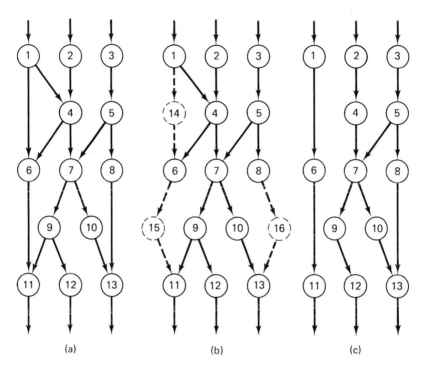

(a)   (b)   (c)

Fig. 8.2.12   An example of a parallel segmentation: (a) a system graph; (b) its associated "ladder graph"; (c) the segmented subgraphs.

This is achieved by finding the *precedence partition* of the reduced system graph. Let C be the connectivity matrix of the graph. (The *connectivity matrix* $C = \{c_{ij}\}$ of a graph G with n nodes is an $n \times n$ matrix whose ijth element $c_{ij} = 1$ if and only if there is a directed arc from node i to node j, otherwise $c_{ij} = 0$.) To find the precedence partition we will first determine the columns in the C matrix with all zeros, i.e., the entry nodes of the graph. Let S_1 represent this set. We delete the rows and columns of the C matrix corresponding to the nodes in S_1. We then determine the columns with all zeros in the remaining matrix. These will be the nodes with input from the nodes in S_1 only. Let these nodes be denoted by S_2. The rows and columns corresponding to S_2 are then deleted. The procedure is then repeated until no more rows or columns are left. The partition of the set of nodes into the subsets S_1, S_2, . . ., S_p forms the precedence partition of the graph. We can see that the predecessors of the nodes in S_i are among the sets S_1, S_2, . . ., S_{i-1}. The sequence of testing of the nodes must be in the order of $(S_1, S_2, . . ., S_p)$, since S_i may depend on the outputs of S_{i-1}. If S_{i-1} is fault-free and s_i is faulty, it implies that S_i is faulty and all the nodes S_1 through S_{i-1} are fault-free. No further testing may continue on, however, until S_i is fixed.

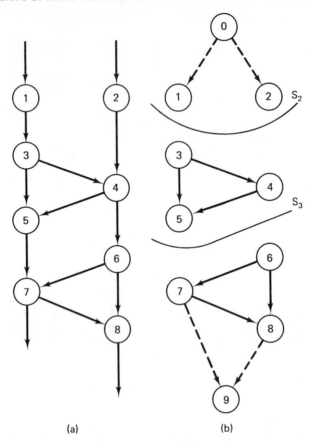

(a) (b)

Fig. 8.2.13 An example of serial segmentation for $P = 3$: (a) the system graph; (b) the segmented form of the system graph.

As an example, consider the reduced system graph in Fig. 8.2.14. The precedence partition is ($\{1,2,3\}$, $\{4,5,6\}$, $\{7\}$, $\{8,10\}$, $\{9\}$, $\{11\}$). Note that the precedence partition is an ordered set. Tests must be conducted in the following sequence: $\{1,2,3\}$, $\{4,5,6\}$, $\{7\}$, $\{8,10\}$, $\{9\}$, $\{11\}$. Note that nodes 1, 2 and 3; 4, 5, and 6; 8 and 10 can be tested in parallel.

Let us now consider the problem of fault location where element failure probabilities are known. Let us first perform the precedence partition of the system into (S_1, S_2, . . ., S_p) and let the relative probability that a failure occurs among the elements corresponding to S_i be P_i, after a fault is detected. P_i can be computed from fault statistics gathered if the system is in operation for a long time. The philosophy of an optimal testing schedule is to minimize the average number of tests required. Fault detection is first performed by using the primary inputs and outputs. After a fault is detected, fault locating tests are performed. If we test the output of S_k using the primary inputs and

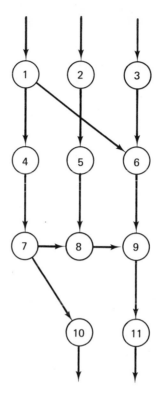

Fig. 8.2.14   An example of a system graph.

if a fault is detected, then the fault must occur among $S_1, S_2, \ldots, S_k$. If no fault is detected, the fault must occur among $S_{k+1}, S_{k+2}, \ldots, S_p$. Therefore the outcome of the test on the output of S_k induces a partition (Q_1, Q_2), where $Q_1 = (S_1, S_2, \ldots, S_k)$ and $Q_2 = (S_{k+1}, \ldots, S_p)$, on the set $(S_1, S_2, \ldots, S_p)$. To minimize the average number of tests, we would like to have maximum fault resolution in every test. Therefore we should choose S_k such that the probability that the fault occurs among Q_1 is approximately the same as that for Q_2. The test on S_k resolves the fault into either Q_1 or Q_2. The same philosophy can be applied by choosing a subsystem S_{q1} (or S_{q2}) among Q_1 (or Q_2) so that the outcome of the test induces a partition on Q_1 (or Q_2) such that the probability of failure of each block in the partition is approximately the same. This adaptive testing procedure will stop when the faulty element is located.

8.2.5.   Microdiagnostics

Microdiagnostics is defined as a set of diagnostic procedures implemented as microprograms on a microprogram-controlled computer [29]. The use of microprogramming in fault diagnosis has certain advantages over conventional methods, which use machine-language programs for fault location and detection. The traditional machine-language diagnostics consist of utility programs and diagnostic monitors performing function tests at the level of machine instructions and data words. Microdiagnostics, however, have much finer fault resolution since the data paths are controlled at the gate level, thus enabling tests at the circuit level. Traditional testing may not provide complete coverage of faults because even using all instruction types may not have tested all the data-sensitive aspects of the functional parts of the computer. On the other hand, each microoperation only activates a specific function of the machine so that the probability of fault cancellation is drastically reduced. Microprograms effectively shorten the time to locate the faults since they are faster and provide better fault isolation and flexibility. Microprograms, which can control the data flow of the machine at the gate level, also have more "intimate" control on the operation of the computer for fault diagnosis. All these factors account for the small size of the hardcore required for microdiagnostics.

Microprogramming also provides other possibilities over machine-coded diagnostics. Microprogrammed diagnostic tests can be interspersed in the regular processing sequences and automatically initiated at the end of regular computing sequences, during idle minor cycles on "idle" hardware. Machine-coded testing is usually initiated by the operator while microdiagnostics can be done automatically. Also in the case of microprogrammed computers, reconfiguration for recovery is possible. For example, in the IBM 360/85, if the hard-wired multiplication unit malfunctions, the operation will be done by an equivalent microprogram without using the faulty multiplication unit.

To test a functional unit F_i a sequence of microoperations are executed to initialize specific data in the registers of F_i and then compare the result to the correct one. Usually a *bootstrapping* strategy is used, i.e., to test a small portion of the hardware initially and then expand the tested area by using the fault-free portions to diagnose untested portions of the hardware. Microdiagnostics are used in several commercial machines, e.g., the IBM 360/30, the IBM 370/145, the Standard Computer MLP-900.

In the IBM 360/30 both machine-coded and microprogrammed diagnostic routines are used [30]. The use of microdiagnostics reduces the size of the hardcore to less than 1 percent of the total CPU logic circuitry, which might exceed 50 percent otherwise. Excluding the manual controls and the circuitry in the CPU for the console typewriter, more than 90 percent of the failures can be detected and located. Further, approximately 85 percent of the failures are resolved to four or less circuit cards (i.e., 0.5 percent fault resolution).

The IBM 370/145 has as its hardcore an external tester called the "console file," which is a small computer that loads the microprogramming store and initiates diagnostic action. As in the IBM 360/30, the microdiagnostics operate in two modes: resident and nonresident. The resident part checks the primary control and data paths. The nonresident part checks the main memory, I/O, etc. Approximately 95 percent of the faults at the CPU are detected and located, with the help of some machine code programs.

The MLP-900 processor has special features and special-purpose micro-instructions design for microdiagnostics [31]. Hence it is possible to locate a fault to a single gate. Because of the vertical microinstruction format used in the machine, writing microdiagnostic programs is very easy. Although the MLP-900 is a rather complex processor (over 20,000 equivalent gates) the running time for the entire fault detection routine is only about 6 ms.

8.2.6   Maintenance Techniques for the IBM/360 Processors

After the discussion of various techniques for fault diagnosis, it may be an appropriate time to examine the maintenance scheme of a commercial machine. Maintenance techniques vary from manufacturer to manufacturer and from model to model. Let us use the IBM 360/50 system as a practical example [11].

During the design of the IBM 360/50 processor, special hardware for testing purposes have been included to provide an extremely complete facility, both to reset the processor to a specified state, and to record its state. This facility is invoked by executing either of two machine functions, called *Scan-In* and *Scan-Out*. Execution of Scan-Out causes the state of every memory element in the processor to be stored in a special fixed area of the main memory. Scan-In performs the reverse operation, forcing the processor to a fixed state by the data stored in that special area of the memory. This facility is extremely powerful. The designer of the diagnostic tests can specify any state to start the test and put the processor into that state by a Scan-In operation. An execution of Scan-Out can save the entire processor state while the restart of a process can be initiated by a Scan-In operation. Other hardware facilities enable the processor to be run in small increments, rather than complete instruction cycles, thus providing better fault resolution. The hardcore is approximately 10 percent of the processor hardware.

The diagnostic tests are derived by one-dimensional path sensitizing and stored on a reel of tape. The testing begins with reading the tape into the memory of the machine. The processor is then set to an initial state with a Scan-In operation. Afterwards the processor is exercised for a few clock cycles. A Scan-Out is performed and the test results are compared with pre-calculated values, by programs. The next test is then selected according to this comparison (adaptive testing). If a fault is detected, diagnostic tests are performed to locate it, hopefully to some replaceable circuit modules. The testing procedure requires human intervention and initialization.

8.2.7. Conclusion

In this section we have discussed a number of fault diagnosis techniques. Each technique has its advantages and drawbacks. Several criteria have been proposed to aid the selection of techniques for a computer system [32]. The "checkout/detection" criterion is assigned on the basis of the test separating the largest number of faulty systems from the good system. This enables rapid fault detection. The "information gain" criterion is a measure of the information obtained from each test. This is useful when full diagnosis is required. Another criterion is the distinguishability criterion, which selects the test that distinguishes among the largest number of pairs of systems. It is useful for efficient fault location.

We must also understand the limitations of the techniques we have discussed so far. All the techniques assume that the system remains a logical system under the faulty condition. Most of the techniques deal with single, nontransient, logical faults of the types of "stuck-at-1" and "stuck-at-0." Not much progress has been made in the diagnosis of multiple faults, transient faults, and nonlogical faults. It seems that a unified mathematical theory of diagnosis is necessary in order to make spectacular advances in this field. The authors feel that a theory based on graph theory concepts seems most promising.

EXERCISES 8.2

1. Find the primitive D-cubes of the following logical functions: NAND, NOR, OR, and EXCLUSIVE OR. (Assume that each logical gate has two inputs.)

2. Determine the minimum fault detection sequences to test all "stuck-at" type of faults in a two-level AND/OR network. Solve the same problem for a two-level NOR/NOR network.

3. Find a test for G_7 s-a-0 and s-a-1 in the following circuit with (a) one-dimensional path sensitizing, (b) the D-algorithm, (c) the Boolean difference method, and (d) the equivalent normal form method.

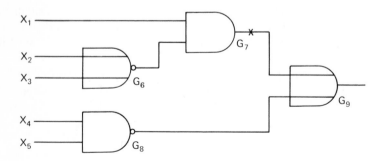

8.3. THE USE OF ERROR-CORRECTING CODES IN FAULT-TOLERANT COMPUTER DESIGN

8.3.1. Introduction

The use of error-correcting codes in communication channels have been known for many years. Within a digital computer the "channel" becomes the collection of data paths and storage devices embodied in the registers, the memories, and associated input-output transfer links. One has also to include the central processor unit, such as the arithmetic units, etc. The evaluation of the performance of an error-correcting code for this type of channel is different from the communication channels because (1) appropriate measures of efficiency may be different and depends on the information redundancy, the circuit cost, and speed of the encoder and decoder in a more complex way; (2) the most probable types of errors (noise) may be different; (3) faults may occur in the decoding logic circuit; (4) the speed requirements of encoding and decoding may be very strict; and (5) if possible, the codes should be compatible in some sense with arithmetic and other computer operations [33]. As a result, the feasible codes for a digital computer are not necessarily the optimal codes for communication.

In general, coding techniques can be used to introduce redundancy to the logic circuitry (by replication) or to the information being processed (signal redundancy). The use of coding techniques in failure-tolerant digital networks is uncommon because it is usually more expensive than other repetition schemes due to the need of redundant decoders [6]. Hence information redundancy is usually employed. The most common types of errors in a digital computer are arithmetic operation errors and noise errors in the transfer of information between input and output devices and the computer. The memory system is also an area that needs error protection. Information redundancy will usually introduce a proportional increase in hardware cost in terms of storage devices, data paths, and processor complexity, besides the need of an encoder and decoder. Another cost introduced by using coding is the delay (time redundancy) caused by encoding and decoding. For data transfer errors, error-correcting codes used in communication can be applied directly. For other errors, usually new codes have to be developed or known codes have to be modified. For arithmetic errors, a special subset of error-correcting codes, called "arithmetic error codes," is used. The readers who are interested in the practical application of coding theory in computer systems are referred to the special issue on coding theory and application in the IBM Journal of Research and Development, July 1970.

8.3.2. Introduction to Error-Correcting and Error-detecting Codes

Since Hamming's paper [35] on parity-check codes in 1950, algebraic error-correcting codes has evolved into an established field in communication theory. Error-correcting codes can be classified according to the types of error they are designed to handle: *random error*, where the errors occur randomly, and *burst error*, where the errors occupy contiguous positions. (Note that there are also other error patterns that the engineer can take advantage of to design an efficient code. An example is the *iterative error* in arithmetic operations, where the error occurs iteratively at the same position.)

The first step in using an error-correcting code is the *encoding* of information, i.e., the transformation of information into coded form. The information to be transmitted is first segmented into *message blocks*: each message block M consists of k information digits. There can be a maximum of 2^k distinct messages. The encoder transforms each input message M into a longer binary sequence C of n digits, which is called the *code word* of M. The set of 2^k distinct code words is called a *block code*. The $(n - k)$ digits added to each message block by the encoder are called *redundant digits*. The design of the encoder is to form these redundant digits to provide information for good error-correcting capability. The ratio $R = k/n$ is called the *code rate*, which is interpreted as the number of information digits per transmitted digit.

Suppose that C is the transmitted code word and R is the sequence received. R may be different from C due to channel noise disturbance. On the basis of R and the channel characteristic the decoder decides the transmitted code word. This process is called *decoding*. Usually the "*maximum likelihood decoding*" principal is used. Upon receiving the sequence R, the decoder computes the conditional probability $P(R \mid C_i)$ for all the 2^k code words. The code word C_t is identified as the transmitted word such that the conditional probability $P(R \mid C_t)$ is the largest.

The above encoding and decoding scheme is only applicable to block codes, where there is no interaction between message blocks. There is another class of code, called *convolution code*, in which there is interaction between the message blocks. The block of n code digits generated by the encoder in a particular time unit depends not only on the block of k message digits within that time unit, but also on the blocks of message digits within a previous span of $N - 1$ time units $(N > 1)$. The advantage of convolution code is that the logic circuitry for implementation is very simple but its disadvantage is that there is a high redundancy. Hence convolution codes are not commonly employed in digital computers, where the data transfer rate is very critical. In this discussion, we will restrict ourselves to block codes, and particularly to a subset of block codes called *linear block code*, where the 2^k n-tuple code words is a subspace of the vector space V_n of all n-tuples.

The (Hamming) *weight* of an n-tuple V, $w(V)$, is defined as the number of nonzero components of V. For example, if $V = (101110010001)$, $w(V) = 6$. The (Hamming) *distance* between two n-tuples U and V, $d(U, V)$, is defined as the number of components in which they differ. For example, if $U = (10010001)$ and $V = (01011101)$, then $d(U, V) = 4$. We can see that under modulo-2 addition, the distance between U and V is just equal to the weight of their vector sum, $U + V$. In the example above, $U + V = (11001100)$ and $w(U + V) = 4$, which is just $d(U,V) = 4$. Given a linear code, we can determine the distances between all possible pairs of code words; the smallest distance is called the *minimum distance* of the code, denoted by d_{min}. d_{min} is also equal to the minimum weight of the nonzero code vectors in the linear code. The minimum distance of a code determines the error-correcting and error-detecting capabilities of the code. A linear code with a minimum distance of d' can detect up to $d' - 1$ errors. It can also be used to correct up to t errors so long as $d \geq 2t + 1$. When it is used simultaneously for error-detecting and error-correcting, it can detect s errors and correct t errors such that $d' \geq s + t + 1$, where $s \geq t$. For a proof of the above statement, refer to any textbook on error-correcting codes, such as Peterson [36].

An (n, k) linear block code is characterized by a $k \times n$ matrix, called the *generator matrix G*. The code word V of a message block m is obtained by multiplying m and G. For example, the generator matrix of the single error correcting $(7, 4)$ Hamming code is

$$
G = \begin{bmatrix}
1 & 0 & 0 & 0 & 1 & 1 & 0 \\
0 & 1 & 0 & 0 & 1 & 0 & 1 \\
0 & 0 & 1 & 0 & 0 & 1 & 1 \\
0 & 0 & 0 & 1 & 1 & 1 & 1
\end{bmatrix}
$$

Therefore the code word for the message $M_1 = (1011)$ is $V_1 = M_1 G = (1011010)$. In a *systematic code* (i.e., the first k digits of the code word are exactly the same as the message block and the last $n - k$ digits are redundant digits) the generator matrix has the following form:

$G = [I_k\, P]$,   where I_k is a $k \times k$ identity matrix and P is a $k \times (n - k)$ matrix

The (n, k) code can also be characterized by a $(k - n) \times n$ matrix, called the *parity check matrix H*. H is orthogonal to the row space of G. H is usually used in the decoding stage. The received code word V^* is multiplied by H^T to get the *syndrome*, which is an $(n - k)$ component vector used for error-detection and correction. A zero syndrome indicates the absence of an error. For example, the parity check matrix for the above Hamming code is

$$
H = \begin{bmatrix}
1 & 1 & 0 & 1 & 1 & 0 & 0 \\
1 & 0 & 1 & 1 & 0 & 1 & 0 \\
0 & 1 & 1 & 1 & 0 & 0 & 1
\end{bmatrix}
$$

If the received code vector $V_1^* = (1011010)$ for V_1 above, then the syndrome is $V_1 H^T = (000)$, indicating no error. If the third bit is corrupted so that $V_1^* = (1001010)$, then the syndrome is (011), which can be used to locate the error. In this case, an error in the third bit is indicated. For a systematic code, the parity check matrix has the form

$$H = [P^T I_{n-k}], \qquad \text{where } P \text{ is the transpose of the matrix } P \text{ of the generator matrix}$$

Most of the research on block codes has been concentrated on a subclass of linear codes called *cyclic codes*, in which any code vector shifting cyclically one place to the right (end-around) is also a code vector. An (n, k) cyclic code can be completely specified by a polynomial called its *generator polynomial*, and the desired code words can be generated by forming multiples of this polynomial mod X^n. (In this case, a code vector is represented by a polynomial.) For example, the G matrix of a $(7, 4)$ cyclic Hamming code is

$$G = \begin{bmatrix} 1 & 1 & 0 & 1 & 0 & 0 & 0 \\ 0 & 1 & 1 & 0 & 1 & 0 & 0 \\ 0 & 0 & 1 & 1 & 0 & 1 & 0 \\ 0 & 0 & 0 & 1 & 1 & 0 & 1 \end{bmatrix}$$

The generator polynomial is $1 + x + x^3$. Cyclic codes have two advantages. The encoding and syndrome calculation can be implemented easily by simple shift registers with feedback connections. This allows serial checking to save hardware cost. Besides, cyclic codes have inherent algebraic structure so that simple and efficient decoding methods can be employed easily. An encoder and a syndrome calculation circuit are shown in Fig. 8.3.1. and Fig. 8.3.2, respectively.

Of all the cyclic codes studied, the Bose-Chaudhuri-Hocquenghem (BCH) codes are most extensively studied. It has been shown that for any positive integer m and $t(t < 2^{m-1})$, a BCH code can be constructed with block length $(2^m - 1)$ to correct t errors. Interested readers should consult the excellent books by Berlekamp [37], Peterson and Weldon [36], or Lin [38].

Many low-cost decoding schemes have been discovered for certain classes of cyclic codes. Error-trapping decoding employs only a very simple combinatorial circuit and is efficient for single or double error-correcting. Another useful decoding method is the majority-logic decoder which uses threshold elements to reduce the cost of combinatorial logic and improve the speed of decoding by using the orthogonality property of the code. Interested readers are referred to Massey [39].

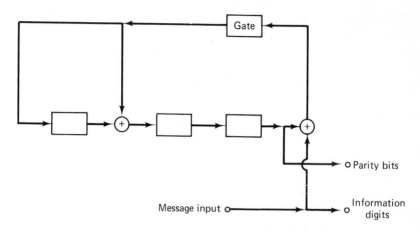

Fig. 8.3.1   An encoder for the (7, 4) cyclic Hamming code.

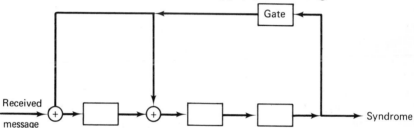

Fig. 8.3.2   A decoder for the (7, 4) cyclic Hamming code.

So far we have been talking about *random-error-correcting codes. Burst-error-correcting codes* are practical in some cases. The number of parity check digits of any b-burst-error-correcting code must be at least 2*b*. It should be noted that random-error-correcting codes can be interlaced or "multiplied" to form burst-error-correcting codes. Some common burst-error-correcting codes are the Fire codes [40].

8.3.3.   Application of Error-Correcting Codes in Memory Systems

The definition of an "optimal" code depends critically on the environment in which the code is to be used. The choice of a code for the memory system is dictated by the following considerations. The increase in cost of storage is directly proportional to the amount of information redundancy. The correction process should not unduly increase the memory access time, which limits the speed of the computer in many cases. The delay introduced should not exceed 5 to 10 percent of the access time. Therefore the error-correcting net should be less than three or four layers deep. For memory words of the order of 40 to 100 bits, the only codes satisfying this requirement economically are the multiple redundancy majority codes and the double redundancy parity codes. Also cell defects are common in the modern integrated memory devices, especially in large scale integration. Some of these cell defects are clustered so that burst-error-correcting codes are suitable. The materials discussed here are mainly taken from Srinivasan [41, 42] and Chien [43].

8.3.3.1. Correction of Cell Defects in Integrated Memories

1. *Error correction without input encoding.*   Let us assume a word-organized memory system with s planes of w words each, and each word has n information bits. Cell defects on a digit line will make the output of the line unreliable. In order to guarantee n information bits per word, k additional bits have to be fabricated.

The simplest error correction scheme is to replace the erroneous digit lines with the redundant error-free lines. Therefore with k redundant lines, one may correct at most k erroneous digit lines per plane.

In reality, we can take advantage of the error distribution to increase the efficiency of the correction. Suppose the defects are well scattered so that not many of the erroneous digit lines have errors along the same word line. Suppose (d_1, d_2, d_3) are three erroneous digit lines, no two of which have cell defects along any given word line, as shown in Fig. 8.3.3. If the same respective information bits are stored along all the three digit lines, i.e., triplicating the information bits of the word, then the majority of their outputs would always equal the stored input value when a word is selected, since there is at most one error per word in this triplet. This triplet is called an "admissible triplet" [41].

By the triplet, we are using two redundant digit lines to correct altogether three digit lines which would be erroneous otherwise. Therefore, if there is a way that we can arrange the erroneous digit lines (lines with at least one defect cell) into triplets so that no two digit lines in the triplet has defective cells along any given word line, k redundant lines can tolerate $3k/2$ erroneous digit lines per plane. Suppose that there are h erroneous lines that cannot be permuted to give admissible triplets, k redundant lines can correct up to $\frac{3}{2}k - \frac{1}{2}h$ erroneous lines. Thus, given the error statistics and patterns, less redundancy is required to be fabricated to give n information bits per word. The idea of admissible triplets can be generalized to any number $(2m + 1)$ instead of 3 by using a $(2m + 1)$-input majority gate. An algorithm to find the largest set of disjoint "admissible subsets" (admissible triplets for the case $m = 1$) with a known error pattern is given in Srinivasan [41].

This idea can also be generalized to the case when an integrated circuit module contains only one information bit per word. Three "erroneous" modules can form an admissible triplet if the cell defects do not occur at the same word address. We can therefore salvage modules which would have to

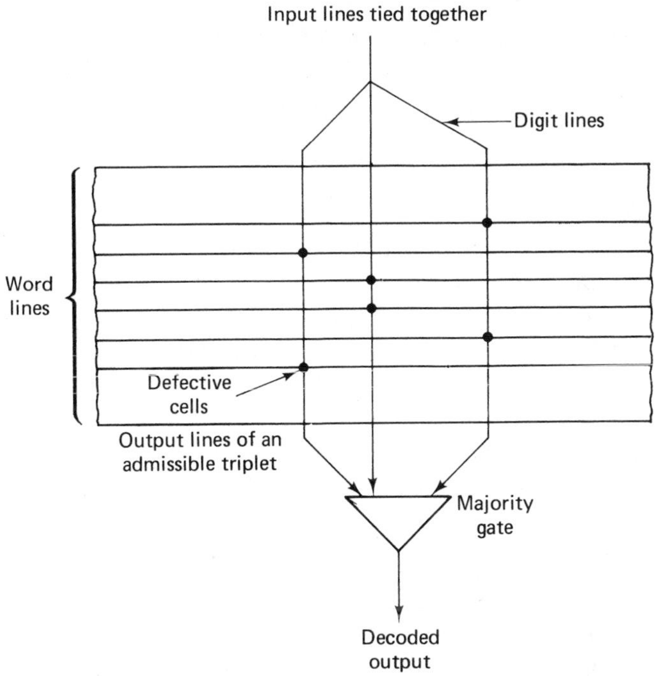

Input lines tied together

Fig. 8.3.3   Illustrating the simple error correcting principle.

be discarded otherwise. This design philosophy may also be important for large scale integration when some cell defects cannot be avoided. Also note that testing of the module is required for this approach in order to determine the error pattern.

2. *Error correction with input encoding.*   The input information bits can be encoded into an efficient burst-error-correcting code. For a word size of n bits, we add n redundant check bits. Let $x_0, x_1, \ldots, x_{n-1}$ be the information bits and $a_0, a_1, \ldots, a_{n-1}$ the check bits. For $0 \leq i \leq n - 1$, let

$$a_i = x_i \oplus x_{i \oplus_n 1}, \qquad i = 0, 1, \ldots, n - 1$$

where $\oplus$ denotes modulo 2 addition and $\oplus_n$ denotes modulo n addition. ($\ominus_n$ is used to denote modulo n subtraction.) The decoded output is

$$x_i = \mathrm{MAJ}\,[(\hat{x}_{i \ominus_n 1} \oplus \hat{a}_{i \ominus_n 1}), \hat{x}_i, (\hat{a}_i \oplus \hat{x}_{i \ominus_n 1})]$$

where the variables with a $\hat{}$ on top indicate the digits read out of a memory, and MAJ is the majority function. Note that if both $\hat{x}_{i \ominus_n 1}$ and $\hat{a}_{i \ominus_n 1}$ are errone-

ous, $(\hat{x}_{i\ominus1} \oplus \hat{a}_{i\ominus1})$ will give the correct result. Also, the MAJ function will
give the correct result if any two of its inputs are correct. Let D_i, called the
neighborhood set, denote the set of bits that will affect the decoding of x_i,
i.e.,

$$D_i = \{\hat{x}_{i\ominus1},\ \hat{a}_{i\ominus1},\ \hat{x}_i,\ \hat{a}_i,\ \hat{x}_{i\oplus1}\}, \quad \text{for } i = 0, 1, \ldots, n - 1$$

Then, for $n \geq 3$, the code defined above will correct all digit errors in a code
word if and only if, for $0 \leq i \leq n - 1$, the neighborhood set D_i satisfies one
of the following three conditions: (1) D_i has ≤ 1 error, or (2) D_i has exactly
three errors, the erroneous bits being either $(\hat{x}_i,\ \hat{x}_{i\oplus1},\ \hat{a}_i)$ or $(\hat{x}_i,\ \hat{x}_{i\ominus1},\ \hat{a}_{i\ominus1})$,
or (3) all five bits in D_i are in error.

By suitable rearrangement of the information and check bits, the code can
correct burst errors. For example, the code for $n = 8$ is given by the following
arrangement of information and check bits:

$$x_0 a_2 x_5 a_7 x_2 a_4 x_7 a_1 x_4 a_6 x_1 a_3 x_6 a_0 x_3 a_5$$

It can be easily verified that no consecutive three bits here contain two bits
belonging to the same neighborhood set D_i. Therefore this code can correct
any burst error of length ≤ 3. In general, such a code with code length equal
to $2n$ can correct a burst error of length up to $\lceil (2n/5) \rceil - 1$, where $\lceil (2n/5\rceil$ is the
least integer $\geq (2n/5)$. The proof and the algorithm to construct the code is
given in Srinivasan [41]. The advantage of this code is the speed of decoding.
The decoder contains only one level of exclusive-or gates and a threshold logic
gate. The code is quite efficient, since theoretically $2n$ redundant bits can at
most correct burst errors of length n. However, the code has a large fixed
redundancy (100 percent) and a variable fault-correction capability. For a system with short burst errors, the code is not feasible because the fixed redundancy dictates the high cost while the extra power is not needed.

8.3.3.2. Correction of Temporary and Catastrophic Errors. Due to the
speed requirement error-correcting codes used in memory systems must have
simple parallel decoding nets, rather than simple serial shift register serial
decoders as in cyclic codes. Therefore they usually belong to a set of codes that
can be decoded easily by majority logic elements. To protect against temporary
errors, the code must be able to correct scattered random errors as well as burst
errors. Bassen [44] has proposed a scheme for parallel decoding of Hamming-
type and Reed-Solomon-type code for burst-error correction by matrix implementation. Srinivasan [42] has proposed a noncyclic burst-error-correcting
code which is derived from the low-density parity check codes introduced by
Gallager [45]. These codes are less efficient than that of Bossen but they are

self-orthogonal and hence have simple threshold decoders for error-correction. Self-orthogonal codes can also be constructed for correcting random errors.

To protect against catastrophic errors a modular memory organization is needed. An error-correcting code can then be used to correct an error due to the failure of any one of the modules. The word is coded and stored in t modules, with m bits in each module. An m-burst-error-correcting code of course satisfies this requirement since the failure of a single module can at most produce a burst error of length m. However, advantage can be taken of the fact that the starting and ending positions of the burst error is known to construct a more efficient code. Srinivasan [42] has proposed such a code which can be decoded by threshold logic.

8.3.3.3. Correction of Errors in Magnetic Tapes.

Magnetic tapes contain spots where the coating material is thin or defective. These spots would usually affect several consecutive symbols, creating burst errors. These errors can also be produced by the misalignment of read and write units, or circuit and background noise. Although the speed requirement of encoding and decoding is not as strict as the primary memory, rapid decoding is still a key requirement.

In the early IBM magnetic tapes, such as the IBM 729 tape units, an extra bit is added to each row and column of data bits to indicate whether the sum of the data bits is odd or even, the so-called *parity check*. The use of the vertical redundancy check (VRC) and longitudinal redundancy check (LRC) provides very efficient error detection since they can detect any odd number of errors along a row or column. However, such parity checks can only correct single errors and therefore data recovery is virtually impossible in practical cases. A third scheme, known as the cyclic redundancy check (CRC) is therefore introduced to the 2400 Tape Series of IBM System/360 [46]. It uses very little redundancy and takes advantage of the existing checking capabilities offered by the system (VRC and LRC).

The IBM 2400 Tapes has eight tracks of data and one parity track. The recording density is 800 bits per inch. The predominant type of error is a burst error along a single track. Let us suppose that there are N 9-bit characters $(C_1, C_2, \ldots, C_N)$ in a tape record. The CRC is an additional character C_{N+1} written at the end of the record. The CRC, together with VRC, can locate the erroneous track and recover the correct data in a second reading of the magnetic tape. The encoding and decoding schemes are very simple.

Encoding involves the calculation of the CRC character. Let every character C_i be represented by a polynomial:

$$C_i = b_{0i}X^0 + b_{1i}X^1 + b_{2i}X^2 + \ldots + b_{8i}X^8$$

Then the CRC character C_{N+1} is calculated as

$$C_{N+1} = \sum_{i=1}^{N} X^i C_i \bmod G$$

where $G = 1 + X^3 + X^4 + X^5 + X^6 + X^9$. This can be done very easily with a 9-stage shift register and exclusive-or gates since addition mod 2 is equivalent to the exclusive-or operation and multiplication by X is equivalent to shifting the content of the shift register by 1 stage.

A burst error in the track with index j can be represented by $X^j E$, where

$$E = \sum_{i=1}^{N} e_i X^i, \quad \text{where } e_i \begin{cases} = 1, & \text{if an error occurs on } C_i \\ = 0, & \text{otherwise} \end{cases}$$

By the assumption of a burst error along a single track, each erroneous data bit will give a VRC error. Therefore in the decoding procedure we will set $e_i = 1$ whenever there is a VRC error. E can therefore be calculated. The decoding process involves the calculation of

$$\text{EPR} = \sum_{i=1}^{N} e_i X^8 \bmod G = X^8 E \bmod G$$

and

$$\text{CRC}' = \{X^j E + C_{N+1} + \sum_{i=1}^{N} X^i C_i\} \bmod G$$
$$= X^j E \bmod G \quad (0 \le j \le 8)$$

The calculation of CRC′ uses the same circuit as the calculation of CRC. The calculation of EPR uses a circuit that shifts every time when a character is read and inputs a 1 at the X^8 position whenever a VRC error is detected. Since E is already known from the VRC test, the remaining of the decoding procedure tries to determine the index of the erroneous track. This is done by shifting CRC′ until its content matches with that of EPR (a maximum of 8 shifts). Suppose this takes k shifts. Then the index of the erroneous track j is calculated as $8 - k$. The correct data are recovered by a second reading by complementing the bit on track j of the character whenever a VRC error occurs.

Let us examine the problem of uncorrectable errors. The index j is calculated from the condition

$$X^{j-k} E = X^8 E \bmod G$$

where k is the number of shifts. This is equivalent to

$$X^{j-k}(1 + X^{8-j+k}) E = 0 \bmod G$$

In order that this is satisfied for $j + k < 8$, G must divide the left-hand side.

The irreducible factors of G are $G_1 = (1 + X)$ and $G_2 = (1 + X + X^2 + X^4 + X^6 + X^7 + X^8)$. Therefore G_2 must divide E if an uncorrectable single-track error has occured. In this case it is very easy to show that CRC′ is equal to 0 or G_2. Therefore if CRC′ is equal to one of these two patterns, an uncorrectable error has been detected and no correction procedure will be attempted. Uncorrectable errors with CRC′ = 0 are distinguished from correct records by the presence of VRC errors.

Therefore the only uncorrectable single-track errors must have G_2 as a factor. All other burst errors of unlimited length can be corrected. Even if an error is uncorrectable, the code can detect them so that no erroneous correction will be performed. The implementation is very economical since the added redundancy is very small. The encoder and decoder are very simple and fast.

8.3.3.4. Correction of Errors in Other Memory Systems.

In a high speed disc file, burst errors along a single track are still predominant. The coding system must serve a single-track file containing long serial records. Fast decoding is also a necessity. The codes suitable for this type of error are the Fire codes [40]. However, the decoding of Fire codes is very slow. Chien [47] has proposed a modified version together with a fast decoding algorithm which will correct most burst errors and detect the rest in a very short time.

Another memory system where coding has been proposed to increase the reliability is the photo-digital mass memory of IEM [48]. The errors are mostly temporary, occuring in multiple bursts or random. The Reed-Solomon codes [75] were found to be efficient in such an environment.

8.3.4. Arithmetic Error Codes

8.3.4.1. Introduction.

Arithmetic error codes are the error-detecting and error-correcting codes which are preserved during arithmetic operations [34]. Given two numbers x, y, an arithmetic operation $*$, and an encoding $f: x \longrightarrow x'$, then f is an *arithmetic-error code* with respect to the operation $*$ if and only if the operation $*$ can be implemented by an algorithm D_* for the coded operands x' and y' such that

$$D_*(x', y') \equiv (x * y)'$$

Arithmetic error codes can provide *concurrent diagnosis*, i.e., real-time detection of transient and permanent faults concurrent with the operation of the computer, without a duplication of arithmetic processors. Besides detecting errors in the arithmetic processors, the codes can also detect errors caused by faulty transmission or storage. The economic feasibility of an arithmetic error code depends on its cost and effectiveness with respect to the arithmetic operations provided and the speed requirement. Before we study the evaluation of the cost and effectiveness of a code, let us briefly survey some of the common arithmetic error codes.

8.3.4.2. Common Arithmetic Error Codes. The use of parity check in arithmetic operations has been known for many years. The most common form is the *diminished base numerical check*, which is the modulo $(b-1)$ check for numbers of base b. For two numbers of base b, it can easily be shown [49] that the residue modulo $(b-1)$ is preserved under addition and multiplication, due to the fact that $xb^n = x \mod (b-1)$, (except for the case that $b = 2$). Many of us have used the modulo 9 check for digital arithmetics in our high school days. The diminished base numerical check avoids the need for carry cognizance but is meaningless for the binary number system. One solution is the *augmented base check*, which can also detect a single error in the arithmetic operation. For a number system of base b, and a number

$$A = \ldots + a_5 b^4 + a_4 b^3 + a_3 b^2 + a_2 b^1 + a_1 b^0$$

the check digit for A is given by

$$(\ldots + a_5 - a_4 + a_3 - a_2 + a_1) \equiv p \mod (b + 1).$$

It can be shown [49] that the parity check is preserved modulo $(b + 1)$ for addition and multiplication. Interested readers should consult the excellent paper by Harvey Garner [49] for examples and proofs. We will soon see that the idea of generalized parity checking is very useful in deriving new arithmetic error codes.

In this section we will study some of the common arithmetic error codes. Arithmetic error codes can be classified into *separate* and *nonseparate* codes [50]. Both of them are usually *residue (modulo) type codes* and possess many common properties, but differ significantly in their implementation. In a separate code the check bits are separated from the number (operand). There is no arithmetic interaction between the number (operand) and the check bits and usually different arithmetic is defined for them. The separate codes are the *residue code* [51] and the *inverse residue code* [52], which is a previously unexplored variant of the residue code. In a nonseparate code, there is no distinction between information and check bits. The nonseparate code considered is the *AN code*.

1. *Separate code.* Peterson [51] has shown that every separate code is a residue code or is isomorphic to a residue code. A separate residue code for a number system N of base b is usually obtained by setting the check digit R of a number n equal to the modulo g residue of n. It can easily be shown that not every number g will be satisfactory. If the number g divides b^{i-1}, then the ith digit is not checked. Therefore for any d-digit base-b number system, g must not divide b^i for $1 \leq i \leq (d-1)$. The necessary and sufficient condition for the existence of a separate base-g checking code for an d-digit base-b number

system N of cardinality M is that $GCD(M, g) = g$ and if $g = g'b^t$ then $GCD(b, g') = 1$. Efficiency requirement dictates that the $GCD(b, g) = 1$. A separate residue code is characterized by the homomorphism $\gamma:N \longrightarrow R$ and the isomorphism $\beta:N/C \longrightarrow R$ where C is an ideal in N (the set of uncoded operands) and R is the set of check digits, i.e., the residue modulo g.

If $GCD(M, g) \neq g$, then it is necessary to extend N to $N' = Z_{M'}$ which contains Z_M, so that $GCD(M', g) = g$. (Z_n denotes the set of integers modulo n.) Therefore sums or products must be taken modulo M' for checking purposes while the correct arithmetic sum or product is obtained modulo M. Extension is always necessary for *radix complement codes* (two's complement) since for these codes $M = b^d$ and g does not divide b^d. For the *diminished radix complement code* (one's complement), where $M = b^d - 1$, extension is not always required. For example, $g \mid b^d - 1$ for all d if $g = b - 1$ (diminished base check) and for all even d if $g = b + 1$ (augmented base check).

An example of a single-error-detecting residue code for a radix complement coded, four-bit, conventional binary number system is to set $g = 3$. N has to be augmented to $N' = Z_{33}$ such that $GCD(33, 3) = 3$. Addition and multiplication of the complement coded operands from N is executed modulo 16 but the modulo 3 check must be applied on the modulo 32 sum or product. If N is a diminished radix complement coded number system then $M = 15$ and no extension of N is required.

In order to get single-error-correcting capability for a v-bit residue code of modulo g, each error pattern must map onto a distinct element of Z_g. This is possible if and only if $2^j \neq 2^k \bmod g$, for all $j, k \in Z_v$ for $v \leq (g - 1)/2$ [50]. Therefore the necessary and sufficient conditions on an odd integer g for a v-bit single-error-correcting code are $g \geq 2v + 1$; the order of 2 in Z_g is not less than v and $2^m \bmod g \neq -1$ for $m < v$. For example, for a 5-bit binary arithmetic a residue code with $g = 11$ has single-error-correcting capability.

The *inverse residue code* is a variant of the residue code specially designed for fault-detection of repeated-use faults. The modulo g inverse residue encoding for a number n sets the check symbol r to g minus the modulo g residue of n, i.e., $r = g - (n \bmod g)$. The inverse residue code is a separate code since it has no arithmetic interaction between n and r. Let z be the result of an arithmetic operation. In the inverse residue code the checking algorithm computes $z \bmod g$ and compares it with the check result. When no error has occurred, the sum of these two numbers is divisible by g.

Many of the ideas developed in residue coding can be used in fault detection in arithmetic operations. A simple extension of the residue code is the *multiresidue code*. A number n in a number system N of cardinality M (i.e., N is a ring of integers modolo M) is coded in multiresidue form as a $(k + 1)$-tuple as follows:

$$X = (n, |n|_{m_1}, \ldots, |n|_{m_k}) = (n, n_1, \ldots, n_k)$$

where $n_i = |n|_{m_i}$ is the ith check and is the residue of n modulo m_i, for $1 \leq i$

$\leq k$. The m_i are called the *check bases* and are usually pairwise relatively prime integers. The addition of multiresidue codewords is performed component-wise. The sum of two numbers X and Y is

$$X + Y = (|x + y|_M, |x_1 + y_1|_{m_1}, \ldots, |x_k + y_k|_{m_k})$$

The addition of the pairs of components are carried out in $(k + 1)$ independent units so that parallel independent checking is possible. Implementation is very easy, especially if the arithmetic unit uses one's complement system (i.e., $M = 2^t - 1$), and the moduli m_i of the checkers are of the type $2^p - 1$, such that p divides t exactly. By choosing the moduli m_i's properly, a separate multiresidue code of arbitrary minimum distance can be derived [54]. Therefore multiresidue codes can be easily constructed for multiple error correction. An example is the biresidue code (N, N_{31}, N_{127}) that has single error-correcting capability for a 35-bit binary adder (i.e., $M = 2^{35} - 1$).

Another useful extension of the idea of residue codes is to build a residue arithmetic unit. Let $m_1, m_2, \ldots, m_n$ be a set of integers so that m_i are relatively prime. Any integer X such that $0 \leq X < \prod_{i=1}^n m_i$ can be uniquely represented by the n-tuple

$$(|X|_{m_1}, |X|_{m_2}, \ldots, |X|_{m_n}),$$

where $|X|_{m_i}$ denotes X modulo m_i. Addition, subtraction, and multiplication in the modular system are done component-wise modulo m_i and is therefore very simple. Division is a more complex operation [55]. However, if Y is divisible by X and X is relatively prime to M, the residue representation of Y/X $= Z$ is easily found. Mandelbaum [56] has shown that single error correction in a residue arithmetic system can be efficiently implemented by adding two redundant moduli.

2. *Nonseparate codes.* The nonseparate AN code is formed by muliplying an uncoded operand n by the check modulus A to give the coded operand An. For simplicity, we will only consider binary arithmetic codes here. Note that

$$An_1 + An_2 = A(n_1 + n_2)$$

Hence the sum of two codewords is the codeword of the sum and it can be used to check for errors. For a base-b number system A and b have to be relatively prime. Therefore for the binary system A should be any odd integer greater than or equal to 3. AN codes with minimum distance greater than 2 can be described in terms of an integer $M(A, d)$, which is defined as the smallest number such that $AM(A, d)$ has Hamming weight less than d [36]. Therefore if N is restricted to the range $0 \leq N < M(A, d)$, then AN has a minimum weight of at least d and hence the AN code has a minimum distance of at least *d.* If we define the addition and multiplication of the code words modulo $AM(A, d)$, then it is not necessary to restrict the sum or product of the uncoded operands to be less than $M(A, d)$. For one's complement arithmetic, it is advantageous to choose $AM(A, d) = 2^n - 1$. Under the operations of addition and multiplication modulo $AM(A, d)$, the code is an ideal in the ring of integers modulo $AM(A, d)$ [50]. An AN binary code has minimum distance 3 for all numbers in the range $0 \leq N < M$ if and only if the residues $\pm 2^j$ modulo A are distinct and nonzero for all j such that $2^j < A(M - 1)$ [36]. An example of a single error correcting AN code is for $A = 19$ and $M(A, 3) = 27$. There is in general no way to determine $M(A, d)$ except by exhaustive computation and some values for $d = 3$ and 4 are listed by Peterson and Weldon [36].

The advantage of cyclic codes have been shown previously. It is therefore desirable to be able to derive cyclic AN codes. It has been shown [59] that an AN code of length n is cyclic if and only if A generates an ideal in R, the ring of integers modulo $2^n - 1$. Some simple cyclic AN codes of minimum distance 3 are generated by a prime for which -2 (but not 2) is a primitive root. The $23N$ code of length 11 (for $0 \leq N < [(2^{11} - 1)/23] = 89$) is such an example.

3. *Implementation of arithmetic-error codes.* Implementations are different for separate and nonseparate codes. For residue codes, the operands x, y and their check digits x', y' enter separate arithmetic units, namely the adder and the checker, respectively, which produce the main result z and the check result z' (see Fig. 8.3.4.). The checking algorithm determines $|z|_g$ and

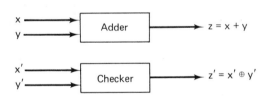

Fig. 8.3.4 Checking system with independent adder and checker for separate codes.

compares it to z'. Any disagreement shows the presence of an error either in the adder or in the checker and supplementary algorithms are used to locate the error. For division $x \div y$ with quotient Q and remainder R, the algorithm computes $|Q|_g$ and $|R|_g$ and obtains the value $|Q|_g \cdot y' + |R|_g$ which is compared to x' for equality.

For the nonseparate AN code the checking algorithm computes $|z|_A$, which should be zero for a correct result. A nonzero $|z|_A$ indicates a fault and for some AN codes the value of $|z|_A$ can locate the error. For the AN code there is no separate checker and the hardware cost is in the greater complexity of the main processor. The complexity of the encoder and decoder is greatly reduced for cyclic AN codes, which can be easily implemented by shift registers. However, in general, separate codes are cheaper to implement than non-separate codes.

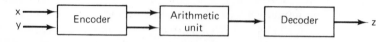

Fig. 8.3.5   Implementation of AN code.

8.3.4.3.   Fault Effects in Binary Arithmetic Processors.   In this section we will discuss the effect of logical faults in the arithmetic processor. In the next two sections we will then discuss the criteria of cost and effectiveness and present some practical arithmetic error codes together with their cost and effectiveness evaluation. Much of the material covered has been presented by Avizienis [34]. We will first investigate the error magnitudes due to the existence of a basic (local, one-use) logical fault in a binary arithmetic processor. A parallel design is assumed, in which the processor is used only once and the faults are single-use faults. Afterwards, we will investigate the error pattern when the processor is used repeatedly.

1.   *Basic faults in parallel arithmetic.*   The set of basic arithmetic operations in a general-purpose processor is listed in Table 8.3.1, together with the error magnitudes $|E|$ and their arithmetic weights generated by a basic fault. The operands are n bits long ($0 \leq i \leq n - 1$), and both the one's complement and two's complement arithmetic systems are considered. All operands and results are treated as unsigned integers for checking purposes.

The results of error magnitudes and weights for (A1), (A7) and (A8) are obvious. Note that the transfer (A1) operation is used in every other algorithm, thus the $|E| = 2^i$ of a transfer may occur in every operation. If the same register is used for the operand and the result, a repeated-use fault may occur. For the complementation algorithm (A7) for the two's complement number system, a "one" has to be added to the digitwise negation of x and so the addition errors of (A6) may also occur. In the round off operation (A8), a bit may have to be added to the kth digit and so the addition error of (A6) may be present.

In (A2)–(A5) the error magnitudes assume the form $c2^j$, where 2^j is the starting position of the error and $1 \leq c \leq 2^{k+1} - 1$ (i.e., the nonzero digits in the error number are contained in at most $k + 1$ adjacent positions.) The arithmetic shifts (A2, A3) are subject to basic faults that affect the values of the end digits. Since the left-end digit x_{n-1} is repeated k times for the k-digit right shift (A3), a fault in x_{n-1} will affect the $k + 1$ left-end digits of the result, giving an error with

$$|E| = \sum_{n-1-k}^{n-1} 2^i = 2^n - 2^{n-1-k} = 2^{n-1-k}(2^{k+1} - 1)$$

Table 8.3.1 ERROR MAGNITUDES DUE TO A BASIC FAULT IN A PARALLEL BINARY PROCESSOR

Number System / Algorithm	$N_1 = 2^n - 1$ ("one's" complement)		$N_2 = 2^n$ ("two's" complement)	
	Error Magnitude $|E|$	Weight W	Error Magnitude $|E|$	Weight W
A1 Transfer (applies also to A2–A7 below)	2^i	1	2^i	1
A2 Left shift, k digits	$2^k - 1$	2	$2^k - 1$	2
A3 Right shift, k digits	$2^{n-1-k}(2^{k+1} - 1)$	2	$2^{n-1-k}(2^{k+1} - 1)$	2
A4 Range extension, k digits	$2^{n-1}(2^{k+1} - 1)$ $2^n(2^k - 1)$	2	$2^{n-1}(2^{k+1} - 1)$ $2^n(2^k - 1)$	2
A5 Range contraction, k digits $(1 \leq c \leq 2^k - 1)$	$c2^{n-k}$ $2^{n-1-k}(2^{k+1} - 1)$	$1 \leq w \leq [k/2 + 1]$ 2	$c2^{n-k}$ $2^{n-1-k}(2^{k+1} - 1)$	$1 \leq w \leq [k/2 + 1]$ 2
A6 Modulo N addition or modulo N subtraction	$2^n - 1 - 2^i$	$2, (i = 0, n - 1)$ $3, (1 \leq i \leq n - 2)$	$2^n - 2^i$	$1, (i = n - 1)$ $2, (0 \leq i \leq n - 2)$
A7 Additive inverse (complementation)	2^i	1	2^i (Also see A6)	1
A8 Roundoff, k digits Also see (A6) for case (a)	2^k	1	2^k	1

*From Avizienis [34]

In the k-digit left shift (A2), k new digits are filled in at the right end. They are equal to x_{n-1} for one's complement system and they are zero for two's complement. In both cases, a fault will give

$$|E| = \sum_0^{k-1} 2^i = 2^k - 1$$

In the k-digit range extension (A4), k identical digits equal to x_{n-1} are attached at the left end. A faulty value of x_{n-1} will give

$$|E| = \sum_{n-1}^{n-1+k} 2^i = 2^{n+k} - 2^{n-1} = 2^{n-1}(2^{k+1} - 1)$$

A fault in the sensing circuit for x_{n-1} will give the error

$$|E| = \sum_n^{n-1+k} 2^i = 2^{n+k} - 2^n = 2^n(2^k - 1)$$

In the k-digit range contraction (A5) is the inverse operation in which k identical digits $(x_{n-1}, \ldots, x_{n-k})$ are removed at the left end when they are equal to x_{n-k-1}. An incorrect removal gives

$$|E| = c2^{n-k}, \quad \text{where } 1 \leq c \leq 2^k - 1$$

An incorrect value of x_{n-k-1} may cause the incorrect removal of k digits, with

$$|E| = \sum_{n-k-1}^{n-1} 2^i = 2^n - 2^{n-1-k} = 2^{n-1-k}(2^{k+1} - 1)$$

The modulo N addition or subtraction (A6) includes the "casting out" of N or $-N$ from the sum or difference, respectively. A basic fault which generates $|E| = 2^i$ will cause an error in the casting out process.

$$|E| = N - 2^i$$

Its weight is 1, 2, or 3, depending on N and i.

2. *Repeated-use faults in binary processors.* Repeated-use faults will occur when algorithms (A1)–(A8) are used in a byte-serial arithmetic processor, and multiplication and division in a parallel processor [34].

In a *byte-serial processor*, the kb digits of the operands enter the processor in a sequence of k bytes, and the digit circuits are used k times. A permanent logical fault will affect the same relative position $h(0 \leq h \leq b - 1)$ within each byte. However, the fault may be ineffective during some of the k uses. In the algorithms (A1), (A2), (A3), (A6), and (A7), the error magnitudes 2^i and $N - 2^i$ become the sets of possible error magnitudes $\{|E_c|\}$ and $\{N - |E_c|\}$, where

$$|E_c| = \sum_{j=0}^{k-1} d_j\, 2^{bj+h}$$

where $d_j = 0$ if the fault is ineffective for the jth byte, $d_j = 1$ for an effective stuck-at-one fault, and $d_j = -1$ for an effective s-a-0. Therefore the maximum magnitude for $|E_c|$ is the case where all d_j are equal to 1 or all d_j are equal to -1. The arithmetic weights W are in the following ranges:

1. for $|E_c| : 1 \leq W \leq k$
2. for $2^n - |E_c| : 2 \leq W \leq k + 1$

and

3. for $(2^n - 1) - |E_c| : 2 \leq W \leq k + 2$

The errors that affect the end digits of the shifts (A2) and (A3), the range manipulations (A4) and (A5), and the roundoff (A8) are not different from the parallel case ($k = 1$, $b = n - 1$) and the results of Table 8.3.1 apply.

In the high speed arithmetic unit, the multiplier is divided into blocks of m bits each and each block is multiplied by the multiplicand to form partial sums. The partial sums are shifted appropriately and added to form the partial produce for that block of the multiplier. Then the partial products are shifted by multiples of the block length m and added to form the product. Therefore the errors in the partial product cased by a local fault in the circuit are the same as those for an addition or shift in a byte-serial processor with byte length m. The effect of a fault is cumulative and iterative, and different positions of the result are affected by successive steps because of the shifting. There are also sources of errors when the multiplicand (or divisor) is shifted left to obtain the multiples 2, 4, 8, etc. to form the partial sums. There are errors when the partial sums are added to form the partial product. The set of possible error magnitudes are $\{|E|\}$ and $\{N - |E|\}$, with

$$E = \sum_{j=0}^{k-1} c_j d_j\, 2^{mj}$$

where c_j is the error pattern in the partial product, and d_j is defined in the same way as in byte-serial adder case. Errors in other algorithms are obtained as the cumulative effect (sum) of the appropriately shifted contributions of the errors in Table 8.3.1.

8.3.4.4. Cost and Effectiveness of Arithmetic-Error Codes.

1. *The criterion of cost.* The introduction of an arithmetic-error code will modify the word length and the arithmetic algorithm, besides adding the step of checking in the arithmetic operation. They represent the cost of the code. The encoding introduces redundant bits to the words and so a propor-

tional hardware increase in the storage devices, data paths, and processor units. The increase is expressed as a percentage of the perfect design and is roughly equal to the code rate (i.e., the number of redundant bits divided by the number of useful information bits). An encoding also often introduces complication to the algorithm for the same arithmetic operation. The cost is expressed by the increase in hardware and the decrease in speed. The checking algorithm tests the validity of every operand and every result in an operation. A correcting operation follows when an error is detected. The cost lies in the hardware complexity and the time for checking.

2. *The criterion of effectiveness.* The effectiveness of an arithmetic-error code in a computer may be expressed in two forms: as a *value effectiveness* inherent in the code, and as a design-dependent *fault effectiveness* [34].

(a) *Value effectiveness:* This includes all the error values that can be detected or corrected by the code, regardless of the logic structure of the computer and the algorithms used. Most arithmetic-error codes are designed to have a value effectiveness of 100 percent detection (or correction) of some types of errors. For example, single error detecting is said to be achieved when all errors of the value

$$\pm cr^i, \quad 0 < c < r, \quad 0 < i < n - 1$$

are detected in an n-digit, radix-r number.

(b) *Fault effectiveness:* Obviously, not all types of errors can occur in a digital system and some errors occur less frequently than the others, depending on the algorithm and the logic implementation of the algorithm. Therefore a code with value effectiveness less than 100 percent may be able to detect all possible occurences of logic faults in the system. In order to correctly evaluate the effectiveness of a code, the "value effectiveness" has to be translated into a measure of "fault effectiveness" for one or more specific types of logic faults. The fault effectiveness of a code k with respect to an algorithm A and a fault f is the percentage of all occurrences of f which will be detected (or corrected) when k is employed. Less than 100 percent fault-effective codes are tolerable when their cost is low because other methods of fault tolerance (especially program restarts) can be used to reinforce the codes. Also some undetectable faults can be made detectable by redesigning the implementation of the algorithm A.

8.3.4.5.   Examples of Some Practical Arithmetic Error Code.   A practical arithmetic error code must have good effectiveness at reasonable cost. For binary numbers, any odd integer $A > 1$ will detect single errors. The choice of A depends on the cost and effectiveness.

1. *Low-cost arithmetic codes.* This is a set of arithmetic codes proposed by Avizienis [58]. These employ check moduli of the form $A = 2^p - 1$, where

p is an integer greater than 1. The parameter p is called the *group length* of the code. The residue is easily obtained without division because of the congruence

$$Kr^i \equiv K \text{ modulo } (r - 1), \qquad r = 2^p$$

Therefore, if the number Z is composed of kp bits, then the residue can be obtained by adding the kp-bit groups in a byte-serial adder with an "end-around carry" addition algorithm, which "casts out $2^p - 1$'s." For example, to calculate the residue of $Z = 110110011010$ modulo 15, we will get $R = 1101 \oplus 1001 \oplus 1010 = 0111 \oplus 1010 = 0010$, without doing any division. The low-cost check moduli $2^p - 1$ are very compatible with binary arithmetic. A complete set of algorithms has been devised for AN-coded operands [58].

(a) *One-use faults:* The check moduli $2^p - 1$ detect all burst errors of length $p - 1$ or less, since their error magnitudes are $g2^j$, with $1 \leq g \leq 2^{p-1} - 1$, which is not divisible by $2^p - 1$. The error pattern of p adjacent bits is undetectable. This is important for the algorithms A2–A5 of Table 8.3.1, which contains error magnitudes of the forms $2^j(2^k - 1)$ and $2^j(2^{k+1} - 1)$. The choice of $p \geq k + 2$ will guarantee fault detection for these algorithms. Some weight—2 error magnitudes will not be detected: for example, an s-a-1 and an s-a-0 fault with a certain separation (multiples of p), giving the error magnitude equal to $2^{rp} - 1$, which is divisible by $2^p - 1$.

(b) *Determinate repeated-use faults:* For operands of k bytes of b bits each, every effective fault detection will be obtained for the choice $p = b$. For a single determinate repeated-use fault all possible $2^k - 1$ error magnitudes (and their 1's complements) are detected by the check modulus $2^p - 1$ for $k < 2^p = 1$. The first undetectable error occurs when $k = 2^p - 1$. For example, if $p = 2$, and $k = 3$, then the repeated-use error pattern $2^4 + 2^2 + 1$ is divisible by $2^2 - 1$ and is undetectable. The check modulus $\alpha = 15$ with byte length $b = 4$ can detect all single repeated-use fault up to $n = 56$.

In general, for any choice (a, b) with word length $n = kb = ca$, it has been shown that the first miss occurs [59] when the word length reaches the value $n' = c'a(2^{a/k'} - 1)$, where $c'a = k'b$ is the L.C.M. of a and b. Therefore, the maximum safe word length is (by setting $k' = 1$)

$$n'_{max} = c'a(2^a - 1) = b(2^a - 1)$$

By setting b equal to a multiple of a, the "safe length" will be increased. For example, $\alpha = 15$ and $b = 8$ allows no misses for words up to 112 bits. The "safe length" is doubled.

(c) *Indeterminate repeated-use faults:* A local indeterminate fault (used m times) will contribute to the error magnitude in one of 3^m possible ways. In every use, its contribution can be 0, 2^i, or -2^i. Given any pair, (a, b), the first undetectable error occurs when the word length exceeds the L.C.M. of

a and b. The maximum safe length n is attained for setting a and b relatively prime. Note that this choice of (a, b) is the least desirable choice for the determinate faults. Therefore, the choice of the values of a and b depends on the relative frequencies of these two types of faults.

(d) *Repeated-use faults in residue codes:* The preceding analysis of repeated-use faults apply to the low-cost AN codes with $A = 2^p - 1$. For the low-cost residue codes in the byte-serial processor, when the check symbol R uses the same digit circuits as the operand x, a logical fault in the circuit may affect both R and x to compensate each other so that no fault will be detected. For example [34], consider the modulo 15 residue encoding.

$$x = 0010, 0011, 0101 \qquad R = 1010$$

An s-a-1 fault sets the rightmost bit to 1 in every byte of x and R to give x^*, R^*:

$$x^* = 0011, 0011, 0101 \qquad R^* = 1011$$

The checking algorithm yields $15|x^* = 1011$, indicating no error.

The compensating miss is eliminated by using the inverse residue code. Consider the following example of modulo 15 inverse residue code:

$$x = 1000, 1101, 0101 \qquad R = 0100.$$

The check gives $15|x + R = 1011 + 0100 = 1111$, i.e., no error. The s-a-1 fault gives

$$x^* = 10001, 1101, 0101 \qquad R^* = 0101$$

The check gives $15|x^* + R^* = 1100 + 0101 = 0010$, indicating an error. The compensating miss does not occur because the change $0 \rightarrow 1$ in R corresponds to the change $1 \rightarrow 0$ in x. All results of the determinate fault are directly applicable to the low-cost inverse residue codes. The result led to the choice of modulo 15 inverse residue codes in the fault-tolerant STAR computer [34].

2. *Codes for correcting iterative error* [60].   Let m be the length of a block in bits and r be the number of blocks; then single *iterative error* E has the form

$$E = \pm 2^k \sum_{i=0}^{r-1} e_i 2^{mi}$$

where $0 \leq k < m$ and $e_i = 0$ or 1 for all i.

A successful correction of error depends on the correct decoding of the polarity, position, and distribution of error. Before presenting the code and the decoding method, let us state some basic theorems. For the proofs of these theorems, please consult Chein and Hong [60].

Theorem 8.3.1

Let

$$E_1 = 2^k \sum_{i=0}^{r-1} e_i \, 2^{mi}$$

Given m and r, if $b < r$ such that the maximum Hamming weight of E_1 is less than $\frac{1}{2}mb$, then the Hamming weight of the error E it less than $\frac{1}{2}mb$ if and only if the polarity of error is positive.

Theorem 8.3.2

Let d be the number of error digits,

$$d = \sum_{i=0}^{r-1} e_i$$

Let S be $E_1 \bmod (2^m - 1)$, then $S \equiv E_1 \equiv 2^k d \bmod (2^m - 1)$. Let $T = (2^m - 1)/(2^x - 1)$, where x is the largest divisor of $m(x < m)$.

For a given d and S, the error position k can be uniquely decided if and only if $r < T$.

Theorem 8.3.3

Let m and r be relatively prime, $E_1 \neq 0$ and $S \equiv E_1 \bmod 2^r - 1$. $S = 0$ if and only if $e_i = 1$ for all i, and when $S \neq 0$, S has d 1's. Furthermore, E_1 can be uniquely decided given k and S.

Theorem 8.3.1 gives the condition for a code so that the polarity of the error can be detected. Theorem 8.3.2 gives us a way to obtain the position of the error and the number of error digits, provided that certain conditions are satisfied. Theorem 8.3.3 shows us how to determine the distribution of the errors.

Now we are ready to describe a single iterative-error-correcting code, called the A_1 code by Chien and Hong [60]. It is an AN code. The generator of the A_1 code is defined as $A = \text{LCM} [(2^{mb} - 1), (2^r - 1)]$, where $r < T$ given in Theorem 8.3.2, $(r, m) = 1$, and b is the smallest integer satisfying the condition given by Theorem 8.3.1. Some of the values of T and $r_{\max}$ for given values of m and b are given in Table 8.3.2. To construct an A_1 code for a given m, one may find a value of r such that $r < T$ from Table 8.3.2, and $(r, m) = 1$, and then one finds the value of b from Table 8.3.2.

Table 8.3.2 VALUES OF GIVEN T AND $r_{\max}$ GIVEN m AND b^*

m	$r_{\max}$							T
b:	1	2	3	4	5	6	7	
3	2	4	7	9	12	14	17	7
4	2	5	8	11	14	17	20	5
5	6	12	19	25	32	38	45	31
6	6	13	20	27	34	41	48	9
7	14	28	43	57	72	86	101	127
8	14	29	44	59	74	89	104	17
9	30	60	91	121	152	182	213	73
10	30	61	92	123	154	185	216	33
11	62	124	187	249	312	374	437	2047
12	62	125	188	251	314	377	440	65
13	126	252	379	505	632	758	885	8191
14	126	253	380	507	634	761	888	129
15	254	508	763	1017	1272	1526	1781	1057
16	254	509	764	1019	1274	1529	1784	257

*From Chien and Hong [60].

The decoding algorithm is given as follows:

Let the corrupted output be $K = AN + E_0$ and let $h(x)$ denote the Hamming weight of the integer x.

Step 1: Let the initial syndrome be $S_0 \equiv K \mod A \equiv E_0 \mod A$. If $h(S_0 \mod 2^{mb} - 1) < \frac{1}{2}mb$, the polarity is positive and otherwise negative (by Theorem 8.3.1). If $S_0 = 0$, there is no error (by Theorem 8.3.2).

Step 2: Let $S_1 = S_0$ if the polarity is positive and let $S_1 = A - S_0$ if the polarity is negative. In either case $S_1 \equiv E_1 \mod A$. (Note that $E_1 = |E_0|$.)

Step 3: Let $S_2 \equiv S_1 = E_1 \mod 2^r - 1$. $d = h(S_2)$ or, if $S_2 = 0$, $d = r$ (by Theorem 8.3.3).

Step 4: Let $S_2 \equiv S_1 \mod 2^m - 1$. Since $2^m - 1$ divides $2^{mb} - 1$ for any $b \geq 1$, $S_3 \equiv S_1 \equiv E_1 \equiv 2^k d \mod 2^m - 1$. Starting with d from the previous step, form $2^i d \mod 2^m - 1$ (cyclic shift of d). When $2^{i'} = S_3$, the error position $k = i'$ (by Theorem 8.3.2).

Step 5: Let E_2 be the distribution of the errors, i.e.,

$$E_2 = \sum_{i=0}^{r-1} e_i 2^{mi}.$$

Now $E_2 \equiv 2^{-k} S_2 \mod 2^r - 1$ (cyclic shift left).
If $S_2 = 0$,

$$E_2 = \sum_{i=0}^{r-1} 2^{mi}$$

If $S_2 \neq 0$, let a_i be determined from the equation

$$2^{-k}S_2 \bmod 2^r - 1 = \sum_{i=0}^{r-1} a_i 2^i, \qquad \text{where } a_i = 0, 1$$

Then E_2 is formed as

$$E_2 = \sum_{i=0}^{r-1} a_i 2(mi \bmod r)m \qquad \text{(by Theorem 8.3.3)}$$

Note that the decoding requires only very simple hardware, essentially three shift registers of length m, r, and mr each, some basic combinatorial threshold logic, and a few constant-divisor divider circuits. An example of the A_1 code and the decoding procedure is now given.

Example 8.3.1

Let $m = 5$. Then $r < 31$ (from value of T in Table 8.3.2). Let us choose $r = 6$ to make the code into a manageable size for illustration purpose. Now $b = 1$, from Table 8.3.2. The generator of the code is given by

$$A = \text{LCM}(2^5 - 1, 2^6 - 1) = \text{LCM}(31, 63) = 1953.$$

A correct code word is

$$C = 01100 \; 11000 \; 10001 \; 00100 \; 10011 \; 10001.$$

Suppose an s-a-1 fault has occurred in the second bit in the adder so that the received word becomes

$$C' = 01110 \; 11010 \; 10011 \; 00110 \; 10011 \; 10011.$$

Therefore, $E_0 = + 2^1 (2^{0m} + 2^{2m} + 2^{3m} + 2^{4m} + 2^{5m})$, $m = 5$. Let us illustrate now how the decoding algorithm gives us E_0.

Step 1: $S_0 \equiv C' \bmod 1953 = 1010110100$. $S_0 \bmod 2^{mb} - 1 = S_0 \bmod 31 = 1010$. Now $h(S_0 \bmod 2^{mb} - 1) = 2 < \frac{1}{2}(5) = \frac{1}{2}mb$. Hence *the polarity is +*.

Step 2: $S_1 \equiv S_0 \equiv 1010110100$.

Step 3: $S_2 \equiv S_1 \bmod 2^6 - 1 = 111110$. $d = h(S_2) = 5$.

Step 4: $S_3 \equiv S_1 \bmod 2^5 - 1 = 1010$. Since $d = 5$ and $2^1.5 = 10_{\text{decimal}} = 1010 = S_3$, $k = 1$. Therefore *the error position is at 2^1*, i.e., 2nd bit.

Step 5: $S_2 \neq 0$ and $2^{-k}S_2 \bmod 2^r - 1 = 11111 \bmod 63 = 11111$. Therefore $a_0 = 1$, $a_1 = 1$, $a_2 = 1$, $a_3 = 1$, $a_4 = 1$, $a_5 = 1$ and $a_6 = 0$.

$$E_2 = \sum_{i=0}^{r-1} a_i \, 2(mi \bmod r)m = 2^{0m} + 2^{5m} + 2^{4m} + 2^{3m} + 2^{2m}$$

Now the decoding is complete. The error is formed by

$$E_0 = +2^1 E_2 = +2^1(2^{0m} + 2^{2m} + 2^{3m} + 2^{4m} + 2^{5m}) = +(2^1 + 2^{11}$$
$$+ 2^{16} + 2^{21} + 2^{26}),$$

which is the correct result.

By the subtraction of the error E_0 from the received word C', we obtain the correct codeword result

$$C = 01100\ 11000\ 10001\ 00100\ 10011\ 10001.$$

8.3.5. Conclusion

The theory of error-correcting codes can be used extensively in fault-tolerant computer design. It can be used in the memory system to increase the "yield" of manufacturing memory devices, especially in semiconductor memories where large integration is employed. It can also be used to increase the reliability of the information stored in the primary memory as well as the secondary memory. It can be used to increase the reliability of the arithmetic unit, which is one of the most complicated and most expensive pieces of hardware in the computer system. Many new arithmetic codes have been proposed and the practical applicability of the low-cost arithmetic code has been demonstrated by the STAR computer in the Jet Propulsion Laboratory in Pasadena, California.

Coding has several attractive features. The redundancy introduced is low compared to other schemes. For example, single error-correction with Hamming code requires redundancy approximately equal to the logarithm of the original system while a replication scheme with voting requires three times the original hardware. In many codes, the information bits and check bits are handled in the same way in an operation. Hence, a uniform design can be used. Coding provides concurrent diagnosis and therefore is able to correct transition errors. Coding also provides automatic fault detection, location, and correction. On the other hand, coding has its drawbacks. Coding introduces time delays due to encoding and decoding, which may be intolerable in some parts of the computer system with strict speed requirements. The different environments of the various subsystems of a computer have different requirements on the code to be used. It is difficult, if not impossible, to find a compatible and efficient code that can be used uniformly in all subsystems of the computer, subject to the speed and cost requirements. Besides, coding cannot correct errors caused by faults in the encoder and decoder, thus increasing the size of the hardcore of the system.

EXERCISES 8.3

1. Use the encoder in Fig. 8.3.1 to code the message (1011). Find the syndromes of all the possible single errors of the encoded message by using the decoder in Fig. 8.3.2.

2. Design the encoder and decoder for the code discussed in Section 8.3.3.3. Then verify their operation by means of an example.

3. Show that an AN code with $A = 19$ can correct all single errors for modulo 27 arithmetic.

8.4. RELIABILITY MODELING AND ANALYSIS OF ULTRA-RELIABLE FAULT-TOLERANT COMPUTERS

8.4.1. Introduction

Reliability, in general, is defined as the probability that a specified function will be adequately performed for a specified time. It is therefore equal to one minus the probability of failure. The reliability of a digital system can be enhanced by improving the reliability of the components and by introducing redundancy. Usually both of these approaches are taken together.

The reliability of the components can be improved by good circuit and hardware design. High quality components have to be used. The "worst case design" principle has to be enforced. The "worst case" device parameters have to be used, taking into account the effects of aging, temperature variation, and manufacturing tolerances. Conservative use of the components should be encouraged in the circuit design so that the devices would not operate at the maximum ratings of current, voltage, power, temperature, etc. Liberal noise margins should be allowed so that the components can function properly in the nonidealistic environment. Simulation can be used extensively to verify our design before manufacture. Intensive testing and evaluation have to be performed on the system before it is put into operation to minimize design and manufacturing errors. The power supplies should be regulated so as to avoid transients which will ruin the components. In the actual physical circuit layout, crosstalks should be minimized in noise sensitive applications. Heat sensitive devices should be located away from "heat generators." Test probes have to be designed into the circuit to increase its test accessibility.

Redundancy can be introduced in different forms (hardware, software, information, time, etc.) and at different levels (components, functional modules, subsystems, whole systems, etc.). Redundancy theory enables us to make reliable computers out of unreliable parts. After presenting some important reliability parameters, we will attempt to model and analyze the reliability of systems with standby replacement redundancy [61], multiple-voting redundancy [2], and hybrid redundancy [62], which is a combination of the first two. Following a brief description of the three systems, the mathematical models and the quantitative evaluations of system reliability of the systems are given. A comparison of these competitive redundancy configurations in terms of cost and some significant reliability measures are then presented.

8.4.2. Reliability Parameters [63]

The reliability of a system is the probability that the system will function correctly over some specified time interval. It is therefore the probability of survival of the system during that time. Although this probability function completely describes the reliability properties of the system, some comparative measures are often more convenient to use. Since reliability is a probability function with respect to time, these reliability parameters generally fall into two major categories, according to whether the comparison is made in the probability domain or the time domain. The first type contains relative comparisons of the reliabilities at a certain time, e.g., the survival probability of a mission, the reliability at the mean life, etc. The second category contains measures of the time that a system can survive with a certain probability, e.g., the mean life of the system, the maximum length of time for which the system has a reliability greater than an acceptable value, etc. Within each category comparisons can be made relative to either the nonredundant (simplex) system or a competitive system. A comparison of systems using stand by replacement redundancy, multiple-voting redundancy and hybrid redundancy in terms of these reliability parameters is given in Table 8.4.1 at the end of this section.

8.4.2.1. Absolute Measures of Reliability.   The absolute measures of reliability are the probability of survival (R), the reliability at the mean life (RMTF), the mean life (MTF), and the maximum mission time for some desired minimum mission reliability (TMAX). The latter two are measures in the time domain.

The mean life, sometimes called "mean time before failure" (MTBF), is the expectation of the time before a failure occurs. It is an average measure and is therefore quite misleading for practical purposes. The reliability at the mean life was proposed to remedy this. However, it was shown [64] that the reliability at the mean life cannot be a satisfactory measure of reliability either due to its asymptotic properties. The measure TMAX gives the time for the system reliability to drop from some reference reliability R2 (usually taken to be 1.0) to some terminal reliability R1. This usually gives the designer a better hint on whether a certain redundancy configuration is suitable to a certain mission.

8.4.2.2. Comparative Measures of Reliability.   Some comparative measures relative to the nonredundant (simplex) design are the following [63]:

1. The normalized mean life, MTF (normalized), is the system mean life divided by the mean life to the simplex system.
2. The simplex time improvement factor SIMTIF is defined to be the ratio of TMAX of a system and the simplex system.
3. The simplex difference SIMDIFF is the difference in reliability relative to a simplex system defined to be R(system) $[t]$ − R(simplex) $[t]$.
4. The simplex gain SIMGAIN is the gain in reliability relative to a simplex system, defined to be R(system) $[t]$/R(simplex) $[t]$.
5. The simplex reliability improvement factor SIMRIF is defined to be $\{1 -$ R(simplex) $[t]\}/\{1 -$ R(system)$[t]\}$.

These measures reflect the improvement of a system with respect to the simplex system. SIMRIF is particularly useful when the two values of reliability are close to each other and both of them are close to 1.0.

Some comparative measures relative to competitive systems are the following:

1. The difference in reliability DIFF is defined to be R2(t) − R1(t).
2. The gain in reliability GAIN is defined to be R2(t)/R1(t).
3. The reliability improvement factor RIF is defined to be $[1 -$ R1(t)]/ $[1 -$ R2(t)].
4. The relative time improvement factor, RATIF is defined to be TMAX2(R1)/TMAX1(R1), where R1 is the minimum mission reliability.

For a specified terminal reliability R1, RATIF states how much more time system 2 will last as compared to system 1.

8.4.2.3. Other Reliability Considerations. Even the most reliable computer will fail eventually. However, the reliability of the system can be restored when the faulty parts are located and replaced. The probability that a failed system will be restored to an operable state within a specified time is called the *maintainability* of the system. It can also be expressed in terms of the mean time to repair a fault in the system (MTRF). A "reliable" system is also a system that can be counted on when needed. Therefore, a reliable system must be "available" most of the time. The *availability* of a system is the probability that the system will be functioning normally at any particular time during its scheduled working period. Therefore,

$$\text{Availability} = \text{percentage of system up-time} = \frac{\text{MTBF}}{\text{MTBF} + \text{MTRF}}$$

The maintainability of the system is related to the speedy repair of and recovery from a failed unit. Therefore, it requires fast error detection, isolation and location, as well as good fault resolution. Concurrent diagnosis and in-process checking are very attractive since the errors are detected as soon as they occur through operational checks. The speedy isolation of faults prevents the propagation of errors, enabling the fault to be located instantly. A number of different techniques can be used, such as coding, threshold detection, etc. Also the system has to provide adequate test accessibility to allow testing of all subsystems and to fully exercise a failed unit. Logic simulators can be used to identify areas where test access and detectability is inadequate. There are other factors that affect the repair time. Good documentation, a complete fault dictionary, unambiguous labeling and terminology all help the repair technician. Plug-in modules also help the actual repair process.

The availability of the system is dependent on the maintainability and reliability of the system. It can be improved by decreasing the mean time to repair a fault and by increasing the mean time before failure of the system. Enough redundancy can be put in the system so that when a fault occurs the fault will be isolated quickly and the system will still have sufficient resources to continue its normal operation while the faulty unit is simultaneously being repaired. Hopefully, the goal of continuous availability can be achieved. The duplication of system elements can be applied at different levels. Usually the lower the level of duplication, the higher the availability and the more complex the interconnections. Note that many of the formulae for reliability analysis are also applicable to availability analysis by substituting availability for reliability and unavailability for failure.

8.4.3. Common Redundancy Configurations

8.4.3.1. Standby-Replacement Redundancy (SR). In this system a number of independent identical units are connected simultaneously to a common input. A failure detector is associated with each unit and a switch is connected to the outputs of the identical units. The output of the system is taken from some one unit until that unit fails, at which time the switching circuits at the output steps to the next unit that is operating satisfactorily. The process continues until the assigned task is completed or all the units fail. This is illustrated in Fig. 8.4.1. If the failure rate of the subsystem is smaller when powered off than powered on, which is usually the case, the standby spares should be powered off until they are used. In this case, a recovery procedure has to take place to put the spare into the appropriate state to continue the process.

8.4.3.2. Multiple-Line Voting Redundancy (NMR)[2]. $N(=2n+1)$ copies of a logical circuit can be made and a voter is placed at their outputs so that the output of the circuit is taken to be the majority of the outputs of the N copies. When the probability of failure of each copy is less than 50 percent, this scheme always produces a more reliable system. The N-tuple-modularly redundant system (NMR) is shown in Fig. 8.4.2. Any odd num-

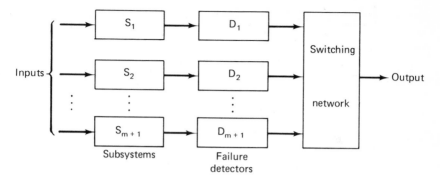

Fig. 8.4.1 A standby replacement system with m standby units.

ber N can be used for the system. The most common configuration has $N = 3$, the so-called triple-modularly redundant system (TMR). The simplex case, with $N = 1$, is the nonredundant system. A fault-detection circuit can also be built into the voter so that the copies with an output different from the majority are identified as faulty elements.

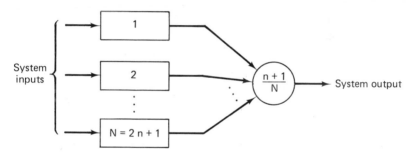

Fig. 8.4.2 An NMR system.

8.4.3.3. Hybrid Redundancy (H). A hybrid system, $H(N, S)$, consists of an NMR core, with an associated bank of S spare units such that when one of the N active units fails, a spare unit is used to replace it and the basic NMR operation continues [62]. This is illustrated in Fig. 8.4.3. Note that the failure rate of components usually increases with the time that they are used. Hence standby parts, which are powered off until used, usually have a smaller probability of failure than used parts.

The physical realization of a hybrid system is shown in Fig. 8.4.4. The disagreement detector (DD) detects if the output of any of the $2n + 1$ active units is different from the system output from the restoring organ. When there is any disagreement, the switching unit (SU) will replace all the units that disagree by switching them out and switching in the spares. If the spare were to fail in the dormant mode and was switched in on demand from the

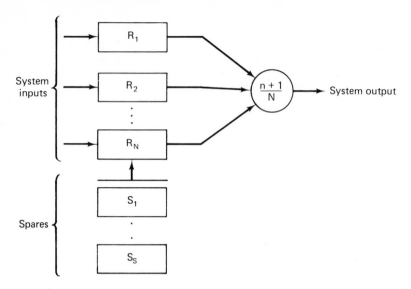

Fig. 8.4.3   A hybrid (N, S) system.

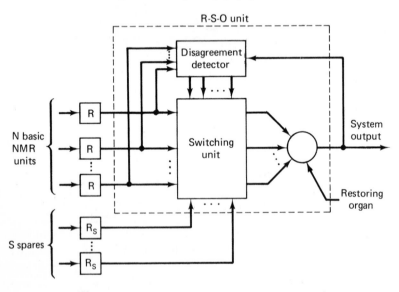

Fig. 8.4.4   Hybrid (N, S) system block diagram [62].

DD unit, the disagreement would still exist and the SU would replace it by one of the spares still unused, until all the spares have been exhausted. Therefore, the system fails upon exhaustion of all the spares and the failure of any $n + 1$ of the basic $2n + 1$ units. Note that a precaution has to be taken against $n + 1$ simultaneous failures in the basic units, in which case all the good spares will be switched out and discarded since the system takes a faulty output as the correct one. When $N = 1$, the hybrid system reduces to a standby-replacement system. When $S = 0$, the hybrid system reduces to the NMR system.

8.4.4. Reliability Modeling and Analysis

Good reliability modeling requires the careful consideration of many factors such as the faults in the system, the behavior of the system under fault conditions, the failure distribution, the level of abstraction, the accuracy and ease of use of the reliability equations, etc. But above all, the most important criterion is the applicability and usefulness of the reliability model in system design. In most reliability models the errors in the system are assumed to be independent. Before we begin the quantitative analysis of different reliability models let us develop a unified notation and discuss some simple reliability calculations.

8.4.4.1. Symbols and Notations. Let $H(N,S)$ denote a hybrid system with N-tuple modular redundancy (NMR) and S spare units. Let NMR denote N-tuple modular redundancy and let TMR stand for triple modular redundant system ($N = 3$). Let $R(\ )$ refer to the reliability of the system as characterized in the parentheses. Therefore, a hybrid redundant system $H(N, S)$ has a reliability of $R(N, S)$. Let R_0 denote the reliability of the simplex system, i.e., the nonredundant system. Furthermore, R_v denotes the reliability of the detection-restoration-switching network for the hybrid system. (Sometimes we can assume $R_v = 1$, i.e., this system overhead has a negligible probability of failure compared to the other parts of the system.)

Let R^* indicate the reliability of the system after the unreliability $(1 - R_v)$ due to the detection-restoration-switching network has been taken into account, i.e.,

$$R^*(N, S) = R_v \cdot R(N, S)$$

8.4.4.2. Reliability of Components. Let us assume that a system will be faulty if there is a failure of one or more components. The failure rate of the system is therefore dependent on the reliability of the components. Since the components of the system are the integrated circuit modules, the experimental failure statistics of these modules are very useful to model the reliability of the system. A typical failure rate curve with respect to time is given in Fig. 8.4.5. The failure rate is the percentage of components that will fail per unit time. It is a function of time.

Such a curve cannot be easily modelled analytically. However, we notice that the curve can be roughly divided into three sections. The first section corresponds to the "burn-in" stage of the components. The failure rate is

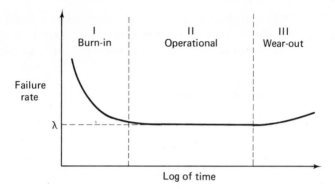

Fig. 8.4.5   Failure rate of integrated circuit modules.

high due to manufacturing errors and operational errors, etc. The last section has a high failure rate because the component is worn out. However, we notice that in the second section, the failure rate remains approximately constant during the entire operational stage. Let the failure rate be equal to a constant λ. Let

$n(t)$ = the number of components that survive after time t in operation

$n_0 = n(0)$ = the number of components at the beginning of the operation

The number of components that fail during the time t to $t + dt = n(t)\lambda \, dt$. Therefore,

$$dn(t) = -n(t)\lambda \, dt$$

$$\frac{dn(t)}{dt} = -n(t)\lambda$$

Since $n(t) = n_0$ at $t = 0$.

$$n(t) = n_0 \exp(-\lambda t)$$

Let us define the reliability of the component at time t, $r(t)$, as the fraction of the original components that survive after time t. Then,

$$r(t) = \frac{n(t)}{n_0}$$

$$= \exp(-\lambda t)$$

Reliability density $= r'(t) = \dfrac{dr}{dt} = -\lambda \exp(-\lambda t)$

Failure density $= (1 - r)' = \lambda \exp(-\lambda t)$

Mean life (MTBF) $= \int_0^\infty t(1 - r)' \, dt = \dfrac{1}{\lambda}$

Therefore, the reliability can also be expressed in terms of the MTBF,

$$r(t) = \exp\left(\frac{-t}{\text{MTBF}}\right)$$

Besides the fact that the exponential failure law is quite accurate in practice, it has useful mathematical elegance. The constant failure rate meant that the probability that a component will fail in a time interval T is independent of the time it has been in operation. The exponential distribution is memoryless. The exponential failure law also gives us mathematical tractability of complex systems. It will be shown later that if a system contains a number of subsystems each with a constant failure rate (exponential reliability) and assuming that all the failures are independent, the reliability of the whole system is still exponential with a constant failure rate equal to the sum of the failure rates of the subsystems.

Usually the active unit has a higher failure rate than the dormant (powered off) unit. From now on, let us denote the failure rate of an active (powered) unit by λ and that of a standby unit (powered off) by μ. Let K be the ratio of λ to μ. Then $1 \leq K \leq \infty$. Also let us denote the time that the system has been put into operation by T. Sometimes T is called the *mission time*. The reliability of a simplex system R_0 is, therefore, $\exp(-\lambda T)$.

8.4.4.3. Some Simple Reliability Analysis

1. *Serial system.* When a system contains N subsystems so that the system operates correctly only if all the subsystems are fault-free, it can be modeled as a serial system, as shown in Fig. 8.4.6. Let us assume that the faults are independent.

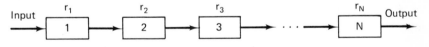

Fig. 8.4.6 A serial system.

If subsystem i has reliability r_i, the reliability of the whole system r is given by

$$r = \prod_{i=1}^{N} r_i$$

Suppose subsystem i has a constant failure rate λ_i, i.e., $r_i = \exp(-\lambda_i t)$,

$$r = \prod_{i=1}^{N} \exp\left(-\lambda_i t\right)$$

$$= \exp\left(-\lambda t\right), \text{ where } \lambda = \sum_{i=1}^{N} \lambda_i$$

Therefore, the failure rate of the system is just the sum of the failure rates of the subsystems. The MTBF of the system is $1/\lambda$.

If the N subsystems are identical, with $\lambda_i = \lambda'$,

$$r = \exp\left(-N\lambda' t\right)$$

and

$$\text{MTBF} = \frac{1}{N\lambda'}$$

Therefore the failure rate is increased by N-fold while the MTBF is $1/N$ that of the simple subsystem.

2.   *Parallel system.*   When a system contains N subsystems so that the system functions normally if one subsystem works correctly, it can be modeled as a parallel system, as shown in Fig. 8.4.7. Assume faults are independent.

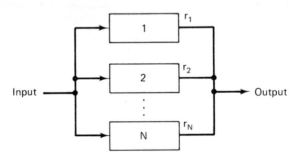

Fig. 8.4.7   A parallel system.

If subsystem i has reliability r_i, the reliability of the whole system r is given by

$$r = 1 - \prod_{i=1}^{N} (1 - r_i)$$

If all the units are identical, each with a constant failure rate λ,

$$r = 1 - \{1 - \exp\left(-\lambda t\right)\}^N$$

and

$$\text{MTBF} = \frac{N}{\lambda} \int_0^\infty \lambda t \{1 - \exp(-\lambda t)\}^{N-1} \exp(-\lambda t) \, d(\lambda t)$$

$$= \frac{1}{\lambda} \sum_{j=1}^{N} \frac{(-1)^{j-1}\binom{N}{j}}{j}$$

$$= \frac{1}{\lambda} \sum_{j=1}^{N} \frac{1}{j}$$

3. *Modeling of a simple computer system.* Suppose a simple computer system has a processor, a core memory, two disks, and three tape drives. Let us assume that the computer needs a disk or two tape drives to function normally with the core memory and processor unit. If the reliability of a single tape drive is r_4 it can easily be shown that the reliability of the whole tape drive subsystem is $3r_4 - 2r_4^3$. The system can therefore be modeled as shown in Fig. 8.4.8. The reliability of the whole system is given by

$$r = r_1 \cdot r_2 \cdot [1 - (1 - r_3) \cdot (1 - r_3) \cdot (1 - 3r_4 + 2r_4^3)]$$

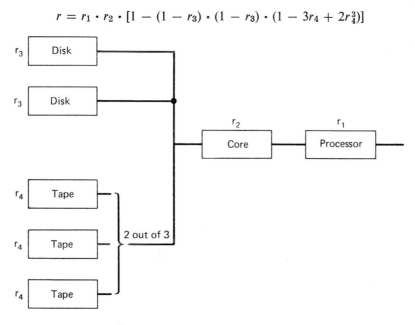

Fig. 8.4.8 A model of the computer system.

4. *Component-wise against system-wise redundancy.* Suppose the system contains n components and we introduce redundancy into the system equivalent to $m - 1$ extra copies of the system. By system-wise redundancy we mean a parallel system with m copies of the system. Therefore it can be modeled as a parallel system with m subsystems each of which is a serial system with

n components, as shown in Fig. 8.4.9. By component-wise redundancy we mean a serial system with m copies of each component. Therefore it can be modeled as a serial system with n subsystems each of which is a parallel system with m components, as shown in Fig. 8.4.10.

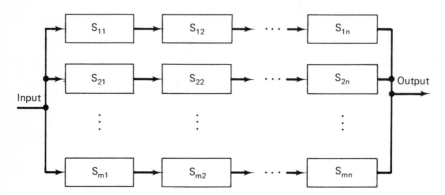

Fig. 8.4.9   System-wise redundancy.

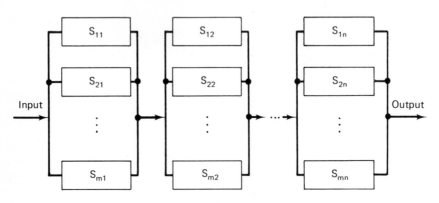

Fig. 8.4.10   Component-wise redundancy.

Suppose each component has a reliability of r. Then

R(system-wise redundancy system) $= 1 - (1 - r^n)^m$

R(component-wise redundancy system) $= [1-(1-r)^m]^n$

We can see that the reliability of the component-wise redundancy system is always greater than the one with system-wise redundancy. However the former has more interconnections and is also more difficult to design.

8.4.5.   Standby-Replacement Redundant System (SR)

Let m denote the total number of replications in the system, i.e., a system with $m - 1$ spares. For perfect failure detection and switching, the reliability of this system is given by

$$R(1, m) = 1 - (1 - R_0)^m$$

which is simply the probability that at least one unit is working correctly.

Let D_a and S_a denote the probability that the failure detector and the switching network, respectively, perform the correct function when failure occurs. Let D_b and S_b denote the probability that the failure detector and the switching network, respectively, will not cause false signals and switching when no failure has occurred. Then it has been shown by Flehinger [61] that the reliability of such a system is

$$R(1, m) = R_0 D_b S_b \frac{1 - \{(1 - R_0) D_a S_a + R_0(1 - D_b)S_a + R_0 D_b(1 - S_b)\}^m}{1 - \{(1 - R_0) D_a S_a + R_0(1 - D_b)S_a + R_0 D_b(1 - S_b)\}}$$

Note that this equation only applies to a single system with standby redundancy. We have not considered the level at which redundancy is applied, i.e., the size of the subsystem where replications are made. From the analysis of the last section, it seems that the smallest unit is desirable. However, the overhead of circuits for fault detection and switching will be excessive. From a reliability viewpoint, a study [65] showed that partition should occur wherever the overhead is smallest. Intuitively, the partition should be done at the level of functional units since the number of signal lines across functional boundaries are usually small and the switching overhead is minimized while the fault detector is easy to design. However, from the point of economy, ease of maintenance, and ease of adaptation, it should be desirable to make the largest possible units redundant. It has been noted that for initially unreliable machines and a moderate degree of redundancy, high reliability is realized only by applying the redundancy to relatively small units. However, for initially reliable machines, the improvement comes primarily from the degree of redundancy rather than the level at which it is applied. The reliability of the system is limited by the reliability of the fault detector and switching network. A large subsystem is usually desirable in this case.

8.4.6. The N-tuple Modular Redundant System (NMR)

An NMR system with $N = 2n + 1$ will function correctly if $(n + 1)$ of the units are functioning correctly. Therefore, its reliability equation is

$$R(N, 0) = R(\text{NMR}) = \sum_{i=0}^{n} \binom{N}{i} (1 - R_0)^i R_0^{N-i}$$

For the TMR case, it reduces to

$$R(3, 0) = R(\text{TMR}) = R_0^3 + 3R_0^2(1 - R_0).$$

The family of curves illustrating its behavior is shown in Fig. 8.4.11, with reliability plotted as a function of normalized time λT.

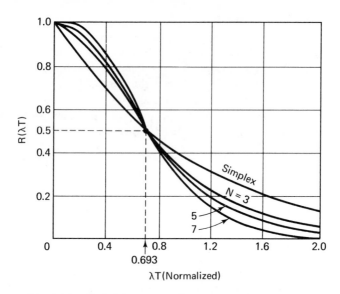

Fig. 8.4.11   Reliability of a NMR system versus normalized time.

An examination of Fig. 8.4.11 shows that for values of R_0 greater than 0.5, the introduction of redundancy improves the reliability of the overall system. However, the use of modular redundancy causes a deterioration of the reliability of the overall system if the simplex system is very unreliable ($R_0 < 0.5$). This is obvious since we are taking the majority of the results as the correct one. If a system is more likely to give an incorrect answer than a correct one ($R_0 < 0.5$), then the more copies of this system that we use, the more likely it is that we will get an incorrect answer, hence the worse the reliability of the overall system. Assuming an exponential law of failure, the reliability of the simplex system will become less than 0.5 after 0.69 of its mean life (MTBF). After this time, the NMR system becomes even more unreliable than the simplex system. Hence the NMR configuration is only feasible for very short mission time. (The reader may also note that the mean life is a misleading reliability parameter since the system is more likely to give an incorrect answer than a correct one after only 0.69 of its mean life.)

The reader is encouraged to plot the reliability curves of the hybrid $H(3, S)$ systems on Fig. 8.4.11 for $S = 1, 2, 3$, and 4. Then it is easy to verify that hybridization enables the system to last for a much longer mission time. We can also observe from Fig. 8.4.11 that the incremental improvement in reliability decreases with the amount of replications introduced. An NMR system with $N = 9$ is not much more reliable than one with $N = 7$. Therefore it seems advisable to use the TMR configuration as the basis and place the additional replications as spares, thus becoming a hybrid $H(3, S)$ system.

Note that, similar to the standby redundancy configuration, the reliability of the system can be increased by partitioning the system into several subsystems, applying NMR at each subsystem, as shown in Fig. 8.4.12. The same considerations have to be applied in order to choose the level of partitioning.

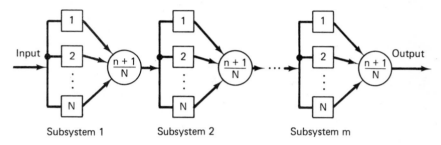

Fig. 8.4.12   A multilevel NMR configuration.

8.4.7.   The Hybrid (*N*, *S*) System

8.4.7.1. The Mathematical Model of the Hybrid (N, S) System [63].   Let *T* denote the mission time. If the mission succeeds, one of the following three cases must occur.

1. All the units (active and standby) survive the mission time T. This event has the probability $R_0^N R_s^S$, where $R_0 = \exp(-\lambda T)$ and $R_s = \exp(-\mu T)$.

2. A spare unit is the first unit to fail at some time t $(0 \leq t \leq T)$, reducing the system to an $H(N, S - 1)$ system for the rest of the mission. The probability of this event is

$$S \int_0^T e^{-N\lambda t} \cdot \mu e^{-\mu t} \cdot e^{-(S-1)\mu t} \cdot R(N, S - 1)\,[T - t] \cdot dt$$

3. An active unit is the first unit to fail and a spare unit is switched on to replace it at some time t, thus reducing the system to an $H(N, S - 1)$ system for the unelapsed time $(T - t)$. The probability of this event is

$$N \int_0^T e^{-S\mu t} \cdot \lambda e^{-\lambda t} \cdot e^{-(N-1)\lambda t} \cdot R(N, S - 1)\,[T - t] \cdot dt$$

Summing up these three cases, the probability that the system functions correctly for the mission is given by

$$R(N, S)\,[T] = R_0^N R_s^S + (N\lambda + S\mu) \int_0^T e^{-(N\lambda + S\mu)t} \cdot R(N, S - 1)[T - t] \cdot dt$$

Note that this integral equation is recursive, i.e., the equation for S spares is defined in terms of the case of a system having $(S - 1)$ spares. By letting $\tau = T - t$, the equation can be rewritten as

$$R(N, S)\,[T] = R_0^N R_s^S \left\{1 + (N\lambda + S\mu) \int_0^T e^{(N\lambda + S\mu)\tau} \cdot R(N, S - 1)\,[\tau] \cdot d\tau\right\}$$

For the case of a single spare $(S = 1)$, the recursive integral equation has the solution

$$R(N, 1)[T] = R_0^N R_s \left[1 + (NK + 1) \sum_{i=0}^{n} \binom{N}{i} \cdot \sum_{m=0}^{i} \binom{i}{m} \frac{(-1)^{i-m}}{(Km + 1)} \left(\frac{1}{R_s R_0^m} - 1\right)\right]$$

Therefore, the general solution for $S > 1$ is given by

$$R(N, S)[T] = R_0^N R_s^S \left[1 + \sum_{j=0}^{S-2} \binom{NK+S}{j+1} \cdot \left(\frac{1}{R_s} - 1\right)^{j+1} + \sum_{i=0}^{n} \binom{N}{i} \binom{NK+S}{S} \cdot \right.$$

$$\left. \sum_{m=0}^{i} \frac{\binom{i}{m}(-1)^{i-m}}{\binom{Km+S}{S}} \left\{\left(\frac{1}{R_s R_0^m} - 1\right) - \sum_{j=0}^{S-2} \binom{Km+S}{j+1} \cdot \left(\frac{1}{R_s} - 1\right)^{j+1}\right\}\right]$$

8.4.7.2. The Hybrid (3, S) System. The most common form of NMR system used is the TMR system $(N = 3)$. In this case, substantial simplification of the reliability equation can be obtained by setting $K = 1$.

$$R(3, S) = 1 - (1 - R_0)^{S+2} [1 + (S + 2)R_0]$$

which is simply the probability that at least any two of the total $S + 3$ units survive the mission duration.

For the H (3, 1) system the relationship between the system reliability R^*, the reliability of the detection-restoration-switching net R_v, and the reliability R of the nonredundant system is illustrated in Fig. 8.4.13. Recall that $R^*(N, S)\,[T] = R_v\,[T] \cdot R\,(N, S)\,[T]$. Let $R_0 = R$. Curve B is the intersection of the plane $R^*(3, 1) = R$ and the surface $R^*(R, R_v)$. The surface A is the region above the intersection bounded by the curve B and indicates the conditions under which $R^*(3, 1) > R$. The curve C is the projection of the intersection on the R, R_v-plane.

From the graph it can be observed that if $R < 0.233$ then $R^*(3, 1) < R$, for all values of R_v. For $R_v < 0.73$ then $R^*(3, 1) < R$, regardless of the value of R. This shows that $H(3, 1)$ redundancy can only be used to increase the reliability of fairly reliable circuits $(R > 0.233)$, when the detection-restoration-switching network is quite reliable $(R_v > 0.73)$. This establishes a bound on the conditions when $H(3, 1)$, and, in general, hybrid redundancy, can be usefully applied. Similar graphical analysis can be applied to the conventional TMR system, and the above two conditions for an $R^*(3, 0)$

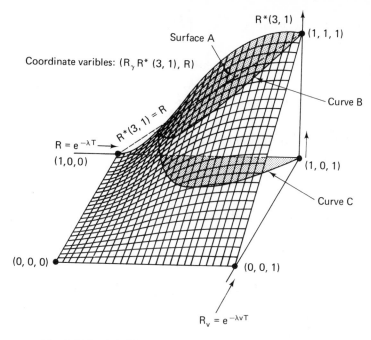

Fig. 8.4.13   Reliability surface of $H(3, 1)$ system versus R and R_v [63].

system can be shown to be $R < 0.5$ and $R_v < 0.89$, respectively. Thus the applicability constraints of a TMR system is even more restricted than that of an $H(3, 1)$ system.

8.4.7.3. Hybrid/Simplex Redundancy.   It may be interesting to know that in a TMR system, upon the first failure of a unit, by discarding one of the two remaining good units together with the faulty unit and allowing the system to operate in a simplex mode, the reliability of the system will in general be increased [66]. The reliability equation for such a system, called TMR/simplex system, is

$$R(3, 0)_{\text{sim}} [T] = R_0^3 [T] + 3 \int_0^T \lambda e^{-\lambda t} [T - t \cdot e^{-2\lambda t} \cdot R] \cdot dt$$

$$= 1.5 R_0 - 0.5 R_0^3$$

Now if a hybrid $H(3, S)$ system is devised which combines standby replacement units with the above replacement scheme, a new scheme called hybrid/simplex redundancy results. By following the same steps as in Section 8.4.7.1, the reliability of the $H(3, S)_{\text{sim}}$ system can be derived as a recursive integral equation of the form

$$R(3, S)_{\text{sim}} [T] = R_0^3 R_s^S + (3\lambda + S\mu) \int_0^T e^{-(3\lambda + S\mu)} \cdot R(3, S - 1)_{\text{sim}} [T - 1] \cdot dt$$

By substituting $\tau = T - t$ the equation can be rewritten as

$$R(3, S)_{\text{sim}} [T] = R_0^3 R_s^S \{1 + (3\lambda + S\mu) \int_0^T e^{(3\lambda + S\mu)\tau} \cdot R(3, S - 1)_{\text{sim}} [\tau] \cdot d\tau$$

The recursive integral equation has the solution

$$R(3, S)_{\text{sim}} [T] = R_0^3 R_s^S \left\{ 1 + 1.5 \left(\frac{1}{R_0^2 R_s^S} - 1 \right) \prod_{i=1}^{S} \left(\frac{3K + i}{2K + i} \right) - \prod_{j=1}^{S} \frac{3K + k}{j} \right.$$
$$\left. \sum_{i=0}^{S-1} \binom{S}{i}(-1)^i \left(\frac{1}{R_s^{S-i}} - 1 \right) \frac{3K^2}{(2K + i)(3K + i)} \right\}$$

For the case $S = 1$, $K = 1$, this equation reduces to

$$R(3, 1)_{\text{sim}} = R_0^4 - 2R_0^3 + 2R_0$$

as compared to the hybrid system

$$R(3, 1) = 3R_0^4 - 8R_0^3 + 2R_0^2$$

Note that the reliability of the hybrid/simplex $H(3, 1)_{\text{sim}}$ system is always greater than the reliability of the hybrid $H(3, 1)$ system, for $0 < R_0 < 1$.

8.4.8.   Comparative Reliability Versus Cost Tradeoffs

The decision to choose a redundant configuration for a certain mission depends on the nature of the mission, the penalty for failure, and the cost of the redundant system. The most important parameter of a mission is the mission time, which determines the reliability of the simplex systems, since an exponential failure law is assumed. Some redundant systems, such as the TMR, deteriorate quite rapidly with mission time and are therefore suitable only for short missions. The minimum reliability required for a mission usually depends on the penalty for failure. If the penalty for failure is very large, a decrease in unreliability for say 10^{-6} to 10^{-8} may be significant, and a more reliable system is required, even at a considerably greater cost.

For practical reasons, one of the most important parameters in any system evaluation is cost. In redundant systems cost is approximately directly proportional to the order of replication of the nonredundant system.

Let us evaluate the cost-reliability tradeoffs between the simplex, NMR, hybrid and standby-replacement systems. One method is to compare the system reliabilities as a function of the degree of replication at a particular

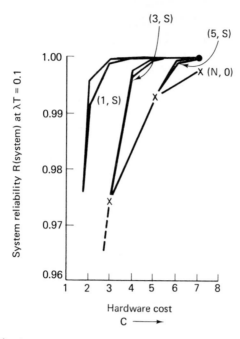

Fig. 8.4.14   System reliability versus cost ($\lambda T = 0.1$) [63].

simplex reliability. This is done in Fig. 8.4.14 for the normalized mission time λT taken to be 0.1, i.e., $R_0 = 0.905$.

Another method to make cost-reliability comparisons of different systems is to fix the total number of replications (and hence the cost) and compare the reliabilities of the different systems under the same conditions (i.e., the same simplex reliability). An allocation of seven units can be used to produce the NMR (7, 0) system, the hybrid H (3, 4) system, the hybrid H(5, 2) system and the standby-replacement SR (1, 6) system. The results of the reliability comparison of these cost-equivalent systems are shown in Table 8.4.1, for a "short" normalized mission time of 0.1 and a "long" mission time of 1.0.

It can be seen from the table that, under the constraints of this analysis, and from a quantitative reliability viewpoint, standby-replacement systems are more cost-effective than the hybrid systems which in turn are superior to NMR systems, for a system with seven replications. The above statement is generally true also for other number of replications. However, the reader must bear in mind that in the standby-replacement scheme, there is no simple way of detecting whether a unit is functioning correctly or not. Hence, the fault detector for a standby-replacement system is more complex, more expensive, and more unreliable than the disagreement detector of the hybrid system. It should also be noted that the hybrid system has the overhead cost and unreliability in the detection-restoration-switching network compared to

Table 8.4.1 COMPUTED VALUES OF RELIABILITY MEASURES ($\lambda T = 0.1$ AND 1.0)*

	Simplex (1.0)	NMR (7,0)	Hybrid (3,4)		Hybrid (5,2)		SR (1,6)	
	$K=1$	$K=1$	$K=1$	$K=\infty$	$K=1$	$K=\infty$	$K=1$	$K=\infty$
Total # of units:	1	7	7	7	7	7	7	7
Cost:	1	7+	7+	7+	7+	7+	7+	7+
R_{sys} §$\lambda T = 0.1$	0.905	0.998	0.999995	0.9999995	0.99986	0.99996	0.9999999	0.9999999
R_{sys} §$\lambda T = 1.0$	0.368	0.23	0.79	0.94	0.51	0.58	0.96	0.99992
SIMDIFF §$\lambda T = 0.1$	0	0.0929	0.0951	0.0952	0.0950	0.0951	0.0952	0.0952
SIMDIFF §$\lambda T = 1.0$	0	0.137	0.43	0.57	0.14	0.21	0.59	0.63
SIMGAIN §$\lambda T = 0.1$	1	1.1027	1.1052	1.1052	1.1050	1.1051	1.1052	1.1052
SIMGAIN §$\lambda T = 1.0$	1	0.63	2.16	2.54	1.38	1.57	2.61	2.72
SIMRIF §$\lambda T = 0.1$	1	42.0	20×10^3	177×10^3	685	1.1×10^3	1.3×10^3	6.4×10^6
SIMRIF §$\lambda T = 1.0$	1	0.82	3.1	9.8	1.3	1.5	15.7	7.6×10^3
MTF (normalized)	1	0.76	1.6	2.2	1.1	1.2	2.6	7.0
R(MTF)	0.368	0.430	0.432	0.44	0.434	0.437	0.42	0.45
LAMPMAX($R_1 = 0.9$)	0.105	0.33	0.79	1.13	0.52	0.57	1.27	3.89
SIMTIF ($R_1 = 0.9$)	1	3.1	7.5	10.7	4.9	5.4	12.1	37.0

*From Mathur [63].

the NMR system. Hence the choice of a redundant configuration depends strongly on the complexity of the nonredundant system and the nature of the mission. For short missions, TMR is the most attractive scheme. For long missions, some form of sparing is absolutely necessary.

8.4.9. Conclusion

This section briefly describes the standby-replacement system, the NMR system, the hybrid and hybrid/simplex redundant system, together with their mathematical models. Some measures of reliability and their cost-performance evaluation are presented. From the analysis it seems that the standby-replacement systems are more cost-reliable than the hybrid systems, which in turn are superior to NMR systems. This can be qualitatively explained from the viewpoint of the number of faulty replications that the system can tolerate. For the system with $M = 2N + 1$ replications, the standby-replacement system can tolerate $M - 1$ failures; the hybrid $H(N, S)$ system can tolerate $(S + [(N - 1)/2])$ failures, which is at most $M - 2$, for $N = 3$; and the NMR $(M, 0)$ system can tolerate only n failures. From the same viewpoint, it should be noted that, for a hybrid system, maximum redundancy should be inserted in the spares bank to allow the tolerance of a larger number of failures. Therefore, in practical implementation, N should equal three, with S as a variable to suit the desired level of mission reliability.

EXERCISES 8.4

1. Plot the reliability curves of NMR (for $N = 3$, 5, 7, and 9) and the hybrid $H(3, S)$ (for $S = 1, 2, 3, 4$, and 5) systems against the reliability of the simplex system. Interpret the results.

2. Find the mean life (MTBF) of the simplex, TMR, and hybrid $H(3, 1)$ systems assuming an exponential failure law.

3. Derive the equations in Sections 8.4.7.1 and 8.4.7.3 and verify the results for $R(3, 1)_{\text{sim}}$ and $R(3, 1)$.

8.5. CONCLUSION

8.5.1. Principles of Fault-Tolerant Computer Design

In this chapter we have discussed different redundancy techniques: fault diagnosis, coding, replication, and standby spares, etc. Usually many of these techniques are used together to provide fault tolerance. The choice of techniques depends on many factors, such as the operating environment of the computer, the nature of the mission, the characteristics of faults to be tolerated, the penalty of an untolerable fault, and above all, the budget for the computer. The design is further complicated by the rapid change of technology, which makes our choice dependent as much on our estimates as on our experience.

In the design of a fault-tolerant computing system, the computational requirements usually establish the architecture of the computer defined under failure-free operation. The fault-tolerant requirements then introduce redundancy into the simplex system. Faults have to be classified and characterized and the extent of tolerance to each class of fault has to be defined. This is a very important phase in the design. Wrong assumptions on the characteristics of faults in the operating environment will lead to the design of an expensive and ineffective machine. Extensive studies have to be made to verify that all the assumptions on faults are correct. Then redundancy is incorporated into the computer to satisfy all the computational and fault-tolerant requirements, together with the cost constraints.

There are essentially two forms of redundancy: static and dynamic. Static, masking, or massive redundancy uses techniques such as component replication, voting, NMR, etc. It is easy to design but expensive. It has the advantages of a small hardcore and concurrent correction of both transient and permanent faults without the need of fault diagnosis and recovery. It is very attractive for systems with a high ratio of transient to permanent faults. However, the prohibitive cost and the inability of self-repair make static redundancy infeasible in many cases.

Dynamic, standby, or selective, redundancy techniques, on the other hand, require three steps in the correction of a fault: fault detection, location, and recovery. Therefore this approach requires several additional features: a system ability to tolerate interruptions for diagnosis and repair, the ability to rollback for recovery of faults, complicated diagnosis procedures, protection of the hardcore, and tradeoff studies between different forms of redundancy [1]. It has the advantages of greater isolation of catastrophic faults, better utilization of hardware, longer survival time of the system, less power consumption, ready adjustability of the size, type, and number of spare units, spare units with lower failure rate (in unpowered state) and easy check-out, and the elimination of circuit-related problems of static redundancy such as the synchronization of separate channels, power consumption, fan-in and fan-out problems, etc. [3]. Cost considerations make dynamic redundancy more attractive.

There are other factors that affect the choice of the redundancy methods. The architecture of the system is an important factor. For example, a microprogrammed computer can take advantage of microdiagnostics over machine-language diagnostics. The hardcore configuration affects the self-diagnosibility of the system. Many commercial machines simply use an *external hardcore*, which is essentially an external processor to diagnose the machine after the system is determined to be faulty. This frequently requires operator intervention. Another configuration is the *centralized hardcore*, as in the STAR computer [3], which is heavily protected and gives the computer the ability of automatic self-diagnosis. The hardcore is a part of the system and monitors the fault detection, location, and recovery procedures automatically. The correct operation of the system depends on the proper functioning of the hardcore. Therefore, it must be heavily protected. Static redundancy is usually employed, such as hybrid redundancy, TMR and voting, component redundancy, duplexing with external supervision, permanently wired-in error-correction capabilities, etc. The cost of protecting the hardcore can be considerably reduced by using a third configuration, the *distributed hardcore*, which involves the partition of the system into a number of nearly disjoint subsystems such that each subsystem is capable of diagnosing at least one other subsystem. The formalization of the theory of self-diagnosibility was published by Forbes et al.[67], and generalized by Preparata et al.[68]. This can be easily implemented in a multiprocessor system.

By employing dynamic redundancy, the ultimate goal is an automatic self-diagnosing and self-repairing computer system. A *modular computer architecture* is very cost-effective to implement such a machine. In a modular organization, the computer consists of a number of functional modules with minimal intermodule connections. The modules are chosen so that when a given module malfunctions the computer can detect the fault and resolve the fault to a module. Standby spares are provided for each module and recovery is effected by automatic switching. For such a computer the level of partitioning of the system into modules is the most important design parameter. The bus, which provides the intermodule communication link, is part of the hardcore of the system. It must be heavily protected to ensure the integrity of the system. Also we must make sure that faulty modules can be disconnected from the system, even in the presence of faults, or else the system will be paralyzed. The rollback of the system must be carried out through the hardcore of the system to make sure that the recovery procedure is correct.

After the preliminary design of the computer system, an evaluation of its reliability has to be performed. This is most conveniently done by using interactive reliability analysis programs, such as REL70 [69], CARE [70], etc. Important reliability parameters can be calculated and different tradeoffs can be studied. The number of spares for each subsystem may be different and these can be calculated and balanced with the aid of these programs. Extensive simulation should also be carried out to verify and debug the logic design. When the machine is being built, the most reliable components and proven techniques of interconnection and packaging should be used, provided that the cost constraints are satisfied. It may also be advisable to build a miniature version of the machine to verify the fault assumptions and operation characteristics, especially if a new technology has been employed. After the machine is built, it has to be carefully and intensively checked out to eliminate implementation errors. This includes the validation of the proper functioning of the redundant features within the system, and the verification of the automatic diagnostic tests and maintenance procedures. Throughout the design, good documentations, including a fault dictionary, have to be kept.

There is an important aspect of fault-tolerant computing that we have left out due to insufficient space. This is the area of software reliability. Interested readers are referred to a brief survey by Elspas et al. [74], and the Record of the 1973 IEEE Symposium on Computer Software Reliability.

8.5.2. Some Examples of Fault-Tolerant Computing Systems

It seems appropriate to conclude this chapter by examining briefly some practical examples to see how the techniques we have discussed are employed in fault-tolerant computer design. In this section we will discuss the highlight of four modern machines: the STAR Computer [3], which is designed for reliability; the ESS [14], which is designed for maintainability; the PRIME [71] system, designed for availability; and SIFT [4], for flexibility. For a survey of other fault-tolerant computers the readers are referred to a survey by Carter and Bouricius [72].

8.5.2.1. The STAR (Self-Testing And Repairing) Computer [3]. The STAR Computer was developed in the Jet Propulsion Laboratory, Pasadena, California, under the direction of Professor A. Avizienis as a tool to investigate and implement fault-tolerant computing techniques. It uses a number of different techniques to achieve tolerance of a wide variety of faults (transient, permanent, and catastrophic). The computer is divided into a number of replaceable functional units, each with its own instruction decoder and sequence generator. Standby spares are provided for each subsystem. Fault detection, location, and recovery are carried out by the "hardcore" test and repair processor (TARP) which is protected by hybrid redundancy (triplication with spares). The TARP monitors the operation of the computer by "bus checkers," which test every word transmitted on the bus for validity, and by examining the status messages sent to the TARP by each functional unit. With the knowledge of the current instruction and its location, the TARP internally reconstructs the proper status code for each unit. Any deviation from normal operation will halt the normal computation and begin a recovery procedure. Transient faults are identified and corrected by the rollback of the program and permanent faults are eliminated by the replacement of the faulty functional units by power switching (units are removed by switching power off and connected by turning power on), followed by a rollback of the program [73]. The words are organized as four-bit bytes, with eight bytes in a word. The data words and the address part of the instruction words are encoded in inverse residue code modulo 15, while the operation code is encoded in a 2-out-of-4 code. Arithmetic operations are therefore checked. Monitoring circuits are provided to supplement the error-detecting codes to verify the proper synchronization and internal operation of the functional units. The ability of concurrent diagnosis makes it very suitable for real-time applications which require fast recovery. The organization of the computer is shown in Fig. 8.5.1.

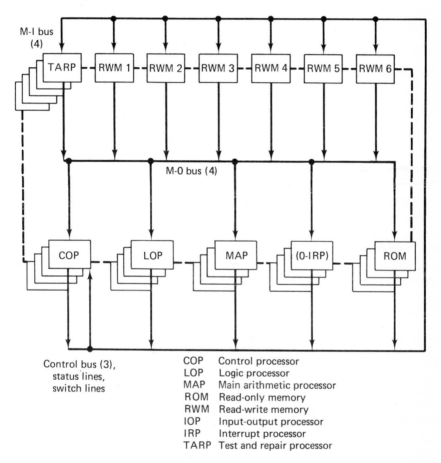

Fig. 8.5.1   STAR computer organization [3].

8.5.2.2. The ESS (Electronic Switching System)[14].   The ESS is like a time-shared multiprogrammed computer operating in real time to perform the basic switching function for the telephone network. The design objective is a highly dependable and maintainable self-diagnosing machine with a downtime of less than 2 hours in 40 years and an error rate of less than 0.02 percent of all calls. A block diagram of a typical ESS is shown in Fig. 8.5.2. The central processor is called the central control. System actions are determined by programs stored in a read-only type of semipermanent memory, called program store, which contains operational programs, translation information, permanent data needed to switch calls, and the maintenance programs. The use of a read-only type of memory prevents the mutilation of important data. Temporary storage of information concerning the calls in progress and administrative information is provided by another memory, the call store.

The basic philosophy employed is the use of stored program and the centralization of the control functions. The major subsystems, i.e., the central control, program stores, and call stores, are duplicated and interconnected by two bus systems. The duplicated central control complexes are run in synchronism while the active achine periodically updates the call records in the call store of the standby machine. The processor is modularized with test points inserted to control and observe the state of the machine. Maintenance circuits are built to compare a number of internal nodes within the two central controls for fault detection. Other circuits also check the hardcore of the system, such as the clock circuitry, power supply, etc. Maintenance circuits are also incorporated for fault diagnosis of the processor and the peripheral devices.

When a fault is detected, usually by the central control match circuit, an interrupt causing a transfer to a fault recognition program will take place. Transient errors are recovered from by a retry. If the error is solid, the fault recognition programs will locate the fault, remove the faulty unit, and switch on the duplicating unit to establish a working configuration. Normal operation will continue while diagnostic programs are run on a time-shared interleaved basis with the normal call processing program to locate the fault in the faulty unit. After the location, the maintenance typewriter will print out the modules to be replaced. The faulty unit can therefore be repaired in a very short time.

Software errors in ESS are handled by data audits and system initialization. Programs to check for consistency within the call store memory are run in an interleaved basis with the normal call processing programs to provide periodic audition of the data. When an error is detected, an attempt to reconstruct the information is performed. When this fails, system reinitialization will take place. Other software defenses are also incorporated in the design of ESS software to make it very reliable.

8.5.2.3.   PRIME—A Fail-Softly System for Time-Sharing Use [71].   The PRIME system is a time-sharing system designed for continuous availability by graceful degradation. Although all functional units in the system appear in multiplicity, they are all potentially active at any time and so there is no functional-unit redundancy. The initial version of PRIME has five processors, 15 disk drives, and 13 memory blocks, connected together by the external access network (EAN). A block diagram is shown in Fig. 8.5.3. Every processor can connect to any disk drive, external device, or other processor. Every processor is connected to eight memory blocks while each memory

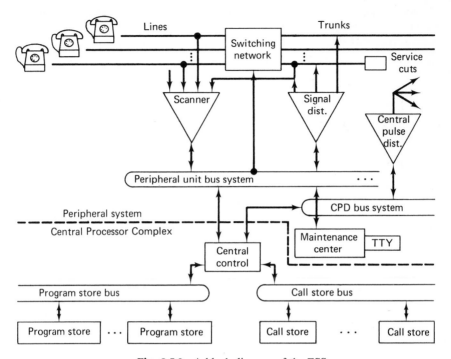

Fig. 8.5.2 A block diagram of the ESS.

block is connected to at least three processors. Each terminal is connected to two processors. One of the processors acts as the control processor (CP) while the rest are problem processors (PP's). Any processor can act as the CP.

In order to degrade gracefully, the system must have a modular architecture with a multiplicity of each functional unit together with the ability to rapidly detect, locate, and isolate a fault and to reconfigure itself to run without the faulty unit. The modular multiprocessor architecture of PRIME is designed to fail softly. The functional units are independent and identical, while the control logic is distributed. The EAN is designed with redundancy so that any internal fault simply manifests itself as a failure of at most two ports. Concurrent fault detection has been incorporated into all the logic external to the processors. However, the PRIME system does not protect against intraprocess errors, although extensive surveillance checks are performed after each job step to detect solid faults in the processor. Interprocess protection is provided to prevent error propagation by having an independent check on every critical function performed by any processor. The operating system is distributed and each PP has a local monitor to dynamically verify decisions made by the central monitor of the CP. Self-diagnosibility is achieved by the distributed hardcore configuration. The first step in the diagnosis procedure after the detection of an error is to assign a fault-free

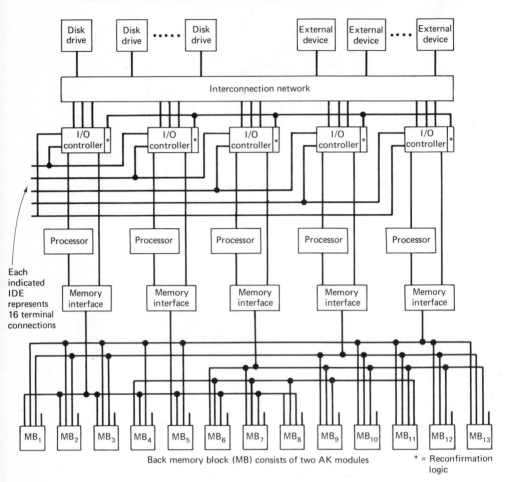

Fig. 8.5.3   A block diagram of the PRIME system [71].

processor as the CP. Usually a neutral processor not involved in the detection of the fault is assigned. However, if the current CP is faulty and refuses to relinquish its role, two PP's can "impeach" the CP to resign. Then the designated CP single-steps the PP's through a set of diagnostic routines through an automated control panel via the EAN. The faulty unit is switched off. In case it is a processor, its associated resources will be shared by the rest of the processors. Each functional unit can be powered off and isolated while the system continues to run, although in a degraded fashion. There is no concurrent replacement of the faulty unit.

8.5.2.4.   SIFT—Software Implemented Fault Tolerance [4].   Contrary to the first three examples, the SIFT system is still in the design stage and has not been built. In this system, software techniques are used for fault detection and correction. Erroneous results are not concurrently diagnosed, but rather at the conclusion of the processing of a task. However, the errors are not permitted to propagate. The system configuration is shown in Fig. 8.5.4. It consists of a number of modules, each composed of a memory and a processing unit. The intermodule bus organization allows a processor to read from but not to write into any other memory units.

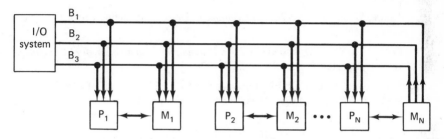

Fig. 8.5.4   A block diagram of the SIFT system.

The basic principle is to break down any computation into a number of tasks. Every task that requires high reliability is carried out in several modules, in an asynchronous fashion. Input data in a module are not destroyed during the computation. After the task has been finished by all the assigned modules, the results are compared by software. Any disagreement among the results will indicate the occurrence of faults. The system can either take the majority of the results as correct or assign more modules to execute the task. The input data can be obtained from the original modules and validated by voting. The results of the computation are again compared and validated after completion of the task by all the assigned modules. The input data in each module are not destroyed until all cooperating processors have read, validated, and used the data. Faulty units can be marked and assigned to no task in the future. Propagation of fault is prevented by the use of read-only connections between processing modules. Hence multiple faults can be tolerated unless they are correlated. Fault tolerance can be varied from task to task while there is no restriction on the design of the hardware.

REFERENCES

1. AVIZIENIS, A., "Design of Fault-Tolerant Computers," *Fall Joint Comput. Conf.*, 1967, pp. 733–743.

2. VON NEUMANN, J., "Probabilistic Logics and the Synthesis of Reliable Organisms from Unreliable Components," *Automata Studies,* Princeton University Press, Princeton, N. J., 1956, pp. 43–98.

3. AVIZIENIS, A., et al., "The STAR (Self-Testing and Repairing) Computer: An Investigation of the Theory and Practice of Fault-Tolerant Computer Design," *IEEE Trans. on Electronic Computers* (Nov. 1971), 1312–1321.

4. WENSLEY, J., "SIFT-Software Implemented Fault Tolerance," *Fall Joint Comput. Conf.,* 1972, pp. 243–253.

5. DALY, W. M., A. L. HOPKINS, Jr., and J. F. MCKENNA, "A Fault-Tolerant Digital Clocking System," *1973 International Symposium on Fault-Tolerant Computing Proceedings* (1973), 17–22.

6. PIERCE, W. H., *Failure-Tolerant Computer Design,* Academic Press, Inc., New York, 1965.

7. TRYON, J. G., "Quadded logic," *Redundancy Techniques for Computing Systems,* Spartan Press, 1962, pp. 205–228.

8. ARMSTRONG, D. B., "On Finding a nearly Minimal Set of Fault Detection Tests for Combinational Logic Nets," *IEEE Trans. on Electronic Computers* (Feb. 1956), 66–73.

9. SCHNEIDER, P. R., "On the Necessity to Examine D-Chains in Diagnostic Test Generation—An Example," *IBM J. of Res. and Dev.* (1967), 114.

10. ROTH, P. J., "Diagnosis of Automata Failures: A Calculus and a Method," *IBM J. of Res. and Dev.* (1966), 278–291.

11. CHANG, H. Y., E. MANNING and G. METZE, *Fault Diagnosis of Digital Systems,* Wiley-Interscience, New York, 1970.

12. MATHUR, F. P., "A Survey of and an Introduction to Fault-Diagnosis Algorithms—with an Extensive Bibliography," *Jet Propul. Lab. Tech. Memo No. 361-16* (Jan. 1972).

13. SELLERS, F. F., M. Y. HSIAO, and L. W., BEARNSON, "Analyzing Errors with the Boolean Difference," *IEEE Trans. on Electronic Computers* (July 1968), 676–683.

14. CHANG, H. Y. and J. M. SCANLON, "Design Principles for Processor Maintainability in Real-Time Systems," *Fall Joint Comput. Conf.* (1969), 319–328.

15. SCHERTZ, D. R. and G. METZE, "On the Design of Multiple Fault Diagnosable Networks," *IEEE Trans. on Computers* (Nov. 1971), 1361–1364.

16. DIEPHUIS, R. J., "Fault Analysis for Combinational Logic Networks," Ph. D. dissertation, Dept. of Electrical Engineering, Massachusetts Institute of Technology, Cambridge, Mass., Sept. 1969.

17. SESHU, S., "On an Improved Diagnosis Program," *IEEE Trans. on Electronic Computers* (Jan. 1965), 76–79.

18. POAGE, J. F. and E. J. MCCLUSKEY, "Derivation of Optimum Test Sequences for Sequential Machines," *Proc. 5th Annual Symposium on Switching Theory and Logical Design* (1964), 121–132.

19. HENNIE, F. C., "Fault Detection Experiments for Sequential Circuits," *Proc. 5th Annual Symp. on Switching Theory and Logical Design* (1964), 95–110.

20. KOHAVI, Z. and P. LAVALLEE, "Design of Sequential Machines with Fault Detection Capabilities," *IEEE Trans. on Electronic Computers* (April 1967) 473–484.

21. SESHU, S. and D. N. FREEMAN, "The Diagnosis of Asynchronous Sequential Switching Systems," *IRE Trans. on Electronic Computers* (1962), 459–465.

22. CHANG, H. Y., "An Algorithm for Selecting an Optimum Set of Diagnostic Tests," *IEEE Trans. on Electronic Computers* (1965), 706–711.

23. KAUTZ, W. H., "Fault Testing and Diagnosis in Combinational Digital Circuits," *IEEE Trans. on Computers* (1968), 352–366.

24. RAMAMOORTHY, C. V., "A Structural Theory of Machine Diagnosis," *Spring Joint Comput. Conf.* (1967), 743–756.

25. RAMAMOORTHY, C. V., "Analysis of Graphs by Connectivity Consideration," *J. ACM* (Apr. 1966), 211–222.

26. MAYEDA, W. and C. V. RAMAMOORTHY, "Distinguishability Criteria in Oriented Graphs and Their Application to Computer Diagnosis—Part 1," *IEEE Trans. Circuit Theory* (Nov. 1969), 448–454.

27. RAMAMOORTHY, C. V. and W. MAYEDA, "Computer Diagnosis Using the Blocking Gate Approach," *IEEE Trans. on Computers* (Nov. 1971), 1294–1299.

28. RAMAMOORTHY, C. V. and L. C. CHANG, "System Segmentation for Parallel Diagnosis of Computers," *IEEE Trans. on Computers* (Mar. 1971), 261–270.

29. RAMAMOORTHY, C. V. and L. C. CHANG, "System Modeling and Testing Procedures for Microdiagnostics," *IEEE Trans. on Computers* (Nov. 1972), 1169–1183.

30. JOHNSON, A. M., "The Microdiagnostics for the IBM System 360 Model 30," *IEEE Trans. on Computers* (July 1971), 798–803.

31. GUFFIN, R. M., "Microdiagnostics for Standard Computer MLP-900 Processor," *IEEE Trans. on Computers* (July 1971), 803–808.

32. BENNETTS, R. G. and D. W. LEWIN, "Fault Diagnosis of Digital Systems–A Review," *Computer* (July 1971), 12–20.

33. KAUTZ, W. H., "Codes and Coding Circuitry for Automatic Error Correction within Digital Systems," *Redundancy Techniques for Computing Systems,* Spartan Books, 1962.

34. AVIZIENIS, A., "Arithmetic Error Codes: Cost and Effectiveness Studies for Application in Digital System Design," *IEEE Trans. on Computers* (Nov. 1971), 1322–1331.

35. HAMMING, R. W., "Error Detecting and Error Correcting Codes," *Bell System Tech. J.* (1950), 147–160.

36. PETERSON, W. W., and WELDON, E. J., JR. *Error-correcting Codes,* 2nd ed. Massachusetts Institute of Technology Press, Cambridge, Mass., 1970.

37. BERLEKAMP, E. R., *Algebraic Coding Theory,* McGraw-Hill Book Co., New York, 1968.

38. LIN, S., *An Introduction to Error-Correcting Codes,* Prentice-Hall, Inc., Englewood Cliffs, N.J., 1970.

39. MASSEY, J. L., *Threshold Decoding,* Massachusetts Institute of Technology Press, Cambridge, Mass., 1963.

40. FIRE, P., "A Class of Multiple-Error-Correcting Binary Codes for Non-Independent Errors," *Sylvania Report RSL-E-2,* Sylvania Electronic Lab., March 1959.

41. SRINIVASAN, C. V., "Codes for Error Correction in High-Speed Memory Systems—Part 1: Correction of Cell Defects in Integrated Memories," *IEEE Trans. on Computers* (Aug. 1971), 882–888.

42. SRINIVASAN, C. V., "Codes for Error Correction in High-Speed Memory Systems—Part 2: Correction of Temporary and Catastrophic Errors," *IEEE Trans. on Computers* (Dec. 1971), 1514–1520.

43. CHIEN, R. T., "Memory Error Control: Beyond Parity," *IEEE Spectrum* (July 1973), 18–23.

44. BOSSEN, D. C., "*b*-Adjacent Error Correction," *IBM J. of Res. and Dev.* (July 1970), 402–408.

45. GALLAGER, R. G., *Low Density Parity Check Codes,* Massachusetts Institute of Technology Press, Cambridge, Mass., 1963.

46. BROWN, D. T., and F. F. SELLARS, Jr., "Error Correction for IBM 800-Bit-Per-Inch Magnetic Tape," *IBM J. of Res. and Dev.* (July 1970), 384–398.

47. CHIEN, R. T., "Burst-Correcting Codes with High-Speed Decoding," *IEEE Trans. on Inf. Theory* (Jan. 1969), 109–113.

48. OLDHAM, I. B., R. T. CHIEN, and D. T. TANG, "Error Detection and Correction in a Photo-Digital Storage System," *IBM J. of Res. and Dev.* (Nov. 1968), 422.

49. GARNER, H. L., "Generalized Parity Checking," *IRE Trans. on Electronic Computers* (Sept. 1958), 207–213.

50. GARNER, H. L. "Error Codes for Arithmetic Operations," *IEEE Trans. on Computers* (Oct. 1966), 763–770.

51. PETERSON, W. W., "On Checking an Adder," *IBM J. of Res. and Dev.* (Apr. 1958), 166–168.

52. AVIZIENIS, A., "Digital Fault Diagnosis by Low-Cost Arithmetical Coding Techniques," *Proc. Purdue Centennial Year Symp. Inf. Proc.* 1 (Apr. 1969), 81–91.

53. BROWN, D. T., "Error Detecting and Correcting Binary Codes for Arithmetic Operations," *IRE Trans. on Electronic Computers* (Sept. 1960), 333–337.

54. RAO, T. R. N. and O. N. GARCIA, "Cyclic and Multiresidue Codes for Arithmetic Operations," *IEEE Trans. on Inf. Theory* (Jan. 1971), 85–91.

55. KEIR, Y. A., P. W. CHENEY, and M. TANNENBAUM, "Division and Overflow Detection in Residue Number Systems," *IEEE Trans. on Electronic Computers* (Aug. 1962), 501–507.

56. MANDELBAUM, D. "Error Correction in Residue Arithmetic," *IEEE Trans. on Computers* (June 1972), 538–545.

57. GARCIA, O. N. "Error Codes for Arithmetic and Logical Operations," Ph. D. dissertation, Dept. of Electrical Engineering, University of Maryland, 1969.

58. AVIZIENIS, A., "A Set of Algorithms for a Diagnosable Arithmetic Unit," *Tech. Rep. 32-546,* Jet Prop. Lab., Pasadena, Calif., Mar. 1964.

59. AVIZIENIS, A. "A Study of the Effectiveness of Fault-Detecting Codes for Binary Arithmetic," *Tech. Report 32-711,* Jet Prop. Lab., Pasadena, Calif., Sept. 1965.

60. CHIEN, R. T. and S. J. HONG, "Error Correction in High-Speed Arithmetic," *IEEE Trans. on Computers* (May 1972), 433–438.

61. FLEHINGER, B. J., "Reliability Improvement through Redundancy at Various System Levels," *IBM J. of Res. and Dev.* (Apr. 1958), 148–158.

62. MATHUR, F. P. and A. AVIZIENIS, "Reliability Analysis and Architecture of a Hybrid Redundant Digital System: Generalized Triple Modular Redundancy with Self-Repair," *Spring Joint Comput Conf.,* 1970. pp. 375–383.

63. MATHUR, F. P., "On Reliability Modeling and Analysis of Ultrareliable Fault-tolerant Digital Systems," *IEEE Trans. on Computers* (Nov. 1971), 1376–1382.

64. MATHUR, F. P., "Reliability Modeling and Architecture of Ultrareliable Fault-tolerant Digital Systems," Ph. D. dissertation, Dept. of Computer Science, University of California, Los Angeles, June 1970.

65. BOURICIUS, W. G., W. C. CARTER, and P. R. SCHNEIDER, "Reliability Modeling Techniques for Self-repairing Computer Systems," *Proc. ACM 1969 Annu. Conf.* (1969), 295–309.

66. BALL, M., and F. HARDIE, "Majority Voter Design Considerations for TMR Computer," *Computer Design* (April 1969), 100–104.

67. FORBES, R. E., D. H. RUTHERFORD, C. B. STREGLITZ, and L. H. TUNG, "A Self-Diagnosable Computer," *Fall Joint Comput. Conf.* (1965), 1073–1086.

68. PREPARATA, F. P., G. METZE, and R. T. CHIEN, "On the Connection Assignment of Diagnosable Systems," *IEEE Trans. on Electronic Computers* (December 1967), 848–854.

69. CARTER, W. C., et al. "Design Techniques for Modular Architecture for Reliable Computer Systems," *IBM Watson Res. Center Report No. 70-208-0002,* March 1970.

70. MATHUR, F. P., "Automation of Reliability Evaluation Procedures through CARE—the Computer-aided Reliability Estimation Program," *Fall Joint Comput. Conf.* (1972), 65–82.

71. BASKIN, H. B., B. R. BORGERSON, and R. ROBERTS, "PRIME—a Modular Architecture for Terminal-oriented Systems," *Spring Joint Comput. Conf.,* 1972.

72. CARTER, W. C., and W. G. BOURICIUS, "A Survey of Fault-tolerant Computer Architecture and its Evaluation," *Computer* (Jan. 1971), 9–16.

73. ROHR, J. A., "STAREX Self-repair Routines: Software Recovery in the JPL STAR Computer," *1973 International Symposium on Fault-tolerant Computing Proceedings* (1973), 11–16.

74. ELSPAS, B., M. W. Green, and K. N. LEVITT, "Software Reliability," *Computer* (Jan. 1971), 21–27.

75. REED, I. S., and G. SOLOMON, "Polynomial Codes over Certain Finite Fields," *J. Soc. Indust. Appl. Math.* (June 1960), 300–304.

9

RADIX ARITHMETIC: DIGITAL ALGORITHMS FOR COMPUTER ARCHITECTURE

David W. Matula
Southern Methodist University
Dallas, Texas

Editor's Note:

This chapter is concerned with the foundations of computer arithmetic with heavy emphasis on the principles of radix arithmetic. Great insights are provided by the author who first develops the algebraic foundation of radix polynomials, and then the mapping between the abstract radix polynomials and their data structures, the digit strings, which are suitable for digital computer processing. In this development, it is pointed out by examples how the presence of redundant representation for numbers can yield simplifications in arithmetic operator design which allow faster execution times; why the carry ripple phenomenon is an inherent attribute of a radix system which is complete and unique; and how multiplication cycle time can be reduced utilizing redundant digit sets and parallelism. Many examples of various digit strings of integer, fixed-point, and floating-point types from programming languages are used for illustration. Overall, the impact of radix arithmetic on computer architecture is brought out explicitly.

The material presented in this chapter could supplement that of Chapter 8 to develop a complete course in the design of fault-tolerant computing systems.

Although a number of algebraic terms are used, they should not hinder the reader's basic understanding of this chapter if ignored. However, for a complete understanding of this chapter, the reader is referred to the following book for information on certain algebraic terminologies used in this chapter.

Birkhoff, G., and S. MacLane, A Survey of Modern Algebra, *2nd ed., The Macmillan Company, New York, 1962.*

9.1. INTRODUCTION

Computer arithmetic deals with the representation of numbers by symbol strings and with the design and analysis of algorithmic symbol string procedures for effecting arithmetic operations on the numbers so represented. When the allowable symbol strings for numeric representation and processing are all restricted to finite length, the arithmetic realized is termed *finite precision arithmetic.* Only finite precision arithmetic is realized on a digital computer.

The initial step in the design of a computer arithmetic system is the choice of a symbol string format for numeric representation. This choice impacts simultaneously on the separate disciplines of computer architecture and numerical analysis, as seen in Fig. 9.1.1.

Syntactically, the choice of symbol string representation interacts with the computer design problem of architecting efficient arithmetic algorithms. Semantically, the choice of symbol string representation along with the finite size of the computer implicitly determines the finite set of representable

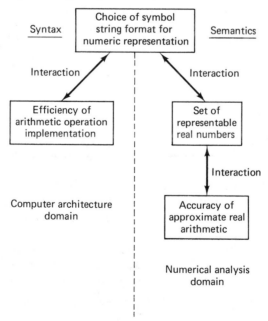

Fig. 9.1.1 The design interactions affecting the choice of a numeric representation system on a computer.

numbers, and, therefore, interacts with the numerical analysis problem of prescribing a suitable finite number system for approximation of real arithmetic. The designer of a computer arithmetic system should keep the full picture of Fig. 9.1.1 in mind. The choice of numeric representation must be based on (1) the computer architectural realities of time and space efficiency as well as (2) the numerical analytic reality of providing a number system with the capability for adequate support of approximate real arithmetic of sufficient accuracy for a wide range of practical applications.

Various tradeoffs must be investigated in the process of selecting a format for numeric representation. For example, the presence of redundant representation [1, 5, 14] for numbers can yield simplifications in arithmetic operator design which allow faster execution times. This beneficial property must be weighed against the resulting loss in storage capacity and the need for additional arithmetic algorithms, e.g., an equality test other than simple identity of representations. The choice of base for radix representation is a much discussed subject [2, 3, 4, 9, 10, 13] resulting in tradeoffs between desirable architecture and desirable accuracy. A larger valued base of the binary family (e.g., 16) provides the convenience of block shifts of bits in the computer design phase, but the relative spacing between successive representable numbers in floating-point number systems exhibit more pronounced variability for larger bases [10] which is generally undesirable from the point of view of numerical analysis.

The computer arithmetic implemented in the hardware of practically all digital computers is based on the principles of radix arithmetic. The most common alternative system discussed in the literature is residue arithmetic [15], and some mention has been made of rational arithmetic [6, 11] and logarithmic arithmetic [2, 8].

The sole concern of this chapter is radix arithmetic, and specifically, those questions about radix arithmetic which impact upon the computer architecture domain.

In Section 9.2 the algebraic foundations of radix polynomials are described. The intent of the presentation is to show that radix arithmetic is based on the standard arithmetic of polynomials whose coefficients are integers. The arithmetic discussed is that of addition/subtraction and multiplication which are closed operations on the ring of polynomials over the integers. Division is not a closed operation and is outside the scope of this presentation. The various options for choice of base and digit values are indicated, and the foundation for investigating redundant radix representation is developed. The primary result discussed is the fact that base β radix arithmetic, for $|\beta| \geq 2$, effects arithmetic on the $|\beta|$-ary numbers $A_{|\beta|} = \{i \mid \beta \mid^j \mid i, j \text{ integers}\}$.

The representation of radix polynomials by digit strings is developed in

Section 9.3. Various forms of digit strings with optional sign and/or radix points are introduced following the precepts of formal languages [see Chapter 1]. Examples of various digit strings of integer, fixed-point, and floating-point type from programming languages are used for illustration. Mappings between radix polynomials and digit strings are developed to provide the necessary link between the abstract radix polynomials and their data structures, the digit strings, which are suitable for digital computer processing. It is emphasized that a digit string explicitly represents a radix polynomial, and only implicitly (through polynomial evaluation) represents a real number. This distinction is of primary importance for the subsequent discussion of redundant number systems. Thus, for example, $943_{[8]}$ and $1143_{[8]}$ are considered to represent distinct octal radix polynomials, although implicitly, through evaluation, they represent the same real number.

In Section 9.4, the spectrum of base and digit set pairs for radix representation is investigated both theoretically and algorithmically. Theory is developed and applied to indicate the variety of unique representation systems possible within the following standard categories: (1) signed-digit, (2) sign-magnitude, (3) negative base, and (4) radix-complement. Letting $\mathscr{P}[\beta, D]$ be the set of radix polynomials with base β and digit values from D, the completeness and uniqueness questions of representation of the $|\beta|$-ary numbers by members of $\mathscr{P}[\beta, D]$ are separately investigated. For D an arbitrary complete residue system modulo $|\beta|$ with $0 \in D$ and any number $b \in A_{|\beta|}$, a "conversion type" algorithm is presented which determines the unique radix polynomial of $\mathscr{P}[\beta, D]$ of value b whenever such a radix polynomial exists. A condition for $\mathscr{P}[\beta, D]$ to provide a unique representation system for $A_{|\beta|}$ is determined and a simple algorithm to test this condition is described.

The theory and basis for algorithm design for the arithmetic of base β radix polynomials whose digit values are limited to D, i.e., the arithmetic of $\mathscr{P}[\beta, D]$, is the subject of Section 9.5. The advantages and deficiencies of signed-digit, sign-magnitude, negative base, and radix-complement systems for various arithmetic operations are discussed. The unary operations of zero detection, sign detection and negation, and the binary operations of addition/subtraction, comparison, and multiplication are each investigated. Inversion and division are not closed operations in $\mathscr{P}[\beta, D]$ and are beyond the scope of this presentation (their inclusion would involve numerical approximation and in justice require a serious foray into the numerical analysis domain). The construction of addition/subtraction tables is described, and the carry ripple phenomenon is shown to be an inherent attribute of any radix system $\mathscr{P}[\beta, D]$ which is complete and unique for the $|\beta|$-ary numbers. The presence of redundancy in the digit set is shown to provide the opportunity for design of arbitrary precision addition in fixed cycle time through parallelism. Multiplication tables and block addition procedures are described which allow imple-

mentation of radix polynomial multiplication in a cycle time proportional to
the sum of the widths of the digit strings of the operands. Utilizing redundant
digit sets and parallelism, it is shown that the multiplication cycle time may
be reduced to the logarithm of the minimum width of the operand digit strings.

In all of our discussion of radix representation in this chapter it is assumed
that the standard decimal digit strings, such as 37 and -46.32, will have their
normal decimal meaning in referring to specific real values without further
elaboration.

9.2. RADIX POLYNOMIALS

9.2.1. Polynomials

To understand radix representation let us first review some of the algebraic
properties of polynomials. Further information on polynomials and polynomial rings may be found in Chapters 3 and 4 of Van der Waerden [16].

Z will denote the set of integers, and a *polynomial* over Z in the indeter-
minant x is a formal expression

$$P(x) = a_m x^m + a_{m-1} x^{m-1} + \ldots + a_1 x + a_0 \qquad (9.2.1)$$

where the coefficient a_i is an element of Z for each $i \geq 0$ with only the (finite
number of) nonzero coefficients explicitly displayed. An *extended polynomial*
over Z in x is an expression

$$P(x) = a_m x^m + a_{m-1} x^{m-1} + \ldots + a_l x^l \qquad (9.2.2)$$

where $a_i \in Z$ for all $-\infty < i < \infty$ with only the (finite number of) nonzero
coefficients explicitly displayed. When all coefficients are zero, $P(x)$ is the *zero
polynomial* and is represented by 0.

The set of all extended polynomials over Z in x will be denoted by $Z^*[x]$
and may be given the algebraic structure of a commutative ring with identity
by defining addition and multiplication as follows. Let

$$P(x) = a_m x^m + a_{m-1} x^{m-1} + \ldots + a_l x^l \in Z^*[x]$$
$$Q(x) = b_n x^n + b_{n-1} x^{n-1} + \ldots + b_k x^k \in Z^*[x]$$
$$p = \max \{m, n\}$$
$$q = \min \{l, k\}$$

For addition let

$$R(x) = P(x) + Q(x)$$
$$= (a_p + b_p)x^p + (a_{p-1} + b_{p-1})x^{p-1} + \ldots + (a_q + b_q) x^q \qquad (9.2.3)$$

where only terms with nonzero coefficients are explicitly displayed except when all coefficients are zero, in which case $R(x) = 0$. For multiplication

$$R(x) = P(x) \times Q(x) = c_{m+n}x^{m+n} + c_{m+n-1}x^{m+n-1} + \ldots + c_{l+k}x^{l+k}$$

$$c_j = a_l b_{j-l} + a_{l+1}b_{j-l-1} + \ldots + a_{j-k}b_k$$

$$\text{for } l + k \leq j \leq m + n \quad (9.2.4)$$

where only terms with $c_j \neq 0$ are displayed except when all c_j are zero, in which case $R(x) = 0$.

If the formal indeterminant x of the extended polynomial $P(x) \in Z^*[x]$ is replaced by the real variable y, then the result, $P(y)$, is an *extended polynomial function*. If x is replaced by a real number a, then $P(x)|_{x=a}$ will denote the real numeric value of the resulting expression. An important consequence of (9.2.3), (9.2.4), and the associative, commutative, and distributive laws of real arithmetic is that formal polynomial arithmetic in $Z^*[x]$ corresponds to the arithmetic of the resulting real numeric values of the polynomials at any fixed real number a. That is:

Extended polynomial equality $\Rightarrow$ real number equality for any real a

$$R(x) = P(x) + Q(x) \Rightarrow R(x)|_{x=a} = P(x)|_{x=a} + Q(x)|_{x=a}$$

$$R(x) = P(x) \times Q(x) \Rightarrow R(x)|_{x=a} = P(x)|_{x=a} \times Q(x)|_{x=a} \quad (9.2.5)$$

For any fixed real number a, let E_a be the *evaluation mapping* which sends each extended polynomial over Z in x into its real numeric value at a, i.e.,

$$E_a(P(x)) = P(x)|_{x=a} \quad \text{for all } P(x) \in Z^*[x] \quad (9.2.6)$$

Algebraically, the implications of (9.2.5) may be formally described as a property of the evaluation mapping.

Theorem 9.2.1

For any real number a, the evaluation mapping, E_a, is a homomorphism of $Z^*[x]$ to the reals.

$Z^*[x]$ is a countable set, so the mapping E_a is not onto the reals. Also, E_a is not one-to-one when a is integral, since then distinct extended polynomials can have the same value at a, e.g.,

$$(9x + 3 + 4x^{-1})|_{x=8} = (x^2 + x + 3 + 4x^{-1})|_{x=8} = 75.5$$

In general, for any given integer a, if $P(x)|_{x=a} = b$ for some particular $P(x) \in Z^*[x]$, then

$$V_a^*(b) = \{R(x) | R(x) = P(x) + (x - a)Q(x) \text{ for } Q(x) \in Z^*[x]\} \quad (9.2.7)$$

is the set of *extended polynomials whose value at a is b*. Hence $V_8^*(75.5) =$ $\{9x + 3 + 4x^{-1} + (x - 8) \times Q(x) \mid Q(x) \in Z^*[x]\}$ is the set of extended polynomials of $Z^*[x]$ whose value at $x = 8$ is 75.5. Algebraically, $V_a^*(0)$ is recognized as a principal ideal for any integer a, and the $V_a^*(b)$ are the elements of the residue class ring $Z^*[x]/V_a^*(0)$.

The significance to computer arithmetic of equations (9.2.5) is that if a is chosen as the base of a radix representation system and if the extended polynomials $P(x)$ and $Q(x)$ are used to represent the real numbers $r_1 = P(x)|_{x=a}$ and $r_2 = Q(x)|_{x=a}$, respectively, then $R(x) = P(x) + Q(x)$ as given by (9.2.3) becomes a representation of the real number $r_3 = r_1 + r_2$, and $R(x) = P(x) \times Q(x)$ as given by (9.2.4) becomes a representation of the real number $r_3 = r_1 \times r_2$. Hence the equalities (9.2.2), (9.2.3), and (9.2.4) provide the foundation for both radix representation and the computational digitwise algorithms for implementation of radix arithmetic. Furthermore, David W. Walkup [17] has pointed out that, algebraically, the set of redundant radix representations of b to radix a is given by $V_a^*(b)$ in (9.2.7), thus allowing the subject of redundant radix representation to be given a firm foundation.

9.2.2. Radix-Polynomials

The process of evaluation of the extended polynomial $P(x) \in Z^*[x]$ at $x = a$ to determine $P(x)|_{x=a}$ may be broken into two steps, as illustrated for $P(x) = 9x + 3 + 4x^{-1}$ and $a = 8$.

Extended Polynomial Evaluation

1. Substitute a for every occurrence of x in $P(x)$ to form a formal expression for $P(x)|_{x=a}$, e.g.,

$$9x + 3 + 4x^{-1} \longrightarrow 9 \times [8] + 3 + 4 \times [8]^{-1} \qquad (9.2.8)$$

2. Evaluate the formal expression for $P(x)|_{x=a}$ to determine the resulting real value, e.g.,

$$9 \times [8] + 3 + 4 \times [8]^{-1} \longrightarrow 75.5$$

It is desirable for discussions of radix arithmetic to assume that a base value a has been fixed for the extended polynomials under discussion so as to clearly specify a particular evaluation mapping E_a and a particular residue class ring $Z^*[x]/V_a^*(0)$ whose members, given by (9.2.7), are then sets of redundant radix representations of the same real number. It is also desirable to recognize the formal expression for $P(x)$ at $x = a$, such as the right-hand side of (9.2.8), as an entity separate from both the extended polynomial $P(x)$ and the real number $P(x)|_{x=a}$. Notationally, such an entity will be denoted by substituting the bracketed value [a] for x, as in $9 \times [8] + 3 + 4 \times [8]^{-1}$, so as to distinguish this "extended polynomial in [8]" from the expression $9 \times 8 + 3 + 4 \times 8^{-1}$, which denotes the resulting real number.

For any integer β such that $|\beta| \geq 2$, $\mathscr{P}[\beta]$ shall denote the *ring of base β radix polynomials* and is composed of the zero polynomial and all extended polynomials over the integers Z in $[\beta]$ of the form

$$P([\beta]) = d_m[\beta]^m + d_{m-1}[\beta]^{m-1} + \ldots + d_l[\beta]^l$$
$$\text{for } -\infty < l \leq m < +\infty, \, d_m \neq 0, \, d_l \neq 0 \qquad (9.2.9)$$

The additive and multiplicative structure of the ring $\mathscr{P}[\beta]$ is that of $Z^*[x]$, with x formally replaced by $[\beta]$, as specified in (9.2.3) and (9.2.4). A member of $\mathscr{P}[\beta]$ is termed a *radix polynomial*.

In (9.2.9), β is the *base* of $P([\beta])$, and the coefficients, d_i, are the *digits* of $P([\beta])$. The integer m indicates the *most significant position* or *degree* of $P([\beta])$, denoted deg $P([\beta])$, and $d_m \neq 0$ is the *most significant digit* of $P([\beta])$. Similarly, l indicates the *least significant position* of $P([\beta])$, denoted lsp $(P([\beta]))$, and $d_l \neq 0$ is the *least significant digit* of $P([\beta])$. It is convenient for the zero polynomial to define deg $(0) = -\infty$, lsp $(0) = +\infty$.

$\mathscr{P}[2]$, $\mathscr{P}[3]$, $\mathscr{P}[8]$, $\mathscr{P}[10]$, and $\mathscr{P}[16]$ denote the ring of *binary, ternary, octal, decimal,* and *hexadecimal* radix polynomials, respectively.

Examples

Radix Polynomial		Ring of Radix Polynomials	Literal Name for Base of $\mathscr{P}[\beta]$
$15 \times [16]^3 + 7 \times [16] + 3 \times [16]^{-2}$	$\in$	$\mathscr{P}[16]$	Hexadecimal
$4\,[\beta]^2 + 3\,[\beta] + 2$	$\in$	$\mathscr{P}[\beta]$	
$5 \times [10]^{-1} + 3 \times [10]^{-2} + 7 \times [10]^{-4}$	$\in$	$\mathscr{P}[10]$	Decimal
$11 \times [8]^3 + 17 \times [8]^2 - 5 \times [8]$	$\in$	$\mathscr{P}[8]$	Octal
$[3]^3 - [3]^2 + [3] - [3]^{-2} - [3]^{-3}$	$\in$	$\mathscr{P}[3]$	Ternary
$7 \times [-8]^3 + 2 \times [-8]^2 + [-8] + 5$	$\in$	$\mathscr{P}[-8]$	Negative Octal
$-3 \times [2]^3 + 4 \times [2]^2 + [2]$	$\in$	$\mathscr{P}[2]$	Binary

Note that our general definition of radix polynomial specifically allows a positive or negative base and positive and/or negative digits whose magnitudes may be larger than the magnitude of the base.

9.2.3. n-ary Numbers

For the radix polynomial $P([\beta]) \in \mathscr{P}[\beta]$, the real numeric value of $P([\beta])$ is denoted by

$$\|P([\beta])\| = P(\beta) \qquad (9.2.10)$$

and

$$\|\mathcal{Q}\| = \{\|P\| \,|\, P \in \mathcal{Q}\} \qquad \text{for any } \mathcal{Q} \subset \mathcal{P}[\beta] \qquad (9.2.11)$$

Thus $\|P([\beta])\|$ denotes the value of the radix polynomial $P([\beta])$ at the integer value β, e.g.,

$$\|17 \times [10]^2 - 3 \times [10] + 5\| = 17 \times 10^2 - 3 \times 10 + 5 = 1675$$

$\|\mathcal{P}[10]\|$ then denotes the set of all real numbers whose value can be represented by a decimal radix polynomial.

For any integer $n \geq 2$, A_n denotes the *n-ary numbers* given by

$$A_n = \{in^j \,|\, i, j \text{ are integers}\} \qquad (9.2.12)$$

where A_n is taken to possess the algebraic structure of the reals restricted to A_n. Specifically, A_n is a commutative ring with the identity 1. Note that A_n is not a field for any n, since $n + 1 \in A_n$, $1/(n + 1) \notin A_n$, although the union $\bigcup\limits_{n=2}^{\infty} A_n$ is a field, the rationals. For several values of n, A_n has an alternative name as indicated below:

A_2	binary numbers
A_3	ternary numbers
A_8	octal numbers
A_{10}	decimal numbers
A_{16}	hexadecimal numbers

Note that $A_2 = A_{16}$, so every binary number is a hexadecimal number and vice versa. Also $A_2 \subset A_{10}$, so every binary number is a decimal number. Further relations amongst the A_n have been investigated in [12].

It is evident that the values of the radix polynomials of $\mathcal{P}[\beta]$ are the real numbers of $A_{|\beta|}$. More importantly, polynomial arithmetic in $\mathcal{P}[\beta]$ corresponds to the arithmetic of the real numbers in $A_{|\beta|}$, as indicated in the following corollary.

Corollary 9.2.1

For any integer β with $|\beta| \geq 2$, the evaluation mapping $E(P) = \|P\|$ for $P \in \mathcal{P}[\beta]$ is a homomorphism, as a commutative ring with identity, of $\mathcal{P}[\beta]$ onto $A_{|\beta|}$.

Proof: Let

$$P = d_m[\beta]^m + d_{m-1}[\beta]^{m-1} + \ldots + d_l[\beta]^l \in \mathcal{P}[\beta]$$

Then

$$\|P\| = d_m\beta^m + d_{m-1}\,\beta^{m-1} + \ldots + d_l\beta^l = i\,|\beta|^l \quad \text{for some integer } i,$$

so

$$\|P\| \in A_{|\beta|}$$

From (9.2.12) for $a \in A_{|\beta|}$, $a = i\,|\beta|^j = k\beta^j$ where the integer $k = i\,|\beta|/\beta$. Now $k[\beta]^j \in \mathscr{P}[\beta]$, and $\|k[\beta]^j\| = k\beta^j = a$, so the evaluation mapping, E, is onto $A_{|\beta|}$. The result that the evaluation mapping is a homomorphism of $\mathscr{P}[\beta]$ to $A_{|\beta|}$ as a commutative ring with identity then follows from Theorem 9.2.1 by taking $a = \beta$. ∎

9.2.4. Redundant Radix Representation

The evaluation mapping $E\colon \mathscr{P}[\beta] \longrightarrow A_{|\beta|}$ partitions the members of $\mathscr{P}[\beta]$ into equivalence classes such that all radix polynomials of a given class have the same numeric value. For any $b \in A_{|\beta|}$, let

$$V_\beta(b) = \{P \mid P \in \mathscr{P}[\beta], \|P\| = b\} \tag{9.2.13}$$

be termed a *redundancy class* of $\mathscr{P}[\beta]$. Thus, for example,

$$P([3]) = 2 \times [3]^2 + 1 \times [3] + 2 \in V_3(23)$$

$$Q([3]) = 1 \times [3]^3 - 1 \times [3] - 1 \in V_3(23)$$

so that $P([3])$ and $Q([3])$ are in the same redundancy class $V_3(23)$, and hence are alternative choices for base 3 radix representation of the number 23.

By elementary properties of polynomials [16] it follows that any extended polynomial function $P(y)$ over Z in the real variable y has a root b such that $P(b) = 0$ if and only if $P(y)$ can be factored to $P(y) = (y - b)\,Q(y)$ for some extended polynomial $Q(y)$ over Z in y. The following lemma is then derived.

Lemma 9.2.1

The redundancy class $V_\beta(0) \subset \mathscr{P}[\beta]$ is the principal ideal of $\mathscr{P}[\beta]$ generated by $([\beta] - \beta)$, i.e.,

$$V_\beta(0) = \{([\beta] - \beta) \times Q([\beta]) \mid Q([\beta]) \in \mathscr{P}[\beta]\} \tag{9.2.14}$$

Furthermore, the $V_\beta(b)$ for $b \in A_{|\beta|}$ are the members of the residue class ring $\mathscr{P}[\beta]/V_\beta(0)$.

Thus the evaluation mapping, E, which is a homomorphism from $\mathscr{P}[\beta]$ onto $A_{|\beta|}$ may be expressed as the composition of two mappings, $E = gf$, where f is the homomorphism of $\mathscr{P}[\beta]$ onto $\mathscr{P}[\beta]/V_\beta(0)$, and where g is an isomorphism of $\mathscr{P}[\beta]/V_\beta(0)$ to $A_{|\beta|}$, as shown in the mapping diagram of Fig. 9.2.1.

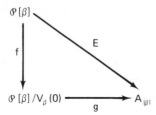

Fig. 9.2.1

In a radix number system it is desired to represent the real numbers of $A_{|\beta|}$ by radix polynomials of $\mathscr{P}[\beta]$ insofar as they represent the classes $V_\beta(b)$. It is well known that for $\beta \geq 2$, $b \in A_\beta$, $b \geq 0$, there is exactly one member $P \in V_\beta(b)$ all of whose digits are in the digit set $\{0, 1, \ldots, \beta - 1\}$, and this is the basis of standard radix representation. In Section 9.4, other digits sets will be shown which yield complete systems of representatives for $\mathscr{P}[\beta]/V_\beta(0)$. Also, redundant radix systems allowing several members from some $V_\beta(b)$ and providing for the development of more efficient digitwise implementation of arithmetic will be discussed.

9.2.5. Radix Integers and Radix Fractions

The *ring of radix integers*, $\mathscr{P}_I[\beta]$, and the *ring of radix fractions*, $\mathscr{P}_F[\beta]$, are given by

$$\mathscr{P}_I[\beta] = \{P \,|\, P \in \mathscr{P}[\beta], \, 1\mathrm{sp}\,(P) \geq 0\}$$
$$\mathscr{P}_F[\beta] = \{P \,|\, P \in \mathscr{P}[\beta], \, \deg\,(P) \leq -1\} \qquad (9.2.15)$$

where the ring structure on $\mathscr{P}_I[\beta]$ and $\mathscr{P}_F[\beta]$ is that inherited from $\mathscr{P}[\beta]$. $P \in \mathscr{P}_I[\beta]$ is a *radix integer*, and is a *normalized radix integer* if $1\mathrm{sp}\,(P) = 0$. $P \in \mathscr{P}_F[\beta]$ is a *radix fraction*, and is a *normalized radix fraction* if $\deg\,(P) = -1$. Any nonzero radix polynomial is then either a radix integer, a radix fraction, or a (disjoint) sum of a radix integer and a radix fraction, so

disjoint sum

$$\mathscr{P}[\beta] = \mathscr{P}_I[\beta] + \mathscr{P}_F[\beta] \qquad (9.2.16)$$

The following additional corollaries to Theorem 9.2.1 are readily derived.

Corollary 9.2.2

For any integer β with $|\beta| \geq 2$, the evaluation mapping is a homomorphism, as a commutative ring with identity, of $\mathscr{P}_I[\beta]$ onto the integers Z.

Corollary 9.2.3

For any integer β with $|\beta| \geq 2$, the evaluation mapping is a homomorphism, as a commutative ring (without identity), of $\mathscr{P}_F[\beta]$ onto $A_{|\beta|}$.

For $P = d_m[\beta]^m + \ldots + d_l[\beta]^l \in \mathscr{P}[\beta]$, the *radix integer part* of P, denoted $\lfloor P \rfloor$, is given by

$$\lfloor P \rfloor = \begin{cases} d_m[\beta]^m + \ldots + d_1[\beta] + d_0 & \text{for } \deg(P) \geq 0 \\ 0 & \text{for } \deg(P) \leq -1 \end{cases} \quad (9.2.17)$$

The *radix fraction part* of P is then given by $P - \lfloor P \rfloor$. Thus for any $P \in \mathscr{P}[\beta]$,

$$\lfloor P \rfloor \in \mathscr{P}_I[\beta]$$
$$P - \lfloor P \rfloor \in \mathscr{P}_F[\beta] \quad (9.2.18)$$

The collection of terminology associated with a radix polynomial is illustrated in Fig. 9.2.2.

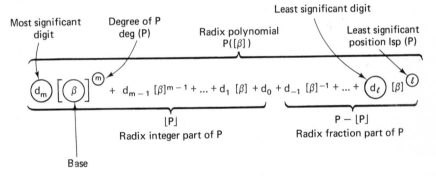

Fig. 9.2.2 Terminology associated with a radix polynomial.

The nonzero radix polynomial $P \in \mathscr{P}[\beta]$ can be factored into the product of two radix polynomials P_1, $P_2 \in \mathscr{P}[\beta]$ where P_1 is a normalized radix fraction or, alternatively, where P_1 is a normalized radix integer, and where P_2 has but a single nonzero coefficient. Specifically, for $P = d_m[\beta]^m + d_{m-1}[\beta]^{m-1} + \ldots + d_l[\beta]^l$, the factored *exponential form* of P is given by

$$P = (d_m[\beta]^{-1} + d_{m-1}[\beta]^{-2} + \ldots + d_l[\beta]^{l-m-1}) \times [\beta]^{m+1}$$
$$(\textit{normalized radix fraction}) \times [\beta]^{\deg(P)+1} \quad (9.2.19)$$

and the factored *scaled integer form* of P is given by

$$P = (d_m[\beta]^{m-l} + d_{m-1}[\beta]^{m-l-1} + \ldots + d_{l+1}[\beta] + d_l) \times [\beta]^l$$
$$(\textit{normalized radix integer}) \times [\beta]^{\text{lsp}(P)} \quad (9.2.20)$$

The factored exponential form (9.2.19) provides the basis for the hardware representation of numeric floating-point data on many computers, most notably the IBM system 360 and 370 series. The scaled integer form (9.2.20) has also been used as a basis for hardware representation of floating-point data on machines such as the Burroughs B-5000 and the CDC-6000 series.

9.2.6. Signed Radix Polynomials

The set of signed radix polynomials in β is given by

$$\mathscr{P}^{\pm}[\beta] = \{P \,|\, P \in \mathscr{P}[\beta] \text{ and all nonzero digits of } P \text{ have the same sign}\} \tag{9.2.21}$$

Any $P \in \mathscr{P}^{\pm}[\beta]$ may be written in factored form as

$$P = \begin{cases} (+1) \times Q \\ \text{or} \\ (-1) \times Q \end{cases} \text{ for some } Q \in \mathscr{P}[\beta] \text{ where all digits of } Q \text{ are nonnegative} \tag{9.2.22}$$

Notationally, the nonzero members of $\mathscr{P}^{\pm}[\beta]$ can be written in abbreviated factored form as $-Q$ or $+Q$ where it is assumed all digits of Q are nonnegative.

$\mathscr{P}^{\pm}[\beta]$ is closed under extended polynomial multiplication as defined in (9.2.4), and it is readily shown that the evaluation mapping $E: \mathscr{P}^{\pm}[\beta] \rightarrow \|\mathscr{P}^{\pm}[\beta]\|$ is a homomorphism, as a multiplicative group, of $\mathscr{P}^{\pm}[\beta]$ onto $A_{|\beta|}$. Note that $\mathscr{P}^{\pm}[\beta]$ is not closed under extended polynomial addition, since $3 \times [\beta] + 1 \in \mathscr{P}^{\pm}[\beta]$, $-1 \times [\beta] - 3 \in \mathscr{P}^{\pm}[\beta]$, and $(3 \times [\beta] + 1) + (-1 \times [\beta] - 3) = 2 \times [\beta] - 2 \notin \mathscr{P}^{\pm}[\beta]$. Thus $\mathscr{P}^{\pm}[\beta]$ is not a subring of $\mathscr{P}[\beta]$.

It is immediate from the proof of Corollary 9.2.1 that $\|\mathscr{P}^{\pm}[\beta]\| = A_{|\beta|}$. Thus

$$V_{\beta}(b) \cap \mathscr{P}^{\pm}[\beta] \neq \varnothing \qquad \text{for } b \in A_{|\beta|} \tag{9.2.23}$$

The members of $\mathscr{P}^{\pm}[\beta]$ provide the basis for computer hardware sign-magnitude numeric representation. The implications of the preceding algebraic discussion of $\mathscr{P}^{\pm}[\beta]$ is that digitwise multiplication may be described independently of the base as in (9.2.4); however, since $P + Q$ may not be in $\mathscr{P}^{\pm}[\beta]$ for $P, Q \in \mathscr{P}^{\pm}[\beta]$, it is necessary to introduce a procedure depending on β to find $R \in \mathscr{P}^{\pm}[\beta]$ such that $P + Q$ and R are both in $V_{\beta}(b)$ for $b = \|P + Q\| = \|R\|$. The details of such a digitwise procedure will be considered in Section 9.5, where radix polynomial representation subject to limits on allowed digit values is discussed.

Subsets of $\mathscr{P}^{\pm}[\beta]$ of particular interest for future reference are the *signed radix integers*, $\mathscr{P}_I^{\pm}[\beta]$, and the *signed radix fractions*, $\mathscr{P}_F^{\pm}[\beta]$, given by

$$\mathscr{S}_I^\pm[\beta] = \mathscr{S}^\pm[\beta] \cap \mathscr{S}_I[\beta]$$
$$\mathscr{S}_F^\pm[\beta] = \mathscr{S}^\pm[\beta] \cap \mathscr{S}_F[\beta] \tag{9.2.24}$$

Both $\mathscr{S}_I^\pm[\beta]$ and $\mathscr{S}_F^\pm[\beta]$ have a closed multiplicative structure that is independent of β, however, their additive structure requires a dependence on β as in $\mathscr{S}^\pm[\beta]$.

9.2.7. Infinite Precision Radix Polynomials

The definition (9.2.9) of radix polynomial requires that any particular radix polynomial have only a finite number of terms with nonzero coefficients, although this number may be arbitrarily large. Thus the expression $\sum_{i=1}^{\infty} 3 \times [10]^{-i}$ is not a radix polynomial. For completeness of terminology, an *infinite precision radix polynomial* will be defined as an expression P of the form

$$P = d_m[\beta]^m + d_{m-1}[\beta]^{m-1} + \cdots \tag{9.2.25}$$

where the integer β is the base, $|\beta| \geq 2$, and d_i is an integer termed a *digit* for all i, $d_m \neq 0$, and where the number of d_i for which $d_i \neq 0$ is infinite. There are many interesting and deep problems associated with the representation of real numbers by infinite precision radix polynomials [7, pp. 176–180], but such problems are outside the scope of our present concern with computer arithmetic.

EXERCISES 9.2

1. For the radix polynomials P and Q as given, determine the following terms.

   $P = 5 \times [\beta]^6 + 3 \times [\beta]^4 + 2 \times [\beta]^3 - 2 \times [\beta]^2$

   $Q = 4 \times [\beta]^3 + 2 \times [\beta]^2 - 6 \times [\beta] - 7 \times [\beta]^{-3} - 3 \times [\beta]^{-4} + 5 \times [\beta]^{-7}$

   (a) $\deg(P + Q)$ (e) $d_{\deg(Q \times Q)}(Q \times Q)$

   (b) $\deg(P \times P)$ (f) $\text{lsp}(\lfloor P + Q \rfloor)$

   (c) $\text{lsp}(P \times Q)$ (g) $\deg(Q - \lfloor Q \rfloor)$

   (d) $d_{\text{lsp}(P \times Q)}(P \times Q)$ (h) $d_{\text{lsp}(P \times Q)}(\lfloor P \times Q \rfloor)$

2. For $P \in \mathscr{S}[\beta]$, $P \neq 0$, show that $\lfloor P \times [\beta]^{-\deg(P)} \rfloor$ is a radix polynomial whose value is the most significant digit of P. Derive a similar formula which determines a radix polynomial whose value is the least significant digit of P.

3. (a) Prove that the ternary numbers is the same set of real numbers as the 9-ary numbers, i.e., that $A_3 = A_9$.

   (b) Prove that $A_{12} = A_{18}$.

   (c) Determine general conditions on p and q such that $A_p \subset A_q$.

4. Prove that $1/(n + 1) \notin A_n$ for any $n \geq 2$.

5. Determine all radix polynomials in the following sets.

(a) $\mathscr{S}^{\pm}_{7}[5] \cap V_5(37)$

(b) $V_{-10}(4) \cap \{P \mid P \in \mathscr{S}_I[-10], \deg (P) \le 2\}$

(c)   All base 8 radix integers of value 3 with degree no greater than 4 and all digit values of absolute value no greater than 7.

6.   Prove Corollaries 9.2.2 and 9.2.3.

7.   Let $\mathscr{S}_t[\beta]$ be the set of all base β radix polynomials with $1\text{sp}\,(P) \ge t$. For $t \ge 0$, show that the evaluation mapping is a homomorphism, as a commutative ring, of $\mathscr{S}_t[\beta]$ into Z.

9.3.   POSITIONAL RADIX DATA STRUCTURES

9.3.1.   Data Structures for Radix Polynomials

The foundations for radix representation and the principle of digitwise arithmetic have been discussed in Section 9.2. The computer implementation of radix arithmetic requires the choice of a data structure to represent radix polynomials.

Consider the radix polynomials

$$P = 6 \times [\beta]^7 + 2 \times [\beta] + 5 \times [\beta]^{-12}$$

$$Q = 3 \times [\beta]^5 + 2 \times [\beta]^4 + 5 \times [\beta]^2 + 7 \times [\beta] \qquad (9.3.1)$$

P and Q could each be represented by a list of (digit value, digit position) ordered pairs $((d_{j_1}, j_1), (d_{j_2}, j_2), \ldots, (d_{j_n}, j_n))$, each list including a pair (d_j, j) for each nonzero digit d_j. Alternatively, P and Q may each be represented by a pair $((d_m, d_{m-1}, \ldots, d_l), m)$ composed of a list of digit values including internal zeros and one index value for normalizing the list. The former representation is storagewise more efficient for P, the latter more efficient for Q. Here, however, the semantics of P and Q will virtually dictate the choice of representation for two reasons.

With the usual restrictions on allowed digit values, a rather dense occurrence of nonzero digit values between leading and trailing terms of a radix polynomial is far more likely to occur in the representations of the numbers utilized in typical numeric computation. Secondly, a radix polynomial such as P in (9.3.1) can quite often (although not always) be acceptably replaced by $P' = 6 \times [\beta]^7 + 2 \times [\beta]$, as there is only a small relative difference between the real numbers by represented P and P'.

A digit list representation for a radix polynomial requires the insertion of internal zeros in the list to indicate proper relative positioning of the terms, such as (3, 2, 0, 5, 7) for Q of (9.3.1). A digit list may also have an appropriate number of preceding and trailing zeros to determine proper absolute positioning of the terms, and also to fill a fixed length field for insertion in a computer word. Thus (0, 0, 3, 2, 0, 5, 7, 0) could be used to represent Q in a computer word assumed to contain an eight octal digit radix integer.

A formal development of digit lists, their relation to radix polynomials, and examples of these data structures in current computer software will now be pursued.

9.3.2. Positional Digit Strings

For any set V, the set V^* is composed of all finite strings of elements of V. The *width*, $w(v)$, is the number of members of the string $v \in V^*$. Let Z be the integers thought of as abstract distinguishable elements termed *digits*, with N the subset of nonnegative integer digits, and $D_d = \{0, 1, 2, 3, 4, 5, 6, 7, 8, 9\}$ $\subset N \subset Z$ the set of *decimal digits*. Then the string $\delta \in Z^*$ is a *digit string*, and $\delta \in D_d^* \subset Z^*$ is a *decimal digit string*.

Thus 00320570 is a decimal digit string, and $7, 15, -3, 2, 0, 0$ is a nondecimal digit string, where, for current purposes of exposition, the individiual elements of a nondecimal digit string are denoted by their standard decimal representations.

For the nonvoid digit string δ, let

$$\delta = a_1, a_2, \ldots, a_n \quad \text{where } a_i \in Z \text{ for } 1 \leq i \leq n = w(\delta) \quad (9.3.2)$$

Then δ is *left-normalized* if the *leading digit* $a_1 \neq 0$, δ is *right-normalized* if the *trailing digit* $a_n \neq 0$, and δ is *normalized* if it is both left- and right-normalized. The void digit string, $\wedge \in Z^*$, is taken as normalized. The maximal normalized substring of $\delta \in Z^*$ is termed the *significand* of δ, and two digit strings with the same significand are *equivalent*.

Thus the decimal digit string 00320570 has the maximal left-normalized substring 320570, the maximal right-normalized substring 0032057, and significand 32057.

A *signed digit string* is a string $\tau \in (N \cup \{+, -\})^*$ of the form

$$\tau = \sigma\mu \quad (9.3.3)$$

where $\sigma(\tau) \in \{+, -\}$ is the *sign* of τ and $\mu(\tau) \in N^*$ is the *magnitude* of τ. The sign, $\sigma(\tau)$, is not considered a digit, so τ is composed of a sign and $w(\mu) = w(\tau) - 1$ digits. τ is left- and/or right-normalized if $\mu(\tau)$ is, however, the *significand* of τ shall mean the unsigned significand of $\mu(\tau)$. Thus the signed decimal digit string -320570 is left-normalized and has significand 32057.

Software Example 9.3.1

The FORTRAN I/O format specification Iw where $1 \leq w \leq C$ (C an implementation dependent constant) denotes

for input:

1. Any decimal digit string δ of width $w(\delta) \leq w$, e.g., $\delta = 047230$ for $w \geq 6$, or

2. Any signed decimal digit string τ where $w(\tau) \leq$ w, e.g., $\delta = +047230$ for w ≥ 7,

for output:

1. Any left-normalized decimal digit string δ, with $w(\delta) \leq$ w, e.g., $\delta = 47230$ for w ≥ 5, or
2. Any signed left-normalized decimal digit string τ with $w(\tau) \leq$ w and $\sigma(\tau) = -$, e.g, $\tau = -3710$ for w ≥ 5.

Software Example 9.3.2

A FORTRAN *integer constant* denotes a signed or unsigned left-normalized decimal digit string subject to a machine dependent limit on size, e.g., 3250 and -74523.

A *positional digit string* is a string

$$\rho = \delta_I.\delta_F \in (Z \cup \{.\})^* \qquad (9.3.4)$$

where the *I-digit string*, $\delta_I(\rho) \in Z^*$, of ρ is followed by the single element string• termed the *radix point* which is followed by the *F-digit string*, $\delta_F(\rho) \in Z^*$, of ρ. The *canonical form* of ρ is the substring determined by deleting leading zeros of $\delta_I(\rho)$ and trailing zeros of $\delta_F(\rho)$. The *significand* of ρ is the significand of $\delta_I\delta_F$, and thus corresponds to deleting the radix point from the canonical form of ρ.

A *signed positional digit string* is a string

$$\psi = \sigma\mu_I.\mu_F \in (N \cup \{+, -,.\})^* \qquad (9.3.5)$$

where $\sigma(\psi) \in \{+, -\}$ is the *sign* of ψ and $\mu_I.\mu_F$ is a positional digit string. The *canonical form* of ψ includes the sign of ψ and is given by $\sigma\rho'$, where ρ' is the canonical form of $\mu_I.\mu_F$, and the *significand* of ψ is the unsigned significand of $\mu_I.\mu_F$.

Example 9.3.3

	Positional Digit String	Signed Positional Digit String
Not in Canonical Form	(a) 00.0039 (b) 1101101.10110 (c) $-7, 12, 5, -14, 0, ., 0$ (d) 7.7700	(i) -00721.40 (j) -0.777 (k) $+, 0, 0, 7, 12, 3, 11, 0,.$ (l) $+, ., 0, 0, 15, 0, 0$
In Canonical Form	(e) 3.14159 (f) 777000. (g) $1, 0, -1, 1, ., 0, -1, 1$ (h) .0039	(m) $-,12, 11, ., 0, 0, 3$ (n) -721.4 (o) $+2.71828$ (p) $+.0000000667$

In Example 9.3.3 note that (h) is the canonical form of (a), and (n) is the canonical form of (i). Also (d), (f), and (j) all have the same significand. In examples (c), (g), (k), (l), and (m) it was necessary to insert commas to distinguish the individual elements of the string. For discussion of practical alternative radix systems, it is convenient to have separate digit symbols for positive and negative integer values for magnitudes through 15. The letters A to F will be used for the integers 11–15 respectively, and barred digit symbols will denote negative digit values in the *digit alphabet*, H, defined by Table 9.3.1.

Table 9.3.1 DIGIT SYMBOLS FOR THE DIGIT ALPHABET H

Digit Alphabet H

Digit Symbol	Numeric Value	Digit Symbol	Numeric Value
0	0	$\bar{1}$	-1
1	1	$\bar{2}$	-2
2	2	$\bar{3}$	-3
3	3	$\bar{4}$	-4
4	4	$\bar{5}$	-5
5	5	$\bar{6}$	-6
6	6	$\bar{7}$	-7
7	7	$\bar{8}$	-8
8	8	$\bar{9}$	-9
9	9	$\bar{A}$	-10
A	10	$\bar{B}$	-11
B	11	$\bar{C}$	-12
C	12	$\bar{D}$	-13
D	13	$\bar{E}$	-14
E	14	$\bar{F}$	-15
F	15		

Utilizing the digit alphabet H, the previous Examples 9.3.3 (c), (g), (k), (l), and (m) become:

(c) $\bar{7}C5\bar{E}0.0$

(g) $10\bar{1}1.0\bar{1}1$

(k) $+007C3B0.$

(l) $+.00F00$

(m) $-CB.003.$

The set of nonnegative digits, H⁺, of H is termed the set of *hexadecimal digits*. Thus (k), (l), and (m) are signed positional hexadecimal digit strings.

Software Example 9.3.4

The FORTRAN I/O format specification Fw.d, where $0 \leq d \leq w \leq C$ (C an implementation dependent constant) denotes

for input:

1. Any signed or unsigned positional decimal digit string ν with $w(\nu) \leq w$, e.g., for $w = 6$, Examples 9.3.3 (h), (j), and (n) (in this case the value of d is ignored), or

2. Any signed decimal digit string τ with $d + 1 \leq w(\tau) \leq w$, e.g., for F7.4, -317416 (in this case a radix point is assumed between elements $w(\tau) - d$ and $w(\tau) - d + 1$ of the string, i.e., between 1 and 7 in -317416 for F7.4), or

3. Any unsigned decimal digit string δ with $d \leq w(\delta) \leq w$, e.g., for F7.4, 23145 (radix point assumed between elements $w(\delta) - d$ and $w(\delta) - d + 1$),

for output:

1. Any positional decimal digit string ρ with $w(\rho) \leq w$, $\delta_I(\rho)$ left-normalized, and $w(\delta_F(\rho)) = d$, e.g., for F7.4, Examples 9.3.3 (d) and (h), or

2. Any negatively signed positional decimal digit string ψ with $w(\psi) \leq w$, $\mu_I(\psi)$ left-normalized, and $\mu_F(\psi) = d$, e.g., for F6.1, Example 9.3.3 (n).

Software Example   9.3.5

A FORTRAN *real constant* in nonexponential form and a PL/I decimal *fixed-point constant* both denote a signed or unsigned positional decimal digit string (subject to an implementation dependent limit on size), e.g., Examples 9.3.3 (a), (b), (d), (e), (f), (h), (i), (j), (n), (o), and (p).

9.3.3. Radix Word and Radix Polynomials

Let ν be a signed or unsigned digit string or positional digit string. Then $\nu_{[\beta]}$ denotes a *radix word* where the *base* β of $\nu_{[\beta]}$ is an integer with $|\beta| \geq 2$. For example, $-27.4150_{[10]}$, $10\bar{1}0.\bar{1}\bar{1}_{[3]}$, and $2F0C3_{[16]}$ are radix words. The substring operators δ_I, δ_F, σ, μ, μ_I, and μ_F applied to $\nu_{[\beta]}$ denote the corresponding operations on ν, e.g., $\delta_I(320.\bar{1}3\bar{4}0_{[10]}) = 320$, $\delta_F(320.\bar{1}3\bar{4}0_{[10]}) = \bar{1}3\bar{4}0$, $\sigma(-270._{[16]}) = -$, $\mu_I(-270._{[16]}) = 270$, $\mu_F(-270._{[16]}) = \wedge$.

Utilizing the right-hand side of a digit string or the radix point of a positional digit string as a reference position, the digits of a radix word $\nu_{[\beta]}$ may be associated with terms of a radix polynomial in $[\beta]$ to determine a unique associated radix polynomial of $\mathscr{P}[\beta]$. If a sign is the leading element of a radix word, then that sign is associated with every term of the radix polynomial. Figure 9.3.1 illustrates this natural association for the various cases.

For every radix word $\nu_{[\beta]}$, the radix polynomial of $\mathscr{P}[\beta]$ associated with $\nu_{[\beta]}$, will be denoted by $\langle \nu_{[\beta]} \rangle$ and is given for

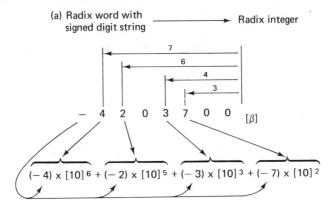

(a) Radix word with signed digit string ⟶ Radix integer

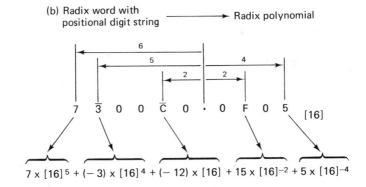

(b) Radix word with positional digit string ⟶ Radix polynomial

Fig. 9.3.1 A radix word and its associated radix polynomial.

$$\delta_{[\beta]} = a_1 \ldots a_{i[\beta]}$$

$$\tau_{[\beta]} = \sigma a_1 \ldots a_{i[\beta]}$$

$$\rho_{[\beta]} = a_1 \ldots a_j \cdot b_1 \ldots b_{k[\beta]}$$

$$\psi_{[\beta]} = \sigma a_1 \ldots a_j \cdot b_1 \ldots b_{k[\beta]}$$

by

$$\langle \delta_{[\beta]} \rangle = a_1 \times [\beta]^{i-1} + \ldots + a_{i-1} \times [\beta] + a_i$$

$$\langle \tau_{[\beta]} \rangle = (\sigma a_1) \times [\beta]^{i-1} + \ldots + (\sigma a_{i-1}) \times [\beta] + (\sigma a_i)$$

$$\langle \rho_{[\beta]} \rangle = a_1 \times [\beta]^{j-1} + \ldots + a_{j-1} \times [\beta] + a_j + b_1 \times [\beta]^{-1} + \qquad (9.3.6)$$
$$\ldots + b_k \times [\beta]^{-k}$$

$$\langle \psi_{[\beta]} \rangle = (\sigma a_1) \times [\beta]^{j-1} + \ldots + (\sigma a_{j-1}) \times [\beta] + (\sigma a_j) + (\sigma b_1) \times [\beta]^{-1} +$$
$$\ldots + (\sigma b_k) \times [\beta]^{-k}$$

where terms on the right with zero digits are deleted unless all digits are zero, in which case the zero polynomial is obtained.

Every radix polynomial $P \in \mathscr{P}[\beta]$ has associated with it a unique radix word denoted $\zeta(P)$, composed of a positional digit sequence in canonical form with the subscript $[\beta]$ given by

$$
\zeta(P) = \begin{cases}
d_m d_{m-1} \ldots d_l \overbrace{00 \ldots 0}^{l}._{[\beta]} & \text{for } \mathrm{lsp}(P) = l \geq 0 \\[2mm]
\underbrace{.00 \ldots 0}_{-m-1} d_m d_{m-1} \ldots d_{l[\beta]} & \text{for } \deg(P) = m \leq -1 \\[2mm]
d_m d_{m-1} \ldots d_1 d_0 \cdot d_{-1} \ldots d_{l[\beta]} & \text{for } \deg(P) = m \geq 0 > l = \mathrm{lsp}(P) \\[2mm]
\cdot[\beta] & \text{for } P = 0 \qquad\qquad (9.3.7)
\end{cases}
$$

Example 9.3.6

	P	$\zeta(P)$
(a)	$7 \times [8]^2 + 3 \times [8]^{-2} + [8]^{-10}$	$700.0300000001_{[8]}$
(b)	$12 \times [7]^4 - 3 \times [7]^3$	$C\bar{3}000._{[7]}$
(c)	$2 \times [-3]^5 + [-3]^3 + 2 + [-3]^{-1} + [-3]^{-4}$	$201002.1001_{[-3]}$
(d)	$6 \times [10]^{-5}$	$.00006_{[10]}$
(e)	$14 \times [16]^{-3} + 7 \times [16]^{-4} + 3 \times [16]^{-5}$	
	$+ 11 \times [16]^{-6}$	$.00E73B_{[16]}$

The relations between radix polynomials and radix words are summarized in the following lemmas.

Lemma 9.3.1

For $P \in \mathscr{P}[\beta]$, $\langle \zeta(P) \rangle = P$.

Lemma 9.3.2

If ρ is a positional digit string, then $\zeta(\langle \rho_{[\beta]} \rangle) = \rho'_{[\beta]}$ where ρ' is the canonical form of ρ.

Lemma 9.3.3

For the digit string ν, and any base β, $\delta_I(\zeta(\langle \nu_{[\beta]} \rangle))$ is the maximal left-normalized substring of ν.

As an illustration of Lemma 9.3.3 note

$$
\delta_I(\zeta(\langle 0320_{[8]} \rangle)) = \delta_I(\zeta(3 \times [8]^2 + 2 \times [8]))
$$
$$
= \delta_I(320._{[8]})
$$
$$
= 320
$$

9.3.4. Numeric Value of Radix Words

A radix word, $\nu_{[\beta]}$, is syntactically a subscripted symbol string. The associated radix polynomial, $\langle \nu_{[\beta]} \rangle$, provides a semantic interpretation of $\nu_{[\beta]}$ relevant to computer architecture and software design; however, the ultimate meaning associated with $\nu_{[\beta]}$ is the real numeric value $\| \langle \nu_{[\beta]} \rangle \|$. Thus $\| \langle \nu_{[\beta]} \rangle \|$ is the *value* of $\nu_{[\beta]}$.

A conventional notation for the value of $\nu_{[\beta]}$ is given by deleting the brackets of the subscript, i.e., ν_β. Thus 372.4_8 denotes the value of $372.4_{[8]}$, and $\| \langle 4\bar{2}1\bar{5}_{[10]} \rangle \| = 4\bar{2}1\bar{5}_{10}$. It should be kept firmly in mind that the subscripted string $372.4_{[8]}$ is a radix word suitable for symbol processing in computer software, whereas the subscripted string 372.4_8 denotes the value of $372.4_{[8]}$, and is a construct of the meta language.

The distinction between the questions (1) "Are two radix words identical?" and (2) "Do two radix words have the same value?" is of critical importance to arithmetic design, since the identity of symbol strings is not a sufficient test for numeric equality in the presence of redundancy. Note that

$$113_{[8]} \neq 93_{[8]} \qquad \text{nonidentical radix words}$$
$$113_8 = 93_8 \qquad \text{equal real numbers} \tag{9.3.8}$$

Also note that the radix polynomials $\langle 113_{[8]} \rangle$ and $\langle 93_{[8]} \rangle$ are not equal, but they are both members of the redundancy class $V_8(75)$. In this previous sentence we have implicitly used at the meta-level the real number equality $93_8 = 113_8 = 75_{10} = 75$.

9.3.5. Floating-Point Words

For any $i \in Z$, a nonzero $P \in \mathscr{P}[\beta]$ may be uniquely factored as

$$P = Q_i \times [\beta]^i \tag{9.3.9}$$

where $\zeta(Q_i)$ and $\zeta(P)$ have the same significand. The factored exponential form and scaled integer form of Eqs. (9.2.19) and (9.2.20) are two instances of (9.3.9). If deg $(P) \ll 0$ or $1\text{sp}\ (P) \gg 0$, then $\zeta(Q_i)$ will have a much smaller width than $\zeta(P)$ for $1\text{sp}\ (P) \le i \le$ deg $(P) + 1$, e.g., $\zeta(5 \times [8]^{12} + 4 \times [8]^{11})$ $= 5400000000000._{[8]}$ has width 14, and $5 \times [8]^{12} + 4 \times [8]^{11} = \langle 5.4_{[8]} \rangle \times$ $[\beta]^{12}$, where $5.4_{[8]}$ has a width of just 3. Scientific numeric computation on a computer quite often leads to a radix representation of a number by a radix polynomial P with deg $(P) \ll 0$ or $1\text{sp}\ (P) \gg 0$, so a data structure for P modeled after the right-hand side of (9.3.9) is desirable.

A *floating-point word* $\omega = (\nu_{[\beta]}, \eta_{[\gamma]})$ is a pair of radix words where $\nu_{[\beta]}(\omega)$ is the *coefficient* radix word of ω, β is the *base* of ω, and $\eta_{[\gamma]}(\omega)$ is the *exponent* radix word of ω, where η must be a signed or unsigned digit string. $\langle \omega \rangle$ denotes the radix polynomial associated with ω and is given by

396 RADIX ARITHMETIC CHAP. 9

$$\langle \omega \rangle = \langle \nu_{[\beta]}(\omega) \rangle \times [\beta]^{\| <\eta_{[\gamma]}(\omega)> \|} \tag{9.3.10}$$

For example,

$$\langle (5.4_{[8]}, 12_{[10]}) \rangle = \langle 5.4_{[8]} \rangle \times [8]^{\| <12_{[10]}\|>}$$
$$= (5 + 4 \times [8]^{-1}) \times [8]^{12}$$
$$= 5 \times [8]^{12} + 4 \times [8]^{11}$$

Note that the base, γ, of the exponent radix word, $\eta_{[\gamma]}$, need not be the same as the base, β, of the floating-point word $\omega = (\nu_{[\beta]}, \eta_{[\gamma]})$. In fact, the value of γ is not recoverable from the radix polynomial $\langle \omega \rangle \in \mathscr{P}[\beta]$.

Although the coefficient, $\nu_{[\beta]}$, and the exponent, $\eta_{[\gamma]}$, of the floating-point word ω are each associated with radix polynomials $P_1, P_2 \in \mathscr{P}[\beta]$ in the factored form $\langle \omega \rangle = P_1 \times P_2$, an important distinction should be kept in mind. $\nu_{[\beta]}$ is associated with the radix polynomial $P_1 = \langle \nu_{[\beta]} \rangle$ by associating digits of ν with digits of P_1, whereas $\eta_{[\gamma]}$ is associated with $P_2 = [\beta]^{\| <\eta_{[\gamma]}> \|}$ by determining the value of $\eta_{[\gamma]}$. The implications of this logical distinction in kind must be appreciated in designing the architecture of radix arithmetic as represented by floating-point words.

Software Example 9.3.7

The FORTRAN I/O format specification Ew.d where $0 \le d \le w - 6 \le C$ (C an implementation dependent constant) denotes for output a floating-point word $\omega = (\nu_{[10]}, \eta_{[10]})$ written as a string $\nu E\eta$, with the base 10 assumed, where η is a signed decimal digit string with $w(\eta) = 3$, and ν is an unsigned or negatively signed (only if $d \le w - 7$) positional decimal digit string with $\delta_I(\nu) = 0$, $\delta_F(\nu)$ left-normalized, and $w(\delta_F(\nu)) = d$. Examples for E11.4 are $-0.3215E+23, 0.1000E-01$, and $-0.4321E+00$. In some implementations the $+$ following the E may be replaced by a blank, as for example in $-0.4321E\ 00$.

Software Example 9.3.8

A FORTRAN *real constant in exponential form* is a floating-point word $\omega = (\nu_{[10]}, \eta_{[10]})$ where ν is a signed or unsigned positional decimal digit string and η is a signed or unsigned decimal digit string with no more than two decimal digits. ω is written as a single symbol string $\nu E\eta$ where the base, 10, is assumed and the symbol E separates the string ν from η. For example, $-31.02E70, 2.100E+3$ and $+.002E-31$ are FORTRAN real constants.

EXERCISES 9.3

1. Determine the canonical forms of the following (signed) positional digit strings and write them using the digit alphabet H.

(a)   0011.010
(b)   0.0739
(c)   +, 7, 3, 0, ., 14, 0, 12, 0
(d)   0, 0, 1, 0, ., 0, −1, −1, 0

(e)   −020.030
(f)   −7, 13, −15, 8, 0, .
(g)   1, 0, −2, 4, −8, 15, .
(h)   0, ., 0, −11, −10, −13

2. Write out the radix polynomials determined by the radix words.

   (a) $\langle 723_{[10]} \rangle$
   (b) $\langle F\bar{C}05.02_{[16]} \rangle$
   (c) $\langle 1\bar{1}\bar{1}.0\bar{1}001_{[3]} \rangle$
   (d) $\langle -E000400.000A_{[16]} \rangle$

   (e) $\langle 1001.001_{[-2]} \rangle$
   (f) $\langle 473000000_{[10]} \rangle$
   (g) $\langle 1A00B00_{[-16]} \rangle$
   (h) $\langle 00.\bar{1}0000\bar{9}_{[8]} \rangle$

3. Write out the radix words determined by the radix polynomials.

   (a) $\zeta\,(3 \times [-8]^4 + 2 \times [-8]^2 + 5 \times [-8]^{-7})$
   (b) $\zeta\,(10 \times [12]^{-2} + 11 \times [12]^{-3} - 10 \times [12]^{-5})$
   (c) $\zeta\,(-5 \times [16]^7 + 15 \times [16]^6 + 15 \times [16]^4 + 3 \times [16]^3)$
   (d) $\zeta\,(12 \times [-16]^{12})$

4. Assuming $\langle \wedge \rangle$ is the zero polynomial, show that for any $P \in \mathscr{P}[\beta]$,
$$\lfloor P \rfloor = \langle \delta_I(\zeta(P))_{[\beta]} \rangle$$

5. Prove that for any $P \in \mathscr{P}[\beta]$, $P \neq 0$,
$$w(\zeta(P)) = \max\,\{\deg\,(P) + 2,\, 1 - 1\text{sp}\,(P),\, \deg\,(P) - 1\text{sp}\,(P) + 2\}$$

6. The arithmetic of radix words can be derived from polynomial arithmetic as indicated in the following examples. Determine the radix word indicated.

   (a) $\zeta(\langle 2.437_{[10]} \rangle + \langle 42.4_{[10]} \rangle) =$
   (b) $\zeta(\langle 210.372_{[8]} \rangle + \langle \bar{2}\bar{1}0.\bar{3}605_{[8]} \rangle) =$
   (c) $\zeta(\langle \bar{2}A3.10\bar{4}_{[16]} \rangle \times \langle 020030_{[16]} \rangle) =$
   (d) $\zeta(\langle 1011.1011_{[-3]} \rangle \times \langle 11011.00101_{[-3]} \rangle) =$

7. Determine which of the following radix words have the same value.

   (a) $\bar{1}9\bar{C}9\bar{2}_{[7]}$
   (b) $1600.160_{[-6]}$
   (c) $\bar{1}4_{[16]}$
   (d) $\bar{3}3_{[-10]}$

   (e) $1\bar{1}1113_{[2]}$
   (f) $\bar{1}A\bar{F}.\bar{9}8_{[8]}$
   (g) $-20.0_{[6]}$
   (h) $1210_{[-3]}$

8. Write out the radix words determined by the floating-point words.

   (a) $\zeta(\langle (3.42_{[8]},\, 12_{[8]}) \rangle) =$
   (b) $\zeta(\langle (AF1703000_{[16]},\, -5_{[16]}) \rangle) =$
   (c) $\zeta(\langle (1.1101_{[2]},\, -11001_{[2]}) \rangle) =$

9. Define PL/I decimal floating-point constants in terms of floating-point words (see Example 9.3.8).

9.4. DIGIT SETS FOR RADIX REPRESENTATION

9.4.1. Digit Sets

A *digit set* $D \subset Z$ is a finite set of integers including zero. The elements of D are termed *digits*. The digit set D is *signed* if $d' < 0 < d''$ for some d', $d'' \in D$, and D is *positive* (unsigned) if $d \geq 0$ for all $d \in D$.

For the base β and digit set D, $\mathscr{F}[\beta, D]$ shall denote the set of all base β radix polynomials all of whose digits are in D, that is,

$$\mathscr{F}[\beta, D] = \{P \mid P \in \mathscr{F}[\beta], d_i(P) \in D \text{ for all } i \in Z\} \qquad (9.4.1)$$

where the ith *digit of P*, $d_i(P)$, is the coefficient of $[\beta]^i$ in P.

The redundancy class $V_\beta(b) \subset \mathscr{F}[\beta]$ was defined in (9.2.13) to contain all base β radix polynomials of value b for $b \in A_{|\beta|}$. In general, $V_\beta(b)$ is an infinite set for each b. For a suitable choice of base β and digit set D, it is possible to show that $V_\beta(b) \cap \mathscr{F}[\beta, D]$ will have exactly one member for each $b \in A_{|\beta|}$, thus providing a *unique representation system* for the $|\beta|$-ary numbers. It is the purpose of this section to determine various base and digit set pairs for which such unique representation is achieved.

The best known digit sets are the *standard β-ary* digit set D_β, for $\beta \geq 2$, and the *balanced β-ary* digit set B_β, for $\beta = 2i + 1 \geq 3$, given by

$$D_\beta = \{0, 1, 2, 3, \ldots, \beta - 1\} \qquad \text{for } \beta \geq 2$$
$$B_\beta = \{-i, -i + 1, -i + 2, \ldots, i\} \qquad \text{for } \beta = 2i + 1 \geq 3 \qquad (9.4.2)$$

Several popular forms of base and digit set combinations for radix representation are given in the following table followed by specific examples illustrating unique representation systems. The historical development of these radix representation forms has been discussed by Knuth [7, pp. 161–180].

Table 9.4.1   CHARACTERISTICS OF SEVERAL RADIX REPRESENTATION SYSTEMS

Radix Representation System	Base	Digit Set	Other Conditions
Signed-digit	Positive	Signed	—
Sign-magnitude	Positive	Positive	Prefix + or − sign
Negative base	Negative	Positive	—
Radix-complement	Positive	Signed	Leading digit signed, other digits nonnegative

Example 9.4.1

Signed-Digit: Balanced ternary representation utilizes base 3 and the balanced 3-ary digit set $\{-1, 0, 1\}$. It is well known that balanced ternary yields a unique representation system for the ternary numbers. $\langle \bar{1}01\bar{1}_{[3]} \rangle$ is the unique member of $\mathscr{S}[3, B_3]$ of value -25.

Sign-Magnitude: Standard octal representation utilizes base 8, the standard 8-ary digit set $\{0, 1, 2, 3, 4, 5, 6, 7\}$, and a $+$ or $-$ sign prefix. It is well known that standard octal yields a unique representation system for the octal ($=$ binary) numbers. $\langle -31_{[8]} \rangle$ is the unique radix polynomial of value -25 in $\mathscr{S}^{\pm}[8, D_8]$.

Negative Base: Negative decimal utilizes base 10 and the standard 10-ary digit set $\{0, 1, 2, \ldots, 9\}$. Negative decimal yields a unique representation system for the decimal numbers, with $\langle 35_{[-10]} \rangle$ the unique member of $\mathscr{S}[-10, D_{10}]$ of value -25.

Radix-Complement: 2's complement utilizes base 2 and the digit set $\{-1, 0, 1\}$. For every nonnegative binary number b, there is a unique radix polynomial of value b with digits from $\{0, 1\}$, and for every negative binary number b, there is at least one radix polynomial of value b with most significant digit -1 and all other digits from $\{0, 1\}$. $\langle \bar{1}00111_{[2]} \rangle$ is one member of $\mathscr{S}[2, \{-1, 0, 1\}]$ of value -25.

Relatively little is known [7, pp. 177–179, 495–497] about properties of radix representation for digit sets other than the standard and balanced type. To appreciate the options available to the computer architect, a preliminary investigation of properties of alternative digit sets is of primary importance. The problem of determining those base β and digit set D pairs for which $V_\beta(b) \cap \mathscr{S}[\beta, D]$ will have exactly one member for each $b \in A_{|\beta|}$ is conveniently separated into the problem of determining those digit sets, D, for which

$$|V_\beta(b) \cap \mathscr{S}[\beta, D]| \geq 1 \qquad \text{for all } b \in A_{|\beta|}$$

termed the *completeness question*, and those digit sets, D, for which

$$|V_\beta(b) \cap \mathscr{S}[\beta, D]| \leq 1 \qquad \text{for all } b \in A_{|\beta|}$$

termed the *nonredundancy question*.

9.4.2. Complete Digit Sets

$\mathscr{S}_I[\beta, D]$ shall denote the set of base β integer radix polynomials whose digits are all in the digit set D, i.e.,

$$\mathscr{S}_I[\beta, D] = \mathscr{S}[\beta, D] \cap \mathscr{S}_I[\beta] \tag{9.4.3}$$

The digit set D is *complete* for base β if

$$\mathscr{S}_I[\beta, D] \cap V_\beta(i) \neq \varnothing \qquad \text{for all } i \in Z \tag{9.4.4}$$

Lemma 9.4.1

Let D be a digit set which is complete base β. Then

$$\mathscr{F}[\beta, D] \cap V_\beta(b) \neq \varnothing \qquad \text{for all } b \in A_{|\beta|} \qquad (9.4.5)$$

Proof: Any $b \in A_{|\beta|}$ can be factored to $b = i\beta^j$ by (9.2.12) where $i, j \in Z$. By (9.4.4) there exists a radix polynomial $P \in \mathscr{F}_I[\beta, D] \cap V_\beta(i)$. Let $Q = P \times [\beta]^j$, and note that the digits of Q are the same as the digits of P. Thus $Q \in \mathscr{F}[\beta, D]$ and $\|Q\| = i\beta^j = b$. ∎

The converse of Lemma 9.4.1 is not valid. For example, by multiplying each digit of each radix polynomial of $\mathscr{F}[3, \{-1, 0, 1\}]$ by the constant 3 and then dividing each resulting polynomial by [3], e.g., $1 \times [3]^3 - 1 \times [3] + 1 \times [3]^{-2} \rightarrow 3 \times [3]^2 - 3 + 3 \times [3]^{-1}$, it is evident that

$$\mathscr{F}[3, \{-3, 0, 3\}] \cap V_3(b) \neq \varnothing \qquad \text{for all } b \in A_3 \qquad (9.4.6)$$

Yet the integer radix polynomials of $\mathscr{F}_I[3, \{-3, 0, 3\}]$ can only have values which are integral multiples of 3, so $\{-3, 0, 3\}$ is not complete base 3. The definition (9.4.4) for a complete digit set base β was chosen in preference to the alternative weaker condition (9.4.5) so as to force a focus on digital the most potentially useful alternatives for representation.

For the next theorem recall that for $n \geq 2$, the residue classes of integers modulo n are determined by $C_i = \{j \,|\, j \in Z, j \equiv i \bmod n\}$ for $1 \leq i \leq n$. A set, $S \subset Z$, of n integers containing exactly one member of each C_i, $1 \leq i \leq n$, is termed a *complete residue system* modulo n. Thus for $n = 3$, $C_1 = \{\ldots, -5, -2, 1, 4, \ldots\}$, $C_2 = \{\ldots, -4, -1, 2, 5, \ldots\}$, and $C_3 = \{\ldots, -3, 0, 3, 6, \ldots\}$ are the residue classes, and $S_1 = \{-1, 0, 1\}$ and $S_2 = \{-5, 8, 6\}$ are both complete residue systems modulo 3. An important relation between complete digit sets for base β and complete residue systems modulo β is obtained in the following theorem.

Theorem 9.4.1

Let D be a digit set which is complete for base β for $|\beta| \geq 2$. Then D contains a complete residue system modulo $|\beta|$.

Proof: For $1 \leq i \leq |\beta|$, let $P \in \mathscr{F}_I[\beta, D] \cap V_\beta(i)$. Then $P = d_m[\beta]^m + d_{m-1}[\beta]^{m-1} + \ldots + d_1[\beta] + d_0$ where $d_0 \neq 0$, since $\|P\| = i$ is not divisible by β. Then $i = \|P\| = d_m \beta^m + d_{m-1} \beta^{m-1} + \ldots + d_1\beta + d_0 \equiv d_0 \bmod |\beta|$, so $d_0 \in D$ and $d_0 \equiv i \bmod \beta$. Since this is obtained for any $1 \leq i \leq |\beta| - 1$, and since $0 \in D$, D contains a complete residue system modulo $|\beta|$. ∎

Corollary 9.4.1

Let D be a digit set which is complete for base β for $|\beta| \geq 2$. Then D contains at least $|\beta|$ digit values.

Again the converse of Theorem 9.4.1 does not hold. Note that $\{-2, 0, 2\}$ is a complete residue system modulo 3, yet $\mathscr{P}_I[3, \{-2, 0, 2\}]$ contains radix polynomials whose values are all even integers, so $\{-2, 0, 2\}$ is not a complete digit set base 3. For the base β with $|\beta| \geq 2$, we shall be particularly interested in investigating those complete residue systems modulo $|\beta|$ which are complete digit sets for β.

9.4.3. Redundant Digit Sets

The digit set D is *redundant* base β if $\mathscr{P}[\beta, D]$ has two distinct radix polynomials with the same value, i.e., if

$$|\mathscr{P}[\beta, D] \cap V_\beta(b)| \geq 2 \quad \text{for some } b \in A_{|\beta|} \quad (9.4.7)$$

D is *nonredundant* base β if it is not redundant base β.

Theorem 9.4.2

Let β be a base, $|\beta| \geq 2$, and let D be a digit set such that $|D| \geq |\beta| + 1$. Then D is redundant for base β.

Proof: Let

$$\mathscr{Q}_n = \{P \mid P \in \mathscr{P}_I[\beta, D],\ \deg(P) \leq n\} \quad \text{for } n \geq 0$$

$$\Delta = \max\{|d| \mid d \in D\} \quad (9.4.8)$$

For $P \in \mathscr{Q}_n$,

$$\Big\| \|P\| \Big\| \leq \Delta(|\beta|^n + |\beta|^{n-1} + \ldots + 1) = \Delta\left(\frac{|\beta|^{n+1} - 1}{|\beta| - 1}\right)$$

thus at most $2\Delta\left(\dfrac{|\beta|^{n+1}}{|\beta| - 1}\right) + 1$ distinct values are available for the members of $\mathscr{Q}_n$. Since $|D|$ values are available for each of the $n + 1$ coefficients,

$$|\mathscr{Q}_n| = |D|^{n+1} \geq (|\beta| + 1)^{n+1}$$

and

$$\lim_{n \to \infty} \frac{\left[2\Delta\left(\dfrac{|\beta|^{n+1}}{|\beta| - 1}\right) + 1\right]}{(|\beta| + 1)^{n+1}}$$

$$= \frac{2\Delta}{(|\beta| - 1)} \lim_{n \to \infty} \frac{|\beta|^{n+1}}{(|\beta| + 1)^{n+1}} = 0 \qquad (9.4.9)$$

so the number of values available to members of $\mathcal{Q}_n$ per member of $\mathcal{Q}_n$ goes to zero as $n \to \infty$. Hence D is redundant base β. ∎

Theorem 9.4.2 shows that a digit set D with more than $|\beta|$ digits is necessarily redundant, but a digit set with as few as three digits can be redundant. For example, note that $1 \times [\beta]^2 + 1 \times [\beta]$ and $(\beta + 1) \times [\beta]$ are distinct polynomials of $\mathscr{P}[\beta, \{0, 1, \beta + 1\}]$ with the same value for any fixed base $\beta \geq 2$. The following theorem provides a condition assuring that a digit set will be nonredundant.

Theorem 9.4.3

Let β be a base with $|\beta| \geq 2$, and let D be a complete residue system modulo $|\beta|$ with $0 \in D$. Then D is a nonredundant digit set for base β.

Proof: Assume P, $P' \in \mathscr{P}[\beta, D]$, $P \neq P'$, $\|P\| = \|P'\|$. Then for $P = \sum_{i=l}^{m} d_i [\beta]^i$, $P' = \sum_{i=l'}^{m'} d_i'[\beta]^i$, let $k = \min \{i \mid d_i \neq d_i'\}$. Then $\sum_{i=k}^{m'} d_i' \beta^i = \sum_{i=k}^{m'} d_i \beta^i$, and multiplying by β^{-k}, $\sum_{i=k}^{m} d_i \beta^{i-k} = \sum_{i=k}^{m'} d_i' \beta^{i-k}$ is an integer. Hence

$$\sum_{i=k}^{m} d_i \beta^{i-k} \equiv d_k \bmod |\beta|$$

$$\sum_{i=k}^{m'} d_i' \beta^{i-k} \equiv d_k' \bmod |\beta|$$

so that $d_k \equiv d_k' \bmod |\beta|$. But D is a complete residue system modulo $|\beta|$, so $d_k = d_k'$, a contradiction. Also D is finite and contains zero, so D is a nonredundant digit set for base β. ∎

Corollary 9.4.2

Let β be a base with $|\beta| \geq 2$, and let D be a subset of a complete residue system modulo $|\beta|$ with $0 \in D$. Then D is a nonredundant digit set for base β.

There are nonredundant digit sets other than those characterized in Theorem 9.4.3 and Corollary 9.4.2; for example, it is easily shown that $D = \{0, 10, 20, 30, 40, 50, 60, 70, 80, 90\}$ is a nonredundant digit set for base 10. However, our primary concern with nonredundant digit sets for base β will be with the investigation of complete residue systems modulo $|\beta|$.

9.4.4. Digital Representation Algorithm

Theorem 9.4.3 assures that there is at most one radix polynomial of $\mathscr{P}[\beta, D]$ of value $b \in A_{|\beta|}$ when the digit set D is a complete residue system modulo $|\beta|$. The following corollary provides the foundation for an efficient computational procedure for determining such a particular radix polynomial when it exists or, alternatively, determining that no such radix polynomial exists.

Corollary 9.4.3

For the base β, $|\beta| \geq 2$, let D be a digit set which is a complete residue system modulo $|\beta|$. For $i \in Z$, let $d(i) \in D$ be the unique element of D such that $i \equiv d(i) \bmod |\beta|$. Then for any $i \in Z$, there exists $P \in \mathscr{P}_I[\beta, D]$ with $\|P\| = i$ if and only if there exists $P' \in \mathscr{P}_I[\beta, D]$ with $\|P'\| = (i - d(i))/\beta$.

Proof: Let $P \in \mathscr{P}_I[\beta, D]$ with $\|P\| = i$. Then $P = d_m[\beta]^m + d_{m-1}[\beta]^{m-1} + \ldots + d_1[\beta] + d_0$, and clearly

$$\|P\| = i = d_m\beta^m + d_{m-1}\beta^{m-1} + \ldots + d_1\beta + d_0 \equiv d_0 \bmod |\beta|$$

so $d(i) = d_0$. Then

$$\frac{i - d_0}{\beta} = d_m \beta^{m-1} + d_{m-2} \beta^{m-2} + \ldots + d_1$$

so $P' = d_m[\beta]^{m-1} + d_{m-1}[\beta]^{m-2} + \ldots + d_1 \in \mathscr{P}[\beta, D]$ with $\|P'\| = (i - d(i))/\beta$.

Conversely let $P' \in \mathscr{P}_I[\beta, D]$ with $\|P'\| = (i - d(i))/\beta$. Assume $P' = d'_n[\beta]^n + d'_{n-1}[\beta]^{n-1} + \ldots + d'_1[\beta] + d'_0$, then let

$$Q = d'_n[\beta]^{n+1} + d'_{n-1}[\beta]^n + \ldots + d'_1[\beta]^2 + d'_0[\beta] + d(i)$$

Thus $Q \in \mathscr{P}_I[\beta, D]$, and

$$\|Q\| = \|P'\| \times \beta + d(i) = \frac{i - d(i)}{\beta} \times \beta + d(i) = i$$

proving the corollary. ∎

Algorithm 9.4.1 (DGT-Algorithm)

Assume given a base β with $|\beta| \geq 2$, a digit set D which is a complete residue system modulo $|\beta|$, and a $|\beta|$-ary number $b \in A_{|\beta|}$. This algorithm either determines that no radix polynomial of $\mathscr{P}[\beta, D]$ has value b, or the unique radix polynomial $P \in \mathscr{P}[\beta, D]$ of value b is explicitly determined.

Step 1: $l \leftarrow 0$, $a \leftarrow b$.

Step 2: If $a = 0$, $d_0 \leftarrow 0$, $m \leftarrow 0$, and go to step 10.

Step 3: If a is not an integer, $a \leftarrow a \times \beta$, $l \leftarrow l - 1$, and repeat step 3. (Since $b \in A_{|\beta|}$, $b = i\beta^j$ for some $i, j \in Z$, so step 3 is finally exited with $a = b\beta^{-l} \in Z$.)

Step 4: If β divides a, $a \leftarrow a/\beta$, $l \leftarrow l + 1$, and repeat step 4. (After this step, $a = b\beta^{-l} \in Z$, where $a \not\equiv 0$ mod $|\beta|$.)

Step 5: $m \leftarrow l$, $i_m \leftarrow a$.

Step 6: Determine $d_m \in D$ (uniquely) such that $i_m \equiv d_m$ mod $|\beta|$, and if $i_m = d_m$, go to step 10.

Step 7: $i_{m+1} \leftarrow (i_m - d_m)/\beta$, $m \leftarrow m + 1$.

Step 8: If $i_m \neq i_j$ for all $l \leq j \leq m - 1$, go to step 6. (Note that if $i_m = i_j$ for some $l \leq j \leq m - 1$, then without this test steps 6 and 7 would cycle.)

Step 9: Stop. There is no polynomial in $\mathscr{P}[\beta, D]$ of value b.

Step 10: Stop. $P = d_m[\beta]^m + d_{m-1}[\beta]^{m-1} + \ldots + d_l[\beta]^l \in \mathscr{P}[\beta, D]$, and $\|P\| = b$. (Note, furthermore, that for $b \neq 0$, $d_m \neq 0 \neq d_l$, so deg $(P) = m$ and lsp $(P) = l$ are explicitly determined by the algorithm.)

The digit set D utilized in the DGT-algorithm is taken to be a complete residue system modulo $|\beta|$. Thus the d_m are uniquely determined in step 6, and by Theorem 9.4.3, the radix polynomial $\sum\limits_{k=l}^{m} d_k[\beta]^k$ realized if and when step 10 is reached is then the unique polynomial of $\mathscr{P}[\beta, D]$ with value b.

Note that the arithmetic utilized in the DGT-algorithm is that of the host system in which $b \in A_\beta$ is originally represented. A different algorithm would be needed if the only arithmetic available were that of the target system determined by the digit set D and base β. The following two examples utilize standard decimal as the host arithmetic, and exhibit proper termination of the DGT-algorithm in step 10.

Example 9.4.2

Consider balanced 5-ary representation, that is, $\beta = 5$, $D = \{-2, -1, 0, 1, 2\}$. Let $b = 317.36 \in A_5$.

Step 3 of the DGT-algorithm gives:

$317.36 \times 5 = 1586.8$

$1586.8 \times 5 = 7934$

So after step 5:

$l = -2 \qquad i_{-2} = 7934$

Iteration of steps 6 and 7 yields the values in the following table:

m	$i_m = \dfrac{i_{m-1} - d_{m-1}}{5}$	$d_m \in \{-2, -1, 0, 1, 2\}$ where $i_m \equiv d_m \bmod 5$
-2	7934	-1
-1	1587	2
0	317	2
1	63	-2
2	13	-2
3	3	-2
4	1	1

Termination in step 10 is achieved with

$$P = 1 \times [5]^4 - 2 \times [5]^3 - 2 \times [5]^2 - 2 \times [5] + 2 + 2 \times [5]^{-1} - 1 \times [5]^{-2}$$

the desired radix polynomial of $\mathscr{P}[5, \{-2, -1, 0, 1, 2\}]$ of value 317.36. In radix string form $\zeta(P) = 1\bar{2}\bar{2}\bar{2}2.2\bar{1}_{[5]}$, so $317.36_{10} = 1\bar{2}\bar{2}\bar{2}2.2\bar{1}_5$.

As an atypical application let $\beta = -3$, $D = \{0, 1, 5\}$, and $b = -63 \in A_3$. Step 4 of the DGT-algorithm gives:

$$\frac{-63}{-3} = 21$$

$$\frac{21}{-3} = -7$$

So after step 5:

$$l = 2, \qquad i_2 = -7$$

Iteration of steps 6 and 7 yields:

m	$i_m = \dfrac{i_{m-1} - d_{m-1}}{-3}$	$d_m \in \{0, 1, 5\}$ where $i_m \equiv d_m \bmod 3$
2	-7	5
3	4	1
4	-1	5
5	2	5
6	1	1

Termination in step 10 is then achieved with

$$P = 1 \times [-3]^6 + 5 \times [-3]^5 + 5 \times [-3]^4 + 1 \times [-3]^3 + 5 \times [-3]^2$$

the desired radix polynomial of $\mathscr{P}[-3, \{0, 1, 5\}]$ of value -63. In radix string form $\zeta(P) = 1551500._{[-3]}$, so $-63_{10} = 1551500._{-3}$.

It is clear that if the DGT-algorithm terminates in step 10, the unique de-sired radix polynomial has been determined. To prove that the DGT-algo-rithm in general behaves as claimed it is necessary to show that the algorithm must terminate after a finite number of steps, and that termination in step 9 implies that the desired radix polynomial of value b does not exist.

Theorem 9.4.4

For a given base β, digit set D which is a complete residue system modulo $|\beta|$, and $|\beta|$-ary number $b \in A_{|\beta|}$, the DGT-algorithm will terminate after a finite number of steps.

Proof: Let $b = i\beta^j \in A_{|\beta|}$. If $b \neq 0$, step 6 of the DGT-algorithm will eventually be reached. From step 7 for $m \geq l + 1$, with $\Delta = \max \{|d| \,\big|\, d \in D\}$,

$$|i_{m+1}| \leq \frac{|i_m| + \Delta}{|\beta|} \begin{cases} < |i_m| & \text{for } |i_m| > \Delta \\ \leq \Delta & \text{for } |i_m| \leq \Delta \end{cases}$$

Thus the integer terms $i_l, i_{l+1}, \ldots$ decrease in magnitude until a term, i_k, is reached with $|i_k| \leq \Delta$. Then $|i_m| \leq \Delta$ for all $m \geq k$, so some term i_n for $k \leq n \leq k + 2\Delta$ must then either equal a value in D (go to step 10), or a pre-vious term i_j for $j < n$ (go to step 9), causing termination of the algorithm. ∎

Theorem 9.4.5

Given the base β with $|\beta| \geq 2$, the digit set D which is a complete residue system modulo $|\beta|$, and the radix polynomial $P \in \mathscr{P}[\beta, D]$, the DGT-algo-rithm applied to β, D and $\|P\|$ will terminate in step 10 with the determination of P.

Proof: The proof is immediate for $\|P\| = 0$, so assume $\|P\| \neq 0$. Let $P = \sum_{k=s}^{t} b_k [\beta]^k$ where $b_k \in D$ for $s \leq k \leq t$, $b_s \neq 0$, $b_t \neq 0$. Applying the DGT-algorithm to β, D and $\|P\|$ yields $l = s$, $i_l = \sum_{k=l}^{t} b_k \beta^{k-s}$, and $d_l = b_l$ on our first pass through step 6. For successive iterations through step 6,

$$i_m = \frac{i_{m-1} - d_{m-1}}{\beta} = \frac{\sum_{k=(m-1)}^{t} b_k \beta^{k-(m-1)} - b_{m-1}}{\beta} = \sum_{k=m}^{t} b_k \beta^{k-m}$$

$$d_m = b_m \in D \qquad \text{for } l + 1 \leq m \leq t$$

Then since $b_t \neq 0$, the radix polynomial

$$\sum_{k=m}^{t} b_k \, [\beta]^{k-m} \neq \sum_{k=j}^{t} b_k \, [\beta]^{k-j} \qquad \text{for } l \leq j < m.$$

Now $i_m = \| \sum_{k=m}^{t} b_k \, [\beta]^{k-m}\|$ and $i_j = \| \sum_{k=j}^{t} b_k[\beta]^{k-j}\|$, and since D is nonredundant for base β by Theorem 9.4.3, $i_m \neq i_j$ for $j < m$. Thus the test for equality of i_m with any i_j, $l \leq j \leq m - 1$, in step 8 of the algorithm always fails, so step 9 is never reached. Since the algorithm is finite we must eventually stop in step 10 (actually after the $t - s + 1$th pass through step 6), thus determining

$$P = \sum_{k=l}^{m} d_k \, [\beta]^k = \sum_{k=s}^{t} b_k \, [\beta]^k \quad \blacksquare$$

Theorems 9.4.3, 9.4.4, and 9.4.5 together prove that the DGT-algorithm always properly terminates for any allowed input. The next example exhibits an instance of the algorithm where the nonexistence of a radix polynomial of a given specified value is verified.

Example 9.4.3

Let the base $\beta = 3$, the digit set $D = \{0, 2, 4\}$, and $b = 11 \in A_3$, and apply the DGT-algorithm. After step 5, $l = 0$ and $i_0 = 11$. Iteration of steps 6 and 7 yields:

m	$i_m = \dfrac{i_{m-1} - d_{m-1}}{3}$	$\begin{array}{c} d_m \in \{0, 2, 4\} \\ i_m \equiv d_m \bmod 3 \end{array}$
0	11	2
1	3	0
2	1	4
3	−1	2
4	−1	

Thus $i_4 = i_3 = -1$, and the DGT-algorithm indicates there is no radix polynomial in $\mathscr{P}[3, \{0, 2, 4\}]$ of value 11, which is evident since clearly $P \in \mathscr{P}[3, \{0, 2, 4\}]$ implies $\|P\|$ is an even integer.

9.4.5.   Basic Digit Sets

The digit set D is *basic for base* β if D is both nonredundant and complete for base β.

Theorem 9.4.6

Let D be a basic digit set for base β. Then D is a complete residue system modulo $|\beta|$.

Proof: $|D| \geq |\beta|$ by Corollary 9.4.1 since D is complete for base β, and $|D| \leq |\beta|$ by Theorem 9.4.2 since D is nonredundant for base β. D must contain a complete residue system modulo $|\beta|$ by Theorem 9.4.1, and since any complete residue system modulo $|\beta|$ has $|\beta|$ elements, the theorem is proved. ∎

The converse of Theorem 9.4.6 is not true, since, for example, $\{0, 2, 4\}$ is a complete residue system modulo 3 which is not a basic digit set for base 3. To further our understanding of radix representation and the alternatives available for computer architecture, it is desirable to characterize those complete residue systems modulo n which are basic digit sets for the base $\beta = n$ and/or $\beta = -n$.

In addition to the practical computational value of the DGT-algorithm, it is now shown that the DGT-algorithm is a valuable theoretical tool in characterizing those complete residue systems which are basic digit sets. The following result provides a simple sufficient condition that prevents a complete residue system from being a basic digit set.

Lemma 9.4.2

Given a base β with $|\beta| \geq 2$ and a digit set D which is a complete residue system modulo $|\beta|$ such that $k(\beta - 1) \in D$ for some $k \in Z, k \neq 0$, then D is not basic for base β.

Proof: Assume such a digit set is basic for base β. Thus $k(\beta - 1) \in D$ and $0 \in D$ are distinct since $k \neq 0$, so $k(\beta - 1) \not\equiv 0 \bmod |\beta|$ since D is a complete residue system modulo $|\beta|$. Thus β does not divide k. Applying the DGT-algorithm to β, D and $-k \in Z$, from steps 5 and 6, $l = 0, i_0 = -k$, and $d_0 = k(\beta - 1)$. Then in step 7, $i_1 = [-k-k(\beta - 1)]/\beta = -k$, so $i_1 = i_0$ in step 8 and the algorithm terminates in step 9 with the conclusion that no radix polynomial of $\mathscr{P}[\beta, D]$ has value $-k$, so D is not basic for base β. ∎

An immediate conclusion of Lemma 9.4.2 is that the standard digit set $\{0, 1, 2, \ldots, \beta - 1\}$ is *not basic* for base $\beta \geq 2$. This occurs for the obvious reason that all radix polynomials of $\mathscr{P}[\beta, \{0, 1, \ldots, \beta - 1\}]$ must have nonnegative values for $\beta \geq 2$. Anticipating sign-magnitude representation, it would appear of interest to also investigate those "semi-basic" digit sets D which are nonredundant and such that $\mathscr{P}_I[\beta, D]$ has a member of value i for every nonnegative integer i. This topic is postponed to Section 9.4.7 where it is shown that the standard digit set is the only possible digit set with such properties!

The following theorem characterizes those complete residue systems which are basic digit sets. The condition given may then be efficiently tested for any given D by utilizing the DGT-algorithm.

Theorem 9.4.7

For the base β with $|\beta| \geq 2$, let D be a digit set which is a complete residue system modulo $|\beta|$. Then D is basic for base β if and only if there exists $P \in \mathscr{P}_I[\beta, D]$, with $\|P\| = i$ for all i such that

$$|i| \leq \left\lfloor \frac{\varDelta}{|\beta| - 1} \right\rfloor,$$

$$\varDelta = \max \{|d| \,\big|\, d \in D\} \tag{9.4.10}$$

Proof: For D basic for base β, (9.4.10) follows by definition. Alternatively, assume D is not basic. Since D is a complete residue system modulo $|\beta|$, by Theorem 9.4.3, D is nonredundant base β, so D is not complete for base β. Thus there exists some $i \in Z$ such that application of the DGT-algorithm to β, D, and i results in termination of the algorithm in step 9. Let $i_l, i_{l+1}, \ldots, i_m$ where $i_m = i_j$ for some $l \leq j \leq m - 1$ be the succession of values generated by step 7 of the DGT-algorithm in this case. Then

$$|i_{k+1}| \leq \frac{|i_k| + \varDelta}{|\beta|} \qquad \text{for } l + 1 \leq k \leq m$$

If $|i_k| > \varDelta/(|\beta| - 1)$, then

$$|i_{k+1}| < \frac{|i_k| + (|\beta| - 1)|i_k|}{|\beta|} = |i_k| \tag{9.4.11}$$

and if $|i_k| \leq \varDelta/(|\beta| - 1)$, then

$$|i_{k+1}| \leq \frac{[\varDelta/(|\beta| - 1)] + \varDelta}{|\beta|} = \frac{\varDelta}{|\beta| - 1} \tag{9.4.12}$$

Since $i_m = i_j$ for some $l \leq j < m - 1$, inequalities (9.4.11) and (9.4.12) imply $|i_m| \leq \varDelta/(|\beta| - 1)$. It is evident that the DGT-algorithm applied to β, D, and this particular i_m must terminate in step 9 indicating no member of $\mathscr{P}_I[\beta, D]$ has value i_m. Thus the condition expressed in (9.4.10) can not hold when the complete residue system D is not basic for base β, proving the theorem. ∎

By separate treatment of positive and negative values of both the i_k and the base β, an extended proof can be established to verify the sharper result achieved by replacing condition (9.4.10) of Theorem 9.4.7 by the following tighter range on i.

$$\left\lceil \frac{-d_{\max}}{|\beta| - 1} \right\rceil \leq i \leq \left\lfloor \frac{-d_{\min}}{|\beta| - 1} \right\rfloor \tag{9.4.13}$$

where

$$d_{\max} = \max \{d \mid d \in D\}$$
$$d_{\min} = \min \{d \mid d \in D\}$$

For our purposes Theorem 9.4.7 is sufficient, so verification of the sharper result is left as an exercise. The next three corollaries follow immediately from Theorem 9.4.7.

Corollary 9.4.4

For the base β with $|\beta| \geq 2$, let D be a complete residue system modulo $|\beta|$ where $i \in D$ for all i such that

$$|i| \leq \left\lfloor \frac{\Delta}{|\beta| - 1} \right\rfloor \qquad \text{where } \Delta = \max \{|d| \mid d \in D\} \qquad (9.4.14)$$

Then D is basic for base β.

Example 9.4.4

The following digit set and base pairs are readily verified to be basic by Corollary 9.4.4.

| Basic Digit Sets | |
Digit Set	Base
$\{-1, 0, 1, 2, 3, 4, 5, 6, 7, 8\}$	± 10
$\{-2, -1, 0, 1, 2\}$	± 5
$\{-5, -3, -1, 0, 1, 3, 5\}$	± 7
$\{-1, 0, 1, 3, 7\}$	± 5
$\{-21, -2, -1, 0, 1, 2, 13, 21, 23\}$	± 9

Corollary 9.4.5

The balanced digit set $\{-\alpha, -\alpha + 1, \ldots, -1, 0, 1, \ldots, \alpha\}$ is basic for base $(2\alpha + 1)$ and base $-(2\alpha + 1)$.

Corollary 9.4.6

Let $D_{\alpha,\gamma} = \{i \mid \alpha \leq i \leq \gamma\}$. For $\alpha \leq -1$, $\gamma \geq 1$, $D_{\alpha,\gamma}$ is a basic digit set for base $(\gamma - \alpha + 1)$ and for base $-(\gamma - \alpha + 1)$.

A digit set D is *normal* for base β if $|d| < \beta$ for all $d \in D$. There is no normal basic digit set for base 2, and the balanced digit set $\{-1, 0, 1\}$ is the only normal basic digit set for base 3. Several normal basic digit sets exist for base 5, namely $\{-3, -2, -1, 0, 1\}$, $\{-1, 0, 1, 2, 3\}$, the balanced digit set $\{-2, -1, 0, 1, 2\}$, and the "odd" digit set $\{-3, -1, 0, 1, 3\}$.

Corollary 9.4.7

For $\beta \geq 3$, there are $2^{\beta-3}$ normal basic digit sets for base β.

Proof: Let D be a normal basic digit set for base $\beta \geq 3$. By Lemma 9.4.2, $(\beta - 1) \notin D$ and $-(\beta - 1) \notin D$, so $|d| \leq \beta - 2$ for $d \in D$. By Theorem 9.4.6, D is a complete residue system modulo β, so $\{-1, 0, 1\} \in D$. In addition D must contain precisely one of $\{i, i - \beta\}$ for $2 \leq i \leq \beta - 2$. There are then $\beta - 3$ binary choices in our description of D, and the resulting $2^{\beta-3}$ sets so described are the normal basic digit sets for base β. ∎

Corollaries 9.4.4–9.4.6 discuss special classes of basic digit sets. For a general base and digit set, the following simple procedure provides a test to determine if the digit set is basic.

Algorithm 9.4.2   (Basic Digit Set Test)

Assume given a base β with $|\beta| \geq 2$, and a digit set D.

Step 1: Verify that D is a complete residue system modulo $|\beta|$, and if so go on to step 2 (otherwise D is not basic).

Step 2: Apply the DGT-algorithm to β, D, and each of the values i such that $|i| \leq \left\lfloor \dfrac{\Delta}{|\beta|-1} \right\rfloor$, where $\Delta = \max \{|d| \big| d \in D\}$. If step 10 is reached in each case, D is basic for base β by Theorem 9.4.13, otherwise D is not basic. ∎

Example 9.4.5

Given $\beta = 3$, $D = \{-1, 0, 7\}$, check if D is basic for base 3.

1. D is a complete residue system modulo 3.
2. The DGT-algorithm is applied to $\beta = 3$, $D = \{-1, 0, 7\}$, and $i = -2$, -1, 0, 1, 2 to determine

$$-2 = \|-1 \times [3]^2 + 7\|$$
$$-1 = \|-1\|$$
$$0 = \|0\|$$
$$1 = \|-1 \times [3]^3 + 7 \times [3] + 7\|$$
$$2 = \|-1 \times [3]^4 + 7 \times [3]^2 + 7 \times [3] - 1\|$$

By Theorem 9.4.7, $\{-1, 0, 7\}$ is basic for base 3.

9.4.6.   Positive Digit Set—Negative Base Pairs

Corollary 9.4.8

For the negative base $\beta \leq -2$, let D be a positive digit set which is a complete residue system modulo $|\beta|$. Then D is basic for base β if and only if there exists $P \in \mathscr{P}_I[\beta, D]$, with $\|P\| = i$ for all i such that

$$0 \leq i \leq \frac{\varDelta}{|\beta| - 1} \qquad \text{where } \varDelta = \max \{d | d \in D\} \qquad (9.4.15)$$

Proof: From Theorem 9.4.7, D is basic for base β if and only if there exists $P \in \mathscr{P}_I[\beta, D]$, $\|P\| = i$ for $|i| \leq \lfloor \varDelta/(|\beta| - 1)\rfloor$. For $-\lfloor \varDelta/(|\beta| - 1)\rfloor \leq i \leq -1$, with $i \equiv d(i) \bmod |\beta|$, $d(i) \in D$,

$$|i'| = \left| \frac{i - d(i)}{\beta} \right| \leq \frac{[\varDelta/(|\beta| - 1)] + \varDelta}{|\beta|} = \frac{\varDelta}{|\beta| - 1}$$

and

$$i' = \frac{i - d(i)}{\beta} \geq 0 \qquad \text{since } i < 0, \beta < 0, \text{ and } d(i) > 0$$

By Corollary 9.4.3, there exists $P \in \mathscr{P}_I[\beta, D]$ with $\|P\| = i$ if and only if there exists $P' \in \mathscr{P}_I[\beta, D]$ with $\|P'\| = i' = [i - d(i)]/\beta$, proving the corollary. ∎

Corollary 9.4.9

For the negative base $\beta \leq -2$, let D be a positive digit set which is a complete residue system modulo $|\beta|$ where $i \in D$ for

$$0 \leq i \leq \left\lfloor \frac{\varDelta}{|\beta| - 1} \right\rfloor$$

where $\varDelta = \max \{d | d \in D\}$. Then D is basic for base β.

Example 9.4.6

The following positive digit set and negative base pairs are readily verified to be basic by Corollary 9.4.9.

Basic Digit Sets	
Positive Digit Set	Negative Base
$\{0, 1, 2, 3, 4, 5, 6, 7, 8, 9\}$	-10
$\{0, 1, 3, 4, 6, 7, 10, 13\}$	-8
$\{0, 1, 2, 3, 4, 22, 23, 29\}$	-8
$\{0, 1, 3, 4, 7\}$	-5

Corollary 9.4.10

The standard digit set $D_\alpha = \{0, 1, 2, \ldots, \alpha - 1\}$ is basic for base $-\alpha$.

9.4.7. Sign-Magnitude Radix Representation

For the positive base $\beta \geq 2$, the digit set D is *positive semi-basic* for base β if D is a positive and nonredundant digit set for base β such that

$$\mathscr{F}_I[\beta, D] \cap V_\beta(i) \neq \varnothing \qquad \text{for all } i \in Z, i \geq 0 \qquad (9.4.16)$$

Thus for D a positive semi-basic digit set for base $\beta \geq 2$, $\mathscr{F}[\beta, D]$ is a subset of the signed radix polynomials $\mathscr{F}^{\pm}[\beta]$ defined by (9.2.21). Furthermore, the set of factored signed radix polynomials (see Eq. (9.2.22)) composed of $+Q$ and $-Q$ for all $Q \in \mathscr{F}[\beta, D]$ provides a unique representation system for the β-ary numbers as demonstrated, for example, by standard decimal representation. It is now shown that the only positive semi-basic digit sets are the standard digit sets.

Theorem 9.4.8

D is a positive semi-basic digit set for the base $\beta \geq 2$ if and only if D is the standard digit set $D_\beta = \{0, 1, 2, \ldots, \beta - 1\}$.

Proof: D_β is a complete residue system modulo β, so by Theorem 9.4.3, D_β is nonredundant for β. The zero polynomial is the only member of $\mathscr{F}[\beta, D_\beta]$ of value zero. Applying the DGT-algorithm to β, D_β, and i for $i \in Z$, $i > 0$, yields $l \geq 0$, $i_l > 0$ after step 5. If $i_j > 0$ for $j \geq l$, and $i_j \equiv d(i_j) \bmod \beta$, $d(i_j) \in D_\beta$, then $i_j \geq d(i_j)$ since D_β contains the smallest nonnegative residue modulo β for each residue class. Hence

$$i_{j+1} = \frac{i_j - d(i_j)}{\beta} < i_j$$

$$i_{j+1} = \frac{i_j - d(i_j)}{\beta} \geq 0$$

For the successive values generated in steps 6 and 7 of the DGT-algorithm, $i_l > i_{l+1} > i_{l+2} > \ldots > i_m \geq 0$, so termination in step 10 with the determination of $P \in \mathscr{F}_I[\beta, D]$, $\|P\| = i$, is assured. Thus the standard digit set D_β is positive semi-basic for base β.

Assume D is positive semi-basic for base $\beta \geq 2$. Let $1 \leq i \leq \beta - 1$, and assume $i \notin D$. Then for $i \equiv d(i) \bmod \beta$, $d(i) \in D$, it follows that $i < d(i)$ since D is a positive digit set. Note that

$$i' = \frac{i - d(i)}{\beta} < 0$$

and no radix polyminial of $\mathscr{F}[\beta, D]$ can have the negative value i'. By Corollary 9.4.3, no radix polynomial of $\mathscr{F}[\beta, D]$ has value i, a contradiction! Therefore, $i \in D$ for $1 \leq i \leq \beta - 1$, and $0 \in D$ since D is a digit set. Since D is also a complete residue system modulo β, $D = D_\beta = \{0, 1, 2, \ldots, \beta - 1\}$. ∎

Corollary 9.4.11

For the base $\beta \geq 2$ and standard digit set D_β, there is exactly one radix polynomial of $\mathscr{P}[\beta, D_\beta]$ of value b for each $b \in A_\beta$, $b \geq 0$.

9.4.8. Radix-Complement Representation

For $\beta \geq 2$, a base β *signed-leading-digit* radix polynomial is either the zero polynomial or

$$P = d_m[\beta]^m + d_{m-1}[\beta]^{m-1} + \ldots + d_l[\beta]^l \in \mathscr{P}[\beta] \quad (9.4.17)$$

where $d_m \neq 0$, $d_j \geq 0$ for $l \leq j \leq m - 1$. The set of all signed-leading-digit base β radix polynomials is denoted $\mathscr{P}^c[\beta]$.

The *complement digit set*, C_β, for base $\beta \geq 2$ is given by

$$C_\beta = \left\{ -\left\lfloor \frac{\beta}{2} \right\rfloor, -\left\lfloor \frac{\beta}{2} \right\rfloor + 1, \ldots, \beta - 1 \right\} \quad (9.4.18)$$

As special cases the *binary complement digit set* is $C_2 = \{-1, 0, 1\}$ and the *decimal complement digit set* is $C_{10} = \{-5, -4, -3, -2, -1, 0, 1, 2, 3, 4, 5, 6, 7, 8, 9\}$. A signed-leading-digit base β radix polynomial with all digit values in C_β is a *complement* radix polynomial. The set of all complement radix polynomials is denoted $\mathscr{P}^c[\beta, C_\beta]$, and the subset of radix integers is $\mathscr{P}_I^c[\beta, C_\beta]$. Thus

$$\begin{aligned} \mathscr{P}^c[\beta, C_\beta] &= \mathscr{P}^c[\beta] \cap \mathscr{P}[\beta, C_\beta] \\ \mathscr{P}_I^c[\beta, C_\beta] &= \mathscr{P}^c[\beta, C_\beta] \cap \mathscr{P}_I[\beta] \end{aligned} \quad (9.4.19)$$

Example 9.4.7

The following radix polynomials are complement radix polynomials as indicated:

$$\langle \bar{1}1001_{[2]} \rangle \in \mathscr{P}_I^c[2, C_2]$$

$$\langle \bar{4}369.24_{[10]} \rangle \in \mathscr{P}^c[10, C_{10}]$$

$$\langle 215.6_{[10]} \rangle \in \mathscr{P}^c[10, C_{10}]$$

$$\langle \bar{8}4FA63_{[16]} \rangle \in \mathscr{P}_I^c[16, C_{16}]$$

Note that the set of nonnegative digits of C_β is the standard digit set D_β, and for $\beta = 2\alpha + 1 \geq 3$, C_β is the union of the standard digit set D_β and the balanced digit set B_β.

An important property of complement radix polynomials is given in the following theorem.

Theorem 9.4.9

Let $P \in \mathscr{S}^c[\beta, C_\beta]$, $P \neq 0$. Then the sign of the most significant digit of P is the same as the sign of the value of P.

Proof: If the most significant digit of P is positive, the result is immediate. If the most significant digit d_m is negative, then

$$\|d_{m-1}[\beta]^{m-1} + d_{m-2}[\beta]^{m-2} + \ldots + d_l[\beta]^l\|$$
$$< (\beta - 1)(\beta^{m-1})(1 + \beta^{-1} + \beta^{-2} + \ldots)$$
$$= (\beta - 1)\beta^{m-1}\left(\frac{1}{1 - \beta^{-1}}\right)$$
$$= \beta^m$$

Thus, since $d_m \leq -1$, $\beta \geq 2$,

$$\|P\| < d_m \beta^m + \beta^m = (d_m + 1)\beta^m \leq 0 \quad \blacksquare$$

Corollary 9.4.12

For the base $\beta \geq 2$, and the β-ary number $b \in A_\beta$, $b \geq 0$, there is a unique radix polynomial $P \in \mathscr{S}^c[\beta, C_\beta]$ such that $\|P\| = b$, and furthermore this polynomial is in $\mathscr{S}[\beta, D_\beta]$.

Proof: Note that $\mathscr{S}[\beta, D_\beta] \subset \mathscr{S}^c[\beta, C_\beta]$, and by Corollary 9.4.11, exactly one radix polynomial $P_b \in \mathscr{S}[\beta, D_\beta]$ has the given value b. Suppose $Q \in \mathscr{S}^c[\beta, C_\beta]$, $\|Q\| = b$. By Theorem 9.4.9, the most significant digit of Q is positive since $b > 0$. Thus all digits of Q are nonnegative and $Q \in \mathscr{S}[\beta, D_\beta]$, so $Q = P_b$. $\quad \blacksquare$

For a negative β-ary number $b \in A_\beta$, there are numerous radix polynomials of $\mathscr{S}^c[\beta, C_\beta]$ of value b. For example, note that

$$-4 = \bar{4}_{10} = \bar{1}6_{10} = \bar{1}96_{10} = \bar{1}996_{10} = \bar{1}9\ldots96_{10}$$

A *canonical* complement radix polynomial for base $\beta \geq 2$ is either the zero polynomial or

$$P = d_m[\beta]^m + d_{m-1}[\beta]^{m-1} + \ldots + d_l[\beta]^l \in \mathscr{S}^C[\beta, C_\beta] \quad (9.4.20)$$

where either $d_m \neq -1$, or $d_m = -1$ and $d_{m-1} \leq \lfloor(\beta - 1)/2\rfloor$. The set of canonical complement radix polynomials for base β is denote $\mathscr{S}^{CC}[\beta, C_\beta]$, and $\mathscr{S}_I^{CC}[\beta, C_\beta] = \mathscr{S}^{CC}[\beta, C_\beta] \cap \mathscr{S}_I[\beta]$.

Theorem 9.4.10

For the base $\beta \geq 2$ and the β-ary number $b \in A_\beta$, there is a unique radix polynomial $P \in \mathscr{P}^{cc}[\beta, C_\beta]$ such that $\|P\| = b$.

Proof: For $b \geq 0$, the result follows from Corollary 9.4.12, so assume $b < 0$. Consider a modification of the DGT-algorithm so as to allow application of the algorithm to β, C_β, and $b \in A_\beta$ by substituting the following step 6' for step 6:

Step 6': If $i_m \in C_\beta$, set $d_m = i_m$ and go to step 10. Otherwise determine $d_m \in C_\beta$, $d_m \geq 0$ (uniquely) such that $i_m \equiv d_m \bmod \beta$.   (9.4.21)

Apply this modified DGT-algorithm to $\beta \geq 2$, C_β, and $b \in A_\beta$, $b < 0$. Note that for $i < - \lfloor \beta/2 \rfloor$, with $i \equiv d(i) \bmod \beta$ for $d(i) \in C_\beta$, $d(i) \geq 0$,

$$i' = \frac{i - d(i)}{\beta} < 0$$

$$|i'| = \left| \frac{i - d(i)}{\beta} \right| \leq \frac{|i| + \beta - 1}{\beta} \qquad (9.4.22)$$

$$= |i| + \frac{(\beta - 1)(1 - |i|)}{\beta} < |i|$$

Thus for the succession of values generated by steps 6' and 7 of the modified algorithm, $i_l < i_{l+1} < i_{l+2} < \ldots < i_m < 0$, so step 10 is reached and $i_m = d_m \in \{-\lfloor \beta/2 \rfloor, - \lfloor \beta/2 \rfloor + 1, \ldots, -2, -1\} \subset C_\beta$. Thus a radix polynomial of $\mathscr{P}^c[\beta, C_\beta]$ of value b is determined. Note that $i_{m-1} < - \lfloor \beta/2 \rfloor$, so $i_{m-1} \leq - [\beta + 1/2]$, and if $d_m = i_m = - 1$,

$$d_{m-1} = - \beta i_m + i_{m-1} \leq \frac{\beta - 1}{2}$$

Hence the radix polynomial so determined is a canonical complement radix polynomial. ∎

An illustration of the application of the DGT-algorithm with the modified step 6 is shown in the next example.

Example 9.4.8

Consider 8's complement representation, that is, $\beta = 8$, $C_8 = \{-4, -3, -2, \ldots, 6, 7\}$, and let $b = -2377$. Applying the modified DGT-algorithm through step 5 yields

$$l = 0, \qquad i_l = - 2377$$

Iteration of step 6' (see (9.4.21)) and step 7 yields the values in the following table:

m	$i_m = \dfrac{i_{m-1} - d_{m-1}}{8}$	$d_m \in C_8$ $d_m \geq 0$ except for final digit
0	-2377	7
1	-298	6
2	-38	2
3	-5	3
4	-1	-1

Termination in step 10 is then achieved with

$$\langle \bar{1}3267_{[8]} \rangle \in \mathscr{S}\mathscr{f}^{\,c}[8, C_8]$$

the desired 8's complement representation of -2377.

For $\beta \geq 2$, let d be a negative integer of C_β, so $-\lfloor \beta/2 \rfloor \leq d \leq -1$. Then $d, -\lceil \beta \rceil + (\beta + d)$, and

$$-\lceil \beta \rceil^m + (\beta - 1)\lceil \beta \rceil^{m-1} + (\beta - 1)\lceil \beta \rceil^{m-2} + \ldots + (\beta - 1)\lceil \beta \rceil + (\beta + d)$$
$$\text{for } m \geq 2$$

are all members of $\mathscr{S}^c[\beta, C_\beta]$ of value d. Any radix polynomial of $\mathscr{S}^c[\beta, C_\beta]$ with the most significant digit $-(\beta/2) \leq d_m \leq -1$ may be extended similarly yielding other radix polynomials of $\mathscr{S}^c[\beta, C_\beta]$ of the same value; for example,

$$\left.\begin{array}{l} \langle \bar{3}241_{[10]} \rangle \\ \langle \bar{1}7241_{[10]} \rangle \\ \langle \bar{1}97241_{[10]} \rangle \\ \langle \bar{1}997241_{[10]} \rangle \\ \langle \bar{1}9\ldots 97241_{[10]} \rangle \end{array}\right\} \in \mathscr{S}^c[10, C_{10}] \cap V_{10}\,(-2759)$$

The following theorem is then derived.

Theorem 9.4.11

For any $\beta \geq 2$ and any $P^* \in \mathscr{S}^{cc}[\beta, C_\beta]$ such that $\|P^*\| < 0$, there is for each $k > \deg(P^*)$ a radix polynomial $P \in \mathscr{S}^c[\beta, C_\beta]$ with $\|P\| = \|P^*\|$ where $\deg(P) = k$, $d_k(P) = -1$.

A variation of radix-complement representation has appeared in computer arithmetic design under the name *diminished radix-complement.* Specifically, for a binary system, the term is *l's complement.* Diminished radix-complement utilizes the same radix polynomials as radix-complement for the representation of nonnegative values. For the negative values the complement radix polynomial is effectively diminished by one unit in the least significant position to form the appropriate diminished complement radix polynomial. A primary advantage of this system is the ease of determining the radix polynomial of value $- \|P\|$ given P.

Note that the process of diminishing by one unit in the least significant position is not uniquely reversible, so a separate indication of the digital position for diminishing must be preserved. This may be accomplished by working with radix strings where zeros on the right side of the string convey the appropriate information. Peculiarities occur in effecting arithmetic for diminished radix complement representation, and a full treatment of this subject is outside the scope of our present concern.

9.4.9. Alternative Unique Representation Systems

In the initial Table 9.4.1 of this section four types of base and digit set pairs for radix representation were described, namely: signed-digit, sign-magnitude, negative base, and radix-complement. It was demonstrated in this section that numerous digit sets can be combined with a given base such that the resulting radix polynomials provide a unique representation system; the overall results are summarized in the following table.

Table 9.4.2 BASE AND DIGIT SET PAIRS THAT PROVIDE UNIQUE REPRESENTATION SYSTEMS FOR THE $|\beta|$-ARY NUMBERS†

Radix Representation System	Base	Digit Set	References
Signed-digit	$\beta \geq 2$	Balanced: B_β for odd β Many others	Theorem 9.4.7 Corollaries 9.4.4–9.4.7
Sign-magnitude	$\beta \geq 2$	Standard: D_β No others	Theorem 9.4.8
Negative base	$\beta \leq -2$	Standard: D_β Many others	Corollaries 9.4.8–9.4.10
Radix-complement	$\beta \geq 2$	Complement: C_β with radix polynomials in $\mathscr{P}^{cc}[\beta, C_\beta]$ (Others not investigated)	Theorem 9.4.10

†All digit sets referred to in the table are subject to the additional constraint that no nonzero multiples of the base are allowed as digit values.

EXERCISES 9.4

1. Determine all radix polynomials of $\mathscr{P}[4, \{\bar{2}, \bar{1}, 0, 1, 2, 3\}]$ whose degree is no greater than four and whose value is 36.

2. Determine which of the following digit sets are redundant and which are non-redundant for the base indicated.
   (a) $\{\bar{3}, \bar{1}, 0, 1, 3, 5\}$ for base 7
   (b) $\{0, 3, 6, 9, 12\}$ for base -5
   (c) $\{\bar{3}, \bar{2}, \bar{1}, 0, 1\}$ for base 4
   (d) $\{\bar{4}, \bar{1}, 0, 1, 3, 7\}$ for base 8

3. Apply the DGT-algorithm to the following base, digit set, and number triples, and interpret the result.

	Base	Digit Set	Number
(a)	5	$\{\bar{2}, \bar{1}, 0, 1, 2\}$	106725.
(b)	-8	$\{0, 1, 2, 3, 4, 5, 6, 7\}$	62.1953125
(c)	7	$\{\bar{5}, \bar{3}, \bar{1}, 0, 1, 3, 5\}$	3721.
(d)	4	$\{\bar{2}, 0, 1, 3\}$	$-335.$
(e)	3	$\{\bar{1}, 0, 4\}$	$-17.$
(f)	3	$\{\bar{1}, 0, 7\}$	5.

4. Apply the DGT-algorithm as modified for complement digit sets to the following cases.

	Base	Digit Set	Number
(a)	2	C_2	-4127
(b)	16	C_{16}	-5391.75
(c)	10	C_{10}	-32.476

5. Modify the DGT-algorithm to allow a base β and a digit set D that is a subset of a complete residue system modulo $|\beta|$, so that a radix polynomial of $\mathscr{P}[\beta, D]$ of value $b \in A_{|\beta|}$ will be determined if it exists. (Another stopping condition will be needed.) Apply your modified algorithm to the following cases.

	Base	Digit Set	Number
(a)	8	$\{\bar{2}, 0, 1, 2, 3, 7\}$	186.75
(b)	-3	$\{0, 1\}$	-51
(c)	16	$\{0, 1, 2, 3, 4, 5, 6, 7\}$	183.375

6. Utilizing either the theoretical conditions developed in this section or the basic digit set test (Algorithm 9.4.2), determine which of the following digit sets are basic for the base indicated. Note that one application of step 2 of the basic digit set test can result in several critical values of i being confirmed as representable by radix polynomials, so additional efficiencies are possible.

	Base	Digit Set
(a)	10	$\{\bar{7}, \bar{3}, \bar{1}, 0, 1, 2, 4, 5, 6, 8\}$
(b)	5	$\{\bar{1}, 0, 1, 2\}$
(c)	6	$\{\bar{8}, \bar{1}, 0, 1, 14, 15\}$
(d)	-8	$\{\bar{4}, \bar{3}, \bar{2}, \bar{1}, 0, 1, 2, 3, 4\}$
(e)	-5	$\{0, 1, 2, 4, 8\}$
(f)	7	$\{\bar{5}, \bar{3}, \bar{1}, 0, 1, 3, 9\}$

(g)	6	$\{\overline{14},\ \overline{3},\ 0,\ 8,\ 13,\ 17\}$
(h)	−4	$\{0,\ 9,\ 14,\ 19\}$
(i)	3	$\{\overline{1},\ 0,\ 7\}$
(j)	−8	$\{0,\ 3,\ 7,\ 12,\ 17,\ 26,\ 30,\ 69\}$

7. Extend Theorem 9.4.7 by proving the result derived by replacing Eqs. (9.4.10) by Eqs. (9.4.13).

8. Prove that the radix polynomial $P \in \mathscr{S}^c[\beta,\ C_\beta]$ whose existence is asserted in Theorem 9.4.11 is actually uniquely determined.

9. Suppose D is a digit set whose nonnegative digits form a complete residue system modulo β for a particular $\beta \geq 2$. Develop an algorithm to test if $\mathscr{S}^c[\beta,\ D] \cap V_\beta(b) \neq \varnothing$ for all $b \in A_\beta$.

10. Let $W_\beta \subset Z$ be the set of all integers excluding the nonzero multiples of β, i.e., $W_\beta = Z - \{\pm\beta,\ \pm2\beta,\ \pm3\beta,\ \ldots\}$. Let $\mathscr{S}\ [\beta,\ W_\beta]$ be the set of all radix polynomials of $\mathscr{S}\,[\beta]$ all of whose digits are in W_β. Prove that for any $b \in A_{|\beta|}$, all radix polynomials of $\mathscr{S}\ [\beta,\ W_\beta] \cap V_\beta(b)$ have the same least significant position.

11. Let D be a basic digit set for the base β, with $|\beta| \geq 2$ and $\varDelta = \max\ \{|d|\ |\ d \in D\}$. For $i \in Z$, let $P_i \in P_I\,[\beta,\ D]$ be the unique radix polynomial such that $||P_i|| = i$. Prove

$$\left\lfloor \ln\left(\frac{|i|(|\beta|-1)}{\varDelta}\right) \middle/ \ln|\beta| \right\rfloor \leq \deg\,(P_i) \leq \left\lfloor \frac{\ln|i|}{\ln|\beta|} \right\rfloor + 2\left\lfloor \frac{\varDelta}{|\beta|-1} \right\rfloor + 2$$

Research Questions:

12. Show that the digit set $D = \{-19,\ -13,\ 0,\ 1\}$ is complete for base 3 and that no proper subset of D is a complete digit set for base 3.

13. Find the smallest $j > 0$ such that $\{-1,\ 0,\ j\}$ is basic for base 3 and not basic for base -3.

14. Let $T_k = \{-1,\ 0,\ 3k + 1\}$ for $k \geq 0$. Note that T_0 and T_2 are basic for base 3. T_k is not basic for base 3 for any odd $k = 2i + 1 \geq 1$, since then $3k + 1 = 6i + 4 = 2\,(3i + 2)$, and this digit is a nonzero multiple of $\beta - 1 = 3 - 1 = 2$ (see Lemma 9.4.2). Determine those T_k for $k < 50$ which are basic for base 3.

9.5. RADIX ARITHMETIC

If $Q \in \mathscr{S}[\beta]$ is the result of a unary arithmetic operation on $P_1 \in \mathscr{S}[\beta,\ D] \subset \mathscr{S}[\beta]$ or of a binary arithmetic operation on $P_1,\ P_2 \in \mathscr{S}[\beta,\ D] \subset \mathscr{S}[\beta]$, then arithmetic in $\mathscr{S}\ [\beta,\ D]$ shall mean the determination of a radix polynomial $Q' \in \mathscr{S}[\beta,\ D]$ of the same value as Q or an indication that none exists. Thus for each arithmetic operation a procedure is desired having P_1 or $(P_1,\ P_2)$ as input and as output either some member of $V_\beta(||Q||) \cap \mathscr{S}[\beta,\ D]$ or an indication that this set is void.

It is the purpose of this section to develop a variety of efficient algorithmic procedures for implementing arithmetic for sets of radix polynomials whose digit ranges are limited, particularly for those radix systems characterized as signed-digit, sign-magnitude, negative base, and radix-complement.

Unary arithmetic operations to be considered are zero-detection, sign detection, and negation. Binary operations are addition/subtraction, equality testing, comparison, and multiplication. Division is not closed in $\mathscr{S}[\beta]$ and is outside the scope of this presentation.

Properties necessary to allow efficient architecture for these operations will be shown to limit the range of [base, digit set] pairs of practical interest. The properties of redundant digit sets which provide the opportunity for more efficient architecture of arithmetic operations through parallelism will be stressed.

Our description of arithmetic architecture will be solely through the development of algorithms at the digit by digit level. The logic design for hardware realization of these digital algorithms will not be considered.

9.5.1. Zero Detection

In [1] Avizienis showed that if the digit set D had all digit values of magnitude strictly less than $|\beta|$, then $\mathscr{S}[\beta, D]$ has a unique zero, the zero polynomial. The following theorem shows that zero has a unique representation under far less restriction on D.

Theorem 9.5.1   (Uniqueness of Zero)

For the base β, let D be any digit set with no nonzero member of D divisible by β. Then the zero polynomial is the only polynomial of $\mathscr{S}[\beta, D]$ of value 0.

Proof: Let the digit set D contain no nonzero multiple of the base β. Let $P \in \mathscr{S}[\beta, D]$ be a radix polynomial of value zero other than the zero polynomial. Then $\| P \times [\beta]^i \| = 0$ for any i, so we may assume, without loss of generality, that P is a radix integer with $\mathrm{lsp}(P) = 0$, i.e., $P = d_m[\beta]^m + \ldots + d_1[\beta] + d_0$, $d_0 \neq 0$. Then

$$\| P \| = 0 = d_m\beta^m + \ldots + d_1\beta + d_0 \equiv d_0 \bmod |\beta|$$

But $d_0 \equiv 0 \bmod |\beta|$ contradicts the condition that D has no nonzero members divisible by β. Thus the zero polynomial is the only member of $\mathscr{S}[\beta, D]$ of value 0. ∎

The implication of Theorem 9.5.1 is that zero will have a unique representation even in the presence of considerable redundancy for other values and a simple test for zero is straightforward. The presence of redundancy to any extent necessitates a general test for equality other than the identity of symbol strings representing the radix polynomials. Presupposing the design of a procedure for effecting subtraction in $\mathscr{F}[\beta, D]$, can be reduced to testing $P_1 - P_2$ for zero. Hence Theorem 9.5.1 is an important result for architecting arithmetic in the presence of redundancy.

9.5.2. Sign Detection

By Eq. (9.2.22), $P \in \mathscr{F}^{\pm}[\beta]$ may be written in factored form as $+Q$ or $-Q$ where Q has all nonnegative digits. Sign-magnitude representation utilizes this factored form and therefore has an indicator available to check for sign determination. For signed-digit, negative base, and radix-complement radix representation systems, the following theorem is of primary relevance to the problem of sign determination.

Theorem 9.5.2

Let D be a normal digit set for base β, i.e., $|d| < |\beta|$ for any $d \in D$. Let $P \in \mathscr{F}[\beta, D]$ have $\deg(P) = m$. Then

$$\| P \| > 0 \Longleftrightarrow d_m \beta^m > 0 \qquad (9.5.1)$$

Proof: For $P \in \mathscr{F}[\beta, D]$ with D normal for β and

$$P = d_m[\beta]^m + d_{m-1}[\beta]^{m-1} + \ldots + d_l[\beta]^l$$

where $d_m \neq 0$, $d_l \neq 0$, then

$$|(d_{m-1}\beta^{m-1} + d_{m-2}\beta^{m-2} + \ldots + d_l\beta^l)|$$
$$\leq (|\beta| - 1)|\beta|^{m-1}(1 + |\beta|^{-1} + |\beta|^{-2} + \ldots + |\beta|^{l-m+1})$$
$$< (|\beta| - 1)|\beta|^{m-1} \left(\frac{1}{1 - (1/|\beta|)} \right) = |\beta|^m$$

Since $d_{m-1}[\beta]^{m-1} + \ldots + d_l[\beta]^l$ has a value whose magnitude is strictly less than the value of a unit in the most significant position of P,

$$\| P \| > 0 \Longleftrightarrow \| d_m[\beta]^m \| > 0 \Longleftrightarrow d_m \beta^m > 0 \quad \blacksquare$$

Corollary 9.5.1

For the base $\beta \geq 2$, the complement radix polynomial $P \in \mathscr{F}^c[\beta, C_\beta]$ with $\deg(P) = m$ has

$$\| P \| > 0 \Longleftrightarrow d_m > 0 \qquad (9.5.2)$$

For any positive base β and any digit set D which is normal for β, it follows in general from Theorem 9.5.2 that the sign of the most significant digit of any $P \in \mathscr{P}[\beta, D]$, $P \neq 0$, is the sign of the value of P, thus providing a simple procedure for sign detection. For [negative base, positive digit set] radix systems a quite different property is utilized for sign detection.

Corollary 9.5.2

For the base $\beta \leq -2$ and positive digit set D which is normal for β, let $P \in \mathscr{P}[\beta, D]$, $P \neq 0$. Then

$$
\begin{array}{ll}
\| P \| > 0 & \text{if } \deg(P) \text{ is even} \\
\| P \| < 0 & \text{if } \deg(P) \text{ is odd}
\end{array}
\tag{9.5.3}
$$

Table 9.5.1 PROPERTIES ALLOWING SIMPLE PROCEDURES FOR SIGN DETECTION FOR THE SPECIFIC RADIX SYSTEMS INDICATED

Radix Representation System	Base	Digit Set	Sign of Value of Radix Polynomial is Given by
Signed-digit	$\beta \geq 2$	Normal	Sign of leading digit
Sign-magnitude	$\beta \geq 2$	Positive	Sign
Negative base	$\beta \leq -2$	Normal, positive	(deg (P)) mod 2 $\left\{ \begin{array}{l} + \text{ if } \deg(P) \text{ is even} \\ - \text{ if } \deg(P) \text{ is odd} \end{array} \right\}$
Radix-complement	$\beta \geq 2$	C_β	Sign of leading digit

For $\beta \geq 2$, note that if $d_0 = -\beta - 1 \in D$, $d_1 = 1 \in D$, then $P = d_1[\beta] + d_0 \in \mathscr{P}[\beta, D]$ has value -1 even though $d_1 = 1 > 0$. Thus for digit sets which are not normal for β, the problem of sign detection can necessitate inspection of several digits of the radix polynomial.

The practical restriction in the choice of digit set, whether nonredundant or redundant, to digit sets which are normal for base β is primarily to aid in the problem of sign detection rather than in zero detection.

Presupposing the design of a procedure for effecting subtraction in $\mathscr{P}[\beta, D]$, the comparison test to determine the larger of P_1, $P_2 \in \mathscr{P}[\beta, D]$ can be reduced to testing for the sign and/or zero value of $P_1 - P_2$. The results summarized in Table 9.5.1 are therefore of value for architecting an implementation of the comparison operation.

9.5.3. Negation

For $P \in \mathscr{P}[\beta, D]$, the problem of determining a radix polynomial $Q \in \mathscr{P}[\beta, D]$ such that $\| P + Q \| = 0$ can always be resolved by the binary operation of subtracting P from the zero polynomial. For many radix representation systems a more direct procedure is available.

In sign-magnitude representation the sign indicator is merely switched to effect negation. For signed-digit representation an important class of digit sets admits a simple algorithm for negation. A digit set D will be termed *balanced* if $-d \in D$ if and only if $-d \in D$.

Theorem 9.5.3

Let D be a balanced digit set. For $P \in \mathscr{P}[\beta, D] \subset \mathscr{P}[\beta]$, let $(-1) \times P = Q \in \mathscr{P}[\beta]$. Then $Q \in \mathscr{P}[\beta, D]$, and $\| P + Q \| = 0$.

Proof: The result is immediate for P the zero polynomial, and if

$$P = d_m[\beta]^m + d_{m-1}[\beta]^{m-1} + \ldots + d_l[\beta]^l$$

then

$$Q = (-1) \times P = (-d_m)[\beta]^m + (-d_{m-1})[\beta]^{m-1} + \ldots + (-d_l)[\beta]^l$$

and $Q \in \mathscr{P}[\beta, D]$ since D is balanced, and $\| P + Q \| = 0$. ∎

The simple procedure of determining the negative of each digit value thus provides a negation algorithm for $P \in \mathscr{P}[\beta, D]$ when D is balanced.

For a radix-complement system, negation is also possible on a digit by digit basis. For $\beta \geq 2$ and $P \in \mathscr{P}^c[\beta, C_\beta]$, the *negative complement* of P is the radix polynomial $N(P) \in \mathscr{P}^c[\beta, C_\beta]$ determined as follows:

$$N(P) = 0 \qquad \text{for } P = 0$$

and otherwise $N(P)$ has digits d_i', $1\mathrm{sp}(P) \leq i \leq \deg(P) + 1$, given by

$$d'_{1\mathrm{sp}(P)} = \beta - d_{1\mathrm{sp}(P)}$$

$$d_j' = \beta - 1 - d_j \qquad \text{for } 1\mathrm{sp}(P) + 1 \leq j \leq \deg(P) - 1$$

$$d'_{\deg(P)} = -d_{\deg(P)} - 1 \qquad \text{for } d_{\deg(P)} \leq \left\lfloor \frac{\beta}{2} \right\rfloor - 1 \qquad\qquad (9.5.4)$$

$$\left.\begin{array}{l} d'_{\deg(P)} = \beta - 1 - d_{\deg(P)} \\[4pt] d'_{\deg(P)+1} = -1 \end{array}\right\} \quad \text{for} \quad d_{\deg(P)} \geq \left\lfloor \frac{\beta}{2} \right\rfloor$$

Example 9.5.1

P	$N(P)$
(a) $\langle 3724_{[10]} \rangle$	$\langle \bar{4}276_{[10]} \rangle$
(b) $\langle \bar{1}23.077_{[8]} \rangle$	$\langle 054.701_{[8]} \rangle$
(c) $\langle \bar{1}22012_{[3]} \rangle$	$\langle 000211_{[3]} \rangle$
(d) $\langle A742.F0B_{[16]} \rangle$	$\langle \bar{1}58BD.0F5_{[16]} \rangle$
(e) $\langle 3881004_{[9]} \rangle$	$\langle \bar{4}007885_{[9]} \rangle$
(f) $\langle 0237000_{[10]} \rangle$	$\langle 0\bar{3}63000_{[10]} \rangle$

(g) $\langle \bar{1}1101.1100_{[2]} \rangle$ $\langle 00010.0100_{[2]} \rangle$

The following lemmas follow readily from the definition of the negative complement.

Lemma 9.5.1

If $\beta \geq 2$, $P \in \mathscr{P}c[\beta, C_\beta]$, then

$$\| P + N(P) \| = 0 \tag{9.5.5}$$

Lemma 9.5.2

If $\beta \geq 2$, $P \in \mathscr{P}c[\beta, C_\beta]$, $P \neq 0$, then

$$1\text{sp}(N(P)) = 1\text{sp}(P) \tag{9.5.6}$$

Lemma 9.5.3

If $\beta \geq 2$, $P \in \mathscr{P}c[\beta, C_\beta]$, $P \neq 0$, then

$$\deg(N(P)) \leq \deg(P) + 1 \tag{9.5.7}$$

Lemma 9.5.4

If $\beta \geq 2$, $P \in \mathscr{P}cc[\beta, C_\beta]$, then

$$N(N(P)) = P \tag{9.5.8}$$

In general for $P \in \mathscr{P}c[\beta, C_\beta]$, $N(N(P))$ is the canonical complement radix polynomial with the same value as P. Thus $N(N(\langle \bar{1}22012_{[3]} \rangle)) = \langle \bar{1}012_{[3]} \rangle$.

It should be noted that if a radix word representation $\delta_{[\beta]}$ of a complement radix polynomial $P = \langle \delta_{[\beta]} \rangle$ has zero digits on the right and/or left as in Examples 9.5.1 (f) and (g), then these digits are not changed in determining $N(P)$ as are the zero digits falling between the most and least significant positions in P. Thus an algorithm for implementation of negative complement in a fixed length computer word containing a digit string which may possess right or left zeros must scan in from both sides to find the most and least significant digits. Hence Eqs. (9.5.4) cannot be truly implemented in parallel for such a computer representation, and a serial implementation with resulting time sequencing delay is necessary.

An alternative implementation of negative complement for such fixed length computer words subtracts all digit values, including leading and trailing zeros, from $\beta - 1$, and then adds $-\beta$ to the leftmost digit and unity to the rightmost digit, propagating carries.

Thus for the radix word of Example 9.5.1 (f), the digit by digit subtraction yields $0237000_{[10]} \rightarrow 9762999_{[10]}$, and the subsequent additions after carries yields $9762999_{[10]} \rightarrow \bar{1}763000_{[10]}$. Note that the resulting complement radix polynomial achieved by this procedure is not necessarily canonical. The inevitable conclusion is that for a fixed length computer word format, an algorithm for negation in radix-complement representation cannot operate independently on each digit in parallel as was possible for the sign-magnitude and the balanced signed-digit representations.

The negative base system also suffers from the lack of a parallel digit by digit procedure for negation, with subtraction from zero a viable but more time-consuming implementation procedure.

9.5.4. Addition Tables

The addition table is the fundamental tool for effecting addition of radix polynomials having limited digit values. This table describes a mapping which gives the sum and carry digits resulting from the addition of pairs of specific digit values. For the digit set C, termed the *carry digit set*, and the digit set S, termed the *sum digit set*, the *base β addition mapping* $\alpha: C \times S \to C \times S$ is defined so that if $(c_1, s_1) \in C \times S$ and $\alpha(c_1, s_1) = (c_2, s_2)$, then

$$c_1 + s_1 = c_2\beta + s_2 \tag{9.5.9}$$

The digit $s_2 \in S$ is referred to as the *sum digit* and $c_2 \in C$ is referred to as the *carry digit* of the base β addition mapping of c_1 and s_1. If $C = S$ the addition mapping is termed *regular*.

The base β addition mapping may be displayed in table form as an *addition table*, where each entry (c, s) of the table is written as a string, cs. Table 9.5.2 shows the familiar addition tables for standard decimal $C = S = D_{10}$, standard binary $C = S = D_2$, and balanced ternary $C = S = B_3$, all of which are regular.

Table 9.5.2 ADDITION TABLES FOR (A) STANDARD DECIMAL, (B) STANDARD BINARY, (C) BALANCED TERNARY

(a) Base 10

C \ S	0	1	2	3	4	5	6	7	8	9
0	00	01	02	03	04	05	06	07	08	09
1	01	02	03	04	05	06	07	08	09	10
2	02	03	04	05	06	07	08	09	10	11
3	03	04	05	06	07	08	09	10	11	12
4	04	05	06	07	08	09	10	11	12	13
5	05	06	07	08	09	10	11	12	13	14
6	06	07	08	09	10	11	12	13	14	15
7	07	08	09	10	11	12	13	14	15	16
8	08	09	10	11	12	13	14	15	16	17
9	09	10	11	12	13	14	15	16	17	18

(b) Base 2

C \ S	0	1
0	00	01
1	01	10

(c) Base 3

C \ S	$\bar{1}$	0	1
$\bar{1}$	$\bar{1}1$	$0\bar{1}$	00
0	$0\bar{1}$	00	01
1	00	01	$1\bar{1}$

A radix system with the negative base $\beta \leq -2$ and standard digit set $D_{|\beta|}$ requires a carry digit of -1 in any addition mapping, so no regular addition mapping exists. With $S = D_{|\beta|}$, $C = D_{|\beta|} \cup \{\bar{1}\}$, a negative base addition mapping can be defined. In fact, whenever the digit set S contains a complete residue system modulo $|\beta|$, a suitable choice of digit set C with $S \subset C$ can always be made such that a base β addition mapping $\alpha \colon C \times S \to C \times S$ can be constructed. Table 9.5.3 shows addition tables for the standard base negative four radix system and for the base 3 addition mapping on the digit set $S = \{\bar{1}, 0, 7\}$ which was shown in Example 9.4.5 to be basic for base 3.

Table 9.5.3 NONREGULAR ADDITION TABLES FOR (A) THE STANDARD BASE NEGATIVE FOUR RADIX SYSTEM (B) THE UNIQUE BASE 3 ADDITION MAPPING $\alpha \colon C \times S \to C \times S$ WHERE $S = \{\bar{1}, 0, 7\}$ AND $C = \{\bar{3}, \bar{2}, \bar{1}, 0, 1, 2, 3, 4, 5, 7\}$

(a) S Base -4

C	0	1	2	3
$\bar{1}$	13	00	01	02
0	00	01	02	03
1	01	02	03	$\bar{1}0$
2	02	03	$\bar{1}0$	$\bar{1}1$
3	03	$\bar{1}0$	$\bar{1}1$	$\bar{1}2$

(b) S Base 3

C	$\bar{1}$	0	7
$\bar{3}$	$\bar{1}\bar{1}$	$\bar{1}0$	$\bar{1}7$
$\bar{2}$	$\bar{1}0$	$\bar{3}7$	$2\bar{1}$
$\bar{1}$	$\bar{3}7$	$0\bar{1}$	20
0	$0\bar{1}$	00	07
1	00	$\bar{2}7$	$3\bar{1}$
2	01	$1\bar{1}$	30
3	$1\bar{1}$	10	17
4	10	$\bar{1}7$	$4\bar{1}$
5	$\bar{1}7$	$2\bar{1}$	40
7	20	07	$5\bar{1}$

For the base β, let S be a digit set which is a complete residue system modulo $|\beta|$, and let $\alpha \colon C \times S \to C \times S$ be a base β addition mapping. For $\alpha(c_1, s_1) = (c_2, s_2)$ it follows from the defining Eq. (9.5.9) that $c_1 + s_1 = c_2\beta + s_2$. The conditions $s_2 \in S$ and S a complete residue system modulo $|\beta|$ uniquely determines s_2, hence also c_2. Thus the base β addition mapping on $C \times S$ must be unique. The minimal C with $S \subset C$ for which α is defined can be determined by first computing all carry digits resulting from $c_1 + s_1 = c_2\beta + s_2$ for $c_1, s_1 \in S$, and then recursively extending C until no new carry digits are encountered. It is readily shown that no carry digit with magnitude greater than the largest magnitude of the digits of S can be generated by this procedure, so the process must terminate. The following theorem is then derived, a detailed proof being left as an exercise.

Theorem 9.5.4

For $|\beta| \geq 2$, let S be a digit set which is a complete residue system modulo $|\beta|$. Then there is a unique minimal carry digit set C with $S \subset C$ where

$\max \{|d| \big| d \in C\} = \max\{|d| \big| d \in S\}$, for which there exists a base β addition mapping $\alpha: C \times S \to C \times S$, and this addition mapping is unique.

Corollary 9.5.3

For the base β, let S be a digit set which is basic for base β. Then if a regular base β addition mapping $\alpha: S \times S \to S \times S$ exists, α must be unique.

If S is a redundant digit set for the base β, then several distinct regular base β addition mappings on $S \times S$ can exist. Table 9.5.4 shows two regular base 3 addition mappings for $S = B_5 = \{\bar{2}, \bar{1}, 0, 1, 2\}$.

Table 9.5.4   THE ADDITION TABLES FOR TWO REGULAR BASE 3 ADDITION MAPPINGS, α AND γ, ON $B_5 \times B_5$

α B_5 / B_5	Base 3 $\bar{2}$	$\bar{1}$	0	1	2
$\bar{2}$	$\bar{1}\bar{1}$	$\bar{1}0$	$\bar{1}1$	$0\bar{1}$	00
$\bar{1}$	$\bar{1}0$	$\bar{1}1$	$0\bar{1}$	00	01
0	$\bar{1}1$	$0\bar{1}$	00	01	$1\bar{1}$
1	$0\bar{1}$	00	01	$1\bar{1}$	10
2	00	01	$1\bar{1}$	10	11

γ B_5 / B_5	Base 3 $\bar{2}$	$\bar{1}$	0	1	2
$\bar{2}$	$\bar{1}\bar{1}$	$\bar{1}0$	$0\bar{2}$	$0\bar{1}$	00
$\bar{1}$	$\bar{1}0$	$0\bar{2}$	$0\bar{1}$	00	01
0	$0\bar{2}$	$0\bar{1}$	00	01	02
1	$0\bar{1}$	00	01	02	10
2	00	01	02	10	11

9.5.5. Radix Polynomial Addition

Base β addition mappings may be extended to pairs of base β radix polynomials by applying the addition mapping simultaneously on a digit by digit basis. Let $\alpha: C \times S \to C \times S$ be a base β addition mapping. Then the corresponding *radix polynomial base β addition mapping* $\boldsymbol{\alpha}: \mathscr{P}[\beta, C] \times \mathscr{P}[\beta, S] \to \mathscr{P}[\beta, C] \times \mathscr{P}[\beta, S]$ is defined so that if $P_0 \in \mathscr{P}[\beta, C]$, $Q_0 \in \mathscr{P}[\beta, S]$, and $\boldsymbol{\alpha}(P_0, Q_0) = (P_1, Q_1)$, then the digits of P_1 and Q_1 are determined by

$$\alpha(d_i(P_0), d_i(Q_0)) = (d_{i+1}(P_1), d_i(Q_1)) \qquad \text{for all } i \qquad (9.5.10)$$

The iterative application of $\boldsymbol{\alpha}$ to absorb carries is defined by the n-fold composition mapping $\boldsymbol{\alpha}^{[n]}$ for $P \in \mathscr{P}[\beta, C]$, $Q \in \mathscr{P}[\beta, S]$ by

$$\boldsymbol{\alpha}^{[0]}(P, Q) = (P, Q)$$
$$\boldsymbol{\alpha}^{[n]}(P, Q) = \boldsymbol{\alpha}^{[n-1]}(\boldsymbol{\alpha}(P, Q)) \qquad \text{for } n \geq 1 \qquad (9.5.11)$$

From the definitions of a base β addition mapping (9.5.9), the corresponding radix polynomial addition mapping (9.5.10), the composite mapping (9.5.11), and the algebraic structure of real arithmetic, the following fundamental theorem is derived.

Theorem 9.5.5

Let $\boldsymbol{\alpha}\colon \mathscr{P}[\beta, C] \times \mathscr{P}[\beta, S] \to \mathscr{P}[\beta, C] \times \mathscr{P}[\beta, S]$ be a radix polynomial base β addition mapping. If $P_0 \in \mathscr{P}[\beta, C]$, $Q_0 \in \mathscr{P}[\beta, S]$ and $\boldsymbol{\alpha}^{[n]}(P_0, Q_0) = (P_n, Q_n)$, then

$$\| P_0 + Q_0 \| = \| P_n + Q_n \| \qquad \text{for any } n \geq 0$$

Example 9.5.2

Let α_{10} be the standard base 10 addition mapping as shown in Table 9.5.2. Let $P = \langle 372.091_{[10]} \rangle \in \mathscr{P}[10, D_{10}]$, $Q = \langle 4665.320_{[10]} \rangle \in \mathscr{P}[10, D_{10}]$.

$$\alpha_{10}^{[0]}(P, Q) \longrightarrow \left\{ \begin{array}{l} 4665.320_{[10]} \\ 372.091_{[10]} \end{array} \right.$$

$$\alpha_{10}^{[1]}(P, Q) \longrightarrow \left\{ \begin{array}{ll} 4937.311_{[10]} & \longleftarrow \text{ sum digits} \\ 00100.10_{[10]} & \longleftarrow \text{ carry digits} \end{array} \right.$$

$$\alpha_{10}^{[2]}(P, Q) \longrightarrow \left\{ \begin{array}{ll} 4037.411_{[10]} & \longleftarrow \text{ sum digits} \\ 01000.00_{[10]} & \longleftarrow \text{ carry digits} \end{array} \right.$$

$$\alpha_{10}^{[3]}(P, Q) \longrightarrow \left\{ \begin{array}{ll} 5037.411_{[10]} & \longleftarrow \text{ sum digits} \\ 00000.00_{[10]} & \longleftarrow \text{ carry digits} \end{array} \right.$$

Thus $\alpha_{10}^{[3]}(\langle 372.091_{[10]} \rangle, \langle 4665.320_{[10]} \rangle) = (0, \langle 5037.411_{[10]} \rangle)$, and by Theorem 9.5.5 it is evident that $\langle 5037.411_{[10]} \rangle \in \mathscr{P}[10, D_{10}]$ is the desired sum satisfying the digit range limitations.

Example 9.5.3

Let $\alpha_{\bar{5}}$ be the standard base -5 addition mapping with the addition table shown. Let $Q = \langle 304142_{[-5]} \rangle \in \mathscr{P}[-5, D_5]$, and let $P = \langle 421431_{[-5]} \rangle \in \mathscr{P}[-5, D_5 \cup \{\bar{1}\}]$.

C $\diagdown$ S	Base -5				
	0	1	2	3	4
$\bar{1}$	14	00	01	02	03
0	00	01	02	03	04
1	01	02	03	04	$\bar{1}0$
2	02	03	04	$\bar{1}0$	$\bar{1}1$
3	03	04	$\bar{1}0$	$\bar{1}1$	$\bar{1}2$
4	04	$\bar{1}0$	$\bar{1}1$	$\bar{1}2$	$\bar{1}3$

$$\alpha_{\bar{5}}^{[0]}(P, Q) \longrightarrow \left\{ \begin{array}{l} 304142_{[-5]} \\ 421431_{[-5]} \end{array} \right.$$

$$\alpha_{\bar{5}}^{[1]}(P, Q) \longrightarrow \left\{ \begin{array}{l} 220023_{[-5]} \\ \bar{1}0\bar{1}\bar{1}0_{\ [-5]} \end{array} \right.$$

$$\alpha_{\bar{5}}^{[2]}(P, Q) \longrightarrow \left\{ \begin{array}{l} 4214423_{[-5]} \\ 1001100_{\ [-5]} \end{array} \right.$$

$$\alpha_{\bar{5}}^{[3]}(P, Q) \longrightarrow \left\{ \begin{array}{l} 14220423_{[-5]} \\ 0000\bar{1}000_{\ [-5]} \end{array} \right.$$

$$\alpha_{\bar{5}}^{[4]}(P, Q) \longrightarrow \left\{ \begin{array}{l} 14210423_{[-5]} \\ 00000000_{\ [-5]} \end{array} \right.$$

Thus $\langle 14210423_{[-5]} \rangle \in \mathscr{P}[-5, D_5]$ is the desired sum of $\langle 304142_{[-5]} \rangle$ and $\langle 421431_{[-5]} \rangle$ that satisfies the digit range constraints and by Theorem 9.5.5 has the correct value.

For the radix polynomial base β addition mapping $\boldsymbol{\alpha}:\mathscr{P}[\beta, C] \times \mathscr{P}[\beta, S] \to \mathscr{P}[\beta, C] \times \mathscr{P}[\beta, S]$ and any $P \in \mathscr{P}[\beta, C]$, $Q \in \mathscr{P}[\beta, S]$, the *carry length* $K_\alpha(P, Q)$ for the sum of P and Q by $\boldsymbol{\alpha}$ is the minimum n such that

$$
\begin{aligned}
\boldsymbol{\alpha}^{[n-1]}(P, Q) &= (P_{n-1}, Q_{n-1}) \text{ with } P_{n-1} \neq 0 \\
\boldsymbol{\alpha}^{[n]}(P, Q) &= (0, Q_n)
\end{aligned}
\tag{9.5.12}
$$

or, if no such $n \geq 0$ exists, then $K_\alpha(P, Q) = \infty$. Thus from Example 9.5.2, $K_{\alpha_{10}}(\langle 372.091_{[10]}\rangle, \ \langle 4665.311_{[10]}\rangle) = 3$, and from Example 9.5.3, $K_{\alpha_5}(\langle 421431_{[-5]}\rangle, \langle 304142_{[-5]}\rangle) = 4$. It is important to note that whenever the carry length $K_\alpha(P, Q)$ is finite,

$$
\boldsymbol{\alpha}^{K_\alpha(P, Q)} = (0, R)
\tag{9.5.13}
$$

so that $R \in V_\beta(\|P + Q\|) \cap \mathscr{P}[\beta, S]$ is the desired sum of P and Q satisfying the digit range constraints for addition in $\mathscr{P}[\beta, S]$.

Nonstandard digit sets can lead to rather large finite or infinite carry lengths as seen in the following examples.

Example 9.5.4

Let α be the base 3 addition mapping on $\{\bar{3}, \bar{2}, \bar{1}, 0, 1, 2, 3, 4, 5, 7\} \times \{\bar{1}, 0, 7\}$ with addition table as given in Table 9.5.3(b). The following shows, $K_\alpha(\langle -1_{[3]}\rangle, \langle 7_{[3]}\rangle) = 6$.

$$
\boldsymbol{\alpha}^{[0]}(\langle -1_{[3]}\rangle, \langle 7_{[3]}\rangle) \longrightarrow \left\{ \begin{array}{l} \quad\quad 7_{[3]} \\ \hline \quad\quad \bar{1}_{[3]} \end{array} \right.
$$

$$
\boldsymbol{\alpha}^{[1]}(\langle -1_{[3]}\rangle, \langle 7_{[3]}\rangle) \longrightarrow \left\{ \begin{array}{l} \quad\quad 0_{[3]} \\ \hline \quad\quad 2_{[3]} \end{array} \right.
$$

$$
\boldsymbol{\alpha}^{[2]}(\langle -1_{[3]}\rangle, \langle 7_{[3]}\rangle) \longrightarrow \left\{ \begin{array}{l} \quad \bar{1}\ 0_{[3]} \\ \hline \quad\quad 1_{[3]} \end{array} \right.
$$

$$
\boldsymbol{\alpha}^{[3]}(\langle -1_{[3]}\rangle, \langle 7_{[3]}\rangle) \longrightarrow \left\{ \begin{array}{l} \quad 7\ \bar{1}\ 0_{[3]} \\ \hline \quad\quad \bar{2}_{[3]} \end{array} \right.
$$

$$
\boldsymbol{\alpha}^{[4]}(\langle -1_{[3]}\rangle, \langle 7_{[3]}\rangle) \longrightarrow \left\{ \begin{array}{l} \quad 7\ 7\ \bar{1}\ 0_{[3]} \\ \hline \quad \bar{3}_{[3]} \end{array} \right.
$$

$$
\boldsymbol{\alpha}^{[5]}(\langle -1_{[3]}\rangle, \langle 7_{[3]}\rangle) \longrightarrow \left\{ \begin{array}{l} \quad 0\ 7\ 7\ \bar{1}\ 0_{[3]} \\ \hline \quad \bar{1}_{[3]} \end{array} \right.
$$

$$
\boldsymbol{\alpha}^{[6]}(\langle -1_{[3]}\rangle, \langle 7_{[3]}\rangle) \longrightarrow \left\{ \begin{array}{l} \bar{1}\ 0\ 7\ 7\ \bar{1}\ 0_{[3]} \\ \hline \quad 0_{[3]} \end{array} \right.
$$

Example 9.5.5

Let α be the base 3 addition mapping on $\{\bar{2}, \bar{1}, 0, 1, 2, 3, 4\} \times \{\bar{1}, 0, 4\}$ with the addition table shown, and note that $K_\alpha(\langle -1_{[3]}, -1_{[3]}\rangle) = \infty$.

Base 3

	$\bar{1}$	0	4
$\bar{2}$	$\bar{1}0$	$\bar{2}4$	$\bar{1}\bar{1}$
$\bar{1}$	$\bar{2}4$	$0\bar{1}$	10
0	$0\bar{1}$	00	04
1	00	$\bar{1}4$	$2\bar{1}$
2	$\bar{1}4$	$1\bar{1}$	20
3	$1\bar{1}$	10	14
4	10	04	$3\bar{1}$

$$\alpha^{[0]}(\langle -1_{[3]}, -1_{[3]}\rangle) \longrightarrow \left\{\begin{array}{l} \bar{1}_{[3]} \\ \hline \bar{1}_{[3]} \end{array}\right.$$

$$\alpha^{[1]}(\langle -1_{[3]}, -1_{[3]}\rangle) \longrightarrow \left\{\begin{array}{l} 4_{[3]} \\ \hline \bar{2}_{[3]} \end{array}\right.$$

$$\alpha^{[2]}(\langle -1_{[3]}, -1_{[3]}\rangle) \longrightarrow \left\{\begin{array}{l} 4\,4_{[3]} \\ \hline \bar{2}_{[3]} \end{array}\right.$$

$$\alpha^{[3]}(\langle -1_{[3]}, -1_{[3]}\rangle) \longrightarrow \left\{\begin{array}{l} 4\,4\,4_{[3]} \\ \hline \bar{2}_{[3]} \end{array}\right.$$

$$\vdots$$

The following fundamental theorem guarantees the suitability of the use of addition tables to implement addition in $\mathscr{P}[\beta, D]$ when D is a basic digit set for base β. The general proof is too involved for inclusion here, but several special cases of interest are treated in the exercises.

Theorem 9.5.6 (Carry Absorption Theorem)

Let D be a digit set which is basic for base β. Let C be the minimal carry digit set for which an addition mapping $\alpha: C \times D \to C \times D$ is defined. Then for $P, Q \in \mathscr{P}[\beta, D]$, $P \neq 0$, $Q \neq 0$,

$$K_\alpha(P, Q) \leq \max\{\deg(P), \deg(Q)\} - \max\{1\mathrm{sp}(P), 1\mathrm{sp}(Q)\} + k_D \qquad (9.5.14)$$

where k_D is a constant depending on D but independent of P and Q.

The carry absorption theorem guarantees the finiteness of radix polynomial addition for basic digit sets, so the next question concerns the inherent efficiency of this procedure. The carry ripple phenomena observed for standard decimal representation when 1 is added to 99 . . .9 is now shown to be an inherent property for addition in $\mathscr{P}[\beta, D]$ when D is basic for base β.

Theorem 9.5.7 (Carry Ripple Theorem)

Let D be a digit set which is basic for base β. Let C be the minimal carry digit set for which an addition mapping $\alpha: C \times D \to C \times D$ is defined. Then for any $n \geq 1$, there exist radix integers $P, Q \in \mathscr{P}_I[\beta, D]$ such that $\deg(P) \leq n$, $\deg(Q) \leq n$, and

$$K_\alpha(P, Q) \geq n + 2 \qquad (9.5.15)$$

Proof: For a particular $d \in D, d \neq 0$, let $R_i \in \mathscr{P}_I[\beta, D]$ be a radix integer of value id for each $i \geq 1$. Since D is basic for base β, these R_i are uniquely determined. Note that $R_1 = d \times [\beta]^0$, so $\deg(R_1) = 1\mathrm{sp}(R_1) = 0$. For $n \geq 1$, let j be the largest index such that $\deg(R_i) \leq n$ for $i \leq j$, so then $\deg(R_{j+1}) > n$. Let $K_\alpha(R_1, R_j) = m$, and since $\| R_i \| = id$ for all $i \geq 1$,

$$\boldsymbol{\alpha}^{[m]}(R_1, R_j) = (0, R_{j+1})$$

Let

$$\boldsymbol{\alpha}^{[k]}(R_1, R_j) = (P_k, Q_k) \qquad \text{for } 0 \leq k \leq m - 1$$

Since D is basic for base β, the addition mapping $\alpha\colon C \times D \to C \times D$ must have $\alpha(0, d) = (0, d)$ for all $d \in D$. It follows that

$$\deg(P_k) = 1\mathrm{sp}(P_k) = k \qquad \text{for } 0 \leq k \leq m - 1$$
$$\deg(Q_k) = \deg(R_j) \leq n \qquad \text{for } 0 \leq k \leq \deg(R_j)$$
$$\deg(Q_k) < \deg(P_k) \qquad \text{for } \deg(R_j) < k \leq m - 1$$

Hence

$$n < \deg(R_{j+1}) \leq \max \{\deg(P_{m-1}), \; \deg(Q_{m-1})\} \leq \max \{m - 1, n\}$$

so $m \geq n + 2$, that is, $K_\alpha(R_1, R_j) \geq n + 2$. ∎

For both standard base β sign-magnitude and radix-complement radix representation the carry ripple phenomenon is known to occur upon addition of unity to an integer, $\beta^n - 1$, composed of n digits of value $\beta - 1$ for any n. When a basic digit set is used for signed-digit or negative base radix representation, theorems 9.5.6 and 9.5.7 imply that the carry ripple phenomenon will still be present to restrict worse case add time to an amount depending on the number of digits in the operands. Thus the joint conditions of completeness and nonredundancy in radix representation are sufficiently restrictive so that serial delays will always be expected for addition. If the nonredundancy condition is relaxed, the situation is remarkably different!

Example 9.5.6

Let α and γ be the base 3 addition mappings on $B_5 \times B_5$ with addition tables as shown in Table 9.5.4.

$$Q \longrightarrow \qquad 2\,\bar{1}\,0\,2\,0\,1_{[3]}$$
$$P \longrightarrow \qquad \underline{\bar{1}\,\bar{2}\,2\,2\,0_{[3]}}$$

$$\boldsymbol{\alpha}(P, Q) \longrightarrow \left\{ \begin{array}{l} \bar{1}\,1\,1\,1\,\bar{1}\,1_{[3]} \longleftarrow \text{sum} \\ \underline{1\,\bar{1}\,\bar{1}\,1\,1\,0_{[3]}} \longleftarrow \text{carry} \end{array} \right.$$

$$\gamma(\boldsymbol{\alpha}(P, Q)) \longrightarrow \left\{ \begin{array}{l} 1\,\bar{2}\,0\,2\,2\,\bar{1}\,1_{[3]} \longleftarrow \text{sum} \\ 0\,0\,0\,0\,0\,0\,0_{[3]} \longleftarrow \text{carry} \end{array} \right.$$

Thus $\langle 1\bar{2}022\bar{1}1_{[3]} \rangle \in \mathscr{S}[3, B_5]$ is a radix polynomial whose value is the sum of the values of $\langle 2\bar{1}0201_{[3]} \rangle$ and $\langle \bar{1}\bar{2}220_{[3]} \rangle$.

Example 9.5.6 is an instance of an important result due to Avizienis [1]. It is evident from the addition table for α in Table 9.5.4 that if $P_0, Q_0 \in \mathscr{S}[3, B_5]$ with $\boldsymbol{\alpha}(P_0, Q_0) = (P_1, Q_1)$, then $P_1, Q_1 \in \mathscr{S}[3, B_3]$. Furthermore, the addition table for γ then guarantees that $\gamma(P_1, Q_1) = (0, R)$ with $R \in \mathscr{S}[3, B_5]$. Thus the redundancy in the digit set has provided the opportunity to construct a two-step addition process which allows completion of addition in a time independent of the number of digits in the operands.

In general, the choice of $\beta + 2$ appropriate digit values for base $\beta \geq 3$ can allow such a parallel digit by digit two-step implementation of addition for arbitary precision in fixed cycle time. The following theorem is derived from the work of Avizienis [1].

Theorem 9.5.8

For $\beta \geq 3$, and $-\beta + 1 \leq d_{\min} \leq -2$, let $D = \{d_{\min}, d_{\min} + 1, d_{\min} + 2, \ldots, d_{\min} + \beta + 1\}$. There exist base β addition mappings $\alpha: D \times D \to D \times D$ and $\gamma: D \times D \to D \times D$ such that for any $P, Q \in \mathscr{S}[\beta, D]$,

$$\gamma(\boldsymbol{\alpha}(P, Q)) = (0, R) \qquad \text{where } R \in \mathscr{S}[\beta, D] \qquad (9.5.16)$$

Proof: The digit set $D' = \{d_{\min} + 1, d_{\min} + 2, \ldots, d_{\min} + \beta\}$ is basic for base β by Corollary 9.4.6. Thus the addition mapping $\alpha: D \times D \to D \times D$ can be uniquely determined by requiring that α map $D \times D$ into $\{-1, 0, 1\} \times D'$. The addition mapping $\gamma: D \times D \to D \times D$ can then be defined so that $\gamma(c, s) = (0, c + s)$ for any $c \in \{-1, 0, 1\}, s \in D'$, the rest of γ agreeing with α. Then for arbitrary $P, Q \in \mathscr{S}[\beta, D]$,

$$\boldsymbol{\alpha}(P, Q) = (P_1, Q_1) \qquad \text{where } P_1 \in \mathscr{S}[\beta, B_3], Q_1 \in \mathscr{S}[\beta, D']$$
$$\gamma(P_1, Q_1) = (0, R) \qquad \text{where } R \in \mathscr{S}[\beta, D] \qquad \blacksquare$$

Example 9.5.7

The addition tables for the decimal addition mappings α and γ for the redundant decimal digit set $D = \{-2, -1, 0, 1, 2, 3, 4, 5, 6, 7, 8, 9\}$ where $\gamma(\boldsymbol{\alpha}(P, Q)) = (0, R)$ for any $P, Q \in \mathscr{S}[10, D]$ are shown along with an application. Only the relevant portion of γ is shown.

α D Base 10

D	-2	-1	0	1	2	3	4	5	6	7	8	9
-2	$\bar{1}6$	$\bar{1}7$	$\bar{1}8$	$0\bar{1}$	00	01	02	03	04	05	06	07
-1	$\bar{1}7$	$\bar{1}8$	$0\bar{1}$	00	01	02	03	04	05	06	07	08
0	$\bar{1}8$	$0\bar{1}$	00	01	02	03	04	05	06	07	08	$1\bar{1}$
1	$0\bar{1}$	00	01	02	03	04	05	06	07	08	$1\bar{1}$	10
2	00	01	02	03	04	05	06	07	08	$1\bar{1}$	10	11
3	01	02	03	04	05	06	07	08	$1\bar{1}$	10	11	12
4	02	03	04	05	06	07	08	$1\bar{1}$	10	11	12	13
5	03	04	05	06	07	08	$1\bar{1}$	10	11	12	13	14
6	04	05	06	07	08	$1\bar{1}$	10	11	12	13	14	15
7	05	06	07	08	$1\bar{1}$	10	11	12	13	14	15	16
8	06	07	08	$1\bar{1}$	10	11	12	13	14	15	16	17
9	07	08	$1\bar{1}$	10	11	12	13	14	15	16	17	18

γ Base 10

	-1	0	1	2	3	4	5	6	7	8
-1	$0\bar{2}$	$0\bar{1}$	00	01	02	03	04	05	06	07
0	$0\bar{1}$	00	01	02	03	04	05	06	07	08
1	00	01	02	03	04	05	06	07	08	09

$$Q \longrightarrow \quad 3\ 2\ \bar{5}\ 6\ \bar{2}\ 4_{[10]}$$

$$P \longrightarrow \quad \underline{9\ 6\ 8\ 3\ \bar{2}\ 1_{[10]}}$$

$$\alpha(P, Q) \longrightarrow \quad \begin{cases} 3\ 1\ 1\ 7\ \bar{1}\ 6\ 5_{[10]} & \longleftarrow \text{ sum} \\ 0\ 1\ 1\ 0\ 1\ \bar{1}\ 0_{[10]} & \longleftarrow \text{ carry} \end{cases}$$

$$\gamma(\alpha(P, Q)) \longrightarrow \quad \begin{cases} 4\ 2\ 1\ 8\ \bar{2}\ 6\ 5_{[10]} & \longleftarrow \text{ sum} \\ 0\ 0\ 0\ 0\ 0\ 0\ 0_{[10]} & \longleftarrow \text{ carry} \end{cases}$$

Limiting the redundancy to the presence of just one extra digit, it is still possible to complete radix polynomial addition in just three steps. The following theorem is also based on Avizienis [1].

Theorem 9.5.9

For $\beta \geq 2$, and $-\beta + 1 \leq d_{\min} \leq -1$, let $D = \{d_{\min}, d_{\min} + 1, \ldots, d_{\min} + \beta\}$. There exist base β addition mappings $\alpha: D \times D \to D \times D$, $\gamma: D \times D \to D \times D$, and $\theta: D \times D \to D \times D$ such that for any $P, Q \in \mathcal{P}[\beta, D]$,

$$\theta(\gamma(\alpha(P, Q))) = (0, R) \qquad \text{where } R \in \mathscr{S}[\beta, D] \qquad (9.5.17)$$

Proof: Let $D' = D - \{d_{\min}\}$, $D'' = D - \{d_{\min} + \beta\}$, and note that both D' and D'' are complete residue systems modulo β. Let α and γ each be uniquely determined by requiring that α be into $\{-1, 0, 1\} \times D'$ and γ be into $\{-1, 0, 1\} \times D''$. Let $\theta(c, s) = (0, c + s)$ for $c \in \{0, 1\}$, $s \in D''$, the rest of θ agreeing with α. Then for arbitrary $P, Q \in \mathscr{S}[\beta, D]$,

$$\alpha(P, Q) = (P_1, Q_1) \qquad \text{where } P_1 \in \mathscr{S}[\beta, B_3], Q_1 \in \mathscr{S}[\beta, D']$$

$$\gamma(P_1, Q_1) = (P_2, Q_2) \qquad \text{where } P_2 \in \mathscr{S}[\beta, \{0, 1\}], Q_2 \in \mathscr{S}[\beta, D'']$$

$$\theta(P_2, Q_2) = (0, R) \qquad \text{where } R \in \mathscr{S}[\beta, D] \quad \blacksquare$$

Example 9.5.8

The addition tables for the binary addition mappings α, γ, and θ for the redundant binary digit set $B_{[3]} = \{-1, 0, 1\}$ where $\theta(\gamma(\alpha(P, Q))) = (0, R)$ for any $P, Q \in \mathscr{S}[2, B_{[3]}]$ are shown along with an application. Only the relevant portion of the addition tables for γ and θ are shown.

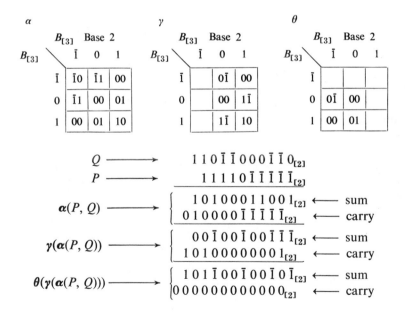

The implications of Theorems 9.5.8 and 9.5.9 for the arithmetic computer architect are important. By implicitly trading off some storage capacity to redundant representation, it is possible to gain the ability to utilize parallelism on a digit by digit basis so as to effect arbitrary precision addition in fixed cycle time.

9.5.6. Radix Polynomial Subtraction

Subtraction in $\mathscr{P}[\beta, D]$ can be implemented utilizing the theory of base β addition mappings. For the digit set D let $\bar{D} = \{-d \mid d \in D\}$. Subtraction in $\mathscr{P}[\beta, D]$ will utilize the base β addition mapping $\alpha \colon C \times S \to C \times S$ where $\bar{S} \subset C$. In particular, if $C = \bar{S}$, then the addition mapping $\alpha \colon \bar{S} \times S \to \bar{S} \times S$ is termed a *regular base β subtraction mapping*. Addition tables for the standard binary and octal subtraction mappings are shown in Table 9.5.5.

Table 9.5.5 ADDITION TABLES FOR THE STANDARD (A) BINARY AND (B) OCTAL SUBTRACTION
MAPPINGS

(a)

$\bar{D}_2$	D_2 Base 2	
	0	1
$\bar{1}$	$\bar{1}1$	00
0	00	01

(b)

$\bar{D}_8$	D_8 Base 8							
	0	1	2	3	4	5	6	7
$\bar{7}$	$\bar{1}1$	$\bar{1}2$	$\bar{1}3$	$\bar{1}4$	$\bar{1}5$	$\bar{1}6$	$\bar{1}7$	00
$\bar{6}$	$\bar{1}2$	$\bar{1}3$	$\bar{1}4$	$\bar{1}5$	$\bar{1}6$	$\bar{1}7$	00	01
$\bar{5}$	$\bar{1}3$	$\bar{1}4$	$\bar{1}5$	$\bar{1}6$	$\bar{1}7$	00	01	02
$\bar{4}$	$\bar{1}4$	$\bar{1}5$	$\bar{1}6$	$\bar{1}7$	00	01	02	03
$\bar{3}$	$\bar{1}5$	$\bar{1}6$	$\bar{1}7$	00	01	02	03	04
$\bar{2}$	$\bar{1}6$	$\bar{1}7$	00	01	02	03	04	05
$\bar{1}$	$\bar{1}7$	00	01	02	03	04	05	06
0	00	01	02	03	04	05	06	07

Let $\alpha \colon \bar{S} \times S \to \bar{S} \times S$ be a regular base β subtraction mapping. For P_1, $P_2 \in \mathscr{P}[\beta, S]$, the determination of $Q \in V_\beta(\|P_1 - P_2\|) \cap \mathscr{P}[\beta, S]$ proceeds by applying α to the pair $-P_2 \in \mathscr{P}[\beta, \bar{S}]$, $P_1 \in \mathscr{P}[\beta, S]$.

Example 9.5.9

Let $\alpha_8 \colon \bar{D}_8 \times D_8 \to \bar{D}_8 \times D_8$ be the standard octal subtraction mapping with addition table shown in Table 9.5.5. Let $P_1 = \langle 423602_{[8]} \rangle \in \mathscr{P}[8, D_8]$, $P_2 = \langle 327711_{[8]} \rangle \in \mathscr{P}[8, D_8]$.

$$\alpha_8^{[0]}(-P_2, P_1) \longrightarrow \begin{cases} 4\,2\,3\,6\,0\,2_{[8]} \\ \bar{3}\,\bar{2}\,\bar{7}\,\bar{7}\,\bar{1}\,\bar{1}_{[8]} \end{cases}$$

$$\alpha_8^{[1]}(-P_2, P_1) \longrightarrow \begin{cases} 1\,0\,4\,7\,7\,1_{[8]} \longleftarrow \text{sum} \\ 0\,0\,\bar{1}\,\bar{1}\,\bar{1}\,0_{[8]} \longleftarrow \text{carry} \end{cases}$$

$$\alpha_8^{[2]}(-P_2, P_1) \longrightarrow \begin{cases} 1\,7\,3\,6\,7\,1_{[8]} \longleftarrow \text{sum} \\ 0\,\bar{1}\,0\,0\,0\,0_{[8]} \longleftarrow \text{carry} \end{cases}$$

$$\alpha_8^{[3]}(-P_2, P_1) \longrightarrow \begin{cases} 0\,7\,3\,6\,7\,1_{[8]} \longleftarrow \text{sum} \\ 0\,0\,0\,0\,0\,0_{[8]} \longleftarrow \text{carry} \end{cases}$$

Thus $Q = \langle 73671_{[8]} \rangle \in \mathscr{S}[8, D_8]$ is the desired result.

For sign-magnitude representation it is necessary to know that $\| P_1 - P_2 \| \geq 0$ for the procedure of Example 9.5.9 to terminate, that is, for $K_\alpha(-P_2, P_1)$ to be finite. This may be checked by a separate comparison of P_1 and P_2, providing that a separate algorithm for this process is available. An alternative is to simultaneously compute for each n both $\alpha^{[n]}(-P_2, P_1)$ and $\alpha^{[n]}(-P_1, P_2)$, and the first (and only) to terminate determines the result and indicates the appropriate sign for the sign-magnitude representation.

It may be necessary to extend the carry digit set C beyond $\bar{S}$ in order to allow an addition mapping $\alpha: C \times S \to C \times S$ to be defined for effecting subtraction in $\mathscr{S}[\beta, S]$. The procedure for determining such a C and α is the same as for addition mappings as described prior to the statement of Theorem 9.5.4.

Example 9.5.10

Let $\alpha_{\bar{4}}: C \times D_4 \to C \times D_4$ be the addition mapping for effecting subtraction in $\mathscr{S}[-4, D_4]$ given by the addition table shown. For $P_1 = \langle 3201_{[-4]} \rangle \in \mathscr{S}[-4, D_4]$, $P_2 = \langle 303_{[-4]} \rangle \in \mathscr{S}[-4, D_4]$, $P_1 - P_2$ is computed in $\mathscr{S}[-4, D_4]$ as follows.

Thus $\langle 130312_{[-4]} \rangle \in V_{-4}(\| \langle 3201_{[-4]} \rangle - \langle 303_{[-4]} \rangle \|) \cap \mathscr{S}[-4, D_4]$ is the desired result.

Note that the utilization of a balanced digit set obviates the need for separate addition tables to affect addition and subtraction. A redundant balanced digit set such as B_5 for base 3 thus allows for a single addition/subtraction table and, through parallelism, for arbitrary precision addition/subtraction in fixed cycle time. Similarly the balanced digit set B_{11} for base 10 has these properties. Since decimal arithmetic is generally implemented with four bits available to encode each digit, the space is already available to encode a redundant decimal digit set and thereby simplify the arithmetic architecture.

9.5.7. Block Addition

Let $D^{(n)}$ be the n-dimensional Cartesian product of the digit set D. An *n-dimensional base β addition mapping* α is a mapping of $D^{(n)}$ to $D^{(2)}$ such that if $(s_1, s_2, \ldots, s_n) \in D^{(n)}$ and $\alpha(s_1, s_2, \ldots, s_n) = (c, s)$, then

$$s_1 + s_2 + \ldots + s_n = c\beta + s \qquad (9.5.18)$$

The corresponding *n-dimensional radix polynomial base β addition mapping* $\alpha : \mathscr{P}[\beta, D]^{(n)} \longrightarrow \mathscr{P}[\beta, D]^{(2)}$ is defined so that if $(P_1, P_2, \ldots, P_n) \in \mathscr{P}[\beta, D]^{(n)}$ and $\alpha(P_1, P_2, \ldots, P_n) = (T_1, Q_1)$, then the digits of Q_1 and T_1 are determined by

$$\alpha(d_i(P_1), d_i(P_2), \ldots, d_i(P_n)) = (d_{i+1}(T_1), d_i(Q_1)) \qquad \text{for all } i \quad (9.5.19)$$

It follows immediately from the definitions and the structure of real arithmetic that if $\alpha(P_1, P_2, \ldots, P_n) = (T_1, Q_1)$, then

$$\|P_1 + P_2 + \ldots + P_n\| = \|T_1 + Q_1\| \qquad (9.5.20)$$

Example 9.5.11

For $\mathscr{P}[3, B_3]$, a unique 4-dimensional base 3 addition mapping $\alpha : B_3^{(4)} \rightarrow B_3^{(2)}$ is determined by Eq. (9.5.18). Let $P_1, P_2, P_3, P_4 \in \mathscr{P}[3, B_3]$ be given as shown, and $\alpha(P_1, P_2, P_3, P_4) = (T_1, Q_1)$ is thus computed.

$$
\begin{aligned}
P_1 &\rightarrow & 1\,0\,\bar{1}\,\bar{1}\,\bar{1}_{[3]} \\
P_2 &\rightarrow & 1\,\bar{1}\,\bar{1}\,1_{[3]} \\
P_3 &\rightarrow & 1\,\bar{1}\,1\,\bar{1}\,0\,1_{[3]} \\
P_4 &\rightarrow & \underline{1\,0\,1\,\bar{1}\,1\,1_{[3]}} \\
\alpha(P_1, P_2, P_3, P_4) = (T_1, Q_1) \qquad Q_1 &\rightarrow & \bar{1}\,0\,0\,\bar{1}\,\bar{1}\,\bar{1}_{[3]} \leftarrow \text{sum} \\
T_1 &\rightarrow & 1\,0\,1\,\bar{1}\,0\,1_{[3]} \leftarrow \text{carry}
\end{aligned}
$$

The 4-dimensional addition mapping of Example 9.5.11 may then be applied to $T_1, Q_1 \in \mathscr{P}[3, B_3]$, it being assumed that when less than four arguments occur, the others are taken to be the zero polynomial. Thus $\alpha(T_1, Q_1) = (0, \langle 1\bar{1}1\bar{1}\bar{1}0\bar{1}_{[3]}\rangle)$, and the addition is completed.

The existence of a large class of n-dimensional base β addition mappings $\alpha : D^{(n)} \rightarrow D^{(2)}$ for a variety of n, β, and D are established in the following theorem.

Theorem 9.5.10

For $-\beta + 1 \leq d_{min} \leq -1$, $d_{max} = d_{min} + \beta - 1$, let $D = \{d_{min}, d_{min} + 1, \ldots, d_{max}\}$, so that D is basic for base β. Then there exists an n-dimensional base β addition mapping $\alpha : D^{(n)} \longrightarrow D^{(2)}$ for $2 \leq n \leq \beta + 1$.

Proof: For $(s_1, s_2, \ldots, s_n) \in D^{(n)}$, let $k = s_1 + s_2 + \ldots + s_n$. Then $nd_{min} \leq k \leq nd_{max}$, and let c, s be chosen so that $k = c\beta + s$ for $s \in D$. Then

$$c = \frac{k - s}{\beta} \leq \frac{nd_{max} - s}{\beta} \leq \frac{\beta d_{max} + (d_{max} - s)}{\beta} \leq d_{max} + \frac{\beta - 1}{\beta}$$

$$c = \frac{k - s}{\beta} \geq \frac{nd_{min} - s}{\beta} \geq \frac{\beta d_{min} + (d_{min} - s)}{\beta} \geq d_{min} - \frac{\beta - 1}{\beta}$$

Thus $d_{min} \leq c \leq d_{max}$, so $c \in D$. Hence $\alpha : D^{(n)} \longrightarrow D^{(2)}$ exists and is uniquely determined for $2 \leq n \leq \beta + 1$. ∎

Let $\alpha : \mathscr{P}[\beta, D]^{(n)} \longrightarrow \mathscr{P}[\beta, D]^{(2)}$ be an n-dimensional radix polynomial base β addition mapping, and let $P_1, P_2, \ldots, P_m$ be a string of radix polynomials with $P_i \in \mathscr{P}[\beta, D]$ for $1 \leq i \leq m$. Then the application of α to the string $P_1, P_2, \ldots, P_m$ shall mean the application of α to the initial n terms of the string yielding (T_1, Q_1) to which the remainder of the original string is concatenated. Thus

$$\alpha(P_1, P_2, \ldots, P_m) = T_1, Q_1, P_{n+1}, P_{n+2}, \ldots, P_m \qquad (9.5.21)$$

and for composite application

$$\alpha^{[0]}(P_1, P_2, \ldots, P_m) = P_1, P_2, \ldots, P_m$$

$$\alpha^{[k]}(P_1, P_2, \ldots, P_m) = \alpha^{[k-1]}(\alpha(P_1, P_2, \ldots, P_m)) \qquad (9.5.22)$$

Thus if α is 4-dimensional and is applied recursively to a string of length eight,

$$\alpha(P_1, P_2, P_3, P_4, P_5, P_6, P_7, P_8) = T_1, Q_1, P_5, P_6, P_7, P_8,$$

$$\alpha(T_1, Q_1, P_5, P_6, P_7, P_8) = T_2, Q_2, P_7, P_8$$

$$\alpha(T_2, Q_2, P_7, P_8) = T_3, Q_3.$$

Example 9.5.12

Let $\alpha : B_3^{(4)} \longrightarrow B_3^{(2)}$ be the unique 4-dimensional base 3 addition mapping. Let $\boldsymbol{\alpha}$ be applied to the string $P_1, P_2, \ldots, P_8$ of radix polynomials of $\mathscr{P}[3, B_3]$.

$$
\begin{array}{rl}
P_1 \rightarrow & 1\ 0\ 1\ \bar{1}\ 1_{[3]} \\
P_2 \rightarrow & 1\ 1\ 0\ \bar{1}_{[3]} \\
P_3 \rightarrow & 1\ 1\ 1_{[3]} \\
P_4 \rightarrow & \underline{1\ 0\ 1\ \bar{1}\ \bar{1}_{[3]}}
\end{array}
$$

$$
\boldsymbol{\alpha}(P_1, P_2, P_3, P_4) \rightarrow \begin{cases} Q_1 \rightarrow & \bar{1}\ 1\ 1\ \bar{1}\ 0_{[3]} \leftarrow \text{sum} \\ T_1 \rightarrow & 1\ 0\ 1\ 0\ 0_{[3]} \leftarrow \text{carry} \end{cases}
$$

$$
\begin{array}{rl}
P_5 \rightarrow & 1\ 1\ \bar{1}\ \bar{1}\ \bar{1}_{[3]} \\
P_6 \rightarrow & \underline{1\ 0\ \bar{1}\ 1\ 1\ 0_{[3]}}
\end{array}
$$

$$
\boldsymbol{\alpha}(T_1, Q_1, P_5, P_6) \rightarrow \begin{cases} Q_2 \rightarrow & \bar{1}\ 0\ \bar{1}\ 1\ \bar{1}\ \bar{1}_{[3]} \leftarrow \text{sum} \\ T_2 \rightarrow & 1\ 0\ 1\ 0\ 0\ 0_{[3]} \leftarrow \text{carry} \end{cases}
$$

$$
\begin{array}{rl}
P_7 \rightarrow & 1\ 0\ 0\ \bar{1}\ \bar{1}_{[3]} \\
P_8 \rightarrow & \underline{1\ 1\ 1\ 1\ 0\ 0_{[3]}}
\end{array}
$$

$$
\boldsymbol{\alpha}(T_2, Q_2, P_7, P_8) \rightarrow \begin{cases} Q_3 \rightarrow & 1\ 0\ 0\ 0\ \bar{1}\ 1\ 1_{[3]} \leftarrow \text{sum} \\ T_3 \rightarrow & 0\ 0\ 1\ 0\ 1\ \bar{1}\ \bar{1}_{[3]} \leftarrow \text{carry} \end{cases}
$$

$$
\boldsymbol{\alpha}(T_3, Q_3) \rightarrow \begin{cases} Q_4 \rightarrow & 1\ 1\ 0\ 1\ 1\ 0\ 1_{[3]} \leftarrow \text{sum} \\ T_4 \rightarrow & 0\ 0\ 0\ 0\ \bar{1}\ 0\ 0_{[3]} \leftarrow \text{carry} \end{cases}
$$

$$
\boldsymbol{\alpha}(T_4, Q_4) \rightarrow \begin{cases} Q_5 \rightarrow & 1\ 1\ 0\ 0\ 1\ 0\ 1_{[3]} \leftarrow \text{sum} \\ T_5 \rightarrow & 0\ 0\ 0\ 0\ 0\ 0\ 0_{[3]} \leftarrow \text{carry} \end{cases}
$$

Hence

$$
\boldsymbol{\alpha}^{[3]}(P_1, P_2, \ldots, P_8) = (\langle 101\bar{1}\bar{1}0_{[3]} \rangle, \langle 1000\bar{1}11_{[3]} \rangle)
$$

and

$$
\boldsymbol{\alpha}^{[5]}(P_1, P_2, \ldots, P_8) = (0, \langle 1100101_{[3]} \rangle)
$$

Note that if $\boldsymbol{\alpha}$ is an n-dimensional base β addition mapping for $n \geq 3$ and if $\boldsymbol{\alpha}$ is applied recursively to a string of radix polynomials of length m, then $\boldsymbol{\alpha}^{[k]}$ must reduce this string to length two for

$$
k = \left\lceil \frac{m - 2}{n - 2} \right\rceil
$$

The additional number of steps to reduce this string to one radix polynomial can depend on the number of digits in the resulting radix polynomials if a basic digit set is used, or it can be completed in a fixed number of addition steps if redundancy is present and different addition mappings exploiting the redundancy are utilized as previously described.

Parallelism may be utilized to further reduce the cycle time for adding a string of radix polynomials as illustrated in Fig. 9.5.1 for a 4-dimensional addition mapping applied to a string of 16 radix polynomials.

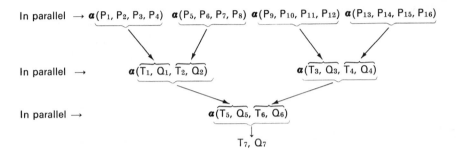

Fig. 9.5.1 Reduction of the sum of 16 radix polynomials of $\mathscr{P}[\beta, D]$ to the sum of two radix polynomials of $\mathscr{P}[\beta, D]$ by a series of three parallel groups of applications of the 4-dimensional base β addition mapping $\alpha: D^{(4)} \to D^{(2)}$.

In general, if $\lceil m/n \rceil$ simultaneous applications of the n-dimensional addition mapping α are made to a string of radix polynomials of length m, then the sum of these m radix polynomials is reduced to the sum of $\lceil m/n \rceil \times 2$ radix polynomials.

Thus, through parallelism, the sum of m radix polynomials can be reduced to the sum of two radix polynomials in a cycle time proportional to log m and this is obtained whether a basic or redundant digit set is used. To further reduce this sum to a single radix polynomial requires a cycle time proportional to the number of digits in the radix polynomials if a basic digit set is used, or a fixed cycle time if appropriate redundant digit sets are utilized.

9.5.8 Multiplication Tables

The fundamental tool for effecting multiplication of radix polynomials having limited digit values is the multiplication table. This table describes a mapping which gives the product and carry digits resulting from the multiplication of pairs of specific digit values. For the digit set C, termed the *carry digit set,* and the digit set S, termed the *product digit set,* the *base β mul-*

tiplication mapping $\chi\colon S \times S \to C \times S$ is defined so that if $(s_1, s_2) \in S \times S$ and $\chi(s_1, s_2) = (c, s)$, then

$$s_1 \times s_2 = c\beta + s \qquad (9.5.23)$$

The resulting digit $s \in S$ is referred to as the *product digit* and $c \in C$ is referred to as the *carry digit* of the base β multiplication mapping of s_1 and s_2. If $C = S$, the multiplication mapping is termed *regular*.

The base β multiplication mapping may be displayed in table form as a *multiplication table*, where each entry (c, s) of the table is written as a string, cs. Table 9.5.6 shows the familiar multiplication tables for standard octal $C = S = D_8$, standard binary $C = S = D_2$, and balanced ternary $C = S = B_3$, all of which are regular.

Table 9.5.6 MULTIPLICATION TABLES FOR (A) STANDARD OCTAL, (B) STANDARD BINARY, (C) BALANCED TERNARY

(a) D_8 Base 8

D_8	0	1	2	3	4	5	6	7
0	00	00	00	00	00	00	00	00
1	00	01	02	03	04	05	06	07
2	00	02	04	06	10	12	14	16
3	00	03	06	11	14	17	22	25
4	00	04	10	14	20	24	30	34
5	00	05	12	17	24	31	36	43
6	00	06	14	22	30	36	44	52
7	00	07	16	25	34	43	52	61

(b) D_2 Base 2

D_2	0	1
0	00	00
1	00	01

(c) B_3 Base 3

B_3	$\bar{1}$	0	1
$\bar{1}$	01	00	0$\bar{1}$
0	00	00	00
1	0$\bar{1}$	00	01

Note that the carry digits are all zero for both standard binary and balanced ternary. It is this feature which allows the simplified recursive shift and add implementation of multiplication for standard binary and the recursive shift and add/subtract implementation of multiplication for balanced ternary.

For nonbinary negative base radix systems the multiplication table is nonregular. The base $\beta \le -3$ multiplication mapping $\chi\colon D_{|\beta|} \times D_{|\beta|} \to C \times D_{|\beta|}$ requires that $C = D_{|\beta|} \cup \{(\beta + 2), (\beta + 1), \ldots, -1\}$. The multiplication table for the standard base -4 radix system is shown in Table 9.5.7, along with the multiplication table for a base 3 multiplication mapping $\chi\colon B_5 \times B_5 \to B_5 \times B_5$ for a redundant balanced ternary system.

Table 9.5.7 MULTIPLICATION TABLES FOR (A) STANDARD BASE NEGATIVE FOUR, (B) BALANCED REDUNDANT TERNARY

(a) D_4 Base -4

D_4	0	1	2	3
0	00	00	00	00
1	00	01	02	03
2	00	02	$\bar{1}$0	$\bar{1}$2
3	00	03	$\bar{1}$2	$\bar{2}$1

(b) B_5 Base 3

B_5	$\bar{2}$	$\bar{1}$	0	1	2
$\bar{2}$	11	1$\bar{1}$	00	$\bar{1}$1	$\bar{1}\bar{1}$
$\bar{1}$	1$\bar{1}$	01	00	0$\bar{1}$	$\bar{1}$1
0	00	00	00	00	00
1	$\bar{1}$1	0$\bar{1}$	00	01	1$\bar{1}$
2	$\bar{1}\bar{1}$	$\bar{1}$1	00	1$\bar{1}$	11

9.5.9. Radix Polynomial Multiplication

The extension of base β multiplication mappings to pairs of radix polynomials will be considered in two steps. First let

$$\mathscr{S}'[\beta, D] = \{P \mid P \in \mathscr{S}[\beta, D], \deg(P) = 1\mathrm{sp}(P)\} \qquad (9.5.24)$$

that is, $\mathscr{S}'[\beta, D]$ is the set of radix polynomials of $\mathscr{S}[\beta, D]$ possessing just one term, $d[\beta]^i$. Let $\chi: D \times D \to C \times D$ be a base β multiplication mapping. Then the corresponding *radix polynomial base β multiplication mapping* $\pmb{\chi}$: $\mathscr{S}[\beta, D] \times \mathscr{S}'[\beta, D] \to \mathscr{S}[\beta, C] \times \mathscr{S}[\beta, D]$ is defined so that if $P \in \mathscr{S}[\beta, D]$, $d[\beta]^i \in \mathscr{S}'[\beta, D]$, and $\pmb{\chi}(P, d[\beta]^i) = (T, Q)$, then the digits of T and Q are determined by

$$(d_{j+1}(T), d_j(Q)) = \chi(d_{j-i}(P), d) \qquad \text{for all } j \qquad (9.5.25)$$

From these definitions and the structure of the real numbers it follows that if $\pmb{\chi}(P, d[\beta]^i) = (T, Q)$, then

$$\|P \times d[\beta]^i\| = \|T + Q\| \qquad (9.5.26)$$

Example 9.5.13

Let χ be the standard octal multiplication mapping with the table shown in Table 9.5.6, and let α be the standard octal addition mapping.

$$
\begin{array}{rl}
P \to & 3\,2\,4\,7_{[8]} \\[4pt]
d[\beta]^i \to & \underline{\quad 5\,0_{[8]}} \\[4pt]
\pmb{\chi}_8(P, d[\beta]^i) \to & \left\{ \begin{array}{l} 7\,2\,4\,3\,0_{[8]} \\ 1\,1\,2\,4_{[8]} \end{array} \right. \\[10pt]
\alpha_8^{[11]}(\pmb{\chi}(P, d[\beta]^i)) \to & \left\{ \begin{array}{l} 1\,0\,4\,0\,3\,0_{[8]} \\ \underline{0\,1\,0\,1\,0\,0_{[8]}} \end{array} \right.
\end{array}
$$

$$\alpha_8^{[2]}(\mathbf{X}(P, d[\beta]^i)) \longrightarrow \quad \begin{cases} 2\,0\,5\,0\,3\,0_{[8]} \\ 0\,0\,0\,0\,0\,0_{[8]} \end{cases}$$

Thus $\mathbf{X}$ is applied to P and $d[\beta]^i$ to reduce the product to a sum of two radix polynomials, and α is applied recursively to this sum until the single radix polynomial $\langle 205030_{[8]} \rangle$ is determined.

Now $\chi: D \times D \longrightarrow C \times D$ shall be extended to $\mathscr{P}[\beta, D] \times \mathscr{P}[\beta, D]$. Let $\mathscr{P}[\beta, D]^*$ be the set of finite strings of members of $\mathscr{P}[\beta, D]$. Then the corresponding radix polynomial base β multiplication mapping $\mathbf{X}: \mathscr{P}[\beta, D] \times \mathscr{P}[\beta, D] \longrightarrow \mathscr{P}[\beta, C \cup D]^*$ is defined so that for $P_1, P_2 \in \mathscr{P}[\beta, D]$, with

$$P_2 = d_m[\beta]^m + d_{m-1}[\beta]^{m-1} + \ldots + d_l[\beta]^l$$

$$\mathbf{X}(P_1, P_2) = \mathbf{X}(P_1, d_m[\beta]^m), \mathbf{X}(P_1, d_{m-1}[\beta]^{m-1}), \ldots, \mathbf{X}(P_1, d_l[\beta]^l) \quad (9.5.27)$$

Let $\mathbf{X}(P_1, d_{m+1-i}[\beta]^{m+1-i}) = (T_i, Q_i)$ for $1 \leq i \leq m + 1 - l$, then Eq. (9.5.27) may be written as the string

$$\mathbf{X}(P_1, P_2) = T_1, Q_1, T_2, Q_2, \ldots, T_{m+1-l}, Q_{m+1-l} \in \mathscr{P}[\beta, C \cup D]^* \quad (9.5.28)$$

It then follows that

$$\|P_1 \times P_2\| = \| T_1 + Q_1 + T_2 + Q_2 + \ldots + T_{m+1-l} + Q_{m+1-l} \| \quad (9.5.29)$$

Thus the determination of the product of two radix polynomials of $\mathscr{P}[\beta, D]$ has been transformed into the determination of the sum of a string of radix polynomials of $\mathscr{P}[\beta, C \cup D]$, the length of this string being twice the number of digits in the second operand of the product. The second operand may be taken to have the smaller number of digits.

This resulting string of radix polynomials may be efficiently added by the previously described block addition procedures.

Example 9.5.14

Let $\chi: B_5 \times B_5 \longrightarrow B_5 \times B_5$ be the base 3 multiplication mapping defined by Table 9.5.7(b), where actually χ maps into $B_3 \times B_3$. Let $\alpha: B_3^{(4)} \longrightarrow B_3^{(2)}$ be the four-dimensional addition mapping utilized in Example 9.5.11, and let $\gamma: B_5 \times B_5 \longrightarrow B_5 \times B_5$ be the base 3 addition mapping as defined in Table 9.5.4.

$$P_1 \longrightarrow \quad\quad 2\,1\,\bar{2}\,0\,1\,2_{[3]}$$

$$P_2 \longrightarrow \quad\quad \underline{2\,1\,0\,2\,1_{[3]}}$$

$\chi(P_1, 1[\beta]^0) = (T_1, Q_1) \rightarrow$
$\begin{cases} \bar{1}\,1\,1\,0\,1\,\bar{1}_{[3]} & \leftarrow \text{product} \\ 1\,0\,\bar{1}\,0\,0\,1_{[3]} & \leftarrow \text{carry} \end{cases}$

$\chi(P_1, 2[\beta]^1) = (T_2, Q_2) \rightarrow$
$\begin{cases} 1\,\bar{1}\,\bar{1}\,0\,\bar{1}\,1\,0_{[3]} & \leftarrow \text{product} \\ 1\,1\,\bar{1}\,0\,1\,1_{[3]} & \leftarrow \text{carry} \end{cases}$

$\chi(P_1, 1[\beta]^3) = (T_3, Q_3) \rightarrow$
$\begin{cases} \bar{1}\,1\,1\,0\,1\,\bar{1}\,0\,0\,0_{[3]} & \leftarrow \text{product} \\ 1\,0\,\bar{1}\,0\,0\,1_{[3]} & \leftarrow \text{carry} \end{cases}$

$\chi(P_1, 2[\beta]^4) = (T_4, Q_4) \rightarrow$
$\begin{cases} 1\,\bar{1}\,\bar{1}\,0\,\bar{1}\,1\,0\,0\,0\,0_{[3]} & \leftarrow \text{product} \\ 1\,1\,\bar{1}\,0\,1\,1_{[3]} & \leftarrow \text{carry} \end{cases}$

$\alpha(T_1, Q_1, T_2, Q_2) = (R_1, R_2) \rightarrow$
$\begin{cases} 1\,0\,0\,\bar{1}\,\bar{1}\,0\,0\,\bar{1}_{[3]} & \leftarrow \text{sum} \\ 0\,1\,\bar{1}\,0\,1\,0\,1\,0_{[3]} & \leftarrow \text{carry} \end{cases}$

$\alpha(T_3, Q_3, T_4, Q_4) = (R_3, R_4) \rightarrow$
$\begin{cases} 1\,0\,0\,\bar{1}\,\bar{1}\,0\,0\,\bar{1}\,0\,0\,0_{[3]} & \leftarrow \text{sum} \\ 0\,1\,\bar{1}\,0\,1\,0\,1\,0\,0\,0\,0_{[3]} & \leftarrow \text{carry} \end{cases}$

$\alpha(R_1, R_2, R_3, R_4) = (R_5, R_6) \rightarrow$
$\begin{cases} 0\,\bar{1}\,\bar{1}\,0\,1\,1\,1\,0\,1\,1\,0\,\bar{1}_{[3]} & \leftarrow \text{sum} \\ 0\,1\,0\,0\,1\,\bar{1}\,0\,0\,\bar{1}\,0\,0\,0_{[3]} & \leftarrow \text{carry} \end{cases}$

$\gamma(R_5, R_6) = (0, R_7) \rightarrow$
$\begin{cases} 0\,1\,\bar{1}\,\bar{1}\,1\,\bar{2}\,1\,1\,\bar{1}\,1\,1\,0\,\bar{1}_{[3]} & \leftarrow \text{sum} \\ 0\,0\,0\,0\,0\,0\,0\,0\,0\,0\,0\,0_{[3]} & \leftarrow \text{carry} \end{cases}$

Thus χ is applied to P_1, P_2 to generate a string of eight radix polynomials to be summed, and α is applied three times to reduce this string to the sum of two radix polynomials, and finally γ is applied to reduce the sum to a single radix polynomial $\langle 1\bar{1}\bar{1}1\bar{2}11\bar{1}1101\bar{1}_{[3]}\rangle \in \mathscr{F}[3, B_5]$.

Thus radix polynomial multiplication in $\mathscr{F}[\beta, D]$ may be efficiently implemented through the use of multiplication tables and block addition techniques. The cycle time to reduce multiplication to the sum of two polynomials is proportional to the smaller number of digits in the operands by a serially repetitive procedure. Through parallelism, this may be reduced to the logarithm of this number. The final addition can require a cycle time proportional to the number of digits if the digit set utilized is nonredundant; so to improve the order of performance of multiplication through use of parallelism, the use of redundancy in the digit set is required.

EXERCISES 9.5

1. Determine the negative complement, $N(P)$, for the following complement radix polynomials.

(a) $\langle \bar{1}2021.110_{[3]} \rangle$ (d) $\langle \bar{1}77023_{[8]} \rangle$

(b) $\langle 1100.11_{[2]} \rangle$ (e) $\langle \bar{5}AF7.3D_{[16]} \rangle$

(c) $\langle \bar{4}369.202_{[10]} \rangle$ (f) $\langle 5270_{[10]} \rangle$

2. Give proofs of Lemmas 9.5.2 and 9.5.3.

3. Suppose a simple procedure for conversion of a standard negative base β radix polynomial to a sign-magnitude radix polynomial with base $|\beta|$ and vice versa is available. Discuss the following negation algorithm for $P \in \mathscr{P}[\beta, D_{|\beta|}]$ where $\beta \leq -2$.

Step 1. Convert P to $Q \in \mathscr{P}^{\pm}[|\beta|, D_{|\beta|}]$ with $\|Q\| = \|P\|$.
Step 2. Shift the digits of Q one place to the left, i.e., multiply by $|\beta|$, forming $Q' \in \mathscr{P}^{\pm}[|\beta|, D_{|\beta|}]$.
Step 3. Convert Q' to $P' \in \mathscr{P}[\beta, D_{|\beta|}]$ with $\|P'\| = \|Q'\|$.
Step 4. Shift the digits of P' one place to the right, i.e., divide by β, forming $P'' \in \mathscr{P}[\beta, D_{|\beta|}]$. Claim $\|P''\| = - \|P\|$.

4. Construct addition tables for the following digit set D and base β pairs, or show that none exists.
   (a) $D = \{0, 1, 2, 3, 4\}$, $\beta = 5$
   (b) $D = \{0, 1\}$, $\beta = -2$
   (c) $D = \{\bar{7}, \bar{5}, \bar{3}, \bar{1}, 0, 1, 3, 5, 7\}$, $\beta = 9$
   (d) $D = \{\bar{3}, \bar{2}, \bar{1}, 0, 1, 2, 3\}$, $\beta = 8$
   (e) $D = \{\bar{4}, \bar{3}, \bar{1}, 0, 1, 2, 5\}$, $\beta = 7$

5. Extend the discussion in the text to a full proof of Theorem 9.5.4.

6. Carefully describe an algorithm which takes as input a base β and a digit set which is a complete residue system modulo $|\beta|$ and gives as output the minimal carry digit set C with $S \subset C$ and the addition table for the uniquely determined addition mapping α: $C \times S \to C \times S$.

7. Utilize the algorithm of Exercise 6 to construct addition tables for the following digit set D and base β pairs.
   (a) $D = \{\bar{1}, 0, 1, 6\}$, $\beta = 4$
   (b) $D = \{0, 2, 7\}$, $\beta = -3$
   (c) $D = \{\bar{4}, 0, 1\}$, $\beta = 3$

8. How many different regular base 3 addition mappings α: $B_5 \times B_5 \to B_5 \times B_5$ are there?

9. Let α_β: $D_\beta \times D_\beta \to D_\beta \times D_\beta$ be the standard base β addition mapping for $\beta \geq 2$. Determine the following carry lengths.
   (a) $K\alpha_2(\langle 1101110_{[2]} \rangle, \langle 10_{[2]} \rangle)$
   (b) $K\alpha_{10}(\langle 37.94_{[10]} \rangle, \langle .062_{[10]} \rangle)$
   (c) $K\alpha_4(\langle 3.21032_{[4]} \rangle, \langle 130.12302_{[4]} \rangle)$
   (d) $K\alpha_{16}(\langle AF.B23_{[16]} \rangle, \langle 110.29_{[16]} \rangle)$

10. Utilizing the addition tables given in Table 9.5.3,
    (a) Find $P, Q \in \mathscr{P}[-4, D_4]$ such that $K_\alpha(P, Q) \geq 6$.
    (b) Find $P, Q \in \mathscr{P}[3, \{\bar{1}, 0, 7\}]$ such that $K\gamma(P, Q) \geq 8$.

11. Prove the Carry Absorption Theorem 9.5.6 for the following digit set and base pairs:
    (a) $D = D_\beta, \beta \geq 2$
    (b) $D = D_\beta, \beta \leq -2$
    (c) $D = B_\beta, \beta = 2i + 1 \geq 3$

12. A base β addition mapping $\alpha: C \times S \to C \times S$ is *stable* if $(0, s) = (0, s)$ for all $s \in S$. Show that if α is stable and $\boldsymbol{\alpha}^{[n]} (P_0, Q_0) = (P_n, Q_n)$, then $\mathrm{lsp}(P_n) \geq \mathrm{lsp}(P_0) + n$.

13. Let $D = \{\bar{1}, 0, 1, 2\}$. Construct addition mappings α, γ and θ each mapping $D \times D$ into $D \times D$ such that $\theta(\gamma(\alpha(P, Q))) = (0, R)$ for any $P, Q \in \mathscr{P}[3, D]$. Apply the composite mapping $\boldsymbol{\theta\gamma\alpha}$ to $P = \langle 20112.112_{[3]}\rangle$, $Q = \langle 1212. 2122_{[3]}\rangle$.

14. Construct the addition table for the standard decimal subtraction mapping $\alpha: \bar{D}_{10} \times D_{10} \to \bar{D}_{10} \times D_{10}$.

15. Construct the addition table for subtraction in $\mathscr{P}[3, \{\bar{1}, 0, 7\}]$, that is, the table for $\alpha: C \times \{\bar{1}, 0, 7\} \to C \times \{\bar{1}, 0, 7\}$ where C is minimal such that $\{\bar{7}, 0, 1\} \subset C$.

16. Discuss the existence of n-dimensional base β addition mappings for the following digit set and negative base pairs.
    (a) digit set $D_{|\beta|}, \beta \leq -2$
    (b) digit set $B_{|\beta|}, \beta \leq -3, \beta$ odd

17. Apply the 4-dimensional base 3 addition mapping α of Example 9.5.12 to the same radix polynomials with the string in the order P_6, P_8, P_7, P_3, P_1, P_5, P_2, P_4. Also determine $\boldsymbol{\alpha}^{[n]} (\boldsymbol{\alpha}(P_6, P_8, P_7, P_3), \boldsymbol{\alpha}(P_1, P_5, P_2, P_4))$ for $1 \leq n \leq 4$.

18. Let χ and α be the unique base 5 multiplication and 6-dimensional addition mappings on $B_5 \times B_5$. Determine the minimum n in each of the following.
    (a) $\boldsymbol{\alpha}^{[n]}(\boldsymbol{\chi}(\langle 20\bar{1}_{[3]}\rangle, \langle \bar{1}\bar{2}021_{[3]}\rangle)) = (0, R)$
    (b) $\boldsymbol{\alpha}^{[n]}(\boldsymbol{\chi}(\langle 212\bar{2}\bar{2}.21_{[3]}\rangle, \langle 12012.\bar{2}_{[3]}\rangle)) = (0, R)$
    (c) $\boldsymbol{\alpha}^{[n]}(\boldsymbol{\chi}(\langle \bar{1}2200.\bar{2}2_{[3]}\rangle, \langle .02\bar{2}\bar{2}\bar{2}12_{[3]}\rangle)) = (0, R)$

REFERENCES

1. AVIZIENIS, A., "Signed-Digit Number Representations for Fast Parallel Arithmetic," *IRE Trans. Electronic Computers* EC-10 (1961) 389–400.

2. BRENT, R. P., "On the Precision Attainable with Various Floating-Point Number Systems," *IEEE Trans. on Computers* C-22 (1973) 601–607.

3. BROWN, W. S. and P. L. RICHMAN, "The Choice of Base," *Comm. ACM* 12 (1969) 560–561.

4. CODY, W. J., "Static and Dynamic Numerical Characteristics of Floating-Point Arithmetic," *IEEE Trans. on Computers* C-22 (1973) 598–601.

5. GARNER, H. L., "Number Systems and Arithmetic," *Advances in Computers*, 6, Academic Press, New York, 1965, pp. 131–194.

6. HENRICI, P., "A Subroutine for Computations with Rational Numbers," *JACM* 3 (1956) 6–9.

7. KNUTH, D. E., *The Art of Computer Programming 2, Seminumerical Algorithms,* Addison-Wesley Publishing Co., Reading, Mass., 1969.

8. MARASA, J. D. and D. W. MATULA, "A Simulative Study of Correlated Error Propagation in Various Finite-Precision Arithmetics," *IEEE Trans. on Computers* C-22 (1973) 587–597.

9. MATULA, D. W., "A Formalization of Floating-Point Numeric Base Conversion," *IEEE Trans. on Computers* C-19 (1970) 681–692.

10. MATULA, D. W., "Significant Digits: Numerical Analysis or Numerology," *Proc. IFIPS-71,* North-Holland Publishing Co., Amsterdam, 1972, pp. 1278–1283.

11. MATULA, D. W., "Number Theoretic Foundations of Finite Precision Arithmetic," in *Applications of Number Theory to Numerical Analysis,* ed. by S. K. Zaremba, Academic Press, New York, 1972, pp. 479–489.

12. MATULA, D. W., "Towards an Abstract Mathematical Theory of Floating-Point Arithmetic," *Proc. AFIPS* 34 (1969), 765–772.

13. MCKEEMAN, W. M., Representation Error for Real Numbers in Binary Computer Arithmetic," *IEEE Trans. on Computers* EC-16 (1967), 682–683.

14. ROBERTSON, J. E., "The Correspondence between Methods of Digital Division and Multiplier Recording Procedures," *IEEE Trans. on Computers* C-19 (1970), 692–701.

15. SZABO, N. S. and R. I. TANAKA, *Residue Arithmetic and its Applications to Computer Technology,* McGraw-Hill Book Co., New York, 1967.

16. VAN DER WAERDEN, B. L., *Modern Algebra,* Ungar, New York, 1953.

17. WALKUP, D. W., private communication.

PART IV MODELING

10 PARSING NATURAL LANGUAGE VIA RECURSIVE TRANSITION NET

Terry Winograd
Department of Computer Science
Stanford University
Stanford, California

Editor's Note:

This chapter introduces the concept of an augmented recursive transition net as a model of automata for the recognition of natural language. The author proposes the question as to what is needed in order to recognize an English sentence, and proceeds to develop formalisms as they are needed. Both the approach and the results are refreshing and interesting. The concept of a recursive transition net, which consists of a set of finite automata together with a pushdown store with a highly restrictive accessing function, seems to be more natural for the recognition of context-free language than a pushdown automata. However, the generalization does not seem to extend to the context-sensitive case.

The only prerequisite for this chaper is the notion of context-free and context-sensitive languages introduced in Chapter 1.

10.1. INTRODUCTION

In this paper, I want to show how a rather common-sense approach to understanding English can lead us into many of the formal mechanisms of automata theory. In particular, transition nets are developed as a general formalism for grammars, and their advantages over more traditional forms, such as context-free and transformational rewrite rules are discussed. There is also a discussion of the general shortcomings of syntactic formalisms in trying to deal with a communication system whose basic structure is oriented towards conveying semantic meanings.

Rather than following an axiomatic development, we will proceed by asking the question "What do we need to know to recognize an English sentence?" and develop formalisms as they are needed to represent that knowledge. We will begin by accepting without discussion the fiction that it is indeed possible to give sensible answers to this question in purely syntactic terms. This implies a kind of strong modularity in the structure of language, dividing its structure into separable components labelled *syntax* and *semantics*, or *meaning*. In the concluding section, we will discuss some of the difficulties produced by this assumption.

Our task then can be simply stated as producing a mechanism which can accept a string of symbols as input, and produce as output a judgment as to whether it is or is not an English sentence. Many current views of language demand additional output from a grammar, in the form of a "structural description" of the sentence. We will see that this follows in a direct way from having the ability to perform the simple recognition task.

10.2.   MAIN RESULTS

10.2.1.   Patterns, Programs, and State Diagrams

As a first naive approach to the problem of recognizing the sentences of a language, we might consider simply matching candidates against a list of acceptable sentences. Taken in its simplest form, this would only work if we had a complete list of possible symbol sequences. Indeed, we might believe that this sort of straightforward recognition is used in natural languages for recognizing utterances such as "How do you do!" and "I'll be damned!"

But for most sentences of the language, two obvious factors make a small number of patterns cover a much larger number of sentences—word classes and internal structure. Clearly it seems uneconomical to have two separate patterns for "Fat giraffes munch leaves" and "Brainy rabbits nibble carrots." For many thousands of years, linguists have noted that languages are organized around classes of words, with labels traditionally given like *noun*, *verb*, and *adjective*. Instead of specifying the patterns of the language in terms of individual words we can specify patterns of word classes, like:

Adjective Noun Verb Noun

There are many difficult problems in trying to give tight formal criteria for assigning words to classes, and a great deal of linguistic study has gone into various approaches to these problems. For our current purposes, we will take a simplistic view, assuming that a language contains a small number of distinct classes, and that every word can be clearly assigned membership in one or more of them.

The second economy comes in recognizing that there are many patterns in the grammar which exhibit strong similarity, and that the similarities can easily be expressed in a slightly richer notation which allows options and repetitions. For example we might have two patterns:

Adjective Noun Verb Noun
Adjective Noun Verb

Where the first corresponds to sentences like "Fat giraffes munch leaves," and the second to sentences like "Wooly bears grunt." We can collapse these into a single pattern with a notation allowing a symbol to represent "or," as in:

Adjective Noun (Verb Noun   v   Verb)

Similarly, we notice that some elements can be repeated an indefinite number of times. If we want to represent the structures of *"bears. . .," "wooly bears . . .," "ferocious wooly bears. . .," "hungry ferocious wooly bears. . .,"* etc., it is unsatisfactory to have a set of patterns:

Noun . . .
Adjective Noun . . .
Adjective Adjective Noun . . .
Adjective Adjective Adjective Noun . . .
. . .

We can adopt another notation to represent iteration, and combine these into:

Adjective* Noun . . .

These notations are motivated by noticing certain kinds of regularities in the language, but of course they have been put in this form to correspond to the formalism for *regular sets* as described in any introduction to automata theory. By letting the elementary symbols correspond to word classes in the input stream, we can directly represent our observations about language so far.

Up to this point, we have not asked just how these patterns are to be used. If there is a simple list of literal patterns, we might have a process which just went through them sequentially testing their identity with the input. With this more expanded notion of an *allowable sentence pattern* we need a more elaborate process. One of the fundamental theorems of automata theory gives an excellent answer: Corresponding to any regular set, there is a *finite state machine* which operates under simple rules to either accept or reject any input string as a member of the set. Transitions can be labelled either with particular input words, or with word classes. We might represent a slightly expanded version of our patterns (accounting for *Determiners* like *the*) as in Fig. 10.2.1.

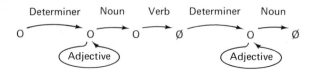

Fig. 10.2.1   A finite state transition net.

This kind of state diagram can be called a *transition network* or *transition net*, to emphasize the importance of the different *transitions* or *arcs* which describe the possibilities for going from one state to another. The operation of such a net is exactly as described in any elementary introduction to finite state machines. We adopt the convention of using the symbol $\bigcirc$ to represent a state, and $\varnothing$ to represent an accepting state.

10.2.2.   Constituent Structure and Recursive Transition Nets

10.2.2.1. Recursive Structures.   The transition net as described in the previous section can represent a potentially infinite number of different sentences, and gives a straightforward procedural mechanism for recognizing them. However, there are still some things it is obviously missing. One of the fundamental organizing principles of language is the presence of *constituent structure*. We can think of a sentence as a structure built up of separate substructures, each of which can be described in its own terms. Each substructure plays a particular *function* in the overall structure, and has a specific internal *form* describing how it in turn is built up.

To some degree, the internal form of a constitutent is not dependent on its function in the larger structure. We can describe how to recognize it independently of the context in which it appears. For example, in the network above we note that there are two different appearances of the sequence shown in Fig. 10.2.2.

In examining the overall grammar of English, we will find this particular grouping at a number of places, in a number of other structures. It seems reasonable to give it a name, and specify the entire combination in the network by a transition arc specifying that name. If we name our original network S for *sentence*, and our subgroup NP for *noun phrase*, we now have the net shown in Fig. 10.2.3.

We may want such groupings to be recursive, in the sense that a particular constituent can have, as one of its internal constituents, something of the same

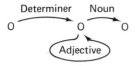

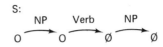

Fig. 10.2.2 Subsequence of transition net.

Fig. 10.2.3 Recursive transition net for simple sentences.

type. For example the noun phrase "the purple bottle in the top drawer" has as one of its constituents the noun phrase "the top drawer." We can capture this by extending our NP network to that of Fig. 10.2.4.

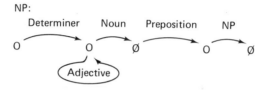

Fig. 10.2.4 Recursive transition net for noun phrases.

The same sort of analysis immediately shows that the combination Preposition NP occurs in many places, and deserves to be labelled as a grouping in its own right, which we will call PREPP (prepositional phrase).

Transition nets extended in this way to include entire groupings as transitions are called *recursive transition nets*. Although they are based on ordinary transition nets, their formal properties are quite different. First, there is no longer a straightforward connection between the network description and the process of analyzing an input. In the simpler networks, it is always possible to decide whether a given transition is possible by comparing the symbol of the arc to the next word in the input string. In recursive transition networks, the correspondence is more complex. In order to see whether an arc can be taken, it is necessary to call the entire recognition process recursively, with the current string as its input, and with its network specified by the name on the arc. If this second process succeeds at recognizing the desired constituent, as indicated by going into an accepting state, then processing returns to the original network, going to the state at the end of the transition, and continuing with the input string that is left after removing the elements "used up" by it.

The implementation of such a process requires a stack of some sort to remember what networks are currently being processed, so they can be continued when their constituents are completed. It is easy to demonstrate that they are formally equivalent to a nondeterministic pushdown automaton.

10.2.2.2.   The Equivalence Between RTN and PDA.   We can build any set of networks into a PDA with the following instructions:

States: The set of states is the union of all the states in the separate nets making up the grammar.

Symbols: The set of initial input symbols corresponds to the word classes, and the set of symbols for writing on the tape consists of a symbol for each arc in the grammar.

Instructions:

Begin in an initial state of the network for Sentence.

If an arc specifies a word or word class, and it matches the current input word, go to the state at the end of that arc, and remove the word from the input.

If an arc specifies the name of a network, place the arc name on the stack, and go to the initial state of that network.

If you are in an accepting state, and there is an arc-name on the top of the stack, go to the state at the end of that arc.

The recognition succeeds whenever the PDA is in an accepting state for the Sentence network, the stack is empty, and the input string has been completed.

Fig. 10.2.5   Correspondence between RTN and PDA.

It is important to note that these are instructions for a *nondeterministic* PDA. There will be cases where more than one of these rules apply at a given time. For example, we may be in a state of some network which is an accepting state, but has arcs leading out of it. We must try both the alternative of following the arcs, and of popping to the state named on the top of the stack. More simply, there may be several arcs leading out of the same state, which must be followed separately. Note that this can happen even if they are transitions based on word classes, since a single word can belong to more than one class. (For example *love* is both a verb and a noun).

The properties of nondeterministic PDAs have been explored extensively, and one of the basic results demonstrates their equivalence to *context-free grammars*.

Example 10.2.1

A simple context-free language like the set of strings of the form $a^n b^n$ can easily be expressed as a transition net like:

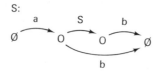

Example 10.2.2

The syntax of a programming language is often defined by a set of context-free rules. It could equivalently be represented by a recursive transition net, which would then provide the basis for a parser. A fragment of an imaginary language might look like:

Iterative Statement:

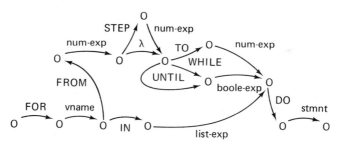

where vname = variable name, num-exp = numerical expression, boole-exp = Boolean expression, list-exp = list expression, and statement = executable statement or block.

10.2.2.3. The Advantages of RTN Formulations over CFG. The usual description of the properties of English we have discussed so far takes the form of a set of context-free rewrite rules which specify the same set of sentences. Although they are formally equivalent, it makes sense from a heuristic standpoint to compare the advantages of context-free rewrite rules and recursive transition nets.

The major difference is that RTN's make it possible to indicate explicitly the connections between rules. For example, the network for NP given above would be represented in a context free grammar as in Fig. 10.2.6.

Fig. 10.2.6   Context-free grammar.

| NP → Determiner NP2 |
| NP2 → Adjective NP2 |
| NP2 → Noun |
| NP2 → Noun Preposition NP |

The information in the net has been separated into a group of individual rewrite rules. Although the formal content is equivalent, there is no direct way to look at a set of rules and determine their structure—the fact that at a certain point there is a set of alternatives, or that there is a loop indicating an indefinitely long string of adjectives before the noun, etc.

From the point of view of writing and understanding grammars, this additional *explicit* information about the connections can be extremely useful. One of the fundamental uses is the recognition of groupings which have meaningful functions. In the context-free representation, no distinction is made between a constituent like NP which is a basic structural ingredient of the language, and a symbol like NP2 which is being used to represent the structure of all the NP except the initial *Determiner*. In the network representation, a clear distinction is made between having a separate network for a constituent or simply representing it as a particular state within a network. Of course we could write a RTN which ignored this, by setting up a new net for every state, but the extra information provided by the distinction between networks and states can be of advantage both in using the analysis (for example in determining the meaning of a sentence) and in extending its power, as described in Section 10.2.3.

10.2.3.   Context Sensitivity and Augmented Transition Nets

By progressing from simple patterns to transition nets to recursive transition nets, we gain the ability to represent the sentences of a language in a much more perspicuous way. However, there are other aspects of natural language structure for which this is not enough. As a simple example, take the problem of subject-verb agreement in English. We say "he *plays*" but "they *play*" with the form of the verb corresponding to whether the subject is singular or plural. If our networks are to describe exactly the set of sentences in the language, they must make this distinction. There needs to be some way to make the transition corresponding to the Verb arc conditional on its agreeing with the NP.

An obvious way to do this is to *augment* the formalism by allowing a set of *conditions* to be attached to any arc. The transition along that arc is taken only if it satisfies all the normal conditions for a recursive transition net, and the specific conditions are met as well. Our sentence network might be augmented by adding to the Verb arc the condition: The verb must be singular if the NP is singular, and plural if the NP is plural.

This is far too vague; in order to make the conditions part of an algorithm for accepting sentences we must be much more careful about the sorts of things specified by terms like "the NP" or even "is singular." In some sense, we need to specify a programming language for the conditions. One approach is to allow the use of a general-purpose programming language, like LISP, restricting the content of a condition only in that it must be a valid construct in the language. This is easy solution from the programming point of view, if we are actually implementing the parser in such a language. However, it leaves questions from both a formal and a linguistic viewpoint. Formally, it is clear that allowing arbitrary computations gives our *augmented transition networks* the power of a Turing machine. We might ask whether there is some more restricted augmentation which can serve the necessary purposes for language. From a linguistic viewpoint, we may not want to limit the theoretical power of the formalism, but are interested in seeing specifically what types of operations and entities are called for. As an analogy, we could do arithmetic with a formalism involving only a simple concatenation operator on strings of a single symbol, but we gain much more understanding by explicitly recognizing the presence of operations like plus and times, and objects which correspond to integers, fractions, etc.

The formalism which has been best explored for ATN grammars is the use of explicit *registers* associated with each use of a particular net. These registers correspond to the bound variables of programming languages, and are set by explicit *actions* associated with transitions.

Example 10.2.3

Taking a formal example, we might use an ATN to parse strings of the form $a^n b^n c^n$. One way to do this would be by adding registers named A-COUNT, B-COUNT, and C-COUNT to the following S network, and augmenting the arcs as described in Fig. 10.2.7. Note that an initialization of the counts to zero must be explicitly included. There are various simple mechanisms for doing this. At first glance, this grammar seems almost like cheating—by expressing the count of each constituent directly in a register, it avoids all the problems of writing grammar rules. This is exactly the point of augmented transition nets. When a grammar has some property which can be captured directly by a simple procedure, the ATN makes it possible to put this procedure directly into the net. For real languages, the reason such regularities exist is usually that they are connected to some aspect of the meaning of the strings, and by expressing the special features explicitly we have a much better handle on deciding what the string means.

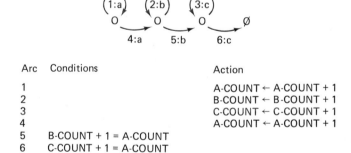

Arc	Conditions	Action
1		A-COUNT ← A-COUNT + 1
2		B-COUNT ← B-COUNT + 1
3		C-COUNT ← C-COUNT + 1
4		A-COUNT ← A-COUNT + 1
5	B-COUNT + 1 = A-COUNT	
6	C-COUNT + 1 = A-COUNT	

Fig. 10.2.7   Augmented transition net.

Returning to our sentence network, we might have a register for Number. This could be set by actions associated with the arcs for Determiner and Noun. If the Determiner arc is taken by using the input word *a*, the Number register would be set to Singular. If the Determiner were *all*, it would be Plural. Note that *the* does not specify the number, since we can say both *the cat* and *the cats*. There could be a condition on the Noun arc, specifying that it must not disagree with the Determiner, and an action specifying that if the Determiner hasn't set the Number register, it should be set according to whether the Noun is singular or plural. Of course all this involves knowing which in-

put words are singular and plural, as would be done in some sort of dictionary associated with the grammar.

We now want to put a condition on the Verb arc which checks the Number
register of the NP which precedes it. But what sense does it make to talk
about "the NP." We have described our networks as instructions to a kind of
automaton—almost exactly like programs. In analyzing a sentence, we may
call the NP network, and it may use a set of internal variables (registers).
However, when it is done it simply returns an answer to the arc which called
it. It either recognizes a constituent of the proper type, or fails to. The result
of its efforts is reflected only in this decision and in having possibly removed
some words from the input string.

It appears that in doing this, we are throwing away a good deal of useful
structural information. It would be easy to view a "trace" of the process as
a description of the syntactic structure which was parsed. In order to get
structural trees like those produced by context-free grammars, we need only
add to each network a register named Structure, with the following general
conditions on arcs:

When you enter a network, set the Structure register to an empty list.

When you make a transition involving an input symbol, add that
symbol to the end of the Structure list for the current network.

When you make a transition involving a recursive call to a network,
add a new item to the end of the Structure list for the network which
calls it. This item should be labelled with the name of the network called
by the arc, and should contain the Structure list resulting from that call.

In a sense this is just a trace of the parsing process which the network
caused. However it can also be seen as a tree structure corresponding to the
parsing for that sentence. This particularly simple relationship between the
parsing process and the structure exists because of the context-free nature of
the RTN. If we use the symbol $*$ to represent the structure built for the arc
just taken, our extended grammar now looks like Fig. 10.2.8. The function
GETR gets the value of a register associated with a particular structure, so
(GETR $*$ NUMBER) has the value of the Number register of the structure
just built.

Once we have adopted the idea of using registers to build a structure corresponding to the input, we can use this power to improve our grammar in
several ways. One possibility is to use registers for explicit information about
properties of the constituents, for example the Plural associated with an NP.
The conditions on other arcs could then test these in a simple direct way.
Another possibility would be to use structure-building operations to produce
a description more akin to the underlying "deep" structure of the input. One
of the basic observations of recent linguistic theory has been that many sentences which differ substantially in their superficial ordering of words (surface

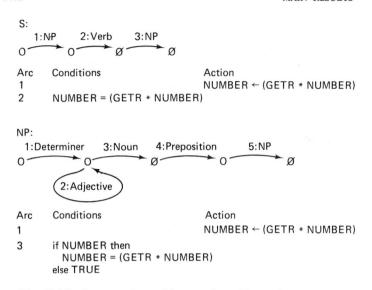

Fig. 10.2.8 Augmented transition net for subject-verb agreement.

structure) may in fact represent a much greater similarity at a deep level. For example, "A cat chased my rat" and "My rat was chased by a cat" both represent a deep structure in which the cat is the actor and rat the object of the chase. We can put explicit structure-building operations on the transitions which find the object NP and "by" prepositional phrase. These can put the cat in the appropriate place in the structure in both cases, thus capturing the appropriate generalizations about the similarity between the two sentences. The resulting sentence network is shown in Figure 10.2.9.

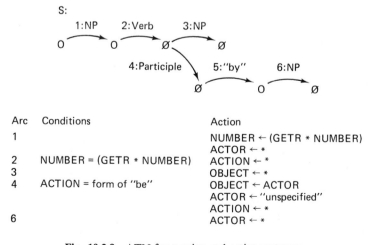

Fig. 10.2.9 ATN for passive and active sentences.

Much of the work on augmented transition net grammars has been oriented towards using the structure-building relations to produce "deep" analysis
of the sentences parsed. Early work [4] concentrated on structures like those
of transformational grammar, while later versions [3] have been oriented
towards more general representations.

Example 10.2.4

Even in cases where the augmentation is not necessary from a formal viewpoint, it may be a better representation. Above we wrote a simple recursive
transition network for the strings $a^n b^n$. We could also do this with an augmented transition net parallel to the one above:

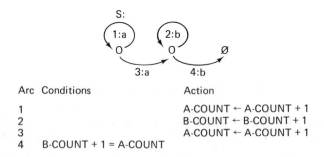

Arc	Conditions	Action
1		A-COUNT ← A-COUNT + 1
2		B-COUNT ← B-COUNT + 1
3		A-COUNT ← A-COUNT + 1
4	B-COUNT + 1 = A-COUNT	

The choice between the two different network grammars for the same language is dependent on what the strings really are. If this grammar represented
parenthesis nestings, the original net is better, since it indicates the recursive
structure directly, showing that a proper nesting can either be made up of a
matched pair of parentheses, or by a pair with a further nested structure between them. On the other hand, if it were a grammar of "symmetric page divid-
ers" of the form:

→→→→→→→→→→→→→→→→→←←←←←←←←←←←←←←←←←

we would be better off with the simple counter which checks to see if the
numbers are the same, and doesn't go through a more complicated structure.

10.2.4.   Nondeterminism, Ordering, and the Parsing Process

In describing the connection between a finite-state transition diagram and
the process of parsing a string, we talked in simple terms of "following" the
arc indicating the appropriate transition. As long as there is only a single such
arc in any state, this makes sense. However, if there are multiple possible arcs,
the process must be able to follow up more than one possibility. If there are
two possible paths through the network for the same input, both ending in a

final state, then it is ambiguous. However, even if no two full paths exist, there may be partial paths leading through some sequence of states before fizzling out. If we follow one of these in the obvious sense, we lose the chance to find the correct one along a different route.

It can easily be shown that for finite-state networks this is no problem, since for any nondeterministic process, we can construct an equivalent completely deterministic net (one for which there is never more than one possible path from a state for a given input word).

But when we go to recursive and augmented transition nets, the problem becomes more serious. It is not the case that there is an equivalent deterministic network, and the parsing process must deal directly with the problem of multiple possibilities. Various strategies can be adopted, the most obvious of which are *depth-first with backup*, and *parallel breadth-first*. In the depth-first method, whenever there is more than one possible transition to be taken, the parser simply chooses one and takes it, temporarily ignoring the others but noting their presence on some sort of stack. If at any point the process reaches a state in which nothing can be done, it goes back to the last place a decision was made, undoing everything which has happened since then, and tries an alternative. This could either be the result of having hit a dead end in trying to parse the sentence, or in having finished it successfully and going back to look for alternative parsings.

In the breadth-first approach, we simulate a machine which has the power to create multiple copies of itself to try different things at the same time. Whenever it reaches a choice, it starts up one copy for each alternative, setting the new copies off down their respective paths simultaneously. Each one continues (sprouting successors when new alternatives are hit) until it either reaches a dead end, and is discarded, or completes a successful parsing.

These strategies are equivalent in the set of possible parsings they will find, but quite different in behavior such as the amount of time until a parsing is found, the order in which they will be found, etc. If we were to treat them only as formal systems, this might not be of much interest, but there are two reasons why this kind of flexibility in "scheduling" the networks is interesting for natural language.

The first is that for many applications it might seem feasible to allow the parser to proceed until it finds a single parsing, and then to go ahead and use that parsing without checking to see if there are other possibilities. Transition nets give us ways to control what that initial parsing will be. For example, one possibility is to follow the depth-first strategy, but to order the arcs from any node in some a priori way, so that the arc taken is the one most likely to get the correct parsing. Another possibility is to combine breadth-first and depth-first strategies (perhaps with arc ordering as well) to tailor much more directly the order in which possibilities are explored.

A second reason for having an interest in this is the potential of using a transition net formalism to explain the actual empirical properties of human parsing. This goes beyond the formal determination of which sentences are accepted, considering in addition data like the length of time a human takes to parse a particular sentence, and the likelihood of particular mistakes. It may be possible to build an appropriate strategy model for a transition net which explains in detail the behavior of human parsing systems. See Kaplan [3] for a discussion of many of the issues involved.

10.2.5. Formal Properties

Recursive transition nets were shown above to be equivalent in power to context-free grammars. It is clear that augmented transition nets as we have described them are equivalent to Turing machines. We can think of the net as a flowchart for a program, with the computation being done by the arbitrary conditions and actions on the arcs. There may be, however, reasonable ways to limit the formal power of the nets in an interesting way. For example if the amount of computation which can be done on any one arc is bounded, then the whole network will in fact be recursive, since the number of arcs which can be taken is limited by the number of terminal symbols in the input. In order to be sure of this, we must adopt two conventions. First, in some forms of transition network formalism there are "lambda-arcs" which have a condition and action like other arcs, but do not involve actually removing an input symbol from the string, or calling another network recursively. These are very useful for specifying optional elements, since we can have two arcs connecting a pair of nodes, one of which finds the element, and the other of which doesn't but takes the appropriate corresponding actions and checks for the appropriate conditions under which the element can be missing. If we want to maintain the boundedness provided by the finite length of the input string, we can prohibit closed loops of lambda-arcs in the networks. This includes prohibiting nets containing lambda-arcs in such a way that they could produce a loop through recursion, for example, by beginning with a lambda-arc followed by a call to the same network. Note that in some sense we are being too strict. There may be cases in which there looks like there might be a closed loop, but in fact the conditions on those arcs make it impossible that the loop would ever be taken. In general it will be undecidable whether that is the case (since we allow arbitrary computation), but by avoiding even the possibility of such loops, boundedness of the process is guaranteed.

In the grammars developed so far, these restrictions are easily met. There are no cases where linguistic considerations even tempt the grammar writer to write actions and loops of the sort which could lead to unbounded computations. It is interesting to speculate whether this sort of naturalness criterion can be extended to produce tighter formal results.

EXERCISES 10.2

1. Draw a transition net to represent the expressions for the time of day in English. The basic word categories will be *hour-number* (one, two, . . ., twelve), *minute-number* (one, two, . . ., fifty-nine), *fraction* (quarter, half), and specific connectives like *to, past, after, 'till.*

2. Write a formal definition of the pushdown automaton which corresponds to the RTN of Figs. 10.2.3 and 10.2.4.

3. Write a context-free grammar corresponding to the recursive transition net of Example 10.2.2.

4. Write an ATN grammar which extends that of Fig. 10.2.9 to handle direct and indirect objects, as in "I gave my love a cherry." "This mobile was given to me by a friend." etc. Note that the registers will now include ACTOR, ACTION, OBJECT, RECIPIENT and that these roles are signalled both by the order of the NP's and by the presence of prepositions like "to" and "by."

5. Give an example of an ATN (possibly with lambda-arcs) for which the set of strings defined is recursively enumerable but not recursive.

10.3. ADDITIONAL DISCUSSION

10.3.1. The Problems of Natural Communication

In exploring the structure of natural language, we find many phenomena which are not easily explainable or describable from a formal automata theory point of view, but whose origin is deeply entwined with the function of language as a communication system. Sentences are not really arbitrary symbol strings, as are the objects of formal automata theory. They are designed to convey meaning from one intelligent being to another, and in doing so they take advantage of the knowledge and reasoning power of the language users.

Examples of such phenomena can be found in conjunction and ellipsis. If our grammar is to account for the way in which conjunctions like "and" can appear, it must accept the fact that at almost any point in the structure of a sentence, we can insert an "and" and a constituent which combines in some way with the previous one. Thinking in transition net terms, this means that there is an arc from almost every node, labelled "and," going back to some previous point in the same network. Even worse, there are often several possibilities, as in the conjoined sentences:

She gave them a bowl and I gave them a spoon.
She gave them a bowl and took nothing in return.
She gave them a bowl and me a spoon.
She gave them a bowl and a spoon.
She gave them a bowl and spoon.

It seems that the behavior of such conjunctions can be characterized in a rule stating more directly: "Whenever you run across 'and', try to parse a constituent which matches some part of one you are in the process of building." Even with precise definitions for what is meant by "a part" and "in the process," it is not clear how to integrate such an algorithm into the transition net formalism without simply grafting it on.

Ellipsis is similar. Asked "Do you want a piece of apple pie?," I can reply "Bring me a piece" or "Bring me a piece of pecan" or "Bring me pecan" or "Bring me two." All of these are natural forms in English, and the grammar must worry in detail about just when things can be left out. Again in the straightforward transition net formalism, this would involve having a multitude of lambda-arcs, bypassing each element which might be deleted. It seems much more satisfying to express the deletion as a separate algorithm which works in conjunction with the more usual transition network mechanisms.

One of the interesting future possibilities for work with transition nets lies in specifying more clearly just how such additional processes can be added on without losing the clarity of the nets. One of the prime advantages of a network formalism is that is gives a clear and explicit statement of the alternatives which are possible at any point in the parsing of an input. This is not true for arbitrary programs, and we want to be particuarly careful about putting in layers of "hidden" processing.

Finally, it is not easy to decide how semantic considerations should be intermixed with the strategy component of a transition net parser. We discussed earlier the possibility of modelling human parsing performance through specific search strategies for following the alternatives in the grammar. If human strategies make significant use of meaning, then there must be some way to add these considerations to the more straightforward considerations of search. As is the case with most formalisms for natural language, there is little understanding of how to intermix the syntactic and semantic considerations in a satisfying way. One of the main justifications for transition nets is that by making explicit the structure of choices available in the syntactic form of language, they provide a good tie-in point from which to extend the analysis.

Acknowledgments

I would like to thank Ron Kaplan of the Xerox Palo Alto Research Center for a number of enlightening discussions about the nature and problems of transition net formalisms.

REFERENCES

1. BOBROW, D. and B. FRASER, "An Augmented Sta̋te Transition Network Analysis Procedure," in *Proceedings of International Joint Conference on Artificial Intelligence,* ed. by Walker and Norton, 1969, pp. 557–568.

2. KAPLAN, RON, "Augmented Transition Nets as Psychological Models of Sentence Comprehension," *Artificial Intelligence* 3: 2 (Summer 1972), 77–100.

3. KAPLAN, RON, "A General Syntactic Processor," in *Natural Language Processing*, ed. by Rustin, Algorithmics Press, New York, 1973.

4. THORNE, J., P. BRATLEY, and H. DEWAR, "The Syntactic Analysis of English by Machine," in *Machine Intelligence*, ed. by D. Michie, American Elsevier, New York, 1968.

5. WOODS, WILLIAM, "Transition Network Grammars for Natural Language Analysis," *Comm. ACM* 13(1970), 591–602.

11

AUTOMATA THEORETICAL APPROACH TO VISUAL INFORMATION PROCESSING

David Waltz
*Department of Electrical Engineering and
Coordinated Science Laboratory
University of Illinois
Urbana, Illinois*

Editor's Note:

This chapter represents a detailed probe of ways in which certain regularities in pictures can be formulated in terms of automata and language theory. Concepts introduced in this chapter are well illustrated with examples.

Material covered in this chapter together with that of Chapter 4 could form the core for a course in syntactic scene analysis.

The notions of finite automata and context-free grammar are all that is needed to understand this chapter.

11.1. INTRODUCTION

This chapter deals with ways in which certain regularities in pictures can be mathematically formalized and thus can be handled by computer programs. In what follows, the actual organization of programs to realize the processes will not be considered (see Shirai [9] and Waltz [10] for details, or Waltz [11], Winston [12,13] for overviews of program organization). Here we will be principally concerned with the nature of line drawing representations and the relations of these drawings to real world objects, or *scenes*.

11.2. SCENES

In what follows, we will make a careful distinction between parts of a *scene*, which is three-dimensional and parts of a *line drawing*, which is a two-dimensional projection of a scene.

Definition 11.2.1

A *scene* is a collection of three-dimensional objects. For the purposes of this chapter we will always assume that the objects are opaque polyhedra. (For a recent treatment of simple curved objects, see Chang [2].)

We will first describe various parts of *scenes*, and then establish a correspondence between these scene parts and the parts of a line drawing. Basically, we will define a scene to be made up of *faces*, *edges*, and *vertices*.

Definition 11.2.2

In a *scene*, a face is a maximal *physically connected* portion of a plane. (*Note:* By *physically connected*, we will mean physically connected in an obvious common-sense way. For example, we will consider objects 1 and 2 in Fig. 11.2.1 to be physically disconnected, even though they might conceivably be glued together.)

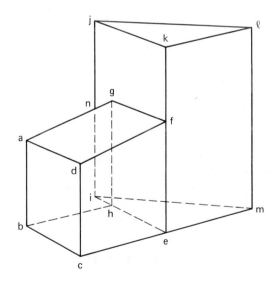

Fig. 11.2.1

Example 11.2.1

Assume that Fig. 11.2.1 depicts a scene with two objects sitting on a table

or support surface. There are twelve faces in this scene. The surface supporting the objects is one face, and the others are: a-b-c-d, c-d-f-e, a-d-f-g, a-b-h-g,
e-f-g-h, b-c-e-h, i-j-k-e, j-k-l, e-k-l-m, i-j-l-m, and e-i-m.

Definition 11.2.3

An *edge* is the intersection of two or more faces in a scene, where the number of faces which intersect remains constant over the entire length of the
edge.

Example 11.2.2

In Fig. 11.2.1 there are 20 edges: a-b, b-c, c-d, d-a, a-g, d-f, c-e, b-h, g-f,
f-e, e-h, h-g, h-i, i-j, j-k, k-f, k-l, j-l, e-m, and i-m. Notice that k-f and f-e are
different edges, since k-f is the intersection of two faces whereas f-c is the intersection of four faces. Similarly h-i, the intersection of three faces, and e-h, the
intersection of five faces, are different edges.

Definition 11.2.4

A *vertex* is a point in a scene where three or more edges intersect.

Example 11.2.3

Each vertex in the scene of Fig. 11.2.1 is marked with a letter, a through m.
Notice that edges a-g and i-j do *not* form a vertex at n, since no edges intersect
at the apparent crossing point of the edges.

Definition 11.2.5

A *trihedral vertex* is a vertex where exactly three faces intersect.

Example 11.2.4

The following vertices in Fig. 11.2.1. are trihedral: a, d, j, k, l. All the rest
are nontrihedral. For example, at vertex b four faces intersect, namely a-b-
c-d, b-c-e-h, a-b-h-g, and the support surface. Seven faces intersect at vertex
e: the support surface, c-d-e-f, e-f-g-h, b-c-e-h, e-i-j-k, e-i-m, and e-k-l-m.

EXERCISES 11.2

1. Find the number of faces which intersect at vertices c, f, g, h, i, and m in Fig.
   11.2.1.
2. Can you imagine a scene where every vertex is trihedral? Where no vertex is
   trihedral?

11.3. LINE DRAWINGS

Various techniques can be used to obtain line drawings of a scene. While these techniques have some mathematical interest, we will not consider them here in detail.

Basically an imaging device such as a TV camara or image dissector (see Horn [7]) produces electrical signals which can be digitized to obtain a digital picture. A line drawing can be obtained from the digital picture by finding *feature points*, or points in the digital picture where the spacial derivative is greater than a certain threshold, and then connecting these feature points to form *lines* (see Duda and Hart [4]).

Let us make the following initial assumptions:

1. All scenes will consist only of opaque polyhedra; thus all lines in a line drawing will be straight lines, since the projection of a straight line in 3-space is a straight line in 2–space.

2. All line drawings are perfect; i.e., all unobstructed edges and vertices in a scene map into lines and line intersections in the line drawing of the scene.

3. Scenes are shadow-free, so every line in a line drawing of a scene represents an edge in the scene.

4. Line drawings are obtained from a position in scene space called a *general position*. A general position is one where small changes in eye position do not result in changes of image topology.

Example 11.3.1

The line drawing in Fig. 11.3.1 does *not* satisfy the general position requirement, since a small eye movement changes the line drawing topology to that of Fig. 11.3.2.

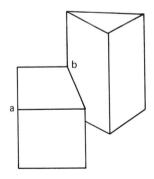

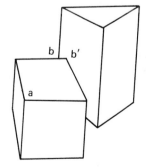

Fig. 11.3.1 A line drawing which does not satisfy the general position assumption.

Fig. 11.3.2 Topology changes as the eye move to the left; changes at a and b have been exaggerated for clarity.

Let us formally define what a line drawing is:

Definition 11.3.1

A *line drawing* is a simple, undirected planar graph, where every vertex of the graph lies on some circuit (see Definition 11.2.4). Moreover, the first assumption above tells us that every arc of a line drawing of a scene is a straight line.

Definition 11.3.2

A *junction* is a point in a line drawing where two or more lines intersect. (Thus a junction is a vertex of a graph; however, we will reserve the term "vertex" to refer only to an intersection of edges in the scene domain. See Definition 11.2.4)

Example 11.3.2

In Fig. 11.3.3, the junctions are a, b, c, d, e, f, g, n, j, k, l, and m. You may recognize Fig. 11.3.3 as a line drawing of the scene in Fig. 11.2.1.

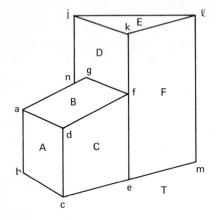

Fig. 11.3.3

Definition 11.3.3

An ordered pair of lines is called *right adjacent at a junction* if, when one enters the junction on the first line, the second line is the rightmost path leaving the junction. A *region* is a member of the set of all simple circuits in a line drawing such that each simple circuit consists only of lines which are right adjacent at each junction on the circuit.

Example 11.3.3

{((e, f), (f, k)), ((k, f), (f, g)), ((g, f), (f, d)), ((d, f), (f, e))} is the set of all right adjacent lines at junction f in Fig. 11.3.3. The figure has seven regions: A, B,

C, D, E, F, and T.

Definition 11.3.4

A *line drawing of a scene* is a *line drawing* which is the projection at some point in scene space of a scene.

Example 11.3.4

This means that we will not be considering line drawings like those of Fig. 11.3.4. For a treatment of such line drawings, see Huffman [8]. In this paper titled "Impossible Objects as Nonsense Sentences," Huffman demonstrates methods which enable one to decide whether a given *line drawing* can possibly be a *line drawing of a scene.*

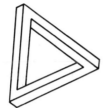 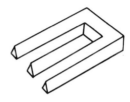

Fig. 11.3.4

Let us now sketch the correspondence between parts of scenes and parts of line drawings. (From here on in we will take *line drawing* to mean *line drawing of a scene.*)

1. Each *line* in a line drawing corresponds to some scene *edge* or portion of a scene edge (part of an edge may be obscured). In most scenes, not all edges map into lines in the line drawings of these scenes, e.g., one cannot see all edges of a cube for any single point.

2. Each *region* of a line drawing corresponds to some face or portion of a face in a scene.

3. There are two types of *junctions* in a line drawing, those which correspond to *vertices* and those which do not.

Example 11.3.5

In Fig. 11.3.5, junctions a, b, d, e, f, g, h, i, k, n, o, p, q, s, t, and u in the line drawing each correspond to a scene vertex. Junctions c, j, l, m, and r in the line drawing do *not* correspond to scene vertices. (I have assumed the obvious interpretation of the line drawing as a scene with two objects, one L-shaped with a hole in it, the other a brick.)

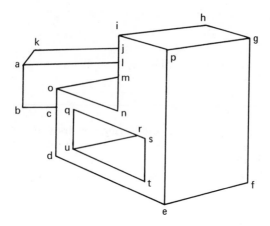

Fig. 11.3.5

The mapping from scenes to line drawings is many-to-one, i.e., there is in general more than one scene which can correspond to a single line drawing. Before examining this phenomenon, it will help to have some more precise terminology.

Definition 11.3.5

An *exposed face* in a scene is a face every point of which is visible from some eye position.

Definition 11.3.6

A *hidden face* in a scene is a face, no point of which is visible from any eye position.

Definition 11.3.7

A *partially exposed face* is a face, part of which is visible and part of which is not visible from any eye position.

Notice that all three types of face are defined in the scene domain, and that the definitions are thus independent of the particular eye position used in obtaining a line drawing.

Example 11.3.6

In Fig. 11.3.6, faces A, C, D, E, G, H, and I are *exposed faces*. Faces F, J, and K are *hidden faces*. Faces B and T are *partially exposed faces*. We can now use these definitions to aid in understanding the nature of the various scenes which can give rise to the line drawing in Fig. 11.3.7 in the following important example.

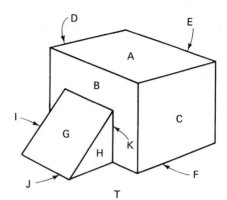

Fig. 11.3.6   Types of faces.

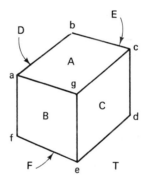

Fig. 11.3.7

Example 11.3.7

Consider the simple line drawing in Fig. 11.3.7. We will enumerate some possible scenes which can give rise to this line drawing (assuming a reasonable completion of the invisible portions of the scene; for instance we assume that there are no other objects in the scene, etc.)

Case 1: If we assume that the object in Fig. 11.3.7 is not supported at all, i.e., that this is a line drawing of a cube in orbit or in free fall, then all the junctions represent *trihedral vertices*. (See Definition 11.2.5.) In this case, all faces in the scene are exposed faces.

Case 2: If we assume that Fig. 11.3.7 represents a cube sitting on a table T, then junctions a, b, c, and g represent trihedral vertices; junctions f, e, and d represent nontrihedral vertices, since four faces intersect at each of these vertices. In this case faces A, B, C, D, and E are exposed faces, F is a hidden face, and T is a partially exposed face.

Case 3: If we assume that the figure represents a protrusion from a surface T, then all the junctions represent trihedral vertices, and all faces A, B, C, D,

E, and T in the scene are exposed faces. Notice that in this case there is no face F, since the "object" is connected to and part of T; this explains why T is not a partially exposed face, but an exposed face.

Case 4 and 5: If we assume that the figure represents a cube sitting against a wall, then either the vertices corresponding to junctions f, a, and b are non-trihedral (case 4) or the vertices corresponding to junctions b, c, and d are nontrihedral (case 5). To make these cases clearer, rotate the figure 90 degrees clockwise (case 5) or counterclockwise (case 4), and think of T as the floor. (We have said nothing about the direction of gravitational force, or whether there *is* a gravitational force assumed to be present in the scene.) In case 4, faces A, B, C, E, and F are exposed faces, D is a hidden face, and T is a partially exposed face. In case 5, faces A, B, C, D, and F are exposed faces, E is a hidden face, and again T is a partially exposed face.

Cases 6 and 7: The figure could also represent a protrusion from a wall which faces either right (case 6) or left (case 7). In both these cases, all the junctions correspond to trihedral vertices. In case 6 there is no face D and in case 7 there is no face E; in both cases all the faces in the scene are exposed faces.

Cases 8, 9, and 10: The figure can represent a brick emerging from a hole in a horizontal surface (case 8), a wall facing right (case 9), or a wall facing left (case 10). For case 8, d, e, and f are nontrihedral vertices, A and T are exposed faces, and B, C, D, and E are partially exposed faces.

Comment: Note that in the case of a real scene, we would be able to get additional information about the correct interpretation of the scene from shading, region brightness, and our knowledge of gravity. It is important to note that this line drawing as it stands is essentially ambiguous; without more information, we cannot choose which, if any, of the cases describes the scene which is the source of the line drawing. It would be more obvious which case is true if we were to add shading and redraw some of the edges to suggest connection or lack of connection. Later in Section 11.8 we introduce formalisms which allow us to easily describe each case.

EXERCISES 11.3

In each of the subfigures of Fig. 11.3.8 assume (1) that a gravitational force is present and directed downward, and (2) that the background of each line drawing represents a horizontal face.

1. If the background is an exposed face (i.e., the bottom objects are protrusions of the background region *T*), which junctions in each portion of Fig. 11.3.8 correspond to trihedral vertices?
   Which junctions do not correspond to trihedral vertices?

2. If the background is a plane, partially exposed face, which junctions *do not* correspond to trihedral vertices?

A

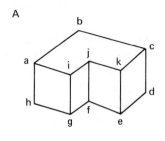

B

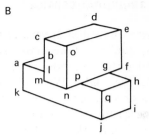

C

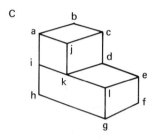

D

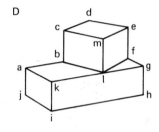

E

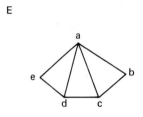

F

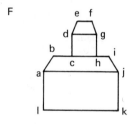

G

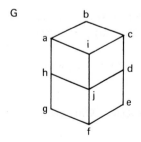

H

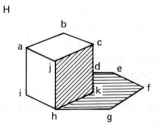

Fig. 11.3.8

11.4. TRIHEDRAL VERTICES

How many trihedral vertices are physically possible? How could we enumerate them? First we know that since we can have only three faces at a trihedral vertex, no more than three planes can intersect at such a vertex. Consider Fig. 11.4.1. We can imagine that various sectors are filled with solid material or are empty. Let us classify vertices according to how many of the eight space sectors at a vertex are filled. We will distinguish as different only those vertices which cannot be obtained by rotation and translation of other vertices. I will call these sectors *octants*, though the planes need not be at right angles, so the sectors will not be true octants.

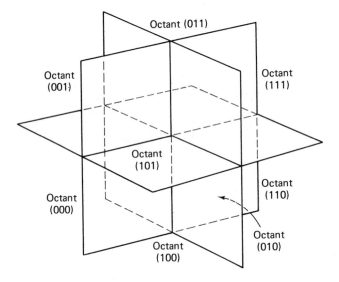

Fig. 11.4.1

Type I vertex [see Fig. 11.4.2(a)]:

There is only one possible type I vertex (one in which only one octant of space is filled); it corresponds to any vertex of an unsupported cube.

Type II vertices [see Fig. 11.4.2(b)]:

There are three distinct ways to fill two octants of space. None corresponds to a trihedral vertex.

Type III vertices [see Fig. 11.4.2(c)]:

There are four ways to fill three octants of space. Only type IIIA can be trihedral.

Type IV vertices [see Fig. 11.4.2(d)]:

There are six possible type IV vertices, none of which is trihedral.

Type V vertices [see Fig. 11.4.2(d) and 11.4.2(e)]:

There are seven possible type V vertices. Of these only type VC can be trihedral.

Type VI vertices [see Fig. 11.4.2(e) and 11.4.2(f)]:

None of the three type VI vertices can be trihedral.

Type VII vertex [see Fig. 11.4.2(f)]:

There is only one type VII vertex and it can be trihedral. So in summary, types I, IIIA, VC, and VII are all the possible trihedral vertices.

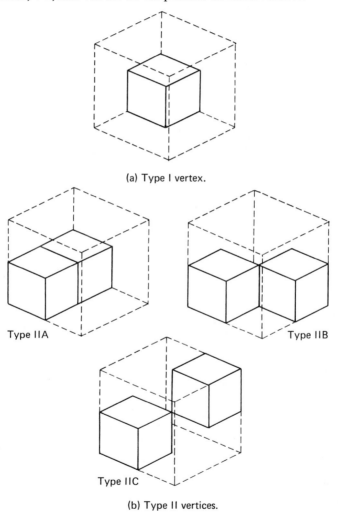

(a) Type I vertex.

Type IIA   Type IIB

Type IIC

(b) Type II vertices.

Fig. 11.4.2

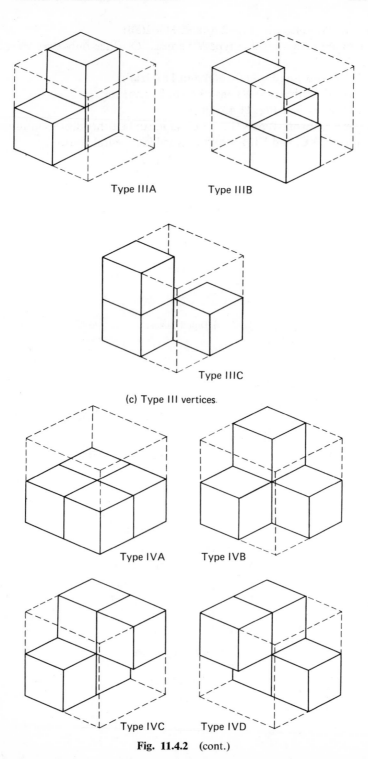

Type IIIA   Type IIIB

Type IIIC

(c) Type III vertices.

Type IVA   Type IVB

Type IVC   Type IVD

Fig. 11.4.2   (cont.)

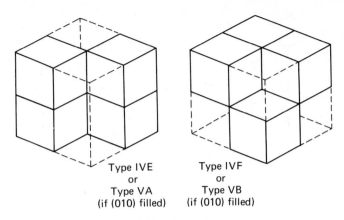

Type IVE
or
Type VA
(if (010) filled)

Type IVF
or
Type VB
(if (010) filled)

(d) Type IV vertices.

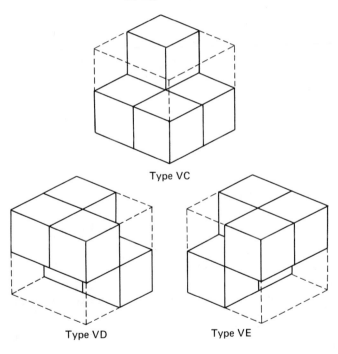

Type VC

Type VD   Type VE

Fig. 11.4.2   (cont.)

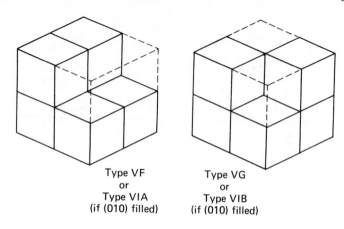

Type VF
or
Type VIA
(if (010) filled)

Type VG
or
Type VIB
(if (010) filled)

(e) Type V vertices.

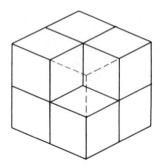

(f) Type VII vertex or Type VIC vertex (if (010) is not filled).

Fig. 11.4.2   (cont.)

EXERCISE 11.4

1. For each junction in Fig. 11.3.8 identify the vertex type, using the classifications of Fig. 11.4.2.

11.5. VERTEX VIEWS

Let us begin by giving names to various junction types. These names are due to Guzman [5] and are illustrated in Fig. 11.5.1.

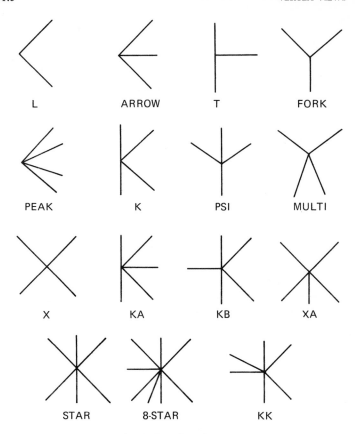

Fig. 11.5.1 Junction types.

Now consider which of the types of junctions the various vertices can map into. We will begin with the trihedral vertices; pick the standard representations from Fig. 11.4.2 and imagine rotating the vertices in space to obtain all possible views of the vertices.

Type I vertex:

The type I vertex can appear as a FORK, ARROW, or L junction, as shown in Fig. 11.5.2(a). (T junctions are excluded by the general position assumption; see Section 11.3.)

Type IIIA vertex:

The type IIIA vertex can appear as an ARROW, as an L, or as a FORK junction as shown in Fig. 11.5.2(b).

Type VC vertex:

The type VC vertex can appear as an ARROW or an L junction, as shown

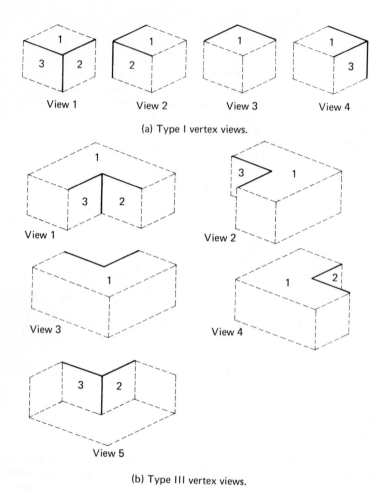

(a) Type I vertex views.

(b) Type III vertex views.

Fig. 11.5.2

in Fig. 11.5.2(c).

Type VII vertex:

The type VII vertex can only appear as a FORK as shown in Fig. 11.5.2(d).

Conclusion: Trihedral vertices in general position can only appear as FORK, ARROW, or L junctions; other junction types correspond to other scene features.

11.6   LINE LABELS

The material in this section was published independently by Huffman [8] and Clowes [1].

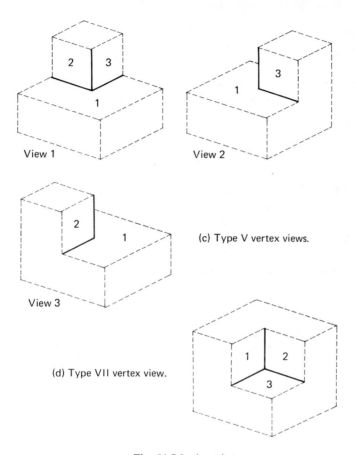

View 1   View 2

(c) Type V vertex views.

View 3

(d) Type VII vertex view.

Fig. 11.5.2   (cont.)

In order to distinguish the different possible views of trihedral vertices, let us first characterize the two possible types of edges which can occur at trihedral vertices. (The term "quadrant" will be used to refer to a sector of space bounded by two planes intersecting at any angle less than 180°.)

Definition 11.6.1

A *convex edge* is an edge where at any point on the edge, one quadrant of space is filled with solid matter.

Example 11.6.1

All the edges of a cube, tetrahedron, or prism are convex edges.

Definition 11.6.2

A *concave edge* is an edge where at any point on the edge, one quadrant of space is *not* filled with solid matter.

Example 11.6.2

All the inside edges of a room are concave edges.

A concave edge can only be seen if both faces which bound the edge are visible. However a convex edge can be seen in two ways:

1. Both faces which bound the edge may be visible.

or

2. Only one face which bounds the edge may be visible.

We will label concave edges with a minus sign (−). If both faces bounding a convex edge are visible, we will label that edge with a plus sign (+). If only one face bounding a convex edge is visible, we will call that edge an *obscuring edge*, and will label the line corresponding to that edge with an arrow. If we imagine standing on the line looking in the direction the arrow points, then the obscuring face will be on our right, and the obscured face on our left. Figure 11.6.1 illustrates these labels for an object assumed to be floating in space, i.e., unsupported.

We can now apply these labels to each of the trihedral vertex views in Fig. 11.5.2, and obtain the set of labels of Huffman and Clowes. These labelings are shown in Fig. 11.6.2(a), and are organized according to junction types.

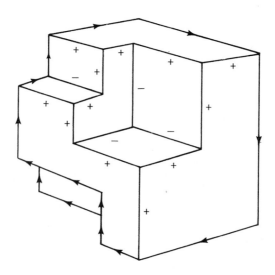

Fig. 11.6.1

The vertex type and view of each is listed below it. In Fig. 11.6.2(b) all the possible ways in which an edge can be obscured are listed. These are not vertices, but must be included in a set of junction labelings in order to completely characterize scenes made up of trihedral vertices.

Example 11.6.3

We can now use these labels to demonstrate the meanings of the trihedral cases in Example 11.3.7 (see Fig. 11.3.7) without resorting to the use of shading. Figure 11.6.3 shows all the possible labelings for the trihedral cases, namely cases 1, 3, 6, and 7. Note that the usual interpretation as a cube on a surface is *not* trihedral.

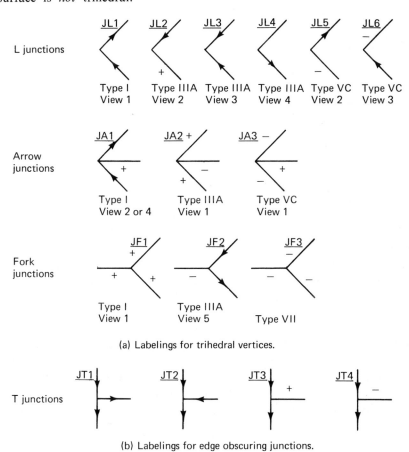

(a) Labelings for trihedral vertices.

(b) Labelings for edge obscuring junctions.

Fig. 11.6.2

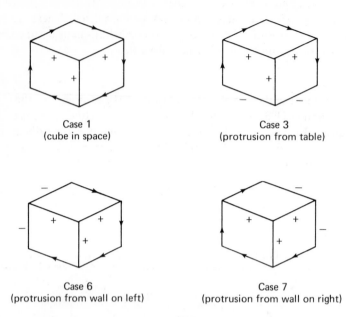

Case 1
(cube in space)

Case 3
(protrusion from table)

Case 6
(protrusion from wall on left)

Case 7
(protrusion from wall on right)

Fig. 11.6.3

Let us distinguish between two terms: *label* and *labeling*. By *label* we mean a label for a single line, e.g. convex, concave, or obscuring. By *labeling* we mean a consistent set of labels for lines at a junction or in a line drawing.

In most of what follows, we will be concerned with the problem of assigning particular labelings to junctions of line drawings. This process is in some ways analogous to the process of assigning semantic interpretations to ambiguous words in a sentence. The following discussion should help to clarify this analogy, and hopefully the analogy itself will help to clarify the labeling process.

If we think of each possible label for a line as a letter in the alphabet, then each junction must be labeled with an ordered list of "letters" to form a legal "word" in the language. Thus each "word" represents a physically possible interpretation for a given junction and thus the 3-dimensional interpretation of the labeling is the *meaning* of the "word." Furthermore, each "word" must match the "words" for surrounding junctions in order to form a legal "phrase," and all "phrases" in the scene must agree to form a legal "sentence" for the entire scene. The knowledge of the system is contained in (1) a dictionary made up of every legal "word" for each type of junction, and (2) rules by which "words" can legally combine with other "words." The range of the dictionary entries defines the universe of the program; this universe can be expanded by adding new entries systematically to the dictionary.

So far we have been discussing the universe of objects made up of trihedral vertices. Figure 11.6.2 constitutes the dictionary for this universe.

What are the conditions under which labelings can combine? Before answering this, we need a definition.

Definition 11.6.3

Two junctions are said to be *adjacent* if they are joined by a line with no intervening junctions.

Example 11.6.4

The set of all adjacent junction pairs in Fig. 11.6.4 is {(a, b), (a, k), (a, i), (b, c), (b, 1), (c, d), (d, e), (d, 1), (e, f), (f, g), (f, 1), (g, h), (g, j), (h, i), (i, j), (j, k), (k, 1)}. Junctions a and c are not adjacent since b intervenes, and b and d are not adjacent since c intervenes.

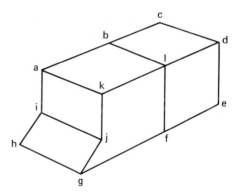

Fig. 11.6.4

The Labeling Rule

Adjacent junction labelings must assign the same label to their common line.

The physical reason for this is that an edge formed by the intersection of planar faces cannot change its nature between adjacent vertices, i.e., a line cannot represent a convex edge at one end and a concave edge at the other if there are no intervening junctions.

Using the labeling rule we can check to see whether a given set of labelings can represent a physically possible interpretation for a line drawing of a scene; moreover we can use the labeling rule to construct the set of physically possible interpretations for a line drawing. Note that we are *not* using the labeling rule to establish that a given line drawing represents a physically possible scene; we assume that each line drawing can arise only from a real scene (see Definition 11.3.4).

Definition 11.6.4

A *physically possible labeling* for a scene is one where the labeling rule is satisfied for every line segment.

Example 11.6.5

Figure 11.6.5 represents a physically possible interpretation for the line drawing, since all the labelings for adjacent junctions match along the joining line segments and each labeling is physically possible.

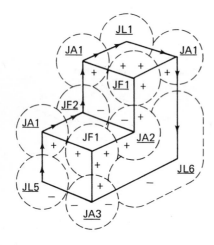

Fig. 11.6.5

From here on we denote the labeling of Fig. 11.6.5 as shown in Fig. 11.6.6; each line segment will be marked with only one label, since each line segment can only have one label.

We can find the physically possible labelings for a line drawing by use of a tree search strategy.

Example 11.6.6

Let us construct the tree for the line drawing of a tetrahedron. First order the junctions as shown in Fig. 11.6.7.

Now starting with J1, let the branches at each level of the tree represent all the possible labelings for that junction as shown in Fig. 11.6.8.

Since the tree rapidly becomes unmanageable, I have pruned it at each ply to eliminate all the labelings which do not satisfy the labeling rule. Thus

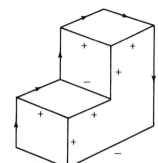

Fig. 11.6.6

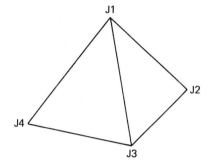

Fig. 11.6.7

at level 2, all but four nodes can be eliminated by applying the labeling rule along line segment J1-J2.

We can then move on to J3. Now there are two line segments which must be checked for satisfaction of the labeling rule, namely line segments J1-J3 and J2-J3. In this case the entire center branch can be eliminated, since none of the possible labelings for J3 can satisfy the labeling rule for all segments given that J1 was assigned labeling JA2.

Now we can label J4. Finally, each labeling that satisfies the labeling rule represents the last piece of a complete labeling for the line drawing. There are three distinct possible labelings; as illustrated in Fig. 11.6.9.

Various tree search strategies can be used to ascertain all the physically possible labelings for a line drawing. A computer program which finds all the Huffman/Clowes labelings for a scene was written by Dowson [3] in the MICRO-PLANNER language.

EXERCISES 11.6

1. Find and verify a physically possible Huffman/Clowes labeling for each of the line drawings in Fig. 11.6.10.

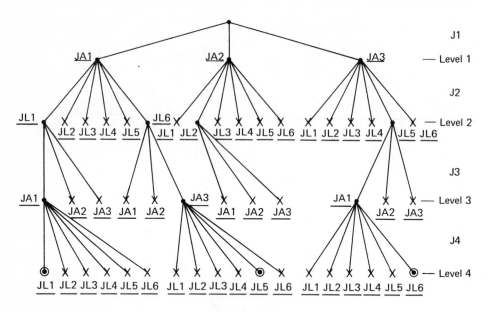

Fig. 11.6.8

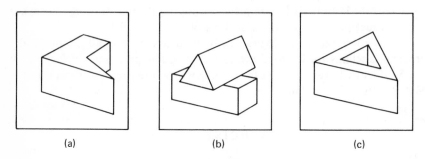

Fig. 11.6.9

Fig. 11.6.10

2. Find all the physically possible Huffman/Clowes labelings for the line drawing from Fig. 11.6.10(c).

11.7. REGIONS OF TRIHEDRAL OBJECTS

This section deals with an alternative method for treating objects made up of trihedral vertices. The last section dealt with *analysis* of polyhedra; this section deals with *synthesis* of polyhedra. Basically we will see that a very simple machine can generate all views of all polyhedra (given enough time of course). Using the language analogy, this machine represents a generative grammar for objects containing only trihedral vertices.

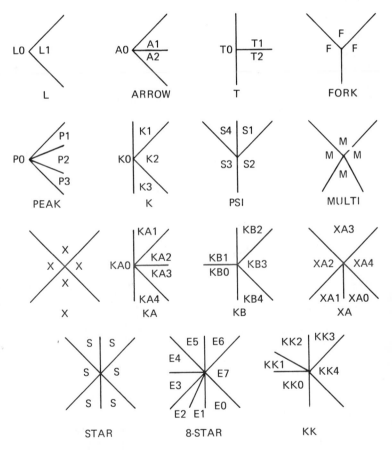

Fig. 11.7.1 Junction segment types.

The basic idea is this: We imagine moving around the lines bounding a region in a fixed direction, namely clockwise when viewed from an interior point of the region. At each junction we note the type of junction segment (see Fig. 11.7.1 for explanation of junction segment types). Only certain ordered pairs of junction segment types can occur physically. These correspond to adjacent junctions which satisfy the labeling rule. When we arrive back at the starting junction segment, we are through.

Example 11.7.1

Suppose we want to find all possible regions which are bounded by type I vertices only. Let us first list all the labelings which can occur around such a region. This list, shown in Fig. 11.7.2, is a subset of the labelings shown in Fig. 11.6.2. Assume for the time being that we only want to generate unobscured regions. Each junction segment which can be part of such a region is shaded in Fig. 11.7.2.

Now suppose that we start with a FORK junction segment, F. If we move clockwise around the line segments, what junction segment type can be encountered next? The answer is: Any junction segment which is shaded and which has a convex $(+)$ labeling as its left bounding line. Thus the next segment must either be A1 or F. Following the same reasoning, we can arrive at the following set of transition rules for a region bounded by type I vertices:

$$L1 \;\longrightarrow\; \{L1, A2, T0\} \qquad \text{(label line} \to \text{)}$$
$$F \;\longrightarrow\; \{F, A1\} \qquad \text{(label line} + \text{)}$$
$$A1 \;\longrightarrow\; \{L1, A2, T0\} \qquad \text{(label line} \to \text{)}$$
$$A2 \;\longrightarrow\; \{F, A1\} \qquad \text{(label line} + \text{)}$$
$$T0 \;\longrightarrow\; \{L1, A2, T0\} \qquad \text{(label line} \to \text{)}$$

This can also be represented graphically as shown in Fig. 11.7.3, where the appropriate line labels are marked on the transitions. The only restrictions on the machine shown are that in order to represent a region, the sequence of junction segment types must contain at least three elements, and the starting segment type must be reachable in one transition from the final segment type. Thus the following sequences represent valid regions:

$\{F, A1, L1, A2\}$ (a face of a cube)
$\{A1, L1, A2\}$ (a face of a tetrahedron)
$\{F, F, A1, L1, L1, A2\}$ (the face of the line drawing in Fig. 11.7.4)
$\{F, A1, T0, T0, L1, T0, T0, A2\}$ (the face of the cube in Fig. 11.7.5)

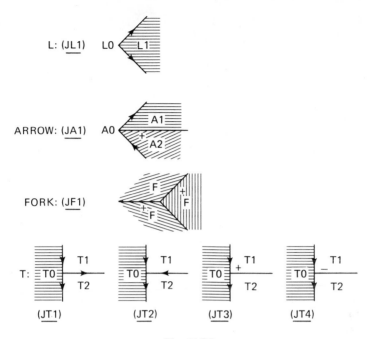

Fig. 11.7.2

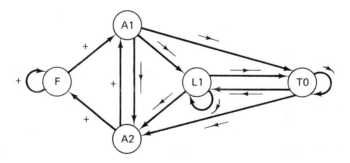

Fig. 11.7.3

Example 11.7.2

The following transition rules represent a machine for generating regions bounded by convex edges and type I or type IIIA vertices.

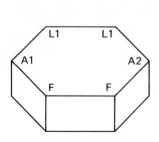

Fig. 11.7.4

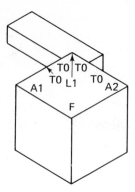

Fig. 11.7.5

L1 $\rightarrow$ {L1, A2, T0, L0}   (label $\rightarrow$)

F $\rightarrow$ {A1, F, L0, A0}   (label $+$)

A1 $\rightarrow$ {L1, A2, T0, L0}   (label $\rightarrow$)

A2 $\rightarrow$ {F, A1, L0, A0}   (label $+$)

T0 $\rightarrow$ {L1, A2, T0, L0}   (label $\rightarrow$)

L0 $\rightarrow$ {L1, A2, T0, L0}   (label $\rightarrow$)

L0 $\rightarrow$ {F, Al, L0, A0}   (label $+$)

A0 $\rightarrow$ {F, Al, L0, A0}   (label $+$)

Two regions generated by this machine are shown in Fig. 11.7.6. Note that regions generated by the machine in the previous example can also be generated by this machine. Hollerbach [6] calls any region that can be generated by such a machine a *projectable region*. By this he means that it is possible to imagine generating an object by moving the face in some direction and filling in all the space through which the face passes.

Example 11.7.3

Suppose we wish to extend the machine in Example 11.7.1 to include the possibility that the region may be partially obscured by other trihedral objects. As we move around a region R in the standard clockwise direction, the first evidence of such obscuring will be that we encounter a type T1 junction segment, and we know that the label for the next line segment must indicate that the region R is obscured. What sequence of junction segments can we now encounter? The answer is that we can encounter any of the junction segments marked with stars in Fig. 11.7.7. Notice that since neither a convex edge marked

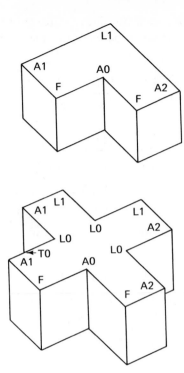

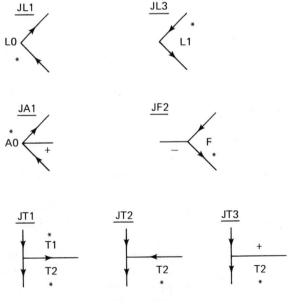

Fig. 11.7.6

Fig. 11.7.7

"+" nor a concave edge can obscure a region, we can eliminate all junction segments which are bounded by either of these edges. The augmented transition rules are:

$$L1 \rightarrow \{L1, A2, T0, T1\} \qquad (\text{label} \rightarrow)$$

$$F \rightarrow \{A1, F, T1\} \qquad (\text{label} +)$$

$$A1 \rightarrow \{L1, A2, T0, T1\} \qquad (\text{label} \rightarrow)$$

$$A2 \rightarrow \{A1, F, T1\} \qquad (\text{label} +)$$

$$T0 \rightarrow \{T0, L1, A2, T1\} \qquad (\text{label} \rightarrow)$$

$$T1 \rightarrow \{T1, T2, F', A0, L0, L1'\} \qquad (\text{label} \leftarrow)$$

$$F' \rightarrow \{T1, T2, F', A0, L0, L1'\} \qquad (\text{label} \leftarrow)$$

$$A0 \rightarrow \{T1, T2, F', A0, L0, L1'\} \qquad (\text{label} \leftarrow)$$

$$L0 \rightarrow \{T1, T2, F', A0, L0, L1'\} \qquad (\text{label} \leftarrow)$$

$$L1' \rightarrow \{T1, T2, F', A0, L0, L1'\} \qquad (\text{label} \leftarrow)$$

$$T2 \rightarrow \{T1, T2, F', A0, L0, L1'\} \qquad (\text{label} \leftarrow)$$

$$T2 \rightarrow \{L1, A2, T0, T1\} \qquad (\text{label} \rightarrow)$$

$$T2 \rightarrow \{A1, F, T1\} \qquad (\text{label} +)$$

EXERCISE 11.7

1. Generate a set of transition rules to describe a region that is bounded by type I and type V vertices, and which is not obscured. Comment on the relationship between these rules and the rules of Example 11.7.1.

11.8.   NONTRIHEDRAL VERTICES

We noted earlier (in Section 11.4) that many common vertices are non-trihedral. For example, recall that whenever an object made up of trihedral vertices is supported by a surface, the vertices where the object touches the surface are nontrihedral, since they are the intersection of four faces: three faces from the object plus the support surface face. A number of nontrihedral vertices are illustrated in Fig. 11.8.1. Notice that each object, taken by itself, is made up of only trihedral vertices.

In this section we will first develop a notation which will allow us to label line drawings like Fig. 11.8.1 appropriately, and then we will show how to enumerate all the junction labelings which are then possible.

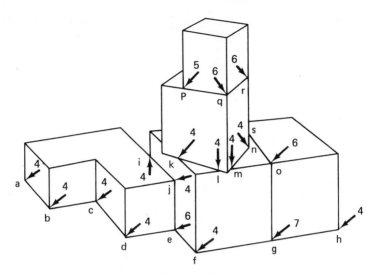

Fig. 11.8.1 Nontrihedral vertices.

Definition 11.8.1

A *crack edge* is an edge where two objects meet in such a way that there are two hidden faces and two coplanar exposed faces *locally* at each point along the edge. By *locally* we will mean that there is some cylinder of nonzero radius in which the definition holds. Note that any of the four faces forming a crack edge may actually be partially hidden.

Example 11.8.1

Lines g-o, o-s, p-q, and q-r in Fig. 11.8.1 represent crack edges in a scene.

Definition 11.8.2

A *two-object concave edge* is an edge which has the same geometry as a concave edge, but which is composed of two objects in such a way that three faces intersect at every point along the edge.

Example 11.8.2

Lines a-b, b-c, c-d, d-e, e-f, f-g, g-h, i-j, j-e, k-l, and m-n correspond to two-object concave edges. (Assuming that the L-shaped object contacts the neighboring brick along both i-j and j-e.)

The labeling conventions for these lines are illustrated in Fig. 11.8.2. Notice that like obscuring edges, crack and two-object concave edges each have an arrow mark; this corresponds to the observation that along these edges one of the two objects comprising the edge obscures the other.

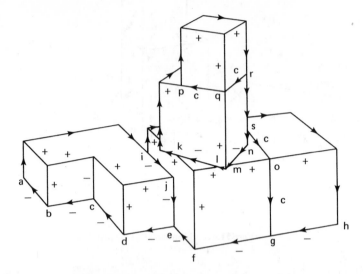

Fig. 11.8.2   Labels for nontrihedral vertices.

We will now proceed to enumerate all the possible scene vertices which can be represented as line drawings labeled from this extended label set. However, we will retain the following restrictions on scenes:

1. Each vertex has associated with it exactly three planes; every face at that vertex must lie in one of the three planes.
2. Every edge at a vertex must map into lines which can be labeled using only the set of labels defined so far.

Example 11.8.3

Figure 11.8.3 illustrates some scene features which violate the above restrictions:

1. We have no labeling for edge a-b.
2. Vertices c and d have faces which lie in four different planes; we have no labeling for edge c-d (it is a "separable convex" edge).
3. We have no labeling for edge e-f.
4. Vertex g has faces in four different planes.
5. Vertices h, i, and j each have four different planes; we have no labeling for h-i or k-j.

We can now refer back to Fig. 11.4.2, and imagine adding separating

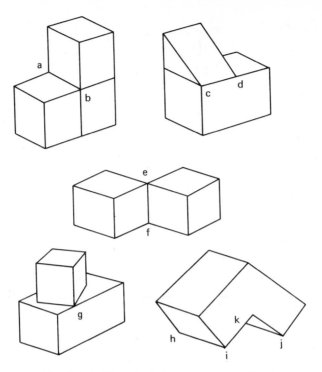

Fig. 11.8.3 Nontrihedral vertices not considered.

planes to the vertices, keeping the restrictions above in mind. The result of this process is the list of labelings in Fig. 11.8.4.

To reiterate what we have done: First we catalogued all the possible vertices which contain only three planes; next we defined trihedral (or three-face) vertices, and noted that these vertices could be characterized by the fact that only three junction types (L, ARROW, and FORK) represented trihedral vertices, and that only three different line labels (obscuring, concave, and convex) were needed to label all views of trihedral vertices; now we have added two new labels (crack and two-object concave) and have catalogued how many vertices we can now label in all possible views, given the extended label set.

It may seem that there are now a great many possible junction labelings. However, the number of ways of labeling a junction that are physically meaningful is only a tiny fraction of the number of ways of labeling a junction without regard to meaning. In terms of the language analogy of Section 11.6, the "words" in our scene language are the ordered combinations of "letters" (or line labels) which make physical sense. Since we have so far defined eight different labels for an edge $(+, \ -, \ \nearrow, \swarrow, \ ^-\!\nearrow, ^-\!\swarrow, \ ^c\!\nearrow, \ ^c\!\swarrow)$ there are $8^3 = 512$ possible "words" of three letters; of these 512 "words" only five "words" represent real scene ARROWS! Table 11.8.1 summarizes the "dictionary"

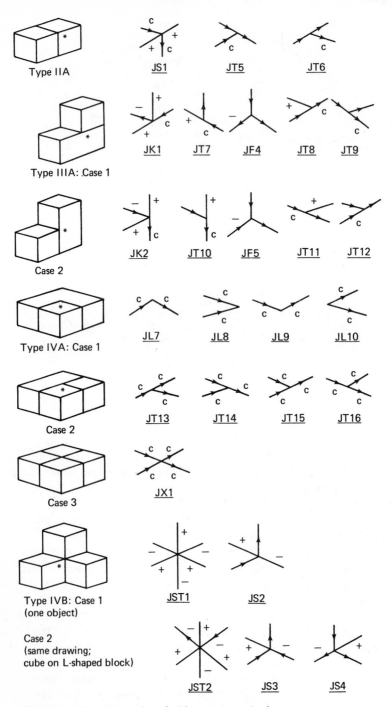

Type IIA

JS1   JT5   JT6

Type IIIA: Case 1

JK1   JT7   JF4   JT8   JT9

Case 2

JK2   JT10   JF5   JT11   JT12

Type IVA: Case 1

JL7   JL8   JL9   JL10

Case 2

JT13   JT14   JT15   JT16

Case 3

JX1

Type IVB: Case 1
(one object)

JST1   JS2

Case 2
(same drawing;
cube on L-shaped block)

JST2   JS3   JS4

(Note: all other cases require a 3-object concave edge.)

Fig. 11.8.4

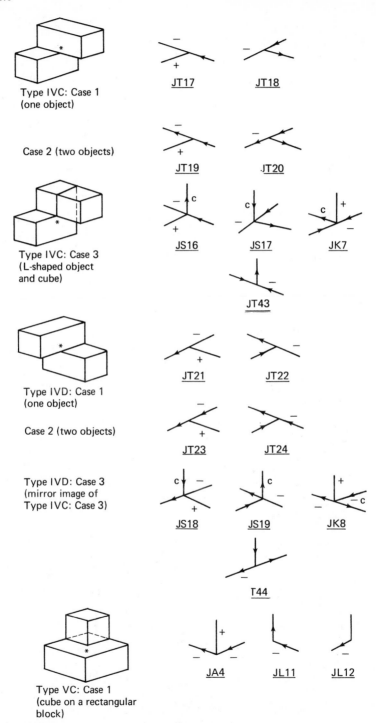

Type IVC: Case 1
(one object)

JT17   JT18

Case 2 (two objects)

JT19   JT20

Type IVC: Case 3
(L-shaped object
and cube)

JS16   JS17   JK7

JT43

Type IVD: Case 1
(one object)

JT21   JT22

Case 2 (two objects)

JT23   JT24

Type IVD: Case 3
(mirror image of
Type IVC: Case 3)

JS18   JS19   JK8

T44

Type VC: Case 1
(cube on a rectangular
block)

JA4   JL11   JL12

Fig. 11.8.4 (cont.)

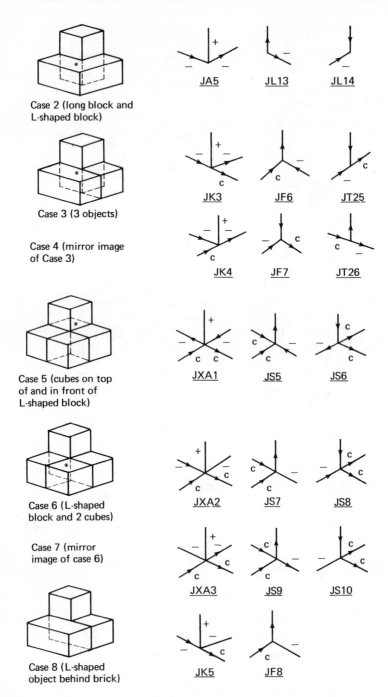

Case 2 (long block and
L-shaped block)

Case 3 (3 objects)

Case 4 (mirror image
of Case 3)

Case 5 (cubes on top
of and in front of
L-shaped block)

Case 6 (L-shaped
block and 2 cubes)

Case 7 (mirror
image of case 6)

Case 8 (L-shaped
object behind brick)

Fig. 11.8.4 (cont.)

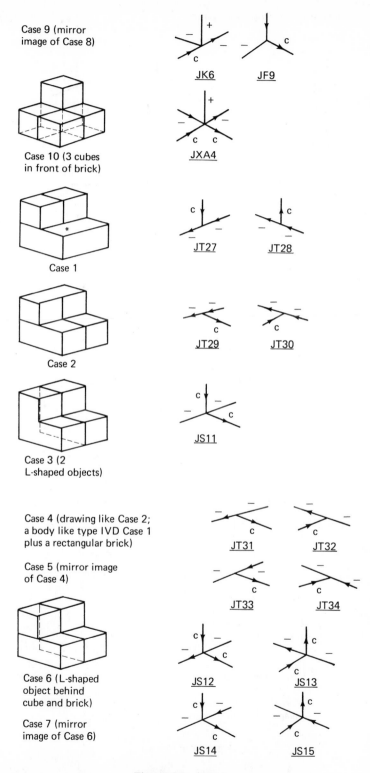

Case 9 (mirror image of Case 8)

JK6   JF9

Case 10 (3 cubes in front of brick)

JXA4

Case 1

JT27   JT28

Case 2

JT29   JT30

Case 3 (2 L-shaped objects)

JS11

Case 4 (drawing like Case 2; a body like type IVD Case 1 plus a rectangular brick)

JT31   JT32

Case 5 (mirror image of Case 4)

JT33   JT34

Case 6 (L-shaped object behind cube and brick)

JS12   JS13

Case 7 (mirror image of Case 6)

JS14   JS15

Fig. 11.8.4 (cont.)

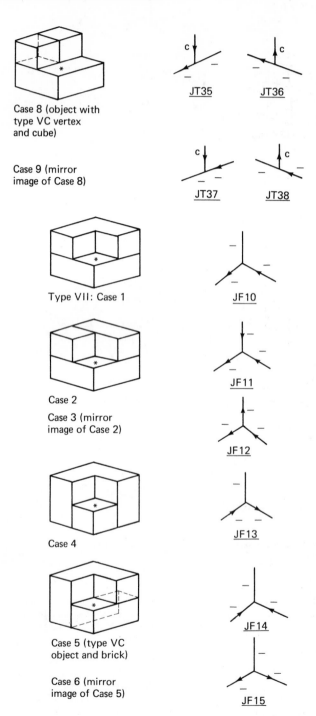

Case 8 (object with type VC vertex and cube)

JT35 JT36

Case 9 (mirror image of Case 8)

JT37 JT38

Type VII: Case 1

JF10

Case 2

Case 3 (mirror image of Case 2)

JF11

JF12

Case 4

JF13

Case 5 (type VC object and brick)

Case 6 (mirror image of Case 5)

JF14

JF15

Fig. 11.8.4 (cont.)

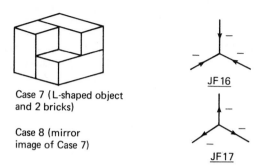

Case 7 (L-shaped object
and 2 bricks)

Case 8 (mirror
image of Case 7)

For completeness, we must also include these apparent vertices:

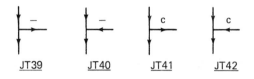

Fig. 11.8.4 (cont.)

entries for the Huffman/Clowes four-letter alphabet and for our current eight-letter alphabet.

A consequence of the relatively small percentage of physically possible labelings is that if we have partial information about a junction, i.e., if we know that one line must be labeled in a particular way, then we can impose strong limitations on the ways that the other lines of the junction can be labeled. In this sense, each labeling contains a great deal of information about the physical world.

Table 11.8.1

Junction Type	Huffman/Clowes		Eight Letter Alphabet	
	Number of Letter Combinations	Number of "Words"	Number of Letter Combinations	Number of "Words"
L	16	6	64	14
ARROW	64	3	512	5
FORK	64	5*	512	47*
T	46	4	512	44
K	256	—	4096	8
PSI	256	—	4096	19
X	256	—	4096	4*
XA	1024	—	32768	4
STAR	4096	—	262144	8*

*Since these junctions are symmetrical, there are more "words" than there are labelings.

EXERCISE 11.8

1.   Label each line of the line drawing of Fig. 11.8.5, assuming that the scene represented consists of objects resting on a plane support surface T. Verify that each
junction labeling is a valid one.

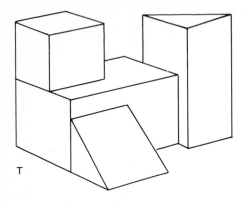

Fig. 11.8.5

11.9.   SHADOWS OF A SINGLE POINT LIGHT
SOURCE

We now come to the final type of edges we will consider, namely shadows.
As noted earlier, shadows give information about whether or not objects
touch, and we will show how to exploit this fact. Throughout this section we
will assume that we have a single point light source, plus a diffuse source, so
that object edges are visible within shadows. This corresponds to outdoor
lighting on a sunny day; the sun is approximately a point source and a blue
sky is a diffuse light source. Diffuse light is *not* present on the moon, so that
shadows on the moon do not contain detail like that shown in the figures of
this chapter. We will make one more assumption throughout this section,
namely that the light source is in *general position*. This is analogous to the eye
being in general position, and requires that small changes in light position do
not change the topology of the line drawing of a scene.

Example 11.9.1

In Fig. 11.9.1(a), it is not possible to decide whether the objects touch,
nor is it possible to tell whether the objects are supported, and how they are
supported. However, if we have shadows as in Fig. 11.9.1(b), we can tell that
the objects touch at a and that they are supported. If we have shadows as in
Fig. 11.9.1(c), we can tell that the objects do *not* touch at a and that the objects

are either unsupported, or supported in a way that cannot be seen (e.g., by small blocks underneath them). Without the shadows, as in Fig. 11.9.1(a), figures are usually highly ambiguous, whereas with them, as in Fig. 11.9.1(b) and 11.9.1(c), there is often a unique interpretation for a line drawing.

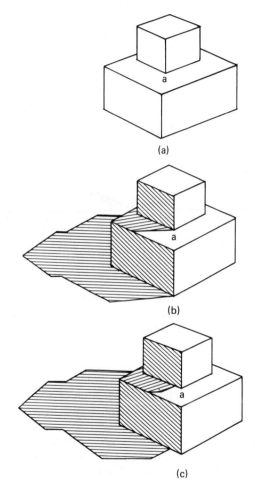

Fig. 11.9.1

Definition 11.9.1

A *shadow edge* is an apparent edge whose existence is solely dependent on light placement.

Example 11.9.2

All the shadow edges in Fig. 11.9.2 are marked with the notation we will use to label shadow edges, ✕. The arrow points from an illuminated region to a region in shadow.

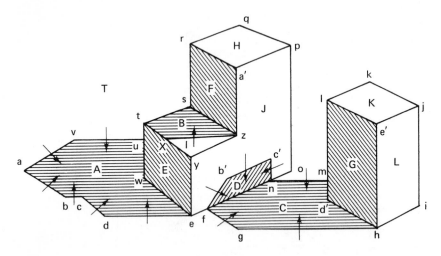

Fig. 11.9.2

The shadow edges are e-d, d-c, c-b, b-a, a-v, v-u, x-z, h-g, g-f, f-b′, b′-c′, c′-n, and n-m. Edges t-u, u-w, w-e, e-y, y-x, x-t, t-s, s-z, z-a′, a′-r, r-s, d′-m, m-1, 1-e, e-h, and h-d are *not* shadow edges, but are normal object edges.

Definition 11.9.2

A *projected shadow area* is a face or portion of a face (1) which is oriented toward the light source, and (2) from every point of which a vector from the face to the light source intersects some solid matter.

(By "oriented away from the light source" we mean that the angle between the outward normal vector of the face and the vector from the face to the light source is greater than 90°; by "oriented toward the light source," we mean that this angle is less than 90°.)

Example 11.9.3

Regions A, B, C, and D in Fig. 11.9.2 correspond to projected shadow areas in the scene depicted.

Definition 11.9.3

A *self-shadowed face* is a scene face which is oriented away from the light source. None of its edges can be shadow edges.

Example 11.9.4

Regions E, F, and G in Fig. 11.9.4 correspond to self-shadowed faces in the scene.

Definition 11.9.4

An *illuminated area* is a face or portion of a face which is oriented toward the light source and which is not a projected shadow area (i.e., there is a clear path from each point of the illuminated area to the light source).

Example 11.9.5

Regions H, I, J, K, L, and T in Fig. 11.9.2 correspond to illuminated areas in the scene.

We will label the regions of a line drawing according to the type of area or face that region corresponds to:

    1. A *type I region* corresponds to an *Illuminated area*.
    2. A *type SP region* corresponds to a *Projected Shadow area*.
    3. A *type SS region* corresponds to a *Self-Shadowed face*.

Definition 11.9.5

A *shadow causing edge* is one which casts a shadow. (I will appeal to your knowledge of the world in stating some of the following lemmas without proof.)

Lemma 11.9.1

A shadow causing edge must always be a convex edge.

Lemma 11.9.2

Every convex edge must always be labeled $+$, $\nearrow$, or $\swarrow$.

Lemma 11.9.3

Every shadow causing edge has an illuminated area on one side and a self-shadowed face on the other side.

Definition 11.9.6

A *shadow causing vertex* is a vertex where one shadow edge and the edge casting that shadow intersect.

Example 11.9.6

The vertices corresponding to junctions e, z, and h in Fig. 11.9.2 are shadow causing vertices. At e, the shadow edge is e-d and the shadow causing edge is e-y. At z, z-a′ causes z-x, and at h, h-e′ causes h-g.

Definition 11.9.7

A region is said to be *obscured with respect to a vertex* if, at the junction corresponding to the vertex, the two lines bounding the region must both be labeled as edges which obscure the region.

Example 11.9.7

In Fig. 11.9.2, region T is obscured with respect to the vertices t, s, r, q, p, l, k, and j.

Lemma 11.9.4

The type of illumination of a region obscured with respect to a vertex cannot be inferred from the labeling of the rest of the vertex.

Lemma 11.9.5

Of the vertices which we have enumerated in Fig. 11.8.4 and in Section 11.5, only vertices with the geometries of type IIIA, IVB, IVC, IVD, and VC (see Fig. 11.4.2) can be shadow causing vertices.

Proof: We have enumerated vertices of the following geometries: I, IIA, IIIA, IVA, IVB, IVC, IVD, VC, VIA, and VII. Since a shadow causing vertex must have at least one convex edge as a shadow causing edge, neither geometries VIA nor IVA nor VII can be shadow causing vertices. Type I and IIA vertices have convex edges, but since they have no concave edges, it is impossible for any convex edge to cast a shadow which intersects the vertex. The views of all shadow causing vertices are enumerated in Example 11.9.8. ∎

Example 11.9.8

First note that each vertex geometry has the same shadow causing properties regardless of whether or not cracks are present at the vertices. Thus we need only consider each geometry once, and we can extend the results to the crack cases trivially. All the views of shadow causing vertices for each non-crack case are listed in Fig. 11.9.3.

Example 11.9.9

Each shadow edge at a shadow causing vertex in Fig. 11.9.3 has also been marked with an L or R, according to whether the arrow on the shadow edge points counterclockwise or clockwise, respectively. The additional labels preclude the possibility of labeling an edge as a shadow caused from both ends. If we did not distinguish shadow edges at shadow causing vertices from other shadow edges in this manner, then it would be possible to label Fig. 11.9.4(a) as shown, with edge a-b interpreted as a shadow edge, caused from

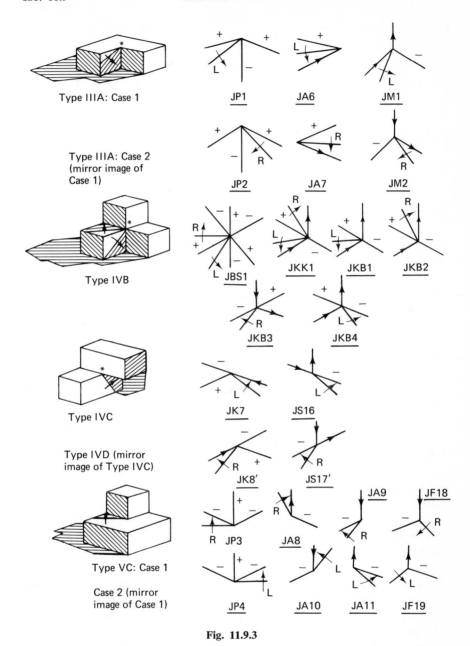

Fig. 11.9.3

both ends! With the L and R appended to the shadow causing vertices, it is impossible to match the two shadow causing vertices, and so a-b cannot be

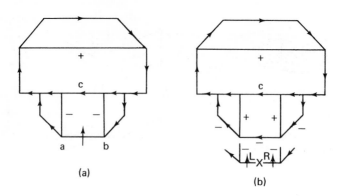

Fig. 11.9.4

interpreted as a shadow edge, as illustrated in Fig. 11.9.4(b). (The L and R are short for left and right, originally used because in case VC, L means lit from the left and R, lit from the right.)

Lemma 11.9.6

At a junction corresponding to a shadow causing vertex one and only one of the following four statements must be true for each shadow causing edge at the vertex:

a. The shadow causing edge is labled "+", and has an illuminated area on one side and a self-shadowed face on the other.

b. The shadow causing edge is labeled as an obscuring edge, and has an illuminated area on the obscuring side and a projected shadow area on the obscured side.

c. The shadow causing edge is labeled as an obscuring edge, and has a self-shadowed face on the obscuring side and an illuminated area on the obscured side.

d. The shadow causing edge is labeled as an obscuring edge, the obscuring side is either a self-shadowed face or an illuminated face, and the obscured side is a region obscured with respect to the vertex.

Proof: Statement a follows trivially from Lemma 11.9.3. In statements b, c, and d, if we can only see one side of the shadow causing edge, then that side must be either illuminated or self-shadowed, again by Lemma 11.9.3. If the shadow causing edge obscures a region that is obscured with respect to the vertex, then statement d is obviously true. Otherwise, the shadow causing edge must obscure a region which is part of the shadow causing vertex. If we can see the illuminated side of the shadow causing edge and if we can also see the shadow edge at the vertex (which we can by definition of a shadow causing vertex) then the projected shadow area must adjoin the shadow causing edge—what could be between them? If we can see only the self-shadowed side, then the adjacent region must be illuminated, or else the shadow causing edge could not cast a shadow at the vertex. ▌

Example 11.9.10

The proof may be clarified somewhat by Fig. 11.9.5. Each statement of Lemma 11.9.6 is illustrated at the shadow causing vertices marked a, b, c, and d.

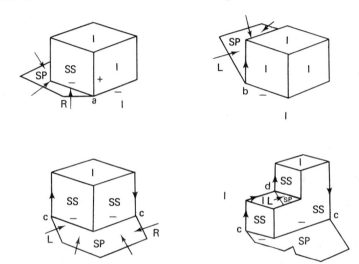

Fig. 11.9.5

Lemma 11.9.7

Two regions, X and Y, separated by a crack edge must always have the same illumination type.

Proof: If X is type SS, then since regions bounding a crack edge are coplanar, region Y must be type SS also, since both have the same orientation with respect to the light source. If X is illuminated, then Y could only be other than illuminated if a shadow edge coincided exactly with the crack edge, but this is precluded by the general light position assumption. A symmetrical argument holds for the case where X is a projected shadow region. ▌

Lemma 11.9.8

A region X, separated by a concave edge or a two-object concave edge from a region Y, is type I if region Y is type I.

Proof: By reasoning similar to that for Lemma 11.9.7. ▌

Lemma 11.9.9

At a shadow causing vertex, if we consider in order the edges which intersect at the vertex, there is exactly one edge of concave geometry between the shadow edge and the edge which causes it. (This assumes that we move in the direction of the arrow on the shadow edge.)

Proof: The line in the scene corresponding to the shadow causing edge cannot lie in the plane of the face on which the shadow is cast, and thus this line must intersect the plane at the shadow causing vertex. Moreover the angle between this line and the normal to the plane must be less than 90°. Thus both faces bounded by the shadow causing edge must form concave edges with the plane on which the shadow is cast, and since we only allow three planes at any vertex, these three planes (the two which intersect along the shadow causing edge and the plane on which the shadow is cast) are the only planes at the vertex, and thus no other edges can intervene between the shadow edge and shadow causing edge. ∎

Theorem 11.9.1

If we can identify a junction as corresponding to a shadow causing vertex, and if we can label each line which intersects at the junction, then we can uniquely specify the illumination types for each region at the junction, except for regions obscured with respect to the vertex.

Proof: We can always by definition label the regions bounded by shadow edges as type I and type SP by definition of these illumination types. What can each of these regions be bounded by? (1) First, whenever the next edge is a crack, we can label the next region trivially, since the illumination types must be the same on both sides of a crack, by Lemma 11.9.7. (2) If the next edge is concave and its bordering region is illuminated, then the next region must also be illuminated, by Lemma 11.9.8. (3) If the next edge is concave and its bordering region is a projected shadow, then the next region must be either a projected shadow or a self-shadowed face by Lemma 11.9.7. But by Lemma 11.9.8, we know that such a concave edge must be the only edge between the shadow edge and the shadow causing edge, and thus the next region must be self-shadowed by Lemma 11.9.3. Furthermore we can then label the next region as illuminated since the other side of a shadow causing edge must be illuminated. (4) If the next edge is an obscuring edge, we can invoke Lemma 11.9.6. [The completion of this proof is left as an exercise for the interested reader.] ∎

We can illustrate the possible illumination combinations for each type of edge as shown in Fig. 11.9.6. For each possible illumination combination

		Illumination of R1		
		I	SP	SS
Illumination of R2	I	✓		
	SP		✓	✓
	SS		✓	✓

For an edge labeled:

R1 $\dfrac{\ }{\ }$ R2   or   R1 $\dfrac{\ }{\ }$ R2   or   R1 $\dfrac{\ }{\ }$ R2

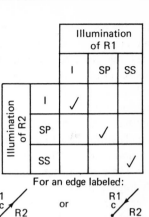

		Illumination of R1		
		I	SP	SS
Illumination of R2	I	✓		
	SP		✓	
	SS			✓

For an edge labeled:

R1 $\dfrac{\ }{c}$ R2   or   R1 $\dfrac{\ }{c}$ R2

		Illumination of R1		
		I	SP	SS
Illumination of R2	I	✓		✓
	SP		✓	✓
	SS	✓	✓	✓

For an edge labeled:

R1 $\dfrac{\ }{+}$ R2

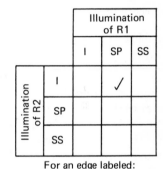

		Illumination of R1		
		I	SP	SS
Illumination of R2	I		✓	
	SP			
	SS			

For an edge labeled:

R1 R2   or   R1 R/R2   or   R1 L/R2

		Illumination of R1		
		I	SP	SS
Illumination of R2	I	✓	✓	✓
	SP	✓	✓	✓
	SS	✓	✓	✓

For an edge labeled:

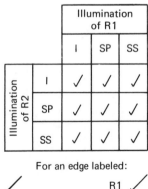

R1 R2   or   R1 R2

Fig. 11.9.6   Possible illumination combinations (✓).

and edge geometry, we will define a new label. Thus we now will have 52 possible labels for an edge: 18 possible obscuring edges, five possible concave edges, ten possible two-object concave edges, seven possible convex edges, six possible crack edges, and six possible shadow edges. In terms of the language analogy, we now have an "alphabet" of 52 "letters." Thus instead of labeling a region directly for illumination type, we will merely label all the edges bounding that region appropriately. This will enable us to demonstrate an extremely simple labeling strategy in the next section. We will not show all the junction labelings that are now possible. Note however that for a T junction with three obscuring edges, we now have $3 \times 3 \times 3 = 27$ new junction labelings in place of one old one, since the illumination of obscured regions is independent of the obscuring region. However, each shadow causing vertex has only one labeling, by Theorem 11.9.1, unless a region is obscured with respect to the junction, in which case there are three labelings.

Example 11.9.11

Why is it desirable to label the regions according to illumination type? Figure 11.9.7 illustrates how this information can cut down the number of interpretations for scene features. Suppose that we have labeled a as a shadow causing vertex as shown. If we do not label R1 as a projected shadow region, then *any interpretation is possible for line c-d*, i.e., c-d can be labeled with any of 52 labels. However, if we know that R1 is a projected shadow region and that R2 is illuminated, then c-d can only be labeled as (1) a shadow edge (c $\underline{\quad}\big|{\scriptstyle\frac{I}{SP}}$ d) or (2) an occluding edge (c $\xrightarrow{\quad}{\scriptstyle\frac{I}{SP}}$ d or c $\xleftarrow{\quad}{\scriptstyle\frac{I}{SP}}$ d). Note that $_c\underline{\quad}^{L}\big|{\scriptstyle\frac{I}{SP}}$ d and c $\underline{\quad}^{R}\big|{\scriptstyle\frac{I}{SP}}$ d are precluded because no T junctions are shadow causing vertices.

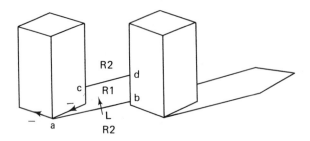

Fig. 11.9.7

Example 11.9.12

In order to complete this treatment of shadows, we must also enumerate all the other junctions that shadows can form which do not correspond to shadow causing vertices. These junctions and their labelings are listed in Fig. 11.9.8.

In Fig. 11.9.8, the junctions marked with numbers correspond to the lettered junctions of Fig. 11.9.2.

(1) corresponds to a, b, v, b′, and c′;

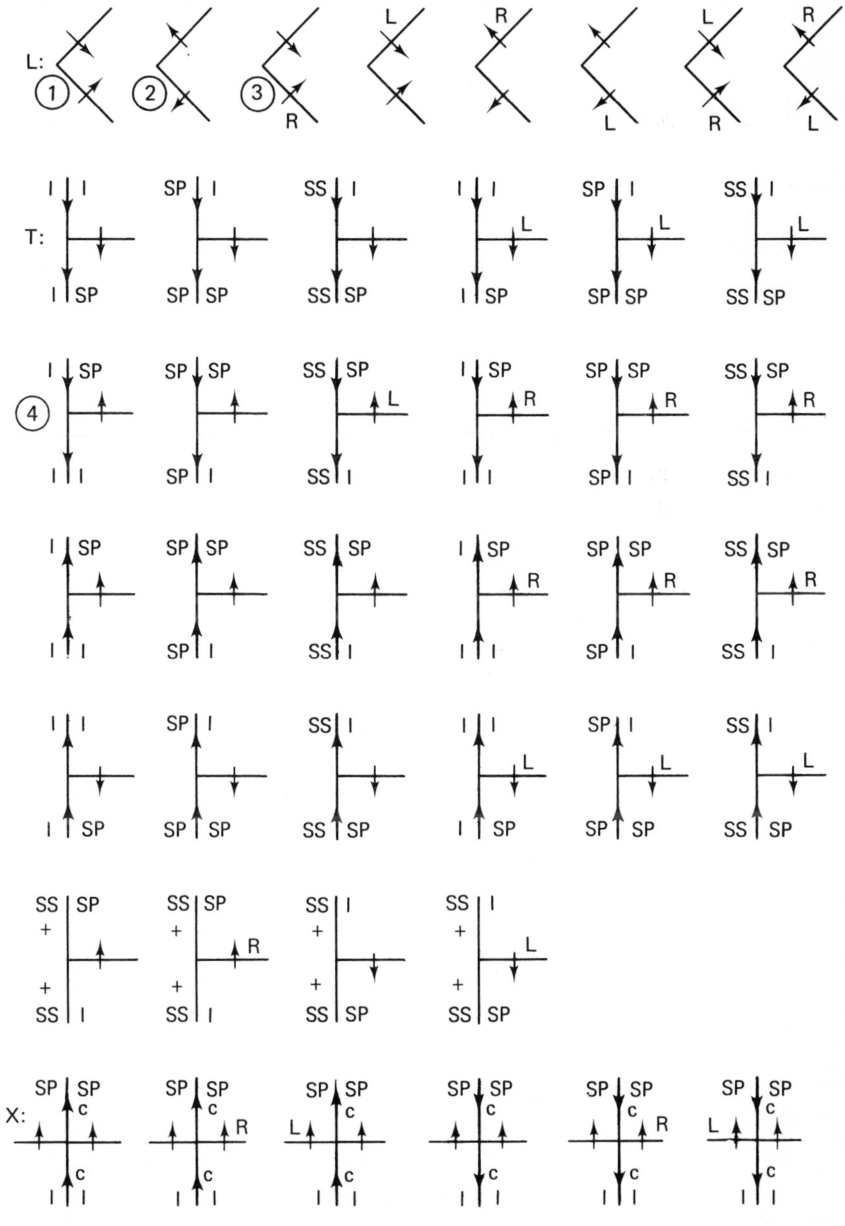

Fig. 11.9.8

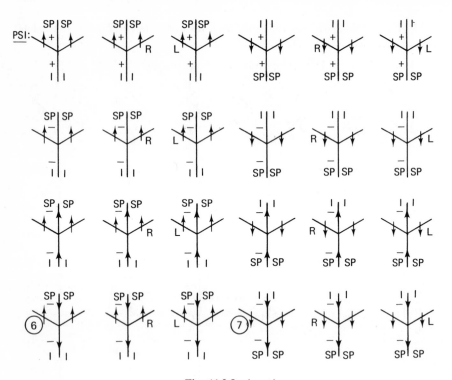

Fig. 11.9.8   (cont.)

(2) corresponds to c;

(3) corresponds to d and g;

(4) corresponds to m and u;

(5) corresponds to x;

(6) corresponds to f; and

(7) corresponds to n.

EXERCISES 11.9

1. Prove Lemma 11.9.3.

2. Complete the proof of Theorem 11.9.1.

3. Draw scenes containing each of the labeled junctions found in Fig. 11.9.9.

4. Construct a machine like those in Section 11.7 which will generate all unobscured shadow regions with shadow causing vertices having shadow edges marked ⊥ᴸ .

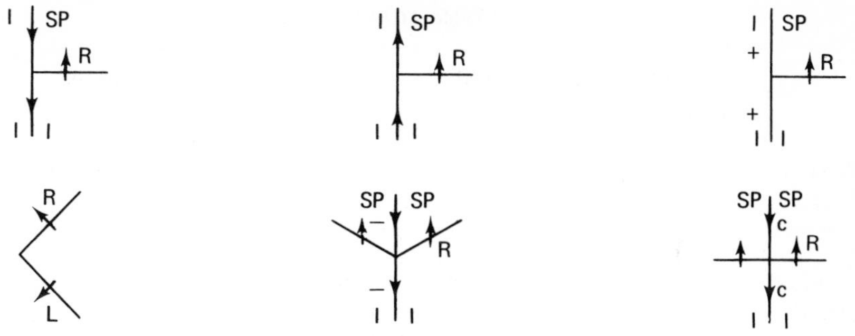

Fig. 11.9.9

11.10. LABELING SCENES WITH SHADOWS

This section presents three major results. First we will show what has happened to the number of junction labelings in going from eight possible labels to 52. Second, we will show how to use some natural assumptions about scenes to reduce the number of labeling choices at junctions around the outline of a scene. Third, we will show that with the more precise descriptions of edges embodied in the new labelings we can use a scheme to label line drawings which requires much less computation than does a tree search algorithm.

Table 11.10.1 summarizes the numbers of junction labelings and compares with the eight-label case, reproduced from Table 11.8.1. There is a dramatic reduction in the *percentage* of the combinatorially possible labelings that actually correspond to real physical scene features. However the *numbers* of labelings are still quite large.

There are many other types of information that can be used to preclude certain line labelings. For example, because two planes can only meet along one straight line, we can eliminate the possibility that a-b and c-d in Fig. 11.10.1 can have different labels; thus by checking for collinear line segments we can eliminate certain ambiguities that remain after the normal labeling process. Similarly, if we know that two regions like R1 and R2 in Fig. 11.10.2 are separated by a shadow edge, then we know that every line which separates the two regions must be a shadow edge, since the two regions must be coplanar, and the only coplanar edge which has an illuminated region on one side and a projected shadow on the other is a shadow edge.

Let us systematize some of the other clues we can use to cut down on the number of possible interpretations of a line drawing.

Lemma 11.10.1

The SP side of a shadow edge is darker than the I side of the edge.

Table 11.10.1

Junction Types	Eight Letter Alphabet			Fifty-two Letter Alphabet		
	Number of Letter Combinations	Number of Actual "Words"	Approx. %	Number of Letter Combinations	Number of Actual "Words"	Approx. %
L	64	14	22.0	2704	82	3.0
ARROW	512	5	1.0	140608	73	.05
FORK	512	47	9.2	140608	357	.25
T	512	44	9.2	140608	460	.33
PEAK	4096	—	0	7.31×10^6	8	1.1×10^{-6}
K	4096	—	0	7.31×10^6	94	1.3×10^{-5}
PSI	4096	19	.5	7.31×10^6	181	2.5×10^{-5}
X	4096	4	.1	7.31×10^6	18	2.5×10^{-6}
MULTI	4096	—	0	7.31×10^6	104	1.4×10^{-5}
KA	32768	—	0	3.80×10^8	10	2.6×10^{-8}
KB	32768	—	0	3.80×10^8	30	7.9×10^{-8}
XA	32768	4	1.2×10^{-2}	3.80×10^8	20	5.2×10^{-8}
KK	262144	—	0	1.97×10^{10}	4	2.0×10^{-10}
STAR	262144	8	3.1×10^{-3}	1.97×10^{10}	72	3.7×10^{-9}
8STAR	1.6×10^6	—	0	5.32×10^{13}	1	1.9×10^{-14}

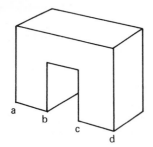

Fig. 11.10.1

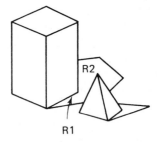

Fig. 11.10.2

Example 11.10.1

Suppose that we wish to label the line drawing in Fig. 11.10.3. Suppose further that we know the region light intensities, and that the order of decreasing brightness is C, D, T, A, B.

Since of the junctions in the scene the smallest percentage of PEAKs is physically possible, let us start by labeling PEAK junction a. There are eight possible cases. Note that all cases label T as illuminated. Case 1 can be immediately ruled out since there is no way to label junction K that is consistent with the labeling at a. In case 2, once we label j, then there is no way to label f, since there is no T which has a shadow edge in the required position. Let us

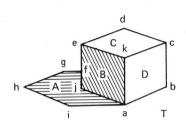

Case 1

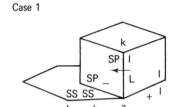

Case 5

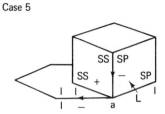

Case 2

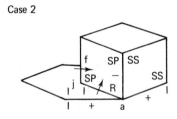

Case 6

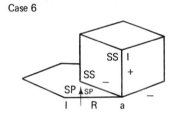

Case 3

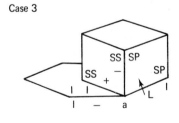

Case 7

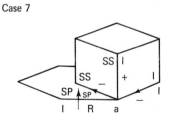

Case 4

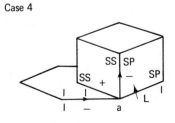

Case 8

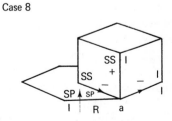

Fig. 11.10.3

now use Lemma 11.10.1; this allows us to rule out cases 3, 4, and 5, since region D is brighter than region T. Cases 6, 7, and 8 are possible interpretations: 6 is an object protruding from T, 7 is a square peg in a square hole in T, and 8 is an object sitting on T.

Given the notation we have developed, it is easy now to take advantage of some natural assumptions about the support surface. Let us assume from here on in that the background (region T in Fig. 11.10.3) is a plane with no holes or protrusions, and that the scene is completely surrounded by background, i.e., no lines intersect the frame of the drawing.

Definition 11.10.1

The *scene/background boundary* consists of the set of all lines except frame lines which have the background on one side.

Example 11.10.2

The scene/background boundary in Fig. 11.10.3 consists of lines a-b, b-c, c-d, d-e, e-f, f-g, g-h, h-i, and i-a.

Let us make one further assumption, that the point light source is located above the support plane so that the background is an illuminated region. We will refer to these assumptions as the *plane background assumptions*.

Theorem 11.10.1

Given the plane background assumptions, only lines labeled from the set of labels can appear on the scene/background boundary. ("B" and "S" are used to identify the regions intended to be parts of the background and scene, respectively.)

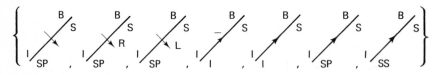

Proof: Since there are no holes or protrusions, there can be no regions joined to the background which are not coplanar with it, so there can be no edges labeled + or − in any illumination combinations. Furthermore, the only way that the background could obscure part of the scene is if part of the scene were below the support surface, which is impossible if there are no holes. Thus B∕S is not a possible labeling for a scene/background boundary line in any of its illumination combinations. Similarly, there can be no cracks on the scene/background boundary, since the presence of a crack would imply either that there is a filled hole in the support surface, or that the background is made up of two or more parts. The latter case is precluded because if the crack does not close on itself as in the case of a hole, then lines corresponding to cracks must intersect the frame in at least two places which we have assumed that no line does. Finally edges from the set

are precluded, since the background is illuminated. This leaves only the claimed line labels as possible interpretations of the scene/background boundary. ∎

Example 11.10.3

Given the plane background assumptions, cases 6 and 8 from Fig. 11.10.3 can also be eliminated as possibilities by applying Theorem 11.10.1, leaving case 7 as the only possible interpretation for the line drawing.

We can use the plane background assumptions to generate a reduced list of junctions which are possible on the scene/background boundary. Table 11.10.2 lists the numbers of labelings possible for each type of junction on the scene background boundary, broken down according to the orientation in which each junction appears. Note that only a fraction of the possible junction types and orientations can appear at all on this boundary.

We can now use all these results to define a new scheme for labeling a line drawing of a scene. Note that there is a considerable problem in using a tree search solution, as was done in the Huffman/Clowes case. While conceptually there is no problem in imagining a tree search solution solving a labeling problem in a finite number of steps, in terms of an actual program, for contemporary computers, a tree with several hundred branches at many of its nodes cannot be searched in a reasonable amount of time. The computational problem can be eased if constraints are employed to reduce the number of combinations to be considered. When I first wrote a program to eliminate such impossible labelings, I stumbled upon an intriguing result. This program operated by the following process P:

P1.   Order the junctions in any manner. (It is most efficient to start with ones on the scene/background boundary.)

P2.   Assign the full list of possible labelings to the first junction.

P3.   At the next junction J, assign a list of labelings by taking the full list and eliminating every labeling which does not match at least one

Table 11.10.2

Junction Type Orientation*	Number of Possible Labelings for Scene/Background Boundary Junction	Number of Possible Labelings for Interior Scene Junction
L/LO	9	82
L/LI	7	82
ARROW/AO	20	73
FORK/F	20	357
T/TO	13	460
T/T1	8	460
T/T2	8	460
PEAK/PO	2	8
PSI/S1	8	181
PSI/S2	4	181
PSI/S3	4	181
PSI/S4	8	181
MULTI/M	6	104
KB/KBO	1	30
KB/KB1	1	30

*These numbers are computed under the assumption that the junction segment specified is part of the background region. See Fig. 13.7.1 for explanation of junction segment types.

other labeling at each adjacent junction that has already been considered.

P4.   Now eliminate any labelings from J's adjacent junctions which do not have labeling matches at J; if any labelings are eliminated at an adjacent junction, repeat this step at that junction; do this recursively until no more reductions are made at any junction; then go to P3.

The net result of this process is to insure that only labelings remain which match pairwise along each line segment of the line drawing. I intended to in this way avoid sprouting tree nodes which would give rise to no daughter nodes, and therefore to cut down the breadth of the tree to be searched. To my amazement, on every line drawing of a scene I have given to this program, only junctions which are part of some total labeling of the scene have survived this pairwise intersection-taking process. Tree search has proved to be simply unnecessary!

Conjecture 11.10.1

For line drawings of scenes satisfying all our listed assumptions, and for the list of junction labelings we have enumerated, we can find exactly the possible interpretations for each junction by applying process P.

Proof or refutation: For many scenes process P results in a unique labeling for each line of the line drawing. Whether or not the conjecture is true for every line drawing, the program has proved to be useful for practical computer vision systems, since the amount of time required to solve each scene increases at a rate roughly proportional to the number of objects in a scene, rather than increasing exponentially, as does a tree search scheme. The reason for this is that reductions in labelings rarely propagate between objects, since objects are usually bounded by obscuring edges, both sides of which can be labeled independently. ∎

Example 11.10.4

If the set of junction labelings is less precise than the one we have developed here, process P will definitely not yield the same result as a tree search. Suppose for example that we are labeling the line drawing in Fig. 11.10.4, and that our labeling list for each junction includes the ARROWs, Ls, and FORKs shown. Then each of these labelings will remain at each junction as a possible interpretation if we apply process P, since each has at least one match at each adjacent junction, even though these junctions cannot give a total labeling for the line drawing (try it!). Now let us add region illumination information, and enumerate all possibilities for these junctions. Notice now that none of the FORKs shown can remain, since no ARROW shown has a match for an edge labeled − SP/SP or − SS/SS, and each FORK label contains one or the other of these labels. Since none of the FORKs can stay, neither can the ARROWs or the L labeling.

Unfortunately it is impossible to show written examples of P in their entirety because of the large numbers of labels involved. (Any ideas for a rigorous proof or refutation of Conjecture 11.10.1 will be welcomed by the author.)

Acknowledgments

I would like to thank Patrick Winston for his support and advice, Robert Chien for his support and encouragement, Richard Gabriel for his aid in preparing and improving this manuscript, and Richard Duda for his careful review and helpful comments on this chapter. This work was supported in part by the Joint Services Electronics Program (U.S. Army, U.S. Navy, U.S. Air Force) under Contract DAAB–07–72–C–0259 with the Coordinated Science Laboratory at the University of Illinois at Champaign/Urbana, and in part by the Advanced Research Projects Agency of the Department of Defense and monitored by the Office of Naval Research under Contract Number N00014–70–A–0362–0003 at the MIT Artificial Intelligence Laboratory.

REFERENCES

1. CLOWES, M. B., "On Seeing Things," *AI Journal* (Spring 1971).

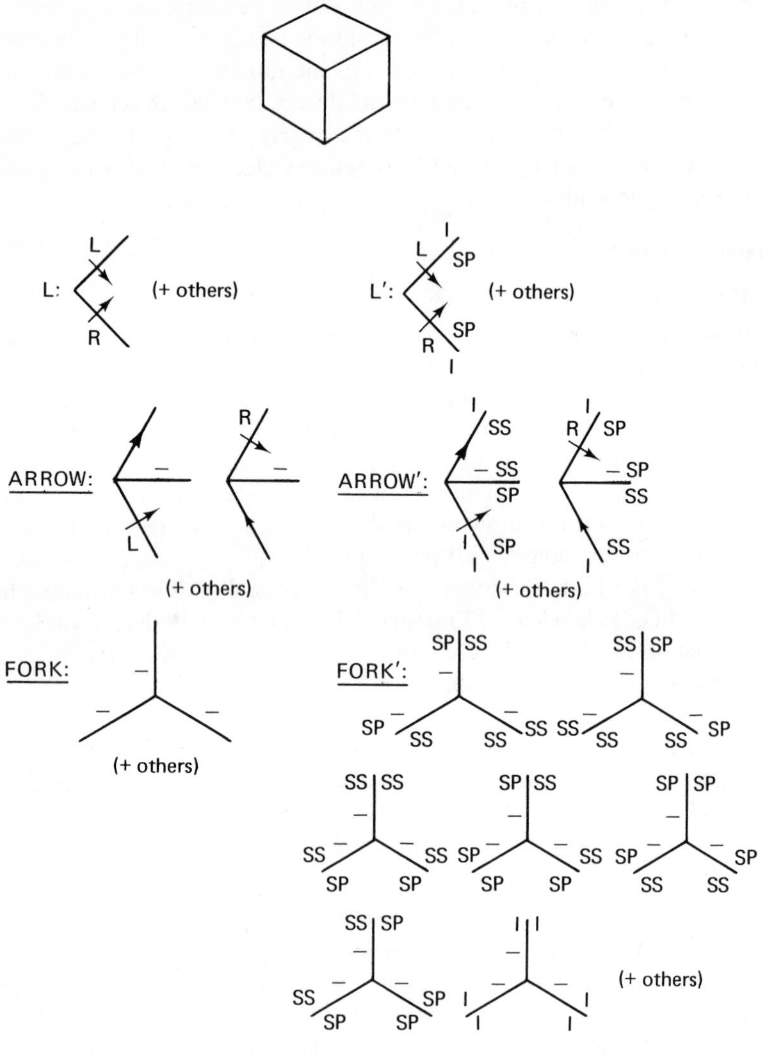

Fig. 11.10.4

2. CHANG, Y., "Machine Perception of 3-D Objects with Curved Surfaces," Ph.D. thesis, Coordinated Science Laboratory, University of Illinois at Urbana/Champaign, Feb. 1974.

3. DOWSON, M., "Progress in Extending the VIRGIN Program," *Vision Flash 20*, MIT Artificial Intelligence Laboratory, Oct. 1971.

4. DUDA, R. D. and P. E. HART, *Pattern Classification and Scene Analysis*, John Wiley & Sons, New York, 1973.

5. GUZMAN, A., "Computer Recognition of Three-dimensional Objects in a Visual Scene," *Technical Report AI-TR-228*, MIT Artificial Intelligence Laboratory, Dec. 1968.

6. HOLLERBACH, J., "The Projective Approach to Object Description," *Vision Flash 37*, MIT Artificial Intelligence Laboratory, Dec. 1972.

7. HORN, B.K.P., "The Image Dissector 'Eyes'," *Memo No. 178*, MIT Artificial Intelligence Laboratory, Aug. 1969.

8. HUFFMAN, D. H., "Impossible Objects as Nonsense Sentences," *Machine Intelligence 6*, Edinburgh University Press, Edinburgh, 1970.

9. SHIRAI, Y., "A Heterarchical Program for Recognition of Polyhedra," *Progress in Vision and Robotics*, ed. by P. Winston, *Technical Report AI-TR-281*, MIT Artificial Intelligence Laboratory, May 1973.

10. WALTZ, D. L., "Generating Semantic Descriptions from Drawings of Scenes with Shadows," *Technical Report AI-TR-271*, MIT Artificial Intelligence Laboratory, Nov. 1972.

11. WALTZ, D. L., "Shedding Light on Shadows," in *Progress in Vision and Robotics*, ed. by P. Winston, *Technical Report AI-TR-281*, MIT Artificial Intelligence Laboratory, May 1973.

12. WINSTON, P. H., "The MIT Robot," *Machine Intelligence 7*, Edinburgh University Press, Edinburgh, 1972.

13. WINSTON, P. H., "Summary of Selected Vision Topics," in *Progress in Vision and Robotics*, ed. by Winston, *Technical Report AI-TR-281*, MIT Artificial Intelligence Laboratory, May 1973.

12 USING FORMAL LANGUAGE THEORY TO MODEL BIOLOGICAL PROCESSES

Gabor T. Herman
Department of Computer Science
The State University of New York at Buffalo

Editor's Note:

This chapter provides a lucid introduction of how to model certain biological processes using language theory. The author artfully brings out how growth processes of many living organisms, especially those in which certain multicellular structures regularly repeat are susceptible to language description. The concept of a developmental system is then introduced and explored for the purpose of describing biological development in terms of cellular actions and interactions.

The chapter is written in plain language with plenty of examples and exercises. For the purpose of keeping the chapter to reasonable length, proofs for most theorems are omitted. However pointers to literature containing them are provided.

The only prerequisite for this chapter would be the concept of context-free grammar introduced in Chapter 1.

One of the important topics of automata theory is the study of "complex" machines built up from "simple" components (automata). In fact, this was considered to be a central problem by early workers in the field (see, e.g., von Neumann [3]). In connection with this, there are two basic questions to be considered.

1. Given a description of the overall behavior of the whole machine what

kind of characteristics of the individual automata and their interrelations are implied?

2. Given the characteristics of the building blocks (and the way they are connected) what kind of overall behavior may one expect?

An area where such questions can be readily studied is developmental biology. We shall view a biological organism as a collection of cells which behave individually in a relatively simple manner, yet in such a way that the behavior of the organism as a whole is much more complicated. The study of biological organisms is desirable since they represent already existing and functioning "machines" rather than theoretical daydreams. These "machines" have many properties which are attractive: ability to adjust quickly to changing environment, ability to achieve their goal in spite of extreme external disturbances, etc. Also, the organization of biological "machines" is in many ways superior to that of our present day computers. They can perform certain tasks (e.g., scene analysis) much faster, even though their basic circuit speed is slower than that of a computer. It should be clear that an automata theoretical study of biological organisms is important not only to the biologist, but also to the computer scientist, who wants to understand how these various desirable characteristics of biological "machines" are achieved.

In this chapter we shall be concerned with how the techniques of automata and formal language theory can be used to describe and discuss the development of biological organisms. We shall find that in order to do this, automata and formal language theory has to be enriched by some new constructs, especially designed to reflect certain aspects of biological development.

Our exposition is based on Herman and Rozenberg [2], the introductory chapter of which gives detailed biological justification of the concepts introduced in this chapter. Here we have to forego such a detailed biological justification for reasons of space, and content ourselves with one example in the first section.

12.1. INTUITIVE INTRODUCTION TO DEVELOPMENTAL SYSTEMS AND LANGUAGES

The purpose of this section is to give the motivation behind some of the concepts discussed more formally in later sections. To do this we will give a biological example.

In many growth processes of living organisms, especially of plants, regularly repeated appearances of certain multicellular structures are readily noticeable. In the simplest cases one observes the same structure being periodically repeated along an axis, such as leaves along a stem. In more complicated cases the entire structure of a previous stage is repeated as part of the organism at a later stage. Thus we have "compound" organisms or organs, such as compound leaves, compound inflorescences, or compound branching structures. In the case of a compound leaf, for instance, some of the lobes (or leaflets), which are parts of a leaf at an advanced stage, have the same shape as the whole leaf has at an earlier stage. One usually notices this relationship when on the same plant some leaves stop in their development earlier than others, and the smaller leaves appear to be identical to portions of the larger ones.

We give an example of a compound branching pattern. The following drawing represents the first sixteen stages of development of a filamentous plant (an alga or fungus).

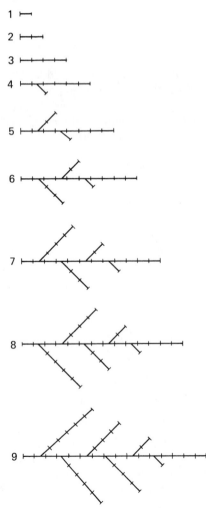

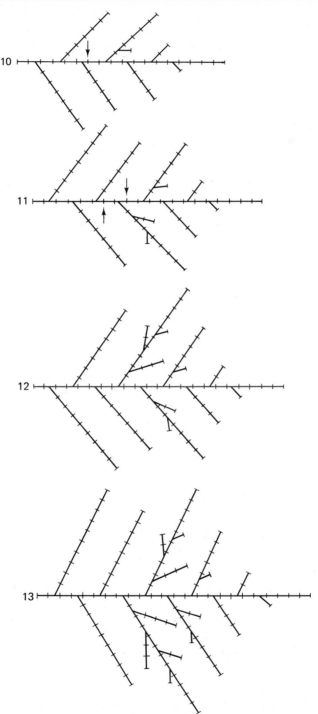

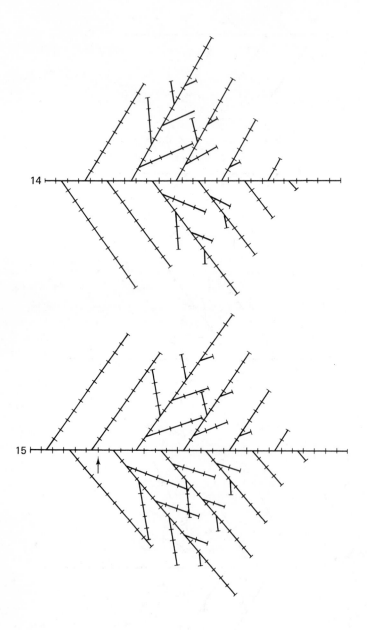

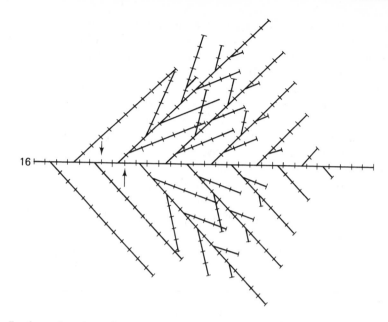

In these drawings the cells are represented by line segments. A somewhat more realistic representation, for example, of stage 7 would be

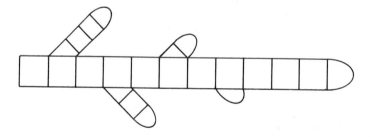

Such developments can be observed in nature. See for example the photograph of a young regenerate of *Callithamnion roseum* Harvey, reproduced in Herman and Rozenberg (Chapter 1, [2]).

Returning to our example, we see that from stage 6 onwards we may divide the organism into two parts. The first six cells (from the left) of the main branch form a *basal* part, while the rest of the cells form an *apical* part. (The points separating the basal and apical parts are marked by an arrow at stages 10 and 15.) Every second cell in the basal part carries a nonbranching *filament*. These filaments develop linearly in time, they repeat at each stage their own previous structure with the addition of one new cell. At stage 6 the lengths of these filaments are 3, 2, and 1, respectively, the longer ones being nearer the base. The apical part at stage 6 consists of four cells without any branches. After this, the apical part at each stage is a repeat of the apical part at the previous stage, together with two new cells at the base end of the apical part. The second of these new cells carried a branch, which is identical to the whole organism six stages previously.

For example, looking at stage 11, the upward arrow separates the basal part and the apical part. To the right of the downward arrow we have the whole of the apical part at stage 10, and between the two arrows we have two cells, the second of which carries a branch identical to the organism at stage 5. The same type of situation is indicated by the arrows at stage 16.

Provided that we know the initial stages of the development, the above description specifies how the organism develops. However, descriptions of this type suffer from all the awkwardness and ambiguity of the English language. It is desirable to give a formal framework within which such descriptions can be given. Such a formal framework will be described in Section 12.3.

In nearly all our studies we shall treat the cell as a basic unit. This allows us to represent the organism in the following way. If we assign different symbols to the different states which the cells of the organism may assume, then, at a particular instant of time, the organism itself may be represented as a string of symbols indicating the states of the cells of the organism, with more complicated geometrical relations between the cells expressed by the appearance of meta-symbols. For example, branching patterns may be described by putting the string representing the states in a particular branch between matching parentheses.

Using this convention the first seven stages of the development described above can be written as follows:

1. c
2. cc
3. $cccc$
4. $cc(c)cccc$
5. $cc(cc)cc(c)cccc$
6. $cc(ccc)cc(cc)cc(c)cccc$
7. $cc(cccc)cc(ccc)cc(cc)cc(c)cccc$

In this description each cell is denoted by a c (i.e., no distinction is made between cells in different states). The beginning of a branch is indicated by a left parenthesis "(", and the end of the branch is indicated by a right parenthesis ")". We have not bothered to distinguish between the sides on which the branch may lie; this could have been done by the use of different types of brackets. When there is a branch within a branch, we can represent this by parentheses within parentheses. For example, stage 10 can be described by

$$cc(cccccc)cc(ccccc)cc(cccc)cc(cc(c)cccc)cc(cccc)cc(cc)cc(c)cccc$$

In this chapter we shall only be dealing with biological phenomena which can be described and discussed in terms of a sequence of strings of symbols. Although, at first sight, this may appear to be a very strong restriction, it has been demonstrated that a variety of organisms can be investigated this way. Also, our simple model has been shown to be useful in discussing some basic problems of theoretical biology.

Once we have a methodology for representing the stages of development of a biological organism by a sequence of strings of symbols, we can formalize our description of a compound development. If we specify the strings which describe the relevant parts of the organism at the early stages, and we give some rules as to how strings representing earlier stages of development are to be put together to describe a later stage of development, then we can compute stage-by-stage the strings representing the organism. We shall formally define in Section 12.3 a *recurrence system* as a collection of such initial stages and rules, designed to describe a compound development.

Whereas recurrence systems are sufficient to generate developmental sequences of the organism as a whole, they give no indication of the cellular mechanism of the development. For example, they do not indicate where cell divisions occur in the organism. To be able to describe the spacing and timing of cellular activities in the course of development, we introduce the idea of a *developmental system*. These systems are designed with the purpose of describing biological development in terms of cellular actions and interactions.

For example, one may ask the following question regarding the compound branching development described above: In order to explain such development on a cellular basis is it necessary to consider the interaction between cells, or is it possible to give an explanation of this type of branching development without cellular interactions? Zoologists refer to development in which what happens to a cell is not influenced by what is going on in the rest of the organism as *mosaic* development. We are now going to show that the branching sequence described above can indeed be achieved mosaically.

For this purpose we need to distinguish between different states that a cell may assume during its development. We distinguish between ten possible states, which we denote by the digits 0, 1, 2, 3, 4, 5, 6, 7, 8, 9. For each state we specify a developmental rule (a *production*) which tells us what happens to a cell if it is in that state. For example, the production

$$0 \rightarrow 10$$

indicates that a cell in state 0 divides into two cells in states 1 and 0. The production

$$7 \rightarrow 3(9)$$

indicates that a cell in state 7 divides into two cells in states 3 and 9, but the cell in state 9 is not along the filament in which the mother cell was, but rather it is the beginning of a new branch.

The complete set of productions for our system is

$$0 \rightarrow 10$$
$$1 \rightarrow 32$$
$$2 \rightarrow 3(4)$$
$$3 \rightarrow 3$$
$$4 \rightarrow 56$$
$$5 \rightarrow 37$$
$$6 \rightarrow 58$$
$$7 \rightarrow 3(9)$$
$$8 \rightarrow 50$$
$$9 \rightarrow 39$$

For the sake of completeness we may also specify productions for the meta-symbols:

$$(\rightarrow ($$
$$) \rightarrow)$$

Given a string of symbols which describe the organism at a certain stage, e.g.,

$$33(339)33(39)33(9)3210$$

the productions can be used to obtain a description of the organism at the next stage. Since each symbol represents a cell, and the cells act independently of each other, this is done by *simultaneously* replacing every symbol in the string by the right-hand side of the production for the symbol. Thus, from the string above we get

$$33(3339)33(339)33(39)33(4)3210$$

If we now specify 4 as the state of the single cell at the beginning of the development we get the following *developmental sequence*.

1. 4
2. 56
3. 3758
4. 33(9)3750

5. 33(39)33(9)3710
6. 33(339)33(39)33(9)3210
7. 33(3339)33(339)33(39)33(4)3210
8. 33(33339)33(3339)33(339)33(56)33(4)3210
9. 33(333339)33(33339)33(3339)33(3758)33(56)33(4)3210
10. 33(3333339)33(333339)33(33339)33(33(9)3750)33(3758)33(56)33(4)3210

If we replace each digit by a c, then we see that this is exactly the developmental sequence described above. It can be proved, by techniques discussed in later sections, that irrespective of how far we go in generating the developmental sequence using the productions, it will always satisfy the global developmental description given at the beginning of the section.

What we have done here is to describe a possible cellular behavior which would lead to the postulated global behavior. It is indeed interesting, although as we shall see not untypical, that such a complicated looking developmental pattern can be achieved without cellular interactions.

Developmental systems, as we discuss them in this chapter, will always operate on strings of symbols. The symbols, which represent the states of the cells, will be the elements of a specified finite set, called the *alphabet*. The justification for assuming a finite set of states is that there usually are threshold values for parameters that determine the behavior of a cell. Thus, with respect to each of these parameters, it is sufficient to specify two conditions of the cell: "below threshold" and "above threshold," although the parameter itself may have infinitely many values. Even in those cases where such a simpler-minded scheme is insufficient, it is usually possible to approximate the infinite set of values by a sufficiently large finite set of values, without any serious detriment to the accuracy of the developmental model.

In addition to its alphabet each developmental system has a set of *productions*. These are the rules which describe the behavior of the cells. Given a string of symbols which describes the organism at a given stage, the description of the organism at the next stage is obtained by *simultaneously* replacing each symbol by a string of symbols.

The developmental system described above was of a particularly simple kind.

First of all, it was a system *without interactions,* i.e., what happened to a cell depended only on the state of the cell itself. Such systems without interactions have also been called *informationless,* since a cell has no information about the state of the rest of the organism. An alternative name that has been used is 0L *system.* ("L system" is an alternative expression for the type of developmental system we are dealing with in this chapter, L abbreviating the name of Aristid Lindenmayer, who first studied such developmental systems in the spirit of our work here. The 0 in 0L system indicates zero-sided interactions, as opposed to one-sided or two-sided interactions.) In Section 12.4

we shall study developmental systems in which what happens to a particular cell may be influenced by several of its neighbors on both sides.

The system of our example is also simple because there is exactly one production for each symbol in the alphabet. Such systems are called *deterministic*. Thus, we call it a D0L system, where the D abbreviates "deterministic." It is often the case that we have to provide alternative productions for the same situation. This may be an expression of our ignorance, or a consequence of the fact that we have lumped together different states of a cell and denoted them by the same symbol. In the rest of this chapter we shall pay at least as much attention to nondeterministic developmental systems as to deterministic ones.

Our example also had another special property: The righthand side of every production was a string of length at least one. Such systems are called *propagating*, and our example is therefore called a PD0L system, where P abbreviates propagating. We shall also study systems with productions whose righthand sides are of length zero. This means that when such a production is used, the symbol to be replaced simply disappears. This, to some extent, reflects the notion of cell death in organisms.

Another way in which our example is simple is that the system operates quite independently of the environment. There are situations in which it is reasonable to have two or more different sets of productions, and in any given step use productions only from one of the sets. For example, one set of productions may correspond to developmental rules during daytime conditions, while the other set is appropriate for describing cellular behavior during the night. Such systems will be mentioned in Section 12.5. There are other types of developmental systems which reflect various biological situations; some of these will also be mentioned in Section 12.5.

So far we have mentioned that a developmental system has an alphabet and a set of productions, which are always to be applied in parallel to all the symbols of a string in order to get the next string in the developmental sequence. An alphabet together with a set of productions will be referred to as a *developmental scheme*. In addition, a *developmental system* specifies one or more starting strings, which we call *axioms*. The system in the example above has the axiom 4.

A given developmental system defines a set of *developmental sequences*. A developmental sequence is a sequence of strings ω_0, ω_1, ω_2, . . . of symbols from the alphabet, such that ω_0 is an axiom, and, for all t, ω_{t+1} is obtained from ω_t by applying the productions in parallel to all the symbols of ω_t.

The *language of a developmental system* is defined as the set of all strings which occur in any developmental sequence of the system. In other words, it is the set of all strings which may be derived from the axioms by repeated parallel applications of the production rules. If the developmental system has been designed with a particular organism in mind, the language of the developmental system should be the set of descriptions of all the possible manifestations of that organism. For any developmental system, the language of the system is a *developmental language*.

Notation

Whenever we have some string of symbols X to describe a particular type of language, we shall use $\mathscr{F}(X)$ to denote the family of all such languages. Thus $\mathscr{F}$(D0L) is the family of all D0L languages.

Given a developmental language, it is always interesting to find out which families it belongs to. Just because a language has been defined using a non-deterministic nonpropagating 0L system, it does not mean that it is not also a PD0L language! Generally speaking, one should always try to describe a biological development with the simplest system which is consistent with the facts as we know them.

12.2. THE BASIC FAMILY: 0L LANGUAGES

In this section we discuss 0L systems. They were introduced to model the development of filamentous organisms in which no interaction between cells takes place. In other words, the action taken by a cell at a given moment of time depends on the state of the cell only. From the biological point of view, "noninteractive" (mosaic) behavior is interesting enough to justify its separate investigation. From the formal language theory point of view, it is natural to study models where the substitution for a symbol does not depend on its context (see, e.g., the context-free grammars of Section 1.2).

Definition 12.2.1

A *0L scheme* is a pair $S = \langle \Sigma, P \rangle$, where Σ (the *alphabet* of S) is a finite nonempty set, and P (the set of *productions* of S) is a finite nonempty subset of $\Sigma \times \Sigma^*$ such that for every a in Σ there exists an α in Σ^* such that $\langle a, \alpha \rangle \in P$.

According to usual conventions of formal language theory, a production $\langle a, \alpha \rangle$ from P will be written as $a \longrightarrow \alpha$, and we shall write $a \underset{P}{\rightarrow} \alpha$ instead of "$\langle a, \alpha \rangle$ is in P."

Definition 12.2.2

Let $S = \langle \Sigma, P \rangle$ be a 0L scheme, let $x = a_1 \ldots a_m$ with $m \geq 0$ and $a_j \in \Sigma$ for $j = 1, \ldots, m$, and let $y \in \Sigma^*$. Then we say that x *directly derives* y (in S), denoted as $x \underset{S}{\Rightarrow} y$, if, and only if, there exist $\alpha_1, \ldots, \alpha_m$ in Σ^* such that $a_1 \underset{P}{\rightarrow} \alpha_1, \ldots, a_m \underset{P}{\rightarrow} \alpha_m$ and $y = \alpha_1 \ldots \alpha_m$.

According to this definition Λ directly derives y if, and only if, $y = \Lambda$. Here and in later sections $\underset{S}{\overset{+}{\Rightarrow}}$, $\underset{S}{\overset{*}{\Rightarrow}}$ and $\underset{S}{\overset{k}{\Rightarrow}}$ are to be interpreted according to the conventions of Section 1.2.

Definition 12.2.3

A 0L scheme $S = \langle \Sigma, P \rangle$ is called *propagating* if there is no production in P of the form $a \to \Lambda$. (A production of the form $a \to \Lambda$ is called an *erasing production*.) Otherwise, S is called *nonpropagating*.

Definition 12.2.4

A 0L scheme $S = \langle \Sigma, P \rangle$ is called *deterministic,* if for every a in Σ there exists exactly one α in Σ^* such that $a \underset{P}{\to} \alpha$. Otherwise S is called *nondeterministic*.

In the sequel we shall write a letter P or D (or both of them) in front of 0L to denote the propagating or deterministic restriction on a given scheme, system or language. For example, a P0L scheme is a propagating 0L scheme.

Definition 12.2.5

A *0L system* is a triple $G = \langle \Sigma, P, \omega \rangle$, where $S = \langle \Sigma, P \rangle$ is a 0L scheme (called the *scheme* of G) and ω (the *axiom* of G) is a word over Σ. G is said to be *propagating* if, and only if, S is propagating and $\omega \neq \Lambda$. G is said to be *deterministic* if, and only if, S is deterministic.

Notation

If $G = \langle \Sigma, P, \omega \rangle$ is a 0L system, and $S = \langle \Sigma, P \rangle$, then we shall often write $\underset{G}{\Rightarrow}$, $\underset{G}{\overset{n}{\Rightarrow}}$, $\underset{G}{\overset{+}{\Rightarrow}}$, and $\underset{G}{\overset{*}{\Rightarrow}}$ instead of $\underset{S}{\Rightarrow}$, $\underset{S}{\overset{n}{\Rightarrow}}$, $\underset{S}{\overset{+}{\Rightarrow}}$, and $\underset{S}{\overset{*}{\Rightarrow}}$. Similar notation will be used without further explanation later on.

Definition 12.2.6

Let $G = \langle \Sigma, P, \omega \rangle$ be a 0L system. The *language generated by G* (or simply the *language of G*), denoted by $L(G)$, is defined as

$$L(G) = \{x \mid \omega \underset{G}{\overset{*}{\Rightarrow}} x\}$$

Definition 12.2.7

A language L is said to be a *0L language* if, and only if, $L = L(G)$ for some 0L system G. If, in addition, G is propagating (and/or deterministic), then L is said to be a *propagating* (and/or *deterministic*) 0L language.

According to the notation introduced above, we abbreviate, for example, "propagating deterministic 0L language" by "PD0L language." Similar notation will be used without further explanation later on.

Example 12.2.1

Let $G = \langle \Sigma, P, \omega \rangle$, where $\Sigma = \{0, 1, 2, 3, 4, 5, 6, 7, 8, 9,), (\}$, $P = \{0 \rightarrow 10, 1 \rightarrow 32, 2 \rightarrow 3(4), 3 \rightarrow 3, 4 \rightarrow 56, 5 \rightarrow 37, 6 \rightarrow 58, 7 \rightarrow 3(9), 8 \rightarrow 50, 9 \rightarrow 39,) \rightarrow), (\rightarrow (\}$ and $\omega = 4$. G is a PD0L system whose behavior has been discussed in the last section.

Example 12.2.2

Let $G = \langle \{a\}, \{a \rightarrow \Lambda, a \rightarrow aa\}, aa \rangle$. G is a 0L system and $L(G) = \{a^{2^n} \mid n \geq 0\}$.

Example 12.2.3

Let $G = \langle \{a\}, \{a \rightarrow aa\}, a \rangle$, then G is a PD0L system and $L(G) = \{a^{2^n} \mid n \geq 0\}$. It is easy to prove (for example using Theorem 1.4.7) that $L(G)$ is not a context-free language. Similarly, it can be shown that the language generated by the PD0L system of Example 12.2.1 is not context-free. Hence we see that even though the productions of a 0L system are "context-free" (in the sense that what a symbol is replaced by is dependent only on the symbol itself), there are 0L languages which are not context-free. The explanation of course lies in the fact that in a derivation by a 0L system all symbols are substituted for simultaneously, while in a derivation by a context-free grammar only one variable at a time is substituted for.

In contrast to Example 12.2.3 we have the following.

Example 12.2.4

Let $L = \{a, aa\}$. L is not a 0L language. This is shown as follows.

First we prove two preliminary results, which are true for an arbitrary 0L scheme $S = \langle \Sigma, P \rangle$ and an arbitrary symbol a in Σ.

1. If $a \stackrel{*}{\Rightarrow} a^2$, then $a \stackrel{*}{\Rightarrow} a^4$.

This is proved as follows. If $a \stackrel{*}{\Rightarrow} a^2$, then $a \stackrel{n}{\Rightarrow} a^2$, for some n. Hence, $aa \stackrel{n}{\Rightarrow} a^4$, and so $a \stackrel{2n}{\Rightarrow} a^4$.

2. If $a^2 \stackrel{*}{\Rightarrow} a$, then $a^2 \stackrel{*}{\Rightarrow} \Lambda$.

This is proved as follows. If $a^2 \stackrel{*}{\Rightarrow} a$, then $a^2 \stackrel{n}{\Rightarrow} a$, for some n. But then $a \stackrel{n}{\Rightarrow} a$ and $a \stackrel{n}{\Rightarrow} \Lambda$. Hence $aa \stackrel{n}{\Rightarrow} \Lambda$.

We now prove that $L = \{a, a^2\}$ is not 0L language. We shall do this by showing for an arbitary 0L system $G = \langle \Sigma, P, \omega \rangle$ that $L \neq L(G)$. We consider three cases.

(a) $\omega = a$. If $a^2 \notin L(G)$, then $L \neq L(G)$. If $a^2 \in L(G)$, then $a \overset{*}{\Rightarrow} a^2$, and hence, by (1) above, $a^4 \in L(G)$, and again $L \neq L(G)$.

(b) $\omega = a^2$. If $a \notin L(G)$. then $L \neq L(G)$. If $a \in L(G)$, then $a^2 \overset{*}{\Rightarrow} a$, and hence, by (2) above, $\Lambda \in L(G)$, and again $L \neq L(G)$.

(c) $\omega \notin L$. Clearly, $L \neq L(G)$.

Since all possibilities have been exhausted, we see that there is no 0L system which generates the finite language $\{a, a^2\}$.

These last two examples can be summarized in the following theorem which shows that $\mathscr{F}$(0L) does not fit nicely into the Chomsky hierarchy (Definition 1.2.4).

Theorem 12.2.1

There exist 0L languages which are not context-free and there exist regular (even finite) languages which are not 0L.

We now state without proof some sample theorems about 0L systems and languages. The reason for not giving proofs is that all our theorems in this chapter (with the exception of Theorem 12.3.4) are proved in Herman and Rozenberg [2].

Theorem 12.2.2

If $S = \langle \Sigma, P \rangle$ is a 0L scheme such that $\#(S) = n$ and a is an element of Σ, such that, for some m, $a \overset{m}{\underset{S}{\Rightarrow}} \Lambda$, then $a \overset{n}{\underset{S}{\Rightarrow}} \Lambda$.

Notation

For any string of symbols x let $|x|$ denote the length of x.

Theorem 12.2.3

Let $G = \langle \Sigma, P, \omega \rangle$ be a 0L system. Then there exists a constant C_G such that, for every word x in $L(G)$, there exists a derivation $\omega = x_0 \underset{G}{\Rightarrow} x_1 \Rightarrow \ldots \Rightarrow x_f = x$ such that $|x_i| \leq C_G \cdot (|x| + 1)$, for every i in $\{0, 1, \ldots, f\}$.

Theorem 12.2.4

There exists an algorithm which for any 0L system $G = \langle \Sigma, P, \omega \rangle$ and for any x in Σ^* decides whether or not $x \in L(G)$.

Theorem 12.2.5

There exists no algorithm which for any two 0L systems G and H decides whether or not $L(G) = L(H)$.

Theorem 12.2.6

The following diagram holds,

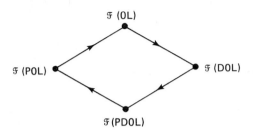

where a solid line denotes strict inclusion (in the direction indicated); and when two classes K_1 and K_2 are not connected by a direct path in this diagram, it means that they are incomparable but not disjoint.

Other theorems about 0L languages are stated in the form of exercises. The exercises marked with an asterisk are not trivial to solve; in nearly all cases their solution can be found in Herman and Rozenberg [2], where they would appear as theorems.

EXERCISES 12.2

*1.   Prove Theorems 12.2.2–12.2.6.

2.   Prove that the following languages are 0L languages.
  (a) $\{a, b\}^+$
  (b) $\{a^{2n-1} \mid n \geq 1\}$
  (c) $\{(ab)^{2n} \mid n \geq 0\}$

3.   Prove that the PD0L language generated by the system of Example 12.2.1 is not context-free.

4.   Prove that $\{a^{2n} \mid n \geq 1\} \cup \{a^3\}$ is not a 0L language.

*5.   Prove that if $G = \langle \Sigma, P, \omega \rangle$ is a 0L system such that $\Sigma = \{a\}$, then $L(G)$ is either of the form $\{a^{ikj} \mid j \geq 0\}$ or $L(G)$ is regular.

*6.   (a)   Prove that for any language L over the one letter alphabet $\{a\}$, the language L^* is a 0L language.
  (b)   Prove that there exists a 0L language L such that L^* is not a 0L language.

7.   Prove that the family of 0L languages is not closed under union, concatenation, the cross operator ($+$), intersection with regular languages, Λ-free homomorphism, and inverse homomorphism.

*8. Let G be a D0L system such that $L(G)$ is infinite. Let ω_0, ω_1, ω_2, ... be the sequence of words generated by this system (i.e., ω_0 is the axiom of G and, for all i, $\omega_i \underset{G}{\Rightarrow} \omega_{i+1}$), and let $\text{Pref}_k(\omega_j)$ denote the word consisting of the first k letters of ω_j. Prove that there exists a positive integer f, such that for every positive integer k there exists a positive integer t such that, for every $j \geq t$ and for every nonnegative integer n, $\text{Pref}_k(\omega_j) = \text{Pref}_k(\omega_{j+nf})$. (This says that the prefixes of some fixed but arbitrary length of the strings of a D0L sequence form an ultimately periodic sequence, and the period depends on the system only.)

*9. Let $S = \langle \Sigma, P \rangle$ be a 0L scheme, and let $G = \langle \Sigma, P, \omega \rangle$ be a 0L system. The *adult language* $A(S)$ of S is defined to be the set of all x in Σ^* such that $x \underset{S}{\Rightarrow} x$ and, for any y in Σ^*, if $x \underset{S}{\Rightarrow} y$ then $y = x$. The *adult language* $A(G)$ of G is defined by $A(G) = A(S) \cap L(G)$. Let $\mathscr{F}(\text{A0S})$ and $\mathscr{F}(\text{A0L})$ denote respectively the family of adult languages of 0L schemes and the family of adult languages of 0L systems. Prove that

(a) $\mathscr{F}(\text{A0S}) \subset L_3$

(b) $\mathscr{F}(\text{A0L}) = L_2$

(The adult language of a 0L system is the set of dynamically stable strings of the system. The contrast between Theorem 12.2.1 and (b) above is very interesting.)

*10. Let $S = \langle \Sigma, P \rangle$ be a PD0L scheme and let $\mathscr{S}$ be a finite sequence $\langle s_0, s_1, \ldots, s_n \rangle$ of strings over Σ^+ such that $s_i \underset{S}{\overset{+}{\Rightarrow}} s_{i+1}$ for all i. Let the *complexity* $\gamma(\mathscr{S}, S)$ of $\mathscr{S}$ with respect to S be defined as the sum of the lengths of all the right-hand sides of the productions in S added to $\sum_{i=0}^{n-1} k_i$, where k_i is the smallest positive integer such that $s_i \underset{S}{\overset{k_i}{\Rightarrow}} s_{i+1}$. Give an algorithm which, for any finite sequence $I = \langle s_0, s_1, \ldots, s_n \rangle$ of strings for which there exists a PD0L scheme such that $s_i \underset{S}{\overset{+}{\Rightarrow}} s_{i+1}$ for all i, will find the PD0L scheme S with this property with respect to which $\mathscr{S}$ has the smallest possible complexity.

12.3. EXTENSION USING AUXILIARY SYMBOLS:
   ## E0L LANGUAGES

   In this section we investigate the effect of allowing auxiliary symbols in 0L systems. That is, similarly to the way languages in the Chomsky hierarchy are defined, we allow the use of symbols in derivations which are not in the alphabet Δ of the language we are generating. We include only those strings in the language of a given 0L system which can be derived from the axiom, but which are also in Δ^*. We call the languages obtained in this way E0L languages.

We also return to the discussion of recurrence systems which have been introduced informally in Section 12.1. We give a formal definition of recurrence systems and of the languages defined by them and show the equivalence of the family of recurrence languages to the family of E0L languages.

Definition 12.3.1

An E0L system is a 4-tuple $G = \langle \Sigma, P, \omega, \Delta \rangle$, where $\bar{G} = \langle \Sigma, P, \omega \rangle$ is a 0L system and $\Delta \subseteq \Sigma$. The *language* of G (denoted by $L(G)$) is defined by $L(G) = L(\bar{G}) \cap \Delta^*$. In such a case $L(G)$ is referred to as an *E0L language*.

Example 12.3.1

$L = \{a^n b^n a^n \,|\, n > 0\}$ is an E0L language. This is because $L = L(G)$, where $G = \langle \Sigma, P, \omega, \Delta \rangle$, with $\Sigma = \{S, A, B, A', B', F, a, b,\}$, $\Delta = \{a, b\}$, $\omega = S$ and P is the set consisting of the productions

$$S \longrightarrow ABA$$
$$A \longrightarrow AA', \qquad A \longrightarrow a$$
$$B \longrightarrow BB', \qquad B \longrightarrow b$$
$$A' \longrightarrow A', \qquad A' \longrightarrow a$$
$$B' \longrightarrow B', \qquad B' \longrightarrow b$$
$$F \longrightarrow F$$
$$a \longrightarrow F$$
$$b \longrightarrow F$$

We demonstrate the operation of this E0L system on two typical derivations.

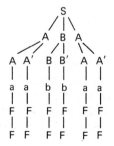
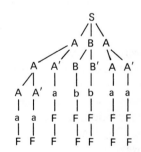

The derivation on the left gave rise to a word *aabbaa* in $L(G)$, but the derivation on the right "went wrong" and did not produce a word in $L(G)$. Since $F \longrightarrow F$, further words in $L(G)$ can never be produced by continuing these derivations.

Recall that it was shown in Example 1.4.4 that L is not a context-free language. In fact, in contrast to Theorem 12.2.1 we have the following result.

Theorem 12.3.1

The family of context-free languages is a proper subset of the family of E0L languages, and the family of E0L languages is a proper subset of the family of context-sensitive languages.

Our knowledge of the position of $\mathscr{F}(\text{0L})$ and $\mathscr{F}(\text{E0L})$ in the Chomsky hierarchy is summarized by the following inclusion diagram.

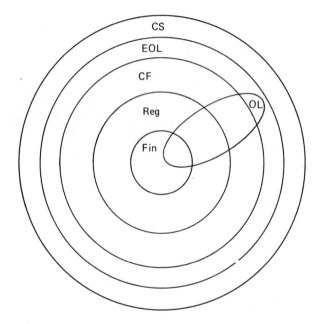

In Section 12.1 we described the development of a compound branching pattern. Although the description specified how the organism develops, it suffered from all the awkwardness and ambiguity of the English language. Recurrence systems have been devised to give a formal framework within which descriptions of the type discussed in Section 12.1 can be given. Description of biological development using recurrence systems is done in the following way.

We specify certain parts of the organism we are trying to describe. For instance, for the example in Section 12.1, we would specify the whole organism W, the basal part B, the apical part A, and the filament part F.

Then we give a set of recurrence formulas which tell us, for each part of the organism at any stage of its development, all the ways it may be constructed from previous stages of its own development and the development of other parts, as well as some "constant" components. For instance, in our example, if W_n, A_n, B_n, and F_n denote the n'th stage of development of each of the whole organism, apical part, basal part, and filament, respectively, then

$$W_n = B_{n-1} A_{n-1}$$
$$A_n = cc(W_{n-5}) A_{n-1}$$
$$B_n = cc(F_{n-2}) cc(F_{n-3}) cc(F_{n-4})$$
$$F_n = cF_{n-1}$$

where the constant c denotes a cell, and the left and right parentheses denote the beginning and end of a branch.

Note that we wrote $W_n = B_{n-1} A_{n-1}$ and not $W_n = A_n B_n$. This is done so that in the formulas the n'th stage of any part is described in terms of earlier stages of other parts.

We must also specify all the possible forms that a particular part of an organism may have at the beginning of its development. For instance, in the example above,

$$W_1 = c$$
$$W_2 = cc$$
$$W_3 = cccc$$
$$W_4 = cc(c)cccc$$
$$W_5 = cc(cc)cc(c)cccc$$
$$A_5 = cccc$$
$$B_5 = cc(ccc)cc(cc)cc(c)$$
$$F_2 = cc$$
$$F_3 = ccc$$
$$F_4 = cccc$$
$$F_5 = ccccc$$

One can use a semi-infinite table to describe the history of the whole organism and its parts. For instance, for the example above we have the following table. Each line of the table is either specifically given as one of the initial stages, or can be obtained from previous lines by the use of the recurrence formulas.

Stage	W	A	B	F
1	c			
2	cc			c^2
3	c^4			c^3
4	$cc(c)c^4$			c^4
5	$cc(c^2)cc(c)c^4$	c^4	$cc(c^3)cc(c^2)cc(c)$	c^5
6	$cc(c^3)cc(c^2)cc(c)c^4$	$cc(c)c^4$	$cc(c^4)cc(c^3)cc(c^2)$	c^6
7	$cc(c^4)cc(c^3)cc(c^2)cc(c)c^4$	$cc(cc)cc(c)c^4$	$cc(c^5)cc(c^4)cc(c^3)$	c^7
8	$cc(c^5)cc(c^4)cc(c^3)cc(cc)cc(c)c^4$	$cc(c^4)cc(cc)cc(c)c^4$	$cc(c^6)cc(c^5)cc(c^4)$	c^8
9	$cc(c^6)cc(c^5)cc(c^4)cc(c^4)cc(cc)cc(c)c^4$	$cc(cc(c^4)cc$ $(c^4)cc(cc)cc(c)c^4$	$cc(c^7)cc(c^6)cc(c^5)$	c^9
.				
.				
.				

In a recurrence system, the number of distinguished parts is called the *width* of the system (this equals the number of columns in the table), while the *depth* of the system is the largest number k such that a part at stage n of its development may depend on a part at stage $n - k$ of its development in a recurrence formula. For instance, in our example, the width is 4 and the depth is 5.

More formally, we can proceed as follows.

Notation

Let N denote the set of *positive* integers and for any x in N, let N^x denote $\{i \mid 1 \le i \le x\}$.

Definition 12.3.2

A *recurrence system* is a 6-tuple

$$S = \langle \Sigma, \Omega, d, \mathscr{A}, \mathscr{F}, \omega \rangle$$

where

1. Σ is a finite nonempty set of symbols (the *alphabet*).
2. Ω is a finite nonempty set (the *index* set).
3. d is a positive integer (the *depth* of S).
4. $\mathscr{A}$ is a function, associating with each $\langle x, y \rangle \in \Omega \times N^d$ a finite set $A_{x,y}$ (of *axioms*), such that

$$A_{x,y} \subset \Sigma^*$$

5. F is a function, associating with each $x \in \Omega$ a nonempty finite set F_x (of *recurrence formulas*), such that

$$F_x \subset ((\Omega \times N^d) \cup \Sigma)^*$$

6. $\omega \in \Omega$ (the *distinguished index*).

Remark

Note that recurrence formulas are strings in which each element is either from Σ or is an ordered pair, the first element of which is from Ω and the second of which is from N^d. Thus, recurrence formulas are not strings of symbols, but are rather strings of elements from various sets. Since all sets involved are finite, there would be no problem to give names to these set elements, but this is not necessary for our proofs.

Definition 12.3.3

Let $S = \langle \Sigma, \Omega, d, \mathscr{A}, \mathscr{F}, \omega \rangle$ be a recurrence system. For $x \in \Omega$ and $y \in N$, we define $L_{x,y}(S)$ as follows.

If $y \in N^d$, $L_{x,y}(S) = A_{x,y}$.

If $y > d$, $L_{x,y}(S) = \{v_0 u_1 v_1 \ldots u_f v_f \mid v_0 \langle k_1, l_1 \rangle v_1 \ldots \langle k_f, l_f \rangle v_f \in F_x$, where for $0 \leq j \leq f$, $v_j \in \Sigma^*$ and, for $1 \leq i \leq f$, $u_i \in L_{k_i, y-l_i}(S)\}$.

$L(S) = \bigcup_{y \in N} L_{\omega,y}(S)$ is said to be the language *generated* by S. A language which is generated by some recurrence system S is said to be a *recurrence language*.

Example 12.3.2

The biological example given above can be described as a recurrence system as follows:

$$S = \langle \{c, \}, (\ \}, N^4, 5, \mathscr{A}, \mathscr{F}, 1 \rangle$$

where

$A_{1,1} = \{c\}$
$A_{1,2} = \{cc\}$
$A_{1,3} = \{cccc\}$
$A_{1,4} = \{cc(c)cccc\}$
$A_{1,5} = \{cc(cc)cc(c)cccc\}$
$A_{2,1} = A_{2,2} = A_{2,3} = A_{2,4} = \emptyset$
$A_{2,5} = \{cccc\}$
$A_{3,1} = A_{3,2} = A_{3,3} = A_{3,4} = \emptyset$
$A_{3,5} = \{cc(ccc)cc(cc)cc(c)\}$
$A_{4,1} = \emptyset$
$A_{4,2} = \{cc\}$
$A_{4,3} = \{ccc\}$
$A_{4,4} = \{cccc\}$
$A_{4,5} = \{ccccc\}$
$F_1 = \{\langle 3, 1 \rangle \langle 2, 1 \rangle\}$
$F_2 = \{cc\,(\langle 1, 5 \rangle)\langle 2, 1 \rangle\}$
$F_3 = \{cc\,(\langle 4, 2 \rangle)\,cc\,(\langle 4, 3 \rangle)\,cc\,(\langle 4, 4 \rangle)\}$
$F_4 = \{c\langle 4, 1 \rangle\}$

Another example of a recurrence system is the following:

Example 12.3.3

$S = \langle \{a, b, c\}, N^4, 1, \mathscr{A}, \mathscr{F}, 1 \rangle$, where
$A_{1,1} = \varnothing$
$A_{2,1} = \{a\}$
$A_{3,1} = \{b\}$
$A_{4,1} = \{c\}$

$F_1 = \{\langle 2, 1 \rangle \langle 3, 1 \rangle \langle 4, 1 \rangle\}$
$F_2 = \{a \langle 2, 1 \rangle\}$
$F_3 = \{b \langle 3, 1 \rangle\}$
$F_4 = \{c \langle 4, 1 \rangle\}$

The first few lines of the semi-infinite table associated with this recurrence system will appear as follows:

	1	2	3	4
1		a	b	c
2	abc	a^2	b^2	c^2
3	$a^2b^2c^2$	a^3	b^3	c^3
4	$a^3b^3c^3$	a^4	b^4	c^4

Clearly,

$$L(S) = \{a^n b^n c^n \,|\, n \in N\}$$

This is the same language as the one in Example 12.3.1. As we shall see below, it is no accident that a language can be generated both by an E0L system and a recurrence system.

A sample result regarding recurrence systems is the following.

Theorem 12.3.2

There exists an algorithm which for any recurrence system S produces a recurrence system T of depth 1 such that $L(S) = L(T)$.

Recurrence systems are an attractive way of describing biological development, both because they are mathematically elegant and because many actual developments can be described by them. However, they give no indication of the underlying cellular or physiological mechanisms. The developmental description of a multicellular filamentous organism, such as *Callithamnion roseum* (see Section 12.1) should account for the spacing and timing of cell divisions, both those along the filaments and those giving rise to new branches. Such descriptions should also include a record of when and where irreversibly differentiated cells arise, i.e., cells which can be recognized by some morphological feature. The problem arises to isolate a feature at the cellular mechanism level which corresponds to global development which can be described by a recurrence system. The theorem below isolates such a feature. Roughly speaking, the result is that a development can be described by a recurrence system if, and only if, it can be generated by a developmental system without cellular interactions. More formally we have the following.

Theorem 12.3.3

1. There is an algorithm which for any E0L system C produces a recurrence system S such that $L(S) = L(G)$.

2. There is an algorithm which for any recurrence system S produces an E0L system G such that $L(G) = L(S)$.

Corollary 12.3.1

A language is a recurrence language if and only if it is an E0L language.

Although this theorem is interesting from a mathematical point of view, its biological significance is not inherent in its statement, but is a consequence of a theorem given below. This is because, even though 0L languages are well motivated from a biological point of view and the creation of a language from another language by intersection with Δ^* is a standard procedure in formal language theory, the intersection of a 0L language with Δ^* does not seem to make any biological sense. After all, why should we exclude certain developmental stages from the language of an organism just because of the appearance of certain cellular states? The answer is provided by the following discussion.

Clearly, the experimental verification of our developmental systems should include, among other features, the identification of the individual cellular states (corresponding to the symbols of the alphabet) which occur in the model. In some cases, no morphological or biochemical distinction can be made among the cells in the course of development, and thus only the temporal and spatial distribution of the cell divisions can be tested against observations. In other cases, there are irreversibly differentiated cells in the organism, and the spatio-temporal occurrences of such cells can be ascertained and compared with those given by the model. It should be the goal of developmental studies that eventually all cellular states, not only the irreversibly differentiated ones, postulated by the models should also be experimentally distinguishable. This goal is however very far from being realized, and in the meantime we must ask the question: What class of developmental systems (class of 0L systems, for instance) will satisfy a certain observed distribution of cell divisions and of differentiated cells? This problem can also be phrased in the following way. Our observations provide us with "images" of the actual developmental sequences. We are trying to find the class of developmental systems which generates a sequence whose "image" is the observed developmental sequence.

For example, in our description of the development of a compound branching pattern in Section 12.1 we denoted each cell by c, i.e., we made no distinction between cells in different states. Even though it is quite possible that experimental observations do not provide us a method by which we can distinguish states, it is clearly reasonable to postulate the existence of different states when trying to explain the development. This is indeed what we have done in Example 12.2.1, where we have proposed a PD0L system with ten different possible cell states. This system is sufficient to explain the observed development, inasmuch that if we replace each digit in the sequence generated by the system by c, then we get exactly the observed sequence. We can formalize this as follows.

Definition 12.3.4

Given two alphabets (i.e., finite nonempty sets) Σ and Δ, a *homomorphism h from Σ to Δ* is a mapping from Σ into Δ^*. The homomorphism h can be extended to sentences and languages over Σ as follows.

$h(\Lambda) = \Lambda$.

For $x = a_1 a_2 \ldots a_n$ in Σ^+, $h(a_1 a_2 \ldots a_n) = h(a_1)\, h(a_2) \ldots h(a_n)$.

For any $L \subseteq \Sigma^*$,

$$h(L) = \{h(x)\,|\,x \in L\}$$

If h is a homomorphism from Σ into Δ such that for every a, $|h(a)| = 1$, then h is called a *coding*.

Our discussion above can now be restated as follows. Due to our lack of ability to distinguish always cells in different states, when presented with a language L describing an organism as observed, we should look not only for systems which generate L, but also for systems which generate a language K such that L is the image of K under a coding. In particular, the family of all languages which are images of 0L languages under coding is in some sense biologically more important than $\mathscr{F}(0L)$ itself.

A major justification for studying E0L languages is provided by the following result of Ehrenfeucht and Rozenberg [1].

Theorem 12.3.4

A language is an E0L language if, and only if, it is the image of a 0L language under some coding.

Example 12.3.4

Consider the PDOL system of Example 12.2.1: $G = \langle \{0, 1, 2, 3, 4, 5, 6, 7, 8, 9, (,)\}, P, 4 \rangle$, where $P = \{ \langle 0, 10 \rangle, \langle 1, 32 \rangle, \langle 2, 3(4) \rangle, \langle 3, 3 \rangle, \langle 4, 56 \rangle, \langle 5, 37 \rangle, \langle 6, 58 \rangle, \langle 7, 3(9) \rangle, \langle 8, 50 \rangle, \langle 9, 39 \rangle, \langle (, (\rangle, \langle),) \rangle \}$.

Let h be the coding such that

$$
\begin{aligned}
h(x) &= c, \quad \text{for } x \in \{0, 1, \ldots, 9\} \\
h(() &= (\\
h()) &=)
\end{aligned}
$$

Then $h(L(G))$ is exactly the recurrence language of Example 12.3.2.

Alternatively, let $\bar{G} = \langle \bar{\Sigma}, \bar{P}, \bar{\omega}, \bar{A} \rangle$ be the EOL system with $\bar{\Sigma} = \{0, 1, \ldots, 9, (,), c, d\}$, $\bar{P} = P \cup \{\langle x, c \rangle \mid x \in \{0, 1, \ldots, 9\}\} \cup \{\langle c, d \rangle, \langle d, d \rangle\}$, $\bar{\omega} = 4$, and $\bar{A} = \{c, (,)\}$. It is easy to show that $L(\bar{G}) = h(L(G))$.

Theorems 12.3.3. and 12.3.4 show that the three rather differently defined families of

1. EOL languages (Definition 12.3.1),
2. recurrence languages (Definition 12.3.3.),
3. images under codings of OL languages (Definitions 12.2.7 and 12.3.4)

are in fact the same family. The latter two definitions have strong biological motivations, and their equivalence is biologically significant. For example, because recurrence systems are a natural and powerful looking way to describe certain observed developments, attempts have been made to describe developments using recurrence systems even though a developmental system with cellular interactions was deemed appropriate. With regard to such attempts Theorem 12.3.4. says: In the case of a development which cannot be explained without cellular interaction, the attempt must fail, and conversely, if the attempt is successful, the proposed developmental system is unnecessarily complicated since one can explain it without cellular interactions.

EXERCISES 12.3

*1. Prove Theorems 12.3.1–12.3.4.

2. For each of the following languages L give an EOL system G, a recurrence system S, a OL system H, and a coding h, such that $L(G) = L(S) = h(L(H))$.
   (a) $\{a, aa\}$ (contrast Example 12.2.4)

(b) $\{a^{2n} \mid n \in N\} \cup \{a^{3n} \mid n \in N\}$

(c) $\{a^i b^j a^i \mid 0 \leq j \leq i\}$

3. Prove that there is an algorithm which for any E0L system G and any sentence x decides whether or not x is in $L(G)$.

4. Prove that there is no algorithm which given an arbitrary pair of E0L systems G and H decides whether or not $L(G) = L(H)$.

5. An E0L system $G = \langle \Sigma, P, \omega, \Delta \rangle$ is said to be *synchronized* if, and only if, for every symbol a in Δ and string β in Σ^*, if $a \overset{+}{\Rightarrow} \beta$, then β is not in Δ^*. Prove that there is an algorithm which for any E0L system G produces a synchronized E0L system $\bar{G}$, such that $L(G) = L(\bar{G})$.

6. Prove that if L_1 and L_2 are E0L languages, then so are $L_1 \cup L_2$, $L_1 L_2$, L_1^+, L_1^* and $h(L_1)$, where h is an arbitrary homomorphism. (Contrast Exercises 12.2.6–12.2.7.)

*7. Prove that the language $K = \{w \in \{a, b\}^* \mid$ number of a's in w is 2^i for some positive integer $i\}$ is not an E0L language. (Note that K has a homomorphic image which is a 0L language; let $h(a) = a$, $h(b) = \Lambda$.)

*8. Place some restrictions on the definition of recurrence systems so that the resulting family of systems generates exactly the family of

(a) 0L languages

(b) D0L languages

(c) P0L languages

(d) context-free languages

*9. Prove that for every D0L system $G = \langle \Sigma, P, \omega \rangle$ such that $\Lambda \notin L(G)$, there exists a PD0L system $\bar{G} = \langle \bar{\Sigma}, \bar{P}, \bar{\omega} \rangle$ and a homomorphism h such that $h(w) = \Lambda$ only if $w = \Lambda$ and

(a) $h(\bar{\omega}) = \omega$

(b) for every x and y in $L(\bar{G})$ if $x \underset{\bar{G}}{\Rightarrow} y$, then $h(x) \underset{G}{\Rightarrow} h(y)$.

That is, every D0L sequence without Λ is the image under a Λ-free homomorphism of a PD0L sequence.)

12.4. SYSTEMS WITH INTERACTIONS

In this section we discuss developmental systems with interactions. These were introduced to model the development of multicellular filamentous organisms in which cells can communicate and interact with each other.

The results obtained in this section point out a large difference between developmental systems with one-sided communication between cells (say always from left to right) and developmental systems with two sided communication. They show the importance of the context which is available for interactions. In particular, they show that within a given amount of context, it is its character (one-sided or two-sided) rather than its distribution that is important.

We also indicate how the notions of synchronization and regulation of multicellular organisms can be discussed within this framework.

Definition 12.4.1

Let k and l be nonnegative integers. A $\langle k, l \rangle$ *system* is a construct

$$G = \langle \Sigma, P, g, \omega \rangle$$

where

Σ is a finite nonempty set (the *alphabet* of G)
ω is an element of Σ^* (the *axiom* of G)
g is an element which is not in Σ (the *marker* of G)
P is a finite nonempty relation (set of *productions* of G)

$$P \subset (\Sigma \cup \{g\})^k \times \Sigma \times (\Sigma \cup \{g\})^l \times \Sigma^*$$

such that

  1. If $\langle w_1, a, w_3, w_4 \rangle \in P$, then
    (a) if $w_1 = \bar{w}_1 g \bar{\bar{w}}_1$ for some $\bar{w}_1, \bar{\bar{w}}_1 \in (\Sigma \cup \{g\})^*$,   then $\bar{w}_1 \in \{g\}^*$;
    (b) if $w_3 = \bar{w}_3 g \bar{\bar{w}}_3$ for some $\bar{w}_3, \bar{\bar{w}}_3 \in (\Sigma \cup \{g\})^*$,   then $\bar{\bar{w}}_3 \in \{g\}^*$,
and
  2. for every $\langle w_1, a, w_3 \rangle \in (\Sigma \cup \{g\})^k \times \Sigma \times (\Sigma \cup \{g\})^l$, such that w_1 and w_3 satisfy conditions (a) and (b) (we say in such a case that $\langle w_1, a, w_3 \rangle$ is *applicable*), there exists a w_4 in Σ^* such that

$$\langle w_1, a, w_3, w_4 \rangle \in P$$

Any $\langle k, l \rangle$ system is also called an *IL system*.

Notation

If $\langle w_1, a, w_3, w_4 \rangle$ is an element of P then we denote this by $\langle w_1, a, w_3 \rangle \underset{P}{\rightarrow} w_4$ or simply by $\langle w_1, a, w_3 \rangle \longrightarrow w_4$.

For any nonnegative integer k, if $w = a_1 a_2 \ldots a_m$ is a word such that $m \geq k$, then $\mathrm{Suf}_k(w) = a_{m-k+1} a_{m-k+2} \ldots a_m$ and $\mathrm{Pref}_k(w) = a_1 a_2 \ldots a_k$.

Definition 12.4.2

If $G = \langle \Sigma, P, g, \omega \rangle$ is a $\langle k, l \rangle$ system, $x = a_1 \ldots a_m \in \Sigma^*$ and $y \in \Sigma^*$, then we say that x *directly derives* y in G ($x \underset{G}{\Rightarrow} y$) if, and only if,

$$\langle g^k, a_1, \mathrm{Pref}_l(a_2 \ldots a_m g^l) \rangle \underset{P}{\rightarrow} \alpha_1$$

$$\langle \text{Suf}_k(g^k a_1), a_2, \text{Pref}_l(a_3 \ldots a_m g^l) \rangle \underset{P}{\rightarrow} \alpha_2$$

$$\bullet$$
$$\bullet$$
$$\bullet$$

$$\langle \text{Suf}_k(g^k a_1 \ldots a_{m-1}), a_m, g^l \rangle \underset{P}{\rightarrow} \alpha_m$$

for some $\alpha_1, \alpha_2, \ldots, \alpha_m \in \Sigma^*$ such that $y = \alpha_1 \ldots \alpha_m$. $\underset{G}{\overset{+}{\Rightarrow}}$ and $\underset{G}{\overset{*}{\Rightarrow}}$ are defined as usual. If $x \underset{G}{\overset{*}{\Rightarrow}} y$, then we say that x *derives* y in G.

Definition 12.4.3

Let $G = \langle \Sigma, P, g, \omega \rangle$ be a $\langle k, l \rangle$ system. The *language* of G (denoted by $L(G)$) is defined as

$$L(G) = \{x \in \Sigma^* \mid \omega \underset{G}{\overset{*}{\Rightarrow}} x\}$$

We also say that G *generates* $L(G)$.

Definition 12.4.4

Let k and l be nonnegative integers. If M is a language such that there exists a $\langle k, l \rangle$ system G for which $L(G) = M$, then M is called a $\langle k, l \rangle$ *language*. Any $\langle k, l \rangle$ language is also called an *IL language*.

If G is a $\langle k, 0 \rangle$ system, for some $k \geq 1$, then G is called a *left- sided system*. If G is a $\langle 0, l \rangle$ system for some $l \geq 1$, then G is called a *right-sided system*. If G is a left-or right-sided system, then it is called a *one-sided system*. If G is a $\langle k, l \rangle$ system for some positive k and l, then G is called a *two-sided system*.

The same names are used for the corresponding classes of languages. The following result is a trivial consequence of the definitions.

Proposition

$$\mathscr{F}(\langle 0, 0 \rangle) = \mathscr{F}(0L)$$

Example 12.4.1

Let $G = \langle \Sigma, P, g, e \rangle$ be a $\langle 2, 1 \rangle$ system, where $\Sigma = \{a, b, c, d, e\}$ and P consists of the following productions:

$$\langle gb, a, b \rangle \longrightarrow babc^2$$
$$\langle gb, a, d \rangle \longrightarrow badc^5$$
$$\langle bb, a, b \rangle \longrightarrow b^2 abc^3$$
$$\langle x, b, y \rangle \longrightarrow \Lambda, \quad \text{for every } x \text{ in } (\Sigma \cup \{g\})^2 \text{ and } y \text{ in } \Sigma \cup \{g\}$$
$$\langle x, c, y \rangle \longrightarrow c, \quad \text{for every } x \text{ in } (\Sigma \cup \{g\})^2 \text{ and } y \text{ in } \Sigma \cup \{g\}$$

$$\langle x, d, y \rangle \longrightarrow \Lambda, \qquad \text{for every } x \text{ in } (\Sigma \cup \{g\})^2 \text{ and } y \text{ in } \Sigma \cup \{g\}$$
$$\langle g^2, e, g \rangle \longrightarrow babc^2$$
$$\langle g^2, e, g \rangle \longrightarrow b^2abc^3$$
$$\langle g^2, e, g \rangle \longrightarrow badc^5$$

Then,

$$L(G) = \{babc^{2n} \,|\, n \geq 1\} \cup \{b^2abc^{3n} \,|\, n \geq 1\} \cup \{badc^{5n} \,|\, n \geq 1\} \cup \{e\}$$

Theorem 12.4.1

The following diagram illustrates the relationships between all the different classes of IL languages.

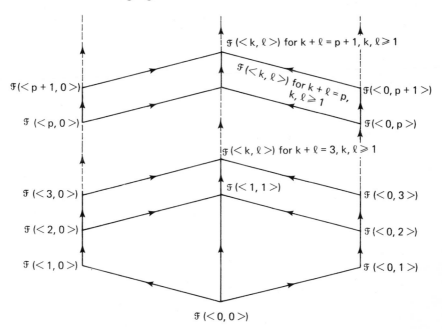

In this diagram a directed solid line leading from class $\mathscr{F}_1$ to class $\mathscr{F}_2$ of IL languages stands for the strict inclusion of $\mathscr{F}_1$ in $\mathscr{F}_2$. The absence of a line between classes $\mathscr{F}_1$ and $\mathscr{F}_2$ stands for the fact that $\mathscr{F}_1$ and $\mathscr{F}_2$ are incomparable but not disjoint classes.

Note in particular the following consequences of this theorem.

1. If $k \geq 1$ and $l \geq 1$, the family of $\langle k, l \rangle$ languages depends only on $k + l$, and not on the actual values of k and l. That is, for two-sided systems,

the total amount of context and not its distribution determines the language generating power.

2. Two-sided systems are inherently more powerful than one sided systems in the sense that $\mathscr{F}(\langle 1, 1 \rangle)$ is not a subset of $\mathscr{F}(\langle k, 0 \rangle)$ for any k, but $\mathscr{F}(\langle k, 0 \rangle)$ is a subset of $\mathscr{F}(\langle k - l, l \rangle)$ for all $l \geq 1$.

Extending the family of IL systems in the same way as we extended 0L systems to get E0L systems, we get the following result.

Theorem 12.4.2

There is an algorithm which for any grammar $G = (N, \Sigma, P, S)$ produces a $\langle 1, 0 \rangle$ system H such that $L(G) = L(H) \cap \Sigma^*$.

Definition 12.4.5

A language L is an *EIL language* if, and only if, there exists an IL system H and an alphabet Δ such that $L = L(H) \cap \Delta^*$.

The following theorem summarizes the relationship between families of developmental languages discussed so far and the Chomsky hierarchy.

Theorem 12.4.3

The following diagram holds

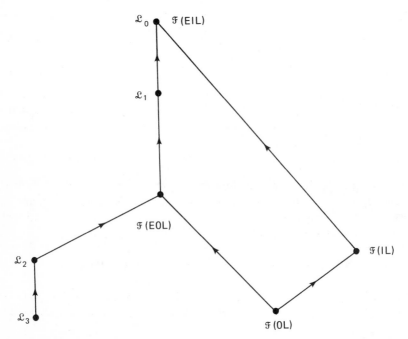

Here a solid line denotes strict inclusion in the direction indicated. If two families $\mathscr{F}_1$ and $\mathscr{F}_2$ are not connected by a direct path in the diagram, then the families are incomparable but not disjoint.

Using systems with interactions we can discuss two particularly attractive properties of biological organisms: their ability to synchronize the action of many cells and their ability to regulate their development in spite of large external disturbances. We discuss these properties in terms of finite one-dimensional iterative arrays of automata each connected to its neighbors. Such arrays can always be represented by a $\langle 1,1 \rangle$ system. On the other hand $\langle 1,1 \rangle$ systems are more general in the sense that they also allow the division of one cell (automaton) into many.

For synchronization we wish to program a finite state automaton in such a way that all the elements of a finite one-dimensional iterative array of such automata will enter a specific state simultaneously, irrespective of the length of the array. This has been referred to as the *firing squad synchronization problem*.

A problem of regulation is the *French flag problem* of Wolpert. Translated into the terminology of iterative automata, this problem is to program a finite state automaton in such a way that a finite one-dimensional iterative array of such automata, initially in identical states, will always turn into a French flag. This means that some of the states will be associated with red, some with white, and some with blue, and the array will eventually be such that the left-hand third is red, the middle third is white and the right-hand third is blue. Furthermore, the automaton has to be programmed so that if the array is broken into two at any point at any time, then *both* of the smaller arrays will turn into French flags. (The problem represents abstractly certain observed biological phenomena. One may think of red as the head, white as the body, and blue as the tail portion of a worm.)

The finished product of a solution to the French flag problem exhibits *polarity*, in the sense that its two ends are essentially different and cannot be taken for each other. Polarity plays a very important role in developmental biology. It is a basic problem whether polarity of the whole iterative array can be achieved without polarity of the individual automata from which the array is built. It has been conjectured that in organisms exhibiting global polarity, the individual cells themselves must possess a polar character.

The notion of polarity translates easily into the terminology of IL systems. Let us use the word *symmetry* to denote lack of polarity at the cellular level.

Definition 12.4.6

1. An IL system $G = \langle \Sigma, P, g, \omega \rangle$ is *deterministic* if, and only if, for every applicable $\langle w_1, a, w_3 \rangle$ there is exactly one w_4 in Σ^* such that $\langle w_1, a, w_3 \rangle \underset{P}{\rightarrow} w_4$.

2. A deterministic $\langle 1, 1 \rangle$ system $G = \langle \Sigma, P, g, \omega \rangle$ is *symmetric* if, and only if, for every $a, b,$ and c in Σ if $\langle a, b, c \rangle \underset{P}{\rightarrow} w$ and $\langle c, b, a \rangle \underset{P}{\rightarrow} \bar{w}$, then

(a) $w = \bar{w}$

(b) w is a palindrome (i.e., it is its own mirror image)

The power of symmetric systems is indicated by the following result.

Theorem 12.4.4

There is an algorithm which for any given Turing machine Z produces a symmetric deterministic $\langle 1, 1 \rangle$ system which simulates Z.

Both the firing squad synchronization problem and the French flag problem can be stated in terms of IL systems. In both cases there are solutions using only symmetric deterministic $\langle 1, 1 \rangle$ systems. In fact such solutions exist even if the arrays are allowed to grow while synchronizing or regulating. Such results show that in spite of the above mentioned conjecture, polarity at the cellular level is not a necessary mechanism for morphogenesis.

EXERCISES 12.4

*1. Prove Theorems 12.4.1–12.4.4.

*2. Prove that $K = \{0, 00, 01\}$ is a deterministic $\langle 1, 1 \rangle$ language, but if a language L is such that $K \subseteq L$, then there exists no deterministic $\langle 1, 0 \rangle$ system G such that $L = L(G)$.

*3. Prove that $\{a^{2u \cdot 3v} \mid u, v \geq 0\}$ is not an IL language.

*4. An IL system $G = \langle \Sigma, P, g, \omega \rangle$ is said to be propagating if, and only if, $\omega \neq \Lambda$ and, for every $\langle w_1, w_2, w_3, w_4 \rangle$ in P, $w_4 \neq \Lambda$. Prove that, for all k_1, k_2, l_1, and l_2, if it is not true that $k_1 \leq k_2$ and $l_1 \leq l_2$, then there exists a propagating $\langle k_1, l_1 \rangle$ system G such that there is no propagating $\langle k_2, l_2 \rangle$ system H such that $L(G) = L(H)$. (Compare this result with Theorem 12.4.1 and the comments following it.)

5. A deterministic IL system G gives rise to a unique sequence of strings $\omega_0, \omega_1, \omega_2, \ldots$, where ω_0 is the axiom, and $\omega_i \underset{G}{\Rightarrow} \omega_{i+1}$. The *growth function* f_G of G is a function from the nonnegative integers into the nonnegative integers defined by: $f_G(t)$ is the length of ω_t. Prove that there is a deterministic $\langle 1, 0 \rangle$ system G such that f_G is not the growth function of any deterministic $\langle 0, 0 \rangle$ system.

*6. State and solve the firing squad synchronization problem and the French flag problem using symmetric deterministic $\langle 1, 1 \rangle$ systems.

7. Suppose that in the definition of an IL system (Definition 12.4.1) we allow instead of one axiom ω a finite set of axioms A, and define language in such a way that any element of A can be used as a starting point of a derivation in Definition 12.4.3. Prove that all the languages generated in this way are already in $\mathscr{F}(\text{IL})$.

*8. Give an algorithm which for any finite sequence $\langle s_0, s_1, \ldots, s_n \rangle$ of strings of symbols produces a deterministic $\langle 1, 1 \rangle$ system G such that, for $0 \le i \le n - 1$, $s_i \underset{G}{\overset{+}{\Rightarrow}} s_{i+1}$.

9. Prove that every finite language is an IL language. (Contrast Theorem 12.2.1.)

12.5. SUGGESTIONS FOR FURTHER READING AND CONCLUSIONS

As we have mentioned before, the material in this chapter is based on some of the topics covered in *Developmental Systems and Languages* by Herman and Rozenberg [2]. We have treated just a few topics in detail, and unfortunately we do not even have space to give a detailed overview of that book. It gives a detailed state-of-the-art account of the subject matter of this chapter, and it is certainly the logical next step for those who are interested in following up this material.

Very briefly, Herman and Rozenberg [2] consist of four parts. The first part is introductory; it discusses developmental systems and languages in their biological context. The second part is a formal treatment of developmental languages; it discusses the family of 0L languages (see our Section 12.2) and its various restrictions and extensions. (This includes the extensions discussed in our Sections 12.3 and 12.4, as well as some others.) Some standard formal language theoretical questions concerning these families of languages are also considered, for example, their closure properties and their relationship to the Chomsky hierarchy. The third part of the book is devoted to the study of developmental sequences (see discussion in Section 12.1). Chapter headings in this part are: "D0L Sequences," "Locally Catenative Sequences," "The Role of Environment," "Syntactic Inference," and "Growth Functions." Some of the topics in the second and third parts are investigated more for their intrinsic formal language theoretical interest than for their relevance to biology. The last part of the book returns to a less formal discussion of topics whose biological motivation is more apparent, such as synchronization of growing filaments, polarity and simulation of developmental processes.

It seems appropriate to consider the question why studies of the type described above should be considered part of Computation Theory. There appear to be three basic reasons for this.

1. The general area is significant to Computer Science, because the understanding of biological organisms may well lead to improvements in artificial computing machines.

2. Our results give further insight into the nature of various concepts traditionally studied in Computation Theory (e.g., the role of context in language generators).

3. Our open problems are such that a background in the Computation Theory appears to be the best preparation for solving them.

There has certainly been a recent upsurge of interest in this topic and a great deal of good work has been done. All the results mentioned in this chapter are less than five years old, and most of them are less than two years old. It is hoped that progress will continue at the present rate and a symbiosis of formal language theory and developmental biology will develop to the mutual benefit of all.

Acknowledgments

The author wishes to express his indebtedness to the two people without whom neither he nor anyone else would know much about the subject matter of this chapter: Aristid Lindenmayer and Grzegorz Rozenberg, both of the University of Utrecht, Holland. Much of the material in this chapter has been taken from joint publications of the author with these gentlemen. Their cooperation is supported by NATO Grant 574, while the author's own research is supported by NSF Grant GJ 998.

The author is also grateful to Professors J. Case, J. van Leeuwen, and H. Pattee and to Messrs. K. P. Lee and A. Walker for reading and criticizing the original manuscript.

REFERENCES

1. EHRENFEUCHT, A. and G. ROZENBERG, "The Equality of E0L Languages and Codings of 0L Languages," *International Journal of Computer Mathematics*, *4* (1974), pp. 95–104.
2. HERMAN, G. T. and G. ROZENBERG, *Developmental Systems and Languages,* North-Holland Publishing Co., Amsterdam, 1974.
3. VON NEUMANN, J. *Theory of Self-Reproducing Automata* University of Illinois Press, Urbana, Ill., 1966.

13

AN AUTOMATA THEORETIC APPROACH TO INTERACTIVE COMPUTER GRAPHICS COMMAND LANGUAGES

Bruce H. Barnes
Department of Computer Science
The Pennsylvania State University

Editor's note:

This chapter uses concepts from automata theory as a descriptive and organizational model for interactive computer graphics control language. The author approaches the problem by means of two examples to illustrate how the essential features of interactive computer graphics control languages can be modeled by means of a sequential machine.
This chapter is self-contained and easily understandable.

The purposes of the chapter are twofold. The first is to demonstrate how automata theory can be useful in organizing the interactive aspects of computer graphics. The second, and probably more important, is to demonstrate that the gap between theory and practice need not exist and that a basic understanding of automata theory is useful to the computer programmer. Automata theory is rapidly becoming the descriptive language for organizing many computer applications. Consequently the emphasis of this chapter will be on the use of automata theory as a descriptive and organizational model rather than as a theoretical model. The value of this approach lies primarily in its ability to model the essential features while ignoring the nonessential aspects of interactive computer graphics control languages.

13.1. INTRODUCTION

That a picture is worth a thousand words is as true in the computer field as any other. For several years high quality sophisticated interactive computer graphics equipment has been available. As a field, however, computer graphics is just beginning to realize some of the impact most of its ardent disciples knew it was capable of achieving. High cost has been a major impediment to its broad usage. However, the cost is now decreasing rapidly and should no longer act as serious deterrent. An equally major barrier has been the difficulty in writing high quality applications programs. The difficulties lie in three major areas;

1. Specifying the interaction between computer and user.
2. Building, maintaining, and using the complex data structures necessary for developing graphic data.
3. The lack of suitable programming languages and techniques, which have required that a user be an accomplished programmer in order to use computer graphics effectively.

In the last few years there have been several improvements in each of these areas. The purpose of this exposition is to indicate how automata theory can be a useful tool in attacking these problems, especially in the design and implementation of interactive computer graphics command languages. An interactive computer graphic command language is a construct for specifying which graphic processes and/or devices are to be activated and what data is to be passed among them.

13.2.   REVIEW OF COMPUTER GRAPHICS

Before we begin our discussion of the application of automata theory to interactive computer graphics, it would be valuable to discuss interactive computer graphics in order to comprehend the difficulties involved and to appreciate the contributions automata theory can make to this vital area of computer science.

An interactive computer graphics system is composed of three major components: a computer, a display, and an assortment of devices whose primary purpose is to allow interaction between the user and the display or computer. See Fig. 13.2.1.

The computer can be one which is used only by the graphics systems, possibly time shared with several graphic terminals or it could be a large computer with a communications link to the graphics system or both. Usually included as interactive devices are a light pen, a console keyboard, a set of function switches, and one or more of the following: foot operated switches, a set of variable control knobs, a joystick, a data tablet, lights, noisemakers, etc. While no system will have all of these, most will include several different types of interactive devices. A graphics system will also have the usual I/O devices

Fig. 13.2.1

available, either through the main computer via the communications link or attached directly to the graphics system. Since we are using graphic data there is an even bigger variety of input/output devices for handling two-dimensional data such as printing the picture on the scope face or photographing the scope face.

Besides the difficulty caused by a wide assortment of hardware, there is an added difficulty in that three programming tasks are going on simultaneously: the user program, the display buffer, and the interrupt handler. In some graphics display systems these three functions are intertwined adding a superficial complexity.

The display buffer is in effect a list of instructions describing what images are to be drawn on the face of the CRT. The graphic terminal will continuously scan through the display buffer and draw the desired images on the face of the scope. If one wishes to modify the picture on the scope face, one needs to change the instructions in the display buffer.

The interrupt handler varies considerably among machines. It can be viewed as a list of device names and corresponding instructions such that if one of the devices in the list is activated then the corresponding instructions are executed. The list of devices will vary according to which ones are active at any point in the program.

The program will run continuously interacting with the I/O devices, the interrupt handler, and the display buffer. Thus, the program is like other interactive programs with the additional complexity of having to be concerned with the display buffer and a greater variety of I/O devices. This and most other aspects of computer graphics is discussed in Newman and Sproull [12].

Due to these programming complexities there have evolved three types of programmers: systems programmers, application programmers, and console users. The console user is primarily interested in gaining insight into his problem with the least difficulty and shortest delay. Thus, he should not have to do or know any programming or be concerned with devices other than those which he needs for his particular application. His knowledge and expertise is concentrated in the application area. The applications programmer writes the programs that the console user uses. He must have a general knowledge of the area as well as broad training in the computer graphics systems. He usually will program in a higher level language and might not be an expert in the detailed operation of the machine. On the other hand, the systems programmer will be an expert in the computer graphics system. He will write the programming system and languages used by the applications programmer. His knowledge will be concentrated on the computer and display terminal.

Added to these programming difficulties is the problem of building the picture on the face of the scope (really it is built in the display buffer, but we will view it as if it is built on the face of the scope or as if it were being drawn on an off line plotter). Each line has to be inserted one at a time by specifying where the ends of each line must be placed on the scope. For an interesting and useful picture this could include as many as 1000 lines. Without some procedure to create pictures from subpictures this task is exceedingly difficult and will be abandoned except in the most important applications.

Out of all this morass have come programming techniques which have made significant progress in bringing computer graphics to the point where it is now and in a short while it should be at the point where an applications user will be able to employ computer graphics with almost the same ease with which they can now use most interactive packages. This progress has been accomplished in part by the application of automata theory to these challenging and interesting problems.

13.3.   AN EXAMPLE OF COMPUTER AIDED DESIGN

The area of computer aided design is a good one to demonstrate what is involved in using a computer graphic systems in an interactive mode. While there is no universally accepted definition of computer aided design, we will use it to describe the processes where the console user uses the computer graphics terminal as an input device. The computer will use this data to analyze the design and output the analysis. The designer will then modify his design and resubmit the data for analysis. This procedure will continue until the console user is satisfied.

For example, suppose we wanted to use a computer graphic system to design a finite automata to accept a given set of tapes. The transition function could be specified by either a next state table or a state transition graph. Although experience has shown that both methods are effective, it is more in keeping with the spirit of computer graphics to use the state transition diagram. For simplicity it will be assumed that the states are numbered 1, 2, 3, . . ., etc. The states will be located by having a rectangular grid displayed on the face of the scope. The designer uses the light pen to decide where each state is to be located and uses the console keyboard to enter its name. After all the states have been entered, he will switch mode of operation to enter the transitions. This could be accomplished, for example, by pushing one of the function keys. In this phase, he would specify the edge in the state transition graph by locating two states with the light pen and entering the edge weight from the console keyboard. When all of the transitions have been specified the automata would be submitted to the computer for analysis.

After the analysis is completed, the results are given to the designer. They could be displayed on the screen, printed on the console typewriter, printed on the terminal printer or if the graphics terminal has a data link to a larger computer it could be output on any of the output devices available on that computer. Through the use of function keys or other devices the designer could have a choice of one or more of these output mediums.

If the designer wished to make changes in the automata, he could have it redisplayed and set the program to operate in change mode. Edges, states, etc. could be removed or added by a combination of light pen and/or function key interactions. When he is satisfied that he has made the correct modifications, he would resubmit the automata for analysis. The automata will again be analyzed and the results returned to the designer. This cycle can be repeated as many times as necessary, until the designer is satisfied that he has the correct automata.

13.4. THEORETICAL BACKGROUND

At this point it is appropriate to introduce some of the theoretical ideas that will be used in the development. A finite state transducer or sequential machine is a finite state control attached to an input tape and an output tape. It is operated by reading an input and depending on the symbol read and the current state of the finite control, it transfers control to a new state and outputs a symbol from the output alphabet. Formally, it is defined as follows.

Definition 13.4.1

A sequential machine is a 5-tuple $M = (S, \Sigma, \Delta, \delta, \omega)$ where,

1. S is a finite nonempty set of "states"
2. Σ is a finite nonempty set of "inputs"
3. Δ is a finite nonempty set of "outputs"
4. δ is a function of $S \times \Sigma$ into S, called the next "state function"
5. ω is a function of $S \times \Sigma$ into Δ, called the output function

The sequential machines moves are determined by δ and its output is determined by ω.

Sequential machines were originally designed as models for sequential switching circuits and used in the design of digital computers. This area has received considerable interest and there are several good books available [2, 7, 15] and also some very good bibliographies [9, 13, 17]. Since our interest is in the area of programming application we will direct our study of sequential machines toward that end.

Sequential machines can be a very useful and descriptive tool for organizing discrete time simulations of continue problems. For example, Ullmann [16] has used sequential machines on pattern recognition problems.

Let us consider the simulation of a traffic tunnel as an example of the application of automata theory. The number of vehicles in the tunnel at any given instant is a function of the previous number of cars in the tunnel and the number of entering vehicles. It would also be a function of the rate of traffic, the density of vehicles, etc. In order to model this type of problem on a computer, it is necessary to break time down into discrete steps. We can associate an input with each time step. In this case, the input is the number of cars that have entered the tunnel since the last time step. The internal states are the number of cars in the tunnel at each time. The next state function depends basically on the number of cars in the tunnel and the number of entering cars. The output in this case is simply a recording of the number of cars in the tunnel, or it could be an analysis of the tunnel behavior.

13.5. APPLICATION OF THEORY TO COMPUTER GRAPHICS

The correspondence between a sequential machine and a graphic terminal are straightforward and have been used by several designers, although some authors did not realize they were using the ideas of automata theory (see, for example, [11, 14]). The application program in conjunction with the interrupt handler serves as the finite control. The various interactions with the terminal input devices play the role of the inputs and the changing of the instructions in the display buffer and other systems responses serve as outputs. The following example illustrates in a simplified manner how a sequential machine can be utilized as an effective model of the interactive display building process.

Recall the problem of using the display terminal to design a finite automata. The main program starts in the initial state. At this time it will only accept inputs indicating that the designer desires to create a new automata or that he wishes to modify an existing one. All other interactions will be blocked. Assume that the designer has decided to create a new automaton. In this case the output from the sequential machine is to create the appropriate images in the display buffer for beginning the design process. One possibility is an array of dots to be used as possible states. The sequential machine will now transfer control to the state indicating that an automaton is to be built.

In this state only a light pen response indicating the selection of a state will be allowed. When the designer chooses a state, this is recorded and control is passed to the state that indicates that the second state in a transition is to be selected. In this state only a light pen detect of another state will be allowed. Next the transition label has to be specified. Thus, in this state only a keyboard response will be accepted. When the transition is labeled, the image of the transition with its label is added to the display buffer and, consequently, to the face of the scope. The process continues in this manner until the designer feels that he has the proper automaton, at which time he transfers control to the analysis program.

The correspondence between the states of the program and the states of a sequential machine are quite obvious and easy to visualize. What then are the advantages? There are at least three for the application programmer and these result in some advantage for the console user. The advantages for the application programmer are simplicity and clarity of design, implementation, documentation, and ease of modification. By isolating which inputs are allowed in each state and which are not minimizes the problem of handling the various possible interactions. Following the flow of control from one state to another helps organize the structural flow of the program. Specifying the appropriate responses as outputs from the sequential machine provides a clean technique for building the display buffer. For these reasons debugging is simplified and gives a straightforward means for documentation.

In summary the design of the control aspects of an interactive computer program could proceed as follows. First list the set of all possible user actions and assign each a different label (numbers work very well). Next list and name the set of all possible input points in the program. This becomes the state set. The system responses are then listed, named, and become the output set. The next step is to complete the next state and output entries in a table defining the next state and output functions. Once this is done implementation, debugging and documentation are straightforward.

Example 13.5.1 :   Circuit Design

In order to better understand the design process let us examine a problem in detail. Consider the problem of circuit design.† Here we have a network

---

† This example and the next are due to Professor Richard Lewallen [8].

of resistors, compositors, inductors, fixed voltages, fixed currents, and grounded wires (for example, see Fig. 13.5.1).

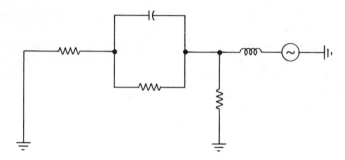

Fig. 13.5.1

The circuit will be drawn on the face of the scope by the use of the light pen and the keyboard will be used to specify values. An input technique known as menu selection will be used to indicate which symbol is to appear in each edge. This is accomplished by displaying on the face of the scope the list of possible symbols called a menu and using the light pen to choose the desired one.

The process begins by displaying an array of points on the face of the scope along with a menu containing DISPLAY, HELP, COMPUTE, REINITIAL-IZE. At this time the only inputs that will be accepted are light pen detects of a node, signifying the selection of the first node of an arc, DISPLAY signifying that the system should display the circuit as far as it has been built, HELP which will cause the operating instructions for the program to be displayed, COMPUTE which will terminate the input portion of the program and transfer control to the analysis portion, or REINITIALIZE which will terminate the current circuit and start the process all over again. Assume that the user selected a node. At this time the only appropriate user actions are to choose a terminal node for an edge in the circuit or to choose a ground. Thus the computer now displays a message to select another node or ground and a menu containing GROUND. If the user chooses another node then the computer will display a menu containing the various elements he might select for an edge, a resistor for example. The only input which will be accepted now is an entry from the keyboard specifying the value of the resistor. At this point we are now ready to either transfer control to the analysis portion of the program or select another edge in the circuit. Thus, we will once again display the array of nodes, the menu containing DISPLAY, HELP, COMPUTE, REINITIAL-IZE, and a message to select the initial node. This process is repeated until the designer is satisfied with his circuit and selects the compute mode.

Let us examine this process from a sequential machine point of view.

There are effectively only 7 different states in the program. These are listed in Table 13.5.1.

Table **13.5.1.** INTERNAL STATES OF CIRCUIT INPUT PROGRAM

State	Interpretation
0	Enter analysis program
1	Control state
2	Initial node selected
3	Terminal node selected
4	Element type selected
5	Display mode
6	Help mode

Except for the keyboard entry of the value for the elements in the circuit all other inputs are light pen detects. To facilitate our design of a sequential machine these inputs will be assigned numbers as specified in Table 13.5.2.

The outputs in this case are the actions to be taken in response to the particular input. The systems response must both update the program variables and change the display buffers. The outputs for this program are listed in Table 13.5.3. The array card is used to record the branches in the circuit for input to the analysis program.

The transition function, which is specified in Table 13.5.4, can be imple-

Table **13.5.2.** INPUTS FOR SEQUENTIAL MACHINE FOR CIRCUIT INPUT

Inputs	User Actions
1	Light pen detect of NODE
2	Light pen detect of DISPLAY
3	Light pen detect of HELP
4	Light pen detect of COMPUTE
5	Light pen detect of REINITIALIZE
6	Keyboard entry
7	Light pen detect of GROUND
8	Light pen detect of RETURN
9	Light pen detect of CHANGE
10	Light pen detect of DELETE
11	Light pen detect of branch
12	Light pen detect of TERMINATE
13	Light pen detect of WIRE
14	Light pen detect of RESISTOR
15	Light pen detect of CAPACITOR
16	Light pen detect of INDUCTOR
17	Light pen detect of FIXED VOLTAGE
18	Light pen detect of FIXED CURRENT

mented as a table driven program or as a program using a construct like, WHEN IN STATE h; IF INPUT m; THEN RESPONSE p and GO TO STATE q. This latter method is useful for documentation, while the first is probably better for debugging and maintenance. The two are, of course, equivalent.

Table 13.5.3.   OUTPUT FOR SEQUENTIAL MACHINE MODEL OF CIRCUIT INPUT PROGRAM

OUTPUTS System Responses

1. Record location of initial node, display message: "SELECT FINAL NODE OR GROUND," and display menu: "GROUND."
2. Record location of final node, display message: "SELECT ELEMENT TYPE," and display menu list provided by analysis program.
3. Display ground symbol at initial node and display message: "SELECT FINAL NODE."
4. Add information entered via keyboard, plus branch and node numbers, to list of CARD's, display message: "SELECT INITIAL NODE," and display menu:"DIS-PLAY/HELP/COMPUTE/REINITIALIZE." Also display branch information entered into array CARD.
5. Display message: "SELECT BRANCH" and menu: "RETURN."
6. Display branch information from array CARD for branch selected and display menu: "RETURN/CHANGE/DELETE."
7. Display message: "KEY IN NEW VALUES" and enable keyboard.
8. Replace old branch information in array CARD with new values entered via keyboard, display new branch information, display message: "SELECT BRANCH," and display menu: "RETURN/CHANGE/DELETE."
9. Return to analysis program to see if deletion is valid for this branch. If invalid, display message to that effect. If valid, delete this branch from scope and data structure, renumber succeeding branches in data structure, and display message: "SELECT BRANCH" and menu: "RETURN."
10. Display message: "SELECT INITIAL NODE" and menu: "DISPLAY/HELP/ COMPUTE/REINITIALIZE."
11. Display system operating instructions and menu: "RETURN."
12. Restore previous display.
13. Return to analysis program to perform computations for this network.
14. Delete all branches and node numbers from display.
15. Perform final housekeeping functions, return to analysis program.
16. Display WIRE (a straight line) between initial and final nodes, number final node same as initial node, display message: "SELECT INITIAL NODE," and display menu: "DISPLAY/HELP/COMPUTE/REINITIALIZE."
17. Display RESISTOR symbol between initial and final nodes, number initial and final nodes, display message: "KEY IN VALUES," and enable keyboard.
18. Display CAPACITOR symbol between initial and final nodes, then duplicate the rest of response 18.
19. Display INDUCTOR symbol between initial and final nodes, then duplicate the rest of response 18.
20. Display VOLTAGE SOURCE symbol between initial and final nodes, then duplicate the rest of response 18.
21. Display CURRENT SOURCE symbol between initial and final nodes, then duplicate the rest of response 18.

Table 13.5.4. TRANSITION FUNCTION FOR SEQUENTIAL MACHINE (ELECTRICAL CIRCUIT ANALYSIS)

Input \ State	1	2	3	4	5	6	7	8	9	10	11	12	13	14	15	16	17	18
1	2/1	5/5	6/11	0/13	1/14	—	—	—	—	—	—	—	—	—	—	—	—	—
2	3/2	—	—	—	—	—	2/3	—	—	—	—	0/15	—	—	—	—	—	—
3	—	—	—	—	—	—	—	—	—	—	—	0/15	1/16	4/17	4/18	4/19	4/20	4/21
4	—	—	—	—	—	1/4	—	—	—	—	—	—	—	—	—	—	—	—
5	—	—	—	—	—	5/8	—	1/10	5/9	5/11	5/8	0/15	—	—	—	—	—	—
6	—	—	—	—	—	—	—	1/12	—	—	—	—	—	—	—	—	—	—

If an application programmer wants to write an interactive computer graphics package for another network problem, for example, PERT networks, control systems, finite automata, etc., then more than half the work is already done. All he needs to do is identify the user responses (input), the system responses (outputs) and change the next state table appropriately.

Example 13.5.2: Layout

In order to solidify our understanding of the relationship between the basic structure of interactive computer graphics programs and the concept of sequential machines, it will be useful to discuss another example. Consider the problem of laying out a design built out of basic components on the face of the scope, for example, laying out a pattern on material, placing trees and shrubs in a landscape, laying out furniture in a room, or arranging equipment in a computer room. The program involves choosing a component and positioning it in space. The various items are selected from a menu of component names similar to the means for choosing electrical components in network problems. The positioning in space can be accomplished by use of a light pen, a curser positioned on the scope face by a joystick, a stylist on a data tablet, or other devices capable of locating an arbitrary point on the face of the scope.

The program begins by displaying the message "INPUT POSITION DATA" and the menu "DELETE/HELP/COMPUTE/REINITIALIZE" on the CRT. As soon as the position data has been entered, the program will switch to a new state and display the menu of items and a message to select a

Table 13.5.5. OUTPUTS FOR COMPONENTS PLACEMENT SEQUENTIAL MACHINE

1. Record positioning data, display message: "SELECT COMPONENT TYPE," and display component menu.
2. Display message: "SELECT COMPONENT TO BE DELETED" and menu: "RETURN."
3. Delete this component from display and data structure, display message and menu as in 2.
4. Display message: "INPUT POSITION DATA" and menu: "DELETE/HELP/COMPUTE/REINITIALIZE."
5. Save current display data, display operating instructions and menu: "RETURN."
6. Restore previous display.
7. Save current display and return to analysis program.
8. Delete all components from display and data structure and perform response 4.
9. Display component 1 according to positioning data, update data structure and perform response 4.
10. Display component 2 according to positioning data, update data structure and perform response 4.
11. Display component 3 according to positioning data, update data structure and perform response 4.
12. Display component 4 according to positioning data, update data structure and perform response 4.

component. The outputs for the system basically describe what is to be displayed on the scope (i.e., which display buffer to process or what modifications are to be made to the display buffers). They are listed in Table 13.5.5.

After the component has been selected it is positioned on the scope according to the positioning data and the program reenters the control state. Thus there are only five states:

(0) analysis program
(1) control state
(2) select component
(3) delete mode
(4) help mode

The inputs for the program are listed in Table 13.5.6.

Table 13.5.6. INPUTS FOR COMPONENT PLACEMENT SEQUENTIAL MACHINE

	INPUTS (User Actions)	
1	Position data	
2	Menu item	DELETE
3	Menu item	HELP
4	Menu item	COMPUTE
5	Menu item	REINITIALIZE
6	Menu item	RETURN
7	Menu item	Component 1
8	Menu item	Component 2
9	Menu item	Component 3
10	Menu item	Component 4
11	Detect of component to be deleted	

The next state function could be specified in program style by:

When in state 1; if input 1, then response 1 and go to state 2
                  if input 2, then response 2 and go to state 3
                  if input 3, then response 5 and go to state 4
                  if input 4, then response 7 and go to state 0
                  if input 5, then response 8 and go to state 1
When in state 2; if input 7, then response 9 and go to state 1
                  if input 8, then response 10 and go to state 1
                  if input 9, then response 10 and go to state 1
                  if input 10, then response 12 and go to state 1
When in state 3; if input 11, then response 3 and go to state 3
                  if input 6, then response 4 and go to state 1
When in state 4; if input 6, then response 4 and go to state 1

13.6. ADVANTAGES OF FINITE STATE APPROACH AND PROGRAMMING CONSIDERATIONS

A systems' programmer could easily write a compiler that would translate this description into a computer program. Writing the input recognition subprograms, programming the system responses, and building the various display menus are the more difficult parts of the program. The interactive inputs and system responses tend to be independent of the particular application and can frequently be built out of standard system subprograms. Thus, another advantage of the sequential machine approach is to separate the application dependent and application independent portions of the program.

In using a sequential machine as a model for designing, implementing, modifying, and maintaining an interactive computer graphics system, the essential key is to delineate the inputs, the outputs, and the states. Construction of the transition table is straightforward. The inputs are the various user interactions or possibly other interactions with devices external to the computer graphics system, for example, a remote sensing device. The input not only involves the use of one of the diverse input devices, but also the particulars as to how these devices are used. The outputs and system responses are more difficult to specify, because the applications programmer has to concern himself with building the appropriate data structures and updating the program variables as well as building the display buffers. This process can be accomplished in two steps. First, specify the system responses in general terms and then as implementations develop the incorporation of more detail. The states contain two kinds of information, current program data and location and what input responses are appropriate at this place in the program's progression.

The advantages of the finite state approach are many. The most important is simplicity and clarity of program design. Other advantages are easy debugging and documentation. The fact that the application independent and dependent portion are separated means that designing and implementing a different, but similar, application are considerably easier, and might prove to be one of the biggest advantages of this automata theoretic approach.

13.7. SYNTACTIC PICTURE GENERATION

Another basic problem in computer graphics is that of creating the appropriate picture on the face of the display. Even a simple picture such as computer room layout will be made up of many separate lines. In order to facilitate the building of such a picture, there has to be some means for building the display image from subcomponents. Once again automata theory can provide a framework and the linguistic machinery to describe the process. This time, however, we will use formal language theory instead of sequential machine theory. Recall that a context-free grammar consists of a set of variables, a set of terminals, a set of productions, and a start symbol. In the translation of arithmetic expressions the operators, literals, and language variables are the terminals, the variables correspond to intermediate results in computation, and the production describes how to parse the expression. In our case, the terminal symbols correspond to lines, circles, squares, or other basic shapes from which an application orientated figure can be constructed, the variables correspond to composite pictures and the productions describe how a display is built out of these components.

For example, consider the application of computer room layout. The layout consists of boxes which have little human activity associated with them, like memory units; units with moderate activity, I/O devices for example; some with high human activity, for instance the operator console and some non-computer components, like furniture. Depending on the application we might also be interested in connecting cables, telephones, etc. Thus, if we let DISPLAY be the start symbol, we have a production of the form DISPLAY → COMPONENTS, I/O DEVICES, CONSOLES, FURNITURE. In this production COMPONENTS, I/O DEVICES, CONSOLES, and FURNITURE are variable, "," is a terminal. A typical production expending the variable I/O DEVICES might be I/O DEVICES → TAPE UNIT, CARD READER, LINE PRINTER. The variable CARD READER would expand into the appropriate basic units to build a picture of a CARD READER. This could be represented as a tree as shown in Fig. 13.7.1.

Using the basic structure of context-free languages one can organize the picture building process in a way that avoids the confusion, is readily documented, and is easily modified. This scheme for organizing computer graphics

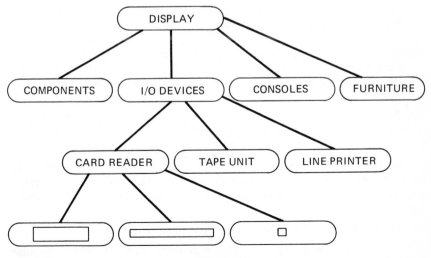

Fig. 13.7.1

data is not new and has been used on several systems [10, 14]. Formal language theory, however, gives one the language and descriptive tools necessary for manipulating these structures.

13.8. CONCLUSION

By now it should be apparent that the contribution that automata and formal language theory give to interactive computer graphics is not so much in theorems and theory as it is in its organization and descriptive power. Just as calculus has become the language of continuous mathematics and set theory the language of discrete mathematics, automata theory is rapidly becoming the language of Computer Science.

EXERCISES 13.8

The exercises are intended as an extension of the text. Even if the reader doesn't work the exercises in detail he should be sure that he understands how they could be done.

1. In the application of laying out a computer room suppose that we wish to do some of the analyses interactively from the terminal. We might wish to check that the doors on the various cabinets can be opened without hitting another cabinet. This could be done by having the image of a door attached to the image of a cabinet. The image of the door could be linked to a variable control knob in such a manner that as the knob is turned the door will open. Thus the console user can open the doors and see if they will intersect another piece of equipment. By using two knobs he could check to see if two doors collide if they are both opened. Which doors are to be opened could be selected by a light pen detection. How could the sequential machine for component layout be modified to incorporate this extension? That is, identify the inputs, the outputs, and how the transition table is to be modified.

    This exercise should demonstrate that the sequential machine approach render the computer program easily modifiable. In computer graphics application this is a very important feature, because immediate interactive feedback supplies the researcher with a whole new environment for gaining insight into his studies, and, consequently, stimulates his imagaination and wets his appetite.

2. The context-free language used to describe the displays for layout of a computer room does not contain any positional data. How could the grammar be augmented to include this information?

    The following exercises are typical of problems that can utilize sequential machines in their organization for computer solution. The key to this kind of organization is usually in recognizing the state set and how the program changes states as time progresses.

3. Use a sequential machine to play the game of tic-tac-toe.

4. Use a sequential machine to simulate population growth. The states might represent the number of organisms in each of three classes: young, reproducing age, and old.

REFERENCES

1. ALLEN, T. R. and J. E. FOOTE, "Input Output/Software for a Man-Machine Communication and Image Processing System," *Proc. AFIPS Fall Joint Computer Conference* 26 (1964), 387–396.

2. GILL, A., *Introduction to the Theory of Finite State Machines*, McGraw-Hill Book Co., New York, 1962.

3. BROWN, S. H., "Conversational Job Control," *IBM Systems Journal*, 7 (1968), 271–280.

4. COTTON, I. W. and F. S. GREATOREX, JR., "Data Structures and Techniques for Remote Computer Graphics," *Proc. AFIPS Fall Joint Computer Conference*, 33 (1968) 533–544.

5. COTTON, I. W., "Languages for Graphic Attention-Handling," in *Advanced Computer Graphics Economics Techniques and Applications*, ed. by R. D. Parslow and R. E. Green, Plenum Press, New York, 1971, pp. 1049–1091.

6. FAIMAN, M. and J. NIEVERGELT (eds.), *Pertinent Concepts of Computer Graphics*, University of Illinois Press, Urbana, Ill. 1969.

7. HARRISON, M. A., *Introduction to Switching and Automata Theory*. McGraw-Hill Book Co., New York, 1965.

8. LEWALLEN, R. A., "A Standardized Approach to Developing Software for Computer Graphics Applications, " Ph.D. thesis, Pennsylvania State University, University Park, Pa., June 1973.

9. MILLER, E. F. and J. H. PUGSLEY, "Bibliography 22: Sequential Machines, *Computing Reviews*, 11: 5 (1970), 303–325.

10. NAKE and ROSENFELD (eds.), *Graphic Languages, Proc. IFIP Working Conference on Graphic Languages*, North Holland Publishing Co., Amsterdam, 1972.

11. NEWMAN, W. M., "A System for Interactive Graphical Programming." *Proc. AFIPS Spring Joint Computer Conference*, 32 (1968), 47–54.

12. NEWMAN, W. M. and R. F. SPROULL, *Principles of Interactive Computer Graphics*, McGraw-Hill Book Co., New York, 1973.

13. RAHIMI, M. A., "Key-word Index Bibliography of Automata, Formal Languages and Computability Theory," *SIGACT News*, 5 (1970).

14. SHAW, A. C., "A Formal Picture Description Scheme as a Basis for Picture Processing Systems," *Information and Control*, 14 (1969) 9–52.

15. TOU, J. T. (ed.), *Applied Automata Theory*, Academic Press, Inc., New York, 1968.

16. ULLMANN, J. R., *Pattern Recognition Techniques*, Crane, Russak & Co., New York, 1973.

17. WOOD, D., "Bibliography 23: Formal Languages Theory and Automata Theory," *Computing Reviews*, 11:7 (1970), 417–430.

14 MODELING OPERATING SYSTEMS WITH AUTOMATA

John Howard
Department of Computer Sciences
Computation Center and Institute for
Computer Sciences and Computer Applications
The University of Texas at Austin
Austin, Texas

Editor's note:

This chapter uses concepts from automata theory to model how processes interact in a multiprogrammed operating system. The approach taken here is to introduce structures on the state set and transition rule of an automaton to obtain the desired model. Concepts such as determinateness and deadlock from operating systems are formalized in automata theoretical terms and carefully analyzed. Plenty of examples are provided here for the benefit of the reader.

The only prerequisite for this chapter is the concept of finite automaton introduced in Chapter 1.

14.1. INTRODUCTION

This chapter uses concepts from the theory of automata to model programs, the processes they define, and the way these processes interact in a multiprogrammed operating system. The strength of this model is that it relates two familiar areas: programs in the form of flowcharts, and automata. It is applied here to analysis of correctness in individual programs and systems of programs, to performance evaluation, and to the formal definition of familiar operating systems terminology.

Operating systems differ from "normal" computer programs in several respects. First, operating systems are large, complex programs containing many concepts, written by teams of programmers. This makes debugging them nearly impossible. Formal or automatic tools for validating operating system correctness are highly desirable.

Second, operating systems make explicit use of parallel processing in order to maximize utilization of system resources and thus hopefully to increase the rate of job completions. Unfortunately parallel processing is a major contributor to the complexity of an operating system. Three problem areas must be dealt with. First, independent tasks must be kept from interfering with each other. Second, processes which do communicate with each other must do so in a disciplined way. These two areas are usually considered together under the name of *determinateness,* which requires that the behavior of individual processes should not be affected by the concurrent interpretation of other processes. The third problem area is *deadlocks,* which are a byproduct of the interlocking rules introduced to obtain determinateness. Intuitively, a deadlock occurs when several processes are mutually and permanently interlocked.

Section 14.2 starts with the general concept of a sequential process, which is an automaton with no restrictions on its state set or transition rules. Subsequent sections develop concepts for relating sequential processes to programs. These concepts include structuring the state into a Cartesian product of components corresponding to programs' memory cells, homomorphisms of processes, and compressing state change information into primitive operations used as transition labels. The discussion of single processes culminates with applications including inductive assertions and sequence checking.

Systems of parallel processes operating asynchronously are introduced in Section 14.12. Discussion starts with completely independent processes, uses them to define "determinateness," and then goes into the problem of allowing dependence between processes without losing determinateness. The model is used to define terms such as "critical section," "resource," and "mutual exclusion." Finally, applications in the areas of system correctness, implementing mutual exclusion, and performance evaluation are discussed briefly.

Since there is a recent and thorough survey of formal models of parallel processing (see Baer [1]), it would be redundant to repeat it here. Readers who are interested in other models are urged to consult Baer's excellent survey. The bibliography at the end of this chapter contains only works directly related to the model presented here.

Finally, it should be noted that this model owes much to the ideas of Dijkstra, and could justly be described an attempt to formalize his "cooperating sequential processes." Dijkstra's cited work is compulsory reading for anyone interested in operating systems.

14.2. SEQUENTIAL PROCESSES

Definition 14.2.1

A sequential process is an ordered pair $P = (Q, R)$ where Q (the *states*) is a nonempty set and R (the *transitions*) is a binary relation on Q.

This is a streamlined definition and omits many considerations usually found in definitions of automata, such as:

The structure of Q. Should Q be finite, a stack, a bounded or an unbounded tape? Later sections will develop a structure for Q appropriate for modeling programs.

Inputs and outputs. How does P receive information from and send information to the "outside world?" In the model to be developed, processes receive inputs by acquiring new state components and produce outputs by releasing components.

Initial and final states. When necessary, the existence of subsets Q_I(initial) and Q_F (final) of Q will be assumed without formal specification.

14.3. STATE GRAPHS

A process can be interpreted as a directed graph whose vertices correspond to states and whose arcs correspond to transitions. The choice of terminology is arbitary. The process terminology will be used here when a dynamic interpretation is intended, and the graph terminology will be used in a static sense. Thus a process is an entity which traverses a state graph, and a state graph is like a program in that it defines what a process may do.

14.4. LABELED ARCS

Processes defined by computer programs change state by performing instructions written in the programs. It is reasonable to reflect this fact by labeling the arcs of the state graph with symbolic tokens of the instructions involved. Therefore let L be a set of *primitive operations,* and extend the definition of R to

$$R \subseteq Q \times L \times Q$$

such that $(a, s, b) \in R$ means that there is a transition (arc) labeled with s from state (vertex) a to state (vertex) b. Interpretations for the primitive operations in L will be defined as the concept of unfolding a program into its state graph is introduced.

14.5. COMPUTATIONS

Definition 14.5.1

A *path* in a state graph is a finite sequence of arcs,

$$(a_0, s_1, a_1), (a_1, s_2, a_2), \ldots, (a_{n-1}, s_n, a_n)$$

which lie head-to-tail. Paths correspond to the possible partial *computations* of a process. Given such a path, a_n is said to be *reachable* from a_0. (By convention, any vertex is reachable from itself *via* a path of length 0.) When considering the state graphs of computer programs, it is reasonable to insist that only states reachable from initial states be considered, and desirable to have some final state reachable from every state considered.

Definition 14.5.2

The sequence $s_1 s_2 \ldots s_n$ of operations along a path is a *trace*. The set of all traces defined by a graph is a language, and will be regular if the graph is finite, or context-free if the graph has an appropriately stack-like structure. Section 14.12 explores an application of the linguistic structure of traces.

Computations, defined as paths in the state graph, reflect the discrete nature of digital computers in two ways. First, the states themselves form a discrete set. Second, the flow of time is broken up into a discrete sequence of transitions with no indication of "how long" each one takes. Only the ordering of events along the computation matters. The assumption of ignorance about the length of time intervals is almost universally accepted by authors of parallel programs. Use of timing information yields programs which are highly machine-and-system-dependent and cannot be modified easily.

14.6. HOMOMORPHISMS AND FOLDING

Analysis of processes requires that their state graphs be manipulated in structure-preserving ways. For example, many programs have infinite state graphs which must be represented finitely. Structure-preserving mappings are usually called homomorphisms. In a state graph, the structure to be preserved is the set of arcs.

Definition 14.6.1

Let $P_1 = (Q_1, R_1)$, $P_2 = (Q_2, R_2)$, and $f : Q_1 \to Q_2$ be a mapping. Then f is a *homomorphism* if and only if

$$(a, s, b) \in R_1 \quad \text{implies that} \quad (f(a), s, f(b)) \in R_2.$$

Definition 14.6.2

A *folding* is an onto homomorphism with the additional property that $(a', s, b') \in R_2$ implies that there exists some $(a, s, b) \in R_1$ such that $a' = f(a)$ and $b' = f(b)$.

Definition 14.6.3

An *isomorphism* is a 1–1 onto homomorphism whose inverse is also a homomorphism. Note that an isomorphism is a folding.

If initial and final states are specified, then homomorphisms must map initial states to initial states and final states to final states, and foldings must have the property that if $a \in Q_{2I}(Q_{2F})$ then there exists some $a' \in Q_{1I}(Q_{1F})$ such that $a' = f(a)$.

Intuitively, a folding is a homomorphism for which the resulting state graph contains no unnecessary vertices or arcs. The term folding is used because the inverse images of vertices in Q_2 are equivalence classes of vertices in Q_1, and f "folds" the vertices in each equivalence class together, preserving arcs as it does so. Note that for any Q_1, R_1, and function f on Q_1, there are unique sets $f(Q_1)$ and $f(R_1)$ (the notation is informal) such that f is a folding onto the state graph $f(P_1) = (f(Q_1), f(R_1))$.

Lemma 14.6.1

Homomorphisms preserve traces.

Proof: Since homomorphisms preserve arcs, they preserve paths. Therefore any trace of P_1 can also be found in P_2 by observation of the image of the path defining the trace. ∎

Note that homomorphisms may introduce spurious traces. An extreme example is the folding of the entire graph into one vertex, with the result that all sequences of instructions become traces.

Example 14.6.1

If the two center vertices of the following graph are folded together,

then the resulting graph is

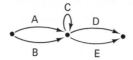

The reader can easily verify that all traces have been preserved and that infinitely many spurious traces have been introduced.

EXERCISE 14.6

1. Null labels are skipped when following paths to generate traces. Under what circumstances can two vertices connected by an arc with a null label be folded together with no effect on the traces generated? Consider the example above, with the C converted into a null label.

14.7.   STATE COMPONENTS

Programs break their state sets into components such as individual variables or groups of variables. The theory of data structures offers a wide variety of methods for building up hierarchies of state components and subcomponents. For the purposes of this discussion, the simple *Cartesian product,*

$$A \times B = \{(a, b) \mid a \in A \text{ and } b \in B\}$$

adequately captures the notion of a state as a group of components. If the program being considered has variables $x, y, \ldots, z$, where the value of x is an element of Q_x and so on, then the state may be written as

$$Q = Q_x \times Q_y \times \ldots \times Q_z, \ Q_x = \pi_x(Q)$$

and if $a = (a_x, a_y, \ldots, a_z) \in Q$ then the x component of a is written

$$\pi_x(a) = a_x$$

The π_x mappings are called *projections.*

It is often the case that a component is used only in portions of a process's lifetime. If x is such a component, and all others are lumped together into a component r, then

$$Q = Q_{r1} \cup (Q_{r2} \times Q_x)$$

where $Q_r = Q_{r1} \cup Q_{r2}$ is a partition of Q_r into the parts that use x and that do not. Unfortunately this notation becomes messy when several dynamically accessed components like x are present. Therefore, introduce a special symbol, ω, to indicate a component not in use, and write

$$Q = (Q_{r1} \times \{\omega\}) \cup (Q_{r2} \times Q_x)$$

This can be abbreviated imprecisely but compactly to

$$Q = Q_r \times \tilde{Q}_x, \quad \text{where } \tilde{Q}_x = \{\omega\} \cup Q_x$$

The partitioning of Q_r is implicit. Note that the projection π_r for the non-dynamic case applies to the dynamic case as well.

14.8.   IGNORING STATE COMPONENTS

Projections can be used to fold state graphs with the result that state components are selectively ignored. Rewriting the definition of folding in terms of a projection, if

$$P = (Q_r \times \tilde{Q}_x, R)$$

then

$$\pi_r(P) = (Q_r, R')$$

where

$$(a, s, c) \in R' \quad \text{iff for some } b, d \in \tilde{Q}_x, ((a, b), s, (c, d)) \in R$$

Ignoring enough state components may reduce a state graph to a manageable size. Unfortunately it can also lose critical information since it may introduce spurious computations. Whether or not simply ignoring components will suffice depends on whether or not the critical control variables (those which must be left unfolded) take a manageably small finite set of values.

14.9.   PRESERVING STATE INFORMATION IN LABELS

It is possible to preserve information about the state component being folded out of the state graph by adding it to the arc labels. In fact, it is precisely for this purpose that arc labels are used. The completely unfolded state graph does not need labels, and folded versions are labeled to indicate how they are to be unfolded. Ultimately the program which defines a process can be considered to be a highly folded version of the state graph with extensive labeling in the form of symbolic statements or instructions. (In the program,

the only state component which remains unfolded is the program counter.)
The basic technique is to convert the transition

$$((a, b), s, (c, d)) \in R$$

to the transition $(a, \text{"} x = b; s; x \leftarrow d\text{"}, c)$ where the label now consists of three
parts: "$x = b$", which is a predicate which must be satisfied if the transition
is to be applied, "s", which is the original label, and "$x \leftarrow d$", which indicates
that the value of x is to be set to d if the transition occurs. This saves all state
information but loses the benefits of state compression, since no arcs are deleted. Fortunately, program state graphs exhibit patterns in such arcs which
allow them to be combined. The best way to define such patterns is to work
them backward, explaining how to unfold certain "primitive operations"
into state graphs for which the component values are explicit.

14.10. PRIMITIVE OPERATIONS

As suggested by the preceding section, arc labels in the form of instructions
can be treated as directions for unfolding the graph. The unfolding rules stated here can also be used as patterns for refolding a state graph while preserving structure. The instructions used here as arc labels are called *primitive
operations*.

Adopting the notation for dynamically accessed components defined in
Section 14.7, let

$$Q = (Q_{r1} \times \{\omega\}) \cup (Q_{r2} \times Q_x) = Q_r \times \tilde{Q}_x$$

where $Q_r = Q_{r1} \cup Q_{r2}$, ω stands for "not in use," and Q_x is the value set of
the component x being unfolded. Let y stand for all of the components which
remain folded. Let $g(x, y)$ be a function and $p(x, y)$ a predicate on $Q_x \times Q_y$,
write $g(x = b, y)$ for the function on Q_y obtained by substituting the constant
parameter b for x in $g(x, y)$, and similarly for $p(x = a, y)$.

14.10.1. Branching Operations: $p(x, y)$

$$(a, p(x, y), c), \qquad \text{where } a, c \in Q_{r2}$$

unfolds into

$$((a, b), p(x = b, y), (c, b))$$

for each b in Q_x for which $p(x = b, y)$ is not identically false. If $p(x = b, y)$
is identically true, it is omitted as a label (identically true predicate labels may
be omitted whenever they occur).

14.10.2. Assignment Operations: $x \leftarrow g(x, y)$ and $y \leftarrow g(x, y)$

$$(a, y \leftarrow g(x, y), c), \qquad \text{where } a, c \in Q_{r2}$$

unfolds into

$$((a, b), y \leftarrow g(x = b, y), (c, b))$$

for each b in Q_x. If $g(x = b, y)$ is the identity function it may be omitted as a label.

$$(a, x \leftarrow g(x, y), c), \qquad \text{where } a, c \in Q_{r2}$$

unfolds into

$$((a, b), d = g(b, y), (c, d))$$

for each b and d in Q_x such that the predicate "$d = g(b, y)$" is not identically false.

14.10.3. Acquisition Operations: Acquire x

$$(a, \text{acquire } x, c), \qquad \text{where } a \in Q_{r1} \text{ and } c \in Q_{r2}$$

unfolds into

$$((a, \omega),, (a, d)) \qquad \text{for all } d \text{ in } Q_x$$

Note that the process reads the acquired component's initial value by branching during acquisition.

14.10.4. Release Operations: Release x

$$(a, \text{release } x, c), \text{ where } a \in Q_{r2} \text{ and } c \in Q_{r1},$$

unfolds into

$$((a, b),, (a, \omega)) \qquad \text{for all } b \text{ in } Q_x$$

14.10.5. Component Not in Use: $y = g(y)$ and $p(y)$

$$(a, s, c) \qquad \text{where } a, c \in Q_{r1}$$

unfolds into

$$((a, \omega), s, (c, \omega))$$

Here s can be any operation which makes no reference to x.

14.10.6. Uninterpreted Operations: A, B, ...

$$(a, A, c), \qquad \text{where } A \text{ is any uninterpreted operation}$$

unfolds into

$$((a, b), A, (c, b)) \qquad \text{for each } b \text{ in } Q_x \text{ (or for } b = \omega \text{ as appropriate)}$$

Uninterpreted operations are useful for marking program steps of special interest for later analysis. The null arc label is treated like an uninterpreted operation.

14.11. UNFOLDING PROGRAMS

The primitive operations defined above are sufficient to express programs as flowcharts. (For the purposes of this work, subroutine calls must be modeled either as uninterpreted operations or by using assignments and conditional branches.) Folded state graphs are not quite flowcharts, because in a flowchart the operations label vertices rather than arcs. However, a flowchart can be converted easily into a flowchart by moving the operations out of the boxes (vertices) onto their emergent arcs.

Example 14.11.1

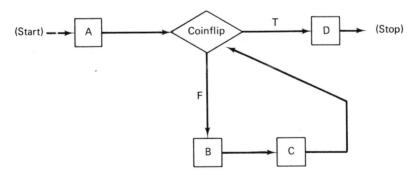

In order to represent nondeterminancy, let "coinflip" be a predicate which is randomly true or false. The flowchart converts into the state graph where asterisks have been used to denote starting and final states. Since all operations in this graph are uninterpreted, no unfolding is possible. The state graph can be interpreted as a finite automaton which generates the regular language $A(BC)^*D$.

Example 14.11.2 The Flowchart

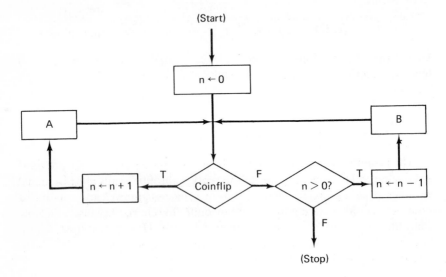

converts into the state graph

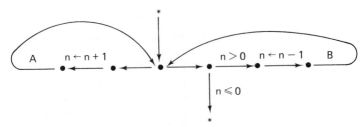

This may be unfolded on n to get the infinite graph

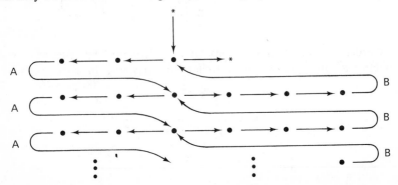

Note that states not reachable from the initial states are omitted.

1. The language defined by the above state graph is context-free. What is it?

2. Use expansion and refolding of a state graph to simplify the program

> **begin integer** i;
> **for** i: $= 1$ **step** 1 **to** 3 **do**
>   **if** $i = 3$ **then** C
>   **else if** $i = 2$ **then** B
>   **else if** $i = 1$ **then** A
> **end**

If the value of i is simply folded out of the state graph, what language is produced? If i is retained, what language is produced?

14.12. APPLICATIONS

The method of inductive assertions consists of attaching assertions about the state to various points in a program and proving that each assertion implies the next assertion reached in the computation. The implication is derived by following the computation and incorporating the state changes at each step in the starting assertion. If every loop is broken by an assertion then this process is finite. Induction is then used to prove partial correctness in the sense that if the program terminates, the assertion at the beginning of the program implies the assertion at the end. Termination itself can be proved by proving a finite bound on a step counter artificially included in the state.

Clearly state graph concepts are an important part of the inductive assertion method. In state graph terminology, an assertion is a description of a subset of the states, and the individual computation following proofs demonstrate that all paths starting in one subset must lead to another in a finite number of steps. The induction step exploits the fact that the "is reached from" relation on subsets is a partial ordering. This viewpoint may be of some use in future development of the inductive assertion method because it unifies the program counter with other state components and because it offers the possibility of more direct termination proofs.

A second application involves analysis of the sequence of operations performed by a program. If a program containing uninterpreted operations is unfolded into its state graph, only the uninterpreted operations remain as arc labels. The set of all traces from starting to ending states in this graph is a language over the alphabet of uninterpreted operations, and characterizes the sequences of such operations performed by the program.

In many cases, not all sequences of operations are legal. Usually the set of legal operation sequences (which is itself a language) is regular. Therefore it is possible to use known techniques from automata theory to verify that the program's language contains only legal sequences. The interested reader is referred to Howard and Alexander [6] for further exploration of this area.

14.13. SYSTEMS OF PROCESSES

Dijkstra has characterized an operating system as a "society of cooperating sequential processes." This and subsequent sections extend the model of single programs as sequential processes to systems of interacting processes running asynchronously. Throughout this and subsequent sections it is assumed that all state graphs have been completely unfolded, so the only remaining transition labels will be uninterpreted operations with no effect on the state.

Definition 14.13.1

Let $P_1 = (Q_1, R_1)$ and $P_2 = (Q_2, R_2)$ be processes. Their *product* is the process $P_1 \times P_2 = (Q_1 \times Q_2, R_1 \times R_2)$ where $Q_1 \times Q_2$ is the ordinary Cartesian product and $((a, b), s, (c, d))$ is an element of $R_1 \times R_2$ if and only if either

1. $a = c$ and $(b, s, d) \in R_2$, or
2. $b = d$ and $(a, s, c) \in R_1$

As usual the product operation has inverse operators, or projections, π_1 and π_2 defined by folding the product back into the component state sets.

Intuitively, the independent product system makes a transition whenever one of the component processes does. "Simultaneous" transitions are forbidden by the view of time as being discrete. No real generality is lost since "simultaneous" computations can appear, interleaved, in the product. Note also that the two processes operate completely asynchronously.

Example 14.13.1

A common way for processes to communicate is for one to produce a series of messages and the other to consume them. This kind of communication has been idealized as the "producer-consumer problem." The content of the messages is irrelevant. Let the uninterpreted operations PRODUCE and CONSUME stand for the actions to be coordinated. One simple solution for the problem uses a shared state variable R (standing for "Ready") which is initially 0 and takes a value of 1 whenever a message has been produced and is ready to be consumed. In this solution, the state graphs are:

P_1:

(a) $\xrightarrow{\quad R = 0 \quad}$ (b) $\xrightarrow{\quad \text{PRODUCE} \quad}$ (c) $\xrightarrow{\quad R \leftarrow 1 \quad}$

P_2:

(x) $\xrightarrow{\quad R = 1 \quad}$ (y) $\xrightarrow{\quad \text{CONSUME} \quad}$ (z) $\xrightarrow{\quad R \leftarrow 0 \quad}$

If these processes are unfolded and irrelevant states ignored, they become:

P_1:   (a, 0) $\xrightarrow{\hspace{3cm}}$ (b, 0) $\xrightarrow{\text{PRODUCE}}$ (c, 0) $\xrightarrow{\hspace{3cm}}$ (a, 1)

P_2:   (x, 1) $\xrightarrow{\hspace{3cm}}$ (y, 1) $\xrightarrow{\text{CONSUME}}$ (z, 1) $\xrightarrow{\hspace{3cm}}$ (x, 0)

The product is a dependent product (see next section) and takes the form

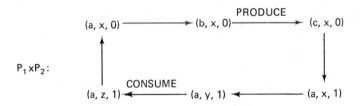

$P_1 \times P_2$:

(a, x, 0) $\xrightarrow{\hspace{3cm}}$ (b, x, 0) $\xrightarrow{\text{PRODUCE}}$ (c, x, 0)

(a, z, 1) $\xleftarrow{\text{CONSUME}}$ (a, y, 1) $\xleftarrow{\hspace{3cm}}$ (a, x, 1)

Clearly each PRODUCE is matched by its following CONSUME. More complex solutions can allow several messages to be buffered.

Example 14.13.2

The producer-consumer problem can be complicated by allowing P_1 to halt at its option, and requiring that it notify P_2 so that P_2 will also halt after consuming any pending messages. To do so, one might try the state graphs

P_1:   (d) $\xleftarrow{\quad E \leftarrow 1 \quad}$ (a) $\xrightarrow{\quad R = 0 \quad}$ (b) $\xrightarrow{\quad \text{PRODUCE} \quad}$ (c) $\xrightarrow{\quad R \leftarrow 1 \quad}$

P_2:   (u) $\xleftarrow{\quad E = 1 \quad}$ (x) $\xrightarrow{\quad R = 1 \quad}$ (y) $\xrightarrow{\quad \text{CONSUME} \quad}$ (z) $\xrightarrow{\quad R \leftarrow 0 \quad}$

Here E is a new state variable, shared, and initially 0. Unfolding and taking the product,

$P_1 \times P_2$:

```
        ┌──────► (d, x, 0, 1) ──────────► (d, u, 0, 1)
        │            ▲
        │            │                        PRODUCE
        │         (a, x, 0, 0) ──────────► (b, x, 0, 0) ──────────────► (c, x, 0, 0)
        │            ▲        CONSUME                                        │
        │         (a, z, 1, 0) ◄────────── (a, y, 1, 0) ◄────────────── (a, x, 1, 0)
        │            │        CONSUME          │                             │
        └──────── (d, z, 1, 1) ◄────────── (d, y, 1, 1) ◄────────────── (d, x, 1, 1) ──────► (d, u, 1, 1)
```

This product displays a bug, since in the $(d, u, 1, 1)$ state both processes have halted but the last message remains unconsumed. The reader should verify that the bug can be fixed either by moving the terminating transition to state b of P_1 or by adding a final test of R to P_2.

It is highly desirable that the component processes of a system should not interfere with each other. In other words, the computations of the individual processes should be unaffected by the presence of other processes. This property is called determinateness, and will be defined more precisely shortly. It is not the same as determinacy, which requires that at most one computation can originate from any given state. The independent product is determinate but nondeterministic.

Saying that P_1 is not affected by the presence of P_2 in the product $P_1 \times P_2$ means that the projection $\pi_1(P_1 \times P_2)$ should be P_1 again. This is only approximately correct, because the transitions of P_2 will still be present in the projection. The product is determinate if these added transitions do not affect the state of P_1, that is, if they are all loops from states in Q_1 back to the same states.

Definition 14.13.2

Let $P_1 \times P_2$ be a product of processes,

$$\pi_1(P_1 \times P_2) = (Q_1, R_1')$$
$$R_1'' = \{(a, s, a) \mid a \in Q_1, \text{ some } (b, s, c) \in R_2\}$$

Then the product is *determinate for P_1* if

$$R_1 \subseteq R_1' \subseteq R_1 \cup R_1''$$

If a product is determinate for all its processes, it is *determinate* (without qualification).

Lemma 14.13.1

The product of independent processes is determinate.

Proof: By symmetry, we need only consider P_1. Take $(a, s, c) \in R_1$. By the definition of the product, for any $b \in Q_2$ $((a, b), s, (c, b)) \in R_1 \times R_2$. By the definition of π_1 as a homomorphism, $(a, s, c) \in R_1'$. Thus the first inclusion is proved. Take any $(a, s, c) \in R_1'$. Since π_1 is a folding, there exists $((a, b), s, (c, d)) \in R_1 \times R_2$ such that $\pi_1(a, b) = a$ and $\pi_1(c, d) = c$. There are two ways such an arc can be in $R_1 \times R_2$:

1. $a = c$ and $(b, s, d) \in R_2$, in which case $(a, s, c) \in R_1''$, or
2. $b = d$ and $(a, s, c) \in R_1$, in which case $(a, s, c) \in R_1$.

Thus the second inclusion is proved. ∎

The definition of determinateness presented here is less stringent than the one usually found in the literature, which requires that each memory cell's sequence of values be invariant. The present definition is more useful since it allows nondeterminism in individual processes and still captures the notion that the processes are unaffected by concurrency.

14.14. DEPENDENT PROCESSES

Two processes are *dependent* if they share state components. Other forms of dependency could be defined, but shared memory is the usual case in operating systems. A pair of dependent processes can be written as

$$P_1 = (Q_1 \times Q_x, R_1)$$
$$P_2 = (Q_2 \times Q_x, R_2)$$

where x is the shared component.

Definition 14.4.1

Let P_1 and P_2 be dependent processes as above. Then their (*dependent*) *product* is

$$P_1 \times P_2 = (Q_1 \times Q_2 \times Q_x, \ R_1 \times R_2)$$

where

$$((a, b, c), s, (a', b', c')) \in R_1 \times R_2$$

if and only if either

1. $b = b'$ and $((a, c), s, (a', c')) \in R_1$, or
2. $a = a'$ and $((b, c), s, (b', c')) \in R_2$.

The corresponding projection functions are

$$\pi_1 (a, b, c) = (a, c)$$

and

$$\pi_2 (a, b, c) = (b, c).$$

Therefore, the requirement for determinateness is that

$$R_1 \subseteq \pi_1(R_1 \times R_2) \subseteq R_1 \cup R_1''$$

where $((a, c), s, (a, c)) \in R_1''$ whenever $a \in Q_1$, $c \in Q_x$, and there exists some $((b, d), s, (b', d')) \in R_2$.

Example 14.14.1

The dependent product is not necessarily determinate. If $((b, c), s, (b', c')) \in R_2$, $c \neq c'$, and $a \in Q_1$, then $((a, c), s, (a, c'))$ is an element of $\pi_1 (R_1, R_2)$ but not necessarily of either R_1 or R_1''.

Lemma 14.14.1

The first inclusion needed for determinateness is valid in the dependent product, i.e.,

$$R_1 \subseteq \pi_1(R_1, R_2)$$

Thus projecting the product does not lose transitions.

Proof: This proof is a trivial modification of the proof of Lemma 14.16.2. ∎

The above example and lemma demonstrate that the dependent product is not determinate because "unexpected" changes in the shared state component are introduced, an unsurprising result.

Example 14.14.2

The producer-consumer system of Example 14.13.1 is not determinate, because $\pi_1(P_1 \times P_2)$ contains the transition $((a, 1),,(a, 0))$ and $\pi_2(P_1 \times P_2)$ contains the transition $((z, 0),,(z, 1))$, neither of which was present in the original process. Of course these transitions are really expected; indeed, they are essential for correct operation.

14.15.   RESOURCES

Adopting the notation of Section 14.7, let

$$P_1 = (Q_1 \times \tilde{Q}_x, R_1),$$

and similarly for P_2, where

$$Q_1 \times \tilde{Q}_x \text{ stands for } (Q_{11} \times \{\omega\}) \cup (Q_{12} \times Q_x)$$

$$Q_1 = Q_{11} \cup Q_{12} \text{ is a partition}$$

and

$$\tilde{Q}_x = \{\omega\} \cup Q_x.$$

Q_{12} is called the *critical section* of Q_1(with respect to x) and x is a *resource* of P_1. Acquire operations lead P_1 from Q_{11} to Q_{12} and release operations from Q_{12} to Q_{11}. All other transitions of P_1 which access x must occur within Q_{12}.

The projection used in this case,

$$\pi_1: Q_1 \times Q_2 \times Q_x \rightarrow Q_1 \times \tilde{Q}_x$$

is defined as

$$\pi_1(a, b, c) = \begin{cases} (a, \omega) & \text{if } a \in Q_{11} \\ (a, c) & \text{if } a \in Q_{12} \end{cases}$$

Thus ω signifies that the x component is not in use and its value is not significant to the state of P_1.

Definition 14.15.1

(*Product with Resources*)
Let P_1 and P_2 be as above. Then the *product* is

$$P_1 \times P_2 = (Q_1 \times Q_2 \times Q_x, R_1 \times R_2)$$

where

$$((a, b, c), s, (a', b', c')) \in R_1 \times R_2$$

if and only if either

    1. $b = b'$, $(\pi_1(a, b, c), s, \pi_1(a', b', c')) \in R_1$, and if $a \in Q_{11}$ or $a' \in Q_{11}$ then $c = c'$, or

    2. $a = a'$, $(\pi_2(a, b, c), s, \pi_2(a', b', c')) \in R_2$, and if $b \in Q_{21}$ or $b' \in Q_{21}$ then $c = c'$.

This definition is easily seen to be the necessary refinement of Definition 14.7.1. The added requirements that $c = c'$ when a or $a' \in Q_{11}$ (b or $b' \in Q_{21}$) mean only that the value of x is changed only within critical sections.

Resources find a variety of uses in operating systems. This section digresses into a summary of commonly encountered resource types with the two purposes of (1) using state graph terminology to make some precise definitions and (2) illustrating the variety of situations with which the model must deal.

A resource is *read-only* if all transitions involving it are of the form $((a, c)$, x, $(b, c))$ and thus do not change its state. Purely read-only resources need not be treated as part of the state since they never change. However, they are useful in that their values parametrize what a process will do. The set of transitions involving c, as above, may be completely different from those involving some $c' \neq c$. For example, an instruction processing unit is a general-purpose process which is parametrized by the programs it interprets.

Resources which are used and reused for scratch storage by various processes are called *reusable*, or *serially reusable*, resources. Typically, the acquiring process has no interest in their value at acquisition. When this is not the case and the value is not properly reset, undesirable nondeterminacies may be introduced in individual processes (the familiar "uninitialized variable" problem.) Typically, processes start and end in their noncritical sections for such resources, and compete for access to them. The competition is resolved by protection and scheduling mechanisms in the system.

Dependence on the value of newly acquired resources is typical of *messages* between processes. Analysis of messages is simplified if they are treated as *consumable resources*, which are used only once in the sense that one process starts out in its critical section relative to the message and eventually defines a value and sends the message with a release operation. The recipient process then receives the message by performing an acquire, and stays in its critical section relative to the message thereafter. Thus messages are single one-way transactions. In practice messages are transmitted through buffers which themselves are reusable resources, acquired by the sending and released by the receiving processes. Both the buffers and the messages they contain must be treated as resources.

The formal definitions given here deal with two processes and a single resource, but the generalizations to many processes and resources are clear. Operating systems have potentially infinite sets of processes and resources, of which only a finite number are active at any moment. The renaming functions necessary to map these infinite sets into the finite set of actual resources of a machine are left out here for simplicity. The mappings can be quite complex. For example, virtual memory systems perform the renaming for main memory.

14.16. MUTUAL EXCLUSION

A system of processes exhibits *mutual exclusion* if at most one process at a time can be in its critical section. Mutual exclusion can be implemented in various ways, such as Dijkstra's semaphores [3]. This section ignores implementation and concentrates on the implications for determinateness.

Definition 14.16.1

The *mutually-exclusive product* of processes is the product with all states (a, b, c) such that $a \in Q_{12}$ and $b \in Q_{22}$, and all transitions involving these states, deleted, and is denoted by $P_1*P_2 = ((Q_1*Q_2) \times Q_x, R_1*R_2)$.

Theorem 14.16.1

The mutually-exclusive product is determinate, provided that each process has a noncritical state.

Proof: $R_1 \subseteq \pi_1(R_1*R_2)$. Take any $((a, d), s, (a', d')) \in R_1$.
Choose any noncritical $b \in Q_{21}$, and choose c and $c' \in Q_x$ as follows:

1. If $a, a' \in Q_{11}$, choose $c = c' \in Q_x$ arbitrarily.
2. If $a \in Q_{11}$ and $a' \in Q_{12}$, choose $c = c' = d'$.
3. If $a \in Q_{12}$ and $a' \in Q_{11}$, choose $c = c' = d$.
4. If $a, a' \in Q_{12}$, choose $c = d$ and $c' = d'$.

Then $(a, d) = \pi_1(a, b, c)$, $(a', d') = \pi_1(a', b, c')$, and $c = c'$ if either a or $a' \in Q_{11}$. Since b is noncritical, (a, b, c) and (a', b, c') are valid states. Therefore $((a, b, c), s, (a', b, c')) \in R_1*R_2$, and $((a, d), s, (a', d')) = (\pi_1(a, b, c), s, \pi_1(a', b, c')) \in \pi_1(R_1*R_2)$.

$\pi_1(R_1*R_2) \subseteq R_1 \cup R_1''$. Take any $((a, b, c), s, (a', b', c')) \in R_1*R_2$. The projections $(\pi_1(a, b, c), s, \pi_1(a', b', c'))$ cover all of $\pi_1(R_1*R_2)$ by definition. Either

1. $b = b'$ and $(\pi_1(a, b, c), s, \pi_1(a', b', c')) \in R_1$, or
2. $a = a'$ and $(\pi_2(a, b, c), s, \pi_2(a', b', c')) \in R_2$, in which case either

2a. $a = a' \in Q_{11}$, in which case $\pi_1(a, b, c) = \pi_1(a', b', c') = (a, \omega)$, and $((a, \omega), s, (a, \omega)) \in R_1''$, or
2b. $a = a' \in Q_{12}$, in which case mutual exclusion implies that $b, b' \in Q_{21}$, so $c = c'$ and $\pi_1(a, b, c) = \pi_1(a', b', c') = (a, c)$, and thus $(\pi_1(a, b, c), s, \pi_1(a, b, c)) \in R_1''$.

Thus in any case $(\pi_1(a, b, c), s, \pi_1(a', b', c')) \in R_1 \cup R_1''$. ∎

Example 14.16.1

A typical operating system resource is a disk with a movable arm which can select one from a number of tracks for data access. Before a track can be read or written, a SEEK operation to position the arm correctly must be performed. The arm position is a shared state component, which may be represented as a variable POS. Thus we may write POS ← i for a SEEK and encode the subsequent data access operation with POS = i, where i is any track number.

It takes little imagination to see that mutual exclusion is necessary as far as POS is concerned. If a second process intervenes between the seek and subsequent access by changing POS, the first process will access the wrong data.

14.17.   SAFETY

There is a significant and subtle flaw in the definition of determinateness used in Theorem 14.16.1, in that it takes the static rather than dynamic viewpoint. In the dynamic approach, the state graph is restricted to those states reachable by finite paths from the starting states. This means that the construction in the first part of the proof, namely that $R_1 \subseteq \pi_1(R_1^*R_2)$, cannot choose b and c arbitrarily because (a, b, c) might not be a reachable state. Therefore the first inclusion is not necessarily true in the dynamic sense, and the dynamic mutually-exclusive product may be missing some transitions and computations when projected.

A simple geometric analogy may help clarify this point. Let a set of points in 3-space be defined by $(x, 0, c)$ for $x < 0$ and $(x, 0, c')$ for $x \geq 0$. Then if $c \neq c'$ this set is a line parallel to the x-axis with a discontinuity at $x = 0$. The projection of this line on the x, y-plane hides the discontinuity. Similarly, the projection used in Theorem 14.16.1 may hide discontinuities.

A stronger criterion for determinateness is needed, to deal with reachable states only and to insist that computations can always be completed within the system.

Definition 14.17.1

Let $P = (Q, R)$ be a process and $a \in Q$. Then
$Q [a]$ is the set of all $b \in Q$ reachable from a
$R [a]$ is the corresponding set of reachable arcs
$P [a] = (Q [a], R [a])$

This notation also applies to products. For example if $P = (Q_1 \times Q_2 \times Q_c, R_1 \times R_2)$ then $P[a, b, c]$ is the portion of P reachable from the state (a, b, c). The product may be mutually-exclusive or not, or may be restricted in other ways. Only the states reachable in whatever product is used will be considered. If a state is characterized simply as reachable, it is reachable from some initial state of the process or system (an initial system state is a product of initial process states.)

Definition 14.17.2

The product is *safe* if it is for each of its component processes, which is the case for P_1 if and only if, for each reachable product state (a, b, c), $R_1[\pi_1(a, b, c)] \subseteq \pi_1(R_1 \times R_2[a, b, c])$. In other words, P_1 is safe in the product if at any reachable system state P_1 can still complete all of its potential computations.

Theorem 14.17.1

$P_1 \times P_2$ is safe for P_1 if and only if (a, b, c) reachable, $(a, d) = \pi_1(a, b, c)$, and $((a, d), s, (a', d')) \in R_1$ imply that $((a, d), s, (a', d')) \in \pi_1(R_1 \times R_2[a, b, c])$. In English, if P_1 has a next step it can take immediately, then in the product it must eventually be allowed to take that step.

Proof: The stated condition is an easy consequence of safety. The reverse implication requires the following lemma.

Lemma 14.17.1

If $P_1 \times P_2$ satisfies the stated condition on immediate steps, and (a', d') is reachable from $\pi_1(a, b, c)$ in P_1, then there exists a state (a', b', c') reachable from (a, b, c) such that $(a', d') = \pi_1(a', b', c')$.

Proof of lemma: Induct on the length of the path from $\pi_1(a, b, c)$ to (a', d') in P_1. For the starting step this path length is zero, so $(a', d') = \pi_1(a, b, c)$ and the conclusion is trivial.

For the induction step, assume that the lemma has been proved for all path lengths of n and that the path from $\pi_1(a, b, c)$ to (a', d') is of length $n + 1$. Then there must be a state (a'', d'') reachable from $\pi_1(a, b, c)$ by a path of length n, and a transition $((a'', d''), s', (a', d')) \in R_1$. By induction there is a state (a'', b'', c'') reachable from (a, b, c) in the product such that $(a'', d'') = \pi_1(a'', b'', c'')$. Since (a'', b'', c'') is reachable, the stated condition implies that the transition $((a'', d''), s, (a', d')) \in \pi_1(R_1 \times R_2[a'', b'', c''])$.

Since π_1 is defined to be a folding, an inverse image of this transition must exist in $R_1 \times R_2[a'', b'', c'']$, that is, some $((p'', q'', r''), s', (p', q', r')) \in R_1 \times R_2[a'', b'', c'']$ such that $\pi_1(p'', q'', r'') = (a'', d'')$ and $\pi_1(p', q', r') = (a', d')$. Thus (p', q', r') is the desired state since it is reachable from (a, b, c) via a path which traverses (a'', b'', c'') and then (p'', q'', r''). ∎

Proof of theorem: Returning to the theorem, assume the stated condition for P_1 and let $((a', d'), s, (a'', d'')) \in R_1[\pi_1(a, b, c)]$. By the lemma, $(a', d') =$

$\pi_1(a', b', c')$ for some (a', b', c') reachable from (a, b, c). Then (a', b', c') is itself a reachable state, so $((a', d'), s, (a'', d'')) \in \pi_1(R_1 \times R_2[a', b', c'])$ by safety. Clearly $\pi_1(R_1 \times R_2[a', b', c']) \subseteq \pi_1(R_1 \times R_2[a, b, c])$ since (a', b', c') is reachable from (a, b, c). This establishes the desired inclusion. ∎

It is easily seen that this result applies to arbitrary products of many processes using many resources, since it does not use any special features of the product.

14.18.   DEADLOCKS

Necessary and sufficient conditions for correct operation of a system of processes have now been established. Reviewing, these conditions are determinateness, which insures that no unexpected transitions occur, and safety, which insures that all expected computations do occur. Furthermore, mutual exclusion is a sufficient condition for determinateness. In the case of mutual exclusion, the criterion for safety can be rewritten as follows:

Lemma 14.18.1

The mutually-exclusive product P_1*P_2 is safe for P_1 if and only if, for each reachable state (a, b, c),

$$((a, \omega), s, (a', c')) \in R_1$$

(that is, P_1 wishes to enter its critical section) implies that for some b' and c', (a, b', c') is reachable from (a, b, c) and b' is noncritical (that is, P_2 eventually leaves its critical section with the desired value in the resource).

The rewritten definition of safety has two requirements: that processes leave their critical sections and that the resources take the expected values. A discussion of the second half is beyond the scope of this chapter. Bredt has suggested that it may be dealt with by viewing the sequences of messages left in resources as a collection of interrelated languages, and Habermann has done so in the finite (regular language) case. Hereafter this chapter assumes that simply leaving the critical sections is sufficient. This is a reasonable assumption for serially reusable resources, for which the value of a resource is insignificant when no process is using it. Formally:

Definition 14.18.1

In a *nonmessage system*, there is a special value x_0 for each resource x, taken whenever x is not in use. This implies that processes enter and leave their critical sections for x with transitions of the form

$$((a, \omega), s, (a', x_0)) \quad \text{and} \quad ((a, x_0), s, (a', \omega))$$

respectively.

A system which contains a mixture of message and nonmessage resources can be brought under this definition by lumping groups of communicating processes (and their message resources) together into single processes.

Definition 14.18.2

A process is *nonpreemptive* if for any state a for which there is a transition

$$((a, \omega), s, (a', c')) \in R$$

(that is, a state just prior to entering a critical section) there are no other transitions from that state. A system is nonpreemptive if all of its processes are.

This is a reasonable assumption to make for practical purposes, and simplifies matters considerably by ruling out conditional entries to critical sections.

Definition 14.18.3

A *deadlock* (in a nonpreemptive system) is a reachable state in which there is some subset of the processes each of which wishes to enter its critical section on a resource held by some other process in the set.

This definition can be extended to preemptive systems but it becomes so complex that the original definition of safety is preferable.

Example 14.18.1

The classical simplest example of a deadlock comes from the mutually-exclusive product of two processes using two resources as follows.

$$P_1: \quad (a) \xrightarrow{\text{acquire } X} (b) \xrightarrow{\text{acquire } Y} (c) \xrightarrow{\text{release } Y} (d) \xrightarrow{\text{release } X} (e)$$

$$P_2: \quad (p) \xrightarrow{\text{acquire } Y} (q) \xrightarrow{\text{acquire } X} (r) \xrightarrow{\text{release } X} (s) \xrightarrow{\text{release } Y} (t)$$

It should be clear that in the product the state (b, q) is reachable, unsafe, and a deadlock.

Theorem 14.18.1

A finite, nonpreemptive, nonmessage, mutually exclusive system in which each process considered alone reliably leaves its critical sections is safe if and only if it has no deadlocks.

Proof: If the system has a deadlock it is not safe, since none of the dead-locked processes will ever be able to enter its critical section. Thus safety implies freedom from deadlocks.

If the system is not safe then by definition there is a state in which some process, say P_1, desires to enter a critical section on some resource x_1 but cannot. This implies that there is some process P_2 which is holding x_1 and will never release it. Since P_2 would release x_1 if not interfered with, any computation of P_2 in the system must be blocked at a state in which P_2 desires to enter a critical section on some resource x_2 and cannot. P_1 is still blocked in this new state. Repeating the above argument, an infinite chain $P_1, P_2, \ldots$ can be built up. Since the system is finite, this chain must eventually repeat a process. The loop thus formed is a deadlock. Therefore, freedom from deadlocks implies safety. ∎

EXERCISES 14.18

1. Prove Lemma 14.8.1.

2. Prove that a nonmessage, mutually exclusive product which involves only one resource is safe if each process, considered individually, always leaves its critical section.

    (*Note*: In working this exercise, the alert reader should have noticed that the presence of only one resource is essential, for if there are two resources x and y, then it is possible that P_1 could be holding x and waiting for y while P_2 is holding y and waiting for x. This is an example of a deadlock, which is defined more precisely in Definition 14.18.2.)

14.19. APPLICATIONS TO OPERATING SYSTEMS

The preceding sections have gone in some depth into the area of system correctness in the sense that the behavior of a system of processes is entirely predictable from analysis of the processes separately.

One of the essential ingredients in this analysis is the mutual-exclusion property. Unfortunately existing computers do not directly provide or enforce mutual exclusion without software support. Since mutual exclusion is closely related to scheduling (both deal with competition for resources by processes) it is not clear that mutual exclusion should be handled entirely by hardware.

Therefore, it is desirable to be able to prove that a given software mechanism does indeed provide mutual exclusion or that processes simulate it properly internally. More generally, it is possible for properly coded processes to be determinate even without mutual exclusion and this should be provable. The folding techniques defined earlier for single processes are applicable to such proofs, using the strategy of ignoring all information private to the individual process and thus reducing the system's state set to a manageable size and complexity.

The discussion so far has ignored all considerations of timing. These can be introduced by associating a traversal time (or time distribution) to each transition and a set of branching probabilities to each nondeterministic branch of the process. Such timing information can be preserved over the various state graph manipulations mentioned in this chapter. Folding, for example, would involve averaging the traversal time distributions and branching probabilities weighted by the flow of probability through the graph.

A particular well-developed instance of this approach may be found in queuing theory. In terms of the model developed here, a queuing network is a set of identical processes which use only one resource (server) at a time. This description suggests that extension of the theory of queues to handle different job types and to allow jobs to hold several resources simultaneously would be welcome. Some results have been established for multiple job types, but at this time holding multiple resources seems to be analytically intractable.

REFERENCES

1. BAER, J. L., "A Survey of Some Theoretical Aspects of Multiprocessing," *ACM Computing Surveys* 5:1 (Mar. 1973), 31–80.

2. COFFMAN, E. G. and P. J. DENNING, *Operating Systems Theory,* Prentice-Hall, Inc., Englewood Cliffs, N.J., 1973.

3. DIJKSTRA, E. W., "Co-operating Sequential Processes," in *Programming Languages,* ed. by F. Genuys, Academic Press, Inc., New York, 1968, pp. 43–112.

4. HABERMANN, A. N., "On the Harmonious Co-operation of Abstract Machines" Ph.D. dissertation, Technische Hogeschool te Eindhoven, Eindhoven, The Netherlands, 1967.

5. HOWARD, J. H., "The Coordination of Multiple Processes in Computer Operating Systems," Ph.D. dissertation, University of Texas at Austin, Texas, 1970.

6. HOWARD, J. H. and W. P. ALEXANDER, "Analyzing Sequences of Operations Performed by Programs," in *Program Test Methods,* ed. by W. Hetzel, Prentice-Hall, Inc., Englewood Cliffs, N.J., 1972, pp. 239–254.

DESCRIPTION OF COURSE: INTRODUCTION OF THE THEORY OF AUTOMATA AND FORMAL LANGUAGE

APPENDIX

I

This course is intended as a one-semester course for upper-division undergraduates in computer science or computing engineering. The prerequisite for this course should be a course in discrete structures.

The purpose of this course is to familiarize students with fundamental theoretical tools to analyze, design, and model computer-related systems. Therefore, theory and applications should be developed in parallel in this course. Since automata theory is already a common descriptive language in a wide spectrum of computer application areas, this course should be a required course for students majoring in computer science and computing engineering.

The prerequisite structure for this course is described by means of a Hasse diagram of a partially ordered set in Fig. I.1.1. Elements of this set are sections of different chapters of the book, and the partial ordering is the relation "to be prerequisite for." The core material of the course, denoted by nodes connected by heavy lines in Fig. I.1.1, explains the basic notions and properties of abstract machines and formal languages. The approach we suggested is to view grammar and automata as devices at the ends of a communication channel for characterizing languages. In order for a grammar-automaton pair to characterize the same language, it is proper to investigate how they are related such that adjustment in one device requires a corresponding adjustment in the other. For example, in order to recognize the language generated by a more powerful grammar, the power of the corresponding automaton must be

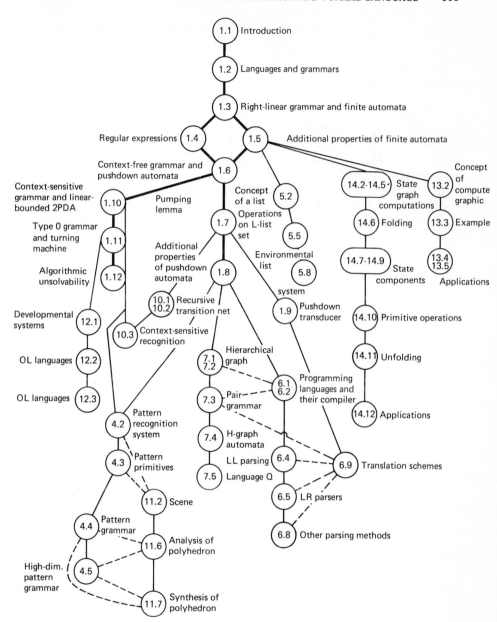

Fig. I.1.1 Prerequisite structure of the course "Introduction to the Theory of Automata and Formal Languages."

increased by means of either increased memory or relaxation of accessing rules to its memory. The concept of computation of an algorithmic process is finally introduced, and that algorithmically solvability is discussed. This material is covered by Chapter 1.

Nodes connected by thinner lines belong to the applications domain, programming language specification, compiler design, operating systems, biological systems, etc. They are selected from various chapters of the book. The instructor can either choose to touch upon many applications as he/she develops the theoretical ideas, or simply select one or two applications and explore them in depth.

Finally, dotted lines indicate desirable but not necessary prerequisites. The Hasse diagram should help the instructor to extract a self-contained program with little effort.

DESCRIPTION OF COURSE:
DESIGN PRINCIPLES OF
PROGRAMMING LANGUAGES
AND COMPILERS

This course is intended for senior or first year graduate students in computer science or computing engineering.

The purpose of this course is to develop certain guiding principles for specific programming languages and compilers utilizing the theory of automata and formal languages. Thus, the course as proposed here first introduces rudiments of language theory. From there, one can either pursue the language definition or compiler specification next. We suggest that the techniques of language definition should be taught before discussing compiler design. In this sequence, while doing the compiler design, students will keep in mind that a compiler should agree with the specification of a given language.

In this course, a programming language is specified by means of a *pair grammar* which generates ordered pairs of sentences, the second one is usually a hierarchical graph representation of the first, the source program. The two component grammars are related by a mapping or translation. If the second grammar were also generating strings, then the corresponding translation specializes to a syntax-directed translation which specifies a compiler. Various parsing techniques are then discussed to realize this translation.

The prerequisite structure for this course is given in Fig. II.1.1. The meaning of the diagram is the same as Fig. I.1.1 as explained in Appendix I.

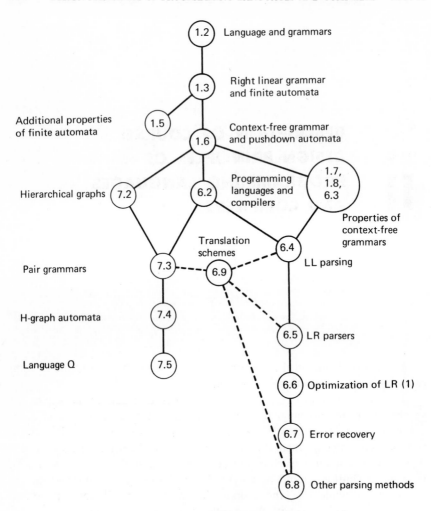

Fig. II.1.1 Prerequisite structure of the course "Design Principles of Programming Languages and Compilers."

DESCRIPTION OF COURSE: DESIGN PRINCIPLES OF FAULT-TOLERANT COMPUTING SYSTEM

III

This course is intended for senior or first year graduate students in computing engineering or computer science. The material for this course should be Chapter 8 of this book supplemented by original literature. The prerequisite for this course should be a course in switching theory and logical design. Courses in computer architecture, discrete structure, and probability are desirable but not necessary. A term project for this course will be very valuable.

The purpose of this course is to survey most of the pertinent techniques for fault-tolerant computing. The course can follow roughly the sequence of material presented in Chapter 8. However, Sections 8.2, 8.3, and 8.4 were written to be quite independent of each other so that the sequence of presenting them can be left to the discretion of the instructor. Starting from different types of faults, the instructor may find it illustrative to show, via circuit diagrams for logic gates, how different types of faults can occur. When time permits, the use of different types of redundancies in circuit design, such as quadded logic, should be covered. The material in Section 8.1 is best illustrated by examples. The instructor should also justify the "stuck-at" model of hardware faults.

After the introduction in Section 8.1, it may be advantageous for the instructor to proceed to Section 8.2 when the student has just learned about different types of hardware faults. Section 8.2 covers different techniques for fault diagnosis of digital systems. Subsections 8.2.2 and 8.2.4 should be covered intensively and slowly. Considerations must be placed on the automation of these diagnosis procedures. Experience shows that the student has most difficulty in understanding the D-algorithm. It may be advisable to illustrate the D-algorithm with several simple examples first before going into the complicated example in the chapter. It may also be illustrative to ask the student to design diagnostic tests for the circuit of a simple hypothetic machine.

Section 8.3 covers the use of error-correcting codes in fault-tolerant computer design. Different error-correcting codes are used in different environments according to the most likely type of errors. The Hamming code is a useful introductory example for error-correcting codes. Different encoding and decoding schemes are best illustrated with examples. The effect of using coding on the architecture of the computer should also be covered.

Section 8.4 covers reliability modeling and analysis of ultra-reliable fault-tolerant computers. A review of probability theory is desirable if the students do not have such a background. The calculation of different reliability parameters should be used as illustrative examples during this review. Depending on the interest of the student the complicated mathematical derivations may be skipped. The advantages and disadvantages of different configurations should be emphasized and the applicability of different reliability models should be compared.

Section 8.5 summarizes different fault-tolerant computing techniques and presents several examples of fault-tolerant computing systems. Depending on the interest of the student, these examples can be covered in detail by referring to the original publications to illustrate how the pressure of economics and efficiency considerations can affect the design.

INDEX